ARMED WITH
ANGER

HOW UK PUNK SURVIVED
THE NINETIES

ARMED WITH
ANGER

HOW UK PUNK SURVIVED
THE NINETIES

Ian Glasper

First published in Great Britain in 2012 by Cherry Red Books
(a division of Cherry Red Records Ltd.), Power Road Studios
114 Power Road, Chiswick, London W4 5PY

Copyright Ian Glasper © 2012

ISBN 978 1 901447 72 9

Design: Nathan Eighty

Front cover image: Pierre from Knuckledust, by Naki

Back cover images: Background: Voorhees, CBGBs 1996, by Richard Corbridge, Left to right: Imbalance, by Naki; Jas Toomer from Urko, by

Martin Jolly; Public Disturbance, by Naki. www.naki.co.uk

CONTENTS

HARDCORE

Standing Strong & Northern Wolfpack

present

IRONSIDE
LAST IN LINE
SUBMISSION
KITO
IMPOUND

Sat 25 July

At the Royalty, Sunderland

(next to Poly)

7.30pm till bust

BLIND MOLE RAT

SPITHEAD

A BENEFIT FOR SHEFFIN SHEFFIELD FREE INFORMATION NETWORK

100% KEROSENE

WED 6TH JULY
HALLAMSHIRE
WEST ST. 8·30 £2·50/£2

A·S·N PRESENT:-

A benefit for Nott's Anti Fascist Action
featuring: THE
CHINEAPPLE PUNX
TRUTH DECAY
combat shock

SAT 25TH APRIL 98

THE OLD GENERAL RadFORD ROad NoTTiNGHAM

£3·00

SAT 23RD MAY 98

zero tolerance

BORN UGLY hatred

THE OLD GENERAL RadFORD ROad NoTTiNGHAM

£3·00

THURSDAY 11th
FRIDAY 12th
SATURDAY 13th JUNE

NoTTiNGHAM
PUNX PICNIC

look out for further details.

NOTTINGHAM

friday 11Th & SaTurday 12th JuNe

THE FUTURE IS OURS

PUNX PICNIC

M RED — PUNK & HARDCORE COLLECTIVE
ADVOCATING THE NON PROFIT PRINCIPLE

SATURDAY 30th JULY AT 4.30pm £2.50

BABY HARP SEAL
TRIBUTE
POLARIS
BROCALI
DECADENCE
WITHIN
SHUTDOWN
BEAU'S COUSIN

TUESDAY 16th AUGUST
ICONOCLAST / BOB TILTON /
COLOURBLIND

THE CITY TAVERN   38 BISHOPGATE ST
BOT FOR FLY POSTIDING   BIRMINGHAM tel 021 643 4394

HOW WE ROCK AND ARMED WITH ANGER
Presents
I IN 12   PA BENEFIT SHOW
WITH
NAILBOMB
IN YOUR FACE HARDCORE
IRONSIDE
BRUTAL HEAVY POWER HARDCORE
at 1 in 12 CLUB CAFE
ALBION STREET
BRADFORD CITY CENTRE
SUNDAY 17th MAY 4.30PM 1992
ONLY A QUID IN!
FIRST BAND ON AT 4.30PM
ALL AGES Veggie/vegan cafe

MOSH!

We know its the same day as FUGAZI.
So why not come over earlier?

HOW WE ROCK AND ARMED WITH ANGER Presents
SUNDAY WORSHIP

CHARITY
BEGINS
AT
HOME.

1 IN 12
PA BENEFIT
SHOW

AFTERNOON SERVICE   WITH

NAILBOMB

IRONSIDE

ALL AGES   Veggie/vegan cafe
ONLY A QUID IN!
1st band on at 4.30pm.
Don't be late   17.5.92

DISCHORD INFERNO PRESENTS
FRIDAY 28TH OF AUGUST
FROM RICHMOND, VIRGINIA

AVAIL

with **ASSERT**
CAMP BLACKFOOT
KILL FOR CHRIST

£4.50 or £4.00 with flyer
doors open 8pm

THE RED EYE
105 Copenhagen St, London, N1 tel: 0171 3874422

Witchfest
real ale camp for the ... it a music from...

Cat
Hip Huggers
Witchknot
Red Monkey
Dominic Waxing Lyrical
Archbishop Kebab

Saturday 19th July '97
1 in 12 Club/Albion St./Bradford
4 pm until midnight £3/£3.50

EPITAFF PRESENTS... GROUND ZERO SIX
MANCHESTER'S TOP POP-PUNK THREE PIECE
GROVER
MELODIC HARDCORE FROM MANCHESTER
ALL BAR NONE

SLOPCORE YANK SELLOUT'S
**FOUR
LETTER
WORD**

SOUTH WALES HARDCORE
**IN
THE
SHIT**

WELLY INC. 1896

AT THE
TRANSPORT
CLUB
GARTH ST, CARDIFF
(NEAR H.M. PRISON)
ON
SATURDAY
23rd MAY
1998
FROM 8pm
'TIL MIDNIGHT
FOR
THREE
QUID
FIRST BAND ON AT 8PM

ALL DAY HARDCORE EVENT
Sat. 1 March 1997

Goober Patrol
SPITE
Four Letter Word
STALINGRAD

Voorhees
GROVER
Cripes
ASSERT

A day of unbridled hardcore and punk fun in the West Country!

The Packhorse, Lawrence Hill, Bristol

4pm till late
£4.50 on the door

Record Stalls ... Any proceeds go to AFA ... Info ring Graham on 0117 9513101

Thursday March 12th

Celebrating the Birthday of Kip

Admission
£1.50

8 till 11

COWBOY KILLERS
FOUR LETTER WORD
IN THE SHIT

AT
THE FROG AND BUCKET
NEWPORT

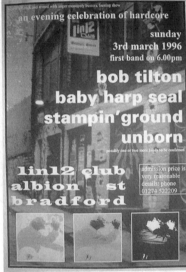

an evening celebration of hardcore

sunday
3rd march 1996
first band on 6.00pm

bob tilton
baby harp seal
stampin' ground
unborn

possibly one or two more bands to be confirmed

1in12 club
albion st
bradford

admission price is
very reasonable
details: phone
01274 522209

TAIN!

AS SEEN
ON
TV!

KENNETH'S TALKING
MACHINE GUN

FRI
23rd
JUN
+
The Bundy Men

AT THE
COACH
HOUSE

STARTS
9PM

£1 A PINT
FREE ENTRY

CITIZEN FISH
SPITHEAD
BENDER

MON 19 JUNE
CITY TAVERN

bishopsgate st - off broad st
a spunky presentation
£3

ALL DAYER WITH...

Blyth Power
Eastfield
SPITHEAD
INTENTION
HOT TORTOISE

P.A.I.N
PROPAGANDA AND INFORMATION OF NATIONS

GENERAL WINTER
PEDIGREE SCUM
Running order to be finalised on the day
BEASTLY

THE MERCAT, BIRMINGHAM
SUNDAY 5th JULY 3 –11pm.

Bradford Street, Behind
Digbeth Coach Station

£3.50 £3 concs

A NIGHT OF BRUTAL HARDCORE

SUN 3RD OCT

PHOBIA
USA
KISMET
(UK)
URKO
BOSTON

£2 DOORS OPEN 8pm

LIVE AT THE INDIAN QUEEN

DOLPHIN LANE BOSTON (01205 360688)

INTRODUCTION

Welcome to, if you'll forgive the conceit, the fourth book in my trilogy about the underground punk and hardcore scene in the UK. After three books dissecting the Eighties – *Burning Britain*, *The Day The Country Died* and *Trapped In A Scene* – it really felt as if that decade had been given the thorough overview it deserved, but it also felt that those books and especially *Trapped In A Scene* which focused on the latter half of the period, left many questions unanswered about what happened next.

Now the Nineties are widely regarded as a soulless vacuum when it comes to punk rock, but – as this book will hopefully demonstrate – they produced many a fine act and more than a few outstanding ones. Some of them went on to genuinely great things, others vanished without a trace. But, as with previous volumes, this book will dig into both the big and the small, the prolific and the one-hit-wonders, the fun-loving jesters and the deadly serious political activists who all played their part in making the punk scene of the Nineties a colourful and eclectic time for alternative music.

Unlike the three books on the Eighties, I didn't have time to include every single band I wanted to, so instead have opted for a good cross-section of all the genres – the best hardcore bands, the best metalcore bands, the best pop-punk bands, the best crusty bands and the best ska-punk bands – with a view to giving the reader an accurate portrayal of the musical and political zeitgeist of Britain's underground punk scene during the Nineties.

It was a desperate and disparate scene, with bands far harder to pigeonhole than previous books. One thing that united most of them was the anger and frustration felt towards not only the government and authorities, that between them ensured the often bleak social conditions that inspired some of these bands to create such intense music as cathartic escapism, but also towards the mainstream music industry, so intent on getting its claws into the best bands the underground had to offer in a bid to tap one of the last fertile veins of latent musical energy.

With the ethics and ideals of punk starting to polarise, not least of all between the drunken punks and the straightedgers, some of that anger was directed towards their peers and their differing lifestyle choices. It all added up to a potent melting pot of passion and fury that gave birth to the bands you're about to meet; armed with anger, they snatched up the glorious baton of UK punk handed down from the Eighties and carried it proudly into a new century.

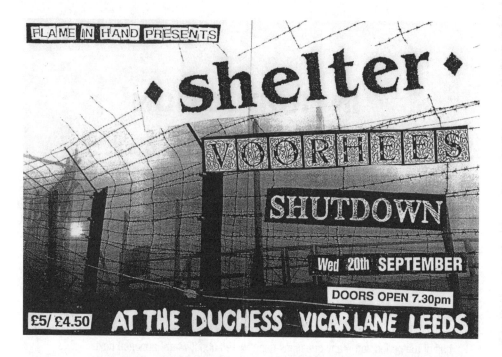

FLAME IN HAND PRESENTS

◆ shelter ◆

VOORHEES

SHUTDOWN

Wed 20th SEPTEMBER

DOORS OPEN 7.30pm

£5/ £4.50 AT THE DUCHESS VICAR LANE LEEDS

FRIDAY 11th JUNE
7 till 11 pm

SATURDAY 12th JUNE
6 till 11 pm

POLICE BASTARD

CRESS
(earth)

NOTTS PUNX PICNIC

PUNK:-
REAL COUNTER CULTURE
OR
JUST ANOTHER POINTLESS
SUBCULTURE.
THE CHOICE IS YOURS!

1999

P.O.A.

HELLKRUSHER
(sweden)

IN THE SHIT

KISMET
(formerly Kismet H·C·)

HUNT SABBATH

£3
(Hopefully) Free Patch and Badge Stall

AT
THE OLD GENERAL,
RADFORD ROAD,
NOTTINGHAM

LEFT FOR DEAD
(hastings)

bastard son of fud
(aberdeenshire)

Plus
Record and T-Shirt Stalls.

£4

Thanks... As always: Jo, Amy, Sam, mum and dad, all my family; Richard, Adam, Iain and all at Cherry Red; Dez; Rid; Welshy; Daren; Rat; Aston Stephens; Rich Corbridge (for the title!); Dewi, Pat, Simon, Dave, Emma, Liam (Fetus Christ) and all at the Combat Academy; Rob Taylor; Big Barr, Silv, Scott, Mobs, Renn and all the old Ledbury punks; Neil 'Veteran' Cox; Sned; Patrick Lawlor; Welly; Pig; Martin Einon and Bristol! Si Godwin and Ade Stokes (but I don't know what for!); Ian Armstrong; Marek Kowalsky; those fuckers in Freebase; Noel Yaxley; Joel McIver; Tom Barry; Louise, Darren, Miranda and all at Terrorizer; all the photographers, especially Naki, Vique, Fraser Scatterty, Scotty, Nick Royles; and, last but not least, all the bands for their time and efforts making this happen, especially those that put up with me face-to-face: Dick Lucas, Lecky and Atko, Sean Forbes, Tony Sylvester, Pete Rose, Paul Catten, Pierre and Ray, the oh-so-patient Ed Wenn... You know who you are. Sorry if anyone's been overlooked – rest assured you've not been forgotten.

In memory of the following, for their unforgettable contribution to the rich musical heritage of UK punk rock:

Dean Uzzell. Always.	**John Peel.**	**Mags.**
Stig.	**Skinny.**	**Andy Crighton.**
Mudgey.	**Jas.**	**Iain 'Corrosive Abuse' Shiner.**

As usual, I should ask that you not write in to complain that your brother's girlfriend's band who had two practices and did a gig down the local youth centre aren't included. I did my best to get all the important – and some not-so-important – bands involved, but sometimes getting an interview out of an old punk band is like pulling teeth. Some of the very first bands I contacted, despite me reminding them and chasing them several times over the next two-and-a-half years, just never found the time to get back to me. Obviously they have people queuing up to talk to them about their illustrious musical career and couldn't fit me into their busy schedules...! Sorry if I sound all twisted up about it – it's because I am.

Every effort has been made to credit photographers correctly wherever possible. If you've not been credited appropriately, forgive me – it probably means I've been given permission to use the image by someone who didn't have the right to give me permission in the first place. Sorry, but shit happens like that in the punk scene.

By the way, it goes without saying that not all opinions expressed in this book are shared by the author. If you're upset by something one of your ex-bandmates has said about you take it up with them, not me.

Ian Glasper, January 2012.

RAPE CRISIS BENEFIT GIG

JAILCELL RECIPES - PLUS: -

A HOST OF THE FINEST ROCK + POP ACTS -

STRENGTH ALONE...

DOWNFALL... IN TOUCH

... WARTORN ... VOORHEES

ORDER OF PLAY TO BE DECIDED ON THE DAY

SATURDAY 1ST FEBRUARY
LEEDS UNI·TARTAN BAR
£2 // £2.50(+ DONATION)
AFTERNOON SHOW!
ALL AGES
1→6 PM

L.U.U. HARDCORE

CHAPTER ONE:
THE NORTHEAST

VOORHEES

Named after Jason Voorhees, the crazed serial killer from the infamous *Friday The 13th* slasher films, Durham's **Voorhees** were unsurprisingly one of the more aggressive UK bands of the Nineties. Their confrontational lyrics and intense live performances quickly won them praise from fans of hardcore punk who were disappointed with the more mainstream direction much of the genre was headed in. You wanted angry? You got it. Wholesale.

"It was what was left over from Steadfast, False Face, Sourface, that kind of thing…mostly kids that were into SXE [straightedge: hardcore kids that didn't drink, smoke or do drugs]; don't forget, [US SXE bands] Youth Of Today and Gorilla Biscuits were still touring at that time," says vocalist Ian 'Lecky' Leck of the Durham scene that spawned the band in 1991. "We grew bored of that scene and wanted to do something a bit different, a bit more like older early Eighties American hardcore; a lot of our friends were all skaters and into that kind of thing. It wasn't a very punk scene at all compared to, say, Newcastle, which was much more to do with crusties and Crass…anarcho punk wasn't very big in Durham!

"I was like Captain SXE for years, that was a big thing for me and I wanted the rest of the world to see that was the right thing to do; I wasn't that pushy about it, but I did sing songs about disliking people that drank and smoked. We just decided we wanted to do something a little different."

Taking their early musical cues from current US hardcore bands of the time like Citizen's Arrest and Born Against, the first line-up of Voorhees saw Lecky joined by guitarist Darrell Hindley and drummer Gary Cousins from False Face and bassist Buzzard (fresh out of prison for GBH!) and played their first gig as Know Your Enemy in 1990. Buzzard quit shortly after ("Because it wasn't very good, to be fair!") and was replaced by David 'Brownie' Brown.

"And then Steadfast broke up about that time, so we decided to get Sean [Readman] in on second guitar," continues Lecky. "Up until then we were still trying to do a SXE sorta thing, a bit like Judge; we didn't have a proper direction and were trying to figure it out, but when Sean joined, at the second practise, he came in and said, 'Right, we're scrapping all those songs and we're doing this style…' and he started playing riffs that sounded like SSD! Really fast like all that early Boston stuff and we all thought, 'Yeah!' A couple of weeks later, he was like, 'I've got a name for the band as well: Voorhees…' and it stuck. He was really into all those horror films of the Eighties, of course, all the video nasties."

The newly named Voorhees played their first gig, with Sourface, at the Durham Rowing Club, in September 1991, before recording the 'Everybody's Good At Something... Except Us!' demo that December and starting to play outside Durham with the likes of Sick Of It All and Rorschach.

"It wasn't supposed to say 'Except us' at the end of the title," reveals Lecky. "The front cover had this still from the *Henry, Portrait Of A Serial Killer* film, of this woman with a Coke bottle stuck in her face and Sean was like, 'Let's call it 'Everybody's Good At Something!' So I went and made the demo covers and stuck 'Except Us' on the end of it... He wasn't happy at the time, he thought I'd totally spoiled what it was meant to mean. But that was always the thing with me and Sean, we had very different ideas. In the early days, just before shows, I'm positive he used to annoy me and wind me up deliberately just to get me angry so I was fired up onstage...

"Anyway, we did it at a community studio in Hartlepool, through the music course I was doing for college because I'd wanted to be a sound engineer. After a few weeks doing this intensive training, I had to record a band to demonstrate what I'd learnt and Voorhees were ready to record at that point. So that was our first demo and my first go at sound engineering. I'm quite proud of it, even though everyone had a go at the desk and every [volume] slide ended up right at the top; everyone wanted to be as loud as possible!"

The band's next recording was another freebie too, when they won two days' recording time at Northern Studios in Consett. Bassist Brownie departed the band just days before they went into the studio ("He vanished off into the rave world and I've never seen or spoken to him since...") so Sean had to play bass *and* guitar during the session and reluctantly covered bass duties while gigging too, until Paul Rugman-Jones, also from Steadfast, stepped into the breach.

"The rehearsal room we used was at the back end of this youth centre, where we used to put on shows, called Fowler's Yard," explains Lecky. "Durham Arts Council had a bit of money left over at the end of year and needed to spend their budget, so they got all the bands who rehearsed there, about 15 in all, to put their names in a hat and they drew two or three winners out to have some free recording time there. Our name just came out the hat; we got lucky for once!"

Lecky moved down to Bradford soon after the recording and it was Bradford-based label Armed With Anger (now *there*'s a good name for a book!) that released it as the 'Violent' EP in April 1993.

"Richard Corbridge from AWA had seen us playing and asked us to do something before I'd even moved down there," reckons Lecky, "so a record was already on the cards. I kinda sorted that out by myself, to do a record with Rich and then told the rest of the band – which didn't sit well with Sean, who wanted to do our own record, but I talked him round to the idea in the end.

"With Steadfast we did the whole record deal thing with Alan [Woods, of First Strike Records] and went down and signed a contract with him, which was really bizarre for a little record label like that, saying he had the rights to us for five years or something equally ridiculous – there was even a clause in there about potential markets on the moon. Seriously. We didn't have a clue about how record labels worked back then, but the fact that he was putting out the Chain Of Strength record in the UK was a big thing for us at the time. And because nothing came of that, and he messed us about for so long, that put Sean off working with other people, I think..."

Voorhees, by Naki

Voorhees, by Naki, Duchess Of York

Voorhees, pic by Naki

Living up to its name, the 'Violent' EP was 10 tracks of pure – ultra-raw – Boston hardcore worship and cut through the band's peers of the time, most of them wallowing in the emerging emocore scene and metaphorically beating themselves up over ex-girlfriends, like a bloody machete through buttered brains. Darrell left for art college after a short UK tour supporting Slapshot and then Gary left after the band recorded 'I'll Survive' and 'Tied Down' for a Negative Approach tribute CD on Canadian label Dysgusher. In true underground punk label fashion, it never came out and the recordings languished unreleased for five years until the project was finally realised by Ugly Pop Records. The line-up stabilised again, though, when 15 year-old Michael Gillham from Sourface joined on drums and Graeme Nicholls became the new lead guitarist and Voorhees recorded their debut album, 'Spilling Blood Without Reason', at Studio 64 in Middlesbrough with Matthew Burke.

"A lot of people say it was the best Voorhees record, but when I listen to it, it seems like there's an awful lot of filler on there," admits Lecky. "I still really like the record, but I know what songs were written and when and how they were written… The idea was, because of the whole *Friday The 13th* thing, we wanted 13 songs on each side of the record, so we had to write 26 songs! We had about 15 or 16 good songs just before we went into the studio and we had to write another 10 and at least six or seven of them were just filler… I'd go to practise and we'd be doing all these cover songs by Negative Approach and Negative FX or whatever and I'd say, 'Right, instead of covering it, let's write a song in that style…' So a lot of it was stolen riffs, with just enough changes to make it our own! Or we'd use a riff in one song and its rhythm in another…whatever it took to get the songs ready in time."

August 1994 saw the band heading over to Europe for the first time to promote the album, a trip that didn't quite go according to plan. "We were all set to go; everyone had booked time off work, we'd sorted out the van hire – Paul had actually sold his motorbike to raise the money for the van – and then Bruno, who'd booked it all, rang us up literally two days before and said that [the other band on the tour] Selfish [from Finland] couldn't do it – did we still want to go? And we said we did, of course, so he said he'd sort out another band to do it instead, which was the drummer from Selfish's other band, Force Macabra.

"He turned up to the first show with his girlfriend, but his band didn't show, so he travelled with us in our van, which was already totally cramped anyway, so that was a bit of a nightmare and then they didn't show up for the next gig either, or the next…and as the tour went on, more and more gigs were getting cancelled. We were supposed to be out there for three-and-a-half weeks, but we only did two. It was quite surprising how organised the squats were there, though; I'd never seen anything like it. In Potsdam, the *whole street* was squatted and on the roof over the road from the venue was a big machine gun on a tripod and everything… I don't even know if they had ammunition for it, or if it even worked, but it looked pretty scary! And there were random plastic letters, about three feet high, that had probably been stolen from the fronts of other buildings that spelled out 'Punks!' Which was pretty cool."

A Peel session was recorded in early 1995, which Lecky doesn't hold much love for ("There wasn't any encouragement or interaction from the engineers, it was just another job for them, so it didn't end up sounding great…"). The same set of songs were re-recorded at Pots'n'Pans in Bradford for a split 7-inch with Stalingrad on Lecky's own Thinking Smart Records.

Early the following year, to coincide with the release of the 'Smiling At Death' discography CD on Grand Theft Audio, Voorhees made it over to North America for their first tour there, with none other than Hatebreed (nowadays one of the biggest hardcore bands in the world) in support. Predictably enough, the trip, organised by Neil Robinson who ran Tribal War Records and sang for Nausea, was an eventful one, from the very first gig in Connecticut…

"We were there playing and some guy jumped up on stage and sat down behind the monitors, which wasn't something I was familiar with 'cos no-one ever did it in England," recalls Lecky. "He sat there with his back to me staring out at the crowd and it wasn't a very big stage, so I kicked him in the arse and told him to move. He just looked at me and looked away, so we started the next song and I jumped in the air and landed on him and he jumped down off the stage and stood there staring at me for the rest of the set. We finished the last song and I turned around to put the mic back on the mic stand; as I turned around he got onstage behind me and grabbed me round the throat…

"Next thing I know, our bass player Paul tried to jump in between us – he still had his bass guitar on and all three of us tripped over the monitors and fell off the stage! And as we hit the floor all the lights went out, so it was pitch black, all three of us swinging fists and kicking each other… When the lights came on – probably 10 seconds later, but it felt like two minutes – Paul had me pinned to the stage by my throat, about to punch me in the face, with my footprint on the side of his head – and the guy who had started it all was nowhere to be seen! But everyone was going around breaking things and Sean got into a fight with someone and cut his arm; it was a really strange night.

"Someone told us the guy was Earth Crisis's tour manager, but I don't know… He came up to me 10 minutes later and threatened me, told me he was going to shoot me and I just laughed in his face and told him to go and get his fucking gun then. The guys from Hatebreed all knew him, he sang for Path Of Resistance or something, but they were quite neutral about it and tried to calm it all down…"

Fisticuffs withstanding, the tour was a great success, but upon their return to the UK Michael and Sean left, throwing the Voorhees line-up into disarray again. "Yeah, it was a good tour, all the gigs went pretty well and we kinda broke even," agrees Lecky. "But you know how it is when you play with all these bands and trade records with them; they all go into a box in the back of the van. We got back to New York and went to separate them all out and Michael had decided he wanted one of everything, even if there wasn't enough copies of them to go round and he and Sean got into an argument over a Mayday 7-inch – Sean ended up slapping him across the face and Michael stormed out.

"He came back a few minutes later and he was the calmest I'd ever seen him, saying, 'I think I needed that, that's sorted me out, has that!' And knowing what Michael's like, that was worrying and I was convinced he'd be slitting our throats in our sleep, so I slept with one eye open that night!

"But Michael had already told us he was leaving the band about halfway through the tour anyway – he'd had enough by that point – and a few weeks after we got back, Sean told me he was as well; he said he'd taken the band as far as he wanted to, so he was done too."

Former Ironside vocalist Richard 'Arms' Armitage took over from Sean on guitar and Michael was replaced behind the kit by Gareth Pugh. Graeme then announced that he was also leaving, to relocate to San Francisco (where he now plays for We Be The Echo) and he was replaced by James 'Atko' Atkinson, a regular customer at Ian's skate shop.

"Lecky gave me a copy of 'Spilling Blood…' to learn the songs," recalls Atko. "I looked at the back cover and there was a picture of all these blokes in Newcastle United shirts and

I thought, 'Fuckin' hell, these guys look like a right bunch...!' But when I got to the first practise, there was only Lecky from that first record I recognised, because Paul had just moved down to Matlock, so I was quite relieved in that respect. If you look at Sean in that picture and imagine being 16 years old and having never met him, he looks a complete psycho! It was completely different to anything I'd ever experienced anyway...

"They gave me the 'Smiling At Death' CD and a list of songs to learn and told me there was a European tour booked. My dad wanted to meet them, so they all had to come down and introduce themselves to him. But he thought they were alright and that was the easiest thing... I'm not sure what they said to him, but he seemed completely happy after they'd left!"

The European tour got cancelled at the eleventh hour, though, due to almost inevitable van problems (the bane of any struggling band's 'career') and Atko made his live debut in Bristol instead. "Like I said, they gave me this list of songs to learn and, at that first gig, the setlist was three sheets of A4 paper taped together," he laughs. "About 30 songs or something, which was pretty daunting, a lot to take in. I didn't know what to expect; it was with Stalingrad and Rich [from Stalingrad] ran across the bar and knocked everyone's drinks everywhere, scared the shit out of everyone... That was an eye-opener; he was so calm and well-spoken in the van on the way down and then he turned into this animal when they played."

The line-up shuffles continued unabated as well; Gareth was displaced by "local student Chris", who himself only managed two gigs (two good ones though: supporting Sick Of It All in Bradford and Agnostic Front in London) before having to return to Greece to do national service. Michael Gillham returned temporarily to undertake the band's second US tour; this time booked by Ben from Drop Dead and Will from Chainsaw Safety Records, it saw Voorhees sharing stages with the likes of Drop Dead, Charles Bronson, Devoid Of Faith and Kill Your Idols. They also took time out to record the (disappointingly synthetic-sounding) 'Fireproof' EP for Chainsaw Safety at Technical Ecstasy Studios in New Jersey, although Lecky fell ill just before the session and had to record his vocals once back in the UK.

Once home, though, Paul moved to London to become an environmental biologist and was replaced by Andrew 'Wrighty' Wright, another ex-Ironside member who had also served time in Unborn, while Michael's place was eventually filled by David Allen from Vengeance Of Gaia. Work began on the '13' album, which was released as a collaboration between Armed With Anger and Californian label Six Weeks. Recorded and mixed at Low Fold Studios, Lancaster, between August 1998 and April 1999, it was admittedly a departure from the traditional Voorhees style but was still a relentlessly intense barrage of noise, let down somewhat by a horrible-sounding triggered snare drum.

It was also the only record that Wrighty played on; he was asked to leave the band soon after due to the heroin addiction that would sadly be the death of him in 2009. His replacement was Steve Stewart, who joined just in time to be credited with playing bass on the split LP the band did with Devoid Of Faith for Dutch label, Coalition, even though Atko played bass as well as guitar on that recording. With Steve in the band, the line-up settled down for a while and this incarnation of the band toured the US in 1999 with Kill Your Idols, the Nerve Agents and the Explosion, before headlining yet another lengthy European jaunt in 2000. By this time Lecky was also fronting Liverpool metallic SXE band Withdrawn as well.

The band became extremely prolific on the recording front as well, issuing split 7-inchs with Radio Alice on Hermit Records, Insult on Balowski Records and Kill Your Idols on Indecision

Records, as well as their own 'Bookburner' 7-inch on THD, a split MCD with Out Cold on Blackfish Records (reissued by Deranged on 12-inch vinyl a year later) and the final Voorhees album, 'Crystal Lake's Legacy'. The last album was released in 2001, in time for the band's final US tour and they played their last show at New York venue ABC No Rio that October.

"We got home after that tour and I was a few weeks later coming home than the rest of the band because I'd stayed over to go on a road trip with my girlfriend, but I *was* expecting to start rehearsing and gigging again," explains Lecky, of the band's unexpected disintegration. "I got a call from Arms saying he wasn't into it any more and he wanted to do something that was more his thing. Even though we'd done two albums and all these splits and 7-inchs and everything with him, whenever we played live the set was all the early stuff, off the first album, because that was what people seemed to want to hear. Arms didn't want to do that any more; he wanted to play material that was more his and I thought, 'Fair enough, we'll get a new guitar player...'

"So I went into work the next day; we shared the space with Out Of Step Records and Steve owned Out Of Step and James worked in Wisdom and I was like, 'So, Arms has quit the band then...' And the next thing, Steve came over and went, 'So it's over then, yeah?' And I was like, 'What? We'll get another guitarist.' And he told me he didn't want to do it any more either..."

"It was weird for me," adds Atko, "because Arms was in the band before me and he'd left and I didn't feel very comfortable with carrying on without him. It was a weird old time; I didn't really know how to deal with the situation, having never been there with a band before, but I could tell that Lecky really wasn't into it the same way he had been when I'd first joined."

"No, I wasn't," admits Lecky. "If you look at those Voorhees records, the first LP was *my* record... I did the layout for it and everything. I wasn't really into the songs on '13'; Arms had taken much more control. I think I only wrote one song on that, I definitely took a back seat. I used to book every single show we played... I was a control freak at the beginning, to be honest; I didn't want to delegate because I didn't trust anyone else to do anything."

Everyone from Voorhees – except Lecky – then started up the Horror with Andy from Imbalance singing ("It stuck in my throat for a long time because it felt like I'd been kicked out my own band," says Lecky candidly), leaving Lecky to eventually start Walk The Plank with Dave Fergusson from Withdrawn on drums. He also played with Cockfight and Meatlocker.

However, like their celluloid namesake, Voorhees did rise from the dead to wreak havoc again on more than one occasion. The first was in October 2004 when the 'Spilling Blood...' line-up (excepting Paul, who lives and works in California and was replaced by Steve Stewart) reunited for the 'Night Of The Living Dead At Sea' gig, booked by SSS vocalist Foxy and held on a Mersey River ferryboat.

A further reunion occurred during April 2010, to coincide with Atko's label Grot Records reissuing 'Spilling Blood Without Reason', although Mother Earth conspired to prevent that line-up reuniting again when the eruption of an Icelandic volcano grounded all flights from the US to the UK, meaning Graeme and Paul couldn't make it over. Voorhees played the two shows – one in Leeds and one in Amsterdam – as a four-piece, with Sam Layzell, from Lecky's latest band, SickfuckinO, on bass.

"Sam's a great bass player and he learnt 30 or 40 songs in two days, which wasn't an easy thing to do because so many of those songs have similar rhythms and start at the same place on the neck, but I don't think we played as well as we would have done if we'd got everyone over for the gig," reckons Lecky. "They were great shows, though; Amsterdam was good, but Leeds was great. We had some of the best UK bands around at the time on with us: the Horror, Deal With It, Torn Apart, Mob Rules, Nowhere Fast…it was Brain Dead's last show as well, which helped pull a few more people out of the woodwork.

"There were people there I hadn't seen in years, people who came down from Durham and all sorts, but the majority of the crowd were young kids who'd never seen the band before, which was a bit weird for me. I always thought that we'd just be forgotten once we'd split!"

Of the other members, Atko remains heavily involved in music, still running Grot Records and playing guitar for not only the Horror, with Arms, Steve and Dave and Rot In Hell, with Nate from xCanaanx and Mark from Area Effect, but also for retro-rockers Gentlemen's Pistols alongside Bill Steer from Carcass. Sean Redman is the guitarist in punk tribute band Mid Life Crisis, Gareth Pugh is drummer in Lowlife UK, Michael Gillham drums for Pellethead and Drunk In Hell, while Darrell Hindley is a professional model painter and Gary Cousins is a police officer. And the whereabouts of David Brown are still unknown!

"We were playing something that wasn't really played by anyone else in the UK at that time," reckons Lecky. "Every other band sounded completely different to us. They were either emocore or metalcore – those two genres were king back then – so we never had an instant fanbase. It was definitely different at the time. The guys from Kill Your Idols actually told us that when Gary took out an ad to start *their* band, he listed Voorhees as one of the bands he wanted them to sound like!

"The lyrics were all about different forms of violence," he concludes. "Everything from being angry at someone and wanting to hurt them, to general violence in the world, like wars and shit. So it was always pretty confrontational, whichever way you looked at it…and I suppose we were a bit more aggressive than most bands of the time. Sean was always snarling when we played live; he was always leaning over the crowd, looking like, 'Anyone come near me, they'll get their head ripped off…' And I'd be leaping around kicking people in the face 'by accident'!

"But it's weird the things people think they remember you doing. Someone came up to me and said, 'I saw Voorhees once and you pulled some guy out of the crowd and beat the shit out of him with the microphone and then threw him back in…' And I'm like, 'What? I've never done that to anybody! I'm sorry to spoil your story, but I didn't.' There were a lot of other instances of random violence against audience members, though, but *most of the time* we were provoked!"

SELECT DISCOGRAPHY:

7-inch:

'Violent' (Armed With Anger, 1993)

'Everybody's Good At Something…Except Us!' (Armed With Anger, 1994) – *flexidisc*

'There's Only One Kevin Keegan' (Thinking Smart, 1995) – *split with Stalingrad*

'What You See Is What You Get' (Crust, 1997)

'Fireproof' (Chainsaw Safety, 1998)

'The World Wanted You Dead' (Indecision, 2000) – *split with Kill Your Idols*

'Bookburner' (THD, 2000)

'DYS' (Balowski, 2000) – *split with Insult*

'Drug Cop' (Hermit, 2004) – *split with Radio Alice*

12-inch:
'Everything You Believed In Was A Lie' (Deranged, 2001) – *split with Out Cold*

LPs:
'Spilling Blood Without Reason' (Armed With Anger, 1994)
'13' (Armed With Anger/Six Weeks, 1998)
'Network Of Friends # 5' (Coalition/Gloom, 1999) – *split with Devoid Of Faith*
'Crystal Lake's Legacy' (Six Weeks, 2001)

AT A GLANCE:
The 'Smiling At Death' CD (Grand Theft Audio, 1996) compiled most of the band's early recordings, while 'The Final Chapter' CD (Violent Change, July 2008) compiles material from the splits and compilation appearances.

IRONSIDE

Bradford's **Ironside** assured their place in the annals of hardcore history with their 1993 EP 'Fragments Of The Last Judgement'. This particularly potent four-tracker helped inform much of the metallic and SXE hardcore that followed in its wake and had an evil enough vibe to get them welcomed with open arms – albeit posthumously – into hardcore's clandestine 'Holy Terror' sub-genre, where they will forever lurk alongside the likes of Integrity, Mayday and Rot In Hell (the latter of whom tellingly covered Ironside's lurching 'Skincrawl' to great effect).

Formed in Bradford in 1992, the band, consisting of aforementioned vocalist Richard 'Arms' Armitage, drummer Nick Royles, bassist Jase Fox (previously in Step One) and guitarists Tom Chapman and Andrew 'Wrighty' Wright, coalesced around the legendary 1 In 12 Club in Albion Street (which has been ran autonomously by its members, an anarchist collective, since 1988) and were an extension of the typically grimy UK take on America's interrelated SXE, skateboarding and hardcore scenes.

"I guess Ironside would never have come together if the reformed Sore Throat and In Touch had not collapsed," begins Nick. "Sore Throat planned to release an EP and played one comeback gig at the 1 In 12 and then imploded. The other guys from In Touch split the band up to revamp another previous band we'd all been in, Nailbomb. In essence I was already doing *my* 'heavier' band with In Touch, which had come back together with the original line-up that split in late '88. Previously that band had been in a Straight Ahead/early Youth Of Today style; the revamped version in 1991 was playing that early-Nineties Victory Records style a la Confront, Face Value, Even Score and Integrity.

"The guys that reformed Nailbomb with the other previous members, Rich from Armed With Anger Records and Rich Militia from Sore Throat, pursued a heavier, more metallic direction like Breakdown, Sheer Terror and Cro-Mags. As I was left without a band, I contacted Richard and we talked about doing something heavy too. We grabbed scene locals Wrighty and Jase, who we'd also known for years. Jase was in the last line-up of No Way Out, which split in 1990 and Wrighty had built up some notoriety with his zine, *Hate Edge*. The last addition was a recent newcomer to the northern scene, Tom, who had moved up from the south to study in Leeds.

"To us, a lot of that late-Eighties wave of generic hardcore had grown stale. It just didn't move us any more and we wanted to take it in a heavier direction. So, similarly to Nailbomb, we also pursued a Breakdown/Cro-Mags path; we actually wanted to be like Chorus or Judge, but we were taking our first tentative steps. We struggled to come up with a name; Jase had a whole list of band names and the only one I can remember was Envocation. Rich wanted to call it Ironweed, but when we were discussing band names in the 1 In 12 cafe I came up with Ironside rather than Ironweed and we thankfully went for that instead.

"A lot of our early-Nineties scene had come together through the hardcore punk skate scene; in fact the two previous bands No Way Out and In Touch were by accident both full-on skate bands with all members skating. The former vocalist of No Way Out, Percy, went on to run the UK's highly respected *Document Skateboard* magazine. Bradford had become the de facto skate capital of West Yorkshire and in the end was where we virtually all ended up living. A grim, northern city with some great skate spots and a cool DIY anarcho space in the 1 In 12 Club.

"At the start of Ironside, Rich and I were both writing material for the band, though Rich was the main songwriter. The first line-up actually recorded our first demo after being together for three weeks. It was all a little rushed and somewhat flawed and, while we thought we were heavy and slow, the music was actually quite fast and very amateurish. We recorded at a practice space that doubled up as a recording studio, across the road from the 1 In 12, where we had originally practiced, but we moved over to these studios and found ourselves sharing the space with [more metal] bands like Chorus Of Ruin, My Dying Bride and Solstice."

"Musically I wanted to stay away from the weaker-sounding straightedge stuff coming out of the US at the time," adds Rich, "and initially took my songwriting influence from Breakdown and Raw Deal, as well as my favourite older bands like Negative Approach. We played slow and heavy and as my voice was pretty deep we got a lot of flattering Sheer Terror comparisons. Once the Clevo [Cleveland] scene started up, we really took on the Integrity influence that defined us, particularly after they did 'Darkness' for that first 'Only The Strong' compilation [Victory Records, 1990].

"Lyrically, I steered clear of straightedge and wrote what now appear to be some self-deprecating morbid lyrics about being messed up that I will no doubt one day regret! There were a lot of people around hardcore in Bradford in the late Eighties and early Nineties. Bradford always had metal fans and after the Cro-Mags played a metalfest with Kreator in Leeds around Christmas 1987 a lot of them crossed over too. When Youth Of Today and Gorilla Biscuits toured here, we rented vans and followed them around the country, meeting the lads who made up the scenes from Newcastle, Liverpool and London for the first time. The 1 In 12 Club helped nurture the scene by providing regular gigs, but there weren't any bands or events of real note, just a bunch of guys that went to gigs and hung out skateboarding. Lots of camo pants, limited edition coloured vinyl 7-inchs, shaved heads and a bit too much testosterone!"

After making their live debut supporting Sick Of It All at the 1 In 12 in March 1992 ("It was their first UK tour and was a big deal for everyone," recalls Rich), bassist Jase left ("He was a committed communist and wasn't happy that we were intending to play with Agnostic Front…!") and was replaced by Andrew 'Bez' Berry, formerly of No Way Out and In Touch, who was also in Nailbomb. He was with the band for several months and numerous shows before deciding he wanted to concentrate on Nailbomb; he was replaced by Doug Dalziel, who relocated from Scotland to join the band.

"There wasn't enough politics in straightedge for me, other than Man Lifting Banner [Dutch 'edgers on Crucial Response Records], at the time," comments Jase, of his departure from Ironside. "Yes, no doubt the easiest pigeonhole for people to put me in back then was 'communist', but I'm a socialist and funnily enough still straightedge and vegetarian to this day. It really was 'true 'til death' with me…which was, I guess, one of the reasons I quit.

"I didn't feel that my values of 'politics' and 'edge' sat well in Ironside after I played bass on the band's first demo, although musically it was exactly where I wanted to be, while totally in awe of people like Breakdown, Nausea and the NYHC revival of the early Nineties…"

Ironside then recorded their second demo, 'Neutered Innocence', at In A City Studios, which they released as a 'cassingle' ("They were all the rage at the time," points out Nick. "I wish we'd allowed Stormstrike to reissue it on vinyl when they offered – but we declined!") and were soon invited to play the first leper festival in Belgium (held back then at the supremely scuzzy Vort'n'Vis venue, it's now an important annual staple of the international hardcore calendar).

"Nick was in touch with people in the Belgian straightedge scene, who asked us to play that first leper fest," Rich adds, of their initial foray on the mainland. "We took our full backline over on the ferry, with Lecky from Voorhees driving our van, plus some mates like Simon Kelly from Liverpool. We went to an outdoor swimming pool when we got to Ieper, where Lecky inevitably got into a scrap with some locals. The Belgians were big into the second wave of East Coast US straightedge bands; they wore stuff like brightly coloured band shirts and hoodies, so we looked a bit different to them and blew all their crummy bands away when we played.

"I introduced us on stage by saying, 'We're a straightedge band from England…does anyone have a problem with that?' It was a joke, but there was still silence until we started playing. People in Belgium still mention this to me even now, which gives you some insight into Belgians and their hardcore scene! I have a T-shirt somewhere with the full line-up of that festival on it, but I know there weren't many bands on that we had heard of or wanted to watch. The scene there seemed a lot younger and cleaner than we were used to… Kelly still mentions seeing kids staying overnight there who were getting into their pyjamas after the gig!"

A third recording followed upon their return, a three-track effort that saw them further defining their virulent sound. "The quality of that recording is quite poor," admits Nick. "But I think you can really see some of our influences emerging more on there than on, say, 'Neutered…' You can easily pigeonhole those songs: 'Modern Myth' is essentially Integrity, 'Forked Tongue' is Ringworm and 'Suffocation' is Raid. I would say that 'Modern Myth' and

Ironside by Tom Chapman

Ironside, Tom Chapman at the 1 In 12 club   Ironside, Rich Armitage at the 1 In 12

BASEMENT SHOW

THE RETURN OF....

SORICIDE

HARDHITTING CLEVELAND HARDCORE

IRONSIDE

WEST YORKSHIRE STRAIGHT EDGE

KITO

GROOVE HARDCORE

SATURDAY 13th JUNE 8.00PM

AT: JASE'S PLACE
51 ROYAL PARK TERRACE
LEEDS

(10 mins from Uni, 2 mins from Hyde Park Cinema).

FREE ALL AGES SHOW

'Suffocation' were most representative of us at that time; 'Forked Tongue' really was a bit of an anomaly, as we were so blown away by the Ringworm demo which, to us, raged like a Slayer meets Cro-Mags mid-paced hybrid. We *were* tempted by that style and pace, but opted for slowness..."

"Yeah, we were getting more and more 'Clevo', with a heavier, pounding sound and an underlaid whispering vocal track," agrees Rich. "'Suffocation' ended up on a 1 In 12 compilation LP [1995's 'Endless Struggle – The Worst Of The 1 in 12 Club Vol 12/13'] and was the nearest I got to writing straightedge lyrics. And obviously within a year of writing an anti-smoking song, I started smoking..."

By the time Ironside recorded the aforementioned 'Fragments Of The Last Judgement' 7-inch for Darlington label Subjugation, they were reaching their musical peak and the four songs on that EP are the most crushingly claustrophobic the band ever wrote, oozing with murderous intent and a slow-burning tension. As debut singles go, it doesn't get much better than this.

Says Rich: "Yeah, they *are* the four best Ironside songs, I think, and I can clearly remember writing them sitting in a damp and dingy Bradford house shared with Doug, Nick and Lecky, listening to Danzig and Slayer. The Integrity influence was totally in evidence and the guitars sound really thick and totally dominate the mix. I still think the riffs are pretty good too, although there are probably too many parts in 'Skincrawl', making the song sound a bit convoluted. The lyrics bear no mention of the usual straightedge clichés which I think prevents it sounding too dated, although the front cover had a picture cut from the London Dungeon guidebook of some guy nailed to an X!

"A few months after it came out, Ian from Subjugation, who I am still mates with, asked us to put a cover together for some spare copies of the vinyl. We drew the most childish cartoon representations of ourselves imaginable – Doug's character was actually called 'Bitchfinder General' – and sent them off, but never saw them again. What I wouldn't give...

"We often played with touring US bands at venues like Bradford Queens Hall or Planet X in Liverpool," continues Rich, of the unfortunately short period when the band were at their prime. "The best gigs for me were at the 1 In 12 and in rooms above pubs in places like Sunderland with other northern UK hardcore bands like Voorhees, Kito, Solace, Wartorn and Last In Line. Fabric and Understand from down south played a bit too. I can't recall much competition between bands and scenes at first, just excitement that there were enough UK bands that could play together without relying on US touring bands to justify someone putting on a gig. I think we only played London once, though, at the George Robey; there was a catfight during our set, which we stopped playing to watch..."

Tom's studies led him to France, so Rich started playing guitar as well as singing, which leeched some intensity from the band's live shows. Then Wrighty left to go travelling and was replaced by Jim Rushby (formerly with the short-lived Ambush) and Tom returned to England and rejoined. However, when the band started to move in a more doom-metal direction, Nick decided to leave and Tom followed soon after.

"I don't think me leaving was really a big deal, but we *had* reached a musical crisis point," explains Nick. "Rich and Doug brought some new material into the practice room one day and it was just like Cathedral...but the bouncy 'Hey, Yeahhhh!' Cathedral and not the oppressive slow style of their earlier material. Surprised by this turn of events, Tom and I couldn't see how this new stuff was going to sit alongside the songs from the EP and, from that ill-fated practice onwards, we had a long spell of not writing anything, a real stalemate.

"Rich and Doug had clear ideas where they wanted to take Ironside – out of the hardcore scene and into the metal scene – while Tom and I preferred to be in the hardcore scene playing metal, but were happy to play metal gigs as well. In fact, one of our last gigs together before the 1 In 12 festival that marked my departure was with Peaceville's Anathema."

Rich, Doug and Jim had no choice but to reinvent the band, recruiting new members from the Bradford metal scene for a second 7-inch – 1994's 'Damn Your Blooded Eyes' for German label Stormstrike – which gave a huge nod to the ponderous riffage of Candlemass and the oppressive atmospherics of early Black Sabbath. "Yeah, we got a full-on metal guy on drums called Shaun Steels," smiles Rich. "I'm not making this up, but one month we were a hardcore band, the next we had a drummer who had never heard a hardcore record, regularly wore a cape and looked like Zorro! And he had double bass drums with 'Iron' screened on one and 'Side' on the other!

"We also got another metal guy on guitar called Clive Hughes; he worked nights at Morrison's in Bradford, so I don't think we ever saw him fully awake. He had a straggly Misfits devil-lock, wore a waistcoat over black long-sleeve shirts with unreadable logos on them and 'played' a BC Rich…just check the photo on the back of the second 7-inch if you don't believe any of this.

"We recorded in early '94, at Academy Studios in Dewsbury where all the Peaceville doom bands like My Dying Bride and Anathema had recorded; Clive didn't play on the record, which was probably for the best. Doom metal generally sounds pretty timeless and I think it holds up within the narrow confines of the sound we were going for. The cover looked suitably grim too.

"The song 'A Woman' was named in tribute to DRI's 'A Coffin' and most people couldn't work out what speed to play it at. We rented a practice room, played a few metal club gigs but mostly hung around boozing in our dilapidated house, which got wrecked every weekend. Our practice room opened out onto a street round the corner from the 1 In 12 and one night a huge drunken tramp kicked the door open, staggered in and told us to play a song for him. He really was intimidating, like I imagine one of those hobo serial killers that ride the rails in the Midwest to be – so after some feeble attempts at telling him we weren't that kind of band and asking him to leave, we played a song and he eventually walked out!"

The summer of 1994 saw the band play a 20-date European tour with US band Chorus Of Disapproval ("It was quite a mismatch, with us boozing and listening to Black Sabbath…a lot of the gigs drew a big SXE crowd that we laid into!") and the last show of that tour, in Ieper, fittingly enough, turned out to be the last Ironside ever played, although the various members went on to populate many important UKHC bands in its wake.

"We split when we got back from Europe. We had a couple of practices – in a church hall where the metal drummer guy had to pick up the keys from the vicar! – and then jacked it in. Believe me, it was the right thing to do. Shaun had apparently been asked to try out for [the hugely successful] Paradise Lost a couple of weeks before, but in an unrivalled display of poor judgement turned them down to stay in Ironside. I then played guitar in Voorhees and am now in the Horror [playing early Eighties-influenced hardcore]. Nick did Unborn, Cracked Cop Skulls and Unquiet Grave and is currently playing with Howl. Wrighty was in Deputy Spade, Blood Simple, Unborn and Voorhees, but unfortunately died in 2009.

Tom played in emo ladyboys Baby Harp Seal, moved to Berlin in 1995 and played in lots of hardcore bands like Battle Royale, Cold War and Miozan [he's relocated back to the UK now and is playing with Geoffrey OiCott!] Jim and Doug moved to Nottingham in 1995 and started Iron Monkey; Jim also played in Hard To Swallow and is now in Geriatric Unit, while Doug also did Dukes Of Nothing. Shaun Steels played drums in Solstice, My Dying Bride and other northern doom-metal bands and Clive Hughes became a DJ and still plays heavy music.

"So, Ironside were in existence for just two years and released just two 7-inchs, but they certainly captured the imagination of the European SXE scene and have proved reluctantly influential in underground circles ever since."

Rich deprecatingly says he would like the band to be remembered as "a reasonable facsimile of the Nineties Clevo metallic hardcore sound, that went strangely wrong," before adding: "for me, the thing with straightedge back then and probably now, is that it provides an instant rent-a-scene because those people will enthusiastically listen to any old shit as long as the band is straightedge. It helped create a buzz around the band very quickly.

"I know it was and imagine it still is, important to Nick, but the rest of us fell off the wagon within a year or two of starting the band. There was a very active straightedge scene in Europe but not much doing in the UK when we started, but it is easy to trace the emergence of the Belgian H8000 straightedge metal bands following the first Ironside gig there, so I think we moved things on from the typical '88' ['old school'] sound. We weren't the first hardcore band to play metal, but there weren't many other hardcore bands playing as slow and heavy as we were, with such deep vocals, at the time."

"I do think we played a part in bringing that really heavy slow sound to the European hardcore scene," adds Nick. "But perhaps, while we *thought* we were fresh at the time, we were really just drawing on all the metallic hardcore punk and anarcho-crust metal that not only came out of the UK in the mid to late Eighties but was worldwide too. There must be something in that because, at the time, UK and US zine reviewers compared Ironside to Amebix, Bolt Thrower and Antisect, as well as all the usual suspects.

"To a degree we were bemused, but I guess you don't always come out sounding how you either think or plan to sound like. And there's nothing wrong with those comparisons; it's just a recognition of the cycles within the hardcore punk scene and the scene in the Nineties eventually became particularly diverse and multifaceted…"

SELECT DISCOGRAPHY:

7-inch:
'Fragments Of The Last Judgement' (Subjugation, 1993)
'Damn Your Blooded Eyes' (Stormstrike, 1994)

AT A GLANCE:
The 1995 'Ecstatic Ritual' CD on Lifeforce compiles most of the Ironside recordings… but good luck trying to track down a copy!

STALINGRAD

Dark. Brutal. Heavy. Fascinating. All adjectives that could quite rightly be attached to **Stalingrad**, a Bradford band that mashed up hardcore, punk and metal and then gave it their own uniquely nasty twist, sometimes with spectacular results. They were pretty damn exciting live as well and, with the benefit of hindsight, could also have been dubbed 'the UK's answer to Integrity'.

"I met Rich [vocals], Mik [drums] and Justin [bass] around '92 or '93," recalls guitarist Russ Schnell. "They had moved over to Bradford from Southport with a few other mates and we found that we had a shared take on hardcore, punk and music in general; we also used to spend a lot of time getting wasted together on shit homebrew and other dubious substances and had been talking the talk about doing a band for ages, but were always stuck for a drummer until Mik came along. I think Mandy from Health Hazard actually came up with our name during a particularly drunken night in the 1 In 12 bar; people used to think we were some communist SXE band or were named after the film *Stalingrad*, which isn't actually true…even though I'm a bit of a World War II history freak!"

"We toyed with the idea of calling ourselves 'Stalinist' at one point," reveals Rich, "because we liked the idea that it suggested we were extreme communists; we liked playing with people's expectations and being slightly ambiguous. Mandy must have known we were thinking along these lines and suggested 'Stalingrad'. It still had that 'communist element' and I am a great believer in those key points in history which are turning points for humanity – and the battle of Stalingrad was one of those…

"Also contrary to what people might think, the Bradford and Leeds scene circa 1992 was pretty small compared to what it is now; we only had the occasional, often badly-attended, gig at the 1 In 12… We're talking about the same 30 or 40 people at every gig, unless there was some big band playing and most people were *over* the age of 25 – compare that to the Leeds scene now!

"Flame In Hand were still putting on bigger bands at the Duchess [Of York pub] in Leeds and I remember seeing the likes of Rancid, Toxic Reasons, Godflesh and SNFU there. There was only really Health Hazard and Wartorn representing hardcore punk in Bradford, although I now understand there were still a few SXE bands kicking about then – but there was still quite a big 'us and them' attitude at the time. The emo/post-hardcore scene in Leeds was just around the corner too, but Leeds was still pretty dead really and there wasn't a great deal going on elsewhere. The scene back then was kept afloat by a small group of hard-working and inspiring individuals basically…namely Sned, Nick Royles, Rich Corbridge, Nick Lauring, Jane Graham, Alec and Sarah, to mention but a few…"

After a "pretty shit" first gig ("But I can't remember where it was…") and a "bloody awful" first demo, Stalingrad began to get a handle on their sound and direction and a much better second demo – "Again recorded at Pots'n'Pans in West Bowling…but with a better drumkit this time!" – began landing them some gigs further afield.

"The punk scene was in a bit of a lull after the whole UKHC thing of the late Eighties," reckons Russ. "And living in Bradford could be pretty bleak at times. I actually stopped going to punk gigs for a couple of years around 1990, 'cos of all the crusty 'brew crew' bullshit – especially in London – and just being burned out with it all. But my then-girlfriend Jane gradually got me back into doing things and I started helping out, putting on gigs again with her and a few others at the 1 In 12.

"Me and my mates mainly looked to Europe and the US for inspiration," he adds. "I was listening to a lot of stuff like Infest, Integrity, Born Against, Man Is The Bastard, Crossed Out, Neurosis, Acme, Antischism, Rorschach etc, but I was also listening to a lot of Am Rep and early Sub Pop bands like Tad and the Unsane and liked all the stuff that Flat Earth was putting out… I even used to have a tab on Sned's [Flat Earth] distro! 'Metallic hardcore' was quite new as well and didn't have the same rubbish connotations it has now.

"Mik was into pretty much the same stuff as me, but he was a lot more nihilistic and misanthropic in his outlook – he just used to listen to Sheer Terror and Dark Throne a lot – while Rich was really into stuff like the Swans, Zoviet France, Crass and a lot of weird noise stuff and Justin was into Big Black, New Model Army, Mudhoney, Gaye Bikers On Acid and early grunge stuff. Rich's lyrics were pretty strange and abstract and he used a stream of consciousness/cut-up technique; I never knew what the fuck he was on about half the time! I did write a few songs about more personal and political issues, but I guess we were never 'political' per se, although we did play a few benefits for stuff like homeless charities, hunt saboteurs and Anti-Fascist Action, as well as supporting the 1 In 12 whenever we could, so we did our bit…talk minus action equals zero, you know?"

"One of the musical catalysts for the band was Russell's record collection," confirms Rich. "He was the person that exposed the rest of us to Integrity, Born Against, Man Is The Bastard and Rorschach. I believe they were our common musical thread and that was all down to Russell. He was buying that stuff direct from America well before anyone else in the Bradford scene and we couldn't believe it when we heard it. It sounded so different to everything else around at the time…

"Apart from those bands, me and Justin never listened to that much hardcore or metal during the existence of Stalingrad. I had always liked experimental noise like SPK, Whitehouse, Throbbing Gristle, Test Dept. and Einstürzende Neubauten and that was obviously an influence on the electronic experimentation with Stalingrad."

Late 1995 and early 1996 saw Stalingrad contributing to two split 7-inchs, both on Jason Kilvo's Caught Offside Records and both shared with hardcore bands, the first with Voorhees, the second with Underclass.

"Yeah, I think a lot of people in the hardcore and punk scenes around here suddenly realised that the 'other side' wasn't actually that bad and we were all actually listening to a lot of the same music anyway," laughs Russ. "I remember us all going to Lecky and Rich Corbridge's house down by Bradford College, when we were just about to do the split with them and meeting them for the first time, which was weird. I actually became good mates with Lecky for a while and he helped us out a lot, fixing the PA at the 1 In 12 and stuff; I also knew Atko through college and am still good mates with him – another bloody comedian! But, contrary to popular belief in certain hardcore circles, Voorhees had a sizeable punk following and didn't spend the whole of the Nineties beating up 'crusty punk scum'! Although we did used to joke that all Lecky's stories ended with the phrase, 'Then I hit him 40 times with my skateboard…'

"We ended up playing a lot with them after that…mainly out of town, 'cos neither band was particularly popular round here. Bristol was always a favourite place…full of crazy, mad bastards! We played a totally off-the-wall gig with Stampin' Ground and Knuckledust at the

Stalingrad vocalist, Rich

Stalingrad, Russ, 1995

Kito
beelzebub roaring for his rum

Polaris
asleep in zero gravity

Stalingrad
sour as social justice, on the wash-house wall

Sunday 19th March
£1
doors 7.30pm

At the
Royal Park Pub,
Leeds 6

Skate And Ride there and also a nuts all-dayer in some biker pub that was off the hook too, with shit getting broken and punks getting whacked by irate bikers…"

"Me and Mik liked the SXE scene because it seemed to upset people at that time and we found it amusing to listen to Slapshot while drunk," adds Rich mischievously. "The SXE scene seemed a lot more exciting than anything else going on in the world of hardcore back then and it also seemed mysterious, because there was very little crossover between punks and straightedgers.

"We were interested in their passion and intensity and also the gang mentality, especially the Northern Wolfpack concept. We wanted to meet up with some of the Bradford straightedgers and I met Lecky on my way to one of our practises; he had heard that 'some punks' were doing US-style hardcore and was interested in where we were coming from. We got on pretty well from that point and soon after we engineered to play an out-of-town gig together.

"Voorhees were not like any other hardcore band around at the time; their members were not your typical scene types. They had a lot of stories that revolved around violence, but they didn't strike me as violent people – they were generous individuals with a large variety of interests outside of the scene, who also enjoyed just messing around and doing dumb stuff. I was always interested in their lyrics; they were so simple and stripped-down, almost to the point of being childish, but were brilliant in their direct, aggressive nature. I got obsessed with 'Death To Pigs' and did a remix of it that was released on a cassette of experimental Stalingrad tracks we did; I also performed the song live with them several times when we played together at the same gigs and that was why I got Lecky to perform on our LP, because I thought our vocals worked well together."

Russ: "As for the split with Underclass, we met those guys through mutual friends in Manchester and Liverpool, who we knew through the squat scene in Hulme; they used to have gigs at the legendary 125 squat there. I can't remember the exact circumstances, but we went on tour with them in Europe which was a right blast; their singer, Pete Dandy, was like a toothless Ricky Tomlinson, a total comedian. We also used to play a lot with Kitchener, who were really good live and Extinction Of Mankind and Pigpile from Buxton, who were well underrated. Me and Jane used to go all over the place for gigs and were pretty familiar faces in the punk scene up here, so getting gigs out of town wasn't too difficult…"

Also in 1996, Stalingrad released 'The Politics Of Ecstasy' 7-inch, a beautiful-looking four-track picture-disc on Armed With Anger that was recorded by Carl Stipetic at In A City Studios and fused the musical and lyrical heaviness of such Eighties anarcho bands as Amebix and Antisect with the dissonant riffing of progressive Nineties thrash and the ponderous rhythms of the post-hardcore and emerging metalcore scenes. It was an immense offering from the band and hinted at a vast well of gnarly potential just waiting to be tapped…which unfortunately wasn't realised by the band's debut album of 1998. Intriguingly entitled 'Patty, We Kind Of Missed You On Your Birthday', the still-convincing material owed much to the likes of Integrity and Prong, but some of the blast-furnace intensity was sucked from the finished release by a tight, overly compressed production.

"I thought the album was a bit rushed as well," offers Russ. "We had a core of good songs, but I remember being quite unwell with back problems at the time, so wasn't at my best guitar-wise and there was quite a lot of filler on there. Rich then went a bit mental on the concept side of things as well, which I didn't really get. I haven't listened to it in a while and personally don't really think it's stood the test of time – but people seemed to like it when it came out, though, so what do I know? It was good having Lecky and Wayne [RIP] from Doom, in on vocals as well [on the tracks 'Traitor' and 'Let It Go' respectively]; local noise provocateurs Smell & Quim even had a hand in things [remixing the song 'Hanged Man']…"

"I disagree with this strongly," counters Rich. "I think the LP was our best release and *did* expand on what we did with the picture disc. It was rushed, but it was always going to be, because of the tight budget. I always felt that our live shows were intense because of that sharing of a physical space with the audience; we couldn't achieve that with a recording, so we experimented instead, like adding analogue synths and guest vocalists…the Lynyrd Skynyrd cover ['Simple Man'] worked better than I ever imagined and I love the instrumental track at the end of the album.

"Also I really enjoyed doing the artwork for the album. I was welding at the time in a place called T&D Industries in Bradford; I was repairing waste containment units and came up with the idea of making a cross for the LP artwork. I did it while no-one was looking and then added the hand-stamped Stalingrad badge later. I listened to the LP again only yesterday and I think it does stand the test of time; we had nice rhythms and it still sounds really heavy."

"But we had our share of bad gigs," says Russ, of some of the road work undertaken to promote the album, "when either we sounded crap or were too pissed/stoned to play properly – or where no-one would turn up 'cos we were such popular chaps. One time in the 1 In 12, I got in a massive strop and drop-kicked my guitar off the stage 'cos it fucked up and stormed off… I then had to get back on the stage a few minutes later and finish the set, pretty shamefaced.

"Another classic was when we played in Niort in France and me and Bri Doom [who had just replaced Mik on drums] had a massive row over two bottles of beer, which ended in a punch-up at the promoter's house and me subsequently leaving the band. I think the best gigs were probably the big hardcore festivals at the 1 In 12… I remember playing on a Sunday with Drop Dead, after drinking and partying for three straight days with all the Bristol lot; it was nuts. We also played with Dystopia there, in '97, which was really good. Some of the gigs in Europe were pretty amazing too and we met some super-cool people both over there and in the UK, like Axel Wittmann and Ralf from Berlin, some of whom I am still friends with to this day…"

"Gigs were everything to us," adds Rich. "It was easily the best part of being in Stalingrad and we would try and get gigs wherever we could and if we hadn't played a particular city before, we would target it to make sure we did play there. Russell told us a story once about how Black Flag would play a gig in front of 10 people like it was a full venue and we always tried to emulate that. At the beginning, all four of us tended to dress in black, wear army boots and have skinheads, which created a strong visual image. We didn't entertain onstage with banter or song introductions and that gave us an intensity that audiences liked. Once we started playing, we would get into people's faces, pushing them to react.

"We played Bristol once at the end of the third European tour and that was the last gig we did with Russell. We had had a tough time on that tour and there had been a lot of arguments; we all believed it would be our last ever gig and we were all exhausted. There was a lot of other bands playing, including Code 13 and quite a large audience.

"A friend who had spent the previous three weeks stuck in a van with us was talking to Code 13 as we were about to go onstage and she said, 'Watch these guys, they are quite good…' We played with an increased intensity and just went crazy; it's hard to describe exactly what happened, but we went for the audience as well as fighting constantly between ourselves. The heightened aggression lasted the whole set, but through it all we also played a tight powerful show…apparently Code 13 looked shell-shocked by the end of it!"

As mentioned above, Russ left the band in 1998, after a third eventful European tour, although they did carry on without him for two years and released a final 10-inch on Scene Police Records.

"Mik left the band first, 'cos he couldn't be arsed any more and wouldn't turn up for practises or invest in a badly-needed drum kit. I think he was just really depressed, though, to be honest, in the light of what I know now…he really hit the booze and drugs hard and was found dead under mysterious circumstances, drowned in the Leeds-Liverpool canal. That affected a lot of us really badly and there was a lot of recrimination between us all 'cos I think we all felt we'd somehow let him down…but these things are an occupational hazard of the punk scene, I guess.

"We had got Bri [Talbot, from Doom] in the band on drums before Mik's death and we did get a lot better, but I for one was having a lot of problems with my health and personal life and was probably a right pain in the arse at times. The internal dynamics of the band could be, let's say, a little 'volatile' now and again. Like I said, me and Bri fell out on tour in France and I left the band after a final gig with Code 13 in Bristol. By this time I felt Stalingrad had run its course really and it was all just getting too hard for me physically, so it was time to pack it in. The others drafted Andy Irvine in from Scatha and Disaffect, released the 'Abandonment' 10-inch on Scene Police and played a couple of gigs. I even offered to teach Andy a couple of new songs I'd written out of goodwill…one of them came out on the 10-inch, but didn't sound anything like I envisaged it, so they fucked that up. Justin then decided to move to Brighton and Stalingrad just fizzled out after that…"

Bri and Rich and Pete from Underclass, formed the Devils, who carried on in a similar musical vein and became pretty notorious for their challenging live performances. Rich also played with the 'Christian noise' act Unicorn Love and went on to become a successful graphic designer, now based in Shipley. Bri joined doom-metal band Khang before playing with Lazarus Blackstar and reforming Doom; he now lives on a boat in Hebden Bridge and runs the 1 In 12 recording studio. Justin still lives in Brighton, where he played in Pico with Lianne from Witchknot as well as a rock band called Burnthouse.

"I moved to Leeds in 1990, 'cos I was sick of Bradford and I had a place at uni," concludes Russ. "I was in a few short-lived bands, like Carbomb, but most of my energy went on doing a university degree in music technology. I also put on a few gigs for the likes of Artimus Pyle and From Ashes Rise, as well as doing bits of live PA work for bands. I now work in the community mental health field, but am still a regular on the punk and hardcore scene and I still do the occasional gig for good touring bands. I think I prefer letting the younger kids with more energy play the music nowadays; I'd rather work on my motorbike than haul amps around!

"I don't really think we were that good in the overall scheme of things," he adds modestly, on the Stalingrad legacy – or lack thereof. "We had a lot of ups and downs and seemed to always be struggling; we'd play a load of gigs and hit a peak, but then sit on our arses 'cos there just wasn't the opportunities to play regularly. But then again we got to tour Europe three times, which was the highlight for me; it's not something I bang on about though and

I don't think I'd play the same style of music again now. I don't understand all these bands that reform to re-live the 'good old days'…

"Bradford was – and *is* – a fucking grim shit-hole and the punk scene today is a lot better than then, so there's some aspects of it I don't miss at all. I'm nearly 45 now, so leave being in bands to the younger kids. I really rate some of the new Leeds and Sheffield bands like Closure, the Afternoon Gents, Cyvoid, Dry Heaves, Jewdis, Host, Etai Kesheki…the Leeds punk scene is better in some respects than it's been in years; a bit hedonistic as opposed to overtly political, but there's still a lot of cool kids getting into it, despite all the trendy hipster bullshit that seems to permeate everything. As long as it remains fun, though, I'll still keep going to gigs…"

"I'd like Stalingrad to be remembered as one of the best live bands of that era," states Rich simply. "I want people to remember they saw us and remember the spectacle; we didn't like 'the average', so we tried to do something different. It was an exciting time, with lots of bands starting out and a lot of interesting individuals and it was good to have been a part of all that. Bloody Kev once told me that after we played Nottingham, he went home, cut off all his dreads and started Hard To Swallow…that's a nice legacy!"

SELECT DISCOGRAPHY:

7-inch:
'Split' (Caught Offside/Thinking Smart, 1995) – *split with Voorhees*
'The Politics Of Ecstasy' (Armed With Anger, 1996)
'Split' (Caught Offside, 1996) – *split with Underclass*

10-inch:
'Abandonment' (Scene Police, 2000)

LPs:
'Patty, We Kind Of Missed You On Your Birthday' (Armed With Anger, 1998)

AT A GLANCE:
The CD version of the album includes 'The Politics…' EP as well, so seems a great place to start.

ONE BY ONE

If anyone wants to hear a perfect example of UK hardcore punk that manages to be immensely heavy without once resorting to heavy-metal histrionics, the 1993 'Fight' EP by **One By One** should be top of their shopping list. In fact, anything by One By One will fit the bill, because the band really managed to seamlessly blend 'the three Ps' – politics, passion and power – into a big flailing maelstrom of invigorating noise. Shame they only did the one album and two EPs, but at least they imploded while still utterly relevant.

"[Drummer] Sned and I had been in Blood Robots and Generic together before he had moved south to Leeds," begins guitarist/vocalist Micky. "I drifted away from music for a while to get more involved in serious syndicalist politics and messed around with various musical projects including a tape released as Scorn…predating Mick Harris's project of the same name. After this I was persuaded to form a band by some friends, Kriss Knights, Jenny Edwards and Gippa [aka Michael Gibson], and Anything But That was born…the name coming from a comment made at one of the other proposed name choices!

"We were unfairly labelled as being 'folk punk' due to having a violinist, but we didn't really fit comfortably into any little pigeonhole. After the first gig, Gippa left and Alec replaced him on bass and we played a few more local gigs before embarking on a tour – of Bradford and Boston [Lincolnshire]! Both gigs were great and we went down a storm, but Kriss decided he wanted to concentrate on his literary career and Alec and I had been talking for a while about wanting to move onto doing something with a harder edge to it. So we parted company and, after a brief discussion about the lack of suitable drummers in Newcastle, Alec and I jumped in a car and headed down to Leeds.

"I'd always kept in touch with Sned and we thought we'd pay him a surprise visit. We'd a rough idea of what we wanted to do: to try and combine the power of Bitch Magnet with the energy of the Dead Kennedys and RKL, with a bit of Black Flag and some Sub Pop chucked in, and somehow it came out sounding like One By One! Our first practice was that very afternoon in the cellar at the legendary Sillyville in Leeds and the rest is history…"

"I suppose it was a strange way to start a band, just turning up on Sned's doorstep unannounced, but it worked out okay," adds Alec. "We had a practice, wrote some songs and it worked, musically, politically and personally. I was on a total high as Generic had always been a big influence on me; they had combined power and intelligent, meaningful ideas with ace tunes, all done in an honest, original way. The '…South Africa' EP and their split LP with Electro Hippies still stand up as fucking great releases and will remain important records to me until I turn my toes up."

After playing their first gig supporting the AK47s ("The AK47s were great…we were poor," deadpans Alec), One By One recorded the blistering 'World On Fire' EP at Studio 64, Middlesbrough, with Christine Adams and Michael Baines at the desk. Mixing insanely fast blasts of hardcore rage ('Tell Me') with immense chugging power ('Mother') and Kennedys-like punk-rock brilliance ('Four Into Nothing'), the EP was released on Sned's Flat Earth label in1991 and remains a very impressive debut with a distinctly 'European' feel to it.

"Originally it was only supposed to be a demo," reveals Micky. "But I think Sned was that surprised by it, he agreed to put out the best bits as a single! I listen to it every now and then and I still think it stands the test of time. It pretty much sounded the way we wanted it to, although the review in *Sounds* compared us to Leatherface, which I still think is quite amusing…"

"Both Mickey and Sned are very strong personalities, with strong ideas of right and wrong," comments Alec, on the band's early chemistry. "Sned is one of the best hardcore punk drummers around, while Mickey had a great, unique voice and managed to write belting riffs that combined tunes and power without going all noodly and heavy metal…and I was the lukewarm water between their fire and ice! But working with them pushed me musically and the whole process was brilliant, frustrating, honest and intense and one of the most creative times of my life.

"None of us, except Karin [who joined later], grew up in a well-balanced nuclear family with a dad around and all of us watched people we cared about and the environment being treated like shit for no good reason. So there was no way we could have been anything *but* angry and political…"

On the undeniable strength of the single, One By One landed themselves a John Peel session, which was broadcast just as they were embarking upon their first – and very eventful – European tour, with Oi Polloi.

"The first gig was in Newcastle at the Dog And Parrot and went well," recalls Micky. "That was the first time I got to meet our tour organiser Arjen, a lovely bloke who is now the second-in-command on a freight barge. The second gig was at the Hell House in Hackney, which was squatted by Ben Sik 'O' War and all his international mates. We were trying to listen to the Peel session outside on the van's radio and there were loads of pissed punks drinking on the street in front of the place. It was an all-day gig and, as always, everything was running late. I know that Dread Messiah got to play and that Coitus were part-way through their set; we were due to play next and were in the process of loading our gear in when the place got busted by the cops…so we loaded our stuff back out and had to drive off in the middle of all the chaos of the eviction.

"I don't remember where we stayed, but the following night was another gig in London and the cops turned up *again* to bust the gig! I was beginning to wonder if we'd ever get to play on the tour at all and was seriously thinking about going home, but my mate Dave, who then lived in London, talked me into carrying on. We got to play a short set in the end, but it wasn't much fun due to the atmosphere; we then drove overnight and ended up in Liege, at the Nabate folks' house, and from there we drove to our first gig in Switzerland – via Gottingen and an ass-prodding at the Swiss/German border!

"We'd refused to pay the Swiss motorway tax, as we were only going to be there for two days, so they let us turn round and told us to go back on the smaller roads. The Germans saw us being turned back and assumed that we'd been refused entry and suddenly became very interested in our car and van. I was in the car and they did all the usual stuff, getting us to get all our stuff out and asking us lots of questions about why we'd been refused entry and where we were going etc. They did the same with the van as well, but when they checked the passports they found that Arjen had skipped bail in Germany for possession of hash and that was it: everyone and everything out, in with the sniffer dogs and off to the inspection room – drop your pants, spread your cheeks, the thwack of a rubber glove being put on…

"Arjen ended up getting banged up in jail, but luckily Sned had a copy of his contacts and our itinerary so we continued without him. We spent hours driving round Switzerland on shitty little roads and got to Zurich really late. Arjen's directions said that the squat we were

One By One, Karin

One By One, Alec

One By One, Micky

playing in had 'Fuck The Police' painted on the road outside…in 10-foot-tall letters as it turned out!"

"Cue lots more eight-hour drives, criss-crossing Europe," adds Alec. "The weather was hot, but the thermostat in the van was knackered and it was leaking oil like a sieve, so we had to have the heater on full-blast to stop the engine over-heating and we literally poached our plums. The bonnet catch and wing mirror were knackered too and held down by some old washing line…

"But getting to meet people who were on the frontline of any number of struggles through touring was a huge education for me and reinforced the importance of trying to do what we did – be it the band, Flat Earth, the 1 In 12, or just living life in general – with as much honesty, passion, intelligence and creativity as we could. It also helped you feel that, although isolated in some ways, you were part of a bigger community of people who were trying to find ways of improving things."

Late 1991 saw One By One record their self-titled LP, at Studio 64 again, which was released by Newport's Words Of Warning Records the following year and continued the fine direction previously established by the EP. Another hard-hitting, cerebral release, it benefited immensely from a thick production – all snarling bass and powerhouse snare hits – and Micky's diverse voice, which was more than able to cope with both the shouty punk bits and the more melodic (sometimes surprisingly so) passages in songs like 'Making Bacon'.

"Somewhat amusingly, we attracted a bit of mainstream record company attention about that time," he recalls. "I can't remember if it was before or after the LP came out, but I got a phone call from Sony asking for a copy of the LP and they couldn't understand why we weren't interested in sending them one down. Apart from the fact that we didn't want to sign to them, I didn't much fancy getting sued by them either!"

By the end of 1992, One By One had been joined on vocals by Karin, a Belgian who had relocated to the UK after meeting One By One on their first European tour and she brought even more intensity and diversity to the already potent mix. She not only changed the direction of One By One but also that of Micky's life…

"I'd spotted this tall blonde chick walking around in the AK47 [Dusseldorf], and for me it was love at first sight," says Micky candidly. "I thought she was German and I was really surprised to find out that she was Belgian and – more disappointingly – Arjen's girlfriend, Karin! I knew she'd be coming round with us on the rest of the tour, but, if you had asked me then, never in my wildest dreams would I have thought that she'd emigrate to the UK, we'd have two kids together and that all of us would then emigrate back to Belgium…

"Looking back on it now, Karin joined One By One the day she got into the van in Düsseldorf, but I don't think that any of us knew it at the time. She was in a band called Pertotal with Vrocker and Sling from Chronic Disease [who now drums for Soulwax]. When she moved to the UK, she didn't join the band straightaway, but at some point we asked her, as the songs were just getting too complex for me to sing and play at the same time. And then she started scaring the shit out of young punk and hardcore boys…"

"I saw One By One and thought they needed something extra on vocals," laughs Karin. "No, seriously, the story as Micky tells it is true. In the first instance, I was quite shook up about the fact that Arjen was being held in jail and that I was going to miss out on my holiday, touring around with him and the band. I decided to go meet these crazy English people anyway, to ask if I could still go on tour with them and that was probably the best decision I had taken in a long while. It turned out to determine pretty much the rest of my life…

"By the time I had moved to Newcastle, I pretty much always went with the band to gigs; I often used to sing One By One songs in the house where we lived with Alec and Sarah and I guess they must have thought it didn't sound that bad, so one day they asked me and I was dead chuffed to be part of the band, the music and the ideas behind it. I'd like to think I added a bit of diversity and tried to explore different methods and vocal sounds; I always really enjoyed the positive comments I received, particularly from other women…but used to get really pissed off with low-level sexist behaviour, which did still sadly exist in the punk and hardcore scene at that time."

Karin made her studio debut with the band on the aforementioned 'Fight' EP, which was recorded during October 1992 and released early the following year by Flat Earth and Nabate, Karin's distinct vocal presence elevating the six songs to a whole new plane. 'Pin In The Atlas' in particular hit a new level of ferocity thanks to her harsh, barked delivery.

"Having a musical vehicle for cranking out political, social and personal ideas was ace, as we were all opinionated sods," reckons Alec. "But the end product wasn't always what we set out to do and generally didn't sit easily into a particular genre. Complex stuff that worked in practices didn't always translate well when playing live, as we had to be firing on all four cylinders to be on it; this was especially tough on Micky when he was singing and guitaring. When it worked, it was fucking magic; when it didn't it was very frustrating, which was all part of the drive to get Karin in.

"She's one of the best female vocalists in punk and playing live always worked better after she joined. She really added a whole new dimension to what we were capable of, musically freeing Micky up to do more clever stuff with the guitar. But, more importantly, having a female singer with a really powerful voice is inherently political, which enhanced the ideas in the lyrics and generally I think we all feel that the 'Fight' EP was the best thing we did."

To promote the EP, One By One predictably headed back to Europe, this time for a lengthy trek with Sedition…that almost cost them their lives! "Far and away our worst experience on the road would have been when we were on that tour with Sedition in Poland, heading towards Poznan," sighs Micky. "We don't know exactly what happened, but we were driving along the motorway in heavy rain and the van aquaplaned and spun round three times in the middle of the road before hitting the kerb and the tyre blowing out. The van then rolled down a grass embankment, turning over completely three times before coming to rest the right way up at the bottom of the bank.

"The tape recorder was still blasting out Terminus singing, 'We're heading for the terminus…', which was a little too close for comfort at the time, so I ripped the recorder out before climbing out of the passenger-side window. I ran up the embankment to get help, only to be met by Sedition running down the bank, expecting to be pulling dead bodies out of the wreckage. We somehow managed to force all of the doors open and get everybody out, physically unscathed and incredibly the only damage to our gear was where someone's knee had gone through the cloth cover on my cab…and that cost me a lot, but that's another can of worms I don't wish to reopen!

"Anyway, we were all shocked by the crash as we really did think that we were going to die and the last thing we expected was for Karin to be arrested by the police for 'the crime' of having an accident. Somewhat unusually – ahem! – the police were really unpleasant; they shouted at us and behaved really aggressively towards us. They kept us waiting for hours without food or water and made no effort to help us in any way. They brought in a translator, which we had to pay for, and he was even more of twat to us than the police were.

"Eventually they got bored of making our lives a misery and made it clear to us that the only way that we were going to leave the police station was if we agreed to pay a fine. We asked what the fine was for and, after being shouted at again, we agreed to pay up and were given some bits of pink paper with numbers on, that looked like the Polish version of raffle tickets, as a form of receipt. Dick Turpin rides again in a white Lada with a blue flashing light…!

"After being dumped at the train station by the Old Billski, we had to find somewhere to stay as we only had one van, but two van-loads of people and a backline. Alec or Sned managed to get in touch with some people from the band Alians, who then managed to sneak us into a student accommodation block. We really did have to sneak in two or three at a time, as there were these right old battle-axes [very stern women!] guarding the door in old-fashioned Soviet-era matron's uniforms.

"Downstairs looked okay, but upstairs was more like being in one of the more chaotic squats we'd played; there was no water or light in the toilets after dark, so a trip to the bog was pretty risky, but the people we stayed with really looked after us; they fed us…and got us some much-needed beer! The next morning we woke up to the sound of pandemonium in the hallways – the water was on…but only for an hour! We all managed to get a shower and then headed off to the train station, where Alec did an amazing job trying to reach the western world; he had to queue in one long queue to eventually be told that he could go and queue in another long queue.

"After hours of patient queuing and endless telephone calls to the UK and dealing with people who didn't seem to understand our predicament or know how to resolve it, we were advised that we were unable to hire any vehicle in Poland that we could take back into the EU or hire any vehicle in the EU that we could take into Poland! So our only choice was to get a train back to Berlin and pick up a hire *car* from there, as apparently there were no Transit vans to hire in the whole of Germany…

"While Alec was doing this, we were all sitting around shell-shocked, getting seriously hassled by Polish drunks and beggars who seemed unable to understand the word 'No' in any language. They did, however, seem to understand 'Fuck off!' Particularly when shouted with the type of built-up anger you get after suffering a near-death experience, highway robbery at the hands of the police and being stuck beyond reach of western communications…"

1994 saw the 'Fight' EP enjoying a limited release in the US through Gern Blandsten, the label ran by Charles Maggio from Rorschach and One By One headed Stateside for a much less stressful string of dates, although even then their van broke down in Kalamazoo. ("Charles, Will and Neil from Tribal War, were awesome though," says Alec, "and very cool about us being disaster magnets!") While in America, the band did a great live session for WMFU Radio, New Jersey, which was ably produced by Charles, who left all the raw, chaotic edges to their sound very much intact, making for one of the band's most memorable and representative recordings.

Although work did begin on a second album when they got home, it was never finished and, with Alec and Sned increasingly busy with Health Hazard, One By One was left on a back burner. For good.

"It just kind of faded away," confirms Micky. "By that time, Karin and I were travelling down from Newcastle to Bradford, where Alec and Sned lived, and we'd be there before them for the practices. It got to the stage where we just felt that no-one else was interested, so we stopped pestering Alec and Sned to practice and got on with doing something else ourselves. My only regret is that we didn't finish off that second LP as it has some good songs on it that never saw the light of day. Perhaps if we'd all been a little more honest with each other about not wanting to continue, we could have harnessed some of our energy into finishing that off."

Micky and Karin cranked up the intensity several notches for Ebola, who released the 'Incubation' LP through Flat Earth in 1996, as well as three 7-inchs, during their six-year existence before Micky teamed up with members of 30 Seconds Until Armageddon to do Jinn, who released several split 10-inchs and LPs and a self-titled album of their own in 2006 on Bristol label Super-Fi.

"Then Karin and I emigrated," he continues. "And since moving to Belgium, I have tried to get a band together over here, but things haven't quite worked out. I sometimes drive over to Gent to jam with Isaac from A Den Of Robbers, but nothing more structured than that. I'm still writing fiction and slowly working on my second book; my first book was a collection of gritty short stories, which delved into my experiences and the dark recesses of my mind, called *Blunt Wound Trauma*…only £7.99 from all good bookshops and Amazon!"

"It's tempting to look back and think that, if we'd been a bit easier on ourselves and each other, we could have practiced more, pushed ourselves more, both musically and politically and really hit our potential," concludes Alec. "But we're all fairly difficult characters (apart from Karin, who coped with our shenanigans brilliantly). I was (and probably still am) pretty up my own arse; driven by a conflicted moral code and guilt about not being a perfect revolutionary and not using the privilege we have in the west well enough, I end up trying a bit too hard and being a bit of a cock. One By One was incredibly important to me at the time and the culmination of years of wanting to make honest, politically driven music. I look back and think we, at least partially, did just that, with naff-all resources other than the goodwill and support of a network of political/punk/DIY folk who actually gave a shit and a knackered old Transit."

SELECT DISCOGRAPHY:

7-inch:
'World On Fire' (Flat Earth, 1991)
'Fight' (Flat Earth/Nabate, 1992)
'Les 40 Ans Du Vieux' (Flat Earth, 1994) – *split with Sedition*
'El Fascista Planeta Tierra' (Victimas Del Progreso, Crimenes De Estado, 1994)

LP:
'One By One' (Words Of Warning, 1992)

AT A GLANCE:
Search out that 'Fight' EP, folks. You won't regret it.

HEALTH HAZARD

Health Hazard were formed in late 1992 when Alec and Sned from One By One teamed up with vocalist Mandy and bassist Chris from Biohazard, all of them looking for another outlet to vent their musical and intellectual frustrations. The band only lasted two years, but in that time they undertook some serious touring and unleashed some memorably pissed-off and noisy hardcore punk.

"We'd known each other for years," explains Alec, "through gigs, hunt sabs and various other anarcho and punk goings-on in Newcastle and Bradford. Mandy and Chris were playing in Biohazard – the *real* Biohazard, mind you, not them cheesy Americans! – that had recorded a couple of things for a '1 In 12' compilation then sort of split up. I'd looked after Flat Earth Records when Sned went to New Zealand [winter '91/'92] and then just sort of carried on helping out after that; we were both playing in One By One, which was great, but quite intense and serious and limited by Micky's job. Frustrated by this, as well as by getting our house broken into and general aggro, Sarah from Witchknot and I had just moved down to Bradford to live the anarcho-punk dream: get more involved in the 1 In 12 and Flat Earth, do more music, weave our own soya milk etc.

"The four of us found ourselves on the dole in Bradford with a burning need to get out there playing something fast, fun and meaningful, without being at all precious about it…which was a good job, as I never have been – and never will be – a guitarist. Mandy kindly lent me her guitar and I made it make noise and we started practicing a couple of old Biohazard songs, some other stuff Chris wrote and some stuff I'd written when fantasising about being in a Finnish hardcore band! Mandy wrote all the lyrics and it was a total blast; we got on great, started and stopped at the same time…it was obviously the right thing to do."

"Bradford was a pretty happening place at that time," adds Chris. "Lots of bands and active people, the catalyst being the 1 In 12, which was a magnet for disaffected types beyond the usual punk crew, so was a great meeting point for ideas and sparks flew off in all directions. There was a lot of creative things going on and the ace thing was that there were loads of bands with a similar attitude, but all sounding very different: Headache, Recussant, Witchknot, Love Chips And Peace, Mash-M etc. We did a '1 In 12 UK tour' with three other Bradford bands, Headache, Mash-M and Recusant, and all four bands sounded completely different to each other.

"Things were happening in a wider scene that was still divided between punk and hardcore, but even though we were obviously at the punk end of the spectrum, playing *gigs* rather than 'shows' (!), we enjoyed and respected the likes of Voorhees, Bob Tilton and Baby Harp Seal and built some links and mutual respect. I just remember it as a very good time in my life in general."

"Touring with Sedition, when I was in One By One, was a huge inspiration," continues Alec. "They were powerful, meaningful and serious enough, but still a great crack and it was the same with Pink Turds In Space and Dawson. Awesome, powerful, magical bands and people and that's what I aspired to, more than sounding like anyone in particular, though obviously we grew up in the anarcho-punk tradition, so that shaped how we did things: keep it honest, as DIY as we could, treat people with respect and try to support good things happening whenever we could. So, without sitting down and actually writing a plan, I think playing intense meaningful gigs, whenever we got the chance, was what we were about. It was a big commitment. Even though we were only going for a short time, everything we'd all been doing for years beforehand was a preparation for doing it 100% with Health Hazard. And for the next few years it *was* pretty much all we did."

After making their live debut on 20 March 1993, at the 1 In 12 with Glue (from Glasgow), Slum Gang, Body Bag (who would later become Kitchener) and Dog On A Rope ("The gig was hilarious," smiles Alec. "We all started and stopped at the same time and made shit loads of noise in-between, even though me and Chris were sometimes playing different songs…!"), Health Hazard recorded the 'Not Just A Nightmare' 7-inch for French label Minstrel at Studio 64 in Middlesbrough and headed out to Europe in support of it. Nine tracks of raw abrasive thrash (a tenth song, 'Man Killing Man', was recorded but rendered unusable for the record when the last verse and chorus were erased in post-production) powered by Mandy's incredibly intense vocal delivery, it was a sterling first release that captured the imagination of the international DIY punk community.

"We squeezed a hell of a lot of travelling into our two years," says Chris, of the relentless touring Health Hazard then undertook. "A tour of France, Spain and Switzerland with Kitchener… A tour of Europe with Drop Dead and MVD… We did a lot of gigs with Witchknot. The worst gig for me was undoubtedly a gig in Villa Amalias in Athens, where I got impetigo from an ear piercing I'd had done just before the tour. My housemate [Birdy from Headache] had bought a piercing gun and I was the guinea pig, but I think my immune system had given up as I started to feel like I had flu as well. I spent a day lying in a corridor with pus dripping down my face and into my ear, hardly able to move, while the others were off at the beach. Had to get up in the evening to play and don't know how I got through it. I had to go to the hospital in the end… Mandy said a few days later that she never thought my ear would look the same again!"

"But the gig was great," Alec picks up the sorry story. "We did an Amebix cover, 'cos everyone we met – including the cops! – seemed big into Amebix. After the gig though, Chris's ear wasn't looking good. We dragged our pasty carcasses up to Thessaloniki and stayed in the brilliant squat there with all these beautiful, tanned, healthy-looking people; Chris was pretty besotted, but unfortunately by this time his ear looked like a pakora and he had to admit the magic herbs he'd been using on it had been defeated and he went and got it looked at. So, as the gig approached, Chris strolled back with his whole head bandaged up and I mean like 'cartoon bang on the head' bandaged. Between the tears of laughter, we could make out a man looking as pissed off and 'don't sit next to me on the bus' bonkers as it's possible to look."

But Chris wasn't the only member to suffer injury while on tour with Health Hazard (that name starts to take on sinister connotations now, doesn't it?) At risk of sounding all *Spinal Tap*, Alec himself fell foul of a bizarre baking accident…

"We were on a death march tour through France heading for Portugal and Spain," he begins. "Every day was the same: get up, drive eight hours, get lost, look for punks near the station, get to the gig, play, do the stall, find food/beer/somewhere to crash, send Chris out to 'make with the party' and repeat. I was the only driver, so tended to get up earlier than everyone else to get my shit together. We were staying with the ace folks who would later become Enola Gay; they didn't speak very much English and we only spoke a bit of French, but we'd managed to have a blast at the gig and get some scran from a supermarché ready

Health Hazard, 1993, Chris, Sned, Mandy, Alec

Health Hazard, Chris

Health Hazard, Mandy

for breakfast, as it was a killer drive to Portugal the next day.

"If I remember rightly, the gig in Toulouse was ace, couldn't-see-the-hand-in-front-of-your-face smoky, but loads of just normal people who really got into the whole jumping-around-to-noisy-bands thing. Anyhow, after a night spent listening to Brazilian death-metal demo tapes and not sleeping much, I got up to get fed and on the road, opened the bag of food and a ninja baguette sprung out, smacking me in the face and suddenly it all goes dark. Half an hour later, when I still can't open my eye and the laughter has died down a bit, we tried to get on the road again, but driving while trying to hold my eye shut and needing help changing gear didn't work out brilliantly, so we turned back.

"Waking up our confused hosts, who thought they'd got rid of the odd smelly Brits who were suddenly back and talking about not being able to drive 'because of bread' and being blind 'because of breakfast' left us looking mental and a bit lost. We eventually found a doctor who bunged some burning goo in my eye, which made it go mental colours, then taped it shut to fester away and hurt like buggery.

"If I'd had two decent eyes to start with, that would have been fine, but I knackered my other eye up years before, so when the second attempt to drive failed, Sned phoned the gig organiser: 'No... Bread... In his eye... Dangerous breakfast... No, we are rough tough hardcore punks, but we can't come because of the bread, the terrible bread...!'"

In among all the touring, Health Hazard popped into Bradford's In A City Studios during spring 1994 to record a self-titled 14-song 10-inch, that they released on Flat Earth later that year. Produced by Brian Talbot from Doom and Carl Stipetic (who also played piano for the jazzy intro to 'Breeding Hatred'), it sounded even gnarlier than the first 7-inch and considerably heavier thanks to some lower-tuned guitars. However, not long after its release, Mandy left (a decision she admits to "regretting on and off for many years after") and the band played their last gig – at the 1 In 12's 'Xmas On Earth '94' festival, alongside Ex-Cathedra, Suicidal Supermarket Trolleys, Sarcasm, State Of Filth, Substandard and Rudimentary Youth (which was basically Mandy from Health Hazard, Brian from Doom and Darron and Steve from the Next World, all doing Rudimentary Peni and Reagan Youth covers!)

Alec, Chris and Sned became Suffer, although they did honour a tour of Spain and Portugal they already had booked, with Max from Headache filling in for the departed Mandy. "Similarly, when Suffer toured with the mighty Drop Dead, Gordy sang a couple of Health Hazard songs with us," says Alec, "but we only did that as it was playing to people who would have never got to see Health Hazard; it was never an attempt to carry on without Mandy. For all of us, it was really important that the band was a platform for Mandy to say what she wanted; punk and hardcore was full of male voices and agendas, but her voice was different and a crucial part of what Health Hazard was about: turning living in a potentially shitty situation into a rejection of accepting the inevitable slide into depression, isolation and being ground down.

"Health Hazard was a celebration of what's possible with a shared vision, a network of friends and enough like-minded conspirators. We started with nothing and in my case almost no ability to play and were somehow lucky enough to end up being part of something worthwhile and having a magic time doing it.

"But playing in Health Hazard was a massive commitment and playing lots at the kind of intensity we did took its toll physically, mentally and emotionally and demanded – particularly of Mandy – absolute 100% dedication. She eventually decided that she wanted to do something other than scream her lungs out, sleep on floors in stinking gig clobber, eat when we were lucky enough to get cooked for and not really have a life outside the band. And without Mandy there was no Health Hazard... Me, Sned and Chris wanted to carry on doing something together, though, so we morphed into Suffer."

"Seeing as I didn't go on to do another band, there's not really anything of musical interest to say about myself," states Mandy. "After leaving Bradford I moved about a bit – Channel Islands, Wales and Oxford – and now I'm back in the northeast. I still listen to a lot of music, go to the occasional gig and am teaching myself to play the digital piano...badly! I think I need lessons! I now enjoy sport and in the past few years I've got quite into cross-country running (I think that singing in HH may have improved my lung capacity) and I've just started to do some open-water swimming."

A final recording was made at In A City in spring '95, which was originally intended for a split release with Poland's Homomilitia on Scream Records, but didn't appear until a few years later as a split single with fellow Geordie thrash troupe, Sawn Off (whom Sned and Chris eventually joined in 2000). A spirited cover of 'Jailbait' was also recorded for a Motörhead tribute EP that never materialised either and that ended up on the 1999 compilation, 'Worst Of The 1 In 12 Club, Volumes 14/15: A Decade Of Dissidence'. A fitting end for a band that appeared – and disappeared – at the club.

"Nothing set us apart; that was the whole point," concludes Alec, on what may or may not have differentiated Health Hazard from their peers. "We were no different from lots of other people around at that time, just lucky to have found a channel for our creativity, anger and frustration and lucky to been involved in the 1 In 12 and to have had Sned who'd put years of work into Flat Earth. The people who end up standing on stages can only do that because loads of other people clean the building, run the cafe, do the bar, do the PA, have boring meetings, organise gigs that people may or may not come to and because some people can be bothered to build something better than the slops they're offered.

"We only did what we did because of trust... Michael and Christine at Studio 64 trusted us to pay them later for the recording of 'Not Just A Nightmare'... Every tour we did was built on trust... All the distros that sold our records were based on trust... It's amazing what you can do!"

SELECT DISCOGRAPHY:

7-inch:
'Not Just A Nightmare' (Minstrel, 1993)
'On A Path To No Tomorrow' (Flat Earth, 1998) – *(posthumous) split with Sawn Off*

10-inch:
'Health Hazard' (Flat Earth, 1994)

LP:
'Discography' (Flat Earth, 1996)

AT A GLANCE:
In May 2010, Flat Earth reissued the Health Hazard 'Discography' LP, 30 tracks, all remastered and sounding as ferocious as the day they were recorded. You need this album in your life.

WITCHKNOT

Witchknot were an unconventional, uncompromising all-girl band with members from all over the northwest of England, but whose activities were primarily focused on the 1 In 12. Just being an all-girl band in a punk scene dominated by males was enough to set them apart, but when you also consider the weird and wonderful noises they made – somewhere between the Mob and Mr Bungle, perhaps? – it becomes apparent why Witchknot had to feature prominently in this book. They challenged preconceptions and shattered stereotypes wherever they went and helped nurture the emerging 'riot grrrl' scene in the northwest.

The band were originally formed as a three-piece when drummer Sarah moved from Telford, where she had been playing with Curse Of Eve, to Bradford and pooled her talents with vocalist Lianne and bassist/violinist Jane Shagstamp.

"Curse Of Eve was based in Telford in the Eighties and was another – mostly! – female band," she begins. "I played drums and Kes played bass, but we never released anything on vinyl; it being the Eighties, we preferred cassettes – proper dole-queue DIY! We were involved in zines, putting on gigs and eventually setting up a venue. Quite a few anarcho-punk bands came to play in Telford back then and we swapped gigs with a few of them, in particular those freaks running wild in the disco, Flowers In The Dustbin. We had no money or van or anything though and I remember hitching in pairs to our first gig in London and waiting ages for the singer who'd got stuck at a service station on the M1.

"We were influenced by bands like the Slits, the Raincoats, the Au Pairs and Poison Girls and through the punk network – which was all letter-writing in those days, no e-mail or text – we were in touch with other women in bands and put out a compilation cassette featuring, among others, Hagar The Womb, Toxic Shock, Youth In Asia, the Sears and also several women punk poets. We did a lot of hitching around, meeting up with people at peace camps, festivals and on demos as much as at punk gigs...

"I moved to Bradford with Alec [who would become guitarist in One By One, Health Hazard and Suffer], mainly due to the 1 In 12 Club, which had been set up as an autonomous venue by the Unemployed Claimants Union in the Eighties. I had been involved in a similar venue called Lion Street in Telford, which eventually got closed down by the council and the 1 In 12 seemed like a good starting point for finding punky lasses to start another band. We arrived at a really good point in time, I think; there were lots of new bands starting who had serious politics but also knew how to have a laugh at the same time. I basically put a poster up in the club and got in touch with a few other women and we started practising in our cellar.

"Lianne was already gigging and doing this solo acoustic stuff, which was amazing and I just couldn't believe what a great voice she had. We liked a lot of the same stuff musically and she got me up-to-date with newer bands while I forced her to listen to dreary old anarcho punk! Basically we loved the Ex, Dog Faced Hermans and Dawson and we tried to aim for a quirky, wonky, slightly disturbed sort of sound rather than thrashing it out. One of our early efforts, 'Udder', scares people to this day apparently. For me I'd always liked punk bands who didn't necessarily just use volume to beat the audience into submission and, as a woman, I didn't really see why I had to copy the way blokes play drums..."

With the aforementioned Jane Shagstamp on board to alternate between violin and bass, Witchknot made their live debut at one of the monthly Docs'n'Frocks events that Sarah was putting on at the 1 In 12, playing the April 1993 Frockfest with various bands that contained mainly female members, including Toxic Shock Syndrome, Suzie Never Barks and Manflesh. With so few females involved in the hardcore and punk scenes, Witchknot were part of a vital attempt to redress the natural balance somewhat and right from the start it was apparent to all concerned that they weren't your average run-of-the-mill thrash band.

"We did put up with a fair amount of nonsense," admits Sarah. "'Why are you an all-women band…are you all lesbians?', 'You can't play – you're shit!' etc etc. I don't suppose any all-male bands get asked if they're all gay and as for judging a punk band on the quality of musicianship…? Having said that, we did find a lot of like-minded bands – of both genders and all points in between – to work with and having the support of Flat Earth, who were releasing so much interesting and challenging stuff, probably encouraged people to give us a listen. Also, having the 1 In 12 as a base for rehearsals and a place to put on gigs, really helped; although there weren't as many women in bands, there were a lot of women involved in running the club and other activities associated with it, so a lot of them supported us and helped with running events, doing stalls or feeding and putting up bands, for instance."

A six-track self-titled demo was recorded at Studio 64, Middlesbrough, which set out the band's stall nice and early, all tribal rhythms and bloody-minded quirkiness and introduced the symbolic image of the sheela-na-gig carving as their logo on its cover.

"The name Witchknot is from an old belief that witches could do healing spells by tying certain knots in hair," explains Sarah, "and at the time we all had long dreads. We adopted the sheela-na-gig as our logo which was the fertility symbol of the earth mother [and, appropriately enough, the female counterpart to the 'hunky punk' grotesques!]; weirdly it was often carved above the door on early churches – perhaps to fool pagans into accepting their new-fangled patriarchal nonsense… I dunno, but it *was* a definite hint that we weren't a cock-rock band!"

After selling the tape at their first few gigs, the band were invited out to Europe for 10 dates with Health Hazard. Although Sarah admits the experience was "pretty nerve-racking", she recalls that first tour of the continent very fondly.

"It was the first time I'd ever played abroad and I couldn't believe the way everything just came together. It was all DIY, no contracts or guarantees of money or riders or owt; we just turned up and played for petrol money. Having said that, we always got fed and watered and got to stay in some of the finest squats in Europe. It is intense being with the same few people every single day and getting progressively more tired, smelly and hungover, but meeting so many other folk just trying to live an honest life and doing stuff for nothing just because they are into it was really inspiring. It was also good that over the years we could return the favour for some of the people who put us on and in turn we put on gigs at the 1 In 12 and had bands stay in our house that we originally met on that tour…or even just friends of friends of people we'd met on tour!

"The high point for me was probably emptying the Vort'n'Vis in Ieper, Belgium – we played in-between Health Hazard and Doom – apart from a small group of women left at the front! And the low point was putting diesel in the petrol engine of the van. 'Gazole' equals diesel in French…doh!"

Upon their return to the UK, Jane left, so Sarah drafted in Kes, the old bassist from Curse Of Eve, who was living in nearby Manchester.

"And, at about the same time, we found out that Alec's sister's flatmate, Marion, used to

Witchknot

Witchknot live, Marian and Sally

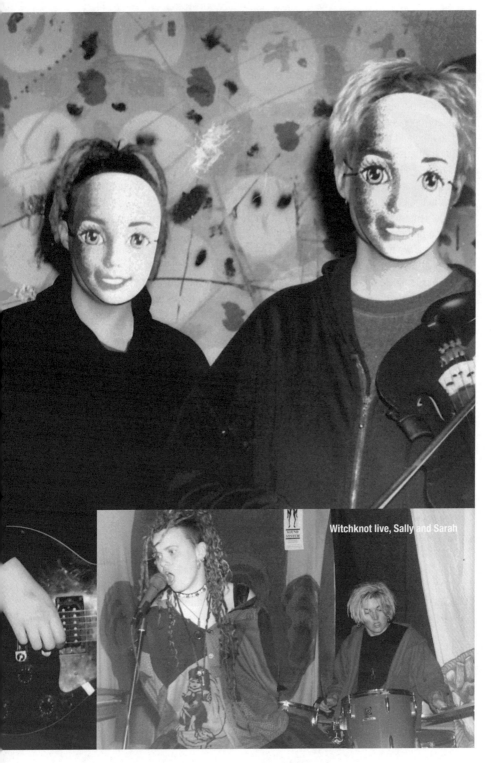

Witchknot live, Sally and Sarah

play fiddle in a ceilidh [Celtic folk] band. I'd also found an ad somewhere for Gaynor, a cello player who was into the Ex and Dog Faced Hermans and somehow we decided to go for another vocalist as well, so that Lianne could do weirder noises on her guitar. We liked what Recusant [another Bradford-based band who had just done a split 7-inch with Headache on Flat Earth] were doing, so borrowed Sally, who was a great live performer…over the years she acquired a number of props, like a silver tinfoil wand to 'zap' people in the audience and a battery-operated toad to help out on backing vocals. It was just what we'd been lacking and so the band doubled in size overnight…"

During August and September, 1994, the new, expanded Witchknot recorded the 'Suck' 7-inch for Flat Earth at Carl Stipetic's In A City Studios. As well as the 'scary' 'Udder' mentioned earlier, with its unnerving shaman-like chants, the single featured three other tracks that all defy easy categorisation, eschewing traditional – read: *predictable* – 'rock' arrangements (verse, chorus, middle eight etc) to build a weighty atmospheric vibe using disconcerting repetition and roaming bass lines.

"Musically we had eclectic influences," states Sarah. "Punk in its many forms, of course – punk, post-punk, anarcho, crust, folk and hardcore – plus indie, grunge, queercore, riot grrrl, dance music, Eastern European stuff, ska, reggae…politically though, the DIY ethic of punk is what motivated us and the network of people that grew out of that enabled us to go on tour and put on gigs. Like anything, there were 'norms' in terms of what a punk band was supposed to sound like, but plenty of people breaking the 'rules' too. Also, the amount of co-operation and trust was incredible.

"We didn't 'write' songs as such," she comments, on the creative process of Witchknot. "We would jam around and record a bit, then jam again and record a bit more (on our trusty old cassette player) and eventually when we had a collection of ideas we would try to put the ones that sounded compatible together and add on maybe an intro or outro. It was a slow process. Also, for us, the band was a social thing and we did waste a fair amount of time eating and talking. No Witchknot practise was complete without a supply of the best samosas ever from Patel's corner shop and when we went on tour we would order a huge boxful.

"The single is probably my favourite release; it was every (not so) young punk's dream come true to release a 7-inch vinyl disc and get it played on John Peel. I like the cowbell riff and the cello zooming along underneath 'Pianist Envy' and 'Udder' *is* still a bit scary; on 'Sabotage', I got to play a dustbin lid and 'Repetitive Beat' sort of sums up that point in time when punk met rave at the free festivals and used to get everyone up dancing."

Witchknot headed back to Europe in 1995 for some dates with Donkey in support of the single. "I loved that tour, as it was mainly in Holland and just short drives between gigs, so plenty of time to hang out in Amsterdam and socialise and listen to new music, mainly courtesy of Grrrt, the soundman for the Ex, who organised the tour for us and put up with seven people and a cello staying with him for over a week. I came back from that tour with a bag full of cassettes of Eastern European bands like Ne Zhdali, Uz Me Doma, Dybbuk, Apolok and Kampec Dolores, all of which just blew me away. These bands were incorporating brass and strings into quirky punky rock/folk/crossover stuff in a way that us 'Knots could only dream of…

"On the nights when we didn't have gigs, we sung for our supper at the squats around Amsterdam, who took turns to do a cheap evening meal for people. We played acoustically, which was hilarious – for us anyway – because the songs sounded wonkier than ever and we couldn't stop laughing…sometimes they'd give us beer just to shut us up!"

Like most dedicated underground punk bands of the Eighties and Nineties, playing their own music was just part of Witchknot's activities and a huge amount of energy was expended propagating the feminist punk scene in the UK and beyond, mainly by organising sympathetic gatherings and furthering cross-pollination of ideas and culture.

"To start with, it was monthly gigs to promote bands which featured women, that weren't necessarily *all* women, that we called 'Docs And Frocks', then, as we got busier with Witchknot, we put on two or three 'Witchfest' all-dayers, once a year at the 1 In 12. We were trying to put on a mixture of women, punk, riot grrrl (Northern Brit style!) and queercore bands and performers and create a slightly different atmosphere from the 'mosh pit' type of gig, to get in a more mixed audience and make it a bit more inclusive. I was thinking back to the Poison Girls' 'Cabaret Of Fools' gigs, which were a mixture of all sorts of stuff, not just 'traditional' punk rock; we had real ale – Witches' Brew and Black Cat, of course – and food and stalls and decorated the whole place with banners and lights…just trying to make more of a festival-type atmosphere.

"I think we succeeded in getting a different crowd of people into the 1 In 12, but getting the balance and timing right was tricky. One time, I put on a cellist from an amazing band called Smart Bombs who also did solo stuff and she got heckled a lot because everything ran a bit late and the drunk punks were coming down from the bar upstairs by the time she came on. If she'd gone on earlier, on the cafe stage, she would have gone down a storm, but I thought that she had such great songs I wanted her to be on the gig floor stage.

"Also, a few of the bands, not being part of the punk DIY scene, would try to insist on guarantees, riders and headline slots etc…how we laughed! The deal was petrol money, a free meal in the cafe, somewhere to sleep if needed and basically (as we learned the hard way) the noisiest band would go on last to drown out all the drunk punks. Oh and the privilege of playing in the best and only autonomous venue in the UK, of course!"

The barrage of bizarre sounds and tempos continued unabated with 1996's 'Squawk' LP, again for Flat Earth. 'Mermaid And Chips' referenced the legendary Birmingham punk venue and, while not as technically advanced as Primus, certainly tapped into their avant-garde otherworldliness. Elsewhere, 'Mad Fairy' and 'Zap' sound like some Sixties detective theme on bad acid, all sassy walking basslines and trippy time signatures, while 'Dried Apple Grandma' is a demented folk western and 'Doris' riffs surreally on the Dead Kennedys' chestnut 'Let's Lynch The Landlord', to great effect.

"Lordy, the LP…" ponders Sarah. "We recorded and mixed down over three days for around £300 and I think we were pushing it a bit, to be honest. If we had been a three-piece band of excellent musicians maybe…but a six-piece shambling outfit of quirksters with too many half-finished songs…? Not a chance! We recorded at In A City again and Carl who runs it is a jazz musician so he didn't try to make everything sound like American-style rock, which suited us fine. Jer from Dawson then did a sterling job of mixing the racket for us and, three sleepless nights and many versions later, we had an LP. I don't know if the right versions ended up on the vinyl, as the editing was done elsewhere and some of my favourite songs didn't sound their best in the studio anyway, but I think that's what Witchknot were: a bit hit and miss, a lucky dip of ideas; some worked better than others, but we never played it safe.

"People seem to love it or hate it!" she adds. "The songs that work best are the ones we'd played most live and the ones that people used to love dancing to – pretty obvious, really – 'Griezzell Greedigutt', 'Mad Fairy', 'Repetitive Beat' (the dance remix!) The lyrics were about protest and freedom, from a feminist perspective, I suppose, but with a few fairytales and love affairs mixed up in there. There's some fairies giggling on it and a gargling mermaid or two, just for good measure. Of course, everybody's doing that sort of stuff now, but we were the first!"

Unfortunately, after touring Europe again, with half of the dates as headliners ("By then people had heard of us and were willing to give us a listen…"), the other half with Scottish band Quarantine, Witchknot wound down quite naturally and without fuss, playing their last ever gig at the 1 In 12 in 1998 with Canada's Submission Hold.

"I think we just came to a natural break when me and Sally were pregnant," reckons Sarah. "We played gigs right up until we were seven or eight months pregnant too, which was fun; I got out of carrying the drums up fire escapes for once. I could feel the baby kicking during the gigs, probably the foetal way of saying, 'Shut up, I'm trying to get some sleep in here!' Sadly, if not unsurprisingly, she's grown up to become a guitarist…

"We didn't plan the split, though; people just got busy with other stuff – life in general – and when Lianne decided to move to Brighton and Marion to London, I guess we knew if we did something else it couldn't be Witchknot without them. I reckon on the whole most bands have a five-year maximum lifespan anyway – then it's time to collaborate with other people and try new ways of doing things or it tends to get a bit stale.

"And our last gig was back where we started, at the 1 In 12. We hadn't been able to rehearse for a while due to being busy with babies, but it still felt like a real celebration. I was expecting it to be a real 'locals' gig', but as soon as I walked in the door some people from the States came up and said, 'We were in Ireland and heard you were playing, so we came over for the gig!' It's humbling when people make so much effort to see your band and you always think, 'I really hope we don't fuck it up!' I never drink alcohol before playing for that very reason. I think bands owe a level of respect to the audience – who are part of the whole experience and who are also usually in other (much better!) bands as well. I don't know if we realised it was our last gig at the time, but as I recall loads of people danced and it was in our favourite venue as well, so a good time was had by all."

Following the demise of Witchknot, Sarah, Sally and Kes teamed up with Cath from Leeds-based Month Of Birthdays to form Baba Yaga (the title of a Witchknot song about an infamous baby-eating Russian witch!) and continued on in the same vein of cooperation, organising exchange gigs with Gertrude from London and Archbishop Kebab from Edinburgh and appearing at some of the weekend-long Ladyfests. Marion relocated to London, where she now plays with a string quartet, while Lianne moved to Brighton and continued her solo career, recording several sessions for John Peel and even having the late, great DJ describe her as 'one of the great English voices!' High praise indeed.

"I'd just like us to be remembered for doing things our own way," Sarah hopes, "being political but also having fun in the process; taking our influences but then trying to do something different, rather than copying a certain formula or style. We certainly didn't make it easy on ourselves; I reckon we would have been much more popular if we'd done emo/hardcore stylee, but it wasn't really where we were coming from. I suppose one of the things that set us apart was that we were sort of between two (or more) 'scenes' in a way: the anarcho/punks and the queercore/riot grrrls. That was an advantage in some respects, because we got to play to very different audiences, but we never totally belonged to, or felt totally accepted by, either one – but hey, how puuunk is that?"

SELECT DISCOGRAPHY:

7-inch:
'Suck' (Flat Earth, 1994)

LP:
'Squawk' (Flat Earth, 1996)

AT A GLANCE:
You'll have to e-mail Sarah and ask her nicely – if you cover her costs, of course – to burn you the Witchknot recordings on CDR: sanda.machenry@virgin.net

CANVAS

Canvas were another of the more challenging UK hardcore bands of the Nineties. Hailing from Leeds, they quickly developed from a bog-standard SXE metalcore band into something completely off the wall and avant garde, all jazz-fusion time signatures and deceptive arrangements. Their second album, 'Lost In Rock', is rightly heralded as a classic of the jazzcore genre, right up there alongside the likes of Converge and Botch.

"It all started when I was about 13, with Guns N'Roses," says guitarist Karl Fieldhouse, recalling his introduction to hardcore music, "which then progressed to the heavier metal bands like Metallica, Pantera, Slayer and Sepultura…but the one defining moment came from a TV show that used to be shown at 3am in the morning on a Wednesday night…well, technically Thursday morning, I guess. That show was called 'Noisy Mothers' and played all kinds of metal and rock videos; it was about a month before my sixteenth birthday and I had recorded the show on the video recorder and got up early so I could watch it before I went to school.

"It was a pretty normal show and I was having my breakfast while watching it and there was a section which had bands that were touring. Sometimes they would play a snippet of a song and video, while the tour dates would be on the TV screen and sometimes they would play a whole song from the band. I remember it playing a snippet of a King's X song that had quite an abrupt stop or break and then the screen changed and it went straight into 'Shades Of Grey' by Biohazard and they played the full video clip and showed all the tour dates.

"I remember being mesmerised by the clip, as it had lots of live footage and just seemed so raw and in-your-face. The song was also just killer: heavy, but full of groove and it sounded

Canvas, by Naki, Dan Kearns, Gareth Brown, Andy Sutcliffe, John Sutcliffe, Karl Fieldhouse, Paul Priest

hard too. I saw that they were playing at Rio's in Bradford on my birthday and so, after seeing that song and watching the video a thousand times, I eventually bought [their second album] 'Urban Discipline' and got tickets for the show, which was the first show I had ever been to. That show changed my life and that is absolutely not an exaggeration; it was Downset, Dog Eat Dog and Biohazard and I remember – during Biohazard especially – that I felt so alive and loved the energy and at some point in their show it hit me like a sledgehammer that I wanted to do what they were doing and make other people feel what I was feeling. I know that sounds quite over the top now – perhaps a bit romantic or cheesy – and some might say that it's just nostalgia, but it's true; it really just hit me and right after that show I went and bought a guitar and started to learn how to play.

"From then on it was just a total free-fall into all that was hardcore. I looked through their CD booklet and read the thanks-list that mentioned all these bands I had never heard of, like Sick Of It All, Madball, Agnostic Front, Cro-Mags, Life Of Agony and Leeway…the whole NYHC scene basically. And 1993 – or was it 1994? – was such an amazing time for those bands coming over here and they'd always bring bands with them you never knew, that got you into more and more different bands; like when Sick Of It All brought Strife out, which then helped me find out about bands like Unbroken, Snapcase, Earth Crisis and Mean Season etc, but I didn't really know much about hardcore in the UK. I think Understand and Above All were the only bands I knew from here and, well, at that age, I didn't think Understand were even 'hardcore' because they didn't sound anything like all the NYHC-type bands I was into.

"Through going to Rio's, I made friends with some people there, which was cool because I would always go by myself, 'cos nobody in Selby liked anything remotely like hardcore. It was always just me hanging out by myself until some kid said hello to me and introduced me to some other people who introduced me to bands like Voorhees, Stalingrad, Hard To Swallow, Ironside, Unborn, Vengeance Of Gaia, Withdrawn and the 1 In 12 Club, the Packhorse, Armed With Anger Records, Flat Earth Records, Sure Hand Records, Subjugation – and a whole host of other things that rumbled below the surface of everything else I knew.

"All of that stuff happened within a few months and hardcore really appealed to me; the music just spoke to me and I did what most teenagers do when they find something that they hook onto so quickly: I disowned everything else and I sold all my metal CDs, everything. Pretty naive, obviously, but hardcore just seemed like it was for me and metal seemed so wrong compared to it. Eventually I bought all that metal stuff back again, of course, because you soon realise what an idiot you are and that you *can* actually like something that doesn't sound like Sick Of It All or Youth Of Today or whatever, but that's how things are when you're a kid. But I was also really attracted to the idea of a community and hardcore really had that, as do so many other genres, which is something you learn with age; it's definitely not the utopia you think it is when you're in your teens, but I still love it. I do find it curious to wonder how my life would have been if I hadn't seen that Biohazard video, or if I'd gone and seen Anthrax as my first show, which I had originally planned to do, but was too chicken to go on my own! Would I have still found hardcore? I have no idea, but I'm glad I did."

Canvas coalesced when Andy Sutcliffe from Schmuck joined Karl in his first band, Blood Green, on second guitar. Blood Green were a 'hardline' vegan SXE band from Sheffield, who only played three gigs before Karl and Andy left to focus on Canvas and the remaining three members – vocalist Nathan, bassist Foster and drummer Craig – started up the even more militant Slavearc.

"I'm not sure what the real goal of the band was, to be honest," admits Karl. "For me it was to play music; there may have been different objectives and agendas for the others, but for me it was the music. The band was initially tagged as a vegan straightedge band, which looking back was so funny because I wasn't even vegetarian when we got together... I'm not even sure if I was vegetarian when we played our first show in Sheffield. The rest of the band was vegan; even in its inception that was the case: three vegans and one meat-eater.

"I'm a little fuzzy on timelines and I'm not sure how long the band existed, but some of the members *were* hardline and there was so much uproar about that viewpoint [due to it being pro-life and apparently homophobic etc] it was eventually the demise of the band, because Andy and I didn't want to have anything to do with that lifestyle belief and didn't want to be tarred with the same brush. So it all ended just as quickly as it began for me, although I remember not being that gutted about it and took it for what it was: other people with fucked-up opinions that I didn't want to play music with any longer."

As well as Karl and Andy on guitars, Canvas comprised Andy's brother John on vocals, bassist Gaz and drummer Dan, who had previously played in a 'jazz lounge band' (!) called Mondo Suave and they wasted little time before playing out.

"The first Canvas show with that line-up was in Leeds; it was probably at the Packhorse and it was probably awesome," laughs Karl. "It's weird, but I don't have any recollection of the details of that first show, like what other bands played or when it was. I remember all my first shows with every band I've been in, except this one. Canvas did play a decent amount of shows and they were mainly in Leeds or Bradford, with a few shows in London, Manchester, Grimsby, Newcastle and the likes, but we played in the Packhorse or the Fenton so many times that I can't remember the first show we did there. I certainly remember shows we played with the likes of Stalingrad, Botch, John Holmes, Imbalance, Iron Monkey, Converge, Hard To Swallow, Area Effect, Narcosis and many more – but not that first one. I have a few things flashing through my mind from it though, like what guitar I played; I have an image of the show and I remember that John and Andy's dad came along, but all the other details are not quite there. I'm sure someone reading this probably remembers it better than me..."

And it was at one of the band's first shows in London that they were seen by Household Name Records, who subsequently released the band's first album in 1998. A self-titled long-player that basically compiled two sessions recorded by Dave Chang at Backstage Studios, the first during July 1997 and the second during July 1998, it was still generic enough ('generic' in the nice sense, that is, of belonging primarily to one genre) to appeal to fans of Earth Crisis, Snapcase and the Belgian H8000 scene. In other words, the band hadn't gone totally crazy with their writing and arrangements yet...that was still to come. One of those early Dave Chang sessions was originally planned for release as a MCD on Sure Hand, but when that never happened the album for Household Name made perfect sense.

"That first release only had three songs on there that I was part of writing," explains Karl, "one of which was a weird instrumental. The other songs had all been written before me joining the band and also used by Schmuck before the name change. The re-recording of those songs took them to a different level, but with regards to the two real new songs that were written as a band and not the odd instrumental; those were written in Andy and John's parents' house, which is where we used to practice. Everything was always set up in what was supposed to be the dining room and we used to practice in the evenings; their parents were great, very supportive and looking back – and knowing how loud it got – it's pretty insane that they even allowed it. But that's where those two songs were written.

"I think Andy wrote 'Unworthy Of Perfection' in its entirety, although we all contributed to the arrangement and structure and I wrote the first half of 'Last Prayer For Judas' and Andy wrote the second half. The writing was very easy; I was lucky to be playing with such accomplished and creative musicians at such a young age. Andy was, I think, two years younger than me and he was just amazing on the guitar and I'm sure he still is and, in honesty, he was my main inspiration when playing. I always wished I could play as well as him and get the tone he had…you always hear about guitar-players that just have that great tone in their fingers, who can make a plank of wood with a piece of string on it sing like a bird; well, Andy was just like that. He played a beat-up BC Rich Warlock, had a shitty amp and a Zoom 1010 effects pedal, but he always sounded amazing…well, at least to my ears he did.

"Dan was a fantastic drummer, capable of a lot of different styles and very open-minded; I was definitely lucky to play with a really good drummer at such a young age, but the problem with that, although it's also a good thing, is that when you go on to play with other people, it makes it very difficult if they're not up to the same standard. Gaz was a fantastic bass player too and also very creative, especially with song structures and the more ambient noise and instrumental-related aspects of Canvas. And John was a hugely diverse vocalist, who could go from a high-pitched squeal to a lowest-of-the-low growl, which no-one would imagine could come from him if you look at his stature. He could also play guitar, drums and bass, making him invaluable in many ways. All of those ingredients made writing songs very easy and very natural."

The album was well received upon release and quickly sold out of its first pressing. Household Name also licensed it for a release Stateside through Prosthetic, who were part of Metal Blade, so there are Canvas CDs out there with the Metal Blade logo on them, which Karl still thinks is "incredibly cool!" Lots of gigs were played to promote the album and the band were gathering momentum, with two split EPs then released the following year, one with John Holmes on Devil Rock (the label ran by Bri from John Holmes) and one with Hard To Swallow on Karl's own Contrition label.

"The record release show for the first album was one of the best gigs we ever played," he recalls. "That was such a packed show and Imbalance [who also played] were really good friends of ours, a great band and good people. I think the room held 120 people and we had 180 paying in, which was insane. Other killer shows included the Converge show in London and any number of shows in the 1 In 12; that place was always awesome and it just had such a great vibe.

"As for the worst shows we did…well, we always enjoyed playing. There may well have been shows where something might go wrong, or people looked at us slack-jawed 'cos they didn't get it, but we always enjoyed playing no matter what. We were pretty young and I didn't have the experience that I have now and I hadn't played all the places I have now, so all the things that happened back then, when first starting to tour and play out, were all met with incredible enthusiasm.

"Due to the success I've had with other bands up to the point of writing this and the extensive touring I've done, I've become quite spoilt with where I've played, but it has to be said, some of the best shows I've ever had were in squats, living rooms of houses…or in Derby with one paying punter! That was a killer show; it was Hard To Swallow, Canvas and another band whose name escapes me and there was one person who paid in…or maybe two? Either way, each band watched the others and rocked the fuck out; it was such a fun show and definitely not what you would expect. So, yeah, I have a lot of fond memories of the shows I played with Canvas."

January 2000 saw the release of the 'Lost In Rock' album and Canvas spectacularly coming into their own and combining an ambitious multitude of moods and momentums, throwing the listener at every twist and turn with yet another whiplash-inducing tangent. Featuring some incredible musicianship and some truly off-kilter ideas, it took the direction hinted at by the material on the split with John Holmes and brought it to daring fruition.

"'Lost In Rock' was the first effort which you could call a proper album and it was our *only* album, really," elaborates Karl. "It was also recorded at Backstage Studios with Dave Chang again, but this time we did it all in five days, which, if you listen to the album, is pretty insane. I distinctly remember us telling Dave everything we wanted to do and him saying it wouldn't be possible. We again recorded by just playing live, but there were so many other elements to record and add that five days really didn't seem enough.

"The album, in my opinion, is perfect, though," he adds, proudly, "especially for what it was then – and even now I think it stands up to the test of time pretty well. There were so many different influences for that record compared to what our previous work contained, we had a very distinct sound and, while we were around at the same time as the likes of Converge and Botch etc, I still think we were original and probably ahead of our time in many ways. If we'd have continued to make music, or had released that album a couple of years later, I think we would have been much bigger than we actually were, due to various expansions in heavy music and certain bands becoming more well-known and accepted. But I think a lot of people couldn't get their head around that record at that time, mainly the ones that liked the self-titled first album so much… I'm not saying everyone that liked that first record couldn't like the second, but I think most were a little surprised with how 'Lost In Rock' turned out.

"We wrote it all in the basement of Gaz and Dan's house in the Hyde Park area of Leeds, which was the central hub of the Leeds hardcore scene. It was very small and had a distinct atmosphere in there and I just remember that we would take all these awesome riffs Andy had written and try to adjust them, chop bits off, work with odd drum patterns and basically try to make everything as abrasive as possible…and also make it as *pretty* as possible at other times. It was a very creative period and it was a lot of fun and the end result was a great record that you either love or hate. It had a great reception from some people, while others were a little disappointed by it. But I loved it, Andy loved it, John loved it, Dan loved it and Gaz loved it and that was all that mattered!"

Unfortunately, only six months after the release of 'Lost In Rock', Karl left the band – due to those inevitable 'musical differences' – and without his steadying influence, Canvas quickly crumbled.

"I left because of how the band was progressing," he admits. "Andy and John were always into a lot of different music which is great; I love a lot of different music too, but I had a very clear vision of what Canvas was and should be and 'Lost In Rock' was, for me at least, what embodied the band…and maybe that was the problem too. At the time we broke up, Andy and John were listening to a lot of Pink Floyd and wanted to take Canvas in that direction and make the band less heavy; I also liked Pink Floyd and loved the idea of having that kind of influence even more present in the music, but not at the expense of what the essence of Canvas was, a *heavy* band.

"That's where the conflict lay: where everyone was once pointed in the same direction, we were now pointed in different directions. I don't think I was the only one to feel that way though; I think both Dan and Gaz had a similar feeling about it, although you would have to ask them for a definite answer as to whether that is accurate as this is just a distant memory now. All I knew was, I didn't want the band to be something it wasn't and taking that heaviness away from Canvas would be like turning Black Sabbath into A-ha or something – which is maybe a little over the top, but true nonetheless!

"And my earlier comment about 'Lost In Rock' embodying the band being the problem is that there was little room for expansion or growth from that album; as it was so very diverse, any evolution would be difficult unless something drastic happened – and something so drastic would probably change the band's essence. It was something people felt strongly about at the time and it caused me to leave and led to the eventual demise of the band. Me leaving the band brought about some odd events, with a few discussions after I left and an argument or two and since then I haven't spoken to John or Andy and vice versa.

"There were talks of perhaps doing a reunion show a few years ago and I was asked if I would play, but I turned it down as it didn't make sense to me; I had other things going on and doing a Canvas reunion seemed pointless and still does, especially when there was no natural bond. Perhaps if we'd all stayed friends and talked, or got back in touch to be friends again, it would have made sense as a fun thing to do, but as it was then it made *no* sense. I'm not sure if they did the show or not, but I have absolutely no regrets with anything that happened in Canvas and I'm very proud of what we accomplished and I think the music was great. We definitely made an impact and wrote some very original material; I had some great times with that band, but ultimately the growth and quick evolution was also the band's downfall…"

While Andy and John went on to play with Human Fly, Karl joined **Thirty Seconds Until Armageddon** (alongside Lindsay 'Lins' Cuscani, Peter Falkous and Andy Moore from Vengeance Of Gaia), with whom he had already released a MCD on Contrition.

"I loved Vengeance Of Gaia," Karl enthuses. "They were the UK version of Mean Season and I still play their demo tape every now and again and still love it. Some things just stick with you no matter how the times change or how dated it may seem. We had played shows together and then they [VOG] broke up and eventually formed Thirty Seconds Until Armageddon and so we played shows together with them as well. I think the first time I saw them was in Manchester and it was then I decided to do the label and they would hopefully be my first release. That [self-titled] MCD [1999] was great; it looked shitty, but the music was awesome. At that time, the music was a little bit Vengeance Of Gaia-like, but also had influences from Cave In, Botch and Converge and it was just really good, solid music that really appealed to my taste at that time and releasing it was all the more sweet because they were friends.

"I'm not entirely sure how I ended up in the band, though, or at least what the deciding factor was. I used to talk on the phone with Pete an awful lot; even when I was at work I'd call him, or he'd call me and we'd end up talking on the phone for an hour! But I guess the first thing was that Andy left, so they only had one guitar player which was Sid [aka Ian Sidaway]; I wasn't in Canvas any more and at some point Pete asked me if I would join the band. They were located in Newcastle and I was located in Leeds, so it was a bit of a trek, but only an hour-and-a-half, so not too bad. I'm not sure that it was any different for me than with

Canvas, apart from when I left TSUA, which was due to a lack of other people not wanting to take it as far as possible and tour as much as possible, we all stayed good friends.

"I distinctly remember Adam [Gowland], who played drums, telling me that when they decided to ask me to join he had pointed out to the others that if they did ask me, they had better be prepared to take it to the next level, because Adam knew exactly what I wanted and how I wanted to do things and how hard I wanted to tour and release records. I guess that fell short somehow…but the overall experience was very similar – good friends making good music and having fun while doing it – and everything in that band was fun. I certainly have no complaints or regrets about it all, I just wish that it would have gone further than it did…"

As well as the self-titled MCD for Contrition, Thirty Seconds Until Armageddon also did a split 7-inch with xCanaanx on Ignition and a split MCD with the Autumn Year (on Contrition), before splitting in 2001. Karl moved to the Netherlands and played with the celebrated Dutch metalcore band Born From Pain until late 2010, releasing some sterling albums and touring like mad dogs all over the world, while Lins joined Break It Up, Sid had a band called Spitfire Down and Pete and Adam both played in Jinn. Pete currently plays in Grace.

"I've been incredibly fortunate to play in bands I love and with people I love," says Karl, gratefully. "I have had a lot of great experiences with Canvas, Thirty Seconds Until Armageddon and Born From Pain; I've toured all over the world and wouldn't change a moment of it. I am currently not playing in any bands and don't have any plans to, although I still pick up my guitar and write songs, but that's just for me. I'm not sure what the future will bring with regards to playing or touring with other people, but I'll always play for myself and always go to shows.

"If Canvas and TSUA are remembered, that'll be enough for me," he concludes. "If one day people still remember the names of those bands and have a positive experience reminiscing about them, then that will do me just fine. Hopefully if people listen to the music again it will still hold up for them and won't be something that they say they once loved but now it sounds shitty, but that sometimes happens and that's how it is. I listen to those releases and songs and it still sounds good to me, but I have a different perspective and memories of those records, which isn't very objective, I guess. I think those bands just did what they did and, in some ways, Canvas were pioneers and maybe a little ahead of our time with what we were doing. Perhaps if we'd stayed together a couple more years, we would have been more successful than we were, due to how the music scene evolved…and maybe not.

"The same thing can actually be said for TSUA, because in many ways we were also doing something drastically different to other UK bands, although it was very US-influenced and perhaps if we'd tried to take it that step further, we'd have done a lot more too – but that's just speculation, of course. It could all just as easily turned into a big piece of shit and I might not remember things with the same fondness that I currently do. But anyway, however any of those bands are remembered, they'll always be special for me and I'm sure the others that played in them too."

SELECT DISCOGRAPHY CANVAS:

7-inch:
'Split' (Devil Rock, 1999) – *split with John Holmes*
'Split' (Contrition, 1999) – *split with Hard To Swallow*

LPs:

'Canvas' (Household Name, 1998)
'Lost In Rock' (Household Name, 2000)

AT A GLANCE:

Gotta be 'Lost In Rock', if you want a taste of Canvas at their perversely unquantifiable best. Meanwhile Thirty Days Of Night issued a complete discography of Thirty Seconds Until Armageddon, aptly entitled 'Everything', in 2009.

HELLKRUSHER

Crustier than a week-old baguette at a punk's picnic, **Hellkrusher** were formed in late 1989 by Ali Lynn, soon after he was asked to leave South Shields metal band Energetic Krusher, and bassist Ian 'Scotty' Scott, who himself had just left Hellbastard. Despite the obvious hybrid name, Hellkrusher was a very different beast to their previous bands.

"My views and beliefs were very different to the rest of the lads in Energetic Krusher," Ali explains on how he came to find himself looking for another band. For me it was never about the money or stardom and still isn't. They were a very good band, but had dreams of making the big time and then made the mistake of talking to a band called Slammer [Bradford thrashers] who had just signed to a major label [Warner Bros]. They wanted me to change my singing style and wear nice clothes to fit in with the image/style they were after for the band, so I left. Which is why, if you look at a lot of the Hellkrusher songs, especially the earlier ones, they're all about money and greed in the music business and the world in general. The members of Energetic Krusher all came from different musical backgrounds; all nice lads, though it's just a shame it ended the way it did, but to be honest with you I much prefer what we did in Hellkrusher to EK anyway…"

"Personally the time I spent in Hellbastard had little or no bearing on my approach to doing Hellkrusher," adds Scotty, "especially musically as the whole point of Hellkrusher was to do something new and move away from the more metallic direction that our former bands were heading in and basically return to our hardcore punk roots, sounding more in the vein of Discharge or the Varukers, who we were heavily influenced by at the time.

"But obviously if I hadn't been in Hellbastard, nor Ali in Energetic Krusher, then Hellkrusher would never have happened in the first place and even though I had known Ali for several years prior to the band, it's doubtful we would have even started a band together at all, let alone formed Hellkrusher, if not for those other bands. Although I had briefly been involved in another band before joining Hellbastard, I served my time with them, learnt to play bass and guitar, gained experience playing and putting on gigs as well as recording, answering mail and making hundreds of contacts all over the world, so we took all that experience with us to Hellkrusher and it was a major help in getting the band off the ground in the early days. So we have to be thankful for that."

Those old contacts came in handy when it was time to start gigging and Hellkrusher made their live debut at Newcastle Riverside on 5 March 1990 supporting Energetic Krusher's old labelmates Bomb Disneyland and northeastern band Drill. As well as Ali and Scotty, the line-up that night consisted of drummer Steve Wingrove, from local band Senile Decay, guitarist Davey Thornburn, who was fresh from auditioning for northeastern metallers Atomkraft ("So we thought he *must* be good!" reasons Scotty) and guitarist Paul Knowles. They started gigging enthusiastically with the likes of Doom, Anarcrust, Sedition and Psycho Flowers, building up a strong local following, before coming to the attention of RKT Records from Leicester, who would eventually issue their 'Wasteland' debut album.

"But by 1990, the punk scene in South Shields and the northeast scene in general was a shadow of its former self compared to at its height in the early to mid Eighties," sighs Scotty. "Especially after the demise of the legendary Station in Gateshead and the Bunker in Sunderland. The gigs we put on in South Shields were a lot less well-attended by the local and old-school punk crowd, so we had to rely on people coming from Newcastle and Gateshead to make up the numbers and not even the likes of Concrete Sox, Disaster or Excrement Of War would pull out all the local contingent. Maybe they had moved on or whatever, but the people who did attend those gigs then were pretty much the new generation of punks, so it was as important to them as it was to us to keep the punk scene alive and kicking in the northeast and there were still some very memorable gigs."

'Wasteland' was actually recorded twice before either band or label were satisfied with the results, with Hellkrusher parting company with Paul between the two sessions.

"The first recording of 'Wasteland' was done at Red Nose Studios in North Shields," explains Scotty. "I had previously recorded there with Senile Decay, so I guess that's why we decided to go there, which looking back probably wasn't the best idea to start with, as it was pretty inadequate as studios go. On the day of the recording, we walked to the studio – with all our gear – from South Shields, through the pedestrian tunnel under the River Tyne…fuck knows why, 'cos it's miles to walk. When we eventually got there, Davey never turned up, as he was on the run from the police for some reason or another, so Paul had to record all of Davey's guitar parts and then Davey had to return on a different day to record the rest. Between them both, they managed to achieve two spectacularly awful guitar sounds, not helped by a terrible mix and production – so bad that RKT refused to touch it and the recording was scrapped.

"Another studio was sought out and we eventually entered Baker Street Studios in South Shields [late September 1990] and recorded 'Wasteland' – mark two! A much more polished affair with superior production and cleaner guitar sound, which really captured Davey's playing at its best. Although we were more than happy with the new recording at the time, especially after the disappointment of the first recording, deep down both myself and Ali knew it wasn't the LP we wanted it to be, mainly due to its metal sound rather than the all-out punk style we had wanted to achieve. But still, looking back, it was a great release for us and more than represented the band and the line-up at that time…"

The album was a solid entry to the punk metal canon and, despite an unconvincing instrumental intro – complete with OTT leads – the title track even managed to sound like Discharge mangling Slayer's 'Chemical Warfare'! The production was probably too calculated for its own good however, some of the band's gnarly snarl smoothed away in the

Hellkrusher, live in Derby, Ali,Scotty, Curry, Scoot

Hellkrusher, Halifax 1991, Davey Thornburn, Steve Wingrove

mix, but 'Wasteland' was still very well received upon release during July 1991, although cracks were starting to show in the band's live performances, which all came to a head at a disastrous gig supporting – ironically enough – Disaster at the Irish Centre in Tyneside on 4 December 1991.

"We had put a lot of time and effort into organising the gig and were all well up for it," recalls Scotty. "But Davey was pissed out of his head and when we went on he had to be prompted before every song and *still* fucked them all up; our set was nothing short of a shambles and an embarrassment, to say the least. I suppose it's funny looking back now, but after all these years I still can't bring myself to watch the video of that gig; it was so bad and we were pretty pissed off afterwards.

"The thing is, Davey was a very accomplished guitarist in his own right back then, so it was a shame it ended like it did. In more recent years we even did a couple of rehearsals with him again and he totally blew us away with his playing – so much so in fact that he was way too good for us anyway and probably should have been playing in some 'name' metal band."

The Tyneside gig was the last straw for Ali, though, who split the band up the very next day…only to reform it in the New Year with a whole new line-up, Scotty moving to guitar, with Andy Turnbull and Ian Curry, the latter from Debauchery, joining on bass and drums respectively.

"In the aftermath of the split, things got really messy, which I personally regret; however that's the way with bands and in our defence the decision Ali made was for the benefit of the band in the long run. The transition from bass to guitar was quite easy for me, to be honest, although I am no musician and have never claimed to be one; I just do what I can and hope for the best and I've been getting away with it ever since! I had been learning guitar before I took up bass in Hellbastard anyway and was playing guitar in both Senile Decay and Anemia at the same time as Hellkrusher, so I was getting plenty of practice.

"Moving onto guitar for Hellkrusher was just the obvious thing to do really; it seemed the only way we were going to get the guitar sound and style we wanted…and I'm still using the same guitar now as I was back then. These days, though, we have two guitarists, which really takes the pressure off me and makes our sound a lot more powerful and I'm more than happy to let Scoot do all the hard work playing lead."

The new-look Hellkrusher wasted no time recording a new demo that demonstrated fire was still coursing through their veins. Fourteen songs, all recorded live and then mixed in one frantic day in Newcastle's Project Studios, this demo captured the raw punk vibe at the heart of the band's sound to perfection, the latent Discharge influences finally coming fully to the fore on tracks like 'Third World Exploitation' and 'Dying For Who?' The band made their London debut during May 1992, at Rails in Euston, with support from Coitus and One By One, which not only saw the band winning over the hearts and minds of the London scene, but also starting a long friendship with anarcho band Dirt. The two bands undertook a UK tour together in September of that year and would go on to play almost 80 gigs together.

"We had a pretty good relationship with Dirt," concedes Ali. "They were nice people and we had both good times and bad. Touring with them was a laugh on the whole, but you have to remember that being with the same people 24/7 is hard work at times. The first tour we did with Dirt was in England [September 1992] and after the first gig in Birmingham we all started to get to know each other and the ice was broken; it wasn't a bad tour either. We then went to Europe [April 1993], the first time for Hellkrusher and had a brilliant time; it was so different to England, more organised and the kids were a lot more enthusiastic. As usual, though, we were dogged with van problems; no matter where we went, we *always* had van trouble. On one van we had, the lights kept turning off, which isn't very good when you're driving round country roads in the middle of the night. Mind you, putting petrol in a diesel tank doesn't help things…"

"Yeah, it was an excellent tour, but not without incident," adds Scotty, "including getting stopped for speeding in Poland – but only getting fined £5, much to our relief. Dirt's van broke down and we had to the end the tour in a hire van and hire cars. After a final gig at Brno in the Czech Republic and a long drive back to catch the ferry to Dover, we found ourselves in the company of One By One and Leatherface; it was good to see some familiar faces, but after a few bottles of vodka courtesy of Leatherface, Curry ended up so drunk he literally vomited all the way from Dover to Newcastle in the back of One By One's van, pissed all over Dirt's belongings, smashed his bottle of duty free and lost his duty-free cigarettes…not to mention entertaining us all with some of the best comedy drunken staggering ever. I know he'll probably want to forget all this, but it was without a doubt the funniest thing I have ever seen and we were laughing so much that, at one point, I thought Gus had actually stopped breathing; funny as fuck and a hilarious end to a great tour."

Meanwhile, Ian Armstrong agreed to release the demo as the 'Buildings For The Rich' album in early 1993 on his SMR label. Around this time two tracks from the album – bolstered by two live songs – also found their way onto a 7-inch for New York label Tribal War and Andy, who would later play in both Aftermath and Demon 340, was replaced on bass by Gary 'Gus' Raine from Armed Relapse and Embittered. Then September '93 saw the band in Middlesbrough's Studio 64 recording the 'Fields Of Blood' EP for German-based Skuld Records, a brutally raw release that would go on to be one of the label's best-sellers.

"Me and Gus virtually wrote every song for that EP one Saturday afternoon in my bedroom at home and the results were brilliant with some really great tracks," agrees Scotty modestly. "The recording itself – in true Hellkrusher fashion – was pretty substandard, to say the least; in fact the record label actually told us it was shit, but released it anyway and it was a good decision because it's been re-pressed so many times…"

After the EP, gig offers were flooding in left, right and centre, including the opportunity to tour America with Dirt for a month in early 1994. Scotty and Curry couldn't work this sort of touring in around their work commitments and when it was decided that the tour would go ahead without them, using temporary stand-ins, they both left and formed Aftermath with former Debauchery vocalist, Grant Taylor-Cain and Andy Turnbull. Gus moved to guitar and Steven 'Moy' Morrow joined on bass, while Martin 'Hairy' Harrison, who had previously played with Energetic Krusher and Hellbastard, became the new Hellkrusher drummer. However, the US tour – with Dirt and Final Warning – that had promised so much, while an unforgettable experience, cost them dearly financially. Undeterred, they headed straight back to Europe in May '94 before recording new tracks for a split EP with Japanese D-beat legends Disclose for Bloodsucker Records.

"Personally, that was the worst Hellkrusher tour," says Ali of the American jaunt. "It was badly organised, with very poor turn-outs and just the travelling itself was horrible, but I suppose you've got to remember it's a fucking huge country! Still, like all touring, we had a few highlights too and a few great gigs. We did a European tour in late '93 just before Hairy joined, with a stand-in drummer [Dave from Surf City Rockers], who couldn't really play our type of music and that was one of the longest months of my life too; it was shit, really, we were terrible and couldn't wait for the tour to end…"

In August 1994, Gus left to join Dirt (he ended up moving to America and doing a stint on guitar for Aus Rotten), closely followed by Moy and Hairy, leaving Ali with no band. When Aftermath finished in 1995, he hooked back up with Scotty and Curry, plus second guitarist Scoot and bassist Rob Morrison from Rampage. After making their live debut, supporting Muckspreader in Nottingham, during September '96, the new-look Hellkrusher headed to Europe for yet another mainland tour (this one being unfortunately cut short when Ali fell ill), before recording their third and arguably best album, 'Doomsday Hour', which was released by Skuld in early '97. Tighter than a hangman's noose and unstoppable in its frantic sonic assault, it remains one of the best 'Discore' albums ever recorded outside of Scandinavia.

"Yeah, 'Doomsday Hour' is a complete contrast to 'Buildings For The Rich'," reckons Scotty. "For starters, it was recorded properly at a decent studio [In A City, Bradford] with a producer that actually knew what he was doing, so the sound and production is way better than all the previous recordings. And as a band we had progressed a lot and brought in a second guitarist, so our sound and style had improved considerably; the songs were more technical, not to mention played better, and at last we had achieved the sound and style we had so wanted from day one…in fact it is the LP that 'Wasteland' should have been all along. Will it stand the test of time? I hope so! There's some great songs on it, but to be honest we've never been a studio band; we've always been plagued with bad luck as far as recordings go and we're a lot happier playing live – releasing records is just something we have had to do…"

Lightning couldn't be bottled twice, though, and the next recording was another disappointment, at least as far as Scotty's concerned, a split 7-inch with Preparation H for Dutch label Wicked Witch that was recorded November 1997 and released in early 1998.

"Returning to In A City, I just assumed the recording would be as good as or even better than 'Doomsday Hour', but unfortunately it wasn't! I just didn't like it from the start, to be honest, although getting blind drunk with Scoot the night before the recording and our van breaking down every half hour en route to the studio probably didn't help matters. The master tape actually got stolen from Rob when he was a motorcycle courier; unfortunately we had a copy or I would have jumped at the chance to re-record it, but such is the way with Hellkrusher – we've never had much luck in the studio and probably never will."

Not long after the split 7-inch dropped, Rob was replaced by Jon Green from Halifax, who played on 1999's 'Victims Of Hate' 7-inch for Skuld. Then Curry left in 2000, only to return in 2001 (Hairy played two gigs back with the band during the interim), just in time for the band to split after a shambolic gig in Barrow-in-Furness. The fat lady still hadn't bellowed 'Decontrol', though, because Hellkrusher reformed six years later for the 2007 Scumfest and they have played sporadically since then, including the 2009 Play Fast Or Don't festival in the Czech Republic. The gig offers keep coming, but the band members have more commitments outside of Hellkrusher now than ever before, so heavy touring is not on the cards, although Scotty definitely still has an itch to scratch.

"The future for Hellkrusher is just to continue functioning as a band," he says cautiously. "However little or much that may be, but hopefully to do as much as we can before we're either too old or unable to continue. There's still a lot of life left in us yet and I feel we still have a lot to give as a band; we definitely haven't got any intentions of throwing the towel in just yet anyway. We're just doing what we can when we can and enjoying doing it.

"Apart from doing gigs, our main aim is to record and release the tracks we were working on before we came grinding to a halt back in 2001. We were working on a lot of songs at the time, some completed, some works in progress, but unfortunately we went into hibernation before getting the opportunity to record them. I'd never gave up on the idea of recording again though and I've always craved the sense of closure from doing another recording, even if it is our final release, but yeah, it's definitely a case of unfinished business on my part and an aim we are desperate to achieve.

"Whether it's our metal-sounding name, not really befitting of a punk band, or our connections to our former bands (no disrespect intended), or the fact we left them and took part of the names with us, who knows? But I guess the saying, 'Too metal for punk and too punk for metal' has always followed us around and there's always been someone waiting to shoot us down for whatever reason or other – tossers! If we are to be remembered for anything though, I would like to think it was for our involvement in the UK punk scene as a whole, however small a part we played and for staying true to the DIY ethic we were brought up on.

"There never was or has been any pretence with Hellkrusher, no plan for world domination – we are way too shit for that! – or to make a living from the band for financial gain; we've never made fuck all anyway and had our own lives and jobs outside the band. We just wanted to play in a punk band, do gigs and get some sort of a positive message across to those who were prepared to listen. Sure, we've upset a few people along the way and let people down at times (what band hasn't?) but we've never strayed from the DIY path we set out on all those years back and have remained sincere as individuals and as a band on everything we've said and done since…surely that's enough to be remembered for?"

SELECT DISCOGRAPHY:

7-inch:
'Dying For Who?' (Tribal War, 1992)
'Fields Of Blood' EP (Skuld, 1993)
'Split' (Bloodsucker, 1994) – *split with Disclose*
'Split' (Wicked Witch, 1998) – *split with Preparation H*
'Victims Of Hate' EP (Skuld, 1999)

LPs:
'Wasteland' (RKT, 1991)
'Buildings For The Rich' (SMR, 1993)
'Doomsday Hour' (Skuld, 1997)

AT A GLANCE:
Belfast Records' recently re-mastered version of 'Doomsday Hour' will tear your face off and piss up your nose.

AFTERMATH

The aforementioned **Aftermath** really should have accomplished much more than they actually did. But the music scene is littered with the dust of wasted potential, so best get used to the bittersweet aftertaste of frustration. Formed in November 1993 shortly after Scotty and Curry left Hellkrusher, the band sounded more like English Dogs or GBH than the crusty thrash of HK, their rough-hewn edges tempered with a degree of old-fashioned tunefulness.

"Aftermath just happened," exclaims Scotty, who was also joined by vocalist Grant Taylor-Kane, previously of Debauchery and bassist Andy Turnbull, himself another victim of the ever-evolving Hellkrusher line-up churn. "After me and Curry left Hellkrusher, we realised we couldn't just stop being in a band; it was all we had done for the past however many years, so forming a new band was the obvious thing for us to do. We were all friends outside the band anyway and had all been in different bands together over the years, but essentially Aftermath was just some close friends coming together and wanting to do something new at a time when we were all available; it was almost like a new start for us.

"At first we weren't really trying to achieve anything as far as comparing Aftermath to our previous bands. We just thought we'd give it a go and see what happened; it was never a case of, 'Let's try and be better than this band or that…' It soon became apparent that we worked well together as a band though and had quite a unique sound and style, so we tried to approach everything as professionally as we could, whereas maybe we hadn't with some of our former bands. We would spend a lot of time putting our songs together and getting the right sound and the results *were* probably quite different to what we'd been involved in before, both musically and lyrically…"

Aftermath made their live debut the following March at the South Shields Top Club with local band Grudge and continued to hone their craft with several more local gigs alongside their friends Rampage before entering Route 26 Studios in Gateshead on 21 May 1994 to record the 'Final Prophecy' demo. A four-track effort that nailed perfectly that authentic crossover vibe of fast melodic punk rubbing angry shoulders with tight thrash metal, it was far too good to remain 'just' a demo for long and was snapped up by Edwin Feenstra for his Dutch label Wicked Witch to release as a 7-inch early the following year.

"Time and financial restraints meant we could only do four songs," sighs Scotty, "but we picked the best ones from our set to record, which meant we spent more time getting them right – something we probably wouldn't have done had we recorded more. Route 26 was a little-known studio in Gateshead; in fact, I'd never even heard of it before, but Gary, the engineer, knew what he was doing and did an excellent job for us. It was quite a relaxed recording session if I remember rightly, no pressure and everything went like clockwork on the day for once, but being well rehearsed definitely helped us.

"The finished product was excellent, I think," he adds, justifiably. "And even we were surprised how good it came out; the mix was perfect, a really good production for a demo, so we were more than happy with it. I still think it's a great recording even now and if I don't listen to it for any length of time I have to say I'm still in awe of it when I do. It's definitely aged well with time and doesn't come across as dated; it sounds as good now as when we tracked it."

Indeed it does, so it's little wonder that Wicked Witch released it as an EP, which was well received upon release and soon sold out of its first pressing before most people even knew it had been released. If it had been repressed and the band had made a greater effort to promote it, Aftermath might easily have had a long and illustrious career.

"Newcastle was shit for gigs at the time and if we wanted to do a gig or see a band we usually ended up organising it ourselves, which was why we played so much locally, but we still got to play with some great bands. We didn't get that many offers to play further afield, to be honest and I really don't know why we didn't organise some sort of tour to promote the EP, but we were limited to what we could do due to [bass player] Andy's work commitments, which always seemed to interfere with our plans. We did manage to get a few dates on the Meanwhile tour but, again, Andy couldn't do one of them and our van fucked up for another, so we ended up just doing the Newcastle date, unfortunately, though that was a blinding gig …"

In early 1995, Aftermath entered Uncle Sam's studio in Newcastle to record their second demo, but not before playing their one and only London gig, on 18 February that year, at the Albion in Stoke Newington with Coitus.

"I was in contact with Coitus at the time – we knew them through gigging with Hellkrusher – so we jumped at the chance to play with them. I think the whole idea was to do an exchange gig, with them playing up in Newcastle as well, but sadly it never happened. The gig itself was great though, one of – if not *the* – best gigs we ever did; packed out and with an atmosphere we hadn't experienced before…though that was probably due to the big following Coitus had, as we were virtually unknown outside the northeast. We went down a storm anyway, played a blinder and they gave us a great reception, which is something we weren't used to and it was nice to be playing to people other than the local audience back home for once."

The second demo showcased not only longer, more technical songs, but also superior playing and production when compared to the 'Final Prophecy' recording, but it also lacked its predecessor's spontaneous spark. Nonetheless, one track, 'The Naked Truth', appeared on Wicked Witch's seven-band compilation EP, 'Co-operation Not Competition', alongside the likes of Larm and Beyond Description. Andy was then replaced on bass by Rob Morrison from Rampage, but the band only played a few more local gigs before splitting when Grant left after a gig supporting English Dogs at the Bensham Working Men's Club in Gateshead on 20 October 1995.

"There was no official decision to call it a day," reckons Scotty. "We'd just done a great gig and then Grant announced he was quitting completely out of the blue. He obviously had his reasons, but I think he might have been disillusioned that things weren't moving as quickly as he would have liked; only he can answer that really, but there was no falling-out or ill feeling over it; we were – and still are – all good friends. We tried to carry on as a band, rehearsing and stuff and even had Curry trying to do vocals, but when that didn't work and a vocalist couldn't be found the band came to a natural end. It was all quite premature concerning the timing of the split, especially after all the work we had put into the band; maybe if we had played more gigs further afield and got the breaks we needed, things might have turned out differently… unfortunately they didn't!"

Following the demise of Aftermath, Scotty and Curry walked straight back into their positions as guitarist and drummer of Hellkrusher, where Scotty has remained to this day

Aftermath, 1995, L-R Grant, Ian Curry, Andy Turnbull, Scotty

(he also did a brief spell as bassist for Submit in 2000; originally known as Death Threat, they later became Deathsite). Curry eventually left Hellkrusher and joined Pitbull (who played their first gig on Halloween, 2000), before reuniting with Grant in Middleman, who split in 2004 after releasing several demos; in more recent years, he drummed for the reformed Rampage Brigade and the Fiend and is now back on the throne for Hellkrusher again. Andy Turnbull, meanwhile, played drums for Demon 340.

"Aftermath came and went in the blink of an eye, somewhat unnoticed and quickly forgotten," concedes Scotty. "We weren't around long enough to make any sort of impact, despite our efforts, but it would be nice to be remembered for the two recordings we left behind in our wake and the few gigs we did. We didn't form the band to prove a point or anything, but it was totally original and unlike anything we had done with our former bands before. We were one of only a few bands in Newcastle during that period of time and we did what we could, but we were just a small band in a big scene and sadly it all came to an end before we had chance to impress on a bigger scale... Oh well, shit happens, as they say!"

SELECT DISCOGRAPHY:

7-inch:
'Final Prophecy' (Wicked Witch, 1995)

AT A GLANCE:
Scotty has exciting plans to release both the Aftermath demos on CD, possibly with brand new recordings of some of the songs they never got round to tracking in the Nineties.

RAMPAGE

If ever there was a Nineties punk band from the UK that sounded like an Eighties punk band from the UK(!), it was Newcastle-upon-Tyne's **Rampage**. Although the band only issued three demos in their own right, they gigged often enough and hard enough to get a flagging local punk scene to rally around them. They were formed in late 1991 by vocalist Gary 'Gasa' Mead, who had never been in a band previously but recruited guitarist David 'Devo' Graig (who had formerly played bass with the Phantoms Of The Underground), bassist Rob Morrison and drummer Kev Bambra, the latter two having just split from the Gunrunners.

"Newcastle had always had a good punk scene," reckons Rob, "but by the Nineties places like the Station that we all used to go to had finished, although the Riverside was putting bands like 999 and the UK Subs on and Toot from the Station was getting bands like the Amebix and Civilised Society on there as well. We also had the Mayfair for bigger bands like the Damned and SLF, but many of the local bands that we used to go and see like the Fiend and Uproar had split up; in fact, most local bands were either turning metal or doing more American-influenced hardcore.

"The Phantoms Of The Underground were a '77-type' punk band that did a couple of Stooges covers as well as their own stuff; me and a couple of mates used to see them quite often as I went to school with the singer. They often played around the northeast and did the Station a number of times, supporting the Skeptix and other bands; they had a good following and did two demos. Gasa used to go to their gigs a lot as well 'cos nearly the whole band lived on the same estate as him, so he knew them pretty well.

"As for me, I learnt to play bass and joined a couple of bands that only managed a few practices before I ended up in a local Killing Joke-style band called Ritual, who I did a demo with. Then I joined the Gunrunners who had been going for a little bit and had just lost their bass player; Kev joined not long after on drums...he had also been singing in a band called Blood And Thunder. Again, the Gunrunners were more '77-style rock'n'roll punk, but it got me my first gigs around the country playing places like London, Oxford and Scotland; we played with the Seers, Snuff, Wilko Johnson, UK Subs, Les Thugs, Mega City 4 and the Crazy Pink Revolvers. And again, I got to do two demos with them.

"We all had a wide-ranging, but similar, set of influences," he adds, on what shaped Rampage's early sound. "As most of us had got into punk in '77 or '78, the obvious ones were the Clash, the Pistols and the Damned. I was at school with Devo, a year or so above him and he got his nickname because he always had the 'We are not men, we are Devo' badges on his blazer. But I don't think there was any one band who influenced our sound; we were into most punk from the Eighties onwards, both British and American, but Kev and me were also into bands like Killing Joke and New Model Army and Devo was even into Jimi Hendrix..."

After playing their first gig at Newcastle's Dog And Parrot pub (basically their 'local'), supporting Surf City Rockers, on 12 June 1992, the band entered Mill Studios in Alnwick on 2 August to record their first demo, 'War – Big Business', a spirited six-track effort that sounded like a cross between the Exploited and the Destructors.

"The studio was being run by members of Hellbastard," elaborates Rob. "I can't really remember who had recommended it, but we knew some of Hellbastard and thought that they would be more likely to know what sound we were after. And yeah, we were very pleased with the result, we had enough songs of our own by then and had picked what we thought were our strongest. I remember we did the whole recording fairly quickly, not because of time or money but just because we only needed a couple of takes to get it all down."

The demo helped land the band some gigs further afield, as well as the shows they were arranging locally and Rob has fond memories of their trips to Liverpool to play with MDM and So77: "We always tried to take as many people with us as possible on the 'Rampage awaydays' and they always turned into a full day of drinking, but I can't say we had any bad gigs, as we tried to enjoy every one we did. One of the funniest ones was probably at Cramlington Old Village; they had a fete and some local live bands on the back of a truck outside the church...someone had dropped out and for some reason we got recommended. So we turned up with a few mates, went to the pub as you do and then we went on after a group of young local kids did their Irish dancing.

"All the parents and grandparents were there watching; we marched up and got told not to swear, but as soon as we went on Gasa turned and shouted something like, 'You fuckin'

Rampage live

ready then?' and as the first note was hit all our mates ran forward and started dancing… before the end of the song parents and everyone else were grabbing kids and leaving. Even a wedding party came out and got some pictures took in front of us on stage…we never got asked back, but a lot of people still remember it to this day!"

A second guitarist was added in the shape of Steve Campbell, who brought a heavier, harder edge to the band's punk-as-fuck second demo, 'Load Up Your Guns', recorded once again at Mill Studio, Alnwick. "There wasn't that much of a progression between the first two demos, as most of the songs were written about the same time," reckons Rob. The song 'Riot', he recalls, was written by "Gasa after he had been sat at home and smelled burning; he thought he had left something on the cooker but looked out his window to see people running riot all over his estate…"

Drummer Kev unfortunately broke his ankle windsurfing, which stopped him drumming for three years and he was replaced by Ian Curry from Aftermath and Hellkrusher. Steve also left and was replaced by Robbie Kennedy. Eventually the new line-up entered Polestar Studios in June '97 – with Rob Blamire from Penetration manning the desk – to record their 'Destroy The Power' demo. With the title track becoming a live favourite, reminiscent as it was of Uproar at their anthemic best, two tracks were included by Bomb Factory Records on their 'Keep It Angry' compilation and gigs were played with the likes of UK Subs, Vice Squad, the Varukers, One Way System and the Casualties. However Devo left the very day of a short UK tour with the Exploited…

"We had a gig to do in Edinburgh with the Exploited which we were all looking forward to," explains Rob. "We met up at my mate Low's tattoo shop, as he was driving us up there and there was no sign of Devo. Now, Devo was always late for everything and would sometimes turn up to gigs just as we were about to go on, but as time went by we knew we had to go and get him. So Gasa and Robbie went round to his place with Low, but, after banging on his door, Devo came down, jacket on, guitar in hand, walked out the door, then said, 'I can't do this!' He turned back round, shut the door and was gone…and no end of knocking, calling or anything got him back out. And that was it, no explanation or anything; years later he would only say he had had enough and didn't want to do it any more, but dope was always a priority with him and in later years his problem would come to a head…"

Devo's replacement was Andrew Ridden, who played on the band's version of '4Q' for Rhythm Vicar's 1998 Blitz tribute album 'Voice Of A Generation'. It was the last ever Rampage recording because, with Gasa becoming increasingly disillusioned and apathetic, the band split up the following year. However, they briefly reformed as Rampage Brigade in 2003 and issued a convincing fourth demo comprising seven new songs and re-recordings of 'Load Up Your Guns' and 'Destroy The Power'.

"At the time me, Curry and Gasa were still meeting up at gigs and in bars and this young local punk band we knew called CS Gas were starting to do gigs at the same places we used to play; they were also doing a cover of 'Destroy The Power'. We were all at one of their gigs and Gasa got up to sing it and the place went mad; I remember Gasa walking off stage past me and Curry and saying, 'We're getting the band back together!' Just like in *The Blues Brothers*!

"So that was it; we got Andy Ridden and Kurt Anderson, from CS Gas, to play guitars, Curry on drums again [for a short time at least; he was replaced by Geoff Pearson from CS Gas before the fourth demo] and me on bass. We wrote a few new songs and had three practices before we did our first gig with CS Gas and attitude-wise there was no difference; Gasa was as manic as always, and having younger people in the band made us all think we were 20 years younger – but even they couldn't keep up with Gasa! Musically I think we just went back to basics and lost some of the metal influences that had crept in before; we got back to the hardcore style that had started us off…"

Kurt subsequently left and was replaced by Carlton Train, but when Andy left as well, leaving Rampage with just one guitarist, Gasa started to lose interest in rehearsing again and Rampage split for good in 2008, playing their final show as support to the Adolescents at Trillians in July of that year. Carlton and Geoff both joined Rob in Ego Zombies, an outfit still going strong today, alongside Jane Scott and Oana Barlow.

"Obviously we would love to be remembered for so much more than what we actually did," sighs Rob, on reflection. "But I hope we get remembered for keeping things going at a time when it seemed that the punk scene in Newcastle was starting to dry up. And after all these years, people *do* still remember the gigs we did and the bands we supported or were supported by. But I also hope that, just as we were inspired to pick up instruments and form a band, that we inspired others to try and do the same, whether they were punks or not. There was nothing pretentious about us and people could see that; we were just four friends who wanted to make our own impact on the punk scene and have lots of fun while doing it."

AT A GLANCE:
Rob will gladly burn the reader a CDR of the three Rampage demos if his costs are covered: chaosbrigade@blueyonder.co.uk

---

KITO

One of the most powerful of the northern UK hardcore bands, the savagely eclectic **Kito** (named after the tribe of cannibals and the island they inhabit in Marino Girolami's low-budget Italian splatter film *Zombi Holocaust*) not only ground out gnarly hardcore punk rock in the vein of Rorschach, they also rocked out like righteous motherfuckers when their muse was so inclined, their material veering chaotically from D-beat thrash via discordant jazzy interludes to epic, chugging, metallic instrumentals.

They formed in and around Middlesbrough in 1991 when guitarists Matt Burke and Stephen Paul McGurk (aka 'SP') left their straightedge band Soricide and were joined by drummer Paul 'Cat' Hirst, bassist Tom Chapman and vocalist Robert Hallowes (aka Rob Kito).

"Early Kito practice sessions highlighted a number of musical influences," reckons SP, "including a mix of those hardcore acts you've mentioned like Rorshach and Infest and heavy rock bands such as Into Another and Soundgarden. One of our first songs, 'Sixteenth Saviour', was basically a Soundgarden riff played the wrong way round…were we the backwards offspring of Seattle grunge? Who knows!"

Kito at 1 In 12, 1993, by Rich Corbridge, Matt and Chris

Kito, Rob, by Rich Corbridge

Kito guitar cases

Kito played their first show on 4 April in Fowler's Yard, Durham, supporting the mighty Born Against from New York City; not a bad bill to make your debut on by anyone's standards, but Paul Hirst left that summer, soon after a show with Hell No at the 1 In 12. He was replaced behind the kit by Matthew Woodward from Sofa Head who brought a unique feel to the band's rhythm section, his heavily syncopated style perfectly complementing the dark brooding riffs. With some potent new songs written, the band wasted little time getting into Studio 64, Middlesbrough, to record their 'Trap Them And Kill Them' demo tape, the title of which was another reference to cult Italian horror; it was the alternative title given to Aristide Massaccesi's low-budget shocker *Emanuelle And The Last Cannibals*. The demo marked the dawning of the definitive Kito sound and style, all abrasive grooves and intriguing time signatures.

"The first four songs we wrote were stereotypical political hardcore rants which I wasn't very happy with," admits Rob. "What happened during that recording shaped the future of the band in many ways. The lyrics were too garbled and long-winded and didn't come out well in recording, so basically I had to go home and write some succinct lyrics that would be more powerful. It's then that I started exploring the more repetitive, minimal, personal, weird, nasty, 'dark history' style of lyric writing that would become a Kito standard. I'm not sure exactly how it happened, but I was much happier with the flavour of the lyrics from then on; they were still very political, but with a dark, historical angle that suited me and the music much more than humdrum rants about vegetarianism or whatever…"

The title track of the demo would be used the following year by Armed With Anger Records on their 'Consolidation' compilation 7-inch, with Kito appearing alongside Submission, Voorhees, Nailbomb, Stand Off, Understand and Ironside. Before then, by the end of summer 1992, Tom had relocated to Lille and was replaced by Chris Coulthard, who had previously been known as the unmistakable and charismatic voice behind One2One. Next to leave was SP that same year; Chris Campbell-Lee then joined the band, fresh from Middlesbrough thrashers Catharsis, with Chris Coulthard switching to guitar and 'the new Chris' taking up the role of bass-player.

"Quite unlike many punk or hardcore bass-players, Chris played without a plectrum," recalls Matt, "and his preferred sound was very bass-heavy. He played hard grooves, first on a weighty Westone bass before then switching to his trademark Fender Jazz in later years and, like the rest of us, was also influenced by an eclectic mix of musical styles."

In late 1993 Chris Coulthard left Kito, relocating to London to study film. By this time, the band were becoming somewhat frustrated with having to cope with the seemingly transient nature of their line-up, but finally, with 1994 approaching, Kito found its hard-sought solidity with new guitarist Stuart Smith from Darlington-based melodicore outfit Slick 50.

"I reckon we were still up and down with live performances," offers Rob, "due to shitty equipment and lack of rehearsals, right up until Stu joined. He had such a solid style and he looked after his gear so well; he also had a passion for experimentation and non-conformity… in other words, he slotted perfectly into the Kito fold."

1994 saw the band heading out to Europe for the first time with Baby Harp Seal before unleashing their debut EP, 'Johnson, Mary: 188897764' (named after the subject of a post-mortem anatomy book), at the end of the year. Wrapped in a cover that depicted images of an autopsy room, zombies and a lobotomy, it was never going to be pretty musically, but few were prepared for the relentless measured intensity of the single, which was reminiscent of

Ironside at their peak and some of the early Doghouse roster.

"One song in particular, 'The Victim's Body Showed Traces of Carnal Violence', became a crowd favourite at our shows," says Matthew, "and, along with the instrumental 'Kito', a signature tune. Arguably more so than the band's demo, the four songs on the EP showed a definite continuity in time, tempo, structure and feel, due in some part to the fact that the songs had been structured from the ground up. In our kitchen at Crescent Road in Middlesbrough, Chris and I wrote full rhythm parts prior to the guitars and voice being added; as a result, the overall sound centred round an even greater development of the groove, creating a more danceable, head-nodding feel to the material. Rob's guttural howls still rode atop the sonic waves below, but his less-is-more approach worked to ever greater effect on the 7-inch."

Of that first European tour with Baby Harp Seal, he adds: "The two bands could not have been at greater polar opposites in stylistic terms, but the tour helped to form strong, long-lasting friendships and would ultimately prove to be an extremely important (some might say life-changing) and memorable trip for all concerned. It was also the first time many of the band members had played shows in places such as France, Belgium and Germany and probably one of the first times English DIY bands had toured Europe together.

"Along with other bands helping to build a meaningful exchange of musical and political interaction across Europe, we wanted to prove that major-label backing and hype were not required for bands to tour successfully in Europe. Bands were more than capable of organising, promoting and managing a tour themselves, without the need for managers, press, media hype or even the internet."

"The real kick was when we started touring Europe," adds Rob. "From Dunkerque, Tongeren and that first Potsdam gig in 1994, I knew that this was the best reason to be in a band..."

The rather raging (in the vein of early Neurosis) 'Rings Of Fear' was contributed to the 'Nothing New' compilation EP on Kwijibo Records, that also featured Bob Tilton, Kitchener, Dead Wrong and Bugeyed. However, before the EP was even out, Matt Burke had left, making way for Tom to rejoin in March 1995, although Rob Holden from Baby Harp Seal stood in for several shows at the beginning of the year. Another European tour with BHS was undertaken, with Manfat also in tow, a three-and-a-half week trek that took in Germany, Belgium, Slovakia, the Czech Republic and Austria. Once home, Tom left again, this time relocating to Berlin where he would go on to play with Real and Battle Royale; he was replaced by Michael Blackwood.

"Michael was undoubtedly the band's most technically accomplished guitarist," reckons Matt, "and was also the fourth member of the band to have previously also been a member of Soricide — between 1988 and 1990. He brought an arguably higher and more reliable standard of playing to the band, alongside Stu's creativity, solid chops and good timekeeping. Chris and myself were a flush, ever-improving rhythm section as well and Kito went from strength to strength during that period."

"We became much more reliable as a live act about then," agrees Rob, "especially after the 1995 tour when Michael joined the band. That was our final line-up and we ended up touring Europe three times together [1996 with Rated R, 1997 with Polaris and 1999 with John Holmes], as well as Ireland in '97 [with Bilge Pump] and were at a high standard of quality, both in our writing and live performances."

By 1997, the band's sound was also evolving, generally becoming more progressive, intricate and melodic, probably as a result of touring with more tuneful post-hardcore bands and being exposed to the wonders of the European circuit on a regular basis.

"The nature of the DIY underground punk movement in the UK and Europe had evolved dramatically," explains Matt. "The picture-postcard punk image now had little to do with real life in squats and clubs throughout Europe. Open minds, evolving communities and changing attitudes towards developing ideologies and musical styles meant that bands with radically different sounds could tour together, play the same venues and be appreciated equally, whether playing grindcore or post-rock. To many of the people involved in the DIY network, the term 'punk' had never been purely representative of an image or a sound, but rather a way of doing things, an act of dissension against corporate greed, a passion for maintaining a strong sense of ethics and equality, of a collective conscience and a development of more proactive, positive, meaningful forms of dissent.

"Styles and sub-genres were merging and crossing over, often bringing streams of opposing musical ideas into contact with one another and the Nineties saw possibly the largest and most profound shift so far in DIY and underground music culture…and Kito were no exception to this. We'd always been into a wide range of styles and genres, but at that time it seemed like there were just a lot of really good, really influential bands who were taking punk and hardcore to the next level; bands like Hoover and all those other awesome Dischord bands, who were essentially still playing loud, raw, emotive music but with much greater sophistication and musicality."

During 1997, Kito recorded a cover of (DC hardcore legends) Government Issue's classic anti-fame anthem 'Hall Of Fame' for One More Than Six Records' 'Caesar's Palace' 7-inch compilation that also featured Manfat, Pellethead and Knieval. Interestingly, the band drafted in Michael Gillham (normally the drummer in Manfat) to play second guitar on the session, as a result of a scheduling mix-up and Michael Blackwood not being present at the recording. They also controversially used an image of Southend band Understand (with their eyes blacked out) for their artwork for the single, as a statement on DIY hardcore bands 'selling out' to major labels, Understand having then just signed to East West/Warner.

The new Kito sound was captured beautifully on their 'The Long Player' LP for Flat Earth in 1998, a strikingly considered album that displayed great depth, confidence and a high level of experimentation for a 'UKHC band'. For the first time in their history they abandoned their total use of distorted guitars throughout, opting for both clean and distorted guitars in an attempt to emulate the creepy atmospherics and dynamics of bands such as Slint and June Of '44. Recorded at In A City in Bradford, with Dale Tomlinson (former Catharsis and Manfat guitarist, then playing in John Holmes) at the engineering helm, the album landed a rave four-star review in *Kerrang!* magazine, where it was accurately described as "Occupying the exact point where anarcho-punk meets sludgecore…"

"Yeah, I think we all had fun during the album recording," recalls Matt. "It was a good atmosphere, very relaxed and also remarkably smooth-running. We felt like we were making a record to be proud of and we stayed in the studio really late, just hanging out, drinking and talking. It was like we were in no hurry to leave; we all felt quite at home there, I think."

Unfortunately it was to be the last Kito release in their own right, with the band splitting after a final tour of Europe (with John Holmes) during spring 1999 because Matt and Chris had relocated – to Leeds and London respectively – late the previous year. Kito rocked their last show at the Fenton pub in Leeds in June 1999, with Canvas and Bob Tilton, a fitting bill to mark an end to the band's journey. "It was an amazing night, really, for a lot of reasons," Matt remembers fondly. "The place was totally rammed and there was definitely an air of excitement. We didn't play that well, at least not by our then-high standards, but it was pretty wild…probably the only time I can ever remember seeing people crowd-surfing in the Fenton. So we went out in a positive way, I reckon…"

Post-Kito, Matt, Michael and Stu went on to form a wholly different-sounding (think post-rock/indie) band, the Dragon Rapide, in the winter of 1999, a band that toured Europe extensively between 2001 and 2005 and issued two albums, 'Meetings With Remarkable Machines' (5nach3 Records, 2003) and 'II' (Chinchillatone Records, 2005). Matt also toured the USA with New Jersey trio the Lapse in 2001 and Europe with San Francisco/Melbourne(!) 'riot grrrl' band, Origami, in 2003. Until recently he was with the Afrobeat/electro/post-punk Cissy, but now plays in Azores with ex-Cissy members Gav Montgomery and Matt Dixon, as well as doing the synth/drums duo Asteroid and a new project, Tooth Fairies, with fellow ex-Kito member Stu Smith.

Rob went on to sing with furious Leeds-based hardcore outfit War All The Time, a band that has toured around the world, including Southeast Asia, while Chris would also play bass with several other bands in London, including a brief stint in Comanechi. Robert Holden did time with Month Of Birthdays and Castles And Car Wrecks, Chris Coulthard in Geoffrey Oi!cott and Michael Gilham in Voorhees and Drunk In Hell.

"One of my friends once asked me, 'How come I really like Kito, even though I hate metal and hardcore music?'" offers Matt. "And that question has always meant a lot to me; it seemed like a validation that we were more than just a hardcore/punk/metal band and that we had the ability to reach people, regardless of genre, scene, clique and musical tags or boxes. As creators and consumers of music, it can be easy for people to get hung up on all that stuff sometimes and I hope we displayed an ability to transcend all that, at least in some way.

"When I think about the band and think about why it was special to me, there are a lot of reasons; there were so many things we all experienced and learned as a result of being in that band, about music, people, the world, ourselves…so it wasn't just special musically, it was really meaningful and it taught us a lot, I think. I'd like us remembered as a good band, but also as one of the bands that helped to cement the idea of the DIY attitude within music and the liberation and empowerment that can be achieved through that."

SELECT DISCOGRAPHY:

7-inch:
'Johnson, Mary: 188897764' (Armed With Anger, 1994)
'Split' (Hammerwerk, 1995) – *split with Konstrukt*

LP:
'The Long Player' (Flat Earth, 1998)

AT A GLANCE:
Matt will burn you a Kito discography CDR if you cover his costs:
mattrapide@hotmail.com

EMBITTERED

Also from Middlesbrough, **Embittered** were formed in late 1989 in the midst of the second wave of UK anarcho punk, but more specifically when vocalist Bri Puplett from Catharsis joined forces with bassist Ash Quinn from One 2 One. Several guitarists were trialled, including Matt from Soricide, before Darren 'Shaggy' O'Hara from Malediction and Cerecloth joined, with local jazz drummer Dave Carr rounding out the line-up that recorded the band's first demo in September 1990.

"The local scene was pretty poor when Embittered started, to be honest with you," reckons Bri. "There were always plenty of indie bands, but nothing that could be considered extreme by any stretch of the imagination; there were one or two thrash-metal bands kicking about, but the only bands that were within the same musical mindset as us were Aural Corpse and Malediction, who were more of a death-metal band.

"Anyway, myself and Ash were the founding members, so to speak and I think all we wanted to achieve initially was to make a racket, play some gigs and possibly record a demo…nothing new there! So, what we did achieve in the time we were going, I am very proud of."

"Our other bands, Catharsis and One 2 One played together in '89 and we realised we had a lot in common," adds Ash. "Bri was based in Middlesbrough and I was in a small town called Guisborough; the 'scene', if you could call it that, was small, but we were all young – 15 to 20 years old – and full of enthusiasm. Between us all, people were into all sorts: straightedge, hardcore, punk, death metal and, more importantly, the animal rights movement, with many of us getting active in local groups and the hunt saboteurs."

After making their live debut at the Black Swan in Guisborough with Soricide and Malediction, Embittered recorded their first demo at Studio 64, Middlesbrough, during September 1990, a brutally raw eight-track effort with all the finesse of a charging rhinoceros but a certain punk charm nonetheless. Darren left soon after its release to concentrate on Malediction and was replaced by Sean from One 2 One, with Anth Palmer also joining as second vocalist.

"I moved up to Middlesbrough in 1990 to continue studying graphic design," explains Anth, "but knew absolutely nothing about the place nor anyone there at all. Myself and Bri, although not knowing each other prior to this, had a mutual buddy called Brob over in Belgium, who previously published *Tilt* zine; he gave me Bri's contact details, so I got in touch and he came to my house a few weeks later, saying that his new band were playing a gig at the local pub. I went along and met the rest of the band and when Ash asked me afterwards what I'd thought of the gig, I told him it was great but thought it would be a whole lot better if they had two vocalists – and I ended up joining shortly after…

"I guess I wanted to take the band slightly away from the stereotypical grind mindset that it had, make it more creative and more influential politically. Pretty much the usual aspirations: to record some good music, put forward our views and opinions on subjects we felt strongly about and try to help raise awareness. We weren't a straightforward 'D-beat band' by any stretch of the imagination; we wanted to explore the musical capabilities of the guys in the band and lyrically tackle subjects that weren't particularly stereotypical either."

One aspect of the band where they definitely strived to differ was in the visual side of their live performances. Several UK punk bands – not least of all Chumbawamba – had employed

Embittered, Anth, 1993

Embittered, Bri and Gus, 1993

various props to enhance their message when playing live and Embittered just took it one step further…and added a spice of danger to proceedings in keeping with their breakneck music.

"The idea was for our gigs to have a more visual element to them," concurs Anth, "to accompany the barrage of noise and add another dimension to what we were trying to convey through the lyrics. So we introduced the fire-breathing and placards and backdrops and such; I had more ideas that unfortunately didn't come to fruition due to my leaving the band…the one that always comes to mind was to have a suit covered in bloodied and decaying dolls to represent the effects of over-population."

"Ah, the props we used," adds Bri. "I remember being too drunk to breathe fire once and swallowing the paraffin…that shit tastes bad! Also being drunk and setting articles of clothing – or my own hands – alight and setting off fire alarms at gigs. I think we enjoyed the aspect of presenting something more than just music and the props definitely added to that… Besides, who the hell could really understand what the fuck message we were trying to get across in the lyrics?"

The 11-track 'And You Ask Why?' demo was recorded in July 1991 and saw the band developing their worship of early Napalm Death into something uniquely their own, incorporating the twin vocal attack of ENT with some vicious blast beats from the heavier, more metallic end of the crusty-punk spectrum, not to mention atmospheric samples and an acoustic intro featuring female vocals courtesy of Anth's then-girlfriend, Annj. Although rather thinly produced (think a whirlwind of top end and distortion!), it's still a well-rounded and articulate example of 'anarcho grind' and it saw the band starting to land themselves some very positive fanzine reviews and gigs further and further afield.

"That was the band finding ourselves musically, lyrically and stylistically," claims Bri, "a 25-minute demo which came with an A4 two-sided fold-out cover, stickers and mini-poster… an anarcho-crust delight! By the time we recorded it, we had sorted a steady line-up, written some good songs, which had a degree of experimentation within them, had a quality logo and a genre all our own which we called 'anarcho grind'! I was very happy with it all, as it really felt like an achievement and something that contributed to the nascent second wave of, er, 'Britcore'. As for how it sounds now? I still think it's great, my only regret being that it never got pressed onto vinyl or CD and all any of us have left of it is a copy or two of the old, old original master cassette."

'And You Ask Why?' brought them to the attention of Louisville label Desperate Attempt, who offered them a split 7-inch with deranged Belgian noise terrorists Hiatus, but by the time they recorded two tracks for it – 'In Case of Opposition' and 'This Utopian Dream' – Dave had been replaced by Mac on drums.

"It must be said that the band went through drummers and guitarists like most people go through toilet paper," laughs Bri, "and during our existence we pretty much had most of the local people in who showed any interest at all in being in a crusty-punk band – and even some who didn't. Middlesbrough was a small place for any extreme music at the time, as the majority of people into 'alternative' music were into bands like Primus or Jane's Addiction, or some of the popular thrash-metal bands, with only a handful of people into anything remotely heavier. If you lived there and had dreadlocks, combat pants and were 'crusty-looking', chances were that you were into the Levellers! It irked me like mad when people used to ask me if I liked those kind of bands…which I obviously didn't."

The single didn't come out for 18 months, by which time Sean had been replaced by Gus on guitar and Embittered had not only undertaken a two-week European tour with Svart Sno and Hiatus but recorded a split album with Dystopia for Misanthropic.

"Human Lethargy from Greece did some of the European gigs as well," recalls Bri, "and, like Hiatus and Svart Sno, were all great people playing great music. As for memorable highs and lows? Just getting out of the UK and going to Europe for the first time was a high, as was getting paid and fed, which was a real rarity in the UK at the time…oh and playing Potsdam, which had the local Russian Army kick-boxing champ coming down to see if there were any contenders; he was built like a brick shit-house and hard as fuck compared to all the weedy punkers who were there. As for lows…nothing that I can really recall – except our driver being a complete pain in the arse!"

Mac left both the band and the northeast when he got home from the tour, closely followed by Saul and when the split with Dystopia took an age to appear as well, Anth also departed, relocating to Leeds and concentrating on his zine, *Duhhh!*

"I left around April 1993," says Anth, "and seem to recall that the guy who stepped up to try and replace Mac couldn't quite cut it. I guess that was the catalyst for an on-going situation of not being able to find someone who could fit that vacancy, no matter how hard we tried; throughout the first few years of the band, we'd had so many line-up changes, it had become too much of a pain in the ass having new people in and them having to learn the songs, etc. To be honest, it was too much of an uphill battle to try and keep a solid line-up going…

"The last gig I played was December 1992 at the 1 In 12, an all-dayer that I personally remember as being one of our best gigs. Bri was fire-breathing throughout the set, managing to set his leg on fire and nearly taking out the front row of the audience and the ceiling; we had some props with placards and shit and just bulldozed through our 17-song set flat out with hardly any gaps. It may have been the same gig where some guy was shouting 'ENT!' at us in some pissy fashion that had Big Ste from Extinction Of Mankind wander over to tell him to shut the fuck up…"

With Ash moving to guitar and Cockney from the Incest Brothers and Co-Exist joining on bass, a new drummer was sought, but when this proved easier said than done Bri bought himself a drum machine – which led to Embittered being put on a back-burner when he formed the evil-sounding industrial band Manfat with Ash and Dale (who himself had briefly played for Embittered very early on, prior to Matt and Shaggy joining).

However, when Michael Gilham from Voorhees and Blessed Realm expressed an interest in drumming for Embittered and Bri wasn't interested in resuming his role as sole remaining vocalist, Ash recruited new bassist Mark Fox from Malediction and no less than *three* new vocalists, Shaun Stephenson (also from Malediction), Neil Harrison and Rob 'Slavery' Ankers (who did *Cod Eye* fanzine). This line-up of the band played several gigs and recorded the pretty-damn-intense 'Choked' 7-inch for German label Ecocentric before splitting in1995 when Mark returned home to Hull and Michael left to join Manfat.

"That final line-up should probably have gone under a different name as only I was now left and even I'd switched to guitar," admits Ash. "But I actually prefer the 'Choked' 7-inch to the split with Dystopia, although it was pretty basic due to my lack of ability on guitar. Michael's drumming was great though and the three vocal thing was great live: a punk, a skin and a long-hair…a real oddity."

Manfat went on release a super-heavy three-track self-titled 7-inch on German label A-Wat in 1994 and a split 7-inch with Hard To Swallow for Flat Earth Records in 1997, before Bri and Dale formed John Holmes with Gords from Hard To Swallow and Sned from Generic, One By One, Health Hazard and a million others. Meanwhile, Ash did Sawn Off from 1996 until 2001 and then Boxed In from 2001 'til 2005 and is currently in War All The Time and Death's Black Riders.

"For me personally it was the essence of taking the elements I'd held on to from the early- to mid- Eighties anarcho-punk scene to where I was as an individual by the early Nineties," offers Anth, who 'retired' from making music after Embittered. "By then I had become far less naive, much more cynical and overly more questioning, not only of the aspects in life that I didn't agree with, but also of the critical thinking I had of ourselves, of a subculture that was entrenched in always assuming that we were right and everyone else was wrong. I didn't want to write clichéd lyrics that merely reflected an opposite viewpoint; I wanted to look at different perspectives of pertinent issues that had long been associated with political punk bands.

"For example, the lyrics penned for 'Two Manipulated Bodies' were intended to question the fact that despite individuals portraying themselves as autonomous free thinkers who upheld equality, they (or rather, we) are just as fallible and prone to negative factors inherent in human nature and that we all have the potential, whether intentional or otherwise, to treat someone else like shit to suit our own gains…"

"Back in the day I suspect we wouldn't have wanted to be different from our peers," adds Bri, on a lighter note, "but I would like Embittered to be remembered for our crust…our noise…and our fire!"

SELECT DISCOGRAPHY:

7-inch:
'Split' (Desperate Attempt, 1992) – *split with Hiatus*
'Choked' (Concentric, 1994)

12-inch:
'Split' (Misanthropic, 1993) – *split with Dystopia*

AT A GLANCE:
Anth will gladly burn off a CDR of all the band's recordings (33 tracks, including the demos) if the interested reader will cover his costs: thirteenthirtytwo@hotmail.com

LEATHERFACE

Having attained a huge cult following over the years, it's safe to say that **Leatherface** are one of the more influential bands included in this book. A claim well supported by the fact that 38 bands from eight different countries were moved enough by the band's music that they wanted to pay homage on the double Leatherface tribute CD compiled by Rubber Factory in 2008.

"We started for the same reasons most other bands start," reckons guitarist/vocalist Frankie Stubbs, who formed the band during August 1988 in Sunderland. "We had no friends, but we happened to play guitars. I also opened practice rooms so people could make their own noises in a place called the Bunker; it was a thankless task, but I did it because I loved it and at the same time we raised money to build a recording studio... I really did love it, too; it would be pissing down with snow and I would walk round to open up for bands to practice!

"One of the positives of the northeast scene about then was the Sunderland Musicians Collective; that is what spawned me and everyone else I loved! The negatives were the competition that it created..."

"There were – and always have been – some good musicians and bands in the northeast," agrees drummer Andrew 'Lainey' Laing, who had previously played with HDQ. "But, especially back then, unless you were from Manchester, or further south, it was hard to get your music noticed. Like most young kids, we just wanted to make a racket. [Other guitarist] Dickie [aka Richie Hammond, also from HDQ] and Frankie both had Gordon Smith guitars [the original line-up rounded out by bassist Stuart Scouler], which was unusual and thought it would be great to have two guitarists to make what Hammond often called 'Bison Power'...

"Frankie always wanted to make at least one memorable tune that would stand the test of time; he even said, 'As long as I can write a song like the Lurpak [butter] advert, I'll be happy!' It really was about writing songs that were good tunes, that people would instantly recognise as Leatherface, as well as remembering them..."

Widely regarded as a cross between Motörhead (mainly due to Frankie's raw, rasping vocal style that somehow still manages to be loaded with pathos, despite its gravelly overtones) and Hüsker Dü (because of their fast, unpretentious songs), Leatherface did indeed have a style all their own from the outset. But when one considers the many weird and wonderful songs they chose to cover during their career, it's apparent that there were more eclectic influences at work as well.

After making their live debut apparently supporting GBH, "who didn't turn up", at the Newcastle Riverside ("We played 20 minutes and then went home," laughs Lainey, "leaving most of the audience stunned...not sure if that was a good or a bad thing!"), Leatherface rapidly grew organically as a band. Building up a loyal following with their strong live performances, they recorded a five-song demo at Desert Sounds, Gateshead and embarked upon a 12-date European tour with Union Morbide ("Crazy Dutchmen!" remembers Lainey) during May 1989, although Dickie couldn't make the trip due to prior commitments with his other band HDQ (he would soon be standing in on bass for the Toy Dolls as well), so the band undertook the gigs as a three-piece.

They then recorded their debut LP 'Cherry Knowle' at Beaumont Street Studios, Huddersfield, during July 1989. Released through Meantime Records (Lainey was in Sofahead with label boss Ian Armstrong at the time), it saw the band cutting through the trappings of the complacent British punk scene like a knife through butter with their fiery delivery and incisive rough-hewn melodies and is widely regarded as a UK punk classic. But bassist Stuart left the band the day after recording it, paving the way for a string of bassists including Rob Bewick and Dick 'Head' Camm.

"Most of the writing was done in Frankie's garage," reveals Lainey. "Me and Frankie tried to repair the leaking roof…but probably made it worse than it was before. We recorded the songs in the garage at first, but then to actually go into the studio and hear the full recording was great. But no, we had no idea it would be hailed as a punk classic when we were writing it…"

Apparently named after the Cherry Knowle mental hospital in Ryhope, Sunderland, songs like 'Sublime' did indeed recall Motörhead at their most tuneful, but elsewhere Leatherface really channelled the spirit of Eighties punk band the Blood, an anarchic yet talented bunch of yobbos who took the huge tunes of the Damned and dirtied them up with some heavy-metal guitars and barked vocals. It also featured high-speed covers of 'Knockin' On Heaven's Door' by Bob Dylan and 'In The Ghetto', which was originally written by Mac Davis and made famous by Elvis Presley, a song about the cyclic nature of generational poverty that has also been covered by everyone from Dolly Parton to Nick Cave…but never with the same intensity as the Leatherface version!

"I remember thinking, 'Dickie has made a mistake here…'" laughs Frankie, "and that I should start to say more about what happened in the band…as in how we record and where we record!"

"I remember when that first Leatherface record came out, as if it were yesterday," reckons Welly, vocalist with Cardiff's Four Letter Word, who recorded all four of their albums with Frankie Stubbs sat at the mixing desk. "We'd all hang out in Marvin [from Chaos UK]'s Autonomy Records in Cardiff on a Saturday afternoon and he'd just got 'Cherry Knowle' in from Meantime when it came out and he was saying how great it was 'cos it sounded 'like a punk Motörhead'. I bought it as I'd been following HDQ and it seemed like a continuation of sorts and from there I followed their output until they split initially and then again after they reformed.

"Marvin put them on at a gig after a punk's picnic here around that time, but everyone got so wasted no-one really remembers much about it. I did leave the picnic for a bit and by the time I got to the gig later, Marvin was drunk and had been beaten up by some northern hooligans who'd brought their dogs with them. He was semi-conscious on the pavement outside the gig and the last time I saw him was at the bar. I asked him if he'd paid the bands and he motioned to the top pocket of his denim jacket with a glazed expression. I fished out a wad of notes, paid the venue and found Frankie and paid him. It wasn't until years later that I told Marvin and he told me he thought he'd lost the money. So it turned out I'd met Frankie years before I actually did; he just remembers wondering how they were ever going to get paid and then someone who wasn't the promoter giving him some money…!"

After playing the first of many gigs with their good friends Snuff, the 'Beerpig' 7-inch was released during early 1990 on Meantime, which featured a rousing cover of Elton John's 'Candle In The Wind' (at that point still a tribute to Marilyn Monroe and nothing to do with Princess Diana) and tours were undertaken of the UK (with FUAL) and Europe (again as a three-piece, without Dickie, although he did play one of the shows with Leatherface when

Leatherface, live at the Knitting Factory, Brooklyn, 2010, pictures by Dave Sanders

they were on the same bill as HDQ in Eindhoven). Upon their return, Leatherface wasted little time signing with the Roughneck Recording Company, a division of London's Fire Records, who issued not only the band's second album, 'Fill Your Boots', in 1990 (with Rob Turnbull from Crane on bass), but also the 'Razorblades And Aspirin' single and the 'Smokey Joe' 12-inch, complete with a superb cover of 'Message In A Bottle' by The Police. All saw the band maturing into a melodic powerhouse to be reckoned with.

However, it was the 'Mush' album, released the following year (with Steven 'The Eagle' Charlton on bass), that most agree is the definitive Leatherface release, where everything finally came together and the Leatherface sound that the band had been threatening to unleash for several long years finally unveiled itself in all its humble splendour. All the sonic ingredients previously employed by the band were present and correct, but on 'Mush' they truly captured in the studio the beautiful honesty at the heart of the band and the deep well of emotion that was the essence of Frankie Stubbs's songwriting. Without pretence or contrivance, he put into achingly simple words so many bitter-sweet experiences we could all relate to and thus reached out and touched everyone that ever listened to 'Mush'.

"Frankie's a great songwriter for sure, but for me Dickie makes Leatherface," argues Neil Cox, a dyed-in-the-wool Leatherface fan and vocalist/guitarist with Shutdown during the Nineties. "He's probably the biggest single influence on my own guitar-playing, for what it's worth and has been since discovering HDQ I first saw Leatherface in the very inauspicious Entertainer in Hereford, with [Kent pop-punkers, also signed to Roughneck] Midway Still and was so inspired I bought a Gordon Smith guitar the next day and decided I had to play second guitar in Shutdown rather than just sing. I've still got the guitar and recently brought it out of retirement – and still listen to Leatherface to this day. They were the band I'd been waiting for to come out of the UK: great lyrics and tunes to die for, with their fair share of intricate guitar-work. Leatherface meant so much to a whole generation of English hardcore kids and long may they flourish. I loved dancing (on my own!) to 'Not Superstitious' at my wedding disco…"

February and March 1992 saw Leatherface trekking around Europe with Wat Tyler in support, a tour that Frankie still rates as the most enjoyable ever ("It was good and bad all at once," he says carefully) and after covering Abba's 'Eagle' for a single on Blackbox and the 'Compact And Bijou' 10-inch for Roughneck, the band recorded the 'Minx' album in Sunderland at the end of that year. Frankie still rates this as his favourite Leatherface release of the Nineties, but to the ears of this scribe, while a towering release by anyone else's standards it sounds somewhat subdued compared to the three albums preceding it.

Similarly, the 'Do The Right Thing' 12-inch that followed broke little or no new ground and the band, having been so brilliantly prolific for so long, seemed to be running out of steam. It came as little surprise when they split following 1994's aptly-named 'The Last' LP, another mellow record that felt as if the band were going through the motions somewhat.

"I was trying to get my head around a specific beat that I was being asked to play in the studio and I just could not get to grips with it," reveals Lainey, who reunited with Ian Armstrong and Graeme Philliskirk of Ran, for Bultaco. "It went on for a hour or two and I just got so low and said, 'That's it, get someone else to play the drums!' Leading up to that, the atmosphere in the band was terrible anyway; we were all doing our own things on tour and the only time it felt like a band was when we got onstage to play the set. Then, at the final gig of the tour in Leeds, Frankie announced that it was the last gig ever; we had no idea he was going to announce the split of the band…

"It was an absolute low-point for me, when we split up," he continues. "We all went our separate ways; we had spent so much time in each others' lives and then it was gone… Empty…no communication…horrible! By comparison, the most memorable time was playing Reading for the first time; we came on and started with 'I Want The Moon' and the crowd surged forward; the security couldn't hold them and the barriers came down, it was crazy!"

Frankie then played in Pope (alongside bassist Andy Crighton from Snuff, who had played on both 'Minx' and 'The Last') and Jesse, who issued a self-titled LP on Rugger Bugger in 1998, while Dickie Hammond formed Dr Bison with Barrie Oldfield from the Abs. Leatherface's reputation refused to quietly lie down and die though and in 1999, Dickie Hammond talked Frankie and Lainey into putting Leatherface back together, albeit without him in the initial line-up. The band's comeback release, with Leighton Evans from Jesse on bass, was a superb split album with Hot Water Music from Gainesville, Florida, for Californian label BYO; opening with the powerful, emotional-kick-in-the-gut 'Andy', dedicated to the late Andy Crighton, who sadly committed suicide in 1998, it quickly established itself as the best Leatherface recording since 'Mush'. With 'Cherry Knowle' being reissued Stateside by BYO as well, the band embarked upon their first US tour, which was a runaway success… Leatherface were back and then some.

"The reunion was just a result of people realising we were friends before anything else… and fucking off the business basically!" reckons Frankie. "And that first American tour was probably the best tour we ever did. Hot Water Music were the most amazing band I ever met; I have never had such an amazing time on such an amazing tour… Discount were with us as well and they helped make it special too. D4 also played a couple of the gigs, along with 6 Going On 7, who were also amazing! That tour was the best ever; ask anyone who was involved…"

"When we signed with BYO in 1997," recalls Four Letter Word's Welly, "they wanted to get someone in the studio with us, 'cos they obviously wanted to make sure they didn't get a shit recording back for their money. They asked Andy Turner [of Instigators fame], who suggested Frankie; Shawn [from BYO] asked me and I thought it sounded a good idea, so they gave me his phone number and we went from there. The first two albums were recorded at the Whitehouse in Weston-super-Mare and because we were recording for seven or eight days and it was in the middle of nowhere, we had to get somewhere to stay and the only local place that was cheap was a caravan holiday park. We did that for two albums, which was fun, so, all in all, I've basically lived with Frankie for a month or so of my life! We had some right laughs in those caravans…

"Anyway, when we were recording the first album, I asked Frankie if there was a Leatherface reunion in the pipeline. He told me that they'd just had their first practice the day before he came down. I mentioned this to Shawn on the phone when I gave him a progress report, who then asked if I could put a word in about their label. Of course, we'd just signed, so we were singing their praises and I was telling Frankie how BYO was one of my favourite labels from when I was a kid and that's how Leatherface came to do those BYO records. Not many people know that…he told me he still holds me personally responsible!

"We had some great times recording with Stubbs. The fact that we got him down to record our fourth album with our own money is testament to that. It was always party time, or 'lager o'clock' as he puts it. It's funny these days, now that Leatherface are virtually living legends. Like, as far as a lot of US punks are concerned, the only bands of note to have come out of the UK since GBH and the Exploited have been Leatherface and possibly Snuff. So it's nuts to see them held up like living deities over there – and here as well to some degree. It's funny how things work out."

Despite a disconcertingly minimalist production, 2000's 'Horsebox' LP demonstrated that the band were back near the peak of their creative powers and included a cracking cover of Cyndi Lauper's 'True Colours', while 2004's 'Dog Disco' (with Davey Burdon on bass) and 2010's 'The Stormy Petrel' (with Graeme Philliskirk on bass and Stefan Musch on drums, Lainey having left in 2005) continuing the high standards and reinforcing the widely-held view that *no-one sounds like Leatherface*. And, much like other classic punk bands such as Bad Religion, that sound is so perfect and such a sincere expression of the individuals involved, why change it?

"We would like to think we have influenced bands and people alike," hopes Lainey, modestly, "just left our mark and gave them a few good times. And – most importantly – we will hopefully be remembered for the songs themselves…"

"I'd like us remembered as being *honest*!" concludes Frankie, in typically blunt fashion. "As for what the future holds for us…? Fuck knows!"

SELECT DISCOGRAPHY:

7-inch:
'Beerpig' (Meantime, 1990)
'Razorblades And Aspirin' (Roughneck, 1990)
'I Want The Moon' (Roughneck, 1991)
'Eagle' (Blackbox, 1992)
'Split' (Clawfist, 1992) – *split with Wat Tyler*
'Little White God' (Domino, 1994)
'Win Some, Lose Some' (Rugger Bugger, 1994)

10-inch:
'Compact And Bijou' (Roughneck, 1992)

12-inch:
'Smokey Joe' (Roughneck, 1990)
'Not Superstitious' (Roughneck, 1991)
'Do The Right Thing' (Roughneck, 1993)

LPs:
'Cherry Knowle' (Meantime, 1989)
'Fill Your Boots' (Roughneck, 1990)
'Mush' (Roughneck, 1991)
'Minx' (Roughneck, 1992)
'The Last' (Domino, 1994)
'The BYO Split Series, Volume One' (BYO, 1999) – *split with Hot Water Music*

'Horsebox' (BYO, 2000)
'Dog Disco' (BYO, 2004)
'The Stormy Petrel' (Major Label, 2010)

AT A GLANCE:

In 1998, Irish label Rejected did issue two Leatherface discography CDs, 'Discography One – Live' and 'Discography Two', that compiled various EP and live tracks from the early Nineties, but to be honest, the curious reader is best advised to pick up 'Mush'. And once you've heard that, you'll go and get the rest of it anyway!

W.O.R.M.

W.O.R.M. may indeed have the worst name in the history of punk rock, but since springing up from the same Chesterfield scene that spawned the likes of Septic Psychos and Criminal Sex, they've racked up 1,000 gigs and are working on their fifth album. Not bad for "Three idiots who just want to play loud fast punk rock..." (their words, not mine!)

"I was playing in local punk band Resurgence," recalls drummer Mark Openshaw, of his earliest forays into making music, "which was myself on drums, Brian Lowens on bass and Neil Anderson on guitar. We formed in 1986 and we played quite a few gigs around the local area, one of the more memorable ones being on top of the multi-story car park, which was eventually stopped by local constabulary. We added Jim Twelves as second guitar for a while and then eventually split up. I can't actually remember why we split; there might have been a falling out (wasn't there always?), but myself and Brian decided to carry on gigging, as playing to no-one and getting paid no money for it seemed to be the ideal career choice..."

With Mark moving to vocals ("I must have been suffering from some 'lack of attention' disorder at the time," he chuckles), John 'Wocko' Watkinson from Blind Attack joined on drums and Rob Webley joined on guitar, the band taking a new name, the Corpse Grinders.

"Mark asked me to join this new band he was putting together after Resurgence split up," recalls Rob. "I wasn't at all sure, but then we went to see some gig together; we had gone to see the support band, but hung around for the headliners, who were very accomplished musicians but wouldn't have known a good tune if it had stood in front of them with a big sign saying 'I'm a good tune!' on it. Anyway, after the drummer did a huge drum solo, he threw his sticks into the audience; Mark caught them, broke them in half and threw them back at him. Instantly, I knew I wanted to be in a band with this guy..."

When Wocko was asked to leave after several disastrous drunken gigs ("He also had a knack of getting himself beat up on a regular basis," laughs Mark. "If he could've played drums as well as he could get himself beaten up, he would have been the world's best drummer!"), Danny Clark from Dog Soldier joined on drums and the band changed their

W.O.R.M. Carl , 1994

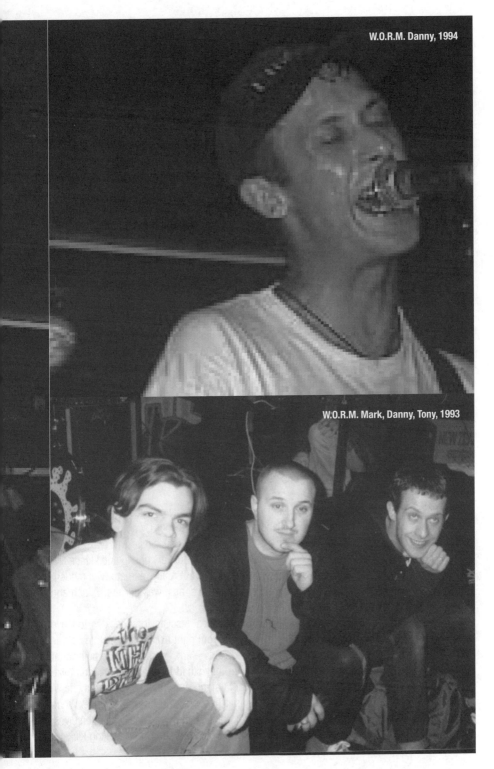

W.O.R.M. Danny, 1994

W.O.R.M. Mark, Danny, Tony, 1993

name to Bunny Heads. Bizarre, I know – from one extreme to another…maybe W.O.R.M. isn't so bad after all?

"The Corpse Grinders had already been together for a year when I joined," reveals Danny. "They had sacked their original drummer, Wocko and I had just been sacked from my old band. I had seen them a couple of times before and thought they were the worst band I had ever seen, but I wasn't really doing anything else at the time. The first release was a self-titled demo recorded on a four-track before I joined; I think I have only ever listened to it twice. The second demo tape, 'My Hovercraft Is Full of Eels', was recorded in a proper studio in Sheffield in 1989 and sold pretty well, while the third demo was a split release with our alter-egos, the Inspiral Cowpats, a kind of Butthole Surfers sort of thing. It only sold to a handful of friends and you'll be lucky to find a copy.

"By then, our name was starting to make people think we were a crusty death-metal band, so we changed it to Bunny Heads…not sure what inspired the name, but we were also considering 'Irate House Bricks'. Anyway, we recorded five more songs in the form of a promo tape to send to lots of record companies, but none of them were interested so we became W.O.R.M."

"I can partly take the blame for the name," admits Rob. "We just had a big list of names to choose from and everyone else liked 'Worm', but I thought it was crap. Later that night I was thinking about bands with animal names and they were all cool animals like The Eagles, Tygers of Pan Tang etc. And we had 'Worm', but then I realised that the band W.A.S.P. were named after a crap animal too, but it looked cool written in capitals with full stops, so at the next practice I said I'd go along with the name 'Worm', but only if it was written 'W.O.R.M.' The rest of the band agreed and to this day are still getting asked what it stands for…"

After playing their first gig during April 1992, at the Saltergate Club in Chesterfield, with Truth Decay from Sheffield, W.O.R.M. recorded two lo-fi demos – 'My Ol' Man's A Mushroom' and 'Die Bastard' – that both sold relatively well at their frequent local gigs before Rob and Brian both left and were replaced by Tony Glover. Two singles then showcased nicely the band's raucous take on speedy pop punk: 1994's 'You've Got To Tow The Line' EP for Spanish label, Victimas Del Progresso and 1995's 'Pray TV'/'FUCK' double A-side for US label Peer Pressure Productions.

"It's not really an exciting story," says Danny, of how their first two releases came to be on international labels. "I just sent demos to labels I found in 'Book Your Own Fucking Life' and got a couple of positive replies. We recorded the tracks in two sessions over two years at Neptune Studios in Sheffield; it was only an eight-track desk, but very cheap and I kinda like the sound of the songs. They have a certain rawness you can't really recreate with modern equipment. I was especially excited with the Spanish release, as it was our first 7-inch and the cover folded out just like they did on all the Crass records…!"

However, after 18 months and much aggro from the local fascists Tony decided to leave and was replaced by Carl Newton from Psychic Dog. "From right back in the Eighties, I was into animal rights, vegetarianism and veganism," explains Mark, "and was quite political at the time; I hated Nazis and still do. I didn't like what they stood for then and still don't like what they stand for now, so it just seemed natural to stand up to them. We did play down in Telford one night, which was Tony's birthday as it happens and he had to drive. When we turned up, the whole crowd was a bunch of seig-heiling Nazis; we really shit ourselves, because we thought we had been set up and we were going to get a right fucking kicking.

We bought cider, we played fucking fast, gave them some abuse and drove off even faster before they killed us…"

"But we were never afraid to speak out and stay true to our beliefs," adds Danny. "We had fascists at some of our early gigs and I always told them what I thought of them. We played at a big anti-fascist gig in town and a lot of trouble kicked off around that. Oddly enough, the organisers of the gig left town the following day – and left us to sort out the mess!

"And after a year-and-a-half of punk rock, touring and acid, Tony decided that being a student might prove to be a more rewarding and safer occupation than being in the band, so it was time to find another guitarist, yet again. And, after auditioning a few, we had a straight choice between a wife-beating lunatic with a restraining order preventing him going within two miles of his missus, or Carl, the guy with the Flying V guitar and blue Docs…well, it was a tough choice but we went with Carl!"

Carl made his debut on the 'Sex, Pies And Sellotape' demo, which the band hawked around various labels for the best part of a year before setting up their own label, SID (Silence Is Deafening), to release the horribly-produced, overly compressed debut album, 'Billynomates', in 1996. Meanwhile, Rugger Bugger was so taken with the song 'FUCK' off the second single, they asked W.O.R.M. to re-record it for inclusion on 'The Swearing EP', which came out in 1997 and also featured Oi Polloi and Wat Tyler.

The band gigged extensively in support of the album, with 'FUCK' in particular becoming a bit of a live anthem for them and entered a period of relative prolificacy, self-releasing the 'Juggling With Poo' CDEP and contributing two tracks – 'Prozac Queen' and 'Another Love Song' – to a split with Raggity Anne for Irritation Records. This was followed in 1999 by the 'Mullet In The Head' LP, a 22-track stormer that remains their fastest, hardest – and best-selling – release to date. But where the band really left their mark – for better and for worse – was on the live circuit, gigging concertedly around the UK every week.

"Yeah, there were loads of fucking bad gigs," sighs Mark philosophically, "but generally they were thankfully outweighed by the good ones. One of our particularly bad ones was when we played in Kendal on a Sunday afternoon; it was on our way home after a mini-tour we did across Scotland. I was suffering from a cocktail of Guinness, whiskey, speed and dope and I'd spent the whole of the night before in a lay-by listening to voices in my head telling me to kill the rest of the band, which might sound funny but was pretty unnerving, to say the least. Anyhow, we got to Kendal in the afternoon in our van from Budget Van Hire and yes, the warning should have been in the firm's name…all the way to Scotland and back in a van which wouldn't go any faster than 40mph!

"Not fucking good, but we eventually arrived in Kendal to hear sirens going all over the place and see people running about pissed and fighting etc, so I decided to have a kip in the van, to try and get my head together before the gig. The next thing I knew Danny was banging on the back door shouting, 'It's all kicking off in the venue…' The gig hadn't even started yet, so I rushed up but, by the time I got there, it had all calmed down. When we came on it all kicked off again; cue fighting, cue glasses being thrown at us, cue a guy in front of me while I was drumming wanting to rip my head off. We played, we came off, we were going to go home…until the landlord asked when we were doing our second set; we said we weren't playing any more stuff and he said if we didn't the crowd would kill us, so we knocked out the fastest, shortest W.O.R.M. set ever!

"The best gig has to be the one we did on the French/Swiss border; it was an outdoor festival in a valley. We'd travelled all night and day, with Road Rage; I think we went on about 1am and there must have been a thousand people there, it was a really great experience.

"The Vic in Derby was always brilliant as well; we used to get really good crowds there… in fact, I think that was the only place we have ever had really good crowds! They were really into us and every gig we did there was loud, sweaty and hectic, with loads of kids jumping about to us. And Boston; how could I forget gigs at the world-famous Indian Queen? That place is totally bonkers and for some reason the guys there always put us on with two Scandinavian death-metal bands, so for about two hours you have some of the heaviest shit to hit the planet, then W.O.R.M. come ambling onto the stage, three idiots singing songs about cats doing drugs and Bob De Niro, but it fucking works. Yeah, that place rocks!"

"There have been too many bad gigs to remember," laughs Danny, before recounting several experiences that will ring bells for anyone who's slogged around the circuit for the love of punk…it can be a thankless task! "Travelling from one end of the country to the other to play in front of just the promoter for five pounds if we were lucky…travelling all day to play for 10 minutes because the other bands on before us had played for too long…waiting all night to go on, only to discover the crowd going home after the local band had been on. And then the local band going home with all the equipment.

"Loads of good gigs too, of course, like whenever we got to play at great, well-organised gigs, or play with our favourite bands. I think playing that open-air punk fest in France has to be the best; partly for the great crowd and partly just because it was an insane couple of days…"

Andy Dickinson was added on second guitar in 2000 to thicken W.O.R.M.'s live sound up, but he only lasted for the one album, that year's 'Vertically Unchallenged Baby'. The following year, Carl ("Who had become such a fuck-up and all-round liability…") was replaced by Rob from the original line-up; the band's drunken roadie Joe Clarkson (from crust band Black Rag) came in to play second guitar, but only lasted a few weeks before he was replaced by Bod Graham. This line-up only managed the 'It Doesn't Have To Be This Way' EP in 2004 before Rob left again to concentrate on his goth band, the Realm.

In 2008, W.O.R.M. entered Danny's own Subzone Studios to record another strong album, 'If You Can't See The Truth, You're Not Looking', which was released by the bizarrely-named Japanese label Fixing A Hole. After an ill-fated Irish tour that saw Bod flying home mid-trip ("After a tequila- and Stella-induced night of mayhem, dancing, fighting and tears," admits Mark), W.O.R.M. were joined by their seventh guitarist, Kyle Schofield from Population Lost, thus arriving at their current line-up. Phew.

"I think up until the present one with Kyle on guitar, the line-up which consisted of myself, Danny and Carl was probably the definitive version of W.O.R.M.," reckons Mark. "We played fast, stripped-down tuneful punk rock, albeit not always in tune, or in time, but the three of us had a really good stage presence.

"Fuck knows where we find the energy to continue in the face of all this adversity," he adds candidly. "I think I must get some sick, perverted pleasure from slogging around the country with five people crammed into Danny's Astra…coming back from Doncaster when it's -9.5 degrees outside and the windows are freezing up on the inside as we drive down the motorway. What's next for W.O.R.M.? Keep recording and keep playing, I suppose and basically just keep doing what we have been doing for the last 20 years…"

"We keep going because we don't know any better," laughs Danny, "and we're not talented enough to do anything else. As we speak, I'm recording the new W.O.R.M. album and putting stuff together for two singles and rarities albums...other than that we just keep gigging.

"We never sold out," he offers, when asked to comment on what sets them apart from their peers. "Mind you, we never really got a chance to sell out either. I wouldn't say we were massively different from our peers, but at least people still come and see us. Maybe because we're loud, fast, friendly and honest?"

SELECT DISCOGRAPHY:

7-inch:
'You've Got To Tow The Line' EP (Victimas Del Progresso, 1994)
'Pray TV'/'FUCK' (Peer Pressure Productions, 1995)
'The Swearing EP' (Rugger Bugger, 1997) – *split with Wat Tyler and Oi Polloi*
'Split' (Irritation, 1998) – *split with Raggity Anne*

CDEPs:
'Jugglin' With Poo' (Silence Is Deafening, 1997)
'It Doesn't Have To Be That Way' (Silence Is Deafening, 2004)

LPs:
'Billynomates' (Silence Is Deafening, 1996)
'Mullet In The Head' (Silence Is Deafening, 1999)
'Vertically Unchallenged Baby' (Silence Is Deafening, 2000)
'If You Can't See The Truth, You're Not Looking' (Fixing A Hole, 2008)

AT A GLANCE:
Until Danny finishes the W.O.R.M. singles compilation mentioned above, readers should start with 'If You Can't See The Truth, You're Not Looking' and work back.

TRUTH DECAY

Truth Decay. Now there's a band name to conjure with! Thing is, these guys came from bands called Dog Soldier, Face First, Bad Blood and – best of all – GGF (short for 'Go Get Fucked'), so they knew a good name when they saw one.

"We started in Sheffield in 1990," recalls bassist Rich. "We were all in various bands in the local scene, so knew each other from playing and going to gigs. I'd been kicked out of Dog Soldier because I robbed the university and our singer worked there and [guitarist] Darren got kicked out of GGF; I don't know why, although he still says he left, but I don't think that's true! Once I started playing in bands though, I was addicted to it, so starting another one was never going to take long. I bumped into [drummer] Jake in town and he said he'd heard we wanted a drummer and he'd just fallen out with the guys in Bad Blood and Face First…so we were basically the people no-one else wanted to play with…"

Taking the best aspects of all their previous bands, Truth Decay were a neat combo of UK82 street punk and early US hardcore, with a shot of gnarly metal for good measure. And the Sheffield scene was thriving during the very late Eighties/early Nineties, so the band had an enthusiastic audience to rally behind them.

"We all liked things each other liked, but we were all into different stuff too," explains Rich, of the band's mixed influences. "Darren was mainly into Slayer, Metallica and Motörhead… stuff like that, but he also had an obsession with Dead Kennedys. I was into GBH, Discharge, English Dogs etc and it was Jake who was more into US stuff like SNFU, Circle Jerks, Black Flag, Bad Brains and so on, so it was all mixed up. Generally when we wrote anything, I'd write a tune, Darren would put something over it that was totally different but still fit and Jake would put it in some kind of order and it just seemed to work; as for lyrics, we couldn't get a singer so I did it in the practice room, just so we could get a gist when writing the music, but ended up doing it all the time because we still didn't have a singer when we got to do our first gig. I used to just shout shit at first, 'cos no-one knew what I was saying anyway, but then I ended up writing proper lyrics later, normally something connected to my depression that I suffer from, as I didn't know what else to write about…

"The first gig was at the Hallamshire Hotel. No-one would put us on anywhere else, so I did it myself; there was us, a shit metal band called Reprobate and a toss PC hippy/punk band that I can't remember the name of. I was amazed at how many people turned out, it was packed; we played last and went down really well, except with the crusties when we played a song about how hypocritical I thought most so-called 'anarchists' were. All that PC stuff was a load of bollocks…and I always wondered why we couldn't get a gig in Leeds or at the 1 In 12! For people who say everyone has the right to say what they want and freedom of speech and all that, they didn't seem to want to listen to my opinion after all – just talk over me and tell me I was full of shit!"

After recording their first demo at the Darnell Music Factory ("It was some community project to help make local unemployed kids creative," recalls Rich, "and Jake was on the dole, so he booked it and we got it for free…"), Truth Decay enlisted the services of Stu Decay on vocals during 1993. This was a move that helped them towards establishing a sound and direction of their own.

"Jake had come up and spoken to me when I'd gone to a gig they were playing at, even though I looked a twat (his words, not mine) as I had a mohican and a leather jacket," laughs Stu. "He was pleasantly surprised when my jacket fell open and he saw I had a Naked Raygun 'Throb Throb' T-shirt on, so we spent a while waffling about our joint love of US punk and then I met Rich through Clive. I used to read a music quiz out in the uni bar and Rich said, 'Do you want to sing for us? You already read the quiz out, so you don't mind talking in public and it's not much different…' He also told me he hated singing (I had noticed he had a habit of shuffling behind the PA stack while he played and sang, hoping you couldn't see him!) so I thought I'd give it a go.

"The first gig was in Scunthorpe, supporting the Scottish Sex Pistols, in front of about 80 blokes in their thirties and forties who just wanted to pretend it was 1976 and they were back at the 100 Club. We were okay, I think; I remember totally shitting myself before we started! After we played, a young kid in a Sepultura T-shirt came up and said he'd loved it, so it all seemed worthwhile; his opinion was way more valid than the time-warp retards who were busy spitting on Johnny McRotten at that point, so we collected our £5 and went home…"

It wasn't long before Truth Decay were over in Europe playing (the continent was still very accessible for UK bands and so much more fun than playing closer to home), their first tour of the Czech Republic in 1994 going so well that they returned there four times during the next three years. Subsequently their first vinyl release was a 10-incher, 'Sole Music', for Czech label Bastard Records, a fine slice of GBH and Exploited-influenced punk, even if Stu's vocals do sound somewhat forced.

"During the first two years or so, I was singing songs already written," points out Stu. "It was almost like being in a covers band, learning 25-plus sets of lyrics, and even when I joined they still wrote songs in the same manner as when they had been a trio. Generally Rich brought finished songs in to practice, complete with words, or Darren brought in a riff and Rich had a huge book of lyrics from which we plucked words… I then had to learn (them) and sing in the way he would have done – which in all honesty didn't fit my voice. It wasn't ideal and it wasn't until he left that I actually worked out my own singing style.

"Anyway, the 10-inch was for Bastard Records in Czech and we recorded 10 or 12 songs at the studio owned by the same guy who made our tour T-shirts…not sure how it came about but somehow we went on tour with 50 T-shirts – 40 in XL and 10 in XXL – to the Czech Republic, where the fattest kid needed – at most – a small size! The 10-inch came in an amazing plastic bag cover, but otherwise sounded like demos, which is very much what it was."

There then followed a dizzying spell of line-up changes, during which Darren was kicked out and replaced by Ade, who was himself kicked out and replaced by Andy from Swampwalk. Founding member Rich was the last to go and was replaced by a returning Ade, making way for new bassist Dave. And somehow, during this confusion, they managed to record the (inconsistent) 'Another Day Wasted' LP for Step-1 that finally saw some of Stu's deranged humour coming out in the lyrics. Just yell if you can't keep up with any of this, won't you?

"I didn't realise when I joined that Truth Decay weren't that classic 'group of friends that formed a band'," sighs Stu. "They actually didn't know each other all that well, so when we went abroad and were cooped up together in a van for long periods of time the tensions rose and all the differences came out… Darren was seriously hard work! Each time we went abroad, he got worse to deal with; at one point on the second tour, Rich drove off and left him on the roadside in Czech, returning five minutes later… Darren thought it was that classic

Truth Decay, Darren, 1996, Czech Republic

Truth Decay, Stu and Jake, Czech Republic 1996

Truth Decay, Rich

tour gag and we'd come back to get him, but Rich just wound the window down, threw his passport at him and drove off again! We had to point out to Rich that we still had about four shows to play and no money to get home without playing them, so this time we did go back and pick him up. On our return to the UK, Rich chucked him out – with our approval – and we asked Ade to join.

"He added a new dimension to us in that now *all* our songs had Test Tubes-style intros! But I liked it as I got on well with him and it helped me to actually start writing full-on lyrics. However, he is one of the world's laziest people; we'd go to pick him up for practice and he'd still be in bed at 7pm waiting for his tea and that would be a reason enough for him to not practice. Once we went to do a gig and he was claiming he was too ill and Rich just couldn't handle it any more, so Ade got binned too.

"Andy joined then, as we had a tour booked; he was a good laugh and fitted in from the off, but things were falling out between the rest of us by then. I was unhappy at the way Ade had been chucked out; fair play, he was rubbish at timekeeping and a lazy fucker, but he was a mate too, so I thought he could perhaps have been given a bit more time. It seemed that Rich had fallen out of love with punk; Feeder and Blur etc were ticking his musical boxes more at that point in time and whenever we played he'd criticise the people who came to see us for having mohicans and leather jackets etc…even though he was basically describing *me* when he did so!

"I wasn't going to practice as much as before, as it just didn't seem to have the same spark. Jake used to come round to mine quite a lot, as we used to listen to records and waffle about music and we both agreed to ask Rich to leave, which we knew would also mean Andy would go, as he and Rich were definitely sparking off each other and enthusiastic about a totally different musical style to us…"

"I wouldn't say 'asked to leave'; I would say more 'kicked out', to be honest," corrects Rich. "It was probably my own fault for being so naive. Jake was always in my ear about Stu's singing, saying how he wanted it to be more melodic and that I was a better singer and he wanted to change the direction of the band; I don't know what he was saying to Stu at the same time, but I listened to him and took it all in. I *didn't* think Stu was the best singer in the world, but he was a good person to have in the band and, at the end of the day we were a punk band and he was a good laugh, so as far as I knew it was Jake who wanted Stu out.

"I got a call saying we were meeting down the pub and when I got there I was told I wasn't in Truth Decay any more, because I wanted to go a different direction and wasn't really into punk enough. I think the thing that miffed me most was that I'd written 90 % of the music, so if that was the case the music would've changed already; plus I learnt to play by copying GBH and Discharge, so my musical abilities weren't that great when trying to play anything else. It wasn't that long after my mother had died either, so I wasn't in the most creative of mindsets, to be honest…"

The thoroughly enjoyable 'Fat Punks Can't Pogo' 7-inch was released in 1998 (think the Exploited or Blitz with a sense of humour) by French label Fight 45, and a European tour with In The Shit followed to promote it, which turned out to be their last trip to the continent. They split upon their return, after kicking Dave out in France (Buffy and Kip from In The Shit helped cover for him at the last two gigs).

"Jake decided to stop touring about then and it seemed pointless carrying on with no original members," explains Stu. "Ade was being a bit flaky again as well; he'd got married and 'forgot' we were going on tour in Germany so had used all his holiday up on his honeymoon…which was fair enough, but he never told us this until the week before we were due to go. And then, once we went on tour and spent some time with him, we realised our bassist Dave was a total sponging git…

"Our 'final' show was an all-dayer in Sheffield that I organised; we knew we were going to split from earlier that year, so the final show was with the Business, the Wernt, In The Shit and about five others.

"However we actually played four more shows after that: in 1990, for a mate's 30th we played a warm-up show and his birthday party, which was good as Rich came back and played it with me, Jake and Ade. We had a good laugh and I think we gave the band a good send-off…but then, a couple of years later, we played Nottingham punks' picnic and another show in Sheffield. That time round, it was me, Rich, Jake and Andy, but I don't remember either show being that great.

"No regrets, though; I'd done way more than I'd ever thought I would and my record-collector insanity was partially sated by us having released a 7-inch, 10-inch and 12-inch, complete with different coloured vinyl pressings. We'd been to Europe not once but multiple times and met loads of great people… So no, I wasn't overly saddened when it ended for good."

"The one thing I can say about the guys I've played and toured with though is they're not just bandmates," reckons Rich, who went on to play in Off Kilter and Bickle's Cab. "After touring together, drinking together, fighting each other and sitting in the van for endless hours, you become more than just bandmates; you grow up together and, apart from the odd person anyway, they become like your family. What do I think about it all now? Well, apart from the birth of my son, playing in bands has been the best time in my life, with the best friends I've ever had."

"On the back of our final show, I went and worked at a club in Sheffield for five years, as their band booker," concludes Stu, "before leaving and setting up a screen-printing company, which is now in its seventh year. So now, after having played with loads of bands I liked, then putting them all on live, I find myself making their merch as well!

"Musically I did nothing 'til 2002, when I learnt bass to join Last Year's Youth. Mainly 'cos they were all good mates…plus I only needed to learn the notes on the E and A-string! We became Burn Subvert Destroy (BSD) and spent the next five years touring and recording etc, getting to the point where we'd got quite well known, probably more so than Truth Decay, in fact, but due to us being a lot older, with kids and jobs etc, after five years we seemed to have exhausted each other's patience.

"The usual turnover of members meant there were only two of us left from the first line-up, so it seemed wise to split up before we totally fell out. We played our final Sheffield show with Bickle's Cab, at *their* final show, as an extension of the somewhat symbiotic relationship that me and Rich seem to have. Indeed, we're both now in the process of once more starting a new band, along with Tommy, the old BSD drummer, so let's see how long that lasts…"

SELECT DISCOGRAPHY:

7-inch:
'Fat Punks Can't Pogo' (Fight 45, 1998)

10-inch:
'Sole Music' (Bastard, 1996)

LP:
'Another Day Wasted' (Step-1, 1997)

AT A GLANCE:
Nothing to report, sorry.

IMBALANCE

Although they were based in the relatively isolated northeastern backwater of Grimsby, **Imbalance** quickly tapped into the vibrant network of friends and acquaintances that comprised the UK's underground hardcore scene and was a great geographical equaliser. They soon hooked up with London label Household Name for their first EP and LP and their modern, intelligent take on the 'old-school hardcore' sound was a breath of fresh air in a scene dominated by metallic beatdowns and macho posturing.

When their band Fold split in 1994, vocalist Andy Bryant (also of Defunkt) and guitarist Bjorn Christensen (also of Kung Fu Joe) hooked up with bassist Rob Collins from the punk band Peroxis and eventually drummer Andy 'Grun' Greenway to form "a hardcore punk-rock band" Andy would soon christen Imbalance.

"Peroxis had lost momentum due to a number of reasons," reckons Rob. "Not least of all my growing realisation that our singer's opinions didn't reflect my own beliefs – or the rest of the band's – leading to me having a big falling-out with him onstage! I'd been hanging around with Andy and Bjorn's circle of friends anyway, as I had more in common with them and ended up jamming with them and a guy called Nick (who I didn't know) on drums.

"Our first practice was at a local rehearsal space – a derelict building! – that was called Sounds Good but known by all as 'Sounds Shit'! From the very start, the band had a very different feeling to the other bands I'd been in and had seen playing around Grimsby. It eventually didn't work out with Nick and, despite my feeling at the time that he was a tit, Grun tried out for us; that's when things really clicked…"

"I never really knew him either," adds Andy, of Grun, "but knew of him; he'd been in a number of bands, I guess the most significant being [thrash-metal act] Mortis. A rumour from our school was that, while on a school holiday to Greece, he'd put a Coke bottle up someone's arse while they were in a drunken sleep and taken a photo… He later clarified to me once in the band though that he'd simply 'rested it between their cheeks'! At this point I ought to mention that, by coincidence alone, Grun, Rob and I all attended Whitgift Comprehensive School, each a year apart. We date the band from the point that Grun joined – October 1995 – and I think I came up with the name about that time too."

"I always considered we had different roles within the band," offers Rob. "Grun was the technical guy, Andy was the intelligent 'thinking man', Bjorn was all about trying new things and I was about the melody."

After honing their chops in Sounds Good for six months, Imbalance played their first gig, at Grimsby's Cartergate Rooms with local death-metal band Crawlspace, on 1 March 1996, before entering Birdsong Studios in Scunthorpe the following month to record their first demo with Steve Bird, who had built a solid reputation as a producer of UKHC working with the likes of Napalm Death and Intense Degree. Featuring six songs and entitled 'Are You In A Good Mood?', it went on to sell over 600 copies and landed the band their first gig outside Grimsby, at the Hull Adelphi with Scarper and Wob, in January '97.

"We really didn't fit on the bill," laughs Rob. "It turned out that they had booked us thinking we were another band with the same name; we didn't even know about them until shortly afterwards, when we received a 'cease and desist' letter from a high-profile showbiz law firm stating that we were using someone else's name. I've never been one to shy away from a fight, so I paid for our own lawyer to write one back telling them to stop using our name, seeing as we had had it for much longer! It worked and we never heard from them again.

"After that we played at Sheffield University with Knuckledust, which was a surreal experience as we had our own security etc…although the next night at the Packhorse in Leeds [with Canvas] was a real bump back to Earth! Through that gig we were invited to play the first Damage Control all-dayer in London [on 5 May 1997, with Knuckledust, Freebase, Area Effect, Withdrawn, Stampin' Ground and Public Disturbance], which to us at the time was a huge thing. We hired a minibus and got a lot of friends to come and had a great day, although it was marred somewhat by one of our friends breaking her leg and ending up in hospital. It was a long night and, after waiting at a London hospital for two or three hours, we told her to 'suck it up' and we drove home without her being X-rayed. It was actually the day after that she found out it had been broken."

It was making an impact at gigs like Damage Control that brought the band to the attention of Lil and Kafren of the aforementioned Household Name, who released their four-track 'March Of The Yes Men' EP in May 1998. Recorded over two days during early February of that year at Birdsong, the single is raw, brash and infectious; taking its primary influences from the States but sounding defiantly British thanks to Andy's honest vocal delivery, it was promoted by a week-long UK tour.

"I haven't listened to the 7-inch for a long time," admits Andy, "but for a 'first record' it's pretty good, I think. I might listen to it in a few years or so, but I can't really be objective about it 'cos it's something I've done. I guess the fondest memory I have of it is sitting in a Travelodge (Rob always did have a thing about hotels!) the night before our first English tour, sticking the middle label of the record on with Pritt sticks… That makes the official release date of the 7-inch the day after – Sunday 24 May 1998 – when we played a weekend festival in Brighton, with, among others, Combat Shock, Assert and Knuckledust."

Imbalance, line-up photo by Naki

Imbalance live, by Naki

Lots more gigs followed, before Imbalance recorded their 'Spouting Rhetoric' album in October, which was eventually released in May 1999. Not the best-produced hardcore album to come out of the UK, for sure, but full of energetic singalongs and throbbing with good intentions, it was packaged in some very eye-catching artwork courtesy of Dan Fenwick and was well received by the hardcore punk underground. A mini-tour of the UK was undertaken (with Ensign from New Jersey) that August, before the band made their first foray into Europe for two Dutch dates in September (with Oil). Upon their return, they decided future releases would not be recorded at Birdsong or released by Household Name.

"We always had a good relationship with Lil and Kafren," Andy is keen to point out, "so it's not that we'd fallen out, or anything as dramatic as that. At the time I certainly thought that the reason it took us so long to get to play on the mainland was the fact that we were on Household… On reflection, I don't think that's the sole reason, but it has to be considered a factor because we then did two releases in succession on different labels – Hermit and Armed With Anger – and we were in Europe almost immediately. I think the thing with Household was that they were like a lot of labels – always looking to the next band/release. They were releasing a lot of records, whereas when we did our next album, Armed With Anger and Hermit just concentrated on that and got it out worldwide…"

Hermit Records was ran by James Beal, joint proprietor of Leeds record shop Out Of Step and a member of the Propagumbhis, who was a close friend of the band and was so enthusiastic about releasing a six-track Imbalance CDEP they simply couldn't refuse him. Another Leeds-based label, Blind Bear, also wanted four Imbalance tracks for a split MCD with, appropriately enough, the Propagumbhis, so the band entered Corby's Premier Studios in January 2000 to record their next two releases in one session, the resulting material showing a marked progression sonically from the slightly muffled Birdsong efforts, not to mention an emerging, albeit subtle, rock influence, with Andy's vocals getting noticeably harsher and less melodic.

"We had always been a little disappointed with the final mix of 'Spouting…'," explains Rob, "so we chose to work with Iain Wetherall at Premier in Corby next, mainly 'cos Vanilla Pod had recorded their last album there; the quality was great and he wasn't that expensive. Working with Iain was completely different to working with Steve; he used different methods and I think that made us less lazy and we learnt a lot from him. I'm very happy with how it turned out."

Another six-date UK tour was undertaken in April to coincide with the new releases, but the band were starting to really yearn for a full European tour, especially after their weekend of Dutch dates had so whetted their appetite for continental hospitality. Once Andy had got married that summer, Imbalance did several UK dates in November with female-fronted USHC act Fast Times before recording their second album, the rather slick 'Wreaks Havoc With The Inner Ear', for Armed With Anger in January 2001.

The album came out six months later and saw the band in fine, focused fettle, confidently mixing powerful dischord and rough-hewn harmony to great effect and finally – after a turbulent few months for Andy, who became a father and relocated to Birmingham with his family – Imbalance undertook that much-anticipated 'full' trek across Europe. To misquote Charles Dickens, it was both the best and worst of times and, despite working so hard to tour on the continent in the first place, at their first gig back in the UK, Andy announced his imminent departure.

"The downside of the European tour, on a personal level, was the amount of effort it had taken to organise and set up and the apparent lack of appreciation from the rest of the band," reflects Rob. "I'd risked my job by spending so much of my work time and resources making fliers and posting out CDs (along with Rich Corbridge from Armed With Anger) and had got into a fair bit of debt to buy better gear for the trip and I think the stress of it all finally got to me when we were over there.

"I had a habit of getting very shouty in order to get things done in the band (it usually worked!) but I had decided that, in order to survive two weeks in a small van, I would try to avoid any conflict and keep myself in control. This worked well until we played in Rožnov in the Czech Republic… I had loaned my bass cab to the band playing before us and they had managed to blow it up. However they never mentioned it to us, or even acknowledged us and I was extremely annoyed. In order to avoid an altercation, I walked out for some fresh air.

"After about 10 minutes I came back in and we rigged something up so that we could play the gig, which turned out to be a real highlight; however, from that point on, things had changed. The other three didn't understand why I walked out – probably still don't – and I became resentful of the fact that they didn't have my back."

"I could wax lyrical forever about stuff that happened on that tour," recalls Andy, with more enthusiasm for the trip, "most of it particularly funny and most of it involving Grun! I know from the experience of that tour that when you have the worst hangover ever and you've only had about three hours sleep on a cold floor, that 'Nellie The Elephant' by the Toy Dolls blasted out at gig volume is the worst way to wake up. I also know that kids who are about 11 years old smoking weed at Zoro's in Leipzig at 8:30 in the morning will not be particularly interested in stealing the torch that is in Grun's bag – despite the fact that he thinks they will be. I also know that Rob Kito and Bjorn narrowly missed being spewed on by Grun from a balcony about 15 stories above them in Graz, Austria… Bjorn said that he imagined that that was what it must have been like attacking a medieval castle.

"In terms of highpoints, a big part of touring for me has always been about the places you go, rather than just the gigs you play and this was my first real experience of the excitement of going from country to country; the low point was the realisation that I couldn't be in the band any more. We had gone through a number of changes in our lives outside the band: firstly Rob left Grimsby, which did alter things, and I followed a couple of years later, about five months before this tour. And yes, I was just a year married and a dad by a couple of months, but it really had no significance in regard to the decision to quit.

"With the benefit of hindsight of being in another band, it is really clear to me now that we spent a significant amount of time just bickering and arguing over the most stupid shit imaginable, but this was almost the culture of the band! That isn't to say we weren't friends or anything, because we were, but we all had very different expectations. I often felt myself being pushed into doing things I didn't really want to do and all of this peaked in the middle of the tour. What I can say, though, is that, if it wasn't for me having the balls to make the first move, that band wouldn't have seen the year out anyway…"

Like the stand-up guys that they are, Imbalance honoured all the gig commitments they had before arranging several farewell gigs for February 2002, playing their final gig at Joseph's Well in Leeds on the 23rd of that month with Vanilla Pod, Oil and Buzzkill in support. Andy almost immediately joined several of the guys from Voorhees in the Horror, who have been terrorising people with their frantic high-speed hardcore ever since, while Rob eventually relocated to the Netherlands.

Imbalance did reform for a strict one-off in early 2005 to play a memorial show for one of their Grimsby friends, Ben Lane from the band Stand, who passed away after a long illness. "The gig itself was obviously very emotional," reckons Rob. "And from a musical point of view it went well enough, although Bjorn had got so drunk he didn't really know where he was, which took the edge off things for me.

"And that was really my last musical outing until the last six months or so, when I started sending music files back and forward with the members of Peroxis which has become a very interesting experience. I'm not sure if Peroxis will ever play live again, but it's really reignited my passion for playing, so I guess I'm looking for a new band – although I'm not sure how many opportunities for fat 38-year-olds there are in Rotterdam!"

"I was a very active participant in the hardcore punk-rock scene during the Nineties," adds Andy. "And while I have become a little less participatory as my priorities have changed, hardcore and punk rock continue to be a significant part of my life. I had a great time with Imbalance and my immersion in the scene, but on reflection I think that, by the end of the decade, hardcore itself had experienced such an identity crisis it didn't even know what to say or how to sound any more. But I would like to think that people got to engage in a bit of escapism when they to came to an Imbalance gig, that we made a few of 'em think and maybe even inspired some of them to just get on with it and do it for themselves."

SELECT DISCOGRAPHY:

7-inch:
'March Of The Yes Men' (Household Name, 1998)

CDEP:
'Imbalance' (Hermit, 2000)

MCD:
'Split' (Blind Bear, 2000) – *split with the Propagumbhis*

LPs:
'Spouting Rhetoric' (Household Name, 1999)
'Wreaks Havoc With The Inner Ear' (Armed With Anger/Hermit, 2001)

AT A GLANCE:
Andy rates the CDEP on Hermit as containing his favourite Imbalance track ever ('Gattaca'), but that second LP is a great place to start too.

CHAPTER TWO:
THE NORTHWEST

WITHDRAWN

After Ironside and alongside Above All, Liverpool's **Withdrawn** were one of the first truly heavy metallic hardcore bands to emerge from the UK; they were also one of the few dedicated vegan SXE bands of the Nineties, so it's safe to say that while their music was hugely enjoyable, it was their message that was of paramount importance to the band.

The conception of Withdrawn can be traced back to December 1993 when drummer Dave Fergusson teamed up with vocalist Neil Schock, guitarist Paul Strangeways and bassist Martin Wainwright as In Touch, blissfully unaware of the Northeast band of the same name that had preceded them! The name probably gives the game away, but they were ploughing the '88 'Youth Crew' furrow with a vengeance, taking their primary inspiration from American old-school SXE bands such as Chain Of Strength and Gorilla Biscuits. Paul was quickly replaced by Martin 'Onion' Von Bargen from Solstice and the band name became Will To Power.

"The first time I saw Onion was outside [legendary Liverpool punk venue] Planet X when we were waiting to see Voorhees and Slapshot play," recalls Dave. "We were sitting on the wall outside and these meat-head straight-edge kids jumped out of a car behind us and started to play baseball with milk bottles, much to the annoyance of the local punks. As well as Onion, I think it was Daz 'Black Pudding' Brooks from Wigan, Walker, Foxy [now vocalist with SSS] and Pete C, who ran the pirate hardcore radio station TCR [Toxteth Community Radio] and got death threats after playing Bad Brains and stuff. I thought they were boss and looked up to them a bit, I suppose.

"Funny thing about that Slapshot gig too, it was the first time I ever saw the long-haired, bearded Lecky sing and I can still remember the impact he made from that day…funny that he later joined Withdrawn too. Anyway, Onion came to my house and we hit it off straight away, especially after he gave me a rare Slapshot hooded top that [ex-Withstand vocalist] Simon Kelly had made in the Eighties; I was fuckin' made up!"

Will To Power made their live debut at Liverpool's Pink Parrot, with Open Mind and Crocodile God, on 17 September 1994, but it was their second show, at the 1 In 12 Club, Bradford, on 8 October that was to prove more inspirational and prompt yet another name-change, this time to Withdrawn. "Yeah, that was the first time I ever saw stalls with animal rights fliers and fanzines," reveals Dave. "And I can't explain how happy I was to come into contact with people like Nick Royles [Sure Hand Records] and Brian [Days Of Fury Records]; it opened up a world of possibilities and excitement about changing things. Other than that, it was the first time Earth Crisis came to the UK [Nick Royles bravely brought them over just to do two dates in Bradford!] and it seemed like the whole of Europe had come to see them. I think they had just released 'Firestorm'? I took my drums to that gig and some cunt from the band Spawn robbed all my cymbals.

"Anyway, we stuck all 10 songs we wrote on a band practice-room tape and never took Will To Power any further than that. The last song we wrote was called 'Violation', which was about rape, and we thought it kind of stepped outside the whole youth crew restraint. Onion and myself started to write some melodies for a side-project called 24 (the number relating to 'X' in the alphabet) and then decided to just incorporate them into the new style. During this time we wrote an instrumental called 'Withdrawn' and decided that was a cool name for the one and only straight-edge vegetarian band from Liverpool…actually it took us a while to convince Onion to jib off eating meat 'cos he was into bodybuilding at the time, but he figured it all out…"

By the end of the year, Withdrawn had recruited a second guitarist in the shape of Shane Byrne from Wallasey and – taking their lead from the likes of Integrity and Mean Season – were steering their music and lyrics into much darker territories. A four-song demo entitled 'Figures' was recorded at Hard City Studios, Liverpool and garnered the band great reviews in *How We Rock* and *Land Of Treason* fanzines and they started to pick up decent supports with touring American bands like Into Another.

Typically enough, just as things were picking up, the line-up fell apart in spectacular fashion. "I remember Shane left the band literally as we were on our way to a gig in the Northeast. We played with Kito, Deadfall and Assert and my favourite memory of that show – apart from the Assert guitarist falling off the stage and cutting their set short! – was that we did a really dark cover of 'Shoplifters Of The World Unite' by the Smiths!

"Shane ultimately decided to leave due to personal battles, I think and both Martin and Neil decided to go too; Martin had just become a dad to Heather, so I think he had a lot on his plate at the time and Neil left after stupidly spraying 'End faggot life' on the wall outside the 1 In 12…he had started flirting with the idea of 'hardline' SXE, but totally got it wrong. Mind you, someone also painted 'Kill all the punks that still eat meat' on that wall as well, which caused much debate in the club; half of the staff wanted to keep it, the other half wanted it covered over!

"Anyway, just as all this happened, I went to the pictures [cinema] with Neil and noticed he had a ton of blood soaking through his pants. When I asked him what had happened, he pulled them up to reveal that he had used a razor blade to cut his 'ONE LIFE DRUG FREE' tattoo from his calf! I think that explains a lot regarding his state of mind at the time. Pity, really, 'cos I always to this day think that he threw away a genuine talent."

This major thinning of the Withdrawn ranks made way for their first really solid line-up. Chris Meadows, the drummer with vegan SXE band Unborn, joined on vocals, Danny McDermott from MDM became second guitarist and, although he didn't join in time to play on their next recording, Mic Foster, who had previously played with Blood Green and Tuneage, took over on bass. This next recording was the 'A Certain Innate Suffering' MCD for Nick Royle's Sure Hand label, recorded in Liverpool's MA Studios during December 1996 with Jamie Cavanagh from respected doom-metal band Anathema helming the desk and Onion handling bass duties.

"I think Chris had an amazing voice," reckons Dave, "and he was the driving force behind

Withdrawn, first vocalist Neil Schock, Middlesbrough 1994

Withdrawn, bassist Phil

Withdrawn live, pic by Naki

Withdrawn, Dave, by Naki

the band becoming fully vegan. We had a song on there called 'Oceans Of Darkness' and it reflected the band's newly focused political assault on vivisection and animal abuse. Things got totally serious with us at this point and I remember one night we went around all the local butchers to glue their locks and chuck shit all over their windows.

"All the songs on the CD had been written with the previous line-up, so they were pretty much ready to record when Sure Hand approached us. Onion had known Nick Royles for a long time by then and the band had always got on with him… I can't remember if Sure Hand approached us or vice-versa, but we fitted in with their politics and were very happy to do a record with them.

"I don't really think the music on the MCD has stood the test of time," he adds. "We still didn't have a fuckin' clue how things worked; there was no Pro-Tools back then and it was recorded onto tape that kept going out of synch. The MCD was slower with a tinny sound and a black metal feel, which was all intentional, but personally I like a more dynamic sound when I listen to a band. I just think none of us wanted to tell the lad from Anathema to do a better job at the time! We were all a bit wet behind the ears when it came to recording and just felt privileged to be in a studio. People still seem to like that release to this day, but personally I think it was a bit of a rushed job and we still had no permanent bass player at the time…"

Striving to be completely vegan and drug-free was a fairly intense commitment involving some fairly intense personalities and this line-up of Withdrawn wasn't destined to last very long, with Chris and Foster soon departing to form Slavearc.

"The band was 100% serious and committed to the subject matter at this time," Dave elaborates. "I even got 'WITHDRAWN' tattooed across my stomach and was really excited about changing things. The only way you could be a member of Withdrawn at this stage was to be drug-free and vegan; there was absolutely no bending on these terms. We just wondered how anyone could take what we were saying seriously or buy into our ideals if the whole band wasn't practising what the lyrics preached.

"We didn't understand how other bands who would say they were a SXE band could have a drummer/guitarist/whoever drinking on stage or sparking up a biffda. Withdrawn was always 100% straight edge and that never ever changed and the heavy music we played just seemed to match the importance of the message to us. We all loved songs like 'Live It Down' by Integrity. They were totally heavy and matched the extreme subject-matter with extreme music; it just made total sense.

"That was the third time the band ended up having to change its line-up; Chris and Foster had formed Slavearc who had a more death-metal and extreme attitude to their sound and politics. Chris also formed Retribute Records, who would later release one of our albums and needed more time for that. Withdrawn always retained a sense of melody and I don't think that was to their taste. As fate would have it, we ended up with the strongest line-up the band ever had. Lecky from Voorhees was on our wish-list to be frontman and luckily he was into the idea too and Phil Smith took over on bass guitar, who was a total force of nature, as anybody that ever saw those early gigs or met him would agree…"

"I didn't see much of a difference between us and bands like Napalm, Doom, Ripcord and Extreme Noise Terror," adds Danny McDermott. "We were basically trying to polish the more grungy sound of Carcass and At The Gates with a more interesting message. The common ethics kind of channelled our energy in the same direction and helped focus creativity without too much distraction. Self-imposed limitation is a common creative technique that often works where you wouldn't expect it to – and, yes, the core ethics and values are still with me to this day for drink and drugs, which means I feel a right tit when socialising… I can't remember the last person I met who had even heard of Minor Threat!"

The new Withdrawn line-up made their studio debut with the '151' demo, recorded at Hard City Records, Liverpool. After playing several very successful all-dayers in the capital, they followed it up with the 'Seeds Of Inhumanity' CD album for London label Household Name, recorded at Andy Sneap's Backstage Studio near Nottingham, with engineer Dave Chang doubling as producer. Lecky's throaty roar lent the band an even more Integrity-like intensity (although there was a strong Slayer influence emerging on the title track) and with everything much faster, tighter and more technical, the band found themselves able to stand their ground against the brutal metalcore that was flowing so prolifically from mainland Europe at the time.

"Dave was fresh from working as an engineer on a Machine Head album, I think, so we were all a bit in awe of him to start with," laughs Phil. "He was amazing and could make any sound you wanted. I remember the first day we went in the studio; he was very quiet and stuff and we were all trying to make a good impression, 'cos our fate was in his hands really. We were sat there all boy-scout-like, good as gold and I noticed something on the floor so decided to be polite and pick it up so it didn't break…and, as I picked it up, it just fell apart in my hands. Not in a good way 'fell apart' either; I mean you could tell it was really broken. I think the first thing I said to him was, 'Hi, my name's Phil and I just broke this!' Not the first impression you wanna make, but he was cool and we were more than happy with the sound he got for us, especially as we only had a week to record, mix *and* master.

"It would have been nice to have had a space between the recording and mastering, where we could have listened to the tracks a bit more and worked on the sound of the album as a whole, but that is just splitting hairs really. I'm still very proud of it."

A cover of 'Hard Times' by the Cro-Mags, featuring guest vocals from renowned Northwest 'edger' Tony Leathers, was also recorded during the sessions for the first album and was included on the Blackfish Records tribute to the Cro-Mags, 'Ushering In A New Age Of Quarrel'. Although the band were unable to tour due to working commitments, a lot of shows were played in support of the album and the band found themselves building a loyal fanbase, but then Lecky left halfway through the writing for the second album, playing his final gig with the band in Wigan with I Fell Sir and Kafka.

Jason Hearne became the new vocalist and the band changed their name to Evanesce, becoming even more metal – if such a thing were possible – than before with their 'Sower Of Sedition' album for their ex-vocalist Chris Meadows' Retribute Records. "When Lecky and me joined the band, the others always said, 'This is it, Withdrawn's final line-up; the next one leaves, we either finish or the name changes'," explains Phil, "and that's basically what happened. We took advantage of the name change to try and change direction too, to try and do some metal shows and just 'be a band', so to speak, not specifically a hardcore band. The music went darker, but was basically the same, if not a bit more technical…only a *bit,* mind – we hadn't advanced *that* much as musicians! The lyrics changed too, I think; I only wrote three sets of lyrics for the second release, but I know I tried to make them more poetic than political. Well, that was the aim anyway… And we decided to be more uniform in our approach too: all in black, no print, no adverts…just trying to make it about the band's image, the band's message and not about the individuals."

During '98 and '99, Phil and Dave also did Xsolution151X, a defiantly straightedge band that played just five shows and also included Area Effect drummer Andy Goddard on bass and Matt Ward from Symbiosis on guitar.

"I kinda felt that Withdrawn could be more 'forceful' with its vegan SXE morals," reckons Phil. "So we decided to start a band that was only about being vegan SXE…although it wasn't a hard-line band; we never went down that route. We decided to tie it in with the whole1x5x1 movement that was going on in the northwest at the time and asked members from the other 1x5x1 bands to help out and it all happened really quickly. Before we knew it, we had done the demo and were playing gigs and then it was over, but it was really important to me personally because it helped me mature as a person and made me start to really think about the flags I was waving.

"It started out trying to put right the injustices we saw animals suffering, but it ended up with me realising I didn't personally see the merit in veganism and my stance was only serving to appease my own conscience without making any impact on the wider world. I think that's the main reason why I didn't do anything to stop the project from splitting up when it did; its purpose was no longer valid for me…"

"I remember when we recorded our only release [for Xsolution151X: the five-track demo 'In These Dark Times The Eye Begins To See']," Dave adds. "We did it in about four hours, including the mixing stage. Just before we left the lad's home studio, it was sounding really powerful and tight, but unfortunately when he came to transfer the music I think he transferred one of the earlier takes of the whole set – including mistakes and a few out-of-time overdubs – and that is the version that we gave away! By the way, good luck finding a copy…"

"The name change always irked me though," confesses Danny, back to the subject of Evanesce. "I got the impression we had some kind of following and respect as Withdrawn, albeit in the SXE niche, but as Evanesce…it felt like we were trying far too hard and overcompensating in some ways, to take on the pure metal kids, which was, in my opinion, always doomed to fail. Things can't stagnate and we had to move forward so maybe it was a necessary step, as in 'you don't get if you don't try', but I know I certainly wasn't technically gifted enough to give most metallers what they've come to expect from a guitarist and didn't have the persona to carry off the aspirational, self-indulgent, rockstar attitude either!

"That was the good thing about Withdrawn and Evanesce; no-one had that fake-ass cock-rock attitude – but was that what was lacking for the next step? I don't think vegan SXE was ever going to be sexy enough for a metal crowd! Partly, I think we just reacted by going more metal with 'Sower Of Sedition' because everyone around us was going 'screamo'!"

Recorded by Dave Chang again, but this time at Philia Studios in Henley-on-Thames, 'Sower Of Sedition' was released by Retribute in early 1999 and the band were even the subject of one of BBC2's *Tribe* programmes about unusual ideologies in youth subcultures. The programme was broadcast on 14 February 2000 and saw Dave gamely debating the benefits of a vegan SXE lifestyle. Unsurprisingly Phil and Danny left before it even aired though, playing their final gig at the Birmingham Foundry in October 1999, both of them unhappy with the band's new direction. Dave and Onion forged on, recruiting Simon Stewart on lead guitar, Jay on vocals and Colin Robertson on bass, for the 'Schemes Of Subversion' split 12-inch with Conquest Of Steel.

Unfortunately, the day before the band was due to travel to Avesta, Sweden, to record the new album at the Black Lounge, Jay and Simon decided to leave. Stubbornly wishing to finish what they had started, Grant Richardson was recruited on vocals and Peter Broom took over from Simon for the 'Secure The Shadow' CD, which, like the split 12-inch before it, was released by West Yorkshire label No Face Records.

No gigs were forthcoming to promote it, however, because Evanesce split in early 2005. "Our last ever gig was at Hannah's Bar in Leece Street [Liverpool], during Summer 2004," says Dave, "and we even played two songs off 'A Certain Innate Suffering' for old time's sake. It was actually a really good gig too, but there was none of the original magic or impetus there. The day after it all finished, I went to a gig in Leeds and that's when Lecky and [skater] Howard [Cooke] asked me to join Walk The Plank, which I did…too fuckin' right! It was just what I needed, back to basics.

"In my mind Evanesce had pretty much been treading water for years and had lost our direction. When you look back to the very beginning of Withdrawn, it was all about introspective politics and adaptable animal rights. By the time we finished, it had kind of morphed into a style of music that became a pointless vehicle for those issues to be heard."

Dave has since become a proud father and, until early 2011, drummed for the aforementioned SSS, a modestly successful and hugely entertaining thrash band signed to the very influential Earache label (his last recording with them being their well-received 'Problems To The Answer' album). After SSS, he teamed up with Russ from Cold Ones and Adam Clarkson from Nowhere Fast to do Salem Rages, "a gloom-punk band in the vein of Samhain or TSOL…" who have so far released two EPs on their own Casket Records.

At the time of writing, Lecky has just fronted Voorhees again for several well-received reunion gigs, Onion is a teacher in Germany and both Phil and Danny still make music, the former currently playing guitar for an urban hip-hop act from Liverpool called KOF.

"And at the moment I'm into tinkering with electronics and circuit-bending for glitchy sounds," reveals Danny. "I play the ukulele more than guitar these days; no performances as yet, but who knows? The big influences for me nowadays aren't musical: Richard Dawkins, Sam Harris, Christopher Hitchens…although I guess I didn't need the academic or scientific approach to atheism when I had the benefit of more direct hardcore lyrics like, 'You picked up a bible and now you're gone' and 'You're full of religion, you're full of shit!'

"My ideal is where politics, ethics and, I guess, the aggressive sound of punk, hardcore or metal mix. Metalcore just seemed to do that for me for a time…now, it seems there just isn't one package that ticks all those boxes."

"I would like Withdrawn to be remembered as part of that Nineties wave of hardcore that took on a darker edge," concludes Dave proudly. "I feel differently about it all now, but at the time I was really proud of the confidence we had in getting the vegan drug-free message out there and I know a lot of people that took the message to their heart. I know it's hard to believe now, but there really was fuck all going on in the north regarding straightedge when we got things going. So I'm proud of maybe being in the first fully vegan straightedge band to have ever come out of Liverpool…"

SELECT DISCOGRAPHY:

MCD:
'A Certain Innate Suffering' CD (Sure Hand Records, 1996)

12-inch:
'Schemes Of Subversion' (No Face, 2003) – *split with Conquest Of Steel – as Evanesce*

LPs:
'Seeds Of Inhumanity' (Household Name, 1999)
'Sower Of Sedition' (Retribute, 2000) – *as Evanesce*
'Secure the Shadow' (No Face, 2005) – *as Evanesce*

AT A GLANCE:
Well, until Dave persuades someone to release 'Seeds Of Inhumanity' and 'Sower Of Sedition' as a double album vinyl set in a gatefold sleeve, start with the former but be sure to check out the latter!

DEAD WRONG

One of the most tragically overlooked bands in the history of UK hardcore, Liverpool's **Dead Wrong** were formed in 1991 when bassist Andy Capper met guitarist Max Linacre and although they only released the one 7-inch on Armed With Anger, they came dangerously close to signing a multi-album deal with metal giants Roadrunner and could probably have been the biggest metalcore band ever from the UK. That said, they wouldn't have been half as awesome if everyone had known about them, would they?

"Max was in a band called Anti-Face with Sean Shea, our unofficial manager/guru/big brother," explains Andy. "He was the guy who booked some of the most important shows in the Northwest at the time and ran a distro; he was also married to Melanie Woods, sister of Alan Woods, of First Strike Records and Alan's [record and skate store in Wigan], where we would all congregate. I thought they were two of the coolest people I had ever met. Sean was the door to so many things in my life: records, books, zines and terrible Japanese snuff films...in fact, I hold him responsible for steering me off the straight and narrow.

"Anti-Face only lasted one gig, though. They had a bassist called Daryl who left to go travelling (he was also the first punk I saw with an eyebrow/septum piercing). I tried to join Anti-Face but was considered not punk enough; this made me even more determined to form my own band, but I knew Max had to be in it. He was a tough scally who used to fight people in the amusement arcades, but had crossed over to hardcore and skating.

"Max introduced me to [Dead Wrong's singer] Jamie Rowe at an ENT gig at the Planet [Planet X, Liverpool's best-loved hardcore venue during the early Nineties]. He was the best-looking guy in punk and wanted to sing like Scott Kelly [from Neurosis] so we knew he had to be in there too. Then Paul Donnelly was one of my best friends in the skate scene; he could kinda play drums and that was the first line-up..."

"Dead Wrong was my first band," recalls Paul. "Before that, as a kid, I played drums in my garden, mostly with big old headphones on, playing along to AC/DC and Motörhead. I started to play drums when I was seven at my uncle's house; he was in a punk band from Southport called Mayhem [see the *Burning Britain* book] and taught me a basic 4/4 beat on the arm of his sofa and then other bits and bobs here and there. He moved to London when I was 10 and left me all of his punk records for a while, which I devoured as a kid; he played gigs with the [Dead] Kennedys and roadied for them and Black Flag.

"I remember watching Mayhem practice as a little kid and all I wanted to be was my uncle; he was so cool and didn't give a shit what anyone thought. Then I got a skateboard and got even more of a 'fuck you' attitude and got into lots more music that I could call my own though the skate videos. I met Andy when I was about 15; skating in a little town, you got to know everyone. Andy was into punk from the first time I met him; he had lots of records and Slapshot T-shirts and was going to all these gigs and telling me about the bands he was watching.

"The scene in Southport was a non-starter; it was a strange place to grow up. Once you understood the mentality, you just wanted to leave…which in a way spawned at least some of my (our) attitude. The friends who stayed in Southport seemed to either turn into everyone else or get massively into smack. All I knew of the Liverpool scene was Planet X and Probe Records, but that was through skating and that all seemed like a different world at that time. I wasn't ever on the scene; I didn't hang out or anything, I was just a kid. I didn't drink and didn't go out to clubs or gigs, I just skated. I knew a bit about the older scene and [legendary Liverpool venue] Eric's from my uncle, but that was it; I knew it was cool, but was a bit daunted, I think."

The first line-up of Dead Wrong made their public debut at Planet X, supporting Burst Of Silence (the Liverpool band, not to be confused with the Canadian SXE act with the same name), before recording an eight-track demo in Vulcan Street Studios with Foz from industrial-metal act RIOT (Recurring Images Of Torture), manning the desk. They soon began honing their distinctly chaotic yet lethally incisive sound, fusing the best of American hardcore with crusty UK punk influences.

"I remember getting the 'Consolidation' EP on Armed With Anger and thinking, 'I want to play shows with all these bands and blow them all off stage!'" laughs Andy. "This was after about five rehearsals and we still sounded like total shit, but had a naive confidence about us that comes from living in a small seaside town your whole life. Only Paul Donnelly could actually play an instrument, but we didn't care; we wanted to make really balls-out, original stuff that didn't sound like anything else. We all loved old DC, Boston and NY hardcore, from the Bad Brains to Minor Threat through all the tough guy stuff like Warzone and Cro-Mags and Sick Of It All… Poison Idea was also a massive thing for me.

"When the ABC No Rio thing happened [New York's legendary DIY punk venue on the Lower East Side], with less huge-looking, more nerdy, skinny kids, I could definitely relate to them more than JJ [John Joseph from Cro-Mags] doing push-ups in Tompkins Square Park. That whole scene was a big influence on us – Born Against, Go!, Citizen's Arrest. There was also a Neurosis show at the Bradford 1 In 12 which totally changed my life – again! It was during the 'Souls At Zero' tour and I have to admit I had what verges on a gay crush on Scott Kelly at that time; he looked like a crust-punk version of River Phoenix in *My Own Private Idaho!*"

"For me there was a kind of 'need' to be in a band," adds Jamie. "Everybody did something,

Dead Wrong, Leicester

Dead Wrong, Manchester squat gig

whether that was putting on gigs, selling records or printing their own zines; we all wanted to be involved and contribute. I think, like a lot of kids who start out, being in a band is like being in a gang. We were no different and we wanted to reflect the stuff we were into at the time. We wanted to do the heavier, gnarlier kind of hardcore, but we wanted to do something a bit different too. We didn't fit the straightedge, crust or generic hardcore punk mould and I think we wanted to kick against those established stereotypes in the scene. We didn't have mohicans or dreads and we didn't felt-tip Xs on our hands. We didn't wear the 'uniform' basically. Don't get me wrong, we were into the British hardcore bands like Doom, ENT and Heresy, but they seemed like they belonged to the generation before us and I don't think we could relate to that. In reality, we probably only missed them by about two years, but when you're a kid that's a long time…"

Stephen 'Ducky' Duckworth from Southport punk act Paradox UK joined on second guitar ("But it didn't work out…probably because he had the wrong stickers on his guitar or something!" admits Jamie) and the 'Rituals' demo was recorded at Pickett Studios. Although obviously still on a sharp learning curve as regards studio technique, the demo saw Dead Wrong already sounding better than most bands do after several albums and captured much of the crazed urgency of their live performances.

"But the engineer was a Rasta who wasn't really feeling what we were trying to do," reckons Andy. "Getting into a proper studio for the first time made me realise how much work we had to do as well. In my mind we always sounded like a crisp blast of honed brutality… in reality, it sounded like some blind people from a remote village in the Himalayas were given some guitars and told to make up shit on the spot."

Ducky was replaced by Rob Holden, a skater from nearby Lancaster who had previously played with Billy Rubin (who had formerly been known as Toast), Dead Wrong finally arriving at their definitive line-up and the one that played on all their vinyl releases.

"He begged me to let him join the band and when he did everything really started working," recalls Andy. "He was an amazing guitarist and brought a lot to the overall Dead Wrong set-up – including some wild moodswings and lots of hash-smoking. It was like when Brian Jones died and the Stones really kicked it up a notch…"

"I was blown away by what Dead Wrong were doing," admits Rob. "Their influences were pretty clear, but the music wasn't derivative and I really dug the lyric writing; it was artful without being pretentious…political without being just slogans. The atmosphere created by the whole thing – the writing and the playing – just made me want in. And my first gig as a member of the group was in Bolton where we played with Bugeyed. I loved it."

Inspired by the aforementioned 'Consolidation' compilation, Andy put together the 'Nothing New' EP in 1993, which was a split release between Bradford label Armed With Anger and Preston's Kwijibo and featured – as well as Dead Wrong, of course – Bob Tilton, Bugeyed, Kitchener and Kito.

"We had a good mix on there," confirms Andy. "Bob Tilton were the new emo kings and our best friends in the scene. We'd play with them a lot and, although they usually headlined, we always blew them off stage. Those gigs we did together were some of my favourite, I always loved those guys. Kitchener were like dirty Manc pop-punk noise stuff and Bugeyed were this gang of older guys from Leeds and Bradford that we really looked up to and wished we were as punk as.

"Kito were kids from Middlesbrough that we liked too; Rob, the singer, was a good character.

He once put us on at a show in Middlesbrough; we, well I, drove four hours in a snowstorm to get there. We played six songs, then drove straight back that night…once again, we'd blown everybody off the stage."

The following year saw the band's only release exclusively in their own name, a self-titled 7-inch on Armed With Anger that still bears up to repeated listens today. Starting to move away from jagged noisecore and into slightly more measured – but still deliciously discordant – alt-rock territory, the EP bears more than a passing resemblance to 'Life Time'-era Rollins Band, with DW finding an abrasive synergy that would surely have produced some unique results had it been given the chance to evolve further.

"The studio we used was in a sort of community business enterprise place in Cheetham Hill [Manchester]," recalls Rob. "Spam and Whitey [from Electro Hippies] recorded us there for the session that made up all the split EP and compilations stuff and we went back for the 7-inch. Listening to all the Dead Wrong recordings lately, I probably enjoyed those three tracks the most; everybody's playing that much better, Jamie's singing had really developed…gigging more had tightened up the band as a whole. I didn't contribute a great deal to the writing of those songs, just a chord progression and a lick in 'The North Room', so listening back it's sort of easier to stand back and appreciate it; the riff Max plays at the opening of 'Cumulus' is an especially great piece of guitar playing. Andy played a sort of 'musical director' role and that's probably why the 7-inch hangs together as a whole thing so nicely…"

Although 'gigging more', Dead Wrong still weren't a touring band by a long stretch of the imagination. But when they did grace a stage with their presence they certainly made an impression with their spontaneous outbursts of manic expression.

"One of my favourite gigs was actually before the single came out," reckons Andy, "at a squat at the old Charles Barry Crescent buildings in Hulme. There were dogs everywhere, a very weird toilet set-up and screaming crackheads wandering around the place. They told us that, by the time our set was finished, somebody would set our car on fire; it was magical. We got some great support slots too, with people like Lungfish, Drive Like Jehu and Neurosis on big-ish stages, but I think my favourite ones were always when we were in the corner of some pub, usually playing with Bob Tilton and trying to outdo each other in the amount of times we could roll around on the floor while still playing guitar. We played a couple of great shows at the 1 In 12 too, which was my personal favourite venue. Our last show was there; Lecky from Voorhees was in the front row dancing and that was a big deal for me.

"But no, we didn't really do a lot of touring," he continues. "We all had very square day jobs and couldn't afford to give them up for a month or whatever it took; in that respect, we were very un-Bohemian. We'd always get, 'I can't believe your drummer works at McDonald's!' And we'd be like, 'Fuck you, go get a job you fucking student!' We were quite snotty towards the more established rules that you were meant to live by. *Personally* I boycotted McDonald's, but if my friend Paul wanted to work there, to pay rent on his tiny flat and occasionally buy stuff for his girlfriend, then I had no problem with that. Living in Southport, there weren't too many vegan co-ops to volunteer at…"

"We did do one small tour actually," Jamie interjects, "with Understand and some band called Jacob's Mouse…about six dates in all. I hitch-hiked to the first gig in Dudley, because I'd spent the previous night in Nottingham; I turned up early so went to a pub and drank… and drank. I spent the whole show staggering around and spitting at people from the stage. Not my proudest moment, for sure. I think the wheels had started to come off…"

Rob: "And there was a short chaotic gig in Northampton that always springs to mind; the stage times got changed and some of us had gone to eat, when Andy came running into this fast-food place and said, 'We're on!' So we all went running back to the Roadmenders looking like a low-rent version of *A Hard Day's Night*, ran in and, with what was left of our allotted time, we just went off on one. I remember Max just ripping the strings off his guitar while I punched mine, with feedback howling around…sort of a best and worst gig for us, really!"

Dead Wrong then contributed the tracks 'Gut' and 'From Prison Diary' to a three-way split 7-inch, 'Electroplating The Dead', for First Strike Records, where they appeared alongside Billy Rubin and Cowboy Killers; also the track 'Time Was' to the 'Autonomy' 7-inch for Subjugation, another compilation this time shared with Bob Tilton, Tribute and Fingerprint. All the positive exposure brought them dangerously close to signing the Roadrunner deal mentioned earlier, but ironically it was all the subsequent pressure and soul-searching that destroyed the band.

"A guy [from Roadrunner] called Miles Leonard came to see us at a couple of shows," explains Andy. "He came to a particularly amazing one in Birmingham at a venue called Sinatra's. I remember all these dodgy white-power guys being there. We gave him one of these photocopied paper business cards that said, 'We Are All Pigs, Fuck You' on them – right next to Jamie's mum and dad's address! He got in touch and we had a couple of meetings and, while we felt slightly flattered by the attention, it was all about five-album deals and going on tour with shitty bands forever and playing the music-industry game and at the time it didn't really appeal to any of us."

"I guess it was a case of different people having different politics," offers Rob, carefully. "The stuff that was going on with underground bands being courted by the big labels at the time was weird because, for some, the bigger labels seemed like a logical step up, but I just saw it as selling out the scene. The independence of that scene meant that the music itself was actually rebellious, rather than something that had been co-opted.

"And musically there were more writers in Dead Wrong than the band probably needed; I certainly didn't conduct myself well when dealing with 'musical differences'… I always felt that my ideas were being overlooked. I *could* just put it down to being young, but I know I've been an egotistical brat loads of times since then as well! The irony is that I enjoyed the bands that everyone did after Dead Wrong. I would have got bored just playing and not writing though and would have kicked up a stink sooner or later, but rather than an 'enfant terrible' I was just terribly infantile…"

"As the chief songwriter, I could feel there were factions developing over the whole 'less rock'/'more rock' debate," claims Andy. "Also, as much fun as I had with our friends in the scene and as much as I loved playing, it had all started to feel a bit stale. I can't stand it when you have to deal with scene politics and rules and all the ensuing arguments and non-fun that entails. Where's the fun if you can't put a few noses out of joint every now and again?

"One guitarist – whose name begins with R! – started to have a really hard time with it all and I think he'd started hanging around in Leeds 6 too much with some guys who were into playing a more pretentious kind of hardcore that involved 'jazz-stylings', while I ideally wanted us to keep sounding like Born Against and Neurosis, only with more of a Sabbath/ Eyehategod thing going on. On the one hand, you had the, 'Let's sound like stoner rock' camp and then the other camp was, like, 'Jawbox are really cool, let's listen to [Miles Davis']

"Bitches Brew" while getting high in our student flat!'

"For me, neither option was workable, so I called Rob Holden up one night after he'd cancelled a practice and we arranged to split the band on a show we had booked at the 1 In 12. At the time I pretended I was into splitting up, but as the set finished it made me feel quite sad; I felt like we were throwing something special away. At the time, there was a big 'emo vibe' coming into the scene, though, so maybe that's what made us behave like such sensitive little bitches?"

After their 50th and final show, Dead Wrong sadly went the way of so many killer bands who disintegrate before realising their full potential and split before even doing a full album. Thankfully the band members carried on making music in the underground hardcore scene, most notably – for this book, at least – Rob who formed Baby Harp Seal with Tom from Ironside.

"I just wish we'd recorded one more time," sighs Jamie. "I thought the 7-inch was great; you know, it was a band that was developing and had ideas. We had *better* material, though; we'd written a whole bunch of songs after putting that single out and we had been playing them live. We were actually booked into a studio to record the new songs; I think it was going to come out on Whole Car Records, which was Tony from Fabric's thing and something to do with Wiija. We loaded up the gear into the rental van and drove down to London; Andy went to the studio door and pressed the buzzer and I remember his ashen face as he walked back to the van. It turns out we *were* booked in, but for the week before and had turned up seven days late! I wish we had recorded those songs, though…they would have been amazing."

"Baby Harp Seal had actually begun before Dead Wrong broke up," corrects Rob. "And we still had a really good friendship with Subjugation [who released their 'Devour' 7-inch and self-titled LP] that continued for [his next band] Month Of Birthdays [and their critically acclaimed 'Lost In The Translation' LP]. Both bands had their run-ins with A&R from major labels and people from the mainstream music press, but they just didn't seem to get it…

"After the Month Of Birthdays ended, I was playing a lot of folk music back in Lancaster but played electric with the Thens, followed by Lee Malvo, before I headed back to West Yorkshire to do Threads with Sned, Cath and Bry. I've well and truly got the country bug these days, playing bluegrass and country at local sessions and twangy Fender stuff with some friends called the Rose Bay Willow Band, although the heavy riffing continues in End Times with Bry – even if we are short of a drummer at the moment…

"But the way Dead Wrong is remembered round here is just fine with me; people still rave about the band. I honestly think we appeared at just the right moment, that little bit ahead of the curve, and then we were gone. Should I just mention that we stood out because we were a fucking good band? Well I have and we were!"

"After Dead Wrong, I went all-out down the stoner rock route," says Jamie, who nowadays lives self-sufficiently on a remote farm. "I was in a band called the Dawn with some friends from Preston. We started gigging with some of my old buddies from the hardcore scene like Fabric; we signed to One Little Indian Records and we supported bands like COC and had a blast for about five years. Soon, though, we started supporting more mainstream rock acts, because the label was trying to get us more exposure. I have no problem with that, in theory, but the nadir came after a 30-date schlep around the country with a band called Thunder who were almost certainly the single shittest band I'd ever heard… I loved the band I was in, but it was so far removed from where I had come from it was time to call it a day."

"I was genuinely lost when Dead Wrong split up, really pissed off," reckons Paul, who now runs a footwear business. "I jumped straight back into another band with Andy and Max, called Des Man DeAblo [who did three singles during '95 and '96, for Whole Car, Simba and Rough Trade]. I was happy to be back in a band situation with the original three guys I had started out with – and with what we knew from DW we got off to a good start and were soon playing shows again. People were eager to see what most of Dead Wrong had become, but I think Des Man surprised a few of them as it was quite different; a few proper punks that used to like DW came to the first few shows, but that quickly stopped. Again, I was really into what we were doing, but I was older and wiser and I had more input. We were offered deals from some big labels; we could have 'made it', whatever that means! We coulda been the next Aerosmith!

"But I moved to Leeds to study instead, where I skated all the time. I made some lifelong friends and avoided the still bustling local hardcore/gig scene like the plague. I didn't want to know, although I would see people from that scene all the time as I lived bang in the middle of it for a long time. I was – and still am – 'the drummer from Dead Wrong' to lots of people…"

"Des Man is still one of the single biggest regrets of my life," admits Andy, who nowadays edits the popular *Vice* magazine. "It happened just around the time I started drinking and taking drugs and the more the band went on, the more drink and drugs I took. We got offered deals all over the place, but it was all just a shambles, both aesthetically and artistically – and it certainly wasn't punk any more.

"As for being remembered? Well, in the spirit of Dead Wrong, I don't give a fuck about that kind of thing, other than we blew everybody else off stage every single time. We are all pigs – fuck you!"

SELECT DISCOGRAPHY:

7-inch:
'Dead Wrong' (Armed With Anger, 1994)
'Electroplating The Dead' (First Strike, 1994) – *three-way split with Billy Rubin and Cowboy Killers*

AT A GLANCE:
The current hardcore scene *needs* a Dead Wrong discography.

AREA EFFECT

In nearby Manchester, **Area Effect** were another quietly influential SXE hardcore band, primarily because of the youthful sincerity they helped bring to the UKHC scene in their early years; their enthusiastic networking certainly helped chip away at the perceived north/south divide as well. The band came together in 1994, coalescing around brothers Mark and Gavin Boardman (on bass and guitar respectively), who had formed Twisted Anger the previous year, but had recruited a second bassist, Gav Scouse, vocalist Mark 'Critch' Critchley and drummer Andy Goddard, with a view to doing something much more hardcore.

"Actually Area Effect was something that formed around Gav and his mate Andy Prescott," corrects Mark. "They'd been learning to play guitar for a few months and talked me into getting a bass; we started messing about and auditioned all our mates to have a go at singing. Our mate Critch was the best of a bad bunch so, with a drum machine, we started working some songs out. I met Gav Scouse in the toilets of a nightclub; he was wearing a Biohazard shirt which, in an indie club in 1993, was pretty weird! We got chatting and he said he played bass, so I told him to come down and try out as a second bass player for us – we knew Godflesh had done it, so why couldn't we? He came down and had a bash, playing the 'high' notes while I played the 'low'!

"Scouse knew a lad who played drums and was into Sick Of It All from going to rock clubs in town, so I met Andy Goddard one night and convinced him to give it a bash; he didn't have a kit so we borrowed one off some death-metal band I'd gone to school with. He seemed into it so we started practicing properly, but then Andy Prescott quit the band 'cos it didn't sound like Oasis!

"We played a few shows around Manchester in September 1995 [the very first being at the Star And Garter on 15 September]; we put on our own gigs 'cos we didn't know anyone else who'd put us on and just flyered all round Manchester. Gav Scouse knocked it on the head after the seventh or eighth gig due to me and him having some 'personal issues' and this 14 year-old kid called Graham [Cox] asked our kid's bird if he could join on second guitar. We started playing with him a few months later, but then Critch left to be with his bird in Lancaster Uni. So Gav decided to pick up the mike [he made his debut at the Star And Garter, supporting Madball and Ignite] and in the space of about half a year we'd gone through a guitar player, a second bass player and a singer! But after that the line-up stayed the same all the way through...well, at least 'til we added Tommy 'Positive' O'Brien on second guitar for the last six months or so."

With their fingers on the pulse of the emerging UKHC scene in the northwest, they started to command a decent following in Manchester, although with a band like Area Effect who were very 'anti' the whole traditional music-industry model, the throng that religiously began turning up at their shows was more a gathering of mates than a fanbase.

"Actually, at the time there wasn't really a hardcore scene in Manchester," reckons Andy. "I guess there was a mohawk cider-drinking *punk* scene and that was it, so to start with it was hard doing shows 'cos there really weren't any other bands doing what we did in Manchester. The main band from Manchester we played shows with was Dog Toffee, who were like rockabilly punk and a good bunch of lads; we must have been playing two shows a week with them at one point! Then, through zines mainly, we started getting in touch

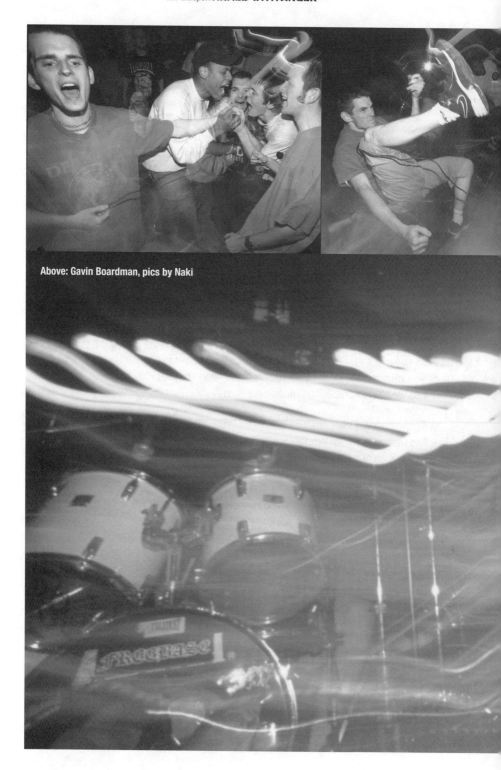

Above: Gavin Boardman, pics by Naki

Area Effect, Mark Boardman live, pic by Naki

with bands across the UK, the first being Stampin' Ground and, I think, Above All. I got into hardcore when I met Mark and Gav really; I was more a full-on metal kid at the time, although I also listened to bands like Biohazard and Sick Of It All…"

"Biohazard was definitely our first influence as a band," agrees Mark. "But then I picked up that Sick Of It All 'Spreading The Hardcore Reality' CD on Lost And Found and we thought, 'Fuck, that's fast…let's add those bouncy Biohazard parts to these Sick Of It All fast bits', and that was pretty much us sorted. We didn't really know what hardcore was at the time and you couldn't Google it – Google hadn't been invented! We were definitely from that *Kerrang!* /Terrorizer school of 'woolly hat hardcore', but I knew a girl who was into pop-punk stuff and she had a few distro lists which she gave to me and I ended up getting records from distros and live tapes from people like Mel Hughes at No Barcodes Necessary. Until then we hadn't realised there were other people still listening to this stuff!

"But as far as we knew there was no hardcore scene in Manchester, so we just did stuff ourselves…we did what the punks do and said, 'Fuck it, it can't be that hard!' We got in contact with bands like Stampin' Ground and Hard To Swallow and put them on in Manchester with us supporting, then we formed a scene of younger kids around us…"

After recording their six-track self-titled demo at Manchester's Spirit Studios during February 1996, Area Effect played at the 1 In 12 Club in Bradford with Strife and Knuckledust, forming a strong alliance with the latter that would extend to sharing a split 7-inch single (which was released in June 1997 on Tom Brandon from Ninebar's label, Black Up) and touring the UK together.

"I first met [Knuckledust vocalist] Pierre at that 'Fuck Reading' show in London that Stampin' Ground, Madball and Refused played," says Mark. "I drove down to that with Heath, the Stampin' Ground singer; it was the day after I'd passed my driving test – so I'm guessing 4 August 1996. I remember having to drive home from London to Bradford 'cos Heath was too tired… I'd only been driving for about 24 hours! Pierre was giving out his little newsletter he did back then, *Time For Some Action*, and I got one and a demo off him and we chatted for a bit. When I got home I listened to that demo and it blew my mind. It said 'Copy and circulate' on it as well…so I did!

"Next time I saw him was when Knuckledust played with us and Strife at the 1 In 12 and it was amazing; I'd been dying to see them and they blew me away. Me, Pierre and [then Touchdown vocalist] Nathan Dean cooked up many schemes for shows across the country and I think that's what pulled that early UKHC scene together. Without Knuckledust, I don't think there'd be much of anything as regards the scene today, because they showed kids around the country how to do it: organise, get off your arse and do it yourself!"

"I think it was a great idea for a northern and a southern band to do the split 7-inch, as I guess there *was* a bit of a north/south divide at the time," continues Andy. "And seeing as we had been doing a lot of shows together, both up north and down south, it seemed a good idea. Then we did the 'UK Brotherhood' tour together when the 7-inch was released; we played from Margate to Glasgow and we played some great shows. The only problem was at the start: the night we arrived in London for the first show; [Knuckledust bassist] Nic had broke his hand and couldn't play!

"The tour had been booked for a good while, so we only cancelled that night's show and Mark, Gav and Graham spent the night with Knuckledust, learning all the bass lines so they could all take it in turns to play for Nic, then we could still play all the other dates. We ended up having a great tour apart from the bit where everyone got food poisoning and a certain person shat himself in a well-known supermarket. It was a time in Area Effect I will never forget for the rest of my life!"

The 'Stand Strong' MCD that followed was the first release by respected London label Rucktion – six tracks of blisteringly raw old school hardcore, seat-of-yer-pants blastbeats spiced with some hard grooves and plenty of singalong, finger-pointing moments. It was quickly taken to heart by the burgeoning UKHC scene and the band enjoyed themselves playing anywhere and everywhere.

"Yeah, we always tried to put on a good show, no matter how many people were there or what kind of crowd it was," agrees Mark. "We played some awesome shows to punk kids in Grimsby before the scene there blew up with Imbalance… London was always a great time too. But I'll always remember the show we put on in Manchester with Knuckledust, Imbalance, Public Disturbance, us and Touchdown; that show was mental and it was great 'cos it was all of our mates' bands on one show. The Star And Garter was literally busting at the seams that night. I can remember a couple of bad shows as well, of course…one where I broke my bass at some metal club in Warrington in front of six people and a tortoise and one at a darts club in Bury with some metal band we knew… The room was so full of dry ice and strobes that I couldn't even see my hand in front of my face!"

Unfortunately Graham started going to university in London and was struggling to make every rehearsal, so the band recruited the aforementioned Liverpudlian, Tommy Positive (aka 'Tommy P'), on second guitar, reasoning that not only would he thicken their sound up, but if ever Graham couldn't make a show they'd still be able to play it with just Tommy. However, Mark had recently became a father and was struggling to reconcile his band and family priorities and Area Effect eventually played their last ever show during August 1999, supporting good friends Knuckledust in New Cross. Mark, Gav and Andy formed Safeguard with guitarist Peter Broom and Tommy P on vocals, but that was relatively shortlived (generating just one eight-track self-titled MCD) and when Gav left to concentrate on a career in mixed martial arts (he still runs the Predators gym in Manchester) he was replaced by second guitarist Teenie.

"Road trip, road trip, road trip!" is how Andy Goddard, who also did a short stint in Solution 151 alongside members of Withdrawn and Symbiosis, remembers the Nineties hardcore scene. "No matter where in the UK, it was always great to jump in a Salford Van Hire van and play with all the great bands we had become friends with over the years. I think the scene was at its strongest during the late Nineties, as the early and mid Nineties were spent striking up relationships with all the bands across the UK and helping build the scene. I think everyone just stuck to their home towns before that, and from our point of view meeting Knuckledust and building up that relationship made all the difference; between Mark and Pierre I think they pretty much started the ball rolling with the north/south thing. I think the all-day shows Pierre used to put on in London were amazing; he would get bands from every corner of the UK and all styles of hardcore, all at one gig…"

"But it was always more than music," states Mark, "and it always will be. We operated outside of the mainstream music industry; we by-passed promoters and stupid tour riders and guarantees. We by-passed the normal venue stranglehold and put gigs on in halls and the upstairs of pubs. We were 19 year-old kids who could roll up in a town 300 miles away in a van and get out and jump around for 20 minutes and thrash our instruments to a bunch of like-minded kids who wanted to jump on each other's heads. I mean how many people can say they could do that?

"To me, that's what punk and hardcore will always be about; it wasn't so much as what food you chose to eat or what chemicals you put into your bodies as it was about just saying 'Fuck you!' to the normal system of bands being fucked over by the clubs, by the record labels, by the promoters. And likewise the kids being fucked over by the bands, the record shops and everyone else! I mean, if we could charge £5 for a CD, how the fuck could HMV charge £12?"

"I would like us to be remembered for the energy and love we used to put into playing," concludes Andy. "We would be the first to admit that we weren't the greatest band out there musically, but I think we played straight-up positive old-school hardcore…"

"And I'd like kids to remember that no matter what, we went all out," says Mark proudly, who has been playing with Rot In Hell, the UK's only 'Holy Terror' hardcore band (and signed to Deathwish Inc) since October 2008 alongside Nathan Dean. "We jumped around and shouted our heads off because we fucking believed in what we were doing. We were totally sincere, it was never an act with us; we loved Side By Side, we loved wearing shorts and we loved meeting new people. People at work ask me, 'Oh, what is it like to be a musician?' I have to laugh and say, 'I'm no musician! I just jump around and twat my bass and sometimes it's the right note!' I'll leave being a muso to people who *don't* think that a 'B Sharp' is Homer Simpson's Barbershop Quartet…"

SELECT DISCOGRAPHY:

7-inch:
'Split' (Black Up, 1997) – *split with Knuckledust*

MCD:
'Stand Strong' (Rucktion, 1998)

AT A GLANCE:
No retrospective releases available, I'm afraid, but you could try e-mailing Mark to see if he'll burn you some Area Effect: xsickpeoplex@gmail.com

EXTINCTION OF MANKIND

Manchester's **Extinction Of Mankind** make no bones about the fact that they worship at the altars of Antisect and Amebix. Yet despite not being the most original punk band in the UK, they've certainly proven themselves one of the hardest-working and – still together 20 years later – most enduring. With a line-up of Ste on vocals, Massimo 'Mass' Centi on guitar, David 'Foz' Foster on drums and 'another Fozz' on bass, the band set off in 1992 as they meant to go on and wasted very little time before they were gigging and recording.

"The first gig was at Magee's in Bolton," begins Ste, "where my mate Mike was the promoter and he really wanted us to play – after just five practices we only had a set of about seven songs. It was with Dr And The Crippens and I can remember shaking like a shitting dog as it was my first gig, but it was really good. We went down really well thanks to all the Manchester punks who turned up – but that could have been the beer talking, as we were all twisted.

"Then we recorded the first demo in Oldham in a church hall ran by these Rastas, which was a bit of a pisser as they didn't know what the fuck they were doing! This was late 1992 and one track off the demo was sent to Loony Tunes Records for one of their compilation LPs. Foz was permanently stoned when we did that recording and it was only after the comp was released that we realised how bad it sounded, so we went off to Big Fish Studios in Manchester, who were mates with Mass, and re-recorded the whole demo...

"It wasn't long after that when Stick [from Doom and Excrement Of War] asked if we would be up for doing a split with Warcollapse from Sweden, so it was time to get our heads together and find a decent studio. I was chatting to my mate Bri from Embittered in Middlesbrough, who recommended a studio up there, so we all piled up in the back of a mate's van (cheers, Tooley!) and recorded two songs in 1993 for Elderberry Records. Soon after that, we were asked if we would do a split with Doom for a forthcoming European tour we had booked with them, during which time Skuld Records got in touch and wanted to release our first full-length EP! So it was off to sunny Bradford where Bri Doom took us to Fulton Street Studios and helped produce all the tracks for the next two 7-inchs in early 1994..."

Phew! Both the split singles and also the 'Weakness' 7-inch, were achingly raw slabs of primal punk rock drawing their primary influences from Scandinavia and the likes of Anti-Cimex or Disfear, although the slower, more metallic sections (usually the dirgy lull before the thrashy shitstorm!) borrowed most obviously from Amebix. The band wasted no time tapping into the underground European circuit during their hefty continental tour with Doom, although on their return bassist Fozzy left and was replaced by Ginny.

"Actually it was all about Antisect!" corrects Ste. "Me and Mass were *heavily* into Antisect and we wanted to form a band along the same lines. But yeah, that first tour abroad was quite an experience, crammed in the back of a van all the way to Dover for the ferry; then we met up with Muskub the tour organiser and from there we had two vans, but both still stinking and full of ale. It was fucking ace and a really good laugh, some long drives and good gigs with great crowds; we met up with Kliester from Skuld, who brought our 'Weakness' EP down for us, which was great to finally get hold of. We were stuck in the attic of a squat somewhere in Hannover folding all the poster sleeves for hours!

"It was hard for Fozzy on tour as he had just had a new-born baby; I think he consoled himself with his two big bottles of brown booze – we never saw him eat, he was just always pulling these bottles of booze out of his pocket…where the fuck did he get it from? And it was a magic bottle 'cos it was always full! Then, when we got back to England, Fozzy's missus saw the state of him, barred him from drinking and whisked him to off to some faraway fairy-tale land in Wales, where he still resides as a cheesemaker today. I think his missus just wanted him to concentrate on bringing up his kids, which was fair enough, but he was a great bloke and I still miss him.

"Anyway we had plans to tour Sweden with Warcollapse in 1995, but Fozzy had said he couldn't do it, so we needed a new bass player. I'd known Ginny for years; I met up with him when we played Oldham next and, after quite a lot of beer and many packets of cigs, he agreed to join EOM."

"I've known Ste since we were small kids, seven or eight years old, living in Salford," confirms Ginny. "I was in a local punk band back in the early Eighties called Demented Ambition; we played a few small gigs, some miners' benefits and even supported the Exploited and GBH. Ste was always at those gigs with his big fuck-off mohican…and I had big bleached spikes in those days too; we were full of soap and studs! I'd moved to Oldham and lost touch a bit, but then started to see Ste round the pubs there; he told me he had a band and I went to see them when they played some Oldham venue. I think it was a hunt sabs benefit. They had all these TVs on stage showing activist videos and the power and energy of the gig really impressed me. I also knew Foz from drinking in the pubs around Oldham and had a passing acquaintance with Mass from gigs around Manchester, so when Fozzy left and Ste asked me if I wanted to go on tour I was well up for it."

However, that's jumping ahead of ourselves and just won't do – not even in a book about punk rock which is meant to be all chaotic and disorderly. Before EOM headed out with the mighty Warcollapse, they recorded the 'Baptised In Shit' LP at Weston-super-Mare's Whitehouse Studios.

"I was never really happy with the outcome," admits Ste, before describing his Whitehouse experience as "A weekend of fucking hell! We just wanted to record and get the fuck out of there; it was all technical bollocks to me, I couldn't stand being in the studio. I wasn't actually arsed how it turned out in the end as the engineer was such a pain and I didn't get along with him. Now I look back and wish we'd gone somewhere else to re-record it as there are some good songs on that LP…"

"When I joined the band they already had three or four songs written," adds Ginny. "So the first few months of being in the band was spent writing songs and practising to get ready for the studio, which was quite exciting for me as I had never recorded anything with Demented Ambition (I also spent a couple of years in a short-lived band in Oldham with Chad, who left to join Feed Your Head, but all we recorded was a demo tape – which was reviewed as 'a cross between Pink Floyd and the Exploited!), so knowing we were gonna do our first real record was a big deal for me…

"And it *was* well recorded, I think – we spent two hours just tuning the drums! Everything was recorded separately, but we prefer to record live these days; it's a better sound for us. Bri Doom had come down to help us with the mix and I don't really think him and [engineer] Martin [Nicholls] saw eye to eye on how it should sound, so it ended up a bit of a compromise. I think it still stands the test of time, though, while being very 'of the time' as well. There are some really strong songs on that album and it was received very well; I'll always remember

Extinction Of Mankind, Tony,
pic by Chris Agitate

Extinction Of Mankind, Scoot,
pic by Chris Agitate.

it came back from the pressing plant while we were on the European tour with Warcollapse and we were all sat in Kleister's flat, folding posters and shoving them in sleeves…"

There's a pattern starting to emerge here – but still DIY to the max, what else? 1996 saw another tour of Europe, this time with Misery from Minneapolis, although Marvin from Chaos UK and the Varukers had to stand in on bass when Ginny couldn't make the trip due to family commitments. Early 1998 saw the band in the Basement Studio with engineer Steve Lloyd recording the four-track 'Scars Of Mankind Still Weep' EP, which Skuld and Profane Existence co-released wrapped in some punky Geiger-ish artwork by Paul Smith. It was however the last EOM release with Foz on drums, who was replaced by Tony in time for a UK tour with Wolfpack.

"It's really hard to remember how and when things came about," sighs Ginny. "There are always conflicts within a band and sometimes small niggles can seem like quite a big problem at the time, but we're all still good friends. Foz is a really unique drummer with a style all of his own and with Tony coming from a metal background his was a more metal style of drumming. But we were playing metal-edged riffs anyway, so it fitted in well and possibly gave us that extra heaviness we'd been looking for. There was sometimes an uneasy atmosphere when we were together as a band, though, and it didn't always feel like you were in a gang. Which is how it was before and how I think a band *should* feel…"

After the tour with Wolfpack, it was decided to bring in a second guitarist to further enhance the band's sonic assault capacity, which opened the door for Scoot from Largactil, Doom and Hellkrusher to join. But things didn't work out and Mass left soon after, so it was back to just one guitar for a Scandinavian tour with Wolfpack and Skit System, a veritable 'wet dream' bill for lovers of D-beat hardcore if ever there was one.

"I remember seeing Ste at gigs long before I actually met him," recalls Scoot of his introduction to the band. "He always had a presence, the funniest person you could meet; anyway, we were friends from 1992 when we met through Bri Doom and while I was in a local band called Largactil, EOM had started the same year and I would see Ste and the lads at the 1 in12, or in Manchester. Then I joined Doom in 1993 and we did lots of gigs together, both here in the UK and in Europe; the tour we did over there in July '94 was my first long tour abroad and two weeks away with Ste was one hell of an experience, to say the least!

"EOM were always a great band to watch live and fun to be with and as time went on we became great friends. During late '94 I joined Hellkrusher so I moved to Newcastle for a year; then in 1995 I left Doom, which wasn't a very happy situation, but we built bridges soon after and I'm happy to say friendships are better than ever now. Anyway, Ste wanted two guitarists in the band – he really wanted a heavier sound – so I joined and by then, I'd seen EOM live well over thirty times, certainly more than any other band…"

"I'm not too sure how into the idea of a second guitarist Mass was," adds Ginny, on why Mass left so soon after Scoot joined. "We had tried it before and it didn't work out, but I was happy at the time to go along with it as I felt it might relieve some of the tension within the band. I can't really remember much about those practices, but things just seemed to fade away and we didn't do anything as a band for a while. Me and Tony were even thinking about doing another band, but we never did and obviously we would see Ste around the pubs of Oldham and talk about getting moving with EOM again.

"Because Mass was based in Manchester, we didn't get to see him much, plus a lot of personal matters were going on for different members of the band and I don't think we talked enough to each other or understood the feelings others were going through, which may have led to some of our behaviour within the band. So, in a similar way to Foz, Mass was replaced; I don't think we really went about it the right way, looking back, but at the time it was the right thing to do.

"We did talk about changing the name of the band, but we had a tour with Wolfpack to do and a split LP planned with Misery and we couldn't really go out on tour with a different name playing EOM songs, so once we had done that and the split album, it just seemed right to keep the name…though these days we rarely play any of the old songs and it's kind of like there is two different EOMs: 'pre-Scoot' and 'post-Scoot'!"

Scoot made his recording debut in 1999, Extinction Of Mankind finally getting round to doing their split album with Misery, a collaboration the two bands had been talking up since their European tour together in 1996. Three cover versions that speak volumes about EOM's strongest influences (Antisect's 'Out From The Void (Part 2)', Discharge's 'Ain't No Feeble Bastard' and 'Sunshine Ward' by Amebix) were also recorded during the same session for the 'Ale To England' EP (the title a friendly pun on Doom's 'Hail To Sweden' EP), although the fruits of these labours were frustratingly slow to emerge on vinyl. The 'Apocalyptic Crust' split LP did not appear until 2001 (initially on Crimes Against Humanity in the US, but then repressed by Sweden's Elderberry Records) and the EP not until 2002 (through Czech label Malarie).

Although the album wasn't out in time for it, EOM headed out to tour the US west coast with Misery in April 2000, returning to hit the east coast and Canada late the following year, when they actually *had* a new record to sell. No-one in the band is especially complimentary of their side of the 'Apocalyptic Crust' split, though, blaming the poor sound on bad mastering at the US pressing plant, but it remains a perfectly serviceable entry to the crust-punk canon, although Scoot remembers the dates undertaken in support of it with much more enthusiasm:

"They were just a great laugh from start to finish; remember, this was mine and Ginny's and Tony's first tour with Misery and we all got along great. We played some great places in Minneapolis, LA, Portland… We did Gilman St in Berkeley and Seattle with Christdriver, one of the heaviest bands I've ever heard, then we did Denver and it was a *long* 18-hour drive back to Minneapolis from there. The back wheel and axle fell off the van – belonging to Jon Misery – on the LA freeway and swerving about in four lanes of traffic was very scary, but luckily no-one was hurt. We did do thousands of dollars' worth of damage to the van, though, which meant we didn't make a penny back from the tour, but there was no way we were going to leave Jon Misery with the debt…"

And that kind of sincerity in the face of adversity is what has ensured EOM's good standing in the punk community to this day. Moving outside the timescale of this particular book, they have not only released their best albums – 2004's 'The Nightmare Seconds…' and 2007's 'Northern Scum' (both released on CD on the band's own label Xtinction and on vinyl by Profane Existence) – but have continued touring around the world on their own terms.

"Mostly it's been pretty good," reckons Ginny, before pondering some of the highs and lows and summarising post-millennium EOM very succinctly: "We bought a van, did a tour round Europe, did a load of gigs, did a few albums, drank a lot of beer, did a lot of festivals, drank a lot more beer, had a little lie down, someone crashed into the van, we got an insurance payout…spent it on beer.

"We went to the Ukraine for this one festival, but the gig the night before was in a little bar and the kids were going mental, really enjoying themselves, it was brilliant. I enjoy those gigs the most: somewhere small, dark and sweaty where people really go for it, like the 007 in Prague or the 1 In 12 in Bradford…basically anywhere the crowd is up for it and not just stood there staring at you. I like the big stages too, but you just don't feel a part of it in the same way.

"The worst place we played by far was some shitty squat in Poland, with a bucketful of shit for a toilet…if you're gonna be anti-system then you'd better learn some skills like basic plumbing! If you've got time to build a bar and play table football and spray graffiti, then at least use some of it to have a level of basic necessities like heat and water – beer and records are *not* basic necessities!"

Strange to hear those words coming from the mouth of an Extinction Of Mankind member, but they did; even stranger given Ginny's closing comment on how he would like the band to be remembered.

"It's not really for us to say how we will be remembered, is it? But 'that band that won the lottery and bought a brewery' would be good, eh? Just as a good down-to-earth set of lads doing their bit, I suppose, not following any trends, just putting out good heavy music with a message; not preaching, just saying honestly how we see things…

"What sets us apart from our peers? I don't know! We're better than some at some stuff and worse than some at other stuff; we just are who we are, we do what we do and we like it that way. If other people like it, great; if they don't like it, so what?"

"Tough question really," adds Scoot. "I personally still hold my anarcho beliefs and values to this very day and I will continue to do everything I can to be a part of the DIY community, no matter how cliquey, bitchy, posey and overly PC certain types can be. We've stood the test of time and fought through a lot of shit that was thrown at us; we are far from perfect – but we don't try to be either. When all's said and done, we love EOM, even though we all get jaded at times, worn out and fed up, moaning about being on tour or whatever… But EOM are still a good laugh – sometimes nihilistic, it's true, yet mostly caring in our own varying ways.

"Ste still loves Antisect; I missed them 'cos I was too young and by the time I first heard of them they were splitting up and boy, does he ever like to keep letting me know that? [Since this interview, of course, Antisect have reformed and Scoot has now seen them play live.] But we just wanted to carry on what they did, simple as that; we wanted to be a part of it and hopefully continue to be. At the end of the day, all I know is that Ste and Ginny are two of the funniest (and Ste can sometimes be the most difficult) people to be in a band with and not having them around would make my life very dull…

"What's next for EOM? Ste's hip replacement, a neck brace for me and Ginny needs his blood pressure checking! We'll hopefully squeeze a few more gigs in around the world, as well as another recording or two… A few more pints wouldn't go amiss either, but who knows? Nothing lasts forever!"

SELECT DISCOGRAPHY:

7-inch:
'Split' (Elderberry, 1993) – *split with Warcollapse*
'Split' (Ecocentric, 1994) – *split with Doom*
'Weakness' (Skuld, 1994)
'Scars Of Mankind Still Weep' (Skuld/Profane Existence, 1998)
'Ale To England' (Malarie, 2002)
'Storm Of Resentment' (Xtinction, 2012)

LPs:
'Baptised In Shit' (Skuld, 1995)
'Apocalyptic Crust' (Crimes Against Humanity, 2001) – *split with Misery*
'The Nightmare Seconds…' (Xtinction/Profane Existence, 2004)
'Northern Scum' (Xtinction/Profane Existence, 2007)
'Split' (Agipunk, 2010) – *split with Phobia*

AT A GLANCE:
In 2008, 'Ale To England' was reissued on CD, complete with a bonus live set, by Mosh Pit Tragedy.

CRESS

Their choice of name may have been misleading, because many people were no doubt expecting some sort of Crass tribute band, but Lowton (Lancashire)'s **Cress** confounded expectations by using a drum machine, keyboards and samples. There *was* a Crass connection there, though, but it ran a lot deeper than just their name, stemming back to Dave, Joe and Pete's first band the Deformed.

"The Deformed were a punk band that were a bit gothy without being goths," explains guitarist/vocalist Pete. "We had a song on one of Crass's 'Bullshit Detector' compilations and we were lucky enough to see Crass live many times and had a lot of conversations and communications with them. They were one of the few bands to make me realise that words are not just something to sing along to – they can be life-changing as well. Same with Subhumans and Flux and Amebix and Hawkwind."

After the Deformed, Pete started the Atomic Space Cakes, a Hawkwind-style free festival rock (and reggae) band, but it wasn't long before he was back writing and recording punk music with Dave and Joe, on bass and vocals respectively, under the banner of Cress. Much of the Atomic Space Cake ethos came with him.

"There was also Stig on keyboards and vocals, Nev on guitar, Hal 2000 – the drum machine! – and Chris doing samples and lighting. We used a huge amount of strobes and psychedelic hippy lights…how un-punk was that? Plus we had two singers with extremely long dreads and one with a beard, which was an endless source of amusement… 'You look like Jesus!' etc. And the Euro punks *hated* it… 'Don't be weird, shave that beard!' Some of the early gig posters were a little worrying, though: stencil-style lettering on old Crass posters and stuff… the last thing we wanted was to be a Crass covers band."

"The early gigs were something to be seen," agrees Dave, "with all the strobes and home-made lights and slides left over from Pete's ASC days; it was like a fucking Hawkwind gig, Chris used to go into total overdrive! We'd cover the venues in smoke and you'd only be able to see us in silhouette, but people loved it and the smoke lowered their inhibitions to dance 'cos no-one could see them; when the smoke finally cleared everyone was up anyway, so no-one cared."

"The first gig was at the Mill, on the Pier in Wigan," continues Pete. "There were about 10 or 12 bands on, all good and local… A few weeks later we supported RDF at the same place, but I think I would say that our first 'proper' gig (top of the bill, so to speak) was at the 1 In 12, with Witchknot. Most people were expecting 'Banned From The Roxy', but they got what would later become our 'Monuments' LP. I always like to see the reaction when the drum machine starts the first song…it's usually one of bewilderment! It's funny and sometimes a little sad, but once the rest of the band start to play the attitude usually changes for the better. Crass cast a big shadow over most early gigs we did and we added to the misconception ourselves by playing 'Big Hands' as our last song…"

Recorded at Pete's house through various formats from cassette to computer, the first Cress demo made its way via the inexorable channels of the underground into the hands of Sned from Flat Earth and Jacko from Worried Sheep Records up in Leven. The latter organised a well-received four-day Scottish tour with Bloodshot and Atkifist and when he said he would finance the recording of a Cress LP and Sned expressed an interest in putting it out, the band hot-footed it into Bradford's In A City Studio with Carl Stipetic and Bri Doom.

"It was winter and there was snow on the ground and it was fucking freezing in that studio," laughs Pete. "We stayed in Bradford with Bri and Wayne from Doom, so there was lots of laughing and drinking and the session went smoothly enough because we were basically recording our live set; all the songs were written well in advance of recording.

"I have lots of zine cuttings about 'Monuments' and it's pretty fair to say that it was well liked. There was a review in *Profane Existence* that said the LP was constantly on the record player in their office, which made me smile. The only bad comments were about the picture of Stonehenge on the front cover, leading people to believe we were hippies, but I never agreed with that label; the picture related to the song 'Monuments' itself, which was about me getting thrown out of Stonehenge by English Heritage for stepping over the barrier!"

Despite *some* obvious Crass references, namely the perfect simplicity of the song structures, the driving rhythms and the chugging guitar riffs, 'Monuments' is lent extra depth by several quieter, more atmospheric passages and even some – dare I say it? – *tunes*. And if it had been released in the Eighties, it would doubtless still be heralded an anarcho-punk classic today.

"When we put out 'Monuments', we started to get a bit more respect," says Dave, proudly. "Up until then we were always dismissed as 'Crass clones', but once they heard the album and read the lyrics it opened people's eyes a bit. With the drum machine and samples and Nev's hypnotic guitar segments, it proved you didn't have to be total hardcore D-beat all the time.

"And I think it's stood the test of time as well, to be honest; loads of the songs are still relevant in today's climate and many people at gigs have told us how much it changed them, for the better, something of which I'm very, very proud."

The band spent the next year playing most of the UK's punk picnics ("Which were chaotic but creative," smiles Pete) and undertaking two extensive European tours. Brian from Doom drove them on the second continental trip, cementing the close friendship started when he recorded the 'Monuments' LP and a split 10-inch with Doom seemed the next logical step. It was another strong release, but the band sacrificed the lovely thick sound of the album for a rougher distorted edge, which was way more punk – but way less enjoyable!

Explains Pete: "I suppose the idea for the Doom split was Sned's, but the original thinking around the split was that it should be recorded by the bands themselves, as cheaply as possible, totally DIY. We recorded our songs at Rehab again [Pete's house!], as lo-fi as we could, to try to capture the rawness of our live set… I think we captured the energy, but not the power."

Jacko from Worried Sheep then talked the band back into In A City ("This time with the heating on," laughs Pete), with Carl and Bri Doom again, to record the bruising 'From Violence To Consumerism' 7-inch. With its relentless stomping beats reminiscent of Exit-stance and a heavy, throbbing production, it's probably the band's most rounded release.

"Jacko used to do a stall at some of our gigs," recalls Pete, "selling our T-shirts and tapes and stuff…we never used to sell a lot, mind you, we gave most of it away. The latter gigs up in Scotland were always good fun; the people up there know how to have a party and myself, Dave and Chris have been known to have the occasional drink! We used to spend so much time up in Scotland, some record reviewers actually thought we lived up there…"

Cress continued touring – and drinking – hard. 'From Violence To Consumerism' would prove to be their last release for over 10 years, with the band going on a lengthy hiatus while the various members took a break from each other – and the punk scene.

"All that touring blurs into one big memory mess," admits Pete. "But during all the down-time between gigs, there were lots of differences of opinion and friendships were tested. In the end I just wanted a break from Cress; I felt like I was preaching to the converted, just going through the motions. There were also a lot of people asking for too much of my time; I wanted to travel, see the world at my own pace and get a job I enjoyed, so I went back to college to do graphic design, travelled round the world with my grant money and long-time girlfriend Karen and had a lot of fun seeing some of the monuments we put on our album cover…"

Musically Pete, Stig and Chris also kept busy playing ambient reggae dub as Lunar Musik (issuing the 'Mixes For Eclipses' double-LP through Skuld), but when their good friend Wayne Southworth from Doom sadly died in March 2005, Cress agreed to reform that July to play the Sozzfest at the 1 In 12 Club ('Soz' being Wayne's preferred abbreviation for 'Sorry'!) Playing alongside the likes of Doom, Boxed In, Gurkha and Extinction Of Mankind, it was a fittingly rowdy celebration of Wayne's life and memory. After another memorial show for another deceased friend, Dek Hill, all personal differences were well and truly set to one side and the band lurched back to life again.

Cress, Dave, Ste and Joe

Cress vocalist Joe.

"The kids are younger, of course, but still full of energy," says Pete, on how they find the scene today. "But I hope they are listening to what we are saying and applying some of it to their everyday lives. There are some very positive people around, like Rob from Burnt Cross, who has really motivated us with his great attitude. We recently did a split single with them, but we don't really have an agenda these days; we are more choosy with our time and other commitments now."

"We've done a few gigs in recent years and been really surprised at how great the reaction was for us," adds Dave, in closing. "It was unexpected, it took us by total surprise. The Punk Illegal festival in Sweden, or the gigs we did in Germany with Extinction Of Mankind, were probably the best for me. We've played with a lot of good bands and never been afraid to play before or after them; it's all about believing in yourself, that's what counts.

"Cress remembered? I hope so! The drum machine and samples always caused quite a stir, just for not being punk in the middle of the punk scene. And it's always good to challenge people's ideas of what they believe punk to be about!"

SELECT DISCOGRAPHY:

7-inch:
'From Violence To Consumerism' (Worried Sheep, 1998)
'Peace Through Superior Fire Power' (Tadpole/Active Rebellion/Loud Punk, 2010) — *split with Burnt Cross*

10-inch:
'Split' (Flat Earth, 1998) — *split with Doom*

LP:
'Monuments' (Flat Earth, 1997)

AT A GLANCE:
The 'Propaganda And Lies' CD on Flat Earth compiles the LP, 7-inch and split 10-inch. There's also a Cress covers album entitled 'Same Shit, Different Arse' (featuring the likes of Wat Tyler, Filthpact and Burnt Cross) that's well worth a listen and plenty of free downloads available from the band's MySpace page: www.myspace.com/cressuk

English Bands!

Manfat
Hard To Swallow
Zum Eisenbahner

Pfarrstr. (S-Bhf. Ostkreuz)

Sonntag 23 Juni

22.00

CHAPTER THREE:
EAST MIDLANDS

HARD TO SWALLOW

Nottingham's **Hard To Swallow** delivered a well-placed boot to the nuts of the UKHC scene at a time when it was at its most stale and complacent and helped change the direction of that scene too, with members of the band going on to form such seminal acts as Iron Monkey, John Holmes, Narcosis and Dead Inside.

"[Andrew] Goy and I had been talking about wanting to do a band for ages," begins vocalist 'Bloody' Kev, "but as we were both useless and talentless, we realised we would have to do the ENT thing and both sing. Goy had just recently got the 'Colossus' LP by Citizens Arrest and it was blowing us away daily; then one evening we went to see our mates' band Substandard playing at the Narrow Boat supporting NOFX… In the middle of the bill that night were a band called Rorschach – and after seeing those guys live we knew what direction we were heading…!"

So, sometime during 1994, the pair recruited drummer Kev Frost, formerly of the Varukers and Cerebral Fix, bassist Paul Boo, from Bloody Lovely and guitarists Sean Duggan, formerly of Killing Floor and Meatfly and Marcus, the latter soon replaced by Stu Toolin from Pitch Shifter. Although the band were rehearsing regularly at the Narrow Boat, the line-up remained unsettled, with Boo being replaced on bass by Alastair 'Gords' Gordon and Kev behind the kit by Scunthorpe drummer Justin Greaves from Mental Seizure and Bradworthy. It was this line-up that played the band's first gig in Corby during May 1995 and within a gig or two, Jim Rushby had also joined on second guitar.

"I'd only just met Gords, who shared a similar – and sick – sense of humour with me," reveals Bloody Kev. "He was also a fuckin' awesome bass player; he'd helped out towards the end of Bloody Lovely and our final gigs. And I'd played in a band with Sean as well; we had toured Europe together, getting on really well and getting into all sorts of shit…

"Anyway, Kev Frost had a lot of touring commitments with Varukers, so we asked a neighbour of mine to stand in. That was Justin Greaves, who was an absolute powerhouse of a drummer and totally revolutionised the band's sound. And Jim was a friend of Justin's who had recently moved to Nottingham; he came in after about the third show, to help fill out the sound during Sean's wild wah-wah solos! The lyrics were just shit about our lives: getting chucked, getting pissed…and a few stolen UFO lyrics too!"

"I remember being asked a few times by Kev and Goy if I wanted to be in the band," says

Hard To Swallow, Amsterdam 1999, pic by Bob Vimto

Hard To Swallow, Jim Rushby, 1 in 12 1996, by Steve Hyland

Hard To Swallow, Birmingham 1995, by Ralph Barklam

Hard To Swallow, Kev, Justin and Peet,
Bielefeld 1999

Gords. "At first I was really not sure; I'd not had the best experience in the Killing Floor, was a bit jaded about playing and was really a bit nonplussed about being involved in the scene again. Still, one night I thought, 'Fuck it!' and said yes; we had a rehearsal later in the week in the Narrow Boat (with pint glasses of stale piss outside one of the other practice-room doors; this place had class!) I remember being totally and instantly blown away with the power we had in the room; we'd all been playing a few years (most of us were in our mid-twenties and with a good few bands/gigs behind us) and the energy in the room was very apparent. Justin was a very hard-hitting, precise and brutal drummer…the band had mojo!

"Songs came together real fast and after a couple of rehearsals we were soon gigging. As Bloody Kev said, a lot of us had been dumped or ended relationships around that time and the band – with this crazy live energy – was the perfect place to let those types of feelings out. We were also at the tail end of the rave thing and all that 'Brit Pap' was beginning; lots of people that were once in the rave/free party scene were coming out of their ecstasy comas and the band certainly tapped into that feeling, against the false friendship bullshit of a lot of ravers…"

"The early stuff we were doing was a lot more straight-up hardcore punky stuff," reckons Goy, "But I got the Citizen's Arrest LP, saw Rorschach at the NOFX gig and also loved a French band called Fingerprint, which basically changed our vocal style. However, with Kev being in the Varukers, we had our first gig booked in Corby and he was on tour. Justin stepped in and we changed overnight, with blast beats and more dynamic structures to our songs. We played fast, but with time changes, so it was not all the same like a lot of fast bands… We were also all massive Sabbath fans and this was how I always saw a lot of our song structures – just quicker. But really the first real secure line-up was when Jim Rushby joined, by about our third gig and he again brought more depth and influence to our sound."

"I moved to Nottingham from Bradford to start Iron Monkey with Justin, who I'd been in a band in Leeds with, several years before that, called Lifeclass," confirms Jim. "I'd also been in Ironside and Wartorn while I was based in Bradford. Anyway, Gords approached me at the first HTS gig and asked if I wanted to fill the sound out; I remember being really excited at seeing the band because I was impressed by their energy, so I agreed to join. As well as Rorschach and Citizen's Arrest and Infest, I was also influenced by the early Nineties West Coast [US] power-violence scene, which had an effect on the songwriting and helped to crystallise the various competing musical directions the band had in it at that time."

Hard To Swallow tracked two demos with Andy Sneap at Backstage Studios during 1995, the second of which became their side of a split 7-inch released by Liverpool label Days Of Fury, shared with Underclass. The band began gigging in earnest, stunning audiences with their ferocious and utterly uncompromising sonic attack, striking a particular chord at the 120 Rats squat in Leeds and the 1 In 12 Club, Bradford.

"The 1 In 12 was right up there with the Narrow Boat for us in the early days," reckons Bloody Kev. "It was like a second home; I used to travel to all the festivals there and always received a warm and friendly welcome…it was the heart of the DIY scene at the time. Plus they used to serve Ayingerbrau D Pils, which helped to fuel our general cuntish behaviour! I saw so many awesome bands there; I have fond memories of Kito, Suffer, Stalingrad, Voorhees, Bob Tilton. The list is endless – and that's just the UK bands."

"The club was a *massive* part of the scene for us," agrees Goy. "Kev and I had been going to the weekenders there a lot before we even started HTS. We made a lot of good friends over the years and it really was a great showcase of all the good and diverse bands at the time. Playing our first festival there on a Sunday was a real big thing for me. Whenever we were asked up, it was never a case of, 'Let's not do this gig because…'; it was such a great chance to hang out and drink the Pils and see the array of great friends' bands. The line-ups at the time were amazing for me, really diverse stuff like Baby Harp Seal, Polaris, Tribute, Underclass, Headache, Curll and so many more."

"I also remember the first few Nottingham shows being great," adds Gords. "A lot of the audience didn't get the shouting/screaming singing and the sheer bloody-minded volume/ style of the band, which was a real buzz, just upsetting people who had this fixed idea of how and what a generic punk band should sound like. Breaking barriers down upset people and that was fine with us.

"Once Goy got told off at the Bull And Gate in London during a soundcheck by the landlord for screaming into the mic! Said landlord stormed into the room and said summat like, 'Pack that up, you feckin' idiot, you'll break the mic!' We all fell about laughing and the landlord soon realised he'd made a tit out of himself. I also remember a landlord at an all-dayer in Birmingham having a similar problem with us; Stu Toolin also broke the PA that night, which was a regular occurrence in those early days. That was also a good show because it was where we first met Manfat and Medulla Nocte. Ivor the Diver [from Visions Of Change] did some great stage-diving that night too; energy was in the room and people really went off to us!

"The band also played a few parties at Bloody Kev's block of flats. This was a set of run-down flats in one of the richest parts of Nottingham, known as The Park. The bohemians and punks were all clustered together on the corner of this well-heeled estate, surrounded by millionaires and well-to do types; the contrast and tension was stark. The size of the rooms made it a perfect venue to have bands playing. I remember playing there (in a very drunk state) two or three times, one show even beginning with me getting a black eye from some trouble-causing macho twat; Goy and Kev were held on their backs above the crowd during the set with the living-room lampshade swinging between them and all sorts of madness happening down the front. The drumkit would often get pushed over at those early shows and those parties were certainly the fun aspect of early HTS and all elements of the Nottingham underground scene descended on the place for them…"

1996 was another busy year gigging for the band; they also recorded a split 7-inch with Manfat that was released by Flat Earth/Enslaved and promoted by a tour of Europe undertaken by both bands that June.

"That first Euro tour was insane," laughs Bloody Kev. "Fallen-through gigs, begging for food, being marched across Berlin by armed police, sofas thrown through windows, a drunken fist-fight between me and Goy in Amsterdam that ended with his shoe in the canal and my trousers and pants around my ankles in front of a load of French tourists… Shoplifting, fights over chocolate, broken bottles, upsetting the band Carol's neighbours, Goy hospitalised in Switzerland with a torn ear, trashing the wrong squat only to find out it was the next day's venue, several members leaving the band only to return later… Oh yeah and I shat myself on stage in Bremen."

"We even stayed at a squatted World War II SS training camp in Potsdam," says Jim, incredulously. "We had to steal potatoes from the kitchen because we hadn't eaten for 24 hours and then we found out later that they were intended for us anyway! I saw grown men cry on that tour, it was fucking gnarly; three weeks of cabin fever, a complete lack of sleep and good hygiene, hunger, heavy drinking and hardcore punk can take its toll on a young man's mind! Every single day was totally ridiculous from start to finish…"

"I remember members of the band sniffing petrol out of sheer boredom when the van was broken down by the side of the road in East Germany," laughs Gords. "Later on, Goy drank so much he fell into the drumkit and bust his ear in Bremgarten; Steve Kerper (RIP) [from Confrontation and Infest], who was on the road with Manfat, took over vocals for the last few shows of the tour.

"On the way home – tour abandoned on account of Goy's ear injury – the van's gear-box died; I remember me and Wes driving overnight, on the long journey home, with no main-beam and only sidelights in the steep snow-covered roads of the Swiss Alps with only two gears. We could only see a few feet in front of the van, with what seemed like sheer drops either side of the road and every other fucker was snoring in the back. That was pure skin-of-the-teeth danger-driving; Justin slept right through it, next to me in the front, as well!

"The van barely got on and off the ferry, as the gearbox had totally given up the ghost, but we eventually got home, courtesy of the AA for the last drive up the UK. The high spirits continued when we were home, though, and we went out for a celebratory curry with the band, John Paul Morrow and various others. There was a fight with four big towny blokes, where I got a kicking; Morrow put a chair over one of their heads and the bloke didn't even flinch. I had to go to hospital and have my head X-rayed; it was a bloody chaotic end to a mad tour…"

During 1997, while writing material for their debut LP – 'Protected By The Ejaculation Of Serpents', released on CD only at first by Household Name in 1998 – Hard To Swallow also toured the UK with two of the most awesome hardcore thrash bands to ever walk the planet, Los Crudos and Drop Dead. Justin missed the Drop Dead dates and Michael Gilham from Voorhees stood in for him on the drums. 1997 also saw members starting or joining other bands, Jim and Justin in Iron Monkey, Gords in John Holmes (with Bri and Dale from Manfat and Sned from Suffer) and Bloody Kev in Helvis and 666 Dead (with Steve and Kalv from Heresy and Meatfly).

By the time HTS recorded the flawed but still ridiculously brutal 'Protected…' album at Birdsong Studios, Scunthorpe, Goy had left and guest vocals came courtesy of Johnny Morrow, although Goy's 'proper' replacement after the album was recorded was Peet from Underclass.

"I had moved to London and already left the band twice before the album, so when it came to recording I was not really 100% with the whole thing," explains Goy. "I remember the band having to explain this to me and at the time I was hurt, but in hindsight it was the correct decision – my heart was really not in it. I liked some of the newer songs, but I think we lost our distinct sound and we were too influenced by other stuff we were listening to. However, that is all water under the bridge now and I am glad to still have these people as close friends."

"Personally I love the songs on the LP, but the recording never did them any justice," offers Bloody Kev. "By the way, the title is from my love for the movie *The Wicker Man*, the [1973] original, not the fuckin' shite Nicolas Cage version. We first used a sample from it on the second 7-inch. There's a scene in it where Sgt Howie reads an inscription on a gravestone out, 'Here lieth Beech Buchannan, protected by the ejaculation of serpents…'"

"When we made that record, we did it in the wrong studio at the wrong time," admits Jim. "There were a few creases that needed ironing out with regards to how tight we were at the time and we really should have toured that material before recording it. The vinyl version (released a year later) has a better sound than the CD and is a lot thicker and warmer as it was remastered by Gords at Porky's cutting plant in London. I listened to that recently and it sounds pretty good, but at the time I don't think any of us liked the CD. That record had lots of great riffs, but none of it really gelled as songs in comparison to the Sneap sessions. For me, my favourite recording was always the split we did with Canvas…"

That split CD came out on Contrition in 1999 and was sadly the band's final release, although at least they bowed out how they deserved, spitting and screaming and raging against the world. Contrition also released a live 10-inch by the band earlier that same year, imaginatively entitled 'Hard To Swallow Live In Leeds'.

"I remember that gig [February 1998] as being just average and the recording was okay at best," says Gords, of the live 10-inch. "Karl from Contrition [and Canvas] kindly offered to put it out on the strength of a tape version of the MiniDisc recording he heard some weeks later. We went into Thumb Studios to mix it and add fucked-up 'Wicker Man' samples and daft folk instruments as a 'bonus track'.

"Basically the whole thing was a bit of a joke at the expense of completist record collectors: 'Porky-prime cut mastering', a limited hand-made homage to the Who/Heresy 'Live At Leeds' version 12-inch card-sleeve, an AC/DC rip-off 10-inch colour inner sleeve and special inserts, all pressed on a range of coloured vinyl with hand-numbered sleeves. Fuck, it even has closed-groove laughter on side one to make the point: you've been had! As a band we had a right laugh doing it and the artwork was done in a single evening by me and Bloody Kev, but whether it captures the live sound of HTS is totally questionable. It *is* good as a comparison to the clear and direct Andy Sneap production on the early recordings, though…

"The European tour in August of 1999 for the 'Protected…' vinyl LP was great," he adds, of some of the more memorable HTS shows. "They largely went off smoothly and we got to play with some great bands this time around. We'd also gelled as a live force once again; after the wilderness of Kev on single vocal duties, Peet brought new energy to the band. We meant business on that tour; we had a lot of merch and records to sell, a set of well-organised shows and places to stay. We also, for the most part anyway, got paid enough money to get around the tour without too much trouble.

"There were certainly not *as many* low points as previously… One show in the south of Germany was not particularly well attended and playing to two people in Roswein was piss-poor. Another low point was in Prague, where we ended up on a ska bill, replete with a load of 'nutty skins' and ska punks as our audience; such a line-up was particularly weird and we went down like a shit in a bathtub. The poker-face audience was priceless. Luckily we got saved at that show when we broke a bass-drum skin early in the set and got the fuck out of there sharpish! The shows at the Leipzig Zoro and another show with Disfear and Wolfpack at the 007 in Prague were totally fucking buzzing and truly great gigs.

"The Holland leg with Insult was a total blast too, especially where we were paid at one show in dodgy stolen ink-stained banknotes – we couldn't spend 'em for ages! Then Germany, taking in one show with Phobia, was also amazing; great times and great shows. Other low points were getting bitten to fuck by some bed-lice in Brussels when sharing the bill with Melt Banana, who in turn got pelted with stale bread rolls while loading the van the next morning…they took it all in good humour and were great people.

"The definitive low point of that tour was counting the band money wrong at the end, so we thought the band was up when it was, in fact, only breaking even! I then gave the band some end-of-tour money in what I thought were Dutch guilders but were in fact Belgian francs and worth a lot less than the Dutch cash. As a result, band members were trying to buy stuff in Maastricht with incorrect currency and I was not a popular guy that day! Still, you live and learn."

By the end of 1999, though, Hard To Swallow ground to a halt under the weight of various personal and musical differences and they played their last ever show, as irreverent as ever – and with all three vocalists present – at the 1 In 12 that November.

"There were always unspoken tensions in the band, but its demise was down to a number of factors, some of which we can talk about here and others are…well, just bloody private," reckons Gords. He continued with John Holmes after HTS and nowadays plays with the mighty Endless Grinning Skulls, who recently issued a self-titled LP on Viral Age Records. "Kev had moved to London, myself and Justin were both new fathers and there were a number of side projects going on, not least of all the Iron Monkey touring machine which occasionally kept us off the road. In many ways, the band just fizzled out after that last 1In 12 gig…by then, we were no longer a new force in the scene and it had become almost obligatory for most underground DIY bands to be extreme in both volume, singing and approach.

"My basic take is that we had run our course. Yes, it was a shame that we broke up when we did and we could probably have done much more, but the mojo had gone and people were not getting it and the underlying problems and tensions took their eventual toll. That said, the positive point is that we all went on to do other bands and have amazing experiences on the road and, like Kev said, I still have life-long, close friendships with some members of the band – they are like my brothers – and we also made some great friends on the international DIY punk scene that continue to support us to this day with our new bands."

"We just didn't give a shit what people thought we were like," summarises Bloody Kev, who continued with 666 Dead and later formed Dead Inside and Regimes (who have a self-released LP out on Keep It In The Family Records). "We just enjoyed playing and meeting and hanging with people…which unfortunately meant there were a lot of missed opportunities too. But I loved the Nineties scene for its diversity and there was a real feeling of belonging to some kinda family."

Justin went on to drum in Varukers, Electric Wizard and Crippled Black Phoenix, while Sean also did time with Varukers, My War and most recently Certified.

"All I want to be remembered for is being a credible and good band of that era – or *any* era of the UK hardcore punk scene," offers Goy. "If we can be looked back on by some people as being as good as the bands I look back fondly on myself, then that is job done for me – why ask for more? I am not sure if we really *stood out* from our peers, though, as the Nineties scene was so diverse and the standards were very high in most of the bands, but it all depended on your taste, I suppose. It was a vibrant time for me and there were so many good bands that all added to the diversity of sounds at shows. It was all built on good DIY ethics and solid friendships, regardless of what your band sounded like. All in all, it was a lot of fun."

"We were playing something quite different to what other bands in the UK were doing at the time," concludes Jim, who went on to form first Armour Of God with Sean and Justin (plus Marvin from Varukers and John Morrow from Iron Monkey) and then Geriatric Unit with Gords, plus Kalv and Steve from Heresy. "And we turned up the fury and the chaos by more than a few degrees. The hardcore scene in the Nineties was a strange place, mind you; it was weird, because collectively the scene seemed to be quite small compared to what had been happening in the Eighties, but there was some really radical stuff going on too, a whole diversity of styles within the boundaries of what hardcore punk was. There was also a strong sense of unity. Having said that, there were a few individuals who wanted a monopoly on the scene and we certainly had our fair share of haters…"

SELECT DISCOGRAPHY:

7-inch:
'Split' (Days Of Fury Records, 1995) – *split with Underclass*
'Split' (Flat Earth/Enslaved, 1996) – *split with Manfat*

10-inch:
'Hard To Swallow Live in Leeds' (Contrition, 1999)

LP:
'Protected By The Ejaculation Of Serpents' (Household Name, 1998)

CD:
'Split' (Contrition, 1999) – *split with Canvas*

AT A GLANCE:
There was a HTS discography CD released by US label Armageddon in 2004.

BOB TILTON

At the opposite end of the sonic spectrum, **Bob Tilton** were quite possibly the most organic and unpretentious 'emo' band to ever come out of the UK. They formed in Arnold, a quiet suburb of Nottingham, during early 1993, when vocalist Simon Fern and drummer Allan Gainer from Downfall met guitarist Neil Johnson and bassist Mark Simms. When Downfall split after one demo and 7-inch because of – wait for it! – musical differences, Bob Tilton, named after the notorious American TV evangelist, was born.

"The TV evangelist thing was stumbled over, to be honest," admits Simon. "It was never given much serious thought, fell into our laps and no-one bothered to cast it off. We had our first show booked in Nottingham supporting Christ On A Crutch and Slum Gang [March '93] and we hadn't decided on a permanent name for the band. Neil and myself were booking the show and decided to cast our own band as one of the supports; the name we had at the time was Static although, personally speaking, I wasn't crazy about it.

"The flyer I constructed showed a picture of Robert Tilton, the evangelist. I was writing stuff at the time on organised religion and religion as business, but also loved religious imagery. I saw Robert Tilton on TV in New Jersey while at a friend's house and was blown away; although horribly disturbing in its execution, disgustingly manipulative and shameful, his performance was so intense and almost comic (with speaking in tongues being a highlight) that it stayed with me. I actually admired the power of performance, like a great actor… but acting was, of course, all it was.

"Anyway, I put him on the flyer, tongue firmly in cheek, with the line 'Bob Tilton presents…' and our band listed as Static. Flyers were initially distributed with this as our band name and it wasn't until shortly before the show that someone suggested we actually use 'Bob Tilton', as it was written on the flyer, as the band name instead. No-one was really passionate one way or another as I recall, but no-one had any better suggestions so the flyers were changed and that was that."

With Mark bringing some indie-rock influences and both Simon and Allan worshipping Born Against and Nation Of Ulysses, not to mention Heroin and Moss Icon, early Bob Tilton was far removed from the more fragile sounds the band evolved towards and nothing really like Slant or Fugazi, the two bands to which BT are most often likened.

"At the band's birth, that wave of US hardcore certainly did make an impression and influenced the shape the band was to take, musically and lyrically," agrees Simon. "Although the influence of Born Against on [the second Bob Tilton album] 'Leading Hotels…' is admittedly far less apparent! Yeah, Fugazi was a band that we were often compared with, but they were never an influence, certainly not as far as I'm concerned. Maybe the other boys brought a little of that in under the radar, but I never even considered that there were any similarities with Fugazi."

After their debut at the Narrow boat, Bob Tilton played another dozen shows in 1993 in places such as Birmingham, Leicester and London, but most significantly one at the Bradford 1 In 12 Club, where their explosive set was thoroughly enjoyed by Ian from Subjugation. This paved the way for the band's first EP, the urgent 'Wake Me When It's Springtime Again', which they actually recorded with massively acclaimed metal producer Andy Sneap on 2 January 1994.

"I don't actually know how the hell that happened," laughs Simon. "I think Neil knew [Andy Sneap's old band] Sabbath's bass player or something? Anyway, he squeezed us in between Poet and Megadeth…only kidding, but somehow I don't think Bob Tilton are on his CV.

"On listening back to that EP years later, I'm pleasantly surprised; I think it still stands up and I'm proud of it. It's the rawest and hardest release we put out, but has a little of the melodic edge that eventually got the upper hand in our sound. And, in retrospect, I wish we had clung to a little more of the anger that was definitely present in some of that early material. I really don't know how it was received at the time, but I think it went through two pressings? Not sure, but it was obviously only reviewed, if at all, in underground hardcore fanzines etc.

"We did actually do a lo-fi recording before the single, but it was only one song recorded onto four-track by Mark Simms at a practice space in Nottingham sometime in 1993. We never put it out as a demo, though; in fact it was a 'limited-edition demo' of one copy I suppose! I made just one copy, constructed a cassette-tape lyric inlay and posted it to Kent McClard at Ebullition, as I had a 7-inch distro and was dealing with him at the time and he said it sounded like Born Against! I never made another copy. The song was 'Well-Hung Christ' and saw the light of day as an extra hidden track on the 'Crescent' CD reissue on Southern. It's hidden *before* the album begins, though, so you would never know it's there! Selling-points were never our strong suit…"

The following year saw a second well-received 7-inch on Subjugation, 'Songs Of Penknife And Pocketwatch', which was promoted by tours of both the UK and Europe. "They were the only two tours we ever undertook as such," reveals Simon. "We had four shows booked with Fabric in March 1995: Liverpool, Glasgow, Kirkcaldy and Manchester. I remember the first two shows as being great and Kirkcaldy as an odd experience, playing with the Newtown Grunts who, I seem to recall, wore bin bags? Manchester never happened, though, because I took ill on arriving at the venue, was vomiting in the car park and had to travel home… real hardcore rock'n'rollers, eh? Three gigs in a row was my physical limit!

"Our second tour was more successful: six shows in Europe during June '95. We did one show in Munster, one in Belgium, with Reiziger and four in Sweden. It was a great experience, although much of this I can no longer remember. Rob from Kito kindly drove us and one prevailing memory I have is of being threatened by a gun-toting, bicycle-riding Swede. A couple of us had wandered off, probably in the early hours of the morning to find a payphone and there was not a soul on the streets. Suddenly this odd, intense-looking guy starts cruising back and forth past us on his bicycle, then rides up and holds aloft a handgun announcing, 'This is fucking power, Englishman!' "Thankfully he decided not to shoot us, nor did he even attempt to steal anything from us, if there actually was anything to steal in the first place. He was gone as quickly as he arrived…perhaps he just wanted to show his weapon to someone? Funny what you remember."

The debut Bob Tilton album, 'Crescent', was recorded in 1996, albeit in a rather unorthodox way and it remains a beautiful, poignant listen even today, at once both noisy and melodic (in a bleak bitter-sweet way), painfully fragile yet naively powerful.

"I wouldn't change anything about it," says Neil, justifiably proud of what is probably the band's definitive recording, "and reckon it'd be pointless to worry about it either. We recorded the instrumental tracks at my parents' house. We wanted to record in the garden, but opted for the lounge; that was all done on a four-track again. The rest was recorded in Lenton,

Bob Tilton, Simon Fern, by Vique Martin

Bob Tilton, Neil Johnson, by Vique

above a friend's flat. We saw that the place was unlocked and borrowed some really primitive recording stuff (eight-track cassette); Mark set it up so we had all the amps and stuff in separate rooms. We put mattresses up against the windows and were just about to go for a take.

"It was a pretty stupid set-up as the landlord worked across the road in a sweet shop and kept all his stuff in the basement (but that's another story); he also had a mosque behind the house. Anyway, just as we were about to record something, he came over from the shop thinking we were squatters. 'What are you doing?' he asked and we said that we were recording an album. He asked how long they took to make and had a look around; we said it would only take a week to record the album and he just said we could go ahead and do it. Amazing, really, as we didn't know the guy and had just set up without his permission. This worked well and gave us more ways of doing things and more time without worrying about the cost. Mark did a great job bearing in mind the stuff we were using too..."

"I haven't listened to this in so long that there is enough distance between us now to enable me to judge it fairly," adds Simon. "I absolutely love it! And it would be unfair of me to offer an opinion on anything I would change in retrospect; at most I would 'un-tame' the vocals a little on a couple of tracks and roar a bit more. But I'm splitting hairs; I am totally pleased with 'Crescent' and I think it pretty much accomplished what we set out to achieve and create from the beginning...for me, at least."

Following the underground success of 'Crescent', Chay Lawrence left the band and was replaced by Ralph Hamilton, although it would be three years before their next release, the much lighter sophomore album 'The Leading Hotels Of The World'.

"Losing Chay was tough," concedes Simon. "We were never the most prolific band, but we had our own momentum; once Chay left we lost that momentum, I think and we were floundering a little. Ralph was a friend who was studying in Nottingham; he used to play in Useful Idiot and was both a lovely guy and a great guitar player.

"We recorded 'The Leading Hotels Of The World' throughout 1998, in bits and pieces basically. Neil tells me it was two weeks recording time spread over one year – which is crazy! – and it was predominantly recorded in the cellar of Mark's house in Leeds where he was based and studying.

"The sound of the band obviously mellowed overall and, listening to it now, I wish I could re-record some of the vocal parts. By that point, though, the writing was becoming harder and didn't feel as natural as it had been. I don't think we ever set out to purposely change direction; it just travelled its own route, but the passage wasn't easy.

"The music [on the second album] is great and personally I am happy with my writing lyrically and wouldn't change a thing, but I was pushing for melody too hard. Some of the rhythms and two-guitar parts were just at odds with the vocal melodies I was trying to force and I wish I had sung it 'straighter' and approached the songs more like the older stuff. Some melodies work, some don't; a case in point is 'You Look Like Sal Mineo'...man, I'd love to re-do *that* one!"

Apart from an instrumental split with Belgians Reiziger on Genet Records, the album was the last thing Bob Tilton put their names to, as they broke up soon after its release. "I think everyone was listening to different music by the late Nineties," reckons Neil, "getting more into the idea of recording exactly how and when we wanted. Our tastes were changing too; there were lots of new and great-sounding bands around and all these things moved us along.

"We split up when Allan left to go and live in London; we were really spread out at that point and it felt like such a struggle. We did consider switching Mark to drums for a few days, but I think it was a good call. So, no regrets re: the band breaking up...but it would still be nice to see more of everyone, though!

"Our last gig *could* have been at the Brixton Academy with Fugazi and Jesus Lizard! But we thought, as it was such an amazing bill, that a band that were going to keep on playing should play instead, so our last gig was actually at the Bunkers Hill Inn in Nottingham; we supported Ligament and Lazarus Clamp opened up. I think it was spring 1999... Everyone came back to mine afterwards and there was a massive argument involving Marc from Plunger, who was living in Nottingham at the time!"

"I think we had somewhat been in decline since 1996," admits Simon. "We certainly played fewer and fewer shows and lost some of the fire in our collective bellies. In retrospect, I think we should've split earlier, but the birth of our second album was so difficult and prolonged that it probably would never have been completed had we split earlier than we did. Having said that, I miss it so very much..."

After Bob Tilton, Simon and Neil played together in Wolves! (Of Greece), who released a self-titled 10-inch in March 2004, before splitting that same year. Neil, who works for a refugee housing organisation and Mark who lives in London and does freelance sound and camera work, both still make music in low-key bands, while Chay now lives in Chicago with his family and Allan is a happily married graphic designer in London. Sadly, Ralph died in a car crash ("We all miss him," offers Neil).

"I would simply like what we did to be remembered," concludes Simon, who still lives in Nottingham with his young family, wistfully. "I touched on this so much in lyrics past, of ageing and memory and leaving your mark and of being someone, or part of something, that mattered. I think this is a common fear. Prints in the earth."

SELECT DISCOGRAPHY:

7-inch:
'Wake Me When It's Springtime Again' (Subjugation, 1994)
'Songs Of Penknife And Pocketwatch' (Subjugation, 1995)
'Split' (Genet, 1999) – *split with Reiziger*

LPs:
'Crescent' (Subjugation, 1996)
'The Leading Hotels Of The World' (Southern, 1999)

AT A GLANCE:
Best pick up the CD version of 'Crescent' on Southern.

SUBSTANDARD

Elsewhere in Nottingham, **Substandard** weren't the most prolific UK punk band of the Nineties, but they were certainly one of the more raging, a feisty fusion of Anti-System and Antisect – and who's going to argue with that? The band reared tentatively to life in 1989 and originally comprised vocalist Stuart Eden, guitarist Andy Hennessey, bassist Craig Howland and drummer Jason Wilson, although Stu only lasted a few rehearsals before he was replaced by Sonia Adams, who herself was soon replaced by Shaun 'Oxo' Oxborough and Debbie.

Debbie didn't last long either (probably because she was an ex-girlfriend of Craig's) and for the first gig, in the basement of a Nottingham squat, Pug (aka Joe Nott from Mortal Terror, Slumgang and the Losers) stood in on bass because Craig was away in Germany. Not the most stable of bands, then, but with much change comes much friction – and friction is always good in punk rock because the songs are usually even more pissed off than normal. And Substandard were *definitely* pissed off.

After adding Pat O'Keefe on second guitar for some extra gnarliness and recording a really intense five-song demo that included a decent cover of Sacrilege's 'Dig Your Own Grave' ("Shaun was so nervous, he hid in a cupboard and sang in the dark," laughs Andy), the band headed for Brixton for their first London gig. Which, predictably enough, was a disaster.

"That was fucking hilarious," recalls Andy. "[Andy's partner] Christine hired a van, paid for the fuel and got the beer in as normal. There was free homebrew for the bands, supplied by Ben [*Raising Hell* fanzine]; Pat was wankered and kept turning his pedal off instead of on, so went 'all Culture Shock' instead of full-on noise and Craig was speeding so thought he was doing fantastic while playing all the wrong songs – backwards!

"Jason was tripping, so had to convince himself his drums weren't spiders trying to scuttle away; I booted Shaun up the arse, he fell off stage and promptly fell asleep on the floor, so Dolby got up and shouted along even though he'd never heard us before. The sound bloke was also deaf in one ear, so turned me nearly all the way off and I was unfortunately sober through it all 'cos we'd hired a van. Christine and Pat then tried to jump out of the van the next day to run the London marathon!"

Following this fiasco, Craig was asked to move from bass to vocals ("He really had no idea how to play it, but Shaun could, so we suggested swapping...") but took great umbrage at this and promptly left the band; however Shaun *did* take up bass duties as planned and Jules (aka Julian Lowery) from Nation Of Bigots joined on vocals, relocating from London to Nottingham to do so.

"Nation Of Bigots was me and Tom Woolford who used to do Sick and Tired distro," he explains. "We had Dave Ferguson on bass for a bit and then he was replaced by Leigh 'Rocker' Wiles [who would later join Excrement Of War and Screamer] who I was in another band with called Fear Of Existence. We didn't play too many gigs and they were all in London...apart from one in Brum. I think the last one may have been playing a birthday party at some British Legion club...although we were obviously only told it was a 'working men's club' or something.

"We arrived after having a few cheekies [sneaky drinks] on the tube over, to be surrounded by brothers and friends of the girl whose birthday it was stressing that no trouble was to be

Substandard, Jules and Pat

Substandard live, Pat, Andy and Jules, 1994

Substandard, Jason in Germany, 1995

had. We proceeded to get hammered and make an absolute racket, with the drumkit doing about 60mph across the shiny floor. Just as an electric keyboard and the picture of the Queen on the wall were going for a burton [about to get trashed], it came to an end. We were asked to leave and the band called it a day.

"After the poll tax march, things were getting kinda hot in London with an over-the-top police presence at gigs and lots of other heavy-handed tactics. I also needed a bit more space to carry on doing more with my label, distribution and putting on gigs. I was thinking of moving up to Nottingham from London anyway and so was chit-chatting with the Substandard and Losers guys at the gig in Brixton and they helped us out with places to stay when we moved…"

"Another big thing happened then," laughs Andy. "Shaun bought a tuner! We'd never used one of them before and thought, 'Bloody hell, that was what it was meant to sound like…'"

A third demo was recorded in 1993 and the following year a split single with Leicester's Nerves released on Inflammable Material, the label ran by Jules and Mike Clarke from Decadent Few. Recorded at Pots And Pans in Bradford, it was a proper UK punk-rock single in every sense of the word – raw and fast and ever so angry – and went on to sell 3,000 copies.

"I haven't played it in a while, but yeah, I think it still stands up well today," says Jules. "The songs on there were very 'of the time'. 'Discount' was basically written when there appeared to be a growing trend of 'Dis-core' bands; some were very good, of course, but some appeared to be coming from a more metal world and looked as if they were just going through the fucking motions, especially with the lyrics…so we wrote a song about getting cheap food from Aldi, as no-one had any money! Then the lyrics to 'Rostock' were mostly written by Bjorn from the Losers and Recharge, about what he was witnessing in Germany before he left, with all the burning of immigrant hostels and stuff and 'Two Nations Panic Stations' was about the criminal justice bill and its threats to stop illegal gatherings of more than 12 people."

A two-week tour of the UK was undertaken with hardcore US punks Defiance before Substandard embarked upon a three-and-a-half week European tour with Social Genocide from Austria and Tuomiopäivän Lapset and Totuus, both from Finland.

"I remember us picking up some young punk kids on the way to Rostock to play a gig," says Andy of that first trip to the continent. "Then noticing swastikas on their jackets…then getting to the gig and there being loads of people there and talking with the venue owner only to be told we'd gone to the wrong venue and it was a massive Nazi do with Europe's biggest Nazi bands! And we were playing down the road '…with the fucking commoners!' Oops!

"I also have 'fond' memories of having to bump start the van over the Czech border and promptly bump it back out again 'cos we were refused entry…maybe something to do with having 10 very drunk people falling out of the van at seven o'clock in the morning? And me having to play a gig off my face and feeling very ill in Switzerland 'cos I'd smoked some smack, thinking it was blow…and what about the police chase and roadblock in East Germany because I was seen drinking beer and driving? Then they realised it was a right-hand-drive vehicle and I was only a passenger! There were plenty of things like that on that tour…"

"[Booking agent] Kleister got us a gig in Stuttgart," adds Jules. "But when we arrived everyone had gone to Holland for some festival, so we phoned around and got a last-minute gig in a gay bar by the docks; they said they'd give us three crates of Beck's and some petrol. And that gig was fuckin' great…lotsa fellas in vests with big 'taches, but absolutely brilliant. It's all very well playing to a punk crowd all the time, but it's so refreshing to play in front of a crowd like that as well."

Shaun then left, but Substandard's relentless punk assault continued unabated with two split singles in 1997 for Dutch label, Wicked Witch, 'USA Meets UK' with Portland's Detestation (and featuring one of this author's favourite Substandard tunes, the metallic Varukers-like chugger 'Annihilate') and 'Germania Meets Britannica' with Pink Flamingos.

"I think Kalv [from Heresy] had some mates over from Holland…" recalls Jules, "Yoss from L'arm, the guys from Seein' Red and Edwin from Wicked Witch Records. We were playing an all-dayer in Bradford and Yoss asked if he could get a lift up with Andy and Christine in their mini; the rest of us went up in a van. I honestly don't remember the gig itself, but it was either the one that erupted into a pitched battle after a misunderstanding with the 'Safeway cider death squad' from Manchester, or some other drunken debacle… Anyway, Joss got back to Nottingham and must have said to Ed something like, 'I've just seen the drunkest bunch of twats ever, why not get them to record for you?'

"So we recorded six songs at Pots And Pans, but then didn't like three of them so used the three we liked for the split with Detestation and recorded three other songs back in Nottingham at the studio we used to practice in [Rubber Biscuit] for the Pink Flamingos thing. Andy played bass on one of the recordings and Eddie Greenaway from Slumgang played on the other…"

Eddie also stood in on bass for the short tour of Germany that followed, during which Jason fell in love with a Berliner and moved out there soon afterwards. "…Which was a bloody shame 'cos he could fucking drum when he wanted to," reckons Andy, "sticking rolls in all over the place. But on the flipside he could also be bloody awful and couldn't play for shit, forgetting that we were even playing gigs and going on tour sometimes."

Jason was replaced by Keith from Suicidal Supermarket Trolleys, who had just moved up to Nottingham, and the 'Consuming Greed' EP was recorded for Inflammable Material in 1999, another potent punk release, with 'Consume' sounding a lot like Conflict at their peak. Goz joined on bass but only lasted for one German tour ("She was a lot younger than us, wasn't drinking at the time either and left when we got back," says Andy) and 'Consuming Greed' turned out to be the last Substandard release as the band had by then went through too many line-up changes to function with any efficiency.

"Nick Harris had a few practices on bass, but we were too fast," explains Andy. "And then Keith left, so Adam [Stevenson, ex-Deviated Instinct] started drumming 'cos he was in Nottingham for a bit, but he soon left, so Pug helped out again, with Eddie back on bass once more. Those two have always helped us out when we needed them, but then Jules moved down to Brighton and Pat started Bomblast Men [and later on the excellent Shithouse] and couldn't do two bands at once, so we stopped for a bit…"

Or at least until 2003, when German label Civilization released a Substandard discography LP, which was reissued on CD in 2006 by Ruin Nation. In 2004 the band did a final tour of Germany to help promote the release, with Jules and Andy being joined by three Combat Shock members: guitarist Malcy, bassist Ben and drummer Sonny. They were joined for the dates by Red With Anger and made their last ever live appearance at a big outdoor anti-fascist festival when the tour culminated in Berlin.

Nowadays Jules, a recent father of twin boys, fronts Constant State Of Terror alongside ex-members of MTA and Combat Shock; he still does his distribution and lends an occasional hand with Inflammable Material. Andy moved to Brittany with Christine, where they now play together in the Flue Sniffers, although quite infrequently as the other two members – vocalist Sally and bassist Len – still live in Brighton and Nottingham respectively.

"Actually, the Flue Sniffers aren't affected by the other two living in the UK any more. We just play as a two, three or four-piece depending upon who can make it at the time, which makes it a bit more dynamic and means we are back doing plenty of gigs. We're doing the same noisy, political shit, but a bit more basic than Substandard," he admits, "and have recorded a couple of CDs at home and just done something in the studio. Most gigs are over here in Brittany, but we do get over to England now and again…

"For years in England I worked with people with a learning disability and fostered as well," he continues, on his current personal and political motivations. "I was working over here at a centre for kids with autism, but the management was so unbelievably corrupt nearly the whole staff team left, so I'm back doing bits of building work (most houses here are made of mud), mechanics, binning for food, making beer…and a racket.

"I've got three daughters at the time of writing; they are five, 16 and 20 and a lad who's 20 too – one of the foster kids who moved in when he was 10 and decided to stay! I will do a bit of session work, or voluntary, probably, but I really don't want anything to do with the shitty way things are run over here. Maybe I'll find a good project to get involved with.

"It's a good [punk] scene over here though; it took a while to find the more political anarcho side of stuff, but we've now met loads of good people in little collectives that put gigs on, with everything *prix libre,* which means you pay what you think or can afford and that can be for the gig, food, beer and often records, pamphlets, T-shirts etc and it *works*. Also we put the odd gig on at ours or other venues, squats, collective buildings, but we never use public buildings or bars. I'm still political (whatever that means), probably more so now, I think, but just older so I think a bit more…but I'm definitely still motivated to do stuff and can't see that ever changing!

"I'd just like Substandard to be remembered as a fast, noisy, political anarcho band," he concludes. "But fun people with a good sense of humour at the same time, who drank far too much for theirs and everyone else's good!"

"Fuck knows how I'd like us remembered," laughs Jules. "We were definitely angry but also knew how to have a laugh. Perhaps for our £2 T-shirts and 30p demos? You don't see those prices these days! But we were just one big dysfunctional family at the end of the day, not afraid of telling it how it was and having a lot of fun and the odd shandy along the way…"

SELECT DISCOGRAPHY:

7-inch:

'Split' (Inflammable Material, 1994) – *split with Nerves*

'USA Meets UK' (Wicked Witch, 1997) – *split with Detestation*

'Germania Meets Britannica' (Wicked Witch, 1997) – *split with Pink Flamingos*

'Consuming Greed' (Inflammable Material, 1999)

LP:
'Discography' (Civilization, 2003)

AT A GLANCE:
Obviously the Substandard discography CD on Ruin Nation… Listening to the band's recorded output as a whole makes you realise how unfortunate it is they never recorded a full album at the peak of their powers. It would have been awesome.

PANIC

Another Nottingham band, **Panic** took the obnoxious simplicity of the Ramones and Dwarves and gave it a filthy English twist to great effect. They undertook a mass of touring that even saw them doubling as Marky Ramone's' 'backing band' for one memorable stint, but never really achieved the kind of popularity to pull respectable crowds in their own right, leading to their eventual demise in 2004.

"I moved from Durham to Nottingham in late 1993 and quickly immersed myself in the local punk rock scene," begins vocalist/guitarist Jamie Delerict (born Jamie Haugh, but now Delerict by deed-poll). "The Narrowboat was definitely the main hang-out spot and it was there that we drank, rehearsed and played gigs; the scene was really vibrant and bands of every genre were all really friendly with each other. This was probably because even the indie/grunge/alternative bands were all seemingly spawned from the hardcore scene of the late Eighties.

"There was garage rock like the Sugar Rays [later to become the X-Rays], indie stuff like Cherry Forever, harder industrial bands like Skin Limit Show, thrash punk like Hard To Swallow and melodic punk like Consumed…and then there was the full-on punk-rock contingent who really 'lived' the punk-rock lifestyle such as the Losers, Slum Gang, Substandard and Concrete Sox. I existed in both camps and, at 18, was by far the youngest guy playing in bands around then. Everybody else seemed to be in their twenties or thirties, yet welcomed me with open arms; this was remarkable to me, because I came from a Durham hardcore scene mainly inhabited by teenagers.

"I lived with and mostly hung around with, the punk-rockers; it's a total cliché, but we were all on the dole, played in bands and shared houses in the lower class suburbs of Forest Fields and Hyson Green. Life was a total blur of cheap cider, parties and gigs. However, probably because of my diverse musical tastes and love of American punk, I also gravitated towards the guys on the other side of town who led slightly more 'normal' lives and – gasp! – even had jobs! I started jamming with a band that included two future members of Bob Tilton, an ex-Concrete Sox guitarist and the future drummer of Panic [Paul 'Tot' Taylor]. Line-ups changed and we only ended up doing two gigs (one in Wakefield and one at the Narrowboat) before going our separate ways; I was disappointed and decided to lay low for a few months, writing and plotting my next move… I also unfortunately sold my amp for beer money!"

Once new gear had been procured, Jamie and Tot hooked up with bassist Mark 'Digs Nothing' Devenport, added Slum Gang drummer Pug Slum (aka Joseph Nott) on vocals and played their first gig as Panic at the Narrowboat in April 1995.

"That first gig was meant to be with the Queers," he sighs. "But they lost all of their luggage en route to Heathrow and had a two-month tour of the UK ahead of them or something crazy like that, so they ended up going home after only a couple of gigs. We were gutted, but the show went ahead anyway; I remember it going really well, though, and being very proud of the impact that we made with the large crowd. We even did a couple of Queers tunes too, just to keep the crowd happy.

"There was a party at my house afterwards and I think I must have played the cassette of our live performance at least 10 times! I still have it somewhere and it actually sounds better than our first record. My high didn't last long, though, as after just one more gig at the Narrowboat, Pug was made to choose between us and Slum Gang and he was forced to step down from his position as lead vocalist. We had gigs booked for the next few months, though, so I *very reluctantly* agreed to step in until we found another singer…and, of course, 10 years later, I was still singing…"

With a sound very reminiscent of the high-energy melodic punk rock of Screeching Weasel, Panic recorded their rather flat-sounding first demo (they still sold a respectable 200 copies, though) at the Warehouse in Nottingham with "Kev, who was a great bloke, but not a very good engineer or producer! The studio was located in a very rough area of town and although it was like a fortress to get into, it was forever getting burgled. While I was laying down some vocals, things went awfully quiet in the control room for quite a while and when I took off my headphones to go and see what was happening, I just caught the tail-end of a scuffle involving Kev and our roadie Sid warding off some young scamps trying to break in. Luckily, our roadie was not only the brother of Pug Slum, but a 20-stone Geordie called 'Sid Security'! He won."

Despite its sonic shortcomings, the demo landed the band a deal. Jamie chose not to release Panic on his own Delerict label, who instead issued 7-inchs by the Nerves and Slum Gang. Panic were signed up by new label Phoenix, run by Stan Smith, the ex-drummer of Anti-Pasti, who released their first EP, the deliciously gonzoid 'Her Family's On Drugs', recorded by Steve Blackman, in May 1995.

"Personally, I think that it sounds like it was recorded in a biscuit tin and I honestly haven't listened to it since the late Nineties," says Jamie of the band's debut release. "The artwork and packaging however, remain something I'm very proud of to this day. Following in the footsteps of Black Flag, using Raymond Pettibone as the artist for every release, this was the first time that we used local artist Noel Sharman, who went on to do all of *our* album artwork.

"We were always very confident in our songs and abilities," he adds. "But even we were surprised when *NME* gave it a great review, *Kerrang!* loved it and we even made Tim Yohannan's Top 10 in *Maximum Rock'n'Roll*. We suddenly seemed to be doing about half a dozen fanzine interviews a week too. The 'limited edition' first run of 500 sold out before any promo copies were mailed out, so I believe another 1,000 were pressed up immediately as well…"

Panic, live in Grimsby 1998,
picture by Jez Goffin

Panic, taken in Nottingham, 2000,
by Nichola Prested

By the time they recorded their first LP for Phoenix, 'Gremlin Generation', Digs had been replaced on bass by Lee Van Cleaver [aka Tim Cleaver] from Slum Gang, who made his live debut with the band at the Leeds Duchess Of York…well, nearly.

"We were invited to play that Leeds gig by a guy called Nat from Dog On A Rope; it was an anti-fascist benefit gig of some description. We were just hanging around outside the venue waiting to soundcheck when we were accosted by about five big men and one gobby woman. They started off friendly enough, asking us questions about the gig that night, but things quickly got weird. Two of them went into the venue, then a couple of minutes later, the doors slammed open and Nat threw them out with an iron bar in his hand! A scuffle broke out in our group and one of the guys CS-gassed me and Nat in our faces.

"I was incapacitated (not that I wanted to fight anyway!) but Nat continued chasing them down the street. The venue staff – unsurprisingly – decided against running the show that night, so the racist thugs ended up winning that one. Not to be deterred, though, we gave our good friends Chopper a call and they were happy to have us play on a bill with them that night at Players Snooker Club in Wakefield, only a 20-minute drive away. Incidentally, very shortly after that crazy night, back home in Nottingham, the council demolished the Narrowboat pub…"

The album itself was recorded at the Jesus And Mary Chain's Drugstore Studio in London with producer Darren Allison, who had previously worked with Jesus Jones, Babybird, Skunk Anansie and Alison Moyet!

"He was a nice guy," reckons Jamie, "but he neglected to mention that he only worked with those artists in an assistant engineer-type role and not as a producer. At the time, we were very happy with it, but in hindsight the production hasn't held up well. I still think there are some really good pop-punk songs on there though and maybe it might benefit from a re-mastering…actually just being mastered at all would have been nice!

"This was where the relationship started to sour between us and the record label; the release date kept getting pushed back and we kept getting fobbed off by Stan and his partner Lee. We had handed in artwork and everything else needed on time, but we were met with constant excuses from those two guys. They were also handling our press and they kept sending out the same interview to all of the fanzines and magazines, infuriating the very people who had got us to where we were at right then.

"They also tampered with my artwork, took off the band's postal address and added an extra song that we'd recorded called 'Parasite' as a hidden track. We were furious with them and I don't think the album came out until about a year later either; it really felt like we'd missed out on a huge opportunity to strike while the iron was red hot. We'd also figured out by then that they weren't going to buy us a van and new amps and guitars as they'd promised!

"At this time, Stan had obviously realised that he was in way over his head; he'd promised a lot of other bands album deals that he couldn't possibly come through with, he'd pissed off the underground press with and now his main act (us!) were trying as hard as we could to distance ourselves from anything that he'd either said or done. I think Lee's interest in Phoenix faded when the new label that he was part of, V2, signed the Stereophonics… and, as they say, the rest is history…"

A rock-solid new 7-inch – 'You Smell Like A Brewery', very reminiscent of the criminally overlooked Automatic 7 – was recorded with Dave Chang at Nottingham's Square Centre and released by Northampton-based Hectic Records ("The guy who put it out worked all summer long in a chicken factory to fund it!"), but it was unfortunately the last release with Lee Van Cleaver, who relocated to Norwich "because he'd fallen in love with the guitarist of all-girl punk band PMT...

"1999 was a tough year for myself and the band; the relationship I was in at the time had gone horribly wrong and I was in a very negative state of mind. I was drinking a lot and felt on the verge of a nervous breakdown on more than one occasion. The pendulum had definitely swung when it came to our 'popularity', too; we were no longer the toast of the town and we'd been surpassed by other bands on our 'level' such as Consumed who'd signed to Fat Wreck. I'm still friends with those guys now, but I don't mind saying that, at the time, I was incredibly jealous! We were definitely in a rut and we needed to hit the 'Refresh' button."

With new bassist Jan Zadora, who would also share lead vocals with Jamie, Panic returned to the Square Centre with Dave Chang to record their second album, 'Movers And Shakers', for Kevin Prested (who had played drums in Jamie's first band, Submission, up in Durham)'s Your Illegal Recording Company. With most of the songs generally longer and slower than previous Panic recordings, it lacked the immediate spark of 'Gremlin Generation' and met with mixed reviews from the underground fanzine press.

"When Jan went AWOL just before a UK tour with the Fux from Allentown, Pennsylvania, he got kicked out of the band, paving the way for Digs' return just in time for a reciprocal three-week US tour with the Fux and the Clap. There was also a brand new EP, 'A Monkey Smoking A Fag', which suffered from not only inadequate distribution but an awful guitar sound.

"A few shows in, I realised that it was going to be similar to any other run of UK dates," comments Jamie on the US tour he had dreamed of for so long. "Peaks and valleys, as they say. I mysteriously started suffering from severe migraines while on this tour, but besides that, I took in and enjoyed every single minute. Even at the poorly attended shows, such as the ones we did in Nashville, Tennessee, there was a little group of die-hard female fans that wanted their Union Jack bags autographed by us!

"We realised that simply by being a British punk band in the US, we were at least getting people's attention. It was and indeed still is, an honour to say that we played CBGB's in New York City, on Independence Day no less. As Ramones disciples, it was incredible to be in that cockroach-infested dressing-room and to use that one disgusting toilet! Another highlight was playing a few shows with Dillinger Four in the Mid West, the best one of those being at the Fireside Bowl in Chicago. That night we stopped with the dude who ran Panic Button Records with Ben Weasel [of Screeching Weasel fame]; he informed us that Ben had really wanted to sign the band, but we had one thing working against us: we were British! This completely confused me at the time, but from a business sense, I actually understand it a little better now. Still, with Tot being the world's biggest Screeching Weasel fan, it was a bit of a bummer!

"We got on really well with the Dillinger guys and they dug our band and loved my lyrics; 10 years on, they are still one of the darlings of the punk underground, so their support meant a lot to us. There were so many highs, to be honest, that any 'lows' just didn't seem to matter. Despite missing our flight and arriving home 24 hours late, we had a fantastic time that we'll all remember for the rest of our lives."

A new deal was inked with Leeds label Crackle for 2001's '...Get Well' album, which was recorded by original Pitchshifter member Johnny Carter and Geffen recording artists

Bivouac's Paul Yeadon and remains their most rounded effort.

"Recording was halted mid-way through the sessions though," recalls Jamie sadly, "as my father passed away very suddenly in unpleasant circumstances. But with a fire in my belly I ploughed through the process and we finished an album that I'm still very proud of to this day. Art, sound and song-wise, we seemed to find our 'sweet spot' on that record…"

But Digs was given his marching orders again after 2003's 'When Monsters Move' EP and it became apparent that the band were in their final cycle, albeit still landing themselves some decent tours. "Yeah, we had some good tours in the early 2000s – with [the German Fat Wreck band] Wizo, [LA legends] the Angry Samoans, [Californians] the Lonely Kings and many others, but most memorable would definitely be the tour we did with Marky Ramone in 2003. Not only did Panic act as main support to Marky's spoken-word tour, but after he was done with his slide show Panic (minus Tot on drums, of course) would perform a 12-song Ramones set with him.

"It was an exhilarating feeling playing in a band with Marky, but he's a very hard man to get along with. One minute he's your best friend and the next he's delusional and paranoid over the Ramones legacy that he somehow thinks is his and his alone. He's a strange man. We knew that before, though, as we'd gone to Europe for a week supporting the Misfits on their 25th anniversary tour and he was drumming for them at the time.

"The gigs on *that* tour were probably the best shows Panic ever played; they had the biggest crowds, we sold lots of merchandise and we were really well looked after by the promoters and, of course, the Misfits and their crew. That's how I choose to remember it anyway. It was miserable for Tot, though, because he was as sick as a dog during that tour and as a diabetic, he probably came close to dying…he played great on stage though! We also managed to get lost on the way to the first gig in Milan and ended up going round and round in circles for hours unable to find the venue. Missing the first gig of your biggest tour yet? That was a bad start!

"We also quickly discovered that the guy who we had replaced Digs with was a total and utter douchebag. Sometimes you only realise these things while travelling in the back of a Transit van in blizzard conditions through the Alps! We had one more bassist after the aforementioned un-named douchebag was fired and did a few more tours, but deep down, I think that Tot and I knew that our time had very probably been and gone…"

In mid 2004, Panic did a final tour of the UK and Ireland, with Birmingham band the Hunchbacks in support and the unanimously poor turn-outs were the final nail in the band's coffin. "The second to last show was actually in Durham. My mother, my uncle, my cousin and one of my old bandmates showed up to see us – and no-one else. A part of me wishes that it'd ended there in my home town; it would have been kinda poetic. But no, the last show ended up being at a total dive of a pub in Hucknall on the outskirts of Nottingham; I played the songs knowing that it was gonna be the last time and to cap it all off, the promoters of the gig were so drunk that they 'forgot' to put anybody on the door, so we didn't get paid. And that just about summed it all up for Panic…"

Tot and Digs still live in Nottingham, the former having apparently hung up his drum sticks for good and the latter enjoying a pretty successful acting career (he starred in *Bronson* with Tom Hardy and…er…the most recent Kwik-Fit advert!) Jamie nowadays lives in South Yorkshire with his partner and daughter, but has never stopped making music and touring, fronting Teenage Casket Company from 2004 to 2009 and playing bass for hard-touring

Irish band the Dangerfields. He's currently singing and playing guitar with JD and the FDCs. And occasionally playing the odd Panic tune to this day.

"I look upon the Nineties as a wonderful part of my life," he concludes fondly. "We had straightedge, emo and scenesters in the punk-rock scene, but it was of course nothing like how it is today. Just like anything *good* and underground, sooner or later it becomes mainstream. Which isn't necessarily a bad thing, but should we all feel proud that we've had a hand in making coloured hair, tattoos and piercings so acceptable in today's mainstream society? I don't know. And as great as the internet is, the magic of arranging tours and gigs by sending out letters was an art form in itself that will never be repeated; there were compilation tapes for those budding record-label owners on a shoestring budget, cut and paste fliers for gigs and many more beautiful little things that are essentially laughed at.

"There was also a really good quality-control element for bands; if you had a CD or a record out, you were to be taken seriously. Nowadays, it's so easy to get a 'studio-sounding' recording and to put it out on CD. Don't get me wrong, the DIY aspect of it all is fantastic and I make full use of it myself. But the fact is that, although it's never been easier to be in a band as it is these days, it's also sadly never been harder to actually be heard…"

SELECT DISCOGRAPHY:

7-inch:
'Her Family's On Drugs' (Phoenix, 1996)
'You Smell Like A Brewery' (Hectic, 1998)

CDEPs:
'A Monkey Smoking A Fag' (Your Illegal Recording Company, 2000)
'When Monsters Move' (Crackle, 2003)

LPs:
'Gremlin Generation' (Phoenix, 1997)
'Movers And Shakers' (Your Illegal Recording Company, 1999)
'…Get Well' (Crackle, 2002)

AT A GLANCE:
That '…Get Well' album is a perfectly-formed pop-punk gem.

SLUM GANG

Slum Gang were only around for a few years, during which time they did just one 7-inch and terrorised Europe on several occasions. But not only did they pen some damn fine tunes that married the raw harmonies of UK punk to the irresistible energy of US hardcore, but Slum Gang members went on to join several important UK punk bands, more than justifying their inclusion in this weighty tome.

The band started in early April 1992, after guitarist Eddie Greenaway's band (the American SXE-influenced) Downfall (who started in 1989 and released the six-track 'Not Your Fault' EP on Godsend in 1992) played with guitarist/vocalist Loyd Sims' band Concrete Sox several times. The pair discovered they had far more in common than not.

"We played with Sox several times," remembers Eddie, "my favourite being at the Rock And Reggae festival, which was a local thing celebrating different cultures with music, food, the usual stuff… This one year they had a 'mohican Magoo' tent which was about 12 punk bands playing all day; it was great playing in a tent with loads of drunk punks dancing about while normal people walked past…the look on their faces was priceless, especially when Sox played and Pug did a striptease!

"After they had played, me and Loyd were having a beer and chatting about doing a band with a heavy Social Distortion influence; we had a couple of jams, but then Downfall went on tour with American band, Born Against. Upon our return Downfall split up due to the old cliché of musical differences [vocalist Simon Fiern and drummer Alan Gainey went on to form Bob Tilton]; it's all water under the bridge now, but at the time I was well fucked off. On the bright side, though, it gave us more time to concentrate on Slum Gang, in which I was playing guitar [he was the bassist in Downfall] and learning new stuff all the time; Loyd was much better on guitar than me (at the beginning!); he gave up Sox to put all his time into it too and Slum Gang were born…"

As well as Social Distortion, Slum Gang embraced the whole snotty-but-tuneful So Cal (Southern California) punk rock sound, as popularised by the likes of DI, Adolescents and Agent Orange and mixed it with shades of the UK bands that had inspired them to pick up instruments in the first place, plus some local colouring.

"The Nottingham scene was awesome in the late Eighties and early Nineties," enthuses Eddie. "But back then, as Loyd puts it, I *was* 'annoyingly positive about everything!' We had Heresy and Concrete Sox, who were both pretty big in an underground kind of way; it seemed like there was a gig every week and we saw some great bands…and some shit ones too. With Nottingham being pretty central in the country, we got people from all over the UK coming here and crashing at our house for the night – or in some cases moving in!

"We quickly built up a network of friends, so whenever travelling away to gigs we'd always have a place to crash and after every punks' picnic here our house would be packed to the rafters. We lived at the end of a row of semis and you had four punks in one side and another four next door… Berridge Road had a bit of a reputation back then, but I've got some great memories of parties and general mad drunken behaviour and I'm still good friends with most people who lived there.

"It was crazy in Forest Fields/Hyson Green at the time; there were punk houses all over the area and, no matter what time of day or night, if you were out and about, you would see a load of like-minded people wobbling around the streets! This was the area that spawned Slum Gang and we soon got into going through skips at the back of shops for food, so we had more giro money for booze. There was a lot of unity too; at Berridge Road, if a party was called, we would all throw money onto the table and it didn't matter if it was £5 or 5p, so long as that was all you had. Then we would liquidise it, sort of 'all for one and one for all'…the punkateers'! Pretty much as close to anarchy as you can get on a giro…"

Joining Eddie and Loyd were bassist Tim 'Lee Van' Cleaver from Real Molesworth Dirt and Joe 'Pug' Nott from Mortal Terror and Slum Children on drums. Loyd called in some favours from his Concrete Sox contacts and Slum Gang actually played their first gig in Liege, Belgium, supporting the Swedish band Svarts Sno, during September '92, staying in Europe for the weekend to also play Ieper and Dordrecht.

"The main thing I remember about the first gig is that we had all been drinking on the ferry and, when we landed in Holland, we promptly split up and wandered off in different directions to various bars," laughs Eddie. "Loyd was trying to pay for drinks with some old American dollars and Tim bed down for the night under a bush, only to wake the next morning with no boots, jacket or socks! So when we got to the gig we not only had to borrow amps, but shoes…the people putting the gig on thought Tim was making some sort of vegan statement, not that he was just a drunken fool who slept in a bush!

"We were all in the one car too, so it didn't help that all Pug took to eat was a jar of hummus and had beer shame the first two nights [he pissed his pants]; we really were stinking, but met some good people too. It wasn't a case of enjoying playing in Europe more than here or anything; it was just exciting. I mean me and Pug had never even been abroad, then suddenly there we were playing gigs in Europe with our band!"

Upon their return, Loyd picked up the 'Slum Mobile' – an old Kawasaki Team Transit van, complete with a horseshoe of red velvet seats ("The van was more popular than us," laughs Eddie) – and the band played anywhere and everywhere, in the time-honoured tradition of DIY punk rock, until early 1993 when they entered the Canning Factory in Nottingham to record their first demo.

"We got the music tracks down, but I think we ran out of time and money, so we ended up with a demo with no vocals on it," explains Eddie. "Then, when we eventually got the money together to finish it, the Canning Factory had shut down! So we went to Sideway Sound, in the picturesque village of Attenborough, where we put down the vocals and did the mix, then set about sending the demo to every promoter and fanzine we could think of. And it was well received in the main, I think, due to it being a bit different to what most other bands were doing at the time…kinda melodic, but political. We did another demo at Sideway and this time we did finish it, vocals and all…but then *that* studio shut down as well – we were starting to get a reputation as studio killers! 'Demo Two' was a bit more tuneful, but still with snotty vocals and biting lyrics…"

September 1995 saw the band back over in Europe for 10 days, on the road with Fermented. "Yeah, it was 10 days of pure alcohol-fuelled chaos," admits Eddie. "Steven Dalley was recruited for driving duties, mainly 'cos he didn't drink but was just as mad as us. We hadn't even left the East Midlands when we got a flat tyre and the exhaust fell off the van! Ten days with no spare wheel and the exhaust held on with shoelaces and bits of wire…and then Dalley went and cracked the windscreen killing a wasp! Sums us up really: falling apart, but together enough to get through the tour.

Slum Gang in Rotterdam, 1995

Slumgang, Ed, Loyd and Tim at the
Narrowboat, Nottingham ▸

"Fermented had a reputation for being a big partying band and so did Slum Gang, so when we met it was chaos. A lot of it's blurred, for obvious reasons, but there were so many high points, including a gig on a site in Hamburg where the crowd were mad for it, so when both bands had finished playing we kinda jammed with various members of each band on different instruments, just banging out covers, and the Slumented Barmy Army was born.

"The last gig of the tour was in Groningen, Holland, which was lovely, so many friends... When we finally hit the stage, Loyd had a Viking helmet on and Pug was topless except for a bra. Another blinder, though, and we have been friends with the Dutch lot ever since... As for low points, there were times when we were hungover, homesick and hungry, but you have to take the rough with the smooth. Customs on the way back was dodgy; we got pulled and they brought out a sniffer dog... We were all bricking it 'cos there had been so much shit imbibed in the back of that van, dubious-looking powder stains all over the amps etc. We needn't have worried though; the dog they brought out was like Scooby Doo and had to be forced into the back of the van, took one sniff of a bag of dirty clothes and got straight back out again! We were stinking!"

Upon their return to England, Slum Gang entered Bradford studio Potz'n'Panz to record their one-and-only single, 'Back In Rags', which was released in 1996 on Delerict Records. Backed by 'Double Crossed' and 'Mickey Don't Get It', it was a wonderfully simple, superbly melodic offering, equal parts Ramones and GBH. But, although another track, 'Pass The Sympathy', was contributed to a benefit EP to raise money for the Zorro squat in Leipzig, the band split up in 1997, soon enough after their single's release on Delerict to leave the label, ran by their mate and roadie Jamie Delerict, with boxes of unsold records.

"Yeah, we felt bad about dropping Jamie in it like that," sighs Eddie. "But there were so many reasons for the split; the main one being that a good friend of ours came to stay with us in Nottingham and he died in the van after partying out in the sticks (RIP Eamon). Loyd and Tim were both there when it happened and as you can imagine it hit them hard. We were also becoming disillusioned with such a supposedly open-minded scene where people all dressed the same and just wanted to see Discharge clones all singing the same old lyrics. It was as if because we were melodic we weren't allowed to sing about politics or have any opinions. Basically I think, after five years of hard partying and touring, we had just burnt out.

"The last gig was at the Old General in Nottingham with Groningen's finest, Mad Punx Disease. Well, *technically* it was just Slum Gang because Mad Punx Disease had been drinking all day and decided to all go walkabout in different directions just before their set and couldn't find the pub in time to play! We were pretty shit that night too, but we didn't know that it would be our last ever gig...and even if we had, would we have been any better? I doubt it!"

Following the premature demise of the band, Loyd ended up in Contempt and Pug in both Panic and Concrete Sox, while Tim played with the Short'n'Curlies and Losers; meanwhile, Eddie, who did stints in Substandard, Concrete Sox and Violent Affray, maintains that its his time in Slum Gang that he remembers most fondly today.

"None of us were ever as happy as we were in Slum Gang; from then on it was get jobs, have kids, move cities and become as normal as four nutters could be. In the grand scheme of things I would like us to be remembered as offering something a bit different; we could play and we had integrity in that what we sang about was what we really were... We rejected the system and, as far as possible, lived outside it – punk as a lifestyle, not just a haircut. But above all we were four best mates who just happened to play different instruments. Thanks to anybody who supported us in any way, far too many to mention by name; let's not forget that it's the crowd that makes the band!"

SELECT DISCOGRAPHY:

7-inch:
'Back In Rags' (Delerict, 1996)

AT A GLANCE:
If you want a no-frills Slum Gang CD, e-mail: eddiegreenaway@googlemail.com

THE X-RAYS

Another seemingly obscure Nottingham band perhaps, but during their short existence, **The X-Rays** actually released 11 singles, three albums and played hundreds of gigs across the UK, Europe and America. And, like so many other Nottingham bands before and after them, they formed in and around the Narrowboat pub.

"At the time, me and [bassist] Coop were living together," begins guitarist/vocalist Gaz X-Ray, "although in those days we rarely *left* the Narrowboat. We had a rehearsal room on the top floor, we'd watch and play gigs on the middle floor and downstairs was the all-important bar area. We had very little experience of being in bands before, but what we did have was a passion for loud, raw, unadulterated garage punk and I ain't talking about that lame-ass Sixties retro shit. We wanted to take what labels like Estrus and Empty were doing, but infuse it with more speed, more energy and give the world high-octane rock'n'roll…

"The only problem was: we had no drummer! But there's an old adage about waiting for a bus and then two show up at the same time; well, in this case, we had three turn up. We happened to bump into [ex-Heresy bassist] Kalv on the way to our local drinking establishment. In conversation he suggested several drummers and, as if by magic, like some crazy episode of *Mr Ben* where the shopkeeper appears from nowhere, suddenly these drummers appeared (no doubt also on their way to the Narrowboat!) We had Kev [now drummer in Spiritualized], Ant [then drummer of Bivouac] and Steve [Charlesworth, also ex-Heresy] all offering their services. Anyway, to cut a long story short, we plumped for Steve, not realising he had sold his kit. How we cobbled together a kit is another story…and one that I believe the Nottingham Constabulary are still interested in!"

The band played their first gig, as a three-piece, in April 1994, supporting the Supersuckers at the Narrowboat, of course; they later expanded to a four-piece when they added 'G-Man' on lead guitar. That they opened for the Supersuckers at their very first show is incredibly apt, though, as the X-Rays bear more than a passing resemblance to the Arizonan hellraisers.

X-Rays line-up: G-Man, Gary, Coop and Steve

X-Rays live: Coop and Gary

"I think the title of the first 7-inch EP ['Booze And Speed'!] sums it up, really," laughs Gaz "Don't try looking for deep and meaningful lyrics like 'Lady In Red', 'cos you ain't gonna find them. But we knew we were onto something right from that very first gig; it was 15 minutes of sweat, blood'n'booze in front of a packed house. I'd certainly like to think we gave the Supersuckers a hard act to follow and showed them how rock'n'roll should be done – the British way!

"As for G-Man joining the band, I am still unsure how it happened. One minute we were a three-piece having a well earned jolly, a boys' outing in Spain; next minute, or should I say several [drinking] 'sessions' later, this Sixties freak-beat ex-scooter boy sweet-talked himself into the band and somehow commandeered my SG guitar. And I still ain't got that fucker back!"

Said first single – and indeed the first LP, 'Speed Kills' – were both released by Lowlife Records, although the aforementioned Seattle label, Empty, couldn't resist such scuzzy, out-of-control punk rock for long and picked the album up for release Stateside.

"I was working at Selectadisc [Records] at the time," explains Gaz. "I used to chat to this guy at Lowlife – he was on telesales – and he happened to ask me what the X-Rays sounded like, so I sent him what at the time I told him was a demo. He told me he loved it, but perhaps it was a bit too raw for the UK market; he wanted to put an album and single out, but wanted it a bit more, in his words, polished. Anyway, after sealing the deal with a boozy night out in Brighton, we managed to convince him to press both a 7-inch and a red vinyl album up without listening to the masters; *he* may not have been too impressed with the end result, but to us that vinyl still sounds awesome – as raw and in-yer-face as when we first recorded it.

"Maybe we should have told Mr Lowlife that the X-Rays didn't do 'demos' and we certainly didn't polish up recordings for anyone. What you got was what was actually recorded, raw and live in the studio at the time. I still love the energy and raw power of those recordings and I think we were vindicated when Empty wanted to put the album out without any talk of trying to clean it up for the supposed mass market."

"And as for Empty picking us up," continues Coop. "I'd just been made redundant and decided to travel round the States for a bit, blowing what little golden handshake I'd been given. We'd already talked about the labels we'd like to be signed to and narrowed it down to a short list of one: Empty, who at that time were releasing most of our favourite records anyway. Armed with a six-track cassette, I made it a mission for me to get to the head honcho of Empty's house in the Ballard area of Seattle, to hand it to him personally. He got quite a shock when he answered his door that morning, but was at least gracious enough to offer me a beer!"

The album was promoted with many eventful gigs, not least of all a UK tour with New Bomb Turks during late '95 and another UK trek, this time with (Epitaph artists) Gas Huffer and Red Aunts, during April '96. Then, by virtue of being signed to a US label (not to mention rocking like motherfuckers!), the X-Rays toured America alongside the Motards and the Fumes as part of an Empty Records package tour.

"By far our best gig in the States was at Gibson's in Seattle," reckons Coop, proudly. "Ask any of the X-Rays and they'll give you the same answer! We tore the place up, watched by just about every Seattle garage- punk luminary in town; members of Zeke, Gas Huffer and Sinister Six filled the audience, with the Supersuckers also turning up…no doubt to pick up a few more pointers! Fuckin' awesome.

"And definitely the most bizarre gig on that tour was in Missoula, Montana, in a saloon bar straight out of Tombstone. Half the crowd were wearing Stetsons and I wouldn't have been surprised if they'd been carrying six-shooters too. It was like walking into a rodeo fuelled by Jägermeister (which was sold by *the pint* on draught!) When the crowd discovered we were English, they automatically assumed we must be the Who and we spent the rest of the night dodging requests for 'Magic Bus'…"

Several more 7-inchs followed before the brilliantly-titled second album in 1997, 'Double Godzilla With Cheese'; recorded – like the first – with Mark Spivey at Track Station in Burton-on-Trent, it didn't look to reinvent the wheel, just to roll it faster, harder and dirtier! By this time, the aforementioned G-Man had joined on lead guitar, lending an extra dimension to that aspect of the band's sound, but apart from that it was (monkey) business as usual and a European tour was duly booked to promote it.

"That was actually our first trip to Europe in '97," clarifies Coop. "We kind of did things arse about face… Having a US label meant we'd toured over there before even considering crossing the [English] Channel! Great memories and some truly bizarre gigs.

"We went down a storm in Holland and Scandinavia, but Groningen stands out as a highlight; the day before having been Steve's birthday and a night 'off'. We were all fairly inebriated from celebrating, but luckily only Steve got arrested for being drunk and disorderly! He spent a night in the cells and only made it to the venue the next night as the booking officer at the local jail was an X-Rays fan and didn't want to sabotage his own planned night out…

"In Oslo we played a squat which was being torn down at 9am the very next day. All the prep work had been done for the demolition job; electrics were literally hanging out the walls and all it needed was an X-Rays gig to bring the place down. The room we were in was rammed, with sweat literally pouring down the walls and down in front was the biggest skinhead I've ever seen who kept dousing us with water. We weren't quite sure what he was doing, but death by electricity seemed to be part of the plan – so, at the end of the set, I confronted him. It transpired he was actually trying to help us; he thought we looked really hot and wanted to cool us down…"

However, as fun as it undoubtedly was, the European tour was the end of that X-Rays line-up, Steve deciding he was burnt out by the relentless pace. The band went on hiatus for six months and then reconvened where they left off, banging out a succession of further 7-inchs during 1998.

"We basically just needed a break," reckons Coop, "Steve more than any of us. We played one last gig at the Wheatsheaf in Nottingham a week after our return from Europe and didn't regroup again until Feb '98. Then we attempted it without Steve, taking on a young drummer from Leicester called Charger in his place. A year later and we figured we'd try things as a five-piece as well, taking on another guitar player, Steve Majors, also from Leicester. We've no regrets, of course, but unfortunately things were never quite the same after Steve left…

"But the 7-inch single is by far the best format," he adds. "So many albums would be so much better if bands had just condensed the contents down to the best couple of tracks and stuck them on a 7-inch single, don't you think?

"One of our favourites of our own has to be 'Grease Monkey Go', which was recorded at Egg Studios, Seattle, with Conrad Uno. We had limited time to do it, as Mr Uno had a game of golf planned for the afternoon of the session and much to his horror we turned up hammered and barely coherent…although, luckily for him, those were the times the X-Rays were typically on their best form! A special mention should probably go to 'Set 'Em Up' as well, purely for the flip-side, 'Erotic Neurotic'. We were asked to record a Saints cover for a Japanese compilation, so I got to record one of my favourite songs by one of my favourite bands…and it just seemed too good to limit it to a Japanese comp."

A third album, 'Going Postal', was released in 1999, with Charger behind the kit ("It didn't really turn out how we wanted it to," admits Coop. "We used a different producer and engineer, which seemed like a good idea at the time, but we should probably have stuck with what we knew…"), before the X-Rays called it a day once and for all, playing their last ever show in support of the New Bomb Turks during September 2002, going full circle and ending as they began, as a three-piece with Steve Charlesworth back on drums.

"Everyone has kept their hand in playing locally and often still together, since," concludes Coop. "Currently me, Gaz and G-Man have a new band on the go called Jameson Shots, which is back to the basic X-Rays style. And Steve is playing in both Geriatric Unit and Endless Grinning Skulls, back to *his* hardcore roots.

"Me and Gaz previously played in Six Killer and me and Steve in God's Chosen Dealers; Steve and G-Man also played together in Metal Gear Solid Madonnas and Mod Fuck Explosion, all of whom had varying levels of success and got out touring at some time or another. Gaz was also the original singer in the Hip Priests.

"We [the X-Rays] were the only band this side of the Atlantic doing that kind of thing at that time. I'd certainly like to think we were an inspiration and influence for bands of that ilk over here who – until then – saw that style as predominantly American-led and I certainly hear our influence in other European bands even today. As is usual, though, we always seemed to have more of an impact overseas than on these shores, but as long as I've left *something* behind to be remembered by, bang on…"

SELECT DISCOGRAPHY:

7-inch:

'Booze & Speed' (Lowlife, 1994)

'Two Ways To Play It Smart In The Sun!' (Get Hip, 1994)

'Wizzin' In The Go-Go!' (Dig The Fuzz, 1995)

'Set 'Em Up' (Dig The Fuzz, 1995)

'PCP' (Dig The Fuzz, 1996)

'Grown Up Drunk' (Ken Rock, 1997)

'Crawling Back To Vegas' (Savage, 1997)

'Snake River Leap' (Sonic Swirl, 1998)

'Fireball #551' (Blue Silver, 1998)

'Whores Are Cool' (Saddle Tramp, 1998)

LPs:

'Speed Kills' (Lowlife/Empty, 1995)

'Double Godzilla With Cheese' (Empty Records, 1996)

'Going Postal' (Saddle Tramp, 1999)

AT A GLANCE:

'Booze & Speed: The 7-inch Singles Collection', a 25-track CD released by Sonic Dirt in 2008, compiles all 11 X-Ray singles onto one disc.

NERVES

Leicester's **Nerves** must surely figure highly on UKHC's extensive list of under-achievers that never realised their full potential. But despite only being together two years and with but two dozen gigs and two pieces of 7-inch plastic to their names, they're still remembered fondly by all that witnessed them in full frantic flight.

The band came together in August 1993, with Tim Brooks (previously of Cornish bands Five Minute Fashion and Totenhaus) on guitar, Iain Blakely on bass, Stu 'WWF' McPherson on drums and Lee 'Misfits' Holford on vocals, all citing the powerful garage-punk of Ohio's New Bomb Turks as a major influence.

"There's really only a few Leicester folk that still call me 'Misfits' these days," laughs Lee, "but basically I was obsessed with that band from about '83 to the early Nineties; I collected all their rare singles and colour vinyl, every leather jacket I ever owned had their logo across the back and I even had the 'devilock' fringe, or the 'Danzig do' hair… It went from the long black 'V' pointed fringe to covering half my face like during his Samhain period – I couldn't see a fucking thing for years! In actual fact, a Leicester punk called Curly had 'the fringe' before me…he used to have to lift it up to light his cigarette!

"I remember a writer, Paul May [of *Problem Child* zine] saying that the only two people he knew who were *that* mad on the Misfits was John March [from Concrete Sox and Heresy], who was into them way before I was and me…and that was about 1984!"

"Looking back now, using a bit of hindsight, the New Bomb Turks seem like just another garage band," adds Tim, of those early influences, "but at the time of all that crappy metallic straightedge and emo they were a bolt out of the blue…fast as shit but with the snot and snarl of the old Killed By Death bands. I saw them play Nottingham and they killed it and when their album came out both me and Lee used it as a reference point. We were/are both super nerds and were really into old UK stuff from the anarcho scene right through to stuff like the Abrasive Wheels, as well as bands like the Big Boys, Dicks, Negative Approach, Antidote, Necros, CIA etc. I think we actually ended up sounding more like a mix of that lot than the New Bomb Turks, to be honest…

"There wasn't really a local 'punk' scene any more, by the time we started; the old bands were gone and, like I said already, most of the new bands were either straightedge or emo – apart from Sarcasm. It didn't really matter, though, as Leicester's position in the middle of the country meant that a lot of bands came through and we were just down the road from Nottingham anyway."

Nerves' first gig was November that year, with Slumgang and various local bands, a 'youth against racism' gig at the Princess Charlotte and things took off quite quickly for the band from there…a month later they were back there again, but this time supporting Rancid!

"Yeah, it was their first ever UK gig," recalls Lee. "We'd had their first LP for a few months by then and loved it, so that was a great little coup. The first gig was fun as well, though; no-one knew what to expect… The crowd was mostly student and alternative types, with a few old punky mates and Slumgang thrown in. A couple of good local mates' bands played, then we went on; with no intro, we ripped into 'Mansize', where we all come in at the same time. We blasted through eight songs, including Angry Samoans and Big Boys covers, during which I was pulled over the rail at the front and had a play fight, while still singing, with our mate Jop who was dancing down the front. Twelve minutes later, it was job done."

The band spent the early part of 1994 gigging around Birmingham, Nottingham and Bradford with the likes of Substandard, Decadent Few, Kitchener, Bob Tilton and their best friends Slumgang and, in March recorded a 10-track demo which they began selling at gigs in London (with Varukers) and Newcastle (with One By One). Gigs in Nottingham with Naked Aggression and SNFU were also highlights and it wasn't long before the band were invited to record a split 7-inch with Substandard for Inflammable Material Records.

"I'd known Ed from Slumgang for two or three years by then," says Lee, "mainly from seeing him and his brother Mick at some old hardcore gigs along with some of the 'newer' (to me anyway) Notts crowd; first at a Gorilla Biscuits gig in London in 1989, then, as I went to more gigs in Notts, I saw them more and more and got to know them. I saw the band Ed was in at the time called Downfall, which was total Born Against-style hardcore; when they split, Si, the singer, formed Bob Tilton and Ed formed Slumgang with Loyd, Pug and Cleaver. I saw them just before we formed and then again when they headlined our first gig. They were just great: full-on, classy, tuneful punk rock with great snotty vocals and hints of early Social Distortion in their guitar sound.

"There was this big house where Ed and Pug from Slumgang, Jamie from Panic and Pat from Substandard all lived next door to each other, where everyone went to drink, hang out, play music and take the piss out of each other; just dole-dossing really, but we had some great laughs there. Once we were just pissing about, singing to tunes and stuff, when I picked up a plate and smashed it over my head; Ed decided he wouldn't be out-done by someone from Leicester, especially someone that didn't drink, so he picked up a shard of plate and sliced his arm open! I don't think he meant to go as deep as he did though and we were all, 'Shit, what you gonna do now, ya daft cunt?' He'd pulled open this bloody great slice nearly down to the bone in his forearm, which he then proceeded to fill *full* of table salt, convinced it would heal quicker!

"And trust me, you do not want to know about Pug and Super-Jawa. That deeply damaged all who witnessed it, believe me, but my lips are sealed. Anyway, at gigs we just used to dance to – and heckle – each other's bands all night, like you do…"

With both bands recording three songs each at Potz'n'Panz in Bradford during August '94, the split was a solid punk-rock release for all concerned and Nerves happily launched it with a gig in Leicester with their heroes, New Bomb Turks. After recording the track 'Caught Out Again' for 'The Boredom And The Bullshit' compilation 7-inch on Refusenik Records, Nerves spent the early part of '95 writing new material for their own 7-inch, '13 Styles Strike', which they recorded back at Potz'n'Panz during that August. Unfortunately they had already unknowingly played their last gig the very week before – at the Abbey Park Festival in Leicester with Panic and Slumgang – because they split soon after its release on Jamie from Panic's Delerict label when drummer Stu left the band.

"I think it was just becoming less and less fun for him toward the end," sighs Lee. "I can't state any real specific reason; he never gave much away, to be honest. But he was a really great drummer and there was no-one we knew at that time in Leicester that even came close; he just fitted in perfectly and more or less defined our style. The only other drummer I saw around that time that blew me away as much was Pete Darlo from Kitchener.

"Of course, me, Tim and Iain wanted to do a 'last gig' in Nottingham, at least, and not finish like that, having already played our last show without even realising it, but Stu just didn't want to. The biggest regret was we'd left Jamie in the shit with our second EP; it wasn't meant to happen like that, we just thought it'd be okay, we'd get rid of them all somehow. But he had no distribution, was – by his own admission – a total pisshead and had no bands playing gigs to help flog them. We gave most of ours away to people who were still writing to us from abroad about the split EP, but all in all I think me and Tim would've liked to have done something else…another EP, perhaps? Or even an album? We had the songs."

"Things had just kinda run their course," explains Tim. "I was in London, Stu was about to go to college… I think Lee was the one who most wanted it to continue, but Stu was irreplaceable; his drumming was one of the things that made the band and it wouldn't have been the same without him. Looking back, though, I wish we'd done more; we had all the time in the world, but we were poor and lazy, so got fuck all done. And I wish we'd helped Jamie sell the second 7-inch and wish we'd done a better job of the recording too. I don't think we would ever have done an LP, though…that might have been a bit ambitious for us, we were more a 7-inch band! But I do wish we had toured Europe like all our pals did…"

The '13 Style Strike' EP wasn't the best note to bow out on either; it was fast and furious, for sure, but lacked much of the raw power that had made everyone sit up and pay attention after the split with Substandard. With Tim having moved to London, Lee tried to get a new Nerves line-up together with Trogg and Iggy from Contempt, but that never got out of the starting blocks. He now resides in Newcastle, where he is trying to get another band together called Out Of Vogue.

Tim eventually moved to San Francisco, where he got married, had kids, wrote for *Maximum Rock'n'Roll*, formed Stockholm Syndrome and currently plays for Young Offenders. Meanwhile, Stu joined Steel Rules Die in the early 2000s.

"Well, the time that we were doing our thing was my favourite period since the early-to mid-Eighties," says Lee, of the Nineties scene. "It was a constant journey of discovery, hearing new bands all the time – nearly every night on John Peel, in fact; buying records, going to gigs, ordering imports on the old Small Wonder and Rough Trade lists…it was great. I'd always check out other stuff, even different genres (and still do) and always went to gigs; I never stopped buying records and never stopped doing my own thing, but that brief early-to-mid Nineties scene was just as special as the early days, as far as I'm concerned. As Keef from the [Suicidal Supermarket] Trolleys said years later, 'That was our scene; we created it'…and we were proud to be a small part of it."

"I always felt I was too late for the Eighties anarcho scene and too early for the hardcore revival," adds Tim. "But looking back, the UK had a really great little scene in the Nineties with bands like Health Hazard, Disaffect, Sedition, One By One, Suffer, Slumgang, Pigpile,

Nerves, Tim and Lee at the
Charlotte, Leicester, 1994

Nerves, Tim and Lee at the Nottingham
Old Angel, 1995

Substandard, Panic, Cowboy Killers etc, who have all stood the test of time. I had some of the best times, saw some of my favourite gigs and made some of my best friends during that period…so it can't have been all that bad!

"One last memory I want to share is that the drives to the gigs were often as much fun as actually playing them. None of the band could drive except me and we used to bring Jono so we could get pissed. Lee always sat up front 'cos it was his dad's van and would sing along to tapes at full volume while banging his knuckles on the dashboard. We would often get to gigs and his voice would be hoarse and his knuckles bloody. The journeys home were always eventful, as the van was chock-full of pissed people; we would stop at the services and trying to herd everyone back into the van would take forever as they stumbled off in all directions into the night…"

SELECT DISCOGRAPHY:

7-inch:
'Split' (Inflammable Material, 1994) – *split with Substandard*
'13 Styles Strike' (Delerict, 1996)

AT A GLANCE:
Can only suggest that you try Tim at: tb666xx@yahoo.com

APOCALYPSE BABYS

With their machine-gun bursts of bubble-gum punk rock, Mansfield's **Apocalypse Babys** were probably the closest the UK punk scene of the Nineties came to having our own Ramones. Despite releasing dozens of records and playing hundreds of gigs, they never really enjoyed the popularity they deserved and they're still soldiering on in the face of ignorant apathy even today.

"I'd been trying to put something together since I'd left school back in the early Eighties," recalls bassist/guitarist/vocalist Asterix Brat (Dave Goodwin). "Unfortunately punk rock was on the wane and all the bands we'd grown up with had either split up or were morphing into metal bands. Then all the music press like *NME* and *Sounds* stopped covering the scene completely, so you really had no clue as to what bands were up to 'cos they just ignored it! All my mates were 'growing up' or getting into other music: Metallica, Slayer, that whole thrash metal scene…certainly no-one was interested in forming a traditional punk-rock band.

"But I was desperate to start something; it seemed like forever, advertising in the local press and national music weeklies for guitarists and drummers and no-one ever got back to me. I remember buying a PA and amps and even a drum kit at one stage, just so if I found anyone

Apocalypse Babys, Kelly, Asterix, Mr Reed, 1991

Apocalypse Babys - Asterix, Kelly, Dutch, The Hippy, 1994

I'd be able to say, 'Look, no problem, we already have all the gear!' Eventually, in '87, I met Kelly [Nigel Kelly] and together with an old schoolmate, The Hippy [Craig Bunyan], we finally started rehearsing…learning to play basically…" "And we spent three years 'learning to play'," adds The Hippy. "A proper 'bedroom band', we'd try all sorts of songs – Rod Stewart, Elvis Costello – so by the time we were ready to play live we were really quite proficient. One of the first songs that lasted longer than a couple of years was 'Dance 'Til You Drop' [it would become the band's first single]. I remember coming up with the opening riff – or 'fanfare', as Asterix called it – during an early rehearsal with Kelly…"

"I can't say that it was any particular band that influenced me," ponders Asterix, on what shaped the band's sound and whether they were particularly inspired by Mansfield's big punk-rock exports of the Eighties, Riot Squad and Resistance 77. "It was just punk rock in general; that was all I ever wanted to do. And the lyrics were never a problem because I'd always written stuff from back when I was at school, so I had a whole drawer full of jotters with loads of words; it was just a case of learning to play guitar and putting the two together. All we knew was that we didn't want to deal in punk clichés; we wanted to express real feelings, not just shout 'Oi! Oi! Oi! Anarchy and chaos!'"

Nigel Reed soon took over from The Hippy (who became the band's loyal roadie) on guitar and Apocalypse Babys made their belated live debut at a bikers' bash – "in this big house in the middle of Derbyshire!" – during November 1990. "We knew nothing about it being a bikers' bash," laughs Asterix. "It was Dutch [Dave Bradford], who later became our bassist, who set it up; we were told it was a house party and the idea was we'd just show up, play a few Ramones covers and then obviously get pissed and shagged! How wrong we were and we certainly didn't expect the Derbyshire chapter of Hell's Angels to show up!

"We got to this house, set our gear up in this big living room and fucked off to the pub for some Dutch courage and when we got back there were these big fucking Triumphs and Harleys outside! The place was full of greasers; Kelly was shitting himself. Anyway, we played 'Chinese Rocks' to 'em a few times and ran off; they were all about a foot away from us, giving us plenty of grief, heckling after every song – a proper 'baptism of fire' – but it hardened us up straight away and after that we never found an audience intimidating again…"

"There was some really obscure venues early on," reckons The Hippy. "There was a club in Matlock Bath where just one person turned up. Dutch mugged three quid off him and he sat there in the middle of this dancefloor on his own, eating his fish supper while the band raced through the set. The best had to be the infamous 'Battle of Black Horse' gig in Somercotes, when we first supported the Subs; the place got completely trashed!"

"A load of skinheads came down from Heanor and started chucking their weight around," adds Asterix. "But they hadn't reckoned on all these lads from local football firms being there. These boneheads started on the wrong people – and got it back!"

Hippy: "They were ripping up chairs for weapons, we were watching it all from the stage; they were smashing all the windows from outside… There was four of 'em kicking shit out of this kid in the road 'til everyone steamed out and chased 'em off."

Asterix: "The funniest thing was, this mate of ours, Gaz, who was tripping off his fucking head, ran 10 miles back to Mansfield thinking these skinheads were chasing him; he literally never stopped all the way home! Everywhere we'd play, we'd get banned; we even used to get accused of nicking gear from the venue, but it's a bit hard to sneak a mixing desk out in your pocket…"

After not only surviving but thriving at several more biker meets ("We used to do 'Ace Of Spades' to keep 'em happy!"), Apocalypse Babys recorded the aforementioned 'Dance 'Til You Drop' single at local studio, Bandwagon (with Dave Lawrence from Slaughterhouse 5 at the desk), which they released themselves in 1992 on ATB ('Asterix The Brat') Records.

"Yeah, we did it all ourselves," says Asterix proudly. "Even saving up our giros and gig money to get 'em pressed! The recording nearly didn't happen, mind you, 'cos me and Dutch had spent the previous night in the cells, drunk and disorderly; we'd legged it from a curry house, got chased by these cop cars and tackled to the ground and bust up really bad by the Old Bill. They let us out about eight in the morning and I went straight to the studio, where we recorded and mixed it all in one day. We all knew our parts and the session went without a hitch; we never double-tracked anything, it was all first take."

The band bombarded the music press and record labels with the single, landing themselves some very positive reviews ('This band play like it's the most important thing in the world!', the *NME* gushed) and radio play from the likes of John Peel.

"I remember our producer Dave Lawrence saying, 'How the fuck did you get in that?'" laughs Asterix, "'cos Slaughterhouse 5 were signed to IRS at the time and were paying a publicist to get them in the weeklies! Anyway, it did really well for us and we thought it was only a matter of time before a major label came knocking... Ah, the naivety of youth!"

Another strong single, 'Shootin' From The Hip', was released in 1993, courtesy of Nottingham's Weird Records, but Mr Reed left soon after ("He kept wearing these fucking sandals; he never quite fitted in – he was our Glen Matlock!") making way for The Hippy to rejoin. Dutch also joined on bass, allowing Asterix to take up rhythm guitar as well as vocals, fattening the band's sound nicely for their debut album, 1995's 'Three Chords To Heaven', for Welsh label Smokin' Troll.

"By the time we were ready to do the album we had more than enough songs," remembers Asterix. "it was just a case of which ones to pick? I basically split them into two albums; one would become 'Three Chords To Heaven' and the other 'Whoops! Apocalypse Babys!' [their 1996 follow-up]."

"We were never really happy with the final product though," adds The Hippy. "We felt the production was muddy, certainly not as sharp as our early singles anyway, but there are some great songs on that album ['Inspiration' being a definite high point] and the reviews knocked us out. We got the thumbs-up from everyone, so we were a bit frustrated at the lack of major label interest..."

Asterix: "We even got a rejection letter from Feargal Sharkey who was an A&R man at the time; he said, 'Sorry lads, too dated!'" "We stopped playing 'Teenage Kicks' after that," deadpans The Hippy. "See, we didn't go along with this idea that punk should always be in the underground; we wanted to be on Sony and sell lots of records and be on *Top Of The Pops* and all that..."

"I remember the Exploited on there and how exciting that was," reasons Asterix. "I didn't want to be on some little indie label that couldn't publicise us. All the music papers were pushing this 'New Wave Of New Wave' thing, bands like Smash and These Animal Men; we saw them support the Ramones and they were fucking awful, so we thought, 'Well, if they can do it...' But Dutch used to say, 'I don't know why you're so bothered about getting signed up anyway; it'd only last about five seconds once they realised what a bunch of twats we are...' Ha!"

As well as the second LP, 1996 also saw Nigel Kelly being replaced by Darren 'Daz' Clay ("He was a great character," guffaws Asterix, "always shitting himself…") The new line-up released the 'Apocalypse Now!' EP on New Life Shark Records and the ludicrously catchy 'I Don't Wanna Be A Nazi' on French label Trisomik. All these releases were promoted with concerted DIY touring across the UK and mainland Europe.

"I remember one time going through Wales, finding this dead sheep and tying it to the bonnet," Asterix recalls some of the things the Babys would stoop to for entertainment while on the road. "We drove through the whole of Wales with this dead sheep on the front; we got lost at one point and asked this local feller for directions and he said, 'Well, boyo, you want to take this road down here…blahblahblah…' But he never once asked why there was a dead animal strapped to the bonnet!

"You do some mad things travelling – it relieves the boredom – otherwise you develop a kind of cabin fever. One time in Holland we'd thrown these sandwiches out the window and just kept going up and down the road about 20 times, flattening 'em and pissing ourselves with uncontrollable laughter…that's not normal, is it?

"We've had such fucking laughs and a lot of our rude shenanigans I can't really divulge 'cos certain ex-members would kill me if their Mrs found out, but one story is so funny I can't resist ! One band member – I won't say who, to save him the embarrassment – had a new camera and there was this girl at this gig who had loads of piercings, studs through her face, rings through her nipples, the lot…and let's just say she was very friendly! Anyway, we asked to borrow his camera and, without him knowing, took pictures of this girl's erm… intimate piercings. We never told him and a week later, unbeknownst to him, his Mrs took the film to be developed at Boots. She gets the pictures back, opens up the envelope and there are all these 6x4 pictures of this girl's twat! She broke his fucking nose when he got home that night!"

1997's 'Local Hero' EP saw the band starting to expand their musical horizons with a keyboard introduction to the song 'Jacqueline', a sonic progression that continued for the melancholic 'Nuclear Rain' (backed by a cover of Abba's 'Does Your Mother Know?') single the following year. 1998's third album, 'What Do You Think Of It So Far?', was also the band's most ambitious full-length release, even though it was recorded in the face of considerable adversity. "Yeah, we made that album through sheer bloody mindedness," agrees The Hippy. "Only a month before we were due to begin recording both Dutch and Daz left the band, leaving us with a bunch of songs that me and Asterix had been working on for the best part of a year. We didn't want to see all that hard work get pissed away, so we called Kelly up and after only three, maybe four, rehearsals we went into the studio.

"Even though Asterix has always brought the songs in, the arrangements were definitely down to both of us working together on that album; I played more on that than anything else we ever recorded. I remember bringing in an acoustic guitar to one recording session…the other two didn't seem to share my enthusiasm. I think I was asked, 'What the fuck do you think you're gonna do with that?' I also helped to engineer and mix it as well…not that I ever got any credit! I know a lot of people hate it though; it's far too eclectic for most people's taste. Rock'n'roll, punky pop…we even had a stab at Fifties-style R&B. Fuck 'em all anyway, I love it!"

Asterix: "One reviewer said at the time that we were 'reaching for something we couldn't quite grasp' and I think that was probably fair 'cos we were going for the big production, putting saxophone on tracks and such like; we started that album with this crooner, 'The Most Precious Thing', which was about as far away from punk rock as you could get, but again, in many ways, was consequently the punkest thing we could probably do. We just wanted to surprise people…"

With The Hippy and Nigel bowing out after the album's release and running low on inspiration and enthusiasm himself, Asterix had to then dig deep to keep the band going. "All the ambition had gone by 1998," he concurs, "but I still wanted to carry on, so I put a completely new line-up together almost straight away, with Rob Kershaw on drums and John Slater on guitar…actually there was two or three other guitarists that were helping us out during this period but were never permanent members: Josh, Rif and Swiss Dave.

"We put a whole new set together and hit the road; unfortunately this line-up only ever recorded the 'Full Metal Racket' EP, which *wasn't* a departure from punk, it was just a play on words. Unfortunately because of the length of John and Rob's hair at the time, a lot of people thought we'd gone 'eavy metal and John *did* eventually leave to join Blaze [Blaze Bayley of Wolfsbane and Iron Maiden's 'solo' project]. John was a bit of a guitar wizard, so he auditioned and got the job; fair play to him really, although I was pissed off at the time 'cos we'd got a tour set up and he didn't even tell us he was auditioning.

"It was weird; there we were one minute playing the Dog And Duck in Scunthorpe with Anal Deathfuck and the next minute he was in Brazil in some stadium supporting Judas Priest!" Rob stuck with the Babys, though, who also got The Hippy back in *again*, albeit this time just as a recording member, in time for the very slick, very poppy fourth album for Smokin' Troll, 'Vive Le Rock'n'Roll'. Rob was replaced in 2001 by Jools 'Ciderman' Zabody, who gave the band a much-needed jolt of energy and attitude and the Apocalypse Babys, while nowhere near as prolific as during the mid to late Nineties, are still turning out damn fine records like 2005's 'The More You Drink…' to this day.

"In all honesty I think it's shrunk to becoming a yearly trip to the seaside," ponders Asterix, commenting on the annual Rebellion festival's domination of the average modern punk's calendar. "At the turn of the millennium, it was in great shape; we were bombing up and down the M1, going from gig to gig, but over the last decade all the fans that came in with Rancid and Green Day seem to have 'grown up' or moved onto something else, because gigs are becoming fewer and fewer. Of course this may all be due to the recession…we'll see!

"I suppose you have to accept the fact that none of us are getting any younger. There are punks we know who just don't go to gigs any more; there's a lot of 'seen that, done that' attitudes in the scene, but I suppose that's only natural as well.

"Punk was pretty quiet in the Nineties, but we were still making a hell of a noise! The problem with the Nineties scene wasn't the standard of the bands, it was the lack of coverage; again, this was before the internet so advertising your shows was harder, today it can all be done online. I personally think that if we'd had the net back then, when there was still a lot of gig-going punks with energy, we could have built up something special again…the actual bands that came through in the Nineties were better musically than a lot of the Eighties bands, just from the wrong decade…"

"I've always thought that we were different from all the other bands [of that period] anyway," The Hippy reckons, "both in terms of musicianship and our actual approach to the songs. We always had quite an open attitude to what we played; we could play straight punk, singalong punky pop, sleazy rock'n'roll and the funkiness of 'Mini Mafia', all in a single night's set and then make albums that included acoustic guitars, slide guitars and synthesisers in the mix… I can't think of anyone else that did any of that, can you?"

"But I couldn't give a fuck how we're remembered," concludes Asterix defiantly. "We know who we are and what we did. We've watched 'em come and watched 'em go; we've always been outsiders, we don't fit into any of the little sub genres. Street punk, Oi!, anarcho? We've always stood alone…and with the never-ending line-up changes we've never had an identifiable image either. It certainly keeps me on my toes. I often turn round on stage and wonder, 'Who's in the band tonight?' We flew the British punk-rock flag throughout the Nineties and we never compromised. And that's why I'm totally proud of the Apocalypse Babys; 20 years is a long time sitting on the fucking wheel arch of a Transit van!"

SELECT DISCOGRAPHY:_

7-inch:
'Dance 'Til You Drop' (ATB, 1992)
'Shootin' From The Hip' (Weird, 1993)
'Apocalypse Now' (New Life Shark, 1996)
'I Don't Wanna Be A Nazi' (Trisomik, 1996)
'Local Heroes' (Underground Medicine,1997)
'Nuclear Rain' (Therapeutic,1998)
'Full Metal Racket' (FUG, 2001)

LPs:
'Three Chords To Heaven' (Smokin' Troll, 1995)
'Whoops Apocalypse Babys!' (Smokin' Troll, 1996)
'What Do You Think Of It So Far?' (Smokin' Troll, 1998)
'Viva Le Rock'n'Roll' (Smokin' Troll, 2000)
'Alcoholacaust' (Vinyl Vera, 2004)
'The More You Drink…?' (Vinyl Vera, 2005)

AT A GLANCE:
The '7-inch Plus!' CD on Nottingham label Vinyl Vera features all the Babys' single releases, 20 songs in total, and is a great introduction to the band.

FREEBASE

Northampton's **Freebase** blundered drunkenly through the UKHC scene of the late Nineties, always way more in control than they seemed to be and always pushing for scene unity – while pissing on your foot! They secured a deal with Danish label Diehard, landing themselves some high-profile European gigs in the process, released two well-received albums and then collapsed in a drunken heap, victims of their own chaotic lifestyles and the revolving-door line-up policy it encouraged.

"[Guitarist] Nick [Lovell] and [original drummer] Jason [Stephenson] were in a covers band called Murderous Intent, doing Suicidal Tendencies stuff and skate-metal songs," explains vocalist Mark Fieldhouse, of the band's musical aspirations prior to Freebase. "They were just schoolmates, playing all these covers and did one gig in a local village hall. I was never in a band before Freebase myself, but me and Nick were mates from about '85 or '86, the tail-end of our school years anyway; that's when we first started knocking around.

"I was a full-on metalhead and into Motörhead, Metallica, all the Eighties thrash stuff and Eighties rock like Kiss and Twisted Sister… Nick was into Maiden too – the first time I met him he had a 'Somewhere In Time' T-shirt on, so it *must* have been 1986 and he got into all the other stuff through that. The other guy, Jason, also liked metal, but he kept on mixing things up; he went through a metal phase, a Cure phase, a punk phase…but when Nick's cousin came over from Australia, she was a full-on punk and we started listening to all this stuff she was listening to, like Mass Appeal, the Hard-Ons, the Spunk Bubbles and we also started getting into GBH, 'cos she was mad about them too.

"I was also getting big into bands like Agnostic Front and Ludichrist through the *Friday Rock Show*… I remember hearing Ozzy Osbourne when he was a guest on there and he played Agnostic Front and the Accused and that weekend I went out and bought 'Victim In Pain'. Metallica were wearing Discharge and GBH T-shirts all the time too, so it was 'okay' for metalheads to listen to punk and the whole crossover thing was in full swing…"

Eventually Nick and Jason asked Mark to join their covers band as vocalist. With him came second guitarist Phil Standen and Jason Westray on bass and Freebase was officially born in August 1995.

"It was me and Phil that came up with the name Freebase, 'cos we used to make a joke about Billy from Biohazard," reveals Mark. "We saw them at the Marquee with Kreator and he was so intense, we were laughing that he must have been freebasing crack round the back of the drumkit. We just thought it would be a good name and we started to find our own direction after that, instead of just doing covers by the likes of Agnostic Front, Helmet, Black Flag, Cryptic Slaughter, Circle Jerks, you know…"

After playing their first local gig supporting Northampton punks Fear And Loathing, Freebase were introduced to Vince Coil, a local punk promoter who really got behind the band from then on and it was Vince who got them their second show a week later, supporting GBH at the Race Horse in Northampton.

By the time the band recorded their first four-song demo during July 1996 (featuring 'Torment', 'The Blame', 'All I Ask' and 'Respect'), Phil had left to set up his own building company, leaving the band as a four-piece; bassist Jason had left to become a father and was replaced by Pete Gordelier from Angelwitch. The demo also featured new drummer Ben.

They quickly became involved with the nascent UKHC scene of the time. "We'd had a couple of record labels come and see us," sighs Mark, "and they'd all said that the drummer was the weak link; we didn't mean to take it that seriously so early on, but we realised that Jason was holding us back, as it were."

They quickly became involved with the nascent UKHC scene of the time. "I think it was Pierre from Knuckledust who wrote to us first and asked for a copy of the tape. He was doing his newsletter, which we'd seen a flyer for when we went down to see Slapshot at the Garage. And then Lil from Household Name got in touch with us and we ended up on a bill in London and it moved quite quickly really; we didn't consciously try to get involved or anything, we just joined in.

"That gig was at the Red Eye down in Islington, one of their Sunday shows; we were the first band on...there was us and Public Disturbance, but I can't remember who else. We started playing London regularly after that and we met more and more people all the time, asking us to play all over."

The next few months saw Freebase travel extensively around the UK, playing shows with the likes of Madball, Peter And The Test Tube Babies, Ignite and English Dogs, to name but a few. Their first full UK tour was in 1998 with US hardcore veterans, Cause For Alarm, the first night being at a sold-out Camden Underworld.

Around this time, Freebase had started to venture into Europe, playing shows in France and also Belgium with Hard Resistance and they were becoming known for their chaotic live shows. Their loud, metallic, punky hardcore was usually a soundtrack for Mark's drunken mischief, the vocalist encouraging the audience to join in not only with dancing and singing but also hurling good-humoured abuse back and forth. He could sometimes be seen staggering sideways off the stage as well as diving forwards into the crowd.

"That actually only happened once, in Birmingham," he laughs, "and I fell about eight feet into a pile of puke! But it's ironic, because when we started none of us drank anything before playing – we just wanted to play as best we could – then some of the punk guys at one of the GBH gigs encouraged us to. We liked to have a good laugh and we had always been 'the boys in the pub that were doing things they shouldn't be doing over in the corner' anyway. We weren't ever not serious about the music, but it was never about trying to change the world or spreading a message; it was all about having a laugh, seeing our friends and playing with all their bands...

"After a while, Nick started to not drink so much, 'cos he had to play guitar, of course and was driving a lot of the time, but I probably went the opposite way; I over-compensated and went off the rails a little bit. We all used to drink a lot and party a lot and it's the same for anyone that does that: sometimes it's good, sometimes it's not good... But the whole essence behind the Freebase show was we wanted everyone to join in, everyone to have fun; it wasn't about perfection, it was more like the punk ethic."

Pete unfortunately couldn't keep up with the band's increasingly hectic gigging schedule and was replaced by Alex Jolly on bass and after contributing the songs '23 Years' and 'Filter' to Household Name's 1997 compilation EP 'Four Way Tie-Up' (that saw them sharing seven inches of throbbing plastic with Public Disturbance, FLS and Lockdown), Freebase also contributed to compilations on Lockjaw and Deck Cheese and had two tracks (one of them the charmingly-entitled 'Smell The Sick') included on HHN's seminal 'UKHC: A Compilation' CD.

Several labels were interested in issuing the band's first album, but when they signed

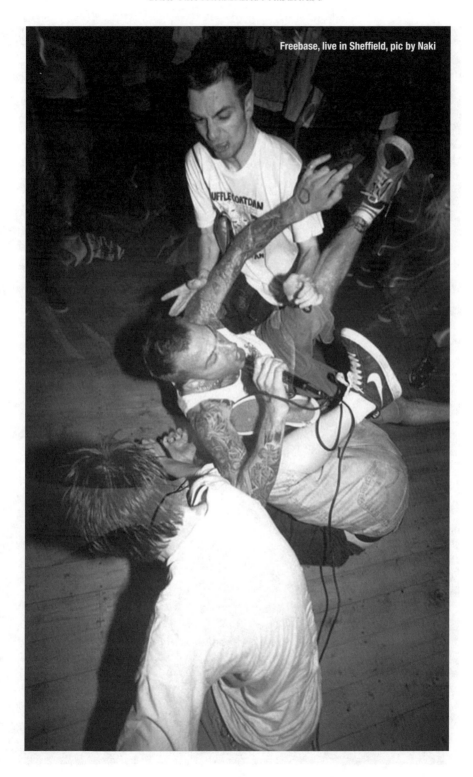

Freebase, live in Sheffield, pic by Naki

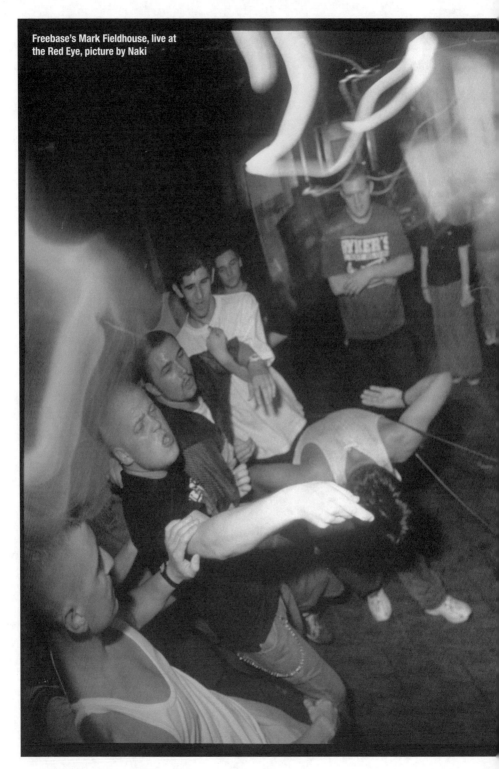

Freebase's Mark Fieldhouse, live at the Red Eye, picture by Naki

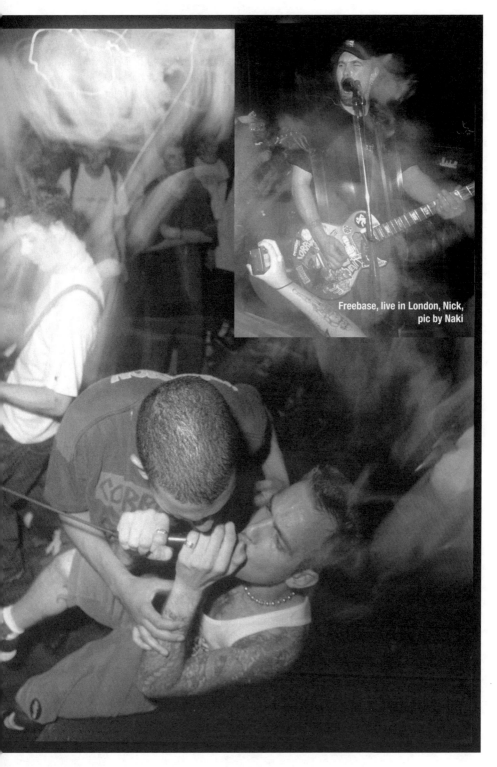

Freebase, live in London, Nick,
pic by Naki

with Danish label Diehard (*not* to be confused with the US white-power label!), Ben was the next line-up casualty. He was replaced by Dave, who lasted several tours but, unable to make the necessary commitments time-wise, was himself replaced by Molly, who played on the 'From One Extreme To Another' split MCD released by Blackfish in 1999 that paired Freebase with Medulla Nocte and the *first* recording of the band's debut album, 'Nothing To Regret'. However, in true Freebase soap opera fashion, Molly's drumming never made it to the finished release, as the band had to re-record it – with Ben back behind the kit again!

"The Diehard deal was thanks to our mates in Barcode," explains Mark. "It was another mate of mine at Earache Records, Al Dawson, who put them in touch with me and we sorted them out a few gigs in the UK…which didn't go too well for them, because their record label billed them as an 'anti-SXE band'! They were just regular guys like us, though, who wanted to have a laugh, they weren't interested in politics…but that's another story, it was just something lost in translation. Anyway, they really liked us and they really liked Knuckledust so they went back home and told Diehard about us. We had four other labels interested in us at that point, but we built a decent relationship with Diehard and they seemed the right ones to go with; they were the ones that would always ring back if we left a message…they were very open, very honest, same as we were, so we got on well.

"We went to Denmark for three weeks, to a studio owned by Anders Lundemark from [Danish death/thrash-metal band] Konkhra, so we were well looked after and – inevitably! – we got severely fucked up. We basically spent three weeks on the piss! The engineer had told me as soon as we got there that our drummer wasn't up to scratch, so there was a bit of friction within the band and the end result was that Alex and Molly went home early and left me and Nick to finish it…

"Then it was sent away to be mixed and about a week later I got a call from the label manager saying, 'Uh, sorry, it's not that good!' And I had to agree we had a problem, 'cos I'd had a week to listen to it as well. So he said, 'What do you want to do?' and I asked if we could use it as pre-production? He said, 'That's a fucking expensive pre-production!'

"But he gave us the benefit of the doubt and we booked in with Dave Chang and got Ben back in on drums and re-recorded the album. So, you can see, it was always pretty hit and miss and there was a lot of booze and a lot of drugs around; looking back, we should probably have taken a break at that point, but we didn't… We'd built up a bit of momentum that we didn't want to lose. We'd concentrated on the live shows and concentrated on recording all those splits, concentrated on doing lots of merchandise, but we hadn't *really* concentrated on doing a full album. In essence I would have liked to have taken a bit of time off before we re-recorded it, to do the songs justice…"

Regardless of Mark's mixed feelings about 'Nothing To Regret', it was a fine debut by most standards, its heavy grooves very reminiscent of Cro-Mags or Biohazard and it saw the band undertaking yet more UK gigs with the likes of Cause For Alarm, Stampin' Ground, Assert and Tribute To Nothing. Not to mention a European tour with Hard Resistance and Backfire! and a stint around Scandinavia with Barcode.

"Most of the bands were thoroughly professional compared to us and we were the party boys they had to put up with," chuckles Mark. "I remember Scott, the Stampin' Ground guitarist, saying, 'There's fucking empty tins of beer everywhere we go on this tour!' And that was the Freebase way really…we got things done, but there was always beer involved: lots of beer and partying."

Of course, the compilation appearances continued unabated and it wouldn't have been Freebase without several more line-up changes. Alex left and the band was back to Mark and Nick yet again, the intrepid duo this time recruiting Liam Durrant from Violation ("He liked beer and metal and was a bit of a naughty boy like us!") on bass and Paul 'Smoka' from Nottingham's Third Stone on drums, in time to record the second – definitive – album, 'My Life, My Rules'. Recorded in Denmark again, this time by Tue Madsen, who did a sterling job and has since become a 'go to' producer in the metalcore genre, the album took all the slamming grooves of the first album and ruthlessly refined and honed the band's attack. Unsurprisingly it garnered great reviews across the board and Freebase looked set to make waves on the international hardcore circuit.

"We were recording the second album when 9/11 [September 2001] went down," remembers Mark. "I was sat watching TV with Jay from Barcode and I said, 'What movie is this?' And he said, 'It's not a fucking movie, it's the news!' And we were just speechless, it really sobered us up quickly; we were both like, 'Fuck! This could be the start of World War III!'

"Two crates of beer a day!" adds Mark, laughing, when asked to describe the progression made between albums. "No, seriously, the second LP was more about the songwriting. I don't think I found my true vocal style until we recorded the second LP either. The first one had some good songs on it, but we didn't capture how powerful they were live. Paul was also the best drummer we'd ever had and Liam was a strong bassist, so it was a good line-up and that was easily our best release. We were way more focused in our approach; I was desperate to make an album I was really happy with."

Things didn't go quite according to plan though (surprise!), as Mark admits that he and Liam were out of control and friction levels within the band's ranks rose to critical levels and Mark effectively walked away from Freebase – but not for long.

"I'd just had enough and was talking to my mates in Dearly Beheaded about doing a new band at that point. I had basically quit, but me and Liam started jamming with a couple of other guys, Jay, the guitarist from Defenestration and his brother Dave and then we picked Freebase back up – but without Nick.

"Mine and Nick's friendship was struggling by then; he was fed up with me drinking so much…and me and Liam *were* being complete arseholes, to be honest. I'm not saying Nick was perfect, though; we were all contributing to the situation in different ways. But we were all tired and pissed all the time.

"Anyway, we toured with Skinlab, then with Labrat; we went to Malta with that line-up and played the European Hardcore Party [in Maastricht] a second time. We were still doing quite a bit and the fun was starting to come back as well, but it wasn't really what the other guys wanted to do, despite it being a great laugh and I wanted to write some more music and record again. So that's when I started talking to Foz from Set Against, who I knew were about to split up themselves; Fozzy, Simon and Sean [*all* from Set Against] joined and Liam moved to guitar, so we had two guitarists again and that was a real good line-up. But that only lasted one 10-date tour of the UK, before I kicked Sean out because…well, we were having problems and I was a bit short-tempered by that time. It was all very volatile, but that was what made it Freebase."

Paul from Northern Ireland's Dissent replaced Sean on guitar and the band continued for another year, even starting to write material for a third album, but when Mark got married in 2003 he took a long, hard look at his behaviour, lifestyle and health ("I was acting like an arsehole at that point, I know that now; I wasn't the most reliable of people…") and decided enough was enough. He needed to take a real break from Freebase. The break lasted almost 10 years, but now, at the time of writing, Mark and Nick have finally settled their differences and Mark and Nick have finally settled their differences and reformed Freebase, alongside ex-members of Stampin' Ground and Assert, to record a brand new 7-inch and play some of 2012's summer metal festivals.

"Hopefully we held our own among the UK and European hardcore scenes," he offers, "and I like to think we helped spearhead the UKHC scene alongside Stampin' Ground and Knuckledust. We did it without being scene police, with a view to being positive and uniting the scene. We used to be backstage with Stampin' Ground and those guys would be doing warm-up stretches and we'd be doing lines of coke! We were very different people, but we were mates as well and that was what it was all about for us.

"I read a blog the other day by Dig from Earache, and he pointed out that Freebase were never your typical narrow-minded hardcore guys…and I'm more than happy to be remembered like that. A lot of bands talk about scene unity, but that's what it really was all about for us."

SELECT DISCOGRAPHY:

7-inch:
'4-Way Tie-Up' (Household Name, 1997) – *split with Public Disturbance, FLS and Lockdown*
'From The Basement' (Dry Heave, 2012)

MCD:
'From One Extreme To Another' (Blackfish, 1999) – *split with Medulla Nocte*

LPs:
'Nothing To Regret' (Diehard, 1999)
'My Life, My Rules' (Diehard, 2001)
'Escalating Unholy War' (Unity Worldwide, 2002) – *split with Eviscerate AD, Set Against and Diction*

AT A GLANCE:
'My Life, My Rules' is still available on CD, so what are you waiting for?

DISGUST

There have been many Discore, or D-beat if you prefer, bands since Discharge wiped the punk-rock slate clean in the early Eighties by boiling the musical equation down to three chords, four lines of lyrics, a thumping fast drumbeat and an insane level of aggression. And who can blame people for trying to capture that magical intensity all over again? 'Trying' being the operative word here, though, as most manage to recreate the *musical* formulae but fail when it comes to that devastating rawness and attitude.

Let's face it, *very* few have even come close to the untamed vibe of the 'Decontrol' 7-inch or the 'Why?' 12-inch and most of those that have are from Sweden, but – against the odds – the UK's own **Disgust** remain about as good as it gets when it comes to pure Discore. Much of which might be attributable to them having one Dave Ellesmere on guitar, who was actually the drummer for Discharge when they committed the seminal 'Why?' record to tape in 1981.

"It all came about during the time I was working at Plastic Head Distribution [in Wallingford] and was a reaction to the latest Discharge release of the time, 'Massacre Divine'," he explains. "Me and Steve [Beatty, the owner of PHD] felt it was such a big disappointment to both the legacy and the fans of Discharge that we decided to put together our own D-beat band to right the wrongs…basically, 'Let's do a band and do the Discharge style the way it *should* be done!' Raw and with the fearsome brutality that was clearly missing on 'Massacre Divine'.

"I was a big fan of Discharge before I joined them and I was a big fan of the band after I left, but that album, with all the slap funk bass and squealing vocals was an embarrassment… and a song called 'Sexplosion'? We were horrified at what they were doing and knew *we* had to do something. As far as adding anything to the classic Discharge sound, though, that's pretty much a strict template that you don't want to mess with. You could say we were more a tribute to the Discharge that wrote 'Decontrol' and 'Hear Nothing, See Nothing, Say Nothing'…"

As well as Steve, who had previously drummed for Mass and Stone The Crowz, on vocals and Dave on guitar, the very first line-up of Disgust also comprised Lee Barrett, another PHD employee, on bass and Andy Baker from the Varukers and Sacrilege on drums. However Andy left after just a few rehearsals, so Steve switched to drums and Barney Greenway from Napalm Death came on board to do the vocals.

A second guitarist was recruited in the shape of Gary Sumner, formerly of Blitzkrieg, the Insane and Blitz, cementing what can only be described as a 'hardcore all-stars' line-up it was no wonder Earache were interested in signing the band before they'd even done a gig! But things didn't work out with Barney on vocals, so he was replaced by Dean Jones, from Extreme Noise Terror, who fronted what would briefly become the classic line-up of Disgust for the 'Brutality Of War' album.

Recorded at Glass Trap Studios by Graeme Tollit and produced by Steve Beatty, 'Brutality Of War' was released by Earache during November 1993 and was basically the Discharge album everyone had been waiting for since 1982, all slavering simplicity and uncompromisingly fast, noisy punk rock. Granted, it was just as generic as all the other Discore clones out there, but at least it was done with passion and precision and apart from Gothenburg's Anti-Cimex no-one had quite nailed the Discharge sound as savagely as this.

"The atmosphere was amazing when we were doing the record," says Steve. "It felt like we were making a proper angry-as-fuck punk record; it felt really good and we were all up for it. When Dean was doing the vocals, he was *really* going for it, all the veins raised on his neck; he looked really serious and I was just sat there thinking that we were doing the best thing ever and finally I was in a band that I really believed in…"

The bleak Discharge aesthetic was also maintained in the lyrics, all of which stuck rigidly to the anti-war theme and the minimalist three-sentence format of Discharge vocalist Cal Morris, and the stark black-and-white artwork, unflinchingly depicting the disturbing aftermath of conflict. Whether you dismiss the band as mere copycats or not, there's no denying the furious primal power of tracks like 'An Horrific End' and 'The Light Of Death'.

The album garnered great reviews across the board and the band played their first gig at the London Garage with Optimum Wound Profile. "We were pretty awful, to be fair," laughs Dave. "Because the album was virtually made up in the studio, we had to rehearse with a CD player in the practice room, listening back to the tracks and then trying to repeat what we'd just heard, which took longer – much longer – than the actual recording of the record itself. The one redeeming factor of that gig is the video that's now all over YouTube!

"It was spontaneous in the fact that we all had some experience with other bands, so we didn't rehearse that much," he adds, on what made the early chemistry of the band so special. "And with the band members being spread out across the UK it was difficult for us all to come together on a regular basis. The rehearsals were more or less just us laying out some ideas before we went into the studio; in fact 90% of the album was written in the studio over one weekend and, even in hindsight, I think we created a classic of the D-beat genre that still sounds powerful today."

"We rehearsed so little, I used to have the song structures scribbled down on a piece of paper by my snare drum when we played live," laughs Steve. "Stuff like ''Thrown Into Oblivion' starts with four thuds on the floor tom!' And once the songs had started, the rest was pretty easy, seeing as it was the same beat the whole way through…"

May 1994 saw the band joining the massive 'Festivals Of Hate' European tour, bizarrely – for such a defiantly *punk* band – supporting popular death-metal acts Samael, Cannibal Corpse and Morbid Angel. Eight tracks recorded live at Huxley's Neue Welt in Berlin were released the following year by German label Lost And Found as a white vinyl 7-inch and MCD entitled 'Thrown Into Oblivion'.

"Yeah, it was a bit weird because we were the opening act on a blatantly metal festival," agrees Dave. "The other bands on the tour didn't really know what to make of us but, by the end of it, most of them were praising us for how much we'd improved each night and Chris from Cannibal Corpse even jumped up one night to sing with us!"

"Dave Vincent from Morbid Angel totally hated us, though," adds Steve, "after we wrote 'Morbid Angel are shit' in felt-tip pen in their dressing room in big letters; we only did it for a laugh, but he took it really badly. 'Disgust? I'm disgusted,' was what he actually said. No sense of humour and all Satan worship and living with your mum and twiddling guitars into the wee hours, no doubt. In the morning he kinda acted all hard and said, 'Which one of you monkeys did this then?' And Dave got right in his face and said, 'I fuckin' did!' And he really backed off…but I think a fight between Disgust and Morbid Angel would have been great, what with us all being peace-loving anti-war types…"

Unfortunately, after the success of the first album, it would take several more years for

Disgust

a follow-up release, during which time it was all change in the Disgust camp, the band swapping labels from Earache to Nuclear Blast, with Kniell Brown and Würzel – from Motörhead! – replacing Dave and Gary on guitars.

"In short, there were two camps in the band," explains Steve: "Dean and Lee [Lee later joined Dean in ENT] on one side and Dave, Gary and myself on the other. We really wanted to do things with the band, but Dean and Lee had their own agendas. Gary got pissed off with the whole thing in the end, as did the rest of us and just walked away from it…"

"And I knew Würzel through my day job at Plastic Head, so when Gary left I asked if he was interested in joining…sadly I then left, before any rehearsals even got underway, to live and work in Holland."

"Which opened the door for Kniell, who was a friend of Lee's from High Wycombe," continues Steve. "He could play the songs so he was in! But working with Earache was a bad experience and by the end of it they wanted rid of us as much as we wanted rid of them, so I guess it worked out best for all concerned. I knew the guys at Nuclear Blast and they wanted to do a record, so we did…and they did a great job. They were really good to work with, hence their position as the world's premier metal label these days."

The band's second album, 'A World Of No Beauty', was released by Nuclear Blast in early 1997. Recorded by respected metal producer Andy Sneap at the Square Centre Studios, Nottingham, it took the raging Discore of the first full length to new heights of lethal execution and metallic fury. It even had a full colour cover, something that was tantamount to complete sacrilege in the D-beat scene of the time, in what seemed a bid to take the genre to a fresh new place.

"I think we were more focused on that second record," reckons Steve, "as we did rehearse and work on the songs a lot more and by that time we kinda really knew where we were at with it. Andy Sneap was always going to make it sound massive and metal, of course and it does, although I now think the songs are just a verse too long and, to be honest, I much prefer the first album. Without Dave in the band, who was our link to old-school Discharge, it wasn't really Disgust anyway. I remember the whole process of doing the second album and sadly it was an even more unpleasant atmosphere than the first – apart from Würzel, who was great to be around. I couldn't help thinking to myself, 'I'm in the studio with an ex-Motörhead member doing a Discore band!' A little odd, to say the least…"

Unfortunately Disgust never played live again and split as soon as the album was released. "We did absolutely *nothing* to promote that record," admits Steve. "By the end of it, Lee and I had had enough of each other…again. The intention was always to just do the album and pack it in; Würzel was in no state to tour anyway and by the end of that record I didn't want anything to do with it any more either. In fact I made a decision there and then never to play drums again, took up the bass and went on to form October File…"

"After the explosion of egos, I'd had enough of playing in bands as well," adds Dave, "and decided to go it alone as an electronic artist. Years later and with more than 30 solo releases on major techno labels from around the world to my name, I don't regret it one bit!"

However, that wasn't the last the world had heard of Disgust, although the Disgust that briefly reared its head in 2002 had very little to do with the original incarnation of the band. Lee Barratt basically recruited a whole new line-up (guitarists Ian and Carlos, drummer Mick and vocalist Joey) and recorded an ultra-fast 16-track album, 'The Horror Of It All', for Crimes Against Humanity Records, at Birmingham's Necrodeath Studios.

"Lee just did it out of spite 'cos I said I was going to do a new record without him," explains Steve. "As far as the original band is concerned, though, that record is an awful legacy born out of our dislike for each other…which pretty much sums us up, sadly!"

Although not as bad as Steve's claiming, 'The Horror Of It All' certainly lacks all the spark of 'Brutality Of War'; it ticks all the right boxes musically, but never quite engages the listener emotionally. "Because it's *not* a Disgust record!" stresses Dave. "It just has our name on the cover…"

The Lee-driven reunion was short-lived, though, and Disgust are now just a memory, albeit still revered in Discore circles for creating one of the best 'Discharge worship' albums ever.

"I would like to hope people thought the albums were good," concludes Steve, who before forming the aforementioned October File played in Brainless with Dave and Wayne Crippen. "I think they are anyway and I like Discharge a lot, so as long as it stands up as being up there with the good records of that genre I'm more than happy…"

"Yeah, we made a record which we were proud of and if other people liked it then even better," offers Dave. "We had really great reviews for the first album in all the relevant press and a feature in the *NME* with a 5/5 review for the album and it's still talked about today as being a classic of the genre. The fact that Max [Sepultura] and Machine Head [on one of their *Kerrang!* covers, no less] wore our shirts for several photo shoots is testament to the fact we made a worthwhile contribution too."

"But Disgust is doing nothing now and will never re-form," states Steve with convincing finality. "Not with me in the band anyway and Dave and I won't do anything unless it involved the both of us…but it's a solid *never ever* from me, I'm afraid. Besides I'm more than busy enough with October File these days and Dave is a very successful techno DJ. Perhaps he'll do a remix album!"

Dave laughs this idea off before asking, "Why re-form when you can do something better and more innovative? Our intention was never to drag it out…"

SELECT DISCOGRAPHY:

7-inch:
'Thrown Into Oblivion' (Lost And Found, 1994)

LPs:
'Brutality Of War' (Earache, 1993)
'A World Of No Beauty' (Nuclear Blast, 1997)
'The Horror Of It All' (Crimes Against Humanity, 2002)

AT A GLANCE:
Metal Mind recently re-released the second album with bonus tracks courtesy of the live Lost And Found release.

CHAPTER FOUR: WEST MIDLANDS

ASSERT

It's safe to say that Telford's **Assert** have always polarised opinion; they are the classic 'Marmite band' you either love or hate. And motormouth front-man Steve 'Britt' Brittain was quite capable of violently swinging the balance one way or the other on any given day of the week, depending upon how confrontational or mischievous he was feeling. But regardless of what light you regard them in, there's no denying they have an intelligent message they've worked damn hard at getting across and some of their records are absolute belters.

The band formed in 1994 and, as well as Britt, the first line-up comprised guitarist Ryan Evans and bassist Johnny 'Sinister' Siviter, who played together in Arrogance and drummer Frank Pendlebury, who had previously kept a relentless pace for Intense Degree.

"There were all sorts of influences at work," reckons Britt. "I have always been into bands such as the Newtown Neurotics, Discharge, the Exploited and Crass, as well as left-wing outfits such as the Redskins and Billy Bragg. Frank was into Black Flag, Heresy, Siege and Slayer, while Ryan and John favoured Sepultura and some thrash metal. It was a real eclectic mix, all thrown in and stirred around.

"Social (and) political lyrics have been a major influence on my own lyrical output and I consider myself a congruent person in so much as I will walk it the way that I talk it; I lead from the front whereas a lot of people in any 'scene' like the sound of their own voice, but are really only in it for the money and the kudos. Bands sing about certain subjects that adhere to a basic hardcore punk ethic, but they certainly don't live their lives that way; a bit more honesty would be more acceptable instead of the usual boring, predictable soundbites.

"Say if two bands go on tour; one gets £1000 a night, the other £100...both have been going for, let's say, 15 years, yet the former talks about 'keeping the scene alive' and the latter picks up their hundred a night and just go about their business. The former charges £10 for a CD and £12 for a shirt, the latter charges a fiver for a CD and £7 for a shirt, or both for a tenner... Which out of those bands adheres to the real ethics of punk and which band are really just professional musicians looking to clear their tax bill and make some money? In their own way maybe they are keeping something alive and some legendary names *can* show the youngsters what it's all about, but they get a decent pay-day for it.

"I don't begrudge anybody anything, but when they start pretending to uphold some ethical values, but it's only in words, I lose all respect; integrity and honesty can never, ever be purchased and liars will always get exposed for who they really are. I state this without jealousy or malice, I really do and I don't think they are *all* fakes and liars; it's a tough business and it's only my opinion, some of the old bands are still legends. And who the fuck cares what I say anyway?

"I can't really remember an early-Nineties Telford punk scene though," he adds, of the scene – or lack thereof – that spawned them. "There were still one or two people around who got a bit upset when we started to organise packed-out pub nights, because it just exposed their lack of competence and support. I always had the drive and determination to create some good nights and we never set out to be stuck in one camp anyway; there were no great numbers of studded jackets and mohawks turning up to our gigs – just ordinary people who had heard by word of mouth that we were worth checking out.

"We did inspire one or two bands from surrounding areas to get off their arses, but, in the end, I think they were looking for the fast track route to the *Kerrang!* magazine cover. For some reason, many bands had the idea that they were lacking authenticity unless featured in the music press on a regular basis.

"There *was* a late Seventies/Eighties Telford punk scene, though, around the 'Guttersnipe' crew of promoters and they put on some fantastic bands such as Angelic Upstarts, the Specials, Dexys [Midnight Runners], the Boomtown Rats and so on. Those people and bands were a major influence on both my life and that of my closest friend Matty, who ended up moving to London and forming the Blaggers. I didn't want Assert to become local heroes; I just wanted to help out bands from outside the area who had helped us get gigs and to acquire some funds for studio time."

After making their live debut, opening for Kuru in Stoke Newington, Assert began gigging in earnest, but Frank was soon replaced behind the kit by Shane 'Spen' Spencer from Hostile and it was this line-up that recorded the 'Assert Yourself' 7-inch at Mad Hat Studios in Walsall with Mark Stuart, which Britt self-released on his Hideous Eye label in 1997. Although the single could have been better produced, it served its purpose and gave the band the perfect excuse – as if they actually needed one– to take their aggressive and unpredictable live performance all over the UK.

"Yes, it was rough around the edges and yes, we could have mixed it better, but so fucking what?" spits Britt. "To me the lyrics, the message, always come first. Hindsight is a wonderful thing, but if we make no mistakes in life we learn nothing. It's okay for us to have made those mistakes anyway, because we never wanted to be perfect; we never wanted a perfect record, because we were raw, imperfect people and inexperienced and naive as far as that process was concerned, which reflected who we were.

"Looking back I should have realised that it was not the early Eighties, it was the late Nineties and the industry and consumers of punk/hardcore were being manipulated into thinking that records needed to have some sort of 'perfect' production. In the press it got mixed reviews, although, even now, people still tell me how much they liked it; I'm indifferent, to be honest, it was a goal which we achieved, then we moved on. You have to realise that we were loners to a certain extent, so didn't have people around us, to guide us and offer us advice; more likely people were watching and waiting for us to 'fail' in some way. In their eyes we 'failed' by putting out a rough 7-inch; in my eyes, we set out our stall: DIY ethics in action and a 'fuck you' attitude, which we have never lost…"

'Assert Yourself' brought the band in contact with Lil and Kafren who ran London label

Assert in Lille

Assert, Ryan and Britt,
Camden Underworld

Assert, Britt and Frank

Household Name, who were from an anarcho-punk background and loved any band that challenged both scene conventions and society's preconceptions. They released the 'More Than A Witness' album in 1998 and the 'Thumb And Four Fingers Fold To A Fist' EP in 1999. Both strong releases lyrically and musically, Assert promoted them the only way they could/ would – by playing anywhere and everywhere that would have them, tearing up and revising the rule book as they went along.

"We were driven by a whole number of things," exclaims Britt. "To get a message across, get in people's faces, to have a laugh, strip naked, be free, to entertain, to piss people off, make them smile, make them scowl, make them walk out… We did it all and so much more; no script, no mimicry of other bands, just a raw expression of who we were. I never knew what I would do each night and the band never knew what I would do either; some people even turned up just for the excitement of not knowing what would happen next. There were no rules, no dress codes and everyone was invited. I started to get a reputation as unpredictable and dangerous, because in reality I suppose I was; others badly wanted that reputation and were probably a bit jealous, but it would never have been who they really were.

"The thing is, I never needed justification from some kid who put out a zine in Leeds or organised all-dayers in Middlesbrough; the self-appointed 'leaders' meant nothing to me. I just did what the fuck I wanted when that mood or idea hit me; it never dawned on me that I had to ask permission from some committee of scenesters or anything. The more people moaned and complained, the worse I got, the more I would take the piss and the more John would put on a dress then cut a hole in it so his arse hung out and Spen would strip off. Other bands just wanted to be Earth Crisis and wear Nike clothes. Even the thought of it makes me yawn; we were embroiled in all sorts of incidents, fights, people shutting off the power… rumours and ridicule wherever we went. It was good fun."

After a multitude of compilation appearances and a second album for Household Name (2000's 'Left Opposition'), Johnny Sinister left the band and was replaced by Adders on bass and drummer Spen was replaced by Chris Burleigh, who proved to be a force of nature behind the kit despite his tender years and added some incredible dynamics to the band's sound and live performances. Gigs continued unabated and Caerphilly label Three Days Dead released the well-received 'Insurrection Rocks' CD album in 2001, with special guest vocals on 'Agitate, Educate' coming from none other than Napalm Death's Barney Greenway. After many forays north of the border, an alliance with Edinburgh's Swellbellys had been forged that was consummated with the 'United Front' split EP on Leven (Fife) label Intimidation in 2001.

"We played in Glasgow so often, they started calling us 'Glasgow hardcore'!" chuckles Britt. "We toured the north and south of Ireland a few times before bands started going over on a regular basis too; we would play anywhere, any time, while others just played 'safe' all-dayers, where they were guaranteed to be liked and told that they were legends. Existing in a nice, safe comfort zone was never for me and, in reality, it shows the fear some of those bands had. *We* were fucking fearless; we would step into environments where they hated us before we even arrived, even though they had never met us or knew anything about us. They had been told that Assert were not representative of 'their' scene and, to be part of 'their' scene, Assert needed to be ostracised and isolated; that was a lot of pressure for those insecure little boys – who by now would have regretted asking us to play – to have coped with. We just played up to it, although, in hindsight, we began to distrust everyone and

I started to be a twat; my view was that you are with us or against us.

"I could get people's backs up very easily and we stopped getting invited to the party, but did this stop us? Did it fuck! I even had the classic, 'You will never play in this town again,' directed toward me; we still played in many towns on a regular basis and would often turn up to hear that all the local bands had dropped out. Self-preservation on their part, I suppose; they needed the scene more than we ever did. Too many rules and too many regulations, just like a corporation in a different guise and the same old names kept slagging us off, trying to impose their rules and gain control; we always came back better and stronger. What superb fuel they were giving me; we turned all the moaning and criticism into a source of energy and just carried on doing our own thing.

"The overly critical tell us more about their fears and insecurities than they realise; the more records we released, the more tours we did, the more press we got, the more 'critics' crawled from under their stones displaying their insecurities and jealousy. Every time we toured with a 'name' band or released another album, it was a success; when people looked at us (the critics often had their own bands) and our 'success', they just saw a reflection of their own perceived failure. They wanted to be safe in their 'all-dayer' comfort zones, where all their friends shared that same space in that small, safe world, scared to expand and grow.

"If we *were* part of a national scene, then we outgrew it very quickly because we needed to do so and had the bravery to do it. Assert had a good, small but loyal following everywhere from Canterbury to Newcastle, Birmingham to Darlington, Limerick to Belfast. We were very lucky to be associated with HHN Records and have an agent who got us some great tours and that created envy and jealousy. We always got on really well with touring bands and they seemed to rate us highly as people and performers; I'm very appreciative of the fact we had those opportunities, but we worked very fucking hard for it and were often totally exhausted. Critics could say we were lucky, but guess what? The harder we worked, the 'luckier' we got.

"I know that there will be bands interviewed for this book who will state that they should have broken away from the scene and signed on the dotted line with whomever and regret not doing so. Now they're out of work, or stuck in a dead-end job, because of loyalty to the scene and all of those 'friends' who they probably never even hear from any more. Our association with 'the scene' could have played a pivotal role in us touring with some legendary bands, so there *were* benefits and I don't want to come across as totally negative about it all. We have always had a strong punk element about us and one of the negatives of that was that the punk scene didn't quite understand why we were associated with the UKHC scene and a lot of hardcore kids thought we were a 'punk' band, so we kind of got caught between the two scenes without ever being fully embraced by either. Hardcore means different things to different people and I just thought of my own band as hardcore punk…

"I've always found a lot of people in the music industry are really up themselves," he continues passionately. "Self-important wankers who seem to have had a humour by-pass operation; those are the kind of people we would irritate the most, because we just don't play the fake game at all. I've smashed monitors to bits, rammed soundmen through doors, pissed in guitar heads and we're talking full bladder release here! Infamously John even shat on stage a few times! I've whacked people with microphones, used cymbal stands as weapons, crashed through stages, had stages literally fall apart under my feet…all sorts.

"I remember a girl pushing her way through to the front and throwing a pint over me;

I waited for the song to finish, grabbed someone's pint, found her and tipped it all over her head; she didn't seem too pleased! The soundmen and bouncers turned the power off once at a gig, because Spen and John got naked, and then the bouncers started to put gloves on, so I got in their faces and just told them to fuck off; I think they thought we would be intimidated by their, 'Let's put our leather gloves on…' routine. A similar scenario took place in Italy once, but to be fair it was an outdoor festival with kids walking around so I told John to put his shorts back on.

"The main reason we never punched fuck out of some of the folk who wanted to mess with us was that I knew they would just wait 'til later and then smash our van up, so they got away with a lot more than they ever should have been allowed to. A few of the scenesters around the UK would have got a serious slapping, believe me; I used to piss myself laughing at some of the folk who thought they were scene tough guys with their laughable local reputation. We preferred to make friends with real people who were not interested in 'the scene' and who liked us for who we were…"

Arguably Assert peaked with the ferocious 'Riotous Assembly' album in 2003 which, apart from one track, 'School Of Assassins' and the occasional intro, was delivered at a relentless breakneck pace throughout and is a very powerful, persuasive piece of agit-punk. It was released on vinyl by Dutch label Suburban and on CD by Danish label Diehard; in the States, enhanced with several bonus tracks, it was licensed by Malt Soda. Unfortunately it was to be the last recording to be blessed with Chris Burleigh's drum talents, as he died shortly afterwards.

"It was unbelievable to lose someone so young and talented," says Britt sadly. "He was smoking hot on that drum stool and I had spent a lot of time with him, nurturing and mentoring him. We were getting ready to play some dates in Europe with F-Minus and MDC, I think, when Ryan knocked on my door and was in bits. Chris had suffered an epileptic seizure and was in a bad way; it was a terrible thing watching his parents going into a room at the hospital and hearing his mother screaming, fucking tragic. I'm just glad that he got to do a number of tours and recording sessions, because it added to his biographical life; there will always be footage of him playing and recordings with him on.

"He is part of our history and what a fucking drummer he was; people were always blown away by his playing. It took us a long time to get over it; we were unsure about carrying on and unsure that we could ever find anyone that good. Our mate Stokesy [Carl Stokes from Cancer] stepped in for a while and kept us ticking over, but I don't think he could handle sleeping on floors and struggling for food and drink, so didn't last very long before he wanted to do his own thing again. We were directly responsible for giving him the desire to reform his old band and he did help us out a lot at the time."

Further tragedy struck when news reached the band that their ex-bassist Johnny Sinister had also died and in rather mysterious circumstances. "Before John quit Assert, he had started to mess around with drink and drugs and couldn't handle the boredom of not touring," recalls Britt. "He got himself into a few shit relationships and couldn't break away from those people. We picked him up to start a tour (the first date was in Belfast) and he just would not go; I knew we needed to get him in the van to save his sanity, but he had smashed his hand up. Later we found out he had fallen out with some woman and his head was in a mess; he didn't see his son very often and was on a downward spiral. A few years later, he had gone missing and they pulled him out the river…which was quite bizarre, because he had managed to get his life together and was then working as a personal trainer.

"John was very special and unique; he loved the band and I wish he had stuck with us longer. Who could ever forget his naked antics? He had a great stage presence and was a true showman. A real shame that we can never have the full, original Assert line-up ever again, but he will never be forgotten. We are lucky that we have film footage of both John and Chris who will remain forever young."

After touring using drum backing tracks for a year, Assert were eventually reunited with original drummer Frank and with a new bassist, Mike Farrant (who had been playing with Snap-Her in the States) and a second guitarist, Ben Elphick from Broken Minds (who replaced Sean 'Sick Boy' Ecclestone), they recorded the 2006 CD album 'Bulletin' for Hideous Eye and the 2009 album 'Laser Tattoo Removal Service' for Italian label Anfibio.

Although Assert have dialled back their touring and recording schedule considerably in recent years and are back to being a four-piece again with just Ryan on guitar, work is under way on their seventh studio album. "The Nineties seem to have been about heavy metal, which for me is not really punk at all," comments Britt, who in recent years also did a stint fronting much-loved Blackpool punk act One Way System. "In some cases, the bands were equipped with even less than punk's traditional 'three chords'. Down-tuned, open-then-close-one-finger playing chugga-chugga style, until it evolved into 'technical' show-off metal. Some bands were entertaining for all of five minutes, then became copycat bands with a lack of originality. A fast-track to the pages of *Kerrang!* or *Metal Hammer* was all the rage and a clamour for recognition from 'journalists' who would not give you the steam off their piss. The Nineties were never as good as the Eighties and the Eighties were never as good as the Seventies and…well, you get the picture!

"Not much long\er and we will have been going for 20 years," he adds proudly, "and that's the aim now. Where are all those fanzines that used to enjoy slagging us off? Did they get to 20 years? I don't think so, mate. I'm happy going out to play for the odd weekend here and there; the thought of long tours doesn't thrill me any more. Playing live used to mean everything to me, but I've found that, as long as I do a bit of boxing and martial-arts training a couple of times a week, I still feel good and have really learned to like people a lot more.

"Assert were always just honest people who were never that interested in fashions or trying to fit in, a band who were leaders rather than followers, who would play any time, any place, anywhere. A band that could always trigger a discussion, were never grey and bland and who added their own uniqueness, both in and out of UKHC. We stuck to our principles and created our own rehearsal space, recording studio and even our own label for a while. Others bleated on about DIY ethics while we put them into action and lived by them.

"We made some people smile and some people grimace, but we never hid behind any façade. What sets us apart is that we have always been willing to stand alone if that's what is needed and we have the bottle to do so. Assert have been like a hydra-headed beast, always coming back stronger with an instinctual desire to survive; every time we were vulnerable, we managed to grow a tougher outer shell and carried on. 'Original' is the one word I would use, but let's not forget we were, are and always will be an anti–Nazi band with a firm left-wing stance."

SELECT DISCOGRAPHY:

7-inch:
'Assert Yourself' (Hideous Eye, 1997)
'Thumb And Four Fingers Fold To A Fist' (Household Name, 1999)
'United Front' (Intimidation, 2001) – *split with Swellbellys*
'Tear It Up' (Hideous Eye, 2002)
'Split' (Stranded, 2004) – *split with Swellbellys*

CD albums:
'More Than A Witness' (Household Name, 1998)
'Left Opposition' (Household Name, 2000)
'Insurrection Rocks' (Three Days Dead, 2001)
'Riotous Assembly' (Diehard, 2004)
'Bulletin' (Hideous Eye, 2006)
'Laser Tattoo Removal Service' (Anfibio, 2009)

AT A GLANCE:
The US version of 'Riotous Assembly' would be as good a place as any to start, with its extra tracks and enhanced video feature. There's also Hideous Eye's 'History Re-Loaded' DVD to check out, with behind-the-scenes footage of the recording of 'Riotous Assembly' and live material from all over the UK.

POLICE BASTARD

Named after a classic Doom song – and how could any punk band really resist such a name? – **Police Bastard** have flown the flag for underground punk in Birmingham for the best part of 20 years. For many avid fans around the world they epitomise the defiant spirit of UK punk rock. Amicable vocalist Stu-Pid will never admit it but he's a veritable punk-rock institution – in a good way, of course! – and the band are still going strong to this day, despite many line-up changes over the years.

"In 1993, I was singing for Contempt and we were offered a slot supporting English Dogs across Europe," begins Pid. "Due to work commitments, Contempt couldn't commit to the tour, but me and [bassist] Trogg still desperately wanted to experience a huge tour of Europe supporting one of the UK's biggest and best punk acts. So we linked up with [drummer] Clive from Filthkick and [guitarist] John from Doom and quickly rehearsed a set of Contempt and Doom songs, as well as rapidly writing the first Police Bastard songs, including 'Race Hate', 'Criminal Justice Bill', 'Kept Down', 'Smash The Face' and 'Payback', and we were ready in a matter of weeks to go on tour."

"They weren't really considering adding me on guitar at first because of my attitude," reckons John Doom. "But Clive, who had been in Cain with me, convinced Pid to get me in.

I remember just wanting to pick up the guitar and play again; plus it was a new challenge just as my old bands were beginning to disintegrate…

"We needed to come up with a name quickly before that first tour of Germany and someone just said 'Police Bastard' at practice one day…it might even have been me! I thought it was maybe a bit cheesy to link our new band to an old Doom song, but liked the 'in-your-face' quality of it so we just went with it.

"The Brummie punk scene has always been full of nice, genuine people, fun characters and no violence or bullshit. The trouble is, musically, it is really disappointing. Most Birmingham bands fall into the category of plodding Oi!-influenced stuff or knuckle-dragging retro street-punk. After witnessing Crass in the early days, then moving onto American hardcore, crust and metal when I wanted punk stuff, I was looking for something more modern, or just some good, heavy, raging crust or thrash-punk. In my opinion there hasn't really been any good hardcore crust or modern forward-thinking punk come out of the Birmingham scene since the demise of [legendary Birmingham venue] the Mermaid. It may sound harsh, but it is largely true…"

Police Bastard played a hasty warm-up gig supporting Velvet Underpants at the Breedon Bar, where Pid promoted weekly punk shows, then their second gig was in Europe with English Dogs. They took to touring in Europe like ducks to water and quickly built a large, loyal following on the continent with their unpretentious mix of hardcore punk and filthy metal.

"When we started to write our own songs, that is when we started pulling in influences from Rudimentary Peni, Conflict, Discharge, Killing Joke, Crass, even Cro-Mags…stuff that had inspired us all as a band," explains John. "Lyrically, I was really passionate about writing honestly and, more importantly, I wanted to write about something a bit more contemporary, not just the typical Eighties 'anarcho' subject-matter. Our first group of songs were just simple and punky, but, when Trogg left and Chris took over, we started writing stuff for the 'Traumatized' album, which began to sound harder, more angry and was getting more interesting lyrically too.

"I wrote the song 'Traumatized' about getting desensitized to violence and war from buying punk records! 'Inferior' was all about supermodels, plastic surgery and body image, which was starting to be everywhere in the media in the early Nineties. We also had songs talking about rave and drug culture which was massive around that time and had taken a lot of people away from the 'thinking' punk scene and more into the hedonistic world of dance music and just getting twatted…

"I was really proud of the way the band was starting to take shape, the mixture of influences; it was modern, lyrically interesting and heavy…very different to other stuff coming from Birmingham at the time."

"All the individuals in Police Bastard were influenced by totally different sounds," adds Pid. "John and Clive definitely came from more of a metal background, which gave Police Bastard its own style. My influences were Crass, Subhumans, Rudimentary Peni, Conflict, Disorder and Chaos UK, as well as the unique guitar sound of Killing Joke…the others will definitely say something different. What we tried to achieve with Police Bastard was to

Police Bastard, Goldsmith Arms, New Cross, London 1997

Police Bastard, Star And Garter,
Manchester,1996

make a difference: going places in the world to promote injustices to same-minded people and playing in places where other bands dared not go like Dresden and Magdeburg, where getting your head kicked in for the colour of your hair by the extreme right-wing skinhead bully boys was an everyday occurrence for the people. Time after time we would hear at our concerts, 'The skinheads are coming!' Oh no, not again!"

After the first European tour, Trogg left to concentrate on Contempt and Chris Crass, who had roadied for them on the tour, joined the band in November 1994. Once the new line-up was broken in live, 16 tracks were recorded during April '95, 11 of which became the 'Traumatized' LP on Inna State Records and nine of which appeared on a split LP with A38 (Bristolian/Oakland punks relocated to Bremen) on German label Barbaren Musi and one, a cover of 'Rain' by Subhumans, was included on the 'Still Can't Hear The Words: The Subhumans Covers Album' on Blackfish. The first 10 tracks from 'Traumatized' were also used for a split CD with Portland's Defiance on Portuguese label Ataque Sonoro (known as Slime Records until 1995).

"The recordings were done at the Clinic in Birmingham by Stevie Young, the nephew of Malcolm and Angus Young from AC/DC and Danny Sprigg, who was working on the Napalm Death record 'Diatribes' at the same time," says Chris. "We recorded on the sound desk from the 'Blow Up Your Video' US tour, which was presented to Stevie as a thank-you for standing in on that tour for Malcolm, who was going through a tough time with alcohol and had some time off to dry out. It was a very big thing for me as AC/DC were my favourite band as a kid!"

After the ominous – and *very* metal – intro, 'The Lie', 'Traumatized' is a whirlwind of speedy crust punk, but elevated above the generic pack by nods towards contemporary influences from the extreme music scenes such as Machine Head and Sepultura, most noticeable in the very aggressive yet accomplished guitar work.

"That recording was okay," adds John, "seeing as we did it in two days for a measly £200. But listening back to it now, it's all played quite slowly and with little energy. The sound was also pretty murky, as me and Clive were left to mix it and ended up getting really stoned with Stevie Young, so the recordings have loads of reverb and echo and ended up sounding a bit too atmospheric and dated. We seemed to get loads of initial support and stuff released quite easily to start with, but unfortunately the material just didn't capture the energy or sound anywhere near our live sets."

With several releases in quick succession to 'promote', Police Bastard spent most of the next two years on tour and didn't record again until Chris left in 1997. "As I remember, all the gigs and tours we did were fun," he says. "Just because the music was dark and the lyrics were morbid didn't mean we didn't have a good time. The most memorable tour for me though was the September 1995 tour of Germany with Maggot Slayer Overdrive. We had so much fun on that tour…how could you not with those guys? Before we'd even got off the ferry in Ostend their singer, Alan, pissed all over himself – and their bass player, Rupert – in the bunk at the back of the van. It just deteriorated from then on! As you can imagine a lot of alcohol was consumed on that tour and not many of us saw a shower, so when the opportunity arose to take a dip, in what we thought was a lake, a few of them jumped at the chance. It wasn't until a very angry, official-looking German guy appeared, shouting at all of us, that we realised we had just been swimming in the main reservoir that fed clean water to most of the villages of the Black Forest region. Christ knows what those poor people found floating in their water for the following few months...

"I became disillusioned with the punk scene around 1997," he adds, explaining why he left the band. "The attitudes and the egos began to grate on me; the mass contradictions that had crept into the scene were starting to destroy what we had and the closure of pubs and clubs made people scatter across the city instead of finding another place they could all call their own. The scene didn't seem united any more, the rot had set in. I left the band soon after and for many years didn't even listen to British punk music; I'd found American hardcore and listened to the likes of Minor Threat, Black Flag, Bad Brains and bands from small independent labels like Gainesville's No Idea Records, Louisville's Initial Records and Revelation Records. It has only been since rejoining in 2007 that I have began to appreciate the English bands and create a connection with the music again."

Chris was replaced by Dee from LD50 and Dan joined on second guitar, for the 1998 four-track 'Gulf War Syndrome' EP on Ruptured Ambitions. This release saw the band moving in an ever more metallic direction – their dirgey punk now being executed with a rhythmic emphasis not dissimilar to Prong or Soulfly – that wasn't sitting too comfortably with Pid, who left in 1999.

"I had been asked to join English Dogs, which I jumped at as they were one of my favourite bands," he explains. "So, coming back off tour with them, Chris had left and been replaced by Dee and then Dan had joined, so I had lost my old mate Chris and the sound was gradually changing too. They were writing a lot of the new songs in my absence and I have to say I really did feel the odd one out and everything was going more and more metal. By then, Police Bastard were musically brilliant, so I guessed they wanted to move forward with things – and, as I was more a traditionalist punk with no ambition for it to be anything more than what it was, I thought parting company was for the best."

Although the band was quite possibly now at their strongest and most powerful and John was a very able vocalist in his own right, Pid's departure spelled the beginning of the end for Police Bastard.

"Pid was basically pushed out of the band in 1999," explains John, "because the new line-up was becoming more and more metally and hardcore, plus the rest of us were listening to all these modern bands like Refused, Hatebreed and even some nu-metal stuff and our songwriting was developing further and further away from straight-up punk. Pid didn't seem to fit into where we were heading and I just told him; there was no animosity, we had just gone in different directions musically. It happens.

"After a rather limp tour of Sweden and Finland with Concrete Sox [during which they recorded a split 7-inch with Unkind for Fight Records], we recorded our final EP, 'Cursed Earth', which was really good in my opinion; very tight and focused and achieving the perfect mix of raging crust and heavy chugginess. All of the band were happy with it, but it was at that point that we decided it didn't feel right to be called Police Bastard any more and we thought it best to change the name to Cursed Earth...and that is when things began to crumble."

'Cursed Earth' was, indeed, 'really good', the band sharpening their punk/metal fusion to near perfection and even covering Slayer's 'Mandatory Suicide' to great, gnarly effect, but the responsibilities of life outside punk rock began impinging on the band members' ability to tour. With John going to university and embarking on a career in radio, Clive and Dan landing jobs in theatre sound production and Dee starting work as a production runner for some big concerts, the decision was made to let 'Cursed Earth' be the band's final release – that is, until Trogg fell terminally ill with cancer and Pid decided to resurrect the band for one last European tour with his old friend.

"Trogg was a special bloke to me," Pid recalls fondly. "He didn't take himself seriously at all; in fact, he just took the piss. He was really funny and people sometimes didn't know how to take him as we would be pissing ourselves laughing at his dry Brummie sense of humour. He was a slave to the DIY scene, playing brilliant bass for over 30 years, now that's dedication for you; first with Sensa Yuma, then in Contempt and then Police Bastard…we were in all three bands together, so we really did work hard together and don't forget, this man could *really* play the bass. When we spoke and he told me he was terminally ill, I knew it was the right time to do Police Bastard again – unfinished business, you might call it – so I spoke to John, Chris and Clive, but they all had work commitments and couldn't do it. But thanks to Max from Sensa Yuma and Gizz from English Dogs, Trogg and myself embarked on our first tour together in over 10 years.

"It was magic, going back to some of the venues we were both inspired by playing years before. The sad thing was, though, Trogg knew it was going to be his last tour and he was the star of the show every night, making us laugh and being daft. Then, on returning to the UK, the cancer had grown to such an extent he couldn't rest his bass on his side – so, without so much of a complaint, he stepped down, giving his bass guitar back to Chris Crass. I never heard him complain once up until his death, either, and he was surrounded by his lovely wife, Tina and his Drongos For Europe and Contempt family; we have enough stories to write a whole book about this man…"

"Trogg was a lovely bloke," confirms John, "warm and laid-back, with a dry sense of humour and a cheeky, playful side. He was loads of fun to be around and, even though he had addiction issues, we didn't really care too much because he wasn't ever untrustworthy or a pain in the ass, even when he disappeared for long periods or was too drunk to play! I have nothing but lovely memories of touring with Trogg; I just regret being a bit musically opinionated around him and dissing his favourite band, the Clash, quite so much."

There was supposed to be a UK tour with the line-up that toured Germany in September 2006 as well, but that was cancelled at the last minute due to ill health on Pid's part. Then Pid and Trogg replaced Max with Pix-E from POA and Gizz with not one but two guitarists: Mark Badger of Last Under The Sun and Seano Porno from Dogshit Sandwich. This line-up only lasted a few months until Trogg's health deteriorated so much he couldn't continue and Chris Crass returned to the fold. Pix-E was then replaced by Simon James behind the kit in late 2008 and finally Police Bastard returned to some semblance of stability in time to record their 'It's Good To Hate…' MCD for guitarist Mark Badger's own Iron Man Records during 2009. Still pushing the band's evolution ever onwards, it even included a powerful and poignant cover of the Mob's 'I Wish'. As good as anything the band released in the Nineties, it was then issued on vinyl as a split with Minneapolis band War/Plague on Profane Existence and ably demonstrates that Police Bastard are still as brutally relevant today as ever. Indeed, they're working on a brand new album for 2012.

"All the reviews for the MCD and recent live performances have been very complimentary," says Chris happily, "way beyond *my* expectations anyway. As we'd been officially inactive for some years, interest could have died off very quickly, especially with the lack of material coming out and all the changes within the band, both musically and personnel-wise over the years. I think Police Bastard are very lucky to have withstood the test of time so well; I'd like to think that it was due to the quality of the music that we've released. I'd also like to think that punkers still revisit the records every now and then 'cos they really like what's held within those records; I'd hate to think we were a band that released an album that was listenable only once then put on a shelf to gather dust amidst all the other second-rate bands that dominated the early Nineties…"

"To be honest, Police Bastard was finished for me after the 'Cursed Earth' EP," admits John. "I was prepared to release the EPs and the songs we have still lying around on a final CD and just forget about it. When I heard that Pid was thinking of putting it back together again, with new people, I was initially a bit pissed off, but after a while I just thought, 'Well if we aren't doing it, then he may as well…' There's no point in getting precious about something that you have let go, is there?

"Anyway, I went to see them a few times and enjoyed watching the songs we'd written but without having to plug my guitar in! I also realised how good some of the stuff was and still is, when watching from the front. They then played me the new EP and asked if I'd do some vocals and, I'll be honest again, I really expected to not want to bother. But when I heard it, it was really good, just like the original band, with that heavy punk/hardcore sound, so I agreed and now we're back in the rehearsal room working on songs for a new album. The line-up now is all great guys too, all Brummie locals, so we can do it for a bit of fun and if I don't want to do it any more, it will be fine. Pid lives in Spain, though, so I think the idea of doing lots of gigs is out of the question; we'll just do it when we can…it's great to be doing a bit of shouting again."

"I think it was always the unique sound we had," concludes Pid, on what set Police Bastard apart from their peers. "It was dirty, aggressive and powerful and politically it was performed with real urgency. We were living in squats, Dee was out living up a tree, hunt saboteuring, protesting…we meant our politics. But most of all we were all decent blokes; we met and partied with, so many people and we made friends wherever we went and so many of the people we met are still good mates of mine even now…and it doesn't get better than that, does it? At the grand old age of 46, I'm just happy I can still do it, although it does get harder the older you get! But I still believe in what we do; we never sold out and I made punk rock my life, along with thousands of other people around the world…"

SELECT DISCOGRAPHY:

7-inch:
'Gulf War Syndrome' (Ruptured Ambitions, 1998)
'Powerless' (Fight, 1999) – *split with Unkind*
'Cursed Earth' (Twisted Chords, 2002)

MCD:
'It's Good To Hate…' (Iron Man, 2010)

LPs:
'Traumatized' (Inna State, 1995)
'Traumatized' (Ataque Sonoro, 1995) – *split CD with Defiance*

'Split' (Barbaren Musi, 1995) – *split with A38*
'Attrition' (Profane Existence, 2011) – *split with War//Plague*

AT A GLANCE:

'It's Good To Hate…' has got to be a good place to start; not only do you get five killer studio cuts but a DVD featuring over 20 live tracks from 2007-2010. Also, the new 'Dead To The World' CD on Iron Man compiles various early EPs and unreleased tracks.

SPITHEAD

Anyone who saw Birmingham's finest ska/punks **Spithead** at the peak of their powers will testify that no one, but *no one*, left one of their gigs without a smile on their face and that, ladies and gentlemen, is reason enough to celebrate their contribution to the UK's underground music scene.

"Love, basically!" smiles vocalist/guitarist John Middleton, when asked what brought him to Birmingham in the first place. "In 1990, I was living on the rather grim Gascoigne Estate in Barking and working for the Royal Mail in Whitechapel. I was hanging around with lots of London Greenpeace/Class War/ALF/squatter-types, as well as being involved in the *Leyton Orientear* football fanzine, which at the time was involved in opposing the BNP's attempts to infiltrate the club. I was also playing in a three-piece anarcho band [with Paul Day, formerly of Monotony Commission and Tim Punter, latterly of Mucho Macho] with the unfortunate name of Stan! Basically, I met Charlotte [Bedford] at a party following a Stop The War march and we decided to move to Brum, where she had spent her teenage years. We knew no-one, but used to go down the Fighting Cocks in Moseley, where lots of punks and crusties hung out… I think the first punk gig we went to in Brum would've been Citizen Fish at the Barrel Organ in 1991…

"Anyway, I eventually saw an ad in a newsagents' window looking for people to form a band. I answered it and it turned out that the bloke who had placed it [bassist Paul Harris] lived across the road; he also had varied musical tastes, including metal and ska. I remember having a conversation with Paul around that time about what we hoped to achieve – all we ever hoped for originally was to do a gig or two…"

Scott Davies then joined on drums, fresh from a long stint with Black Country punks Anorexia and Spithead played their first gig at the Red Lion in Ladypool Road, Balsall Heath, a pub run – and normally frequented – by members of the local Caribbean community.

"The landlord would let people use the back room for free; his only condition was that you gave him some posters to put up… He was always quite insistent on this, otherwise, he didn't give a fuck what you did," laughs John. "We were supporting the other band that Scott was in at the time, SLT [Strawberry Love Truncheon], but I can't remember much else about it, to be honest. We had a set of songs which was very varied in style, but included bits of the punk/ska thing we later grew into. Paul and I came to the band without any real musical direction and Scott with a hankering to do something different to the raging punk-rock assault he'd been playing for the past decade, so with loads of varied influences and tastes, everything we all liked got thrown into the pot…

"Brum had a pretty good punk scene at the time," he adds. "They were exciting days, really. It was pre-Criminal Justice Bill, the peak of Class War, AFA [Anti-Fascist Action] was emerging and there was loads of animal rights stuff…and there were quite a few DIY gigs at places like the Red Lion, the Coach And Horses and Synatra's. We were able to link into all that quite nicely, largely due to Scott being a stalwart of the scene and knowing *everyone*. We started putting on gigs ourselves very early on: Oi Polloi, Tofu Love Frogs, Decadence Within, Terminus, Herb Garden, Blind Mole Rat… We just thought it was better to do that than do the whole 'send off a demo and wait for someone to give you a gig'-type thing. As things developed, Charlotte and Kate started putting on *loads* of punk gigs."

Spithead recorded their first demo, 'Rant Music for Vexed People' in 1992, "in some youth centre in Wordesley, because it was really cheap and we were really broke!" Having recorded and mixed 10 songs in less than two days, it was never going to be a world-class production job, but it nevertheless captured Spithead's earnest energy and one track, 'Fuck The Right To Vote', was included on the 1992 Scumbag compilation album, 'Get Orf Moi Land!'

1993's 'Kill Two Pigs With One Stone' demo was another lo-fi affair, recorded "in some bloke's garage in Bromsgrove," but it saw the band really starting to cement their ska/punk style and brought them to the attention of Martin at Kollusion Records, who released their three-track 'Skascraper' EP the following year, on both black and pink vinyl.

"That was recorded in a decommissioned (not to mention very cold and damp) nuclear bunker in Bearwood," recalls John incredulously. " Again, the bloke who engineered and produced it didn't really get where we were coming from, but I think it's a nice little snapshot of the band before things started changing for us. I'm quite proud of the lyrics on 'Sitting Too Close To The Telly' to this day – one of my finest moments, I reckon. It got a very uncomplimentary review in the *NME* too – which can only be a good thing really!"

"I first heard of Spithead when they contacted me with a copy of the 'Kill Two Pigs…' demo," recalls Martin. "They were enquiring about a show at the Square in Harlow, where I was promoting a monthly punk night at the time. I was impressed by their DIY attitude and constant touring, as well as John 'The Poet Leyton Orient' Middleton's lyrics. Songs about nosey neighbours, Jesus and hard dogs all made an impression on me and, of course, the stand-out lyrics from the track 'Margarine' on the 'Skascraper' EP: 'Even the crumbliest flakiest chocolate rots your teeth and makes you fat, but they never told you that on the pack!'"

Another track, 'Inconvenience', recorded during the same session as 'Skascraper', was included on Red Rosetten's 1995 compilation LP, 'When The Punx And Skins Go Marching In'. "Also around that time, we recorded a cover of the Specials' 'Stupid Marriage', intended for release on Ruptured Ambitions' 2-Tone covers LP. We got our roadie, Paul Carey, to do the spoken intro and asked Charlotte to do vocals…just for a bit of a change really. Charlotte then used to get up and do her bit whenever we played the song live and eventually got incorporated into the line-up full-time. "This was when we were gigging loads with Blind Mole Rat from Sheffield. They did a huge amount of gigs and had a real 'set up, get up and

Spithead live in Harlow

Spithead, drummer Scott

get people dancing' attitude which rubbed off on us a lot. I think they also had that 'go out and get your own gigs' attitude, which reinforced our own approach – hence we rarely did support slots to big bands…and when we were talked into it, we usually ended up wishing we hadn't."

Perhaps burnt out by the relentless gigging, Scott left the band in 1995, eventually going on to play with General Winter and then the Alcohol Licks; he was replaced by Rob Overdrive from Blind Mole Rat, who themselves had just split, also freeing up Tony Baloney (aka Chris Boddington) to join Spithead on organ. "I can't begin to say how gutted we were when Scott left," says John. "Unlike a lot of bands who barely tolerate each other, we were a band who rarely had a cross word said between us. It felt like the end of a relationship, but I think it's fair to say he had just run out of steam with it all and wanted to do something different.

"It just so happened that his leaving coincided with BMR calling it a day. Chris was a very accomplished musician and brought a bit of musicality to the band and Rob's drumming lent itself to a ska sound far more than Scott's much punkier style. So there you have it: we had evolved into our next phase, which meant the band was split between Sheffield and Brum, so we rehearsed less and gigged more, which worked well for us, I think. I suppose this was another BMR influence, because they had been a constantly touring band who had done a ridiculous amount of gigs with a relatively high turnover of members, so were used to a different way of working…"

It was this line-up that recorded the wonderful 'Swag' album at Sheffield's Cage Studios in 1996, with Rob's house mate Roo at the mixing desk; a likeable collection of deliciously catchy rag-tag street urchin anthems, it cemented the band's reputation as one of the best ska punk bands in the UK at the time, right up there alongside the likes of Citizen Fish and Ex-Cathedra.

"We were always very aware that Subhumans/Culture Shock/Citizen Fish were doing that shtick years before us," admits John. "But – although it may not always have sounded like it – we were trying to put our own slant on it. Citizen Fish, to their credit, were always very accepting of bands who followed in their wake, I thought. We played in Bath a couple of times and Bruce Subhuman was doing the sound – which made us feel a bit self-conscious, to be honest – and he came up at the end and said something like, 'I really enjoyed that, it was really original!' And I remember pausing and thinking, 'Is he taking the piss?' but he wasn't.

"Someone said to us a couple of years ago how they thought 'Swag' had been ahead of its time and without wishing to sound big-headed, I think it was. You hear a lot of bands now [Sonic Boom Six, for instance] who are knocking out quite similar stuff and doing very well out of it… and good on 'em, but there's nothing new under the sun, as they say."

"The 'Swag' CD was my favourite release of theirs," reckons Martin, "mainly due to the added keyboards and Charlotte's vocals, but also the great artwork from Boz [Steam Pig/ *Nosebleed* fanzine]. It received enthusiastic reviews in fanzines both here and in the States, where comparisons were made between them and Operation Ivy; this side of the pond the comparison was obvious and they were cited as 'the new Specials'. With their clever lyrics and sharp melodies, they impressed fans and reviewers alike with their political take on Nineties Britain – from a protester's perspective…"

Despite the album being a sonic triumph, Chris had already grown apart from the band to an extent where he left just after it was released. Blame that old chestnut, 'musical differences', of course. Thankfully Paul's partner, Julee Newman, "had had a few piano lessons as a child", so she was in "whether she liked it or not!" Two tracks from the album session, 'Porky' and a cover of the Blind Mole Rat song, 'Some People Want Shootin'', were also released as a split 7-inch with Travis Cut on Suspect Device Records, while Spithead hit the road for some intensive touring. And, as was often the way when 'DIY touring' the various shitholes no mainstream router would dream of putting a band he was taking commission off, they collected hundreds of life-long friends and enough anecdotes to dine out on until Doomsday.

"I used to commute to meet Spithead for gigs from Sheffield," recalls Rob, of some of his touring 'highlights'. "It was really nerve-racking, depending on the generosity of drivers giving me a lift, but I always hitched and never once missed a gig or meet point. We got in a few scrapes; we once drove nine hours while on tour in Europe to the Hotel Fox Squat in Amsterdam [18 August 1996] only to find that the support band, Jilted, had ate all the food that was made for us. We then struggled to get the gear down these narrow stairs to the stage as there were smack casualties who didn't want to move laid out on the steps…there was a huge grate on the ceiling above us when we played and they were chucking beer and ashtray contents through it. I remember Paul jumping up and down throughout the set as usual, but this time shouting, 'I'll get yow, yow cunts…!'

"One time in Wexford, Paul had parked up next to the big lake and I agreed to dog sit and look after the van and also practise some violin. In the morning there were cops all over and a car parked just up from the van had a suicide note left in it. Some woman had thrown herself in the lake – and my screeching violin would have been the soundtrack to her last moments!"

"What about playing somewhere in deepest Cornwall when a shipment of ecstasy had just arrived by boat?" adds John. "And the people who had come to see us going home very early in the evening as the pub filled with people either fighting over the dealing territory or E-ing their tits off? Or playing an absolutely heaving gig in the middle of summer in Brighton and some bloke at the front shouting at Charlotte to dance more – when she was so hugely pregnant she could hardly stand up? Or being vegan and not eating for days in France… then turning up to a little bar in the French countryside that had been decorated all over with drawings of us?

"Ireland was always fucking mental for us too: just mad gigs with people going absolutely nuts. I remember one bloke falling off the top of a bar and breaking his arm so the bone was sticking through and we played a place in New Ross that had a stream coming in the back wall – right next to the electrics. But the overwhelming memory is of the hospitality of people generally, who really tried to make us feel welcome and look after us and of all the fantastic gigs and parties with people and other bands. We never really *toured* with other bands; we just did our own thing, which is a nice way to do it, because it makes you realise the power of the DIY scene… Remember, this was pre-internet days and we used to get letters from Russia, Mexico, US, Yugoslavia…all over the place. Gigs in the UK were a bit more of a hit-and-miss affair than overseas: sometimes packed and kicking, sometimes empty. I think the balance shifted more towards good gigs after the album came out."

The final Spithead single was released in 1996, a split 7-inch (containing the tracks 'Personal' and 'Hard Dog Club') with Irish band Jackbeast and was a joint venture between Kollusion Records and Rejected Records. Soon after its release, Rob left to join the circus (no, really) and focus on his violin-playing; he was replaced by Mike Craycroft from General

Winter, who played the band's last few gigs before they split in 1997.

"Well, we've never actually split up, to be honest," corrects John. "We stopped gigging when Charlotte and myself and Julee and Paul started having babies, but we've done a few occasional gigs over the years since then, with Scott back on drums again, but no-one had the time or inclination to get into the whole slog of doing it 'properly' again. The last time we played together was at Paul and Julee's wedding actually – and we were all that kind of plastered that you only seem to get at weddings and Jules was still wearing her wedding dress and I don't think we played very well!" Chris went on to join Blyth Power and, since Rob finally left the circus, he now performs as Rob Tarana.

"Since the move away from drumming I'd been attempting to become a solo violinist," he explains. "I finished grade seven, but on starting the eighth was put on a section again and found myself in a Sheffield mental ward with my violin but no sheet music, so I just improvised. Later I started singing along with meaningless syllables and it went from there; even though it sounded fucking atrocious, it felt really good and I ended up doing a seven-piece first gig and then having many different players and recording whenever possible. I love that I can let out whatever I feel at any given moment and to me it's more punk than punk." Elsewhere, Paul's still a motor mechanic, Mike works in IT and Charlotte's a lecturer in Australia, with a masters degree in DIY punk(!) and was involved in setting up prison radio. Julee's a solicitor and Scott's a social worker, still drumming with General Winter and the Alcohol Licks.

"I helped to set up a national charity, the Prison Radio Association, which supports and advises prison radio stations across the country," clarifies Charlotte. "As Education Director, I focused on setting up radio broadcasting courses at West Midlands prisons including HMP Birmingham, Brock Hill, Hewell Grange, Swinfen Hall YOI and Long Lartin High Security. I was also education advisor on our flagship project, Electric Radio at HMP Brixton, which was launched by Billy Bragg and Mick Jones and subsequently won six Sony Radio awards. I did my masters on Nineties DIY music and the creative industries while still back in the UK, teach radio and film at a couple of universities over here in Australia, still work in community radio and am just starting my PhD in prison radio."

"I think we tried to practice what we preached," offers John, who tried his hand at performance poetry until about 2002 and then relocated to Australia with Charlotte in 2008, where he is now a psychiatric nurse and active trade unionist. "We were DIY to the core and always tried to treat people decently, including each other. We successfully worked as a collective and largely kept our egos in check. I think we came up with some good tunes and tried to put on a good show without being 'showbizzy'…which was why we tried to stop doing those fake encores where people walk to the side of the stage five minutes before their time is up and wait for a bit of a clap before they come back on and do another song – we always tried to play to our time and go. We put on and played some fucking great gigs and generally had as good, if not better, a time than the audiences – and I think that usually showed in our performances."

SELECT DISCOGRAPHY:

7-inch:
'Skascraper' (Kollusion, 1994)
'Split' (Kollusion/Rejected, 1996) – *split with Jackbeast*
'Split' (Suspect Device, 1997) – *split with Travis Cut*

LP:
'Swag' (Kollusion, 1996)

AT A GLANCE:
It's gotta be that 'Swag' album; crank it up and immerse yourself in some happy tunes.

EASTFIELD

Train-spotting punk rock bands are few and far between, but in the wake of Blyth Power, who were discussed at length in the Zounds chapter of my anarcho book *The Day The Country Died*, came **Eastfield**, themselves named after the famous locomotive depot in north Glasgow. A hard-working and sincere band still making music today, they formed in 1996 when guitarist Jessi Adams relocated to Birmingham from Brighton – via Hackney! – and met up with bassist 'Bambi' Breedon.

"I'd first met Bambi in 1988," he explains, "through our mutual friends in Blyth Power, more specifically [drummer] Joseph Porter. Around this time I found myself travelling with them a fair bit, prostituting myself carrying their broken equipment or looking after their merch stall, just so I could get a lift up to the northeast where my most sought-after freight trains tended to work. Joseph took great delight in recalling that they'd give me a lift to all these gigs but I didn't even like the band…in reality I thought they were okay, but don't tell him that! At the time there were a few of us punky/crusty/hippy trainspotter types; in essence friends that would get together for days, weekends or week-long railrovers out and about on the railways. We'd spend all day 'gricing' travelling round on locomotive-hauled trains, bashing track to weird and wonderful locations or bunking round marshalling yards and engine sheds to photograph the locomotives themselves. Personally, I've always found travel pretty good for the soul and, like any group of friends hooking up, we had a blast.

"We'd all come from a fairly similar perspective, having got into trains and punk music when there was a boom in both pursuits in the late Seventies; however, as we grew up we foolishly stopped going out on trains as it seemed out of kilter with being punk rockers. Then, when we got older, we realised the error of our ways and reversed our actions, drifting back into the railways again. During this time, I also met [vocalist] Elaine [Burton] in 1990 when she started to see DB, one of our gricing mates from Stoke-on-Trent…contrary to popular belief, us trainspotters aren't all single or completely lacking in social skills!

"You'd be surprised at how many people were into both punk music and railways in the late Seventies, albeit to varying degrees. Nowadays we get a fair few people at gigs commenting on the locomotives on our album covers and I suspect there are a load more still to come out of the closet. To some people this might all sound pretty pointless but who are they to judge what people do or don't enjoy? I've had countless discussions over the years stating that surely it's no more pointless than going to see football teams or bands – and besides, trains look, sound and smell far better than any band ever could! When I burned all my punk-rock paraphernalia, I was doing a fair bit of travelling around and as a consequence had already started getting back my appetite for railways, having begun to take more than a passing interest in trains out of the carriage windows. I've always been into the aesthetics of railways and fascinated by associated industrial landscapes, so also got heavily into the photography side of things. As mentioned before, I liked to do this in conjunction with my friends, but also enjoyed the peace and tranquillity of being out by myself, left to my own devices, just travelling around and exploring…

"It would have been great to combine this with Eastfield gigs, but by the time we got the opportunity everything was changing on the railways; the rot set in by privatisation left the network desperately short of its former glory and charisma. Needless to say, I'm still involved with other railway-based projects today…

"But anyway, bandwise, it was only ever Bambi and myself who were really into trains, although when Chris joined in 2003 that made three out of the four of us, which was quorate by anyone's standards. Our current drummer Oddo has also since confessed to owning trainspotting books when he was at school, but that's as far as it goes…"

Joining Jessi and Bambi in that first line-up was drummer Kris Reynolds and the band made their public debut at Chris from Blind Mole Rat's birthday party at Morrissey's in Sheffield on 27 April 1996.

"It also conveniently coincided with an open day at Tinsley locomotive depot just down the road," laughs Jessi. "In addition, an alternative journalist friend had got MTV Europe interested in our railway/punk rock angle and they were booked to film the gig, but then pulled out at the eleventh hour. A shame; it would have made great footage as the place was heaving with loads of people we knew, a lot of them wearing hi-visibility railway vests! We only did a very short, six-song set, though, as by then that was all we'd got rehearsed up with Kris. Nevertheless, it seemed to go down a storm and was a fitting introduction into the world of Eastfield.

"We did actually get filmed for TV three months later and could be seen featured on Channel 4's *Ride On*, a transport-based current affairs programme first broadcast in December 1996. Some people have their 15 minutes of fame, we got our 15 *seconds* – literally! This consisted of a live clip from a gig in Stoke-on-Trent, interspersed with a comment from Bambi (along the lines that we like to travel on trains and annoy other passengers). It looked great on the TV but was probably our least-attended gig ever, having literally been arranged the day before for the benefit of the Channel 4 film crew and fitted onto an existing midweek bill supporting a Seventies glam-rock covers band. Not bad at all for our fifth gig, although the TV/media coverage did weird me out a bit…"

After the first few gigs, Elaine joined as an additional vocalist, bringing the male/female

Eastfield Cambridge
28.4.07 by Grilly Phil

Eastfield, Old Railway, July 1999, photo by Dick Short

'question/answer' vocal arrangements that the band have become renowned for and the 13-track 'Tearing Pages From The Rule Book' demo was recorded by drummer Kris during August 1996. The run of 200 cassettes quickly sold out at gigs and was met with a positive response.

"Bambi suggested the title which comes from a phrase used in enquiries into railway accidents where post-privatisation rail companies were often accused of 'tearing pages from the rule book', cutting corners with regard to general safety and age-old good practice. At the time, cassette was the quickest, easiest and cheapest format to use; up 'til then we'd split any gig money between us after deducting any expenses such as petrol, lost drumsticks or broken guitar strings, but it seemed to make more sense to keep a collective pot to enable us to pay for bigger and better things.

"And the first major lay-out was paying for the cassettes to be 'professionally' duplicated at a unit in Digbeth's Custard Factory; naturally we then photocopied the 'cut'n'paste' inserts ourselves. At the time we were obviously chuffed to put something out that was well received, but in reality it was probably just our friends that bought one. Looking back, it was exactly what it was: rough and ready and done on a shoestring with what resources and equipment we had available to us at that point…"

By the time of the band's next release, a one-sided 7-inch (this format chosen purely due to financial restrictions rather than any desire to be cool and collectable) entitled 'Come To Bevland' (and named after an episode of the popular *Brookside* TV soap opera), which the band issued on their own label, Baszdmeg, in early 1998, Kris had been replaced by Darius Khan on the drum stool. It still captured the band's very British take on the schizoid energy of the Ramones to a tee.

"The literal translation of Baszdmeg is 'Fuck you' in Hungarian," laughs Jessi. "Although that phrase can have fitting connotations as in 'Fuck you, we are going to do this ourselves anyway', it is more the phonetics of the word that appeal to me. I spent a month in Budapest in 1993 and at the time hardly anyone there spoke any English, so I picked up a fair degree of Hungarian in order to get by. Naturally friends are always going to teach you the swear words too…and I just loved the sound of this one!

"From the outset, it was always more about lifestyle choice than just a band," he continues, on what has always driven Eastfield, "and the ethics of DIY culture are firmly ingrained in that. To do everything ourselves was totally a conscious decision, due to both myself and Bambi coming from that DIY background. We wouldn't want it any other way and the fact that it works is a testament to this and surely a reason to carry on in itself. We don't need a record company, agent or manager to tell us what to do or how the band should be run; we make our own decisions and choices…if they work it's great, if not then we can learn from our mistakes.

"I taught myself how to screen-print and as a result have printed thousands of Eastfield T-shirts over the years. Yes, it can sometimes be a pain; printing T-shirts, designing record sleeves and fliers etc yourselves is going to be much harder work but it's worth it as it's much more rewarding when you see the stuff you have made out and about. For us it is very important to have total control over what we put out and what we do; it doesn't mean in the slightest that DIY product has to be inferior, second-rate or not taken seriously – Eastfield produce good quality stuff which sells well at sensible and affordable prices without ripping people off.

"For example, our CDs are properly pressed and exactly the same (or sometimes even better) quality than what you get in the shops that the big bands are charging ridiculous prices for. However, we liaise with manufacturers direct, to cut out the unnecessary middleman or woman. Anyone that deals with Eastfield deals with us in person, which means that we get to know people face to face and also leaves us in a position to pass information and knowledge on to people. These mutual relationships are what form the ethos of what we do and we have since worked alongside other small labels and distros to co-release our stuff.

"We obviously need to make a small profit on everything to help fund the day-to-day running of Eastfield, such as recording, releasing, mending broken equipment or buying petrol to play benefit gigs. But rather than any of this going to a third-party, it all goes back into the collective pot which means that no-one needs to dip into their own pockets. At the same time, no-one makes a living from Eastfield either…if we were doing it merely to line our pockets, then there are much better 'get rich quick' schemes than being in a punk band!"

In early 1998, Eastfield added a lead guitarist, Sam Springer, to their ranks, who made her recording debut on the 1999 album 'Keep It Spikey'. Recorded by Tom Savage at Jigsaw Studios, Frognall, during November and December 1998, it was certainly their most powerful offering to date, something akin to a more earthy Adicts, full of solid – albeit three-chord – punk tunes like 'CI5 Revisited' (a homage to the ITV crime series of the late Seventies, 'The Professionals') and 'Pepper' (hopefully suggesting the police force start testing their pepper spray on each other). To promote it, Eastfield headed out on tour with Blyth Power…well, *as* Blyth Power actually!

"I got a call from Joseph Porter saying that although Blyth Power had recently split up they wanted to honour an outstanding booking to play a mutual friend's wedding," explains Jessi. "With no band at his disposal, he wondered if me and Bambi would be up for learning a set of all their early (and, in our opinion, best) material as a one-off; he thought the Eastfield sound was not too dissimilar to the early Blyth Power sound. We agreed this would be fun and it ended up working out so well that we decided it would be a shame to learn a set solely for the one gig. So why not do three select gigs in places both local to all of us (they now lived in Yorkshire) and where they always used to pull a big crowd? So gigs were booked in Birmingham, London and Leeds with Eastfield also on the bill, which proved to be perfect timing as 'Keep It Spikey' was out around then.

"Soon the grapevine got wind of this and more people came out offering us gigs and the three gigs soon became around a dozen. Eastfield now had our 'tour' to promote the album, albeit spread over a few choice weekends in April and May [1999]. Marvellous, we were now on a roll; we all loved playing out of town and catching up with loads of people we hadn't seen for a while and on the whole this period generally did us a lot of favours, so big respect to Blyth Power for that. From then onwards, Eastfield started to play far more regularly around the country. I also carried on in Blyth Power for a while and often the two bands would play together like one big happy family. However, playing in two bands concurrently is bound to throw up logistical problems and a conflict of interests. No disrespect to Blyth but Eastfield were obviously always going to be my first priority and they in turn already had a ready-made stand-in so my eventual departure was totally amicable; Bambi continued playing in Blyth Power for a good few years, having himself already left Eastfield by this point…"

But Bambi didn't leave until after Eastfield had contributed tracks to the four-band 'Potato

Print' compilation EP (appearing alongside Funbug, Swaktang and Lubby Nugget) and toured the UK with Philadelphia's Violent Society – a tour that ironically enough saw Joseph Porter standing in for *them*, with Darius unable to commit to the gigs. At this point, Jessi felt suitably disillusioned with the band's progress to put it on hold for several months, unfortunately just before they were due to record a second album. However, it wasn't long before he and Elaine had hooked up with drummer Paul Raggity from Raggity Anne and bassist Rhys Jones for a new incarnation of Eastfield that would last nine months and record the 'Opening The Lid Of Todd's Peace Box', which, as the title suggests, featured songs penned by Jessi when he was a member of Todd's Peace Box and was released by Beat Bedsit during early 2001.

"A blazing row at the end of an Italian tour" saw that line-up come to an inglorious end and Paul and Rhys were replaced – respectively – by Sam Fry and Ben Harwood, for a UK tour with (Brighton's) Anal Beard and the long-overdue second album, 'Fanaticos Para Trenes', which Beat Bedsit released in July 2001. After a strong performance on the album, though, Elaine left to devote more time to her family and job and Sam Fry soon followed suit, opening the floodgates for a revolving door of line-ups…

"Drummers came and went, with others filling in when, in true *Spinal Tap* fashion, another had disappeared, got ill or exploded," concedes Jessi wryly. "It *is* rare for a drummer to have been in the studio more than once with us! Those that lasted any length of time were Danny Abrahall, Chris Willsher [who played on probably the band's best album, 2002's 'Roverbrain' for Ruptured Ambitions] and Matt Jockel [who played on 2003's 'One Wrong Can Move A People And A Wronged People Can Move The World' CDEP, again for Ruptured Ambitions]. We gathered a reputation as a hard-working, hard-gigging band, but it probably took its toll on everyone, especially considering we were doing a lot of touring on trains/public transport – and I hate to think of the amount of floors and sofas I have slept on over the years.

"For a few weeks towards the end of 2003, we were all working in various part-time jobs while doing the band fairly full-on; none of us had our own transport or a permanent home and were all fast approaching burn-out. Ben had plans to go off travelling with his girlfriend, Matt had an offer of working on an olive farm in Spain and I was moving up to Lancaster. This seemed like a logical time for a break from it all, so I decided to take a couple of months off. Towards the end of the year we were asked to play a party in Lancaster, though, so Bambi came back, coupled with his wife Trina, who had already done a few gigs with us that year, as a second vocalist, with another old friend Chris Braund on drums [this line-up bringing us the 2005 album, 'Express Train To Doomsville' on Baszdmeg]. In true Eastfield fashion, Chris has since been replaced by Oddo four years ago, which brings us right up to the present day. Having just celebrated our fifteenth anniversary, this is the most stable the band has ever been and long may that continue.

"Inevitably line-up changes will have an effect on intra-band dynamics and chemistry, but this doesn't appear to have had too great an effect on the overall Eastfield sound. Probably because as songwriter, guitarist and singer I have been the only constant and I don't tend to vary too much in what I want to do, or am able to! This hasn't meant that other people haven't played a huge part; they have and a brilliant one too. Inevitably, people are always going to have differing opinions, but on the whole we have all kissed and made up. Some may dismiss my stance as sheer bloody-mindedness, but Eastfield is influenced by my life, ethics, travels, experiences, friends and humour, which is precisely why I can be so damned precious about it. If you believe in something then you have to keep your focus, keep your integrity and always do what you think is for the best. I can honestly say I have always made decisions based on what I believe to be right…though at the same time I'm not so pig-headed to say that I've actually always got it right!"

Since the '…Doomsville' album, Eastfield have issued the 'Loadhaul To Lhasa' CDEP in 2006, a split CD with the reformed Destructors in 2007 and, in among all the gigs, Jessi has even found time to write and record a solo album under the moniker 'Eastfield Derailed'. And, after 'just' six years, a brand new Eastfield full-length is finally in the works as well.

"Eastfield tend not to do 'big' gigs," he offers in conclusion. "Not that we wouldn't relish the opportunity; we just refuse to grovel or prostitute ourselves, so as a result probably get overlooked. However, we're constantly busy and get offered so much that we don't need to be very proactive in chasing gigs ourselves anyway, unless we're filling in existing weekends or piecing together tours with bands we know from overseas. We play similar-sized venues for and with like-minded people up and down the country and that also seems to be the case when we tour abroad. We seem to always draw a similar-sized crowd to our gigs, it's never empty but never hundreds either. Perhaps we have ghettoised ourselves this way? C'est la vie! We've often been told we can transform rooms with the 'Eastfield feel-good factor'… I like that and it's also a compliment when the likes of The Men They Couldn't Hang tell us they enjoy playing with us as it makes them 'raise their game!' We're absolutely as happy and well at home doing smaller festivals such as Glastonwick and Kippertronix etc as we are at Rebellion, where we played most recently in 2009 and the room was full and operating on a one-in/one-out basis…1,000-plus people all upbeat and smiling along with us; I like to think we gave them a lift for the weekend. So, business as usual really…

"And we'll carry on for as long as we continue to have the commitment and self-belief in what we are doing. And for as long as we can stay healthy and out of trouble; who knows how long *that* will be? With regards to being 'relevant', we will *always* be relevant in our hearts and to the people we care about and who care about us. The band has always been based around this mutual co-operation and to this degree, we're constantly communicating and making friends through meeting lots of top people along the way. We have no time for competition, one-upmanship and bickering with our peers, especially when there are more important things in life to worry about.

"It's a horrible word to use, I know, but I consider it a 'success' when I hear that we are frequently looked upon as the 'good guys' (and girls!) We are chuffed that we have managed to do this totally on our own terms, without selling ourselves or shafting anyone else in the process. That would be a fitting epitaph… and that we wrote a load of catchy tunes that people annoyingly couldn't get out of their heads!"

SELECT DISCOGRAPHY:

7-inch:
'Come To Bevland' (Baszdmeg, 1998)
'Potato Print' (PPR, 1999) – *split with Funbug, Swaktang and Lubby Nugget*
'Opening The Lid Of Todd's Peace Box' (Beat Bedsit, 2001)
'Split' (Baszdmeg, 2004) – *split with Confrontation*

CDEPs:
'One Wrong Can Move A People And A Wronged People Can Move The World' (Ruptured Ambitions, 2002)
'Gatecrashing Eurovision' (Baszdmeg, 2005)
'Loadhaul To Lhasa' (Baszdmeg, 2006)

CD albums:
'Keep It Spikey' (Baszdmeg, 1999)
'Fanaticos Para Trenes' (Beat Bedsit, 2001)
'Roverbrain' (Ruptured Ambitions, 2002)
'Express Train To Doomsville' (Baszdmeg, 2005)

AT A GLANCE:
Baszdmeg's 'Urban Rail Punk' is a mammoth two-hours-plus double-CD compilation of everything the band recorded between 1997 and 2005. "143 minutes of the same three chords," scoffs Jessi – and who's going to argue with that?

ROTUNDA

While nowhere near as big as other Birmingham punk exports like GBH, Napalm Death, or even Drongos For Europe, **Rotunda** (named after the infamous Birmingham landmark) are still loved by many and, such is the tight-knit Brummie punk community, are an integral part of the local scene. The self-proclaimed 'punk-rock casualties' are best known for their solid take on the street-punk sound, but started their life as a band intending to be something quite different.

"It all started way back in the summer of 1996, during a good night's drinking, at the now-legendary Birmingham venue known as the Foundry," recalls bassist Dave Cain. "Louis Warren, while talking about the hardcore scene, announced to the table that he wanted to form a new 'power violence' band along the lines of Man Is The Bastard, with a typically 'Brummie'-sounding name and play music that sounded 'like industrial machinery'. Myself, Mark Hawkesford and Dave Burton, who was then guitarist for Intention, all said – pretty much – the same word at once…and that word was 'Rotunda'!"

"The Birmingham scene was good," adds Louis, who, before Rotunda, fronted Depth Charge in the late Eighties and Colourblind during the early Nineties. "There were a lot of bands involved, such as GBH, Contempt, Police Bastard, Intention, Zero Chance, Farse, Spine, POA, Eastfield and Spithead and there was a strong punk community. And there were lots of venues where bands could play, mainly pubs such as the City Tavern, the Jug Of Ale, the Mercat and the Moseley Arms, but particularly the Foundry and most gigs were well attended.

"It was my original idea to form a power-violence band, because that was the kind of music I was into at the time. My idea was for the band to be experimental: to put people together who couldn't necessarily play well, just to make a fucking racket. Then I recruited Pikey into the band and that changed our musical direction completely – because he could actually play and write songs!"

As well as Louis on vocals and Dave on bass, the earliest line-up of Rotunda included the aforementioned Mike 'Pikey' Pike on guitars and Steve Wynne-Jones on drums and they recorded their first demo at a Birmingham studio, Reel To Reel, during March 1997. It featured several songs that would go on to be staples in the band's set – namely 'Neutron Bomb', 'Punk Rocker In Love' and 'Red Sky' – and it wasn't long before Rotunda made their live debut.

"Yeah, the first gig was supporting Snuff and Burnside, on 2 May [1997] at Birmingham's Que Club," says Louis. "We got ourselves on the bill through Greg Hemmings and Debbie Ashmore who were local punk and metal promoters [primarily booking at the Foundry] and good friends of ours. It was particularly nerve-wracking for Dave and Steve, though, because the venue was packed and they'd never played live before, but the gig went down really well."

After playing several local shows that summer, Rotunda entered Magic Garden Studios in Wolverhampton during November 1998 to record their 'My Only Weapon' EP with Gavin Monaghan, which they released on their own Can't Shine Shit Records.

"The name Can't Shine Shit came about following a conversation we had at Magic Garden with Gavin," laughs Louis. "We said to him, 'Can you make anyone sound good?' And he said, 'Well…you can't shine shit!' And we thought that was ace, so we used it as our label name."

In order to thicken their sound up, Rotunda then added a second guitarist to their line-up, in the shape of 20-year-old Jason Webb and began gigging in earnest…including a prestigious gig they *almost* played with the Misfits.

"Yeah, we were really looking forward to that gig and a chance to play with such a legendary band," sighs Louis. "We got there really early, but we weren't allowed a sound check and when the doors opened Whippasnappa were told to go onstage, but they couldn't get any sound out of the mixing desk. Then we were told to go on and the same thing happened to us, which was a bit embarrassing because there were so many people at the gig. Then there was a long wait and Debbie who worked at the Foundry had to go and knock on the door of the Misfits tour bus to tell them it was time to go on. They came in by some back entrance to the Foundry we didn't even know existed and they were in their full regalia. They went onstage to 'Kong At The Gates Of Dawn'; we were standing there as [Misfits bassist] Jerry Only and [their guitarist] Doyle began playing in the backstage corridor next to us as they filed onstage…it was an amazing moment. By the time they went on the crowd were in a frenzy and the sound, of course, was perfect! We wondered afterwards if the Misfits hadn't wanted any support bands in the first place…but even though we were disappointed, it was still a great experience."

During December, 2000, Rotunda recorded their well-received 'The Tribe' CDEP, plus a raucous version of the Conflict classic 'Punk Innit?' for the Blackfish Records compilation, 'Barricades And Broken Dreams: An International Tribute To Conflict'. Matt Pillborough from Sick Puppy then replaced Jason on second guitar, making his live debut at the Station in Redditch on 1 June 2000, supporting the Hard-Ons and Funbug. Sadly he only got the chance to play at the band's beloved Foundry but a few times, as it shut its doors that summer.

"The Foundry was such a brilliant venue," remembers Louis, fondly. "We were very good friends with Greg and Debbie and they gave us some brilliant support slots with touring punk bands. Me, Dave and Pikey even ended up DJ-ing upstairs there on Saturday nights, which helped pay for the 'My Only Weapon' CDEP. The Foundry was brilliant for the Birmingham scene because all the best punk bands played there and when it closed it left a massive gap in the scene, because it was the only independent mid-sized venue where alternative bands could play. We made some really good friends at the Foundry and we were really sad to see it go."

"It really was the band's second home and the place where it all began for us," adds Dave. "So you can imagine how upset we were when rumours began circulating that it was closing its doors for good. Those rumours unfortunately proved true and on 2 July 2001, as the band that had played there the most times, Rotunda were invited to headline the last ever Foundry gig, with support from Farce, Sally and Labrat. Alcohol-fuelled chaos ensued, with people trying to procure souvenirs and at one point during the evening, someone actually attempted to head-butt the condom machine off the wall in the gents' toilet. This same character also got up on stage while Rotunda were playing, wrapped in toilet paper and attempting to set himself on fire. He lived, of course, because as most people with a taste for pyromania know, toilet paper smoulders more than ignites…"

2001 also saw the band playing the Holidays In The Sun festival in Morecambe and appearing as part of the Radio 1 Fringe Festival, supporting Road Rage at Scruffy Murphy's in Birmingham, their set so impressing DJ Steve Lamacq that he played 'Neutron Bomb' on his next *Evening Session* show. But not all their gigs went so well…

"Probably the worst gig we ever did was in Lancaster," laughs Louis. "It was a Halloween party for a friend and some local band wanted to headline, but they were just a covers band so they weren't allowed. Some of the audience were mates with them, though, so they were already pissed off when we played and then the crowd took exception to our song, 'We Don't Like You' and someone punched me in the face as I was singing it. We got threatened with iron bars and had to make a swift exit from the venue, 'cos it was *definitely* going to kick off…!"

On 31 May 2002, Rotunda took a third trip to Magic Garden to record what became known as the 'Out Of Time' EP, which featured a cover of the Soft Cell classic 'Bedsitter' complete with a vocal contribution from Louis' then-fiancée (now wife) Emma Downing. In the latter half of 2002, Matt's friendship with fledgling film-maker Sarah Walker led to Rotunda having one of their songs ('Punk Rock Casualty' from 'My Only Weapon') showcased on the soundtrack to a short 10-minute film which she had written and directed, entitled *420 Seconds Of Love*. On 22 November 2002, Rotunda were invited to attend the Birmingham premiere of the film, which went on to achieve critical acclaim on the UK's independent film festival circuit.

Unfortunately Louis left soon after, due to the usual "musical and personal differences" and formed the Gloaters with Emma and ex-Velvet Underpants bassist Ivan Morris and drummer Rag. However, the band persevered without him, Matt taking over vocal duties for 2003's 'Punk Rock Elite' EP and he re-joined in 2006 in time for Rotunda to contribute to the 'Three-Way Split' on Meltdown Records, alongside Assert and Indecent Assault and to play the ultimate Rotunda gig – at the Rotunda!

Rotunda line-up

Rotunda, Louis live

"This was all due to our involvement with Worcestershire-based author Nick Gaunt's film documentary and accompanying book, *21 Stories*, charting the history of the Rotunda building in Birmingham," says Dave, proudly. "It basically enabled us to do the gig that we had wanted to do since day one, at the Rotunda and [on 12 June 2008], after a hard evening drinking champagne at the opening of the *21 Stories* exhibition in the Three White Walls gallery in Birmingham's Mailbox, we staggered down to the Rotunda and did our thing!"

And it looks as if they'll be 'doing their thing' for some time to come, because they've finally released a proper album, the 26-song 'Chalk It Up', and are sounding better than ever.

"We've somehow still got the same enthusiasm now as we had 15 years ago," concludes Louis, incredulously. "I don't think we ever imagined it would last so long, but it has and that's because we still enjoy gigging and recording. We might not be the biggest band from here, but will hopefully be remembered as Birmingham's punk-rock casualties…rot on!"

SELECT DISCOGRAPHY:

CDEPs:
'My Only Weapon' (Can't Shine Shit, 1998)
'The Tribe' (Can't Shine Shit, 2000)
'Out Of Time' (Can't Shine Shit, 2002)
'Punk Rock Elite' (Can't Shine Shit, 2003)
'Three-Way Split' (Meltdown, 2007) – *split with Assert and Indecent Assault*

CD:
'Chalk It Up' (Can't Shine Shit, 2011)

AT A GLANCE:
Obviously the full-length album would be a good place to start, but the 'You Filthy Rotters' sampler compiles 12 of the best tracks from the band's self-released EPs.
www.myspace.com/punkrotters or look them up on Facebook: Rotunda Punk Rock Casualties

INTENTION

Birmingham's **Intention** were formed in 1995 and featured Jay Malloy on vocals, Dave Burton on guitar, Jonathon 'Banny' Bannister on bass and Ivor Joseph on drums, although most people would agree that the band only started to come into their own when Jay left to start the short-lived but well-respected Ackbar and Ian from LD50 took over the mic.

"The first time I saw Intention, they were supporting 108 and Abinandha at the Hibernian, Birmingham, some time in '95," recalls Ian. "I was very much the anarcho/peace/crust-type punk myself, but would go to pretty much any show that was around. US style hardcore was a bit alien to me, to be honest; it seemed to mainly be metal mixed with punk, played by short-haired blokes in smart jumpers and chinos. That's what seemed to be the case in '95, anyway.

"I still don't know why Jay left them; I just remember him not turning up for a show and Banny singing instead. The next show Intention did, with Banny singing again, was also *my* last show with LD50 and I stepped in to do a few Intention tracks for them. I was gutted when LD50 called it a day – the bassist and main guy, Dee, went on to play in an incarnation of Police Bastard and guitarist 'Little Ian' went to Contempt for a while – but at least I had a new band to go to…a seamless transition, you might say!

"Musically it's always been dependent on the members," he adds, when discussing Intention's ever-changing influences, "but has included everything from blast beats to jazz. The era and bands most of us have had in common though would be the Eighties and Nineties thrash scene and the crossover or 'funk-metal' stuff – if you can call it that? – like Jane's Addiction, Fishbone and Primus. For me, the fave bands that I know shaped our stuff have been Voivod, Sabbat, Primus, Dead Kennedys, Nomeansno, Faith No More, Bad Religion and even Nick Cave. Lyrically it's only ever been myself and I'm a pretty creative guy, even though I say so myself. I like to muck around with imagery, diction and words themselves, just as if I was writing poetry or prose. Very much libertarian or anarchist politically, but with a bit of Buddhism thrown in here and there… Anti-drugs without being straightedge, anti-religion without being full-on atheist… Definitely agnostic – there *is* a difference!"

Playing regularly in and around the Midlands with bands like Spithead, Rotunda, Eastfield, Police Bastard and Contempt, Intention developed their quirky crossover sound – part screamy thrash noise, part funky metallic punk – over several demos they recorded during the mid to late Nineties.

"'Foundation' [1996] was recorded with our mate Crusty Chris [Eastfield's first drummer] in his bedroom," smiles Ian. "Looking back it was pants, but we were really pleased with it at the time. It got one or two good fanzine reviews, but mostly a mediocre response – which was probably pretty fair.

"Then we did 'Opt Out' [1997] at Dudley College with Dave Shaw who was in Banny's other band, Exocet Erection [later renamed Stand To Reason]. That featured my first ever full-on screaming song, 'Self Inflicted', which always went down very well live and shaped our trademark sound – kind of 'Faith No Kennedys' with extra Sabbat demon screams… weird. Next we did 'Hatred Shape' [1998] at a rehearsal space up by Birmingham City Road Hospital, I forget the name, which was more of the same but a bit more arty.

"The turnaround was doing 'Positive' [1999], which we did with Gav Monaghan at Magic

Intention, vocalist Ian, live in Bristol

Intention 2007, Dave, Gaz, Ian and Mothy

Garden. It got 3 out of 5 in *Kerrang!*, which score-wise ain't that great but the write-up was very encouraging. Then we did 'Black Bloc' [2001] at Framework, again in Brum, which one reviewer said was, 'Metal with anarcho lyrics' and they were bang on with that, looking back. That took us up to the early 'Noughties' and we stopped doing demos then as we did our albums instead..."

But before those albums, there were lots more gigs (with everyone from Agnostic Front to Nomeansno), lots more line-up changes (too many to mention) and even a few more demos, 2005's 'Stop The Rot' and 2007's 'Near Dark'. Of the two albums, 'Afraid At The Edges' came out in 2007 on Black Records, through Revolver, and was very fast, very metallic and very political – and, let's face it, there's nothing wrong with records like *that*, is there? By the time the second album landed in 2008 (12 years without an album, then two come along within 12 months!), 'In The Company Of Wolves', the band had reached a definitive sound that saw them distilling their USHC influences through a very English filter, the end result something akin to Assert or Medulla Nocte meets the Dead Kennedys. Again, it's all good.

Nowadays, Intention are still Ian on vocals, only joined by Dave Shaw on guitar, Gaz Armstrong on bass and Jay Tatler on drums, although with half a dozen young kids between them and Jay also playing for English Dogs it's safe to say they'll never be as busy as they were in the Nineties.

"Our hearts were always in the right place," reckons Ian proudly, when pushed as to how he would like Intention remembered. "Always sleeping on floors, or travelling to places like London and Sheffield to do gigs on the train or bus, 'cos we didn't have band member who could drive for many years. We tried and tried and we did to an extent 'keep it real'. We didn't sit easily alongside our peers musically; the fads came and went, but we carried on. There has been a lot of Oi! and street-punk from the West Midlands and we played with all those bands but didn't share their sound. Then there was a lot of slower or more metally stuff as well, lo and behold, just at the time we got faster, twistier and less metal than ever!

"Basically I think we'll be remembered for two songs: 'Stop The Rot' and 'Positive'. Two of the rarest things for us: singalong songs. But I hope someone will one day realise that the line, 'The Noughties ain't that nice' in 'Stop The Rot' was, on the one hand, lamenting the rise of New Labour and on the other, inspired by a cream cake advert by Kenneth Williams!"

SELECT DISCOGRAPHY:

CD LPs:
'Afraid At The Edges' (Black/Revolver, 2007)
'In The Company Of Wolves' (Angry Scenes, 2008)

AT A GLANCE:
Maybe now would be a good time for someone to compile all those demos onto a retrospective CD? Meanwhile you can contact Ian for copies: iantention@hotmail.com

POA

Birmingham's **POA** were only together for four years and released just one EP and album, but they made quite an impact upon the local punk scene with their powerful Antisect-inspired noises and went on to populate several important underground Midlands bands in later years. Guitarist Martin Batt and drummer Pix-E first played together, upon leaving school, in an alternative grunge/rock band called Black Kactus.

"We met through an old girlfriend and as soon as we jammed I knew that something would come of it," reckons Pix-E. "Black Kactus had been going since I was just 13, but we only lasted a few more months after Mart joined. I had a call from the other two guys in the band saying that they were leaving to start a new band in the Brit-pop vein, so I biked it straight up to Mart's and told him the band had split up, but it didn't matter as we could now do our planned side project full-time instead…which was to be a punk band. We were both getting into punk around that time so it seemed a logical step…"

"We started jamming, but didn't have a bass player initially, so we had this girl, Becca, doing bass on a fuckin' keyboard!" laughs Mart. "When we finally got Jon (aka Jon Perverted) to join on bass, none of us had the heart to tell Becca she wasn't needed any more; we just hoped she'd get the message, but in the end Pix was lumbered with telling her."

After toying with various piss-poor names like Nitro and Panik Bratz, the band finally decided on the 'POA' moniker and recruited a second guitarist – Mart's brother, Craig (aka Wig). It wasn't until February 1997 that they played their first gig, though, hiring out Moseley Dance Centre and inviting Farse to support them, quickly tapping into the well-established Brummie punk scene.

"It wasn't until we started gigging that people began asking what POA stood for," reveals Mart. "It was basically just word of mouth among people getting into the band that 'Piss On Authority' stuck. But to be honest, where we were from in Oldbury, on the outskirts of Brum, there was no real *scene*; in fact we thought we were the only punks left on earth! We'd been into the whole early Nineties alternative thing and we'd got turned onto punk by bands like Nirvana and Sonic Youth. I remember reading interviews with those guys and them talking about bands like Black Flag, Hüsker Dü and Scream and instinctively wanting to know more about them. Before I knew it I'd fallen in love with the whole punk thing, which would only escalate when we realised that punk was alive and well and there was this whole network going on around us; it surprised us actually. I remember Pix getting hold of a Ruts tape when we were first discovering punk and that sold it to us a bit more; also, Pix and I saw Rancid at the Foundry in Brum in September '95 and that blew us away… I guess they were quite influential on our early sound."

By the time of that first gig, POA had already recorded three demos, that saw them evolving at a rate of knots, but the third demo was the only one that they even had chance to distribute and was the one that marked their sound crossing over from street-punk to the harder, more politicised style that most people remember them for.

September 1997 saw them supporting Police Bastard in Leamington Spa and two months later they were asked to support PB on a short run of German dates – not bad for a young band with no official release to their name! But that's the self-empowerment of punk rock for you in a nutshell: anyone can get out there and do it if they put their mind to it.

Mart and Wig

POA, Pix-E

"The first stop was Bremen and it was a whole different kettle of fish to what we'd experienced back home," recalls Mart happily. "We were getting free food, free booze, free drugs…it was awesome! We got to the squat where we were playing and then news filtered through that Police Bastard had broken down and wouldn't make the first night, so it turned out we'd be headlining our very first gig in Europe; we shat ourselves! On top of that I turned around after soundcheck to see Wig unconscious! Luckily he recovered in time to play and we seemed to go down okay. I remember losing the rest of the band afterwards and found myself drinking with an Irish punk in some random pub listening to Total Chaos all night; I was in heaven!"

"That first night on tour was my introduction to squatting," says Pix-E, "and I've never looked back since as I've never felt so wanted by any community. It even inspired me to set my own squats up, which I did, and now I help others to do it…"

"The next gig was in Berlin at the Kopi, which Pix now has tattooed on his fingers," continues Mart. "That was a mental gig, our biggest we'd played to date; it was absolutely rammed with about 300 people inside and a load more outside that couldn't get in, lighting bonfires in the car park. Again we went down quite well considering we were still in the early stages of gigging, but when Police Bastard played it totally went off; the whole place was bouncing wall to wall."

"And when we were playing, our driver got left in charge of the lighting while the guy went for a piss," laughs Pix-E. "Big mistake! For the next five minutes we played in complete darkness…" Mart: "Then the last gig of the tour was in Hamburg. Before we played I remember going to the bar to get a beer and the barman asked me, 'Do you smoke?' 'No,' I replied, 'But my friends do…' and the guy reached under the bar and pulled out the biggest bag of weed I'd ever seen. The lads' faces were a picture when I walked back over with that!

"After the gig, the two bands went out into the Reeperbahn part of town and had a wicked night. As soon as we sat down in this one bar, one of our lot came over to our table with a silver tray full of shots of Jägermeister and wraps of speed! We eventually made our way back to the squat above the venue around 5 or 6am and, as we were walking up this spiral staircase, a gang of lads from the squat came charging down, all balaclava'd up with bats and shit. We crapped it for a second until they ran past us…. Apparently someone from the local Turkish community had attacked a punk girl and these guys were off out to sort it!"

Suitably inspired, POA spent the first half of 1998 gigging concertedly, the apparent highlights being when they supported the newly-reformed Subhumans in Birmingham and opening up for Brazilian thrashers RDP at the Bristol Skate'n'Ride. In September of that year, they recorded the four-track 'Let 'Em Burn' CDEP for Staffordshire label Problem Child, although Wig left (he went on to drum for Dogshit Sandwich) and was replaced by Russell (aka Rez) before it was even released. It was an arresting debut nonetheless, with the band demonstrating both their catchy street-punk roots on songs like 'Scapegoat' and their rapidly emerging heavier side, with 'Uniformed Enemy' almost reminiscent of Sepultura.

It brought them to the attention of Blackfish Records, who asked POA to contribute their killer version of 'Subvert City' to the 1999 compilation, 'Still Can't Hear The Words: The Subhumans Covers Album'. Things weren't working out as planned with Problem Child and the band ended up jumping ship to Blackfish for their only album, 'The Fear Of War', which was recorded at Jigsaw Studios in Peterborough by Tom Savage during March 1999 and then re-mastered at the Whitehouse in Weston-super-Mare by Martin Nicholls.

"The guy from Problem Child hadn't even got distribution for the EP," sighs Mart. "We didn't know this until they'd all been pressed and it slowly became apparent he didn't really know what he was doing. It was his first release as well as ours and we certainly didn't know how it all worked, so we trusted him. We couldn't see any form of promotion going on or the EP getting reviewed anywhere…nothing. The alarm bells were ringing and we gave him the benefit of the doubt, but nothing materialised; he talked about possible Peel sessions and stuff like that, but nothing ever came of it.

"At first we were just annoyed by it all and would never have fallen out with him. We already had a verbal agreement to release an album with Problem Child as well, but we knew it would have gone the same way as the EP so after interest from Blackfish Records we pulled the plug on it. The guy freaked out and came to meet us; understandably he was upset as he'd invested money into us but we had no problem with him continuing to sell the EP and making his money back, we just didn't want to put the album out through him. In the end we were contacted by his solicitors, claiming we were liable to pay all costs back to Problem Child; we were fuckin' livid, 'cos this guy had made mistakes, not us. He didn't know how to sell all those copies of our EP and wanted his money back. We could've forked out a load of money and pressed a load of CDs on our own but we trusted he'd know what to do with them.

"We spoke to a solicitor who said it'd be easier to pay up rather than end up incurring court costs and that this guy's word could stand up against ours, despite us never signing any contracts. The guy fucked us over; I know he didn't set out to rip us off or anything, but he stood to lose money through his own negligence and lack of knowledge of the industry, so made us pay instead. We were just kids then, of course and although I can't remember how much we had to pay, we didn't have that sort of money on the jobs we had. It was worth it in the end though as we were all 100% sure that going with Blackfish was the right choice. If it had come out on Problem Child, our friends would have had a few copies, my loft would be more full and my bank account would be emptier…but hey, you live and you learn."

The album was a staggeringly brutal slab of hardcore anarcho punk that by rights should have catapulted POA to the top of the international punk scene. Unfortunately the band split up not long after its release, playing their last gig in Bath during December 1999.

"Why did we split up? It's kind of a weird one to answer as I don't think there is one solitary reason for it," ponders Mart. "It was a lot of things that finished it in the end. I still don't like to phrase it 'splitting up' either, 'cos it wasn't like we all got together and called it a day or anything; it just fizzled out. We had been practising religiously at least three times a week for four-and-a-half years and gigging most weekends for about three years of that. Sometimes we gigged in the week as well and we'd often have two gigs on a weekend with some of them on the same day. Come late '99, we were sick of the sight of each other!

"I think the whole Problem Child episode had an effect as well, paying all that money back in instalments; we weren't little rich kids that could fob it off onto mummy and daddy. Those things take their toll and we became disillusioned. Another big factor was that our loyal driver of the last four-plus years had to leave to care for his missus who had fallen ill; none of us drove and we just couldn't find anyone else to do it. Gigs were coming and going and we just couldn't get to them."

"On top of that I was going through a messy divorce," adds Pix-E. "I got married young, after a whirlwind romance – I think we'd only been together six months – and it got very messy.

She turned out to be a bit psychotic, so I had a lot on my plate around that time…"

"We were still young and very naive," continues Mart. "I don't think we realised our potential at all. We were all getting into loads of different styles of music as well – some good, some bad – and we were curious about experimenting. There was talk of doing something completely fresh but under a different name, so as not to mislead anyone; we were quite fearful of becoming pigeon-holed and stagnating.

"We hadn't done anything for a short while when Pix got asked to do a European tour with Sensa Yuma, which of course he did; he'd just separated from his wife so it came at a good time for him. When he returned, he announced he'd met a girl in France and was moving out there, so that was game over where POA was concerned; Pix and I were the founding members and it would never have felt right with him not in the band."

Pix: "Yeah, I met these squatters in Brittany and it really turned me onto political activism in a much bigger way, so I wanted to stick around." Once Pix-E did eventually return from France, he, Mart and Rez did an experimental alternative band called Kaya (complete with Brit-style MC and DJ), before he and Mart teamed up with Scary Dave from Flyboy and Andy 'Ardcore from Ruin-Nation to form H8-Target. Pix then went on to drum for Police Bastard and Last Under The Sun, while Rez became involved with his dark 'dubstep' project called Zero-One.

Then in late 2006, inspired by the positive response to their belated MySpace page, POA lurched tentatively back to life for a few gigs in Birmingham before going back on hiatus until very recently, when they started to write together again for the long-overdue second album.

"When we started out we didn't have any grand aspirations and, although we didn't shake the scene to its core or anything, the fact we're answering these questions now means we must have done something right," states Mart proudly. "If just one person remembers us for being the band that made them aware of something, or if they maybe formed their own band 'cos they saw a bunch of dimwit Brummies up there doing it and thought, 'Well if they can do it…', or if they just remember having a good night once at a POA gig, then I'm more than cool with that. Hopefully we'll push on from here now we're doing it again…this second album's been a long time coming!"

SELECT DISCOGRAPHY:

CDEP:
'Let 'Em Burn' (Problem Child, 1998)

CD:
'The Fear Of War' (Blackfish, 1999)

AT A GLANCE:
Gotta be 'The Fear Of War', a heaving beast of a punk album if ever there was one!

STEP BACK

Of all the bands that attempted the '88 Youth Crew-style hardcore from Britain, the short-lived but much-loved **Step Back** from Oldbury, Birmingham, were probably the most convincing. They only released the one CDEP, but it's a fairly essential release if you like old school hardcore as per the early Revelation roster and most of their gigs predictably resulted in a good old finger-pointing pig-pile.

"At one point in time, between '94 and '96, there was a small but decent local scene based around the Saracen's Head in Dudley," begins vocalist Dave Goreham, who started writing Step Back material in late '96 when he split from the metal band he was in, Deadlock, "and also the City Tavern in Birmingham. The shows seemed to have some cool line-ups: Hard To Swallow, DDT, Stand To Reason, Intention... The Foundry was another decent local venue, although that was really more suited to bigger touring bands – otherwise the fucker was half empty! Without doubt, my favourite local bands at that time were DDT and Stand To Reason; Banny who sang for STR had an awesome vocal style and wrote great lyrics. Zine-wise the only local one that springs to mind from that era was *Steady Diet...*' [*Of Nothing*, done by Satpal Kalsi] which was good and had a massive variety of musical styles covered.

"I have to say that the 'bigger' UKHC scene that was around at that time, which was mainly bands sounding like Morbid Angel or Slayer, did nothing for me musically; my influences were Bold, Unit Pride, Chain Of Strength, Youth Of Today and Upfront and also some of the older UK bands like Intense Degree and Jailcell Recipes. Lyrically, I'd say the Unit Pride 7-inch or the Wide Awake 7-inch were good reference points. As time went on with the band, I don't think we strayed too much from the original formula and stuck to playing fast, '88-style hardcore. When we first started, it really seemed like there was just a small handful of bands playing the kind of hardcore I was interested in, which was good motivation to do the band and write those songs. By the time we had got a stable line-up and recorded a CD, it seemed like the revival thing had gone crazy and it was totally the opposite. *Way* more bands started playing traditional hardcore..."

As Dave hints in that last sentence, a considerable time lapsed between when he started to write Step Back songs and when the band finally played their first show. Starting as just a two-piece, Dave was joined by Antony 'Dex' Dexter on drums and after trying out several guitarists and bassists, the first Step Back demo was actually recorded by just the two of them.

"That was done in February 1997," explains Dave, "with Banny [aka Jonathan Bannister] and Dave Shaw, who both played in Stand To Reason and were doing a music technology course and could get free studio time at the college. It was awesome that it didn't cost us anything to record, but Dex was set up in a classroom recording the drum tracks and I recorded everything else in the control room. I remember being pretty nervous about recording the vocals, as I'm by no means a vocalist at all; I'd never sang the songs more than a handful of times, so I didn't know how it would sound.

"We were mainly hoping that having a demo out would make it easier to recruit other guys to the band, as well as getting some of the tunes out there. At the time I was really happy with it; in fact I still think it's probably the best thing we recorded, as it's just so simple and raw. Not being able to play live at that point made the demo seem sweeter too, as it gave

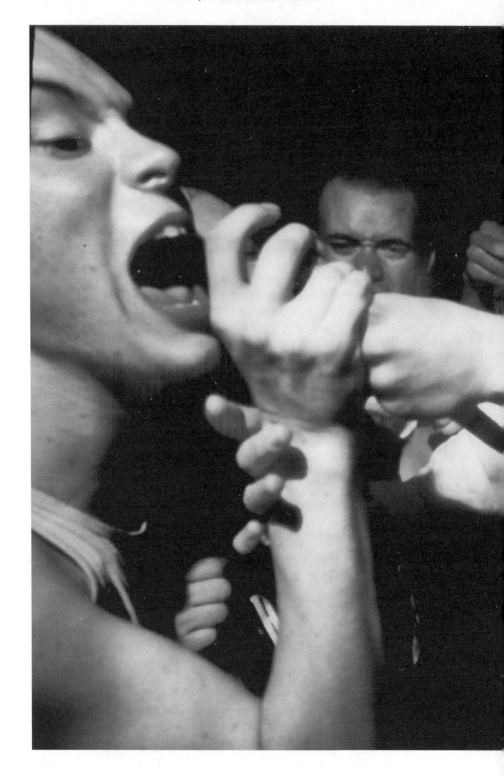

Stepback live, by Naki

Stepback, line-up photo by Naki

269

the band a bit more life. Dave Shaw and Banny recorded and mixed everything, then helped with the back-up vocals and when it was finished we had 50 tapes made; we flyered it at shows all over Brum and in mail-orders and stuff – all the old pre-internet ways – and it really started to sell more than we expected. I think in the end we sold close to 500 of them and got some really good feedback. I also think quite a few people were surprised to hear a band that sounded like us, especially from the UK."

Unfortunately any momentum the band might have established with the demo was counteracted by the fact they didn't have a full line-up and couldn't play live to promote it and it wasn't until January 1998, after they'd recruited guitarist Steve and bassist Rhys, that Step Back finally played their first show. It was at the Flapper And Firkin in Birmingham, with Spine and Farce and once they'd started, they didn't want to stop…

"We played an all-dayer in Leeds the following weekend," recalls Dave. "I don't think there was anybody there that had heard us and we only played a shortish set but sold a ton of demos after and that felt awesome – taking the train to another city, playing, then rushing for the last train back to Birmingham! I think that the first six months of playing shows, from January '98 through that summer, were probably the best gigs we did. For most of them, we took some form of public transport to get there; I think we took a train or a coach to a fair portion of the country, as my car was too old and unreliable to drive four people and gear any reasonable distance. There was a good energy to the band about then, although there were low points as well, of course, like a show at the Old Railway, Birmingham, where about three people showed up… Also our guitar-player Ste getting into a verbal scrap over wearing an England football shirt at a gig. It would have been funny had it not been so cringeworthy.

"But the UKHC scene seemed to take off all of a sudden," he adds. "There were tons of shows happening all the time and there was a fair mix of styles about. I don't think the fast posi-core style of music we played ever *really* took off in the UK, not compared to the amount of bands playing metal; there was only ever a few other bands which were doing it. Touchdown from London were awesome, as were HHH [Peterborough] and Engage [Edinburgh] who came a little later…in 1999, I think? The first time I saw Engage live in Birmingham I was blown away; they played a Dag Nasty cover and sounded like Turning Point…I couldn't believe how good they were. But it seemed like every time you went to a show there was another new zine and another new band and there were some awesome huge distros around too. I remember the first time I saw Touchdown at the Redeye in London; Dave the guitar player was wearing cream Armani jeans…not very Youth Of Today, it has to be said!"

The band recorded the 11-song 'My Own Way' CDEP for Team Spirit Records at UB40's DEP International Studios during May 1998 and it was basically a continuation of the manic Youth Crew hardcore of the demo, although lacking some of the demo's raw energy, no doubt polished off in the confines of a professional studio. Still fast as fuck, though.

"We had Danny Sprig to engineer, who had worked with bands like Napalm Death… I remember me and Dex telling him to make the toms sound the same as Napalm's drum sound! Production-wise, I still think that the recording came out sounding great, but there are a few things I'm not so happy with now, listening back and I really wish someone else could have taken care of the vocals and done a better job than I did. Also I wish I could have recorded all the guitar parts myself, the same as I did with the demo; that's what I was happiest doing, but anyway we recorded all the music live in one room and I did all the second guitar parts. I don't think there were any overdubs on the music at all, then it was a couple of hours to put the vocals down and the whole thing was recorded in one day and we mixed it the following week, again in just one day."

One other song from the session, 'Direction', was included on the 'There's Still A Lot To Say' compilation 7-inch, a split release between two German labels, Give It A Voice and X-Files, that saw them appearing alongside the likes of Reinforce, Highscore and Force Of Change. More gigs were undertaken, but, after a proposed European tour fell through, enthusiasm was waning in the Step Back camp and their cover of 'By Myself' for the Cro-Mags tribute compilation on Blackfish turned out to be the final Step Back release.

"There was never an actual break-up or falling-out which caused the end of the band," explains Dave. "It just seemed to run out of steam; I can't remember if it was late 1999 or 2000? We weren't playing as many shows at that point; Rhys had another punk band going as well by then and was starting to do a fair amount of work as a sound engineer most evenings and it just seemed – to me, at least – that it was nowhere near as much fun as it had been back in the early days. Even writing new stuff was becoming more of a chore.

"The other thing was that I'd been having a few issues with my throat which was making it harder to get through gigs without my voice going. So the split wasn't really planned as such, but I guess it was on the cards; we played a show in Brum and decided to take a few weeks off and we never ended up getting back together. I've no regrets to the timing of it; I think we'd had the best out of the band during 1997 and 1998, those times were really fun."

With his throat shot, Dave played guitar for Approach before reuniting with Dex in 2003 as Affirmation. He and Dex still play killer straight-up hardcore in the vein of Ignite or Uniform Choice even today, as Times Together, who have two EPs available through Anger Battery Records.

"We were around for a relatively short time compared to a lot of other bands," ponders Dave, in closing. "We also never toured as extensively as a lot of other bands, but when we started there was hardly anyone in the UK that played the same style of hardcore as us. I think it would be nice to be remembered as a couple of guys who got together to play hardcore as we liked to hear it, fast and simple and pretend that 1988 had never ended, regardless of what everyone else at the time was doing. No huge agenda; just to have some fun and see what happened along the way…"

SELECT DISCOGRAPHY:

CDEP:
'My Own Way' (Team Spirit, 1998)

AT A GLANCE:
That'll be the EP then, but that demo is also worth a listen if you can hunt it out for download and be sure to check out Times Together too – the spirit of Step Back lives on!

EXCREMENT OF WAR

Dudley D-beat band **Excrement Of War** produced one of the very best 'Discore' albums of the Nineties in the shape of 1993's 'Cathode Ray Coma' and the fact that it contained a good dose of Scandinavian intensity and a vicious male/female vocal attack (and, if you've heard it, you'll know that 'attack' really is the right word!) helped elevate it above the rest of this somewhat cookie-cutter genre. But the first line-up of the band, as realised by guitarist/ vocalist Tom Croft (ex-Genital Deformities), bassist John 'Wonka' Williams and drummer Darren 'Rat' Radburn (ex-Indecent Assault, Depthcharge, Trademark Go! and Semtex) was an all-male three-piece…after they parted ways with their first two vocalists, Adam Kerrigan and Mik Glaze, that is. Indeed the whole Excrement Of War story is one long list of changing personnel.

"The intention originally was to create a racket akin to Disorder or Chaos UK, with lyrics predominantly being in the tried'n'tested Discharge anti-war mould," begins Rat. "At the time we formed [early 1990], Tom was living in a flat that had a bedroom wall adorned with graffiti and I had scrawled several slogans across it…from these, 'Excrement Of War' was chosen as the band's moniker, while others, like 'Rows Of Rotting Soldiers' and 'Maimed And Dismembered' became song titles…

"That early three-piece version of the band recorded the first demo ['Dead In Auschwitz'] in 1990 at Julian Ward Davies' studios, which was basically just a set-up in Julian's council house. Drums were played in an upstairs bedroom, vocals overdubbed by me and Tom and the whole thing linked together with movie extracts from the low-budget horror films that Tom and myself were hooked on, like *Basket Case* and *Return Of The Living Dead*.

"The experience was horrible," he concedes. "We weren't happy with it at all and Wonka seemed to be going the same way as the previous vocalists, basically not as interested as me and Tom. So we discussed a swap-round; I switched to bass and was handling lead vocals as well, Wonka left and Tom decided to ask Stick [aka Tony Dickens from Doom] to help out. We switched from rehearsing in a tiny room in Amblecote to travelling to Brum for practise. The band also took the opportunity to change our style from being a noisy clattering of Riot City label rejects into tight, Swedish-inspired hardcore punk. Stick came up with the names 'Tommi Cimex' and 'Shitty Rat-Licker', an obvious nod to the new sound and inspiration…"

"I got asked to join them as soon as I left Doom," recalls Stick. "I wanted to carry on playing brutal Swedish-style punk and the main reason I left Doom at that time was because it seemed we had lost our direction, or directness anyway, so I actually wanted to re-achieve what I'd already had. We were all a bit new to our instruments, it's true, so it was never going to get too pretentious, which I liked and what we lacked in prowess musically we more than made up for in 'gung ho' spirit…"

After just a few practices, Excrement Of War played their first gig, at the Source in Wordsley with Zygote, before recording another demo, a furiously raw five-track effort, at the Fulton Street youth club where the band practised every Friday night. Stick sent it off to his friends at Swedish label Finn Records, who released four of the songs on one side of a split 7-inch that EOW shared with Dischange.

"We almost had free run of that youth club, which was near to where Tom and Rat lived," reckons Stick. "There was a little studio in there for people to learn on and that's where we did this rough old demo, with five songs on it, one of them a cover of a Doom song ['Relief (Part 3)']. I sent it off to the guys at Finn as they were mates and I just knew it would be up their street and they offered to do a split with Jallo's new band Dischange; their side of the single was a *lot* more polished than ours, of course, but I still think we sounded good."

A second single, 'The Waste…And The Greed' EP, was recorded soon after, this time down at the popular Whitehouse Studio in Weston-super-Mare with Martin Nicholls and released by Mark Bailey from Extreme Noise Terror on his Ragged Trouser Philanthropist label. Limited to just 1000 copies, it was another searing assault on the senses, even though it's hard to take the aforementioned song titles like 'Maimed And Dismembered' or 'Rows Of Rotting Soldiers' completely seriously, given their utter plagiarism of D-beat originators Discharge.

Unfortunately Rat became 'unreliable' and was replaced on bass by Jez, also from Genital Deformities; Mark Bailey joined on second guitar, allowing Tom to concentrate more on the vocals while playing some guitar as well. This line-up only recorded one song – an amazing cover of Discharge's 'Tomorrow Belongs To Us' for the 'Discharged' compilation, released by Rhythm Vicar and also featuring the likes of Extreme Noise Terror and Concrete Sox – before Mark left and the band went into hiatus until they were joined by new bassist Paul 'Mal' Mallen and new vocalists, Leigh Wiles and Margaret 'Mags' Hehir.

"We parted ways with Rat 'cos he had a job and kept blowing gigs out," reveals Stick, before adding, "ironically enough, we chucked him out for that, then couldn't do any gigs as we didn't have a replacement. After that started the revolving door policy that was EOW; people came and went… Tom and myself were the backbone, but bits of the monster kept dropping off. At one point, it was Tom, me and Mal; we'd get together on a Friday night at the youth club and bash out new songs with no real knowledge that dirt were ever gonna get played or recorded. We got quite a stash of material up together, so when Leigh and Mags joined we had plenty of stuff for them to be getting on with…"

"I quit in 1991, although the others may say they kicked me out," counters Rat. "I'd got a lot of stuff going on outside the band, a college course basically, plus I was juggling round other aspects of my personal life; I should have sat down and told the others it was getting difficult, but I'd just not feel like rehearsing, call off the session and go down the pub. I turned up to one rehearsal and Mark was jamming on guitar; he's a smashing bloke, but we'd not even discussed it and I was thinking, 'Hang on, this might well be a good idea, but have I not got a say any longer?' In the end I stayed away and they carried on with Mal on bass, who was one of Tom's mates; then Jez from GD joined as well and I lost touch with it all.

"Looking back it's easy to say you'd have done things differently and ultimately I still ponder why I didn't carry on with it. Stick had done Peel sessions with Doom and ENT and been out to Europe and Japan and we regularly talked about those opportunities being likely for EOW. I loved how the band moved in a different direction by taking Mags on as vocalist too; my biggest regret is that we didn't somehow reconcile our issues and the both of us had recorded something together. I think that would have been the best stuff the band potentially could have put out…"

"I was living in Plaistow, in east London, at the time," says Leigh, picking up the story from his perspective, "sharing a house with John Bryson, who'd left Antisect a few years before and was now concentrating on playing bass with his then-new band Splitpigs. We lived in this housing co-operative called Persons Unknown, along with a group of other people, mostly from the older anarcho-punk scene, including members of Dirt. Most of us hung out

Excrement of War, live

Excrement of War, Mags

together, so I soon became part of that band, mainly driving and doing roadie duties etc, as they had a bit of a visual stage presence with all the TVs playing and banners and stuff. I also became stand-in bassist when needed at practices and I did one gig with them supporting Rudimentary Peni at the Venue in New Cross [London].

"Anyway, we were away with Dirt, doing a two-week UK tour with Hellkrusher, who thought it amusing I get up and sing the cover songs they did at the end of their set every night, One Way System's 'Give Us A Future' and GBH's 'Sick Boy'… I guess it was with reference to my blonde spiked hair similar to Colin from GBH! Stick came along to a few of the gigs too, as Doom played one of the first on the tour; he asked me if I was into auditioning for Excrement Of War, as they were in need of a vocalist and I was really into their two EPs, so was well up for it.

"I'd just started seeing Mags at the time and thought why not suggest dual male/female vocals; the band agreed and I worked a way to combine two singers. Mags was really into the idea but had never sang before; she'd played bass too, but nothing ever came of that band-wise. So I picked her up on the way to the weekend of practice we organised in Birmingham and she was still up drinking from an all-night session the previous evening. We always remember that first practice, where she had the mic in one hand and a two-litre of cider in the other! But what a voice she had…I can't think of anyone that sounded like her at that time, or since, to be honest; she just belted it out, always giving it 100%."

Mags and Leigh joined late in 1992 and early the following year, after first recording a rough 12-song demo in their Wordsley rehearsal room, they recorded the awesome 'Cathode Ray Coma' album for Finn Records – twice! Once at the Icehouse in Dudley and once back at the Whitehouse in Weston…

"I think we were listening to a lot of Japanese stuff about that point and a lot of Swedish stuff as well and it really shows," laughs Stick. "We tried to record it at the Icehouse first, where Doom recorded 'The Greatest Invention', which turned out crap as well, come to think of it! I don't remember *exactly* why it was so bad, but it certainly wasn't good enough to release, so it was back to the Whitehouse.

"A few of the songs had been demo'd already, along with a few re-workings of old, old 'Rat songs' on the 12-track demo that we traded around. I remember when we used to write songs, Tom would play riffs in the practise room then instantly forget them, so I'd be shouting, 'Yeah, that's good,' but Tom would have already forgotten it by then, so it was Mal's job to listen and then play them back to Tom for him to re-learn his own riffs; it was a weird way of doing it, but we got some good stuff. If we had a dry spell for ideas we would get someone's phone number; '0' was an open string, then '1' was the first fret up, '2' the second and so on; we got a few good songs from that method!"

"We were *much* happier with the second version of the album," reckons Leigh, "even though now I still think the sound is a bit flat. Those songs were really good and just how we hoped they'd be, but the sound lets them down a bit; a rawer, noisier, in-your-face punch out of the speakers would have helped dramatically. A sound like the 'Another Religion..' 12-inch by the Varukers would've been just perfect…

"The packaging art could also have been better," he concedes. "Most of it's okay – except for the photo on the front cover of Joe Riot sitting in Stick's floral armchair! Stick and Joe's cover idea was to have a comatose person, sitting hooked up to all these tubes and medical accessories, watching himself on TV…but it just looks like a square cut-out of some bloke in a chair. I guess they didn't really achieve their goal, but, seeing as they'd put a lot of effort into it, Mags and I said nothing."

Finn only brought the album out on CD, though, so Stick and the aforementioned Joe Riot (so-called because he did the Riot fanzine), in true punk rock fashion and because CD players were still a bit of a luxury back then, also put it out as "a proper cassette".

Another split release, this time a split 7-inch EP with Beyond Description from Japan, was recorded soon after, for German label Ecocentric, but again the band nurture reservations about the rather arty finished packaging and sound.

"I remember the guy said he had a great cover idea, which we all went along with without ever seeing it," explains Stick. "It was a picture of a dead bird, but you couldn't see its head and it was crap! The songs we did were good songs, though, which we recorded at the youth club, but the mastering was bollocks, so it sounded awful…"

At the end of 1993, Mal left to concentrate on Doom and Leigh moved to bass, leaving Mags to handle the vocals on her own, a task she was more than capable of, possessing a voice that could flay the hide off a rhinoceros at one hundred yards. This more streamlined version of the band soon set about recording a split LP with Deformed Conscience for French label Sludge.

"Mal just wasn't into it as much any more," says Leigh. "He was more into his motorbike… plus it was getting too much as he was also playing in Doom; EOW often took second place to Doom, what with Stick, Mal and Tom all in that band at one point. That was also probably why the band was never as productive as I'd hoped.

"I was really glad and to a certain point relieved, to just play bass," he admits, "mainly because I was never happy with my voice on those recordings. Mags' voice was far superior and harsher; it really stood out on its own, while mine, at times, was strained to the point of sounding like a strangled Tommy Cooper! The dynamic and chemistry did change as well; Mags and I felt much more a part of it. I still wrote and arranged most of the lyrics, but also had more input with the music. Stick and Tom even came down to London a few times to practice, whereas before we were happy to escape London to practice up in Birmingham…"

Unfortunately the split LP, entitled 'Dogtags And Bodybags', took three years to appear and when it finally did, it had been pressed up on cheap vinyl and the original artwork, courtesy of Squeal who did such awesome work for the Icons Of Filth, had all been changed without the band's permission. It was something of a moot point as, by the time the LP dropped, Excrement Of War had split up, Tom losing interest and leaving and being replaced by Debbie from Dirge and the Suicidal Supermarket Trolleys.

"Yeah, during that time the band played a few gigs, but not many," recalls Leigh. "We all lost a bit of interest because of the release problems and the others were concentrating on Doom tours and recordings. A couple of gigs were hindered by the band not remembering the songs as well, but generally they were pretty good. One journey nearly ended in disaster; we were on our way to play in Bangor, North Wales, travelling in Stick's van, driving through these winding roads on a dark, wet evening. I mentioned to Stick that maybe he should slow down because of the weather conditions, but he didn't.

"A few minutes later the van flew off the side of the road and down a 30-foot drop, the headlights lighting up all the trees and bushes in our path. Sitting in the front seat it was hell of a ride, with amps, guitars, people, all just a mess in the back. My side was smashed in, but luckily we'd narrowly missed the bigger objects and the recovery driver said we'd been really lucky: the ravine had been full of water the day before! Needless to say we cancelled the gig..."

Unfortunately Debbie only lasted a few rehearsals before she dropped her brand new Gibson SG guitar onto the floor, breaking it in half. Everyone agreed EOW was cursed and it was time to call it a day. The LP eventually came out on Sludge in 1997 and the band were so disappointed with the final product they gave Fired Up Records permission to 'officially bootleg' it, to at least see it out there as they intended. They also re-formed – after a fashion – to play the Bristol Punk Festival, but Tom had left by then and Mags had moved home to Cork, so Pete (ex-Spite) and Lisa (ex-Corpus Vile) stood in on guitar and vocals respectively.

"I can't really remember what the motivation was for doing that gig, but it wasn't really what I remember as EOW being about," admits Stick. "And yeah, it certainly felt like we were cursed sometimes; we could write great songs, but seemed to lack the ability to take them out of the practice room and it always felt like one step forwards, two steps back..."

With everyone tending to agree that it 'just wasn't EOW' without Tom and Mags, the Bristol gig proved to be the last, despite talk of a reunion in 2009. Sadly Mags, a mother of two, passed away that year, aged 42.

"Mags and I had lived in both east and north London, sharing both really good and really difficult times in our three or four years together," says Leigh fondly, by way of tribute. "I will always remember her as a really kind-hearted individual, with a great sense of humour, but she wouldn't take shit from anyone. One occasion I returned home to find the local alcoholic tramp sitting on our sofa having a cup of tea with her; she was very accepting of others, no matter who they were. She spent some time at college learning and working as a carer at a home for people with severe learning difficulties; she also learnt and practiced sign language.

"I'm privileged to have known her as I did and I've a lot of fond memories from that time, especially of our involvement in EOW. She did it her way and took it all in her stride and it worked. She enjoyed a good drink and a laugh, she loved punk rock, that whole lifestyle and she will always be lovingly remembered and sadly missed by anyone that knew her. May she rest in peace."

"Once Stick had joined, EOW were one of the better 'Swedish-sounding' punk bands," offers Rat, who didn't play with another band until Indecent Assault reformed in 2005. "Fast, tight and angry, with some brutally unpleasant anti-war lyrics. But I don't think – at least not during my period of the band, anyway – that we had enough output, or gigged enough, to really set ourselves apart from our peers. I'd always consider us good at what we did, but there were a dozen other bands doing the same thing that would be playing the following week too..."

"I was only 22 when EOW recorded 'Cathode Ray Coma'," concludes Leigh, who joined Bristol's Screamer in '97 (and played on their 1999 'Cloven Hoof Blues' CD), before forming Cruelty with Jim Whiteley from Ripcord on guitar and Mike Chaney from In The Shit on drums. He now lives in Sweden and sings for Razored ("A straightforward punk band, 100% crustless and D-beat free!") "It was an exciting time to discover, or be introduced to, all those new/old bands and be influenced by that, but I did feel that scene had been and gone and that EOW was on the tail-end of that thriving and creative period of the Eighties.

"We suffered from not being able to support more good bands and gig attendances had really dropped, but I'm content with our legacy; we were still creative in what we did, we tried to make our own interpretation of that music and not just replicate what had been before like some kind of soulless crust punk idol of today. Just remember EOW as a raw hardcore punk band, that's all…with a curse!"

SELECT DISCOGRAPHY:

7-inch:
'Split' (Finn, 1991) – *split with Dischange*
'The Waste… And The Greed' (RTP, 1991)
'Split' (Ecocentric, 1994) – *split with Beyond Description*

LPs:
'Cathode Ray Coma' (Finn, 1994)
'Dogtags And Bodybags' (Sludge, 1997) – split with Deformed Conscience

AT A GLANCE:
Agipunk Records are apparently planning an official Excrement Of War reissue in the very near future, but until then you need to track down the CD version of 'Cathode Ray Coma' which contains the first two EPs as bonus tracks.

SET AGAINST

Set Against were a convincing hardcore street-punk band from Coventry. They only released the one single in their own right, but, through a succession of demos and compilation appearances, not to mention many, many gigs across the UK, still managed to establish themselves as a vital component of the UKHC scene of the latter Nineties.

"We basically got together because we were so disillusioned with the music scene in Coventry," begins bassist Neil 'Fozzy' Forrest, who was joined in the first line-up by vocalist Simon Nichols, guitarist Kevin 'Yogi' Jones and drummer Steve Brown. "Most local bands were of the old 'shoegazing' indie variety. There were a few metal bands about, of course, but nothing in the way of hardcore bands at that time.

"I had known Simon for years prior to setting up the band – we both came from the punk and goth scenes of the mid-Eighties – and I knew Yogi from playing in a previous band; he was in a metal band that rehearsed next door to us and was friends with a few of the members of my old band.

"We managed to snare Steve because Yogi spotted him walking around Coventry sporting a Sick Of It All T-shirt. Yogi talked to him and he happened to mention that he played drums… totally random, I know! And I was in a band called Treadmill, which was kind of death metal, but had a wide range of musical influences going on among the members. The singer/guitarist was really into his death metal like Bolt Thrower and Death etc; I like loads of different music, but at the time was into Fugazi, Killing Joke, New Model Army and loads of industrial bands like Skinny Puppy and Murder Inc. The other guitarist was into metal ranging from Ratt to Pantera and the drummer was a proper indie kid, but liked a fair bit of metal too…it made for an interesting sound, I can tell you!"

Despite all of the above, Set Against were actually a mixture of old school NYHC and UK street-punk like the Business and the Exploited, with more socially aware lyrics than political. After playing their first gig at the General Wolfe pub in Coventry ("With some prog-rock band…!"), Set Against recorded their first demo, entitled 'Demonstration', at Cued Up Studios during August 1995. A typically flawed debut, it nonetheless captured the band's sincere, angsty vibe and even got them compared to Boston's Slapshot in the well-respected New York fanzine *In Effect*.

"It went really well," offers Fozzy, of that first gig. "We had practiced our asses off for about four months and it really paid off. The headliners thought we had been playing for years and were quite impressed by our overall performance, even if the music wasn't really their cup of tea. I remember being terrified about playing about an hour beforehand, but, once on stage, I really calmed down and enjoyed the show.

"Then we did the demo, which I thought was amazing at the time. The sound that was coming out of the monitors in the studio was awesome; we sounded really big and quite professional. Once I got the recording home and played it through my stereo, it sounded loads different, of course; I wasn't disappointed with it as such, but it certainly gave me a better understanding of what we needed to do to improve the overall sound. These days, I still think the first demo sounds okay, but I'd love to re-record the songs and spend more time over the whole process, because we somehow recorded, mixed and mastered the whole demo in just one day. The production techniques in music and our overall abilities have vastly improved since then, so it would be interesting to see what we would sound like now…"

A second demo was recorded, 'What's Your Beef?', this time at the Lodge in Northampton; with a bigger sound and tighter playing, it was certainly a step in the right direction for the band and featured a rousing cover of Youth Of Today's 'A Time We'll Remember'. But it was the last recording with the original line-up, Yogi and Steve leaving soon after.

"The reason Steve left the band was purely down to work," explains Foz. "He landed a fantastic job that involved him working a lot of odd hours, including nights and weekends. But Yogi's departure wasn't the best; we let him go, because we didn't think he was that committed to Set Against. We felt bad, but knew it would be better for the band as a whole.

"The replacements were quite easy to come across. I knew Simon [Fox] through some other friends and knew he could play drums, so I asked him if he was interested. He was available and was transitioned into the band before Steve finally left. Stuart [North] came on board through word of mouth; we had a few temporary guitarists from other bands, including Nick from Freebase, but Stuart was friends with some of the guys from Silencer 7 [the UK posi-core band who would release the 'Directions On A Compass' LP through Household Name in 2000] and had heard of us. We auditioned him and instantly felt he was a great fit with the band and the next phase of Set Against began, which, in my opinion was the best line-up we ever had…"

Indeed it was this line-up that recorded Set Against's only release in their own right, the

Set Against, pic by Naki.

aforementioned and self-released, 'One True Weapon' 7-inch. Recorded at Mad Hat Studios in Walsall, with backing vocals courtesy of Britt from Assert, it was a classic – and overlooked – slice of no-nonsense hardcore punk, stripped right back to basics with all the surplus fat cut out of it.

"That recording was far better than anything we had done previously," agrees Foz. "Mark [Stuart], the studio owner, had a very good idea of what we were trying to achieve and really helped us get there. I am still very proud of that single.

"The hardcore scene at the time varied depending where you lived," he adds, when asked how the single was received nationally. "Locally, there were some great bands around the Midlands who were incredibly supportive. The London, Welsh, Scottish and northern scenes were all very different, but still supportive and reasonably friendly. Our gigs were usually at the Asylum in Birmingham when playing locally, but, in support of the 7-inch, we played loads of gigs throughout the UK with local and international bands, including Agnostic Front, Murphy's Law, Cause For Alarm, All Out War, Stigmata, 25 Ta Life, Assert, Stampin' Ground, Freebase, Rotunda, Intention, Exploited, UK Subs, Knuckledust, No Redeeming Social Value… and many more.

"The best shows were probably the gigs with Cause For Alarm and Agnostic Front, as we got on really well with them. We played plenty of all-day shows including Uxfest and the Hammerfest at the Garage in London. That show was great; there were some awesome bands on the bill and to top it off, Sacha Baron Cohen turned up dressed as a gay Austrian MTV presenter. He was interviewing loads of people about the hardcore scene as a prank for a TV show; I think it's at the end of one of the Ali G DVDs…

"I remember we played at the Indian Queen in Boston at really short notice. The promoter, Marv, had booked another band that cancelled at the last minute and he was really desperate to get another band in. We turned up on the day; the room was upstairs and quite cramped. The gig started off quite slowly; there were a few local bands on that played great sets. The small crowd was pretty static and I was getting a bit worried that it was going to be crap, but as we were getting ready to go on, the place just filled up. Marv introduced and thanked us, so we ripped into it and the place exploded; I was amazed at all these people going absolutely nuts! They were putting tables in front of the stage to dive off; it was crazy and a fantastic show for us.

"The worst gig was definitely in Worcester; we played at this pub that had stone floors and walls and the sound was terrible. The support band turned up with no gear and expected us to let them use ours; they were complete tools. And we were promised a fair bit of money to play, but the promoter wasn't going to pay us, so we gently persuaded him… I'm not going to tell you how!"

August 1999 saw the band back in Mad Hat to record what would have been their debut album; unfortunately, despite it being their best recording technically and their version of a Cro-Mags classic, 'Street Justice', being used on the Blackfish Cro-Mags tribute, the album never saw the light of day and the band fell apart shortly afterwards.

"I still listen to that recording sometimes and find that it hasn't aged as badly as our previous efforts," claims Foz. "But we were going through the motions a bit and Simon Nichols wasn't particularly happy. He decided to leave the band because it had become a chore instead of being fun and to be fair, he did a lot of the organisation behind the scenes and was just getting tired of it. He was also going through a lot personally.

"Stuart left at the same time to move up north to go to university. The morale obviously wasn't that good at the time, but we knew it was for the best; Simon and Stuart's last gig with us was at the Asylum supporting No Redeeming Social Value. I can't remember the date exactly, but it was a fun show."

After six frustrating months searching for new members, during which Foz and Simon Fox continued rehearsing and writing with just bass and drums, Sean McCann from Dogshit Sandwich was eventually recruited on guitar and Stephen 'Stein' Steinhaus, an American recently relocated to Straford-upon-Avon, joined on vocals.

"Stein sent a previous demo of stuff he had been doing over in Chicago," recalls Foz. "Simon and I were really impressed, so we got him over to go through some of our stuff and it was good. The overall dynamics of the 'new Set Against' were totally different and so was the sound. Sean's guitar style was far smoother and probably a bit more accomplished than Stu's; Stein's vocals were also deeper than Simon's, so it allowed us to move in a slightly darker direction."

Four more songs were recorded at Mad Hat — one of which, 'I Watched Her Die', was included on the 'UKHC' compilation released by Blackfish in 2001 — but Set Against split for good soon after, with Foz, Sean and Simon all briefly joining Freebase, who were also having a turbulent time with *their* line-up.

"Yeah, Stein had a lot of commitments elsewhere and he just could not commit to the band. The recordings we did with him were completed very quickly and didn't end up being as good as they should have; it was quite a frustrating time. Another reason for the split was that Mark from Freebase contacted me and asked if the three remaining members of Set Against wanted to join Freebase; it was a great opportunity for us all and the timing was perfect. And it *was* a great experience, albeit short-lived; I left due to increasing work commitments, Sean was let go and Mark quit the band in the end anyway."

After Set Against, Stuart North went on to do various bands with ex-members of Silencer 7 and he now lives in South Africa. Stein fronts the Dr Teeth Big Band, a hard-touring rhythm'n'blues act with a three-piece brass section and a 2006 album, 'Rhythm Is Our Business' on Big Bear, to their name. Sean went on to play in many bands as well, not least of all Police Bastard, Last Under The Sun and Rubella Ballet.

"I would just like Set Against to be remembered as a good boxer that punched well above its weight," concludes Foz, who has retired from making music and now resides in Canada. "While in the band, I never really knew how we stood among the other bands in the UKHC scene, but after we split there were so many people that were disappointed that we did. It made me incredibly proud that Set Against had that kind of effect on people…but I was also incredibly proud to be part of not just the band, but the UKHC scene as a whole."

SELECT DISCOGRAPHY:

7-inch:
'One True Weapon' (Circlepit, 1998)

AT A GLANCE:
Nothing official, but you might be able to persuade Foz to burn you a CDR of all the band's recordings: neil-forrest@hotmail.com

POLICE BASTARD

SICK On the bus

P O A

SUNDAY 4th OCTOBER

OLD RAILWAY B'HAM

Admission £3.00

2.10.98 - bristol : skate & ride
3.10.98 - worcester : apple tree

CHAPTER FIVE:
THE EAST

PMT

In a scene so heavily dominated by males (despite claims of offering a more representative demographic), all-female punk bands are always a breath of fresh air, especially those laden with as much attitude as Norwich's **PMT**. Anything but shrinking violets, these self-proclaimed 'pissed mouthy trollops' weren't the most prolific of bands, but they're still out there terrorising the lads with their opinionated rants even today.

"Me and Ella [Manning, aka Ella Mental] came up with the idea of doing a band at the start of the Nineties when we were 18 or 19," begins bassist Clara 'Scara' Wiseman. "I learnt to play bass playing along to UK Subs records in my bedroom and Ella could play drums a bit so we thought it would be fun to keep it all girls. We heard Sue [Tebble, aka Spu Terrible] could play guitar, so we arranged a jam in my bedsit; I showed her a song I'd written and luckily it consisted of the only three chords she knew: A, D and E! The day she learnt to play a barre chord was a revolution for our songwriting; it opened up a whole world of opportunities – like B and F! Anyway, Sue brought along her mate Jenny [Preston, aka Jeni Cide] who could play saxophone and there was another mate of ours, Wretch, who was going to be the singer. Turned out she had a raging smack habit and kept nodding off at practices, so we ditched her and decided me and Sue would sing instead…"

"Yeah, I remember it well," adds Spu. "We tried out a few of our friends, who all looked the part, but secretly I wanted to sing anyway. I'd met Wretch in mental hospital and, although she was a brilliant lyricist, she was mad as piss. I was confident that me and Clara could pull it off and, to be honest, didn't really care what anyone else thought. Yeah, the barre chords took a bit of effort, but I persevered; once me and Clara had started there was no stopping us…"

After playing their first gig at the Norwich Oval (15 April 1992, supporting psychobilly band Bad To The Bone), PMT recorded their 'Pretty Mental Tape' at Noisebox Studios ("It stood the test of time for all of two and a half minutes," quips Clara) and started gigging drunkenly in and around Norwich.

"Yeah, we kinda re-kindled the scene in Norwich," reckons Spu. "The Short'n'Curlies had been about for ages and only did the odd gig, but, as soon as we started playing, suddenly all the boys decided to get bands together; they probably couldn't handle the competition! All joking aside, we did shock everyone else into getting their shit together…"

PMT, 1992 (Jenny, Ella, Sue, Clara)

PMT in Germany, Sue, Elaine, Dee and Nikki

"My main influence was Suzi Quatro," she continues. "From the age of seven I'd played guitar and loved her, but it wasn't until I met Clara and we had similar musical tastes that I realised my full potential…up until that point I'd been playing Christmas carols! Which we did capitalise on every Christmas Eve for a few years; we would dress up in tinsel, borrow a mate's dog and go busking in Norwich – punk-rock Christmas carols, with the odd acoustic PMT number thrown in for good measure. We would stay out until we got about 40 quid (which was a lot of money then – more than our giro anyway) and then it would be straight down the pub to get pissed…via the chip shop for a sausage for the dog!"

"During the early Nineties I was mainly listening to '77 and early-Eighties punk," adds Clara. "I loved X-Ray Spex and Vice Squad and was fascinated by women in bands – especially strong, beautiful women like Debbie Harry and Joan Jett. We probably could have jumped on the Riot Grrrl bandwagon that was big at the time, but we were proper punk rockers and wanted to play proper punk rock. When old bands like Peter And The Test Tube Babies and Sham 69 started reforming, it gave us an opportunity to blag some good support slots in Norwich, but we also played loads of gigs with other local bands who were around at the time, like Short'n'Curlies, Braindance, Dump In The Bath and Income Support.

"Our songwriting was limited by our lack of technical ability," she admits. "But we made the most of what we had. We were pretty rough around the edges, but we loved our band: the drinking, the laughs, the showing off, we just got out there and did it. And we wrote some classic catchy tunes like 'Old Cunt', about Old Country, our favourite cider, 'He's Got VD' and 'Mr Howman', all about our dodgy landlord…

"We were all on the dole; I don't think any of us had ever had a job, so we were always totally skint. One night we played a party on Mousehold Heath on the edge of Norwich. After we played, we packed our stuff away in the van, then got pissed and in the morning we discovered our van had been broken into and all our guitars and amps had been nicked. We were gutted. Then we heard about the Prince's Trust, so we applied for a grant and got £1,000 to spend on equipment. We had to have a photo taken for the local papers and, for a laugh, I wore a T-shirt with a massive dick on the front, to see if I could get a bit of porn in the paper… I think that was the only time an erect penis made the *Norwich Evening News*!"

1993 saw Spu fall pregnant with her first son, Jake, a reality check that inspired that year's demo, 'Tunes For The Wombs', recorded at Purple Rain Studios. An excellent cover of 'Heart-Throb Of The Mortuary' by Crass was also recorded for the Crass tribute album put together by Ruptured Ambitions.

"Jenny was appalled at me for getting pregnant, but I never saw a problem with it," laughs Spu, "apart from having to play my guitar 'side saddle' as my stomach expanded, of course. Creatively speaking, we had a whole new experience to write songs about too, although when Jake was born we had to stop for a few months for my stitches to heal, but within three months we were back at it. The band even *helped* me be a mum; just imagine, all that stress and those sleepless nights…but once a week I could play loud guitar and scream my head off. PMT – 'Perfect Mother Therapy'!"

In fact, Jenny left the band that year, closely followed by Ella and they both went on to form Compact Pussycat (an all-girl indie pop/punk band named after Penelope Pitstop's car in the *Wacky Races* cartoon, who are still going strong today), with Elaine 'Elastic' Rayfield being recruited as the new PMT drummer. Also joined by Jenny 'Muff' Divers on saxophone, PMT then recorded their 1994 demo 'In Tomato Sauce' featuring the much more serious song 'It's

Your Problem', which tackled the sexism that the girls were encountering on a daily basis in the so-called 'enlightened' punk scene.

"Yeah, I don't think me having Jake helped Jenny," sighs Spu. "She was hell-bent on fame at the time and saw my pregnancy as a major hold-up. It was kinda musical differences as well; Jen used to wear a wedding dress on stage and we were much more DMs and studded belts – although I used to wear dungarees as well… Clara hated those, but I was going through that whole hippy punk/free festival stage at the time. And once I knew it annoyed Clara so much, I revelled in wearing them; I always knew punk was about a lot more than image…

"Unfortunately we came across a lot of sexism; the punk scene was very male-orientated back then…as it is now, I suppose. Punk is an aggressive form of music and a lot of the girls in the scene were there 'cos their boyfriend was a punk, not because they were…you know the type: dye their hair, wear the right clothes, then, three years down the line, they're working in insurance with a perm. Me and Clara were never like that; we were punks then and still are now. We kinda ignored the sexist bullshit as much as we could; we really didn't care, we were having fun regardless and we always thought it was the boys' problem, not ours. We wrote that song, 'It's Your Problem', though and recorded it for 'In Tomato Sauce'… 'And you scream "Get ya tits out", can't you think of nothing better to shout? Are your minds as small as your dicks? You bore us with your sexist quips!' That says it all!"

In 1995, PMT returned to Purple Rain to record their side of the 'Demolition Derby' split 7-inch for Weird, that they shared with Ipswich's Red Flag '77. Then Elaine got pregnant, so the band had Criss Damage stand in on drums for a UK tour with the Bus Station Loonies and the Filth, by which time other events in the ranks had caused relationships to be strained, to say the least…

"Well, it all went totally tits-up when I hooked up with Sue's boyfriend," admits Clara. "It was very shady behaviour and Sue went mental, but unbelievably we still did the UK tour with the Loonies just after she found out. She held it together for the gigs, but after the last one we had a big hug…then didn't speak again for 10 years.

"I bumped into her about five years later at a gig in Norwich. She'd been drinking all day and was right on one. After the gig she hit me over the head with an empty Grolsch bottle… I guess I had it coming to me. We ended up wrestling in the pub car park; somehow, both of our T-shirts got ripped so we were rolling round with our tits out – not a pretty sight! At one point she had me in a headlock between her thighs…it was the most ridiculous scene. We've now written a song about it called 'Fists Out, Tits Out'!"

"That was a real hard time," says Sue, of the split with Clara. "I was determined to do the tour, but after it was over I knew there was no way we could stay in the band together. I was suddenly stuck in Norwich with a three-year-old son, no boyfriend, no best mate and potentially no band. I spoke to Elaine and Jenny and they both wanted to keep it together, so I asked Niki, a good friend who I knew could play piano, if she fancied playing bass. At the time it wasn't about whether she could play; she was my mate and was up for giving it a go. So she joined and we played at a Norwich punks' picnic that I put on, which ended up a total shambles. We all got mega-pissed, hadn't really practiced that much and completely lost it.

"Jenny then got asked to record with Ex-Cathedra and soon moved to Glasgow, which is where Dee came in. She's a very old mate of mine and we talked a lot about it before she joined; she knew me well and didn't want the band to upset our friendship…which is ironic as when we did split we didn't speak to each other for four years! I should have listened to her. We were a five-piece for a while as well; we got Elaine's sister, Claire, to play second guitar for about a year. I thought it would beef up our sound, but Claire's a gentle soul and I think it was all a bit much for her…she didn't wanna go to Germany either."

With Clara moving to Hackney and going on to play with Zero Tolerance, Intensive Care, Dirty Love and even, albeit briefly, the UK Subs ("All those years playing along to Subs records finally paid off!"), Sue's new PMT line-up recorded the 'Pissed Mouthy Trollops' EP for Weird in 1999 and headed off to Europe for two weeks, with Age Of Chaos from Chichester in support.

"I was pleased with the single, although it was hard not having Clara's input any more," offers Sue. "I've never been totally happy with any of our recordings; I think PMT were always a live band and to capture that in a studio was near impossible. We were all about standing onstage, laughing, taking the piss, drinking and enjoying ourselves; the pressure of a studio is never the same. One of the songs, 'Humble Pie', was a tribute to Dee; we played at a Bristol punks' picnic one year and I ended up getting totally wasted and kicking all of the girls out of 'my band' – and my van! Complete egomania…fuelled by cider and speed! Dee ended up hitching a lift with a dodgy smackhead to her brother's place in Bath. I woke up the next day and didn't even know where she was. The rest of the girls wouldn't tell me either, so, after a long, quiet guilt-ridden and hung-over drive back to Norwich, I had to eat some serious humble pie to all of them, especially Dee.

"The European tour came about after I met Cleaver from Slumgang; he knew Fleas and Lice well and I ended up driving them on a mini-tour around Britain with Slumgang. It was manic, truly punk rock and I ended up with some good European friends; they put me in touch with this German guy, Balo, who then set up the tour with Age Of Chaos. So off we went; four girls in my shitty old van, armed with loads of T-shirts and enthusiasm. The first few gigs were great: free beer, free food and general adoration from the Germans, but it all went wrong in Leipzig where I got horrendously pissed again…well, I was on tour, for fuck's sake! We drove all the way to Freiburg to a squat which had been burnt down by Nazis only three days earlier; the gig was cancelled and the promoters fucked off and left us in the building…

"It was one of the scariest moments of my life, but luckily I was still pissed from the night before, so didn't realise the true horror until the next morning. We left as soon as we could – obviously having a photo opportunity first! – and when we arrived at the next gig we were met by a friend we had made, Cokes, who then reminded me, in front of the others, that he had told me all about Freiburg and the cancelled gig at the Leipzig date! Whoops… so everyone was well pissed off with me! But we finished the tour on a high in Giessen; me and Dee stayed up 'til 5am drinking and then left at 8.30 to drive back to the Hook.

"All I can say is, the van broke down – massively! – but we managed to find a tow, which cost us all of our T-shirt cash. Two of Age Of Chaos wanted to leave us there, which caused a massive argument 'cos Duncan, the good old boy, wouldn't, but we still ended up missing the ferry, crying our eyes out and seven of us sleeping in my van. We were towed onto the ferry in the morning and finally arrived home after 14 days of drink, drugs, arguments and Nazis, courtesy of the AA!"

The PMT soap opera finally ground to a halt when the band played their final gig on 15 April 2000 in Canterbury, although Sue was soon back at it again as well, this time playing bass for Terminal City Ricochet. "The Bowling Green in Wisbech was always a favourite venue of mine," she says, reminiscing on the many memorable gigs played by PMT. "Wisbech is such a backward 'Sticksville' place anyway and to have a classic punk pub in the middle of it was brilliant, but bizarre! My favourite line to start the gigs there was always, 'Hello Wisbech, give me six!'

"We played with everyone there from Pain to Extinction Of Mankind. Me and Mel from Combat Shock always ended up onstage singing with whoever was playing, whether we knew the words or not; it was like one, big, punk karaoke pub with a landlord that always had a shooter at the ready – Wisbech is rough! It all ended during this one all-dayer; we were playing outside on a flat-bed truck… I got too pissed, had a fight with the landlord, called him a cunt and got both myself and my band banned!

"My personal favourite gig though had to be supporting SLF at the Waterfront in Norwich. It was triumph enough to even get on the Waterfront stage – it was one of the big Norwich venues – let alone playing there with my favourite band of all time. I have loved them since I was a young girl…my mum bought me 'Crash Course' by the UK Subs for Christmas when I was 12, but unfortunately she saw the 'explicit lyrics' sticker just before Christmas day, so it went back and 'Inflammable Material' got bought instead. Don't get me wrong, I love the Subs, but from that moment on, SLF were in my soul; I even called my first son Jake.

"And it was a corking gig; as usual I ended up getting slaughtered, but I even gaffer-taped my plectrums to the mic stand in a true professional style. SLF were lovely, gave us a bottle of tequila and treated us like stars. Bruce Foxton was on bass at the time as well, so it was like a double whammy – the Jam *and* SLF! Clara's bass hero was always Bruce Foxton – we used to call him 'Brucey Baby' – so it was a shame she had left by that point 'cos, although I was still very much in hate with her, I knew she would have loved that night…"

"We would just like to be remembered as the pissed, mouthy trollops that we were and are," laughs Clara, in closing. "Sue is a local legend; she's got a big personality and a mouth to match. We were passionate about our band and our music and we weren't afraid to get out there and do it, regardless of the tossers who sneered at us. I'd really like to think we might have inspired other girls to play instruments or start bands; it's such a good laugh, everyone should have a go.

"Me and Sue finally got talking again too, when I moved back to Norwich in 2007. Neither of us were doing anything bandwise, so we had a few pissed-up jams in her kitchen, knocking out the old tunes and writing some new ones; since then we've played a few gigs and who knows, we might play some more…meanwhile, my latest project is the pUKEs – a kind of ukulele anti-society for punks. We meet once a month in a London pub to play punk classics on the uke!"

"Yeah, we realised the old magic was still there," agrees Sue, of the tentative reformation of PMT. "I had missed Clara and the band and it seemed that after all the shit we had gone through it was the perfect ending to all the drama. We've played a couple of gigs now and gone down a treat as well and after all those years of playing we're finally getting pretty good – viva PMT!

"But for now, I'd just like people to have a grin on their face when they think of us; as well as being punk-as-fuck birds, I'd like to think we were entertaining. Obviously being girls in a male-dominated scene made our job harder at times, but we always had a great time and laughed at the sexist comments – and fluttered our eyelashes when we really needed a heavy amp moving!"

SELECT DISCOGRAPHY:

7-inch:
'Demolition Derby' (Weird, 1995) – s*plit with Red Flag '77*
'Pissed Mouthy Trollops' (Weird, 1999)

AT A GLANCE:
Clara might be persuaded to burn you the demos and singles onto a CDR, especially if you cover her costs! thepukes77@gmail.com Meanwhile, the pUKEs have recently issued an amazing 2012 calendar where they have recreated iconic punk album covers from the likes of the Damned, Ramones and Clash in their own image, which is well worth a look, it's so brilliantly realised.

BRAINDANCE

With four albums and some relentless touring in Europe and the States to their name, the aforementioned **Braindance** from Norwich eventually emerged as one of England's finest street-punk bands of the Nineties and if they'd received a little more support from some of their record labels, they could have made an even bigger stamp internationally. Formed in 1989 by schoolfriends Reuben Youngblood (guitar), Matthew 'Chedge' Chedgey (bass), Rob 'Robot' Hedge (drums) and Elliot 'Widge' Savage (vocals), Braindance were spawned in a chaotic environment and that chaos stayed with them throughout their existence.

"I was five years younger than the others," recalls Reuben, "and had already been playing in some bands at school, like Meat and Earth Grind, trying to be AC/DC or the Ruts or something. I even sang for a while – badly! Being so much younger, I was very impressed by the older boys with their mohicans and girlfriends; I left home at 16, moved into Norwich and started to practice daily in bedsits around the city. There was no direction, no plan, no nothing. I have always said that, with no interest in school, learning, or doing as I was told, my options were somewhat limited! I was also crap at football, so guitar seemed the obvious choice to pull girls, but being a spotty long-haired 16-year-old, I personally wasn't hoping to achieve much, but just have a laugh with my mates…

"Norwich was as cool as fuck at the time. I was by far the youngest punk with a lot of my peers being in their early twenties; they had been into it since the late Seventies and early Eighties. There was an infamous club called the Jacquard that various punk bands would play at…the Subs, Exploited, etc. And because of the remoteness of Norwich itself, a lot of the people – including me – were characters from the surrounding towns and villages, mostly nutters starved of entertainment. Norwich has an art college and university, so always had a good mix of students and locals; I can always remember a lot of interesting characters, a lot of facial tattoos and a lot of drinking…a *lot* of drinking! My first bedsit was shared with a half-caste junkie called Paul who had a swastika tattooed on his forehead – so you get the idea… I was taken under the wing by most and basically had license to be as mental as I liked, with a whole army of older mates ready to bail me out; it was fantastic…"

Such was the drunken bedlam of those early gigs, Reuben can't actually remember where or when the first Braindance appearance actually was. "I can remember being told not to swear and to stop spitting and we were always having the power cut a lot back then," he laughs, "which just made us play faster, to try and get as many songs in before they turned us off! And seeing as we would usually be instantly banned afterwards, robbing the bar of beer and smashing things was always on the menu too!

"We did do a gig in North Walsham, which was once a stronghold for some really mental bastards…and my mum came! We played in the back room of the pub and the place got smashed to bits. They had laid a buffet on and we had been booked as a country and western band; it was mayhem, proper *Blues Brothers* stuff. The police got called and soon had to ring for back-up, which had to come from Norwich, 15 miles away. It all ended in tears – and my mum wasn't impressed! I thought it was fuckin' great though and we were the best! And then they asked us back, 'cos the bar had done so well! There were a lot of gigs like that, normally ending in a lot of violence, which – at 17 years old – was very exciting. I have to say, I always did my best to incite as much grief as possible; it was all part of it for me and I loved watching landlords shit themselves when 50 or 60 tattooed nutters walked in…although we were even banned from some pubs before we could even get out of the van in the car park outside the gig! Of course, it was this legacy that would eventually be our downfall, but you need a party with an atmosphere, right?"

Although Widge "looked the part" and was a good mate of Rob's, Braindance eventually parted ways with him during March 1993 ("He just lacked basic timing," sighs Reuben, "and then he moved to London to go to drama college, which made practising difficult…") and he was replaced by David Sloss from local punk act YOB (short for 'Youth Of Britain'), who brought some real power and aggression to the table and even a little range and melody. His joining obviously had a positive effect on the band, because they had landed a record deal with Helen Of Oi and released their first single before the year was out.

Recorded at Purple Studios, Norwich, by Richard 'Hammy' Hammond, the 'Streets Of Violence' 7-inch was an energetic slice of spirited street punk, not dissimilar to the glory days of Red Alert. It was quickly followed by the 'Blind Lead The Blind' EP in early '94, with songs like the driving 'Death Wins' recalling the Exploited's tried-and-tested take on aggro-punk rock. The band were soon in Europe to promote it, but their first trip over there was predictably an eventful one, organised – in true time-honoured fashion – on a wing and a prayer…

"We had agreed to meet a guy in Berlin called Marcus Linda, who was arranging some gigs for us," recalls Reuben, incredulous at how trusting they once were. "I think at that point only Chedge had been abroad before and he was the only one who had a driving license… I don't think Sloss or Rob even had passports! But we said yes anyway, drove to Peterborough, got passports, got on a ferry and headed towards Berlin. We had all told the Social [Department Of Social Security] that we had some job interviews in Scotland and back then they wrote you off for a week and gave you your giro [dole money] early so we were loaded – well, as 'loaded' as you could be on £32 a week!

Braindance, Germany

Braindance, early line-up,
taken at the Oval 1992

"From what I remember, we were halfway there before we realised we didn't have enough money for the petrol and hadn't heard from Marcus and hadn't been able to contact him. Sloss only wrote letters, there was no internet or e-mail then. Anyway, we got to Berlin on stolen fuel and Marcus was true to his word; he had arranged a gig at the Tommy Weisbecker Club with a German punk band called Public Toys. They gave us free beer which had never happened to us before, so we drank it all and took it upon ourselves to be as punk as we could. I thought it was mental we had even got there, never mind that they would be paying us and everything.

"We went on at 2am and played all our songs twice and there was no trouble, no fights; they knew the words to the songs and were really into it. We stayed up all night learning useful German phrases like, 'Do you suck cock?' and 'Do you swallow?', which is all very amusing when you're 19. The barmaid made a big impression on Rob and, although none of us knew at the time, he would end up staying in Germany to live with her when we came back a few months later. I remember we had been asked to do a radio interview or something and the first question from the girl who was interviewing us was, 'So I hear your drummer is coming to live in Germany…?' I nearly shat myself! It was the first I had heard about it! We had the studio booked again for when we got home and a tour to finish, but I guess he was in love, so we came back drummer-less."

Before he went, though, Rob played on the band's debut LP, 'At Full Volume', which was released in 1994 by Helen Of Oi, who also released their sophomore effort, 'Brainiac', featuring new drummer Henry, the following year.

"I honestly can't remember his last name," admits Reuben. "But I met Henry when he was playing at a local venue in Norwich called the Oval; he was playing drums in a really terrible band whose name also escapes me. They were proper shit though – a sort of prog-rock/Zappa thing – but I remember thinking, 'He's got a nice kit and he's really going for it!' He had lots of hair, a bit like Dave Grohl, and after the gig I got talking to him – and realised he was dressed in a pair of waist-high rubber waders – I should have known there and then!

"I told him his band was shit but he had something going on himself and asked if he would like to come for a practice as we were short of a drummer. I gave him a tape of our massive back catalogue, he turned up, played, we hit it off and we fucked off back on tour. Henry was a bit older that most of us with a wife and kids and I think he struggled away from home, especially with me being very young and mental. I would say 'Yes!' to every gig, wherever, whenever and with whoever. The first gig Henry did was an all-dayer in Germany, headlining in front of 2,000 people with local television cameras there and everything; he threw up for two hours, claiming food poisoning, but he got out of the van, cleaned out his pants and played a blinder, so credit where it's due!"

After appearing on a multitude of compilations and releasing what Reuben rates as their best ever single, 1996's 'Gentle Spirit', Chedge left the band and was replaced by their roadie, Sean Wallace. No doubt as a result of their constant touring in Europe, Braindance soon signed to German label We Bite, then home to the likes of GBH and Peter And The Test Tube Babies, for three albums, the first of which was '96's 'Can Of Worms', a strong collection of tunes somewhat compromised by a sterile mix that lacked the band's live power.

"Looking back now, that really should have been our best album," reckons Reuben. "Instead we ended up fuckin' about for days, getting different guitar sounds and doing loadsa overdubs, all sorts of stuff which just made the record sound over-produced and shit. We had two grand to spend on the recording though and we were determined to spend it… when really we should have banged it out in a day for £200 and gone down the pub! Funnily enough, though, a lot of songs on that album went down very well live, especially in America – but poor Rich [at Purple Studios] had to threaten to sue We Bite to get his money for the recording in the end. It left a bitter taste in my mouth and then, to add insult to injury, we didn't get finished copies of the album for months and when we did, they sent us a bill for them. Everyone in Germany, all over Europe in fact, were contacting us saying they couldn't buy the album anywhere.

"Then We Bite said the album wasn't selling because of the cover art, or some such shit; they had already released 7,000 copies of it, but said they would re-package it and release another 8,000…and, like twats, we agreed! I don't honestly know how many did get pressed in the end, but all we got was 25 CDs each…which we paid for ourselves! Someone somewhere made a lot of money. I don't think GBH did much better and the Test Tube Babies told us that they had been to the label's office to demand money but hadn't got any either. Oh well, you live and learn…"

In 1998, Henry left and was replaced by Tom, in time to record the band's fourth and final album, 'Delusions Of Grandeur'. His departure was ushered in by some strange behaviour, to say the least.

"I have kids myself now and wouldn't dream of fuckin' off for eight months in the year, then coming home, totally skint and fucked," reasons Reuben. "So I guess Henry had burnt himself out and just had enough, overindulged, whatever you want to call it; he was a nice guy though and I'm sure he enjoyed himself. He always was a little bit nuts (remember those rubber waders?) and I guess drinking such a lot didn't help. On the plane to Oslo one Christmas, I was in charge of getting Henry and Sean over in one piece, 'cos Sloss had to get an earlier flight. We had a six-hour layover in Amsterdam airport; me and Sean got a bottle of vodka and settled in, but Henry went nuts and I spent an hour trying to stop Sean knocking him out!

"He eventually passed out on the plane with his cock hanging out and after an hour-and-half flight got off the plane and tried to start fighting with machine-gun-armed police at Oslo airport! So then Sean spent half an hour trying to stop *me* from knocking him out on the way to the VIP laid-on meal – where he got even drunker and made a proper cunt of himself. At the gig the next night, Sloss got the 500-strong audience to all chant, 'Henry is a wanker!' He naturally played a blinder…"

Although Braindance then released the 'Last Man Standing' 7-inch through Combat Rock in 1999, the writing was already on the wall for the band, who, truth be told, had been slowly losing their enthusiasm since the debacle with We Bite over 'Can Of Worms'.

"Yeah, after all that grief, we decided to give our fourth album to Knock Out, who had always been good to us in the past. We toured America with the Casualties and Oxymoron in 1997 and that was a really mad tour, a whole book's worth of crazy shit; we did 13 gigs in 14 days and 4500 miles of driving. The last gig was in New York at CBGB's; not the best gig we ever did, but it was a pinnacle and really meant the world to me. I knew it would be hard to top anyway! We got back from America and I was still on the dole and skint and living in Norwich; a bit hard to adjust to.

"We started playing around England again, but there was a lot of violence at the shows; I was a bit older by then and watching people getting glassed in the face wasn't that much of a turn-on. After one gig in Manchester at the Star And Garter, which had ended up in a riot, Sean smashed up the venue, I got a broken nose and our van driver got glassed in the face and nearly lost an eye…and they paid us £46. Sloss pointed out that of the last eight gigs in England we hadn't once finished our set! From a boy that had loved the chaos and mayhem, I was now a man that hated it and, although making money for me was never really a priority, it's hard to swallow when you're on your £32 a week dole money and someone's selling 15,000 copies of your albums for 20 dollars a pop! What did that dead ginger twat [Malcolm McLaren!] used to say? 'Cash from chaos!' Ha bloody ha!

"There was never really a split as such; it all just got to be a chore for everyone, I think… even I started making excuses about why we couldn't do this or that and it's time to end it when your heart's not in it. The last gig was at Morecambe punks' picnic [2000]; it was really good, with lots of people, a good sound and everyone singing along to our songs, a real nice way to finish. I never wanted to be the man hanging on to the last shreds of his mohican, beer gut hanging over his guitar, singing something he's too old to care about and then collecting his grand at the end of the night…"

After Braindance, Reuben helped Sloss re-record an album of YOB songs (entitled, of course, 'Youth Of Britain') and then joined ska/punk band Protection Racket for one album on Combat Rock, before concentrating on a career as a tattooist. Rob plays drums with the reformed Disrupters and Sean sings for Nottingham's furious Certified.

"How would I like Braindance remembered? Fuck me!" laughs Reuben. "I kinda have my own memories; even the bad ones are funny now, looking back. There is nothing I would change and I can honestly say I loved all of it. For anyone that saw us live (the records I can take or leave), I would like to think you saw a bunch of boys who really loved and believed in what they were doing and were up for a laugh, a drink and a fuckin' good time! That sounds cheesy, I know, but that was what it was – pure fuckin' mayhem!"

SELECT DISCOGRAPHY:

7-inch:
'Streets Of Violence' (Helen Of Oi, 1993)
'Blind Lead The Blind' (Helen Of Oi, 1994)
'Gentle Spirit' (Knock Out, 1996)
'Last Man Standing' (Combat Rock, 1999)

LPs:
'At Full Volume' (Helen Of Oi, 1994) – *on 10-inch vinyl*
'Brainiac' (Helen Of Oi, 1995)
'Can Of Worms' (We Bite, 1996)
'Delusions Of Grandeur' (Knock Out, 1998)

AT A GLANCE:
The 'Delusions Of Grandeur' CD also contains the 'Gentle Spirit' 7-inch as bonus tracks and comes highly recommended.

VANILLA POD

Hailing from King's Lynn, Norfolk, **Vanilla Pod** may not be a name you're overly familiar with, but this unassuming melodic hardcore band have released five full-length studio albums – with a sixth on the way – and toured all over the world. Not bad for a band that's original goal when forming was merely to get themselves a gig "out of town"!

"I used to be in a band called the Weatherheads with Gary [Coleman]," explains guitarist Steve Pitcher, of the band's formation during February 1995, "and he was such a good drummer that I wanted to keep his talents with me, so I thought I'd start another band with him. I knew Steve Campion from gigs around Wisbech – he used to sing in a band called Groove Spider that we played with in our old band – and I knew he played bass, so he was an obvious choice too. We were stuck for a singer, though, but Gary knew Paul Davis from his college so we asked him to have a go; we all kinda got along so we set up our first gig in King's Lynn soon after…

"In the early Nineties the punk scene around our way was pretty healthy really, especially in a small town called Wisbech. Sonny and Mel from Combat Shock used to put loads of punk gigs on, which was great; bands like PMT, Short And Curlies, MDM, Contempt, Police Bastard…the list goes on and on. All good times and then we branched out to King's Lynn, putting on gigs whenever *we* could, but like everything else the scene comes and goes, people get complacent with gigs as more and more are put on, so people slowly stop coming. Then the gigs stop, you leave it alone for a while and then everybody says, 'Why aren't you putting on gigs any more?' So you do and then the cycle starts all over again.

"We were influenced by all sorts of things really, when we started out. Steve always loved the Ramones and the Damned so that was in there; I was coming out of my Sub Pop grunge phase and moving onto stuff like Bad Religion, Snuff, NOFX and Green Day. Gary was listening to whatever took his fancy and Paul was a bit of an indie lover, so it took us a while to find our niche really.

We all had a love for a little bit of heavy metal too and I always *loved* the Ruts, so that was a big influence on me personally, but yeah, all that we wanted to achieve initially was to play out of town and have as much fun as possible. And that's still there to this day, 'cos having fun *is* the most important part of being in any band…"

That first gig was at the St Margaret's Club in King's Lynn with Lake Acid Blue ("The name says it all really…" scoffs Steve) and it went well enough for the band to record a four-song demo at Meadowside Studios, Wisbech, to try and secure more gigs further afield. However Paul left to further his education and a *very* young Rob Bunting was recruited in his place.

"Paul decided to go away to university, but he'd been upfront about it and we knew it was going to happen sooner or later fairly early on in the life of the band. Gary was at sixth form and said he knew this kid that was at his school that kept hassling him to come and sing for us [Rob]. He was only 15 years-old, which put us off a bit, but in the end we gave in and he came and had a go. And it just improved the band so much, as he had a really great voice, so we couldn't really refuse him, although trying to get him into clubs was always very interesting – and it was funny picking him up from school to go to gigs, too…!"

1996 saw the band back in Meadowside with Ricko Burrows at the desk, recording their 'Rebound' 7-inch for the aptly-named Off-Shoot Records.

"Actually that recording was originally going to be a six-track demo tape, but Off-Shoot stepped in and released it as a three-track single on yellow vinyl," recalls Steve. "They were called Off-Shoot because they were literally an off-shoot of Norwich label Noisebox, who had bands on their roster like Waddle, the Joeys and Maggoo. I honestly couldn't say what it sounded like now as I haven't heard it for years, but I do know that it was a good stepping stone for us to release it as a 7-inch…"

Indeed; it brought them to the attention of Corby label Them's Good, the punk imprint of 3rd Stone Records (whose Spaceage imprint was the home of Rugby shoe-gazers Spacemen 3).

"Yeah, we sent 'em a single and they came to see us and then decided to add us as the second band on their new punk rock label; their first release on Them's Good was Goober Patrol's 'Vacation' album. And we had a pretty good relationship with them right up until the end; there weren't even any hard feelings when we parted company or anything. It was pretty much a mutual decision for us to leave, as we wanted to move onto a more pro-active label and I think they wanted to finish up Them's Good at about the same time too…

"Anyway, I always felt – and still feel – that 'Trigger' was a bit of a mis-match of stuff, as it wasn't all recorded at the same time. It was basically some of the demo recordings that we did for the first 7-inch release, plus some new stuff that we recorded at Premier Studios in Corby. We were *very* thankful to Them's Good for introducing us to Ian Weatherall at Premier, as he went on to record our next three albums, but in hindsight I really wish we'd recorded *all* of 'Trigger' there…that way it would have sounded more cohesive, but it was still a very exciting time for us, all in all. Really. We had a three-album record deal and an old van to go out and tour in, so we did; we went out and played for fun and would play *anywhere* if someone would put us on."

The band's energetic melodic take on US hardcore was an instant hit with the younger audiences punk rock was starting to attract in the latter part of the Nineties and Vanilla Pod undertook a very successful UK tour in support of the album. Hitting their creative groove, the band wasted no time in getting back into the studio to record a second album for Them's Good, 1998's 'Faster Disco', which they promoted with yet more tireless gigging around the UK and Ireland, ever-larger crowds lapping up their enthusiastic live performances with gusto.

"The 'Faster Disco' was a big step up for us," offers Steve, "as I think we started to find our niche around this time. All the songs were written and recorded together, so it actually felt like a proper album. Again we toured this up and down the country, but found more people coming along to the gigs now. The best thing that sticks out for me about that time was the beginning of the Out Of Spite weekends [the long-running DIY Leeds punk and hardcore festival]. It's been great to see that event grow and grow over the years.

"The name 'Faster Disco' came from someone trying to describe us," he reveals. "'You're kinda like a faster disco', they said, in a heavy Norfolk accent, which made us all laugh – and we decided that was a good enough reason to call the album that!"

Vanilla Pod then became one of the few UK hardcore punk bands to undertake a tour of the Far East (in 2000), although the trip had an adverse effect as well as a beneficial one…

"It was actually a tour of Australia, but we managed to pull in a gig in Hong Kong on the way over. Hong Kong was a great time and was definitely one of the best memories of that tour; it was an all-dayer, with like 10 bands on, but it ran like clockwork and we had everyone

Vanilla Pod, 1997, Steve Campion, Steve Pitcher, Rob Buntin and Gary Colman

The third annual Out Of Spite punk rock spectacular.

Sat.August 12th. Noon start.

Goober Patrol
Southport
One Car Pile Up
Voorhees
FourLetterWord
Douglas
Scuttle
Shooting Goon
Eighty Six
Inside Right
Grampus Eight
Torino 74
Fig.4

Sun.August 13th. Noon start.

Vanilla Pod
Consumed
Wat Tyler
the Propagumbhis
Pylon
the Copperpot
Journals
Grover
Joe Ninety
Otherwise
Southpaw
Dugong

All at Josephs Well, Chorley Lane, Leeds. Two days for ten pounds.
Or six pounds a day. Tickets on the door. For details/directions
Call 0113 2746388 Or email outofspite@hotmail.com

crowd-surfing nicely for our main support slot and we really didn't expect anything like that to happen at all. After the gig we went and watched England beat Germany 1-0 in the Euro championships as well, so a very special night indeed!

"Then off we went over to Oz and played 10 gigs over there; we went all down the east coast and then flew over to Perth to play three gigs on that side. It would have been great, but Steve Campion decided to quit halfway through the tour… I managed to persuade him to stay on and finish the dates, but, as you can imagine, it caused a bit of an atmosphere for the rest of the trip…

"I think he had just had enough, to be honest. It can be very draining out on tour and once you get some doubt in your mind and start questioning if it's all worth it then it's the beginning of the end really. And Steve is the kind of person that, once his mind is made up, then that's it; there's no turning back."

Upon their return to the UK, Leon Muncaster joined on bass, just in time to record the band's third album, 2001's 'Third Time Lucky', which was released by Deck Cheese Records and was the label's first release that *wasn't* a compilation. Another strong entry to the melodicore canon and very reminiscent of US skatecore bands like Ten Foot Pole, Vanilla Pod could easily have been snapped up by a Stateside label like Hopeless or Lookout…

"After we left Them's Good, we *were* obviously looking for a label to put 'Third Time Lucky' out," explains Steve. "But we knew the guys from Deck Cheese, as one of them ran *Big Cheese* [magazine] and they'd put out a couple of compilations called 'The Beast Of British' that we had contributed a track to previously.

"So we asked them if they would be interested in releasing our new album and making us the first proper release on their label and the guys asked us to meet up with them in London to have a chat.

On the way down in the van, we decided that if they took us out to dinner and paid for it then we would go with 'em… Needless to say, the Thai noodles went down very well that day. And that is how cheap Vanilla Pod are to sign!

"Anyway, we recorded 'Third Time Lucky' at Premier in Corby again and we all felt that this album had a real good feel to it. It was another definite progression again, which was reflected in the amount of success we had with it at the time; it got a lot of critical acclaim and we managed to get good airplay with it too, which all led to us getting bigger and better support slots; the biggest probably being with Less Than Jake at the Astoria. Good times."

Vanilla Pod expanded to a five-piece when Steve Campion rejoined on bass and bassist Leon moved to second guitar, where he has remained to this day. Steve's return was but a brief one and he was replaced by Tom Wicks in time for a UK tour with Capdown and Twofold during October 2002. Tom then left in early 2003 and was replaced by another Tom: Tom Blyth from Goober Patrol, who was the bassist on the band's fourth – and probably best – studio album, 'Surrounded By Idiots'.

"Yeah, I love 'Surrounded By Idiots' loads as well, but I don't feel it got the backing that it deserved really; if it had been promoted in the right way and pushed enough in the right places, we could have done some real good things with that record. I think the label tried to grow too fast and was always looking for the next big thing, instead of concentrating on bands that they already had and pushing *them*. But what is done is done.

"I think that just before 'SBI' came out was definitely the best time for us; we had all given up our jobs and were doing the band full-time. Our trip to Europe with MU330 was about that time too and when we got back the copies of 'SBI' were waiting for us and that's always a nice feeling – although it's usually best to get copies of your new album just *before* you go on tour! That trip with MU330 was soooo much fun though; every day was just a Vanilla Pod party everywhere we went – and there ain't no party like a Vanilla Pod party!"

The band went on something of a hiatus then for several years, not least of all because Steve became a father ("Kids are the biggest and best way to keep yourself grounded and humble," he smiles proudly), but lurched back into life to record two new tracks for the 'Gangsta's Corner' compilation CD on Gratuitous Beaver Records, a tribute to the much-loved Norfolk scenester Doug Semtex that also featured Goober Patrol, Red Flag '77 and Toybox Terror etc. Suitably inspired again, a new album was recorded in 2009, 'Poets On Payday' for Boss Tuneage and the band are now working on their sixth full-length, albeit at a much more relaxed pace than they were used to back in the Nineties.

"Now it's all just for fun," reckons Steve. "We have no aspirations to be the next big thing… not that we ever did have, mind you, but we just do what we want to do now. It's still so much fun and we are all good friends, so why would we stop doing it? While people still want to book us and come and see us then I guess we will keep playing whenever we can…and the time it stops being fun is the time we'll stop.

"For now, though, I hope that we will be remembered as just being a decent band that people enjoyed watching and listening to. We never set out to be ground-breaking and we *never* took ourselves too seriously; we just played music that we would like to listen to ourselves. We never wanted to be a massive band or have the biggest tour buses or anything; the main part of it was always to meet like-minded people and just enjoy ourselves.

"But if somebody said to me when I started Vanilla Pod that we would release five albums, tour most of the world and still be playing 15 years later, I would have laughed in their face. So I guess I'm pretty happy with my lot and what we have achieved."

SELECT DISCOGRAPHY:

7-inch:
'Rebound' (Off-Shoot, 1996)
'Mother Stoat Singles Club: September/October' (Mother Stoat, 1999) – *split with Scuttle*
'Once Was Home' (Them's Good, 1999)
'Dead End Town' (Deck Cheese, 2001)

LPs:
'Trigger' (Them's Good, 1997)
'Faster Disco' (Them's Good, 1998)
'Third Time Lucky' (Deck Cheese, 2001)
'Surrounded By Idiots' (Deck Cheese, 2003)
'Poets On Payday' (Boss Tuneage, 2009)

AT A GLANCE:
'Surrounded By Idiots' still comes highly recommended.

GOOBER PATROL

One of the most satisfying 'success stories' in this book, **Goober Patrol** were (or should that be 'are', as the band are still active today) a likeable bunch of drunks from Great Yarmouth who sounded more like a snotty, amped-up version of the Monkees than any other UK punk band, yet managed to sign – without compromising their chaotic sound and carefree approach one jot – to one of the most respected punk labels in the world, San Francisco-based Fat Wreck Chords.

The Goobers actually formed in 1987, so could easily have been included in the *Trapped In A Scene* book that preceded this, but they didn't really hit their stride until the early Nineties, hence them being here.

"We had sort of become obsessed by early Eighties US hardcore like the Dead Kennedys, DI, the Adolescents, Circle Jerks, Scream and Minor Threat," explains drummer Stu Sandall, of their initial conception. "At that point the UK punk scene was dominated by crusty-type bands and we fancied doing something a little different, so we formed the Goobers... plus we just wanted to have fun being in a band, of course.

"The first line-up was me on drums, my brother Si [who had previously played in the short-lived Cautious Approach with Mid from Deviated Instinct] on guitar, a chap called Gary singing and a lad called Simon on bass. Basically we were the *only* people in the area that were obsessive about melodic US punk, so we started a band together and attempted to learn our instruments as we went along. Which again was a bloody good laugh.

"There's no deep hidden meaning to the name though," adds Stu. "Mid from DI started calling us 'the goober patrol' because we looked like hicks with our baseball caps etc [a reference to hillbillies with their own stills for making moonshine] and it just sort of stuck. Odd really, considering we're discussing this 20-plus years later...but good as well; we have had a whale of a time along the way."

After making their public debut at the Brunswick in Great Yarmouth supporting Deviated Instinct and Rhetoric ("It was awful, but we had a great laugh," says Stu. "I remember all the local metal kids trying – 'cos we were so poor! – to headbang to us and just thinking, 'This is brilliant!'"), two suitably ramshackle demos were recorded in Norwich's Rogue Studios.

"Yeah, they were cheap and cheerful," agrees Stu. "But I remember getting a decent review in *MRR* and literally running down the road cheering because we'd got in the 'bible' of punk. It was very exciting for a 17 year-old kid to get his band reviewed alongside the likes of the Dead Kennedys and so on."

Goober Patrol soon evolved into a compact three-piece, with Simon and Stu on guitar and drums being joined by Ian Clitheroe from DI on bass. The band started gigging further and further afield, before hooking up with Boss Tuneage Records for a split 7-inch EP with Boston (UK)'s rampant Vehicle Derek in 1990.

"I remember doing a little mini-tour of Scotland and the north with Deviated Instinct," smiles Stu. "It was brilliant just because we were on tour in a van, like a proper band, eating chips and getting pissed every night. We didn't think it could get any better than that...but it did! A bit later on, we did some gigs with the Mr T Experience and Samiam; these were also memorable for me, as they were probably my two favourite bands of all time at that point and to tour with them was superb, literally like a dream come true..."

"I didn't meet the Goober guys in person until after they had already recorded the split 7-inch for me in January 1990," recalls Aston Stephens, the owner of Boss Tuneage. "I had been in touch with them via mail before that, first with a postal interview for the fanzine I used to write at the time and then Stu sent me a cassette copy of the unreleased 'Jelly On the Sidewalk' 7-inch that they had recorded for Discarded Records that hadn't come out then [and never did!]. Anyway, the guys from Vehicle Derek had organised a show in Boston for Bastro at The Indian Queen and when they pulled out I got on the phone to Stu to see if they could play instead; they could and the two bands hit it off with each other right away and played loads of shows together throughout 1990.

"I remember that summer was really fun: drumkits and vinyl singles and guitar amps chucked into either my old Capri or Si's old Sierra. They even used to drive from Norfolk over to Lincolnshire to pick me up for gigs and would leave the car at my folks' house and borrow my Dad's old van for shows…he even fitted some extra seats in the back from an old Peugeot so everyone had somewhere to sit!

"I have fond memories of that split single with Vehicle Derek because it was the very first release on Boss Tuneage and the first one to get played by John Peel, but it's true to say that over those first couple of years even the band themselves would probably admit that they could be spectacularly brilliant or spectacularly bad when playing live – but it was always fun, regardless. I remember they played at the Harlow Square and you could get the bands filmed with three cameras for £80 there, so I paid to do it so we could put out a live VHS video… Sadly they didn't play very well, so they only let me make 12 copies of the video – just enough to get my money back before it was hastily deleted!

"But even if the live shows were a bit up and down, on record people really liked them and they got great reviews in MRR and all the fanzines of the time. I remember someone called them 'the UK's answer to Green Day', around the time 'Truck Off!' came out, which I remember them being really pleased with! About 20 copies of 'Truck Off' were sent over to Blacklist, MRR's old distro and record shop and it was only later on that we discovered that folks like Billy Joe from Green Day and Dr Frank and Jon Von from the Mr T Experience had bought copies and loved the album – so there was a bit of a buzz building in the Bay Area about them even then…"

December 1990 saw the band in Purple Rain Studios, Great Yarmouth, with Richard 'Hammy' Hammerton engineering and mixing, recording their deliriously raucous debut album, 'Truck Off!' An energetic fusion of the classic punk melodies popularised by the likes of Stiff Little Fingers and the catchy high-speed tunes coming out of the American hardcore scene, 'Truck Off!' was released by Boss Tuneage in 1991.

"Purple Rain was still in Hammy's house when we recorded 'Truck Off!'" recalls Stu. "With hindsight, I quite like the songs…but the drumming mostly makes me laugh! It's fairly poor and a little wacky. The singing is fairly crazy too, come to think of it, but it always makes me smile when I hear it."

The band's second album, 'Dutch Ovens', was recorded with Hammy at Purple Rain as well, during July 1992 and basically saw them honing the direction embarked upon with 'Truck Off!' Faster, catchier, more melodic and, er, stupider (is that a real word? Yes, because in the world of Goober Patrol, anything goes), the album also benefited from a well-rounded production and is widely-regarded as the band's finest moment.

"I just loved the songs on that album," reckons Aston. "It really was true 'pop-punk' before

Goober Patrol, first night in the US, 1996

Goober Patrol, Tom with Jerry A from Poison Idea

Goober Patrol, Stu, 1995

Goober Patrol, Tom's front room.

that became a dirty word. Those early tracks were just so catchy…everything was recorded on a shoestring budget, of course, but both 'Truck Off!' and 'Dutch Ovens' have a naive charm and some kick-ass songs lurking beneath the production. I guess they were learning as a band and I was learning as a label and we were having lots of fun while doing it. Again, 'Truck Off!' holds a special place in my heart as being the first full-length album we released on Boss Tuneage, but 'Dutch Ovens' was when I think they really began to find their feet and develop their own style and sound."

Soon after its release, they were joined by a second guitarist, Tim Snelson, who thickened their sound and opened up a whole new world of options as far as twin guitar harmonies. After a successful tour of France, a split single with the Mr T Experience was released by the band's housemate Ed on his short-lived Punk As Duck label before the Goobers parted ways with bassist Ian. He was replaced by their 'guitar tech' (in the loosest sense of the term) and housemate Tom Blyth, who had played in both Slag Heap and Income Support and joined the Goobers just in time to record a John Peel session and get his picture on the third album.

"It was fantastic," smiles Stu, of the band's French trip, "and a real eye-opener in terms of the way they treated bands, as we got hotels and food and beer and we were just blown away by their hospitality: some great gigs played and some great friends made. This was also about the point that we started to take the band a bit – and I *mean* 'a bit'! – more seriously and stopped just trying to sound like other bands!"

It was also the point that they first met 'Fat Mike' (aka Michael Burkett), proprietor of Fat Wreck Chords, the fast-rising American punk label who would release their third album, 'Vacation', in 1996.

"We put on [Mike's band] NOFX in Norwich – for £100! – in 1994," explains Stu. "Fat Mike said he liked our 'sound' and that if we were to record anything to send it to him. By the time we actually got round to it, Fat had become a big deal and we more or less sent it as a joke. In fact, if I remember rightly, we didn't even send a letter, just a photo of Billie Joe from Green Day on which Tim scribbled, 'That's you, that is!' Two weeks later he phoned to say he liked it and wanted to put it out. It was like the review in *MRR* all over again; we had a cheer and a drink and a month later were on a plane to the US to tour for three months with Tilt…another dream come true for a load of hicks from Norfolk!

"It was incredibly surreal; I remember being at our first gig in America and just wondering what the hell we were doing there, thousands of miles away from home, acting like a 'proper band'. Strange…but if anyone was jealous back home, no-one said anything; I think we got along with most bands in the UK at this point. But then again, they may say otherwise…!"

"People seemed to take us a lot more seriously after we signed to Fat," adds Tom, "even though we were essentially the same band as we had always been. We got on a few good tours as a result and our music and videos got worldwide distribution; another directly positive effect was that we were playing more and more and hence I think we became better musicians out of it. Well, we managed to play better drunk (at least I think we did!). At the time none of us had any particular commitments that weren't more fun than getting out of Norwich and going on tour and we didn't have any high expectations as all gigs differ from place to place. It was just important that we were all close friends and experienced all those good times together…aaahhh!"

Stu: "Yeah, it opened lots of doors and suddenly we were going on tour with 'name' bands and people started to come and see *us* play too. When we rang promoters they actually wanted to put us on, as opposed to sort of being cajoled into it. It was strange because suddenly everything went from being a laugh to being a bit more serious; for a bit we even practiced every day and it more or less became our full-time job. This was a mixed blessing as there was a bit more pressure to be good, but on the other hand it was brilliant in that we all lived together, played together, toured together and had a great time together.

"We stopped trying to sound like other bands and just tried playing what we fancied," he reckons, when thinking back on the 'Vacation' album. "That was the key thing. But we never for a minute thought it was coming out on Fat and that probably helped as well because we were making music we liked, not what we thought Fat Mike or someone else might like. We also practiced loads more and spent much longer writing it. For me, I think it still sounds okay today, but it's hard to tell with your own music…"

The next few years saw the band undertaking some serious touring of the US and Europe, before they recorded their second album for Fat Wreck, 'The Unbearable Lightness Of Being Drunk', at Premier Studios, Corby, with Iain Wetherell during March 1998. A 7-inch single, 'Eight Of Spades', was also released, featuring a fairly hilarious Motörhead homage from Tom as a front cover.

"I think we lost the plot a bit after 'Vacation' and some of the songs lacked tunes and were too long," admits Stu, "We started to try and be too 'show-offy' for some reason. I think it was because we were touring with all these great musicians in the US and Europe and we sort of lost our way a bit. 'Vacation' for me has good, simple songs that have nice tunes and were easy to play when a bit drunk and that's what punk is all about, I think. I haven't really got a least favourite Goober record, though, to be honest, as they always remind me of good times…

"Those US tours were some of the best gigs we ever did, especially the first one with Tilt where we were basically drunk and having the time of our lives for three months. Waking up in a different motel in a different town every day and then moving on to the next town was fantastic and a real experience, 'cos America is such a varied place where you can go from playing DC to somewhere incredibly small and rural like Pensacola, Florida, in a matter of nights. It was basically one massive holiday. Mind you, Europe – on a tour bus! – with Ten Foot Pole was superb…drinking all night while being driven through the Alps and laughing like bastards is such a good memory to have. Also, the gigs in French Canada with Bouncing Souls, Good Riddance and Down By Law really stand out as being another great time.

"We toured the States on three occasions," clarifies Tom. "I remember the look on Fat Mike's wife Erin's face when we arrived at the office after one tour ended; she asked us when us Goobers were ever going to go home and we were all drunk and shouted 'Never!' It was so great seeing the huge mass of those countries and the bands we played with were all fantastic: Me First And The Gimme Gimmes, Bracket, the Nobodys, Neurosis, Strung Out, Diesel Boy, Trigger Happy, Pinhead Circus, Cooter, Lifetime, Swingin' Utters…the list goes on and on really! We met so many great people and I still see a few of 'em nowadays when I am touring with Toy Dolls. It's true that Fat Wreck Chords was like a huge family back then, with all the bands touring together, helping each other out and generally having a great time…"

Things went decidedly quiet with the dawning of the new millennium, although Corby label Them's Good, who had already reissued 'Truck Off!' with bonus tracks lifted from the band's split EP with Vehicle Derek, released the amusingly-titled 'Songs That Were Too Shit For Fat' compilation in 2001 (featuring – just in case you've not figured it out yet – various songs that had been chopped from the Fat albums). After a decade of drunken debauchery, the Goobers then decided to put the band on a back burner to further their educations, although some of their uniquely cheap and cheerful self-produced promo videos would show up on volumes one and three of Fat Wreck's 'Peepshow' series of DVDs in 2002 and 2004.

"We were always touring and drinking and drinking and touring," smiles Tom, "and in between we would get skint and have to take shit jobs, the most recurring of which saw us all at the Colman's Mustard factory in Norwich. This seemed the penance we had to pay for all the good times and it one day occurred to us that if we got some proper education, our job prospects would be better! I wouldn't say we were 'burned out' with the band, but we wanted to do a little bit more with our lives. In fact it was Stu's idea, so cheers, Stu!"

"We basically decided we wanted to do other things and all went to university," Stu continues. "To some extent, I think the pressure of having to be 'good' and thinking that we needed to sound a particular way took some of the fun out of it all and I think that is a large part of why we decided to focus on other things. The others may feel differently, though. Just recently we have been playing together again, but the sound has changed quite considerably and is much simpler and more tune oriented than things like 'The Unbearable Lightness…'. One day we agreed to do an acoustic gig and enjoyed practicing so much that we have just carried on for the sheer fun of it. There really is nothing better than a band practice and a few beers with your mates, I think. We are soon to release a new album, as yet untitled and on which label I don't know. It just needs mixing, but we are really pleased with it…"

While Stu became a history teacher and Simon and Tim got themselves PhDs, Tom achieved a MA in animation and a degree in graphic design before joining Vanilla Pod on bass in 2003 and the Toy Dolls in 2004. Recently the Goobers have lurched back into life as a gigging band again and even have a new album in the can.

"I gave [Toy Dolls main man] Olga a CD of 'Vacation' when I was guitar tech on a Dickies tour in 2003 [Olga was playing bass for them at the time]," explains Tom. "Being in Goober Patrol definitely opened *that* door for me and I really enjoy touring with both Toy Dolls and Vanilla Pod…

"The Nineties were a great time for bands – and a very drunken time for us!" he adds. "There was a core of bands who would always play together: Vanilla Pod, Consumed, One Car Pile Up, Douglas, Dropnose, Travis Cut…it was a really special time. There seemed to be less bands and the internet and all its pros and cons wasn't such a big deal then. I'm sure there have been lengthy opinions expounded elsewhere in this book of how downloading has killed and is killing the sales of CDs, so I won't go into it too much, but what (I hope!) will not change is the live experience… You can see what a band is like on YouTube and what not, but going to an actual gig and enjoying yourself with your mates is second to none!"

"We have basically sold out to 'the man'," laughs Stu. "Other than that it's the usual 'drink and be merry' and going-to-gigs-type stuff. The Nineties was a good decade for music, despite what everyone says; it was also odd that punk became a big deal for a bit and that we were sort of right in the middle of it all, watching the most unlikely people 'get famous'. As for ourselves? I'd just like to be remembered as a group of mates who had a bloody good laugh together…"

SELECT DISCOGRAPHY:

7-inch:
'Split' (Boss Tuneage, 1990) – *split with Vehicle Derek*
'Split' (Punk As Duck, 1991) – *split with Mr T Experience*
'Split' (Snuffy Smile, 1992) *–split with Sprocket Wheel*
'Split' (Lost And Found, 1992) – *split with Gigantor*
'Eight Of Spades' (Fat Wreck Chords, 1998)

LPs:
'Truck Off!' (Boss Tuneage, 1991)
'Dutch Ovens' (Boss Tuneage, 1992)
'Vacation' (Fat Wreck Chords, 1996)
'The Unbearable Lightness Of Being Drunk' (Fat Wreck Chords, 1998)
'Songs That Were Too Shit For Fat' (Them's Good, 2001)
'Mind The Gap' (Hulk Rackorz, 2011)

AT A GLANCE:
The 'Vacation' album on Fat Wreck is probably the best place to start checking out Goober Patrol, it being the band's most popular release and highly representative of their sound and approach, although those first two albums for Boss Tuneage remain eminently listenable too.

COMBAT SHOCK

Although **Combat Shock** formed in Wisbech in October 1994, by the time they split up in late 2006 they had actually relocated to Brighton and released several EPs and a well-received album. As pointed out earlier by Vanilla Pod, Wisbech might be a sleepy market town in the Cambridgeshire fens, but it had a surprisingly vibrant punk scene during the Nineties.

"Yeah, the Wisbech scene *was* quite healthy considering the size of the town," considers drummer Sonny Tyler, who had previously played with PUS "There were a few punk bands around in the Eighties, like Prisoners Of War, Freeborn and Rotten Corpses, but it wasn't until the Nineties that new punk bands were starting to crop up – after the mid-Eighties metal phase had blown over. In Wisbech, we had us lot, Vanilla Pod, Forfeit, Blind Suburbia and PUS, to name but a few. Mel [the Combat Shock vocalist] and I were putting on regular punk gigs at a pub called The Bowling Green, which, after a lot of hard work, became quite established on the circuit. It also doubled up as the Combat Shock rehearsal room for a while. In the end, we had people travelling to the gigs from Nottingham, Boston, Birmingham and London.

"Vanilla Pod also put many gigs on at the time and the local scene was a healthy mix of punks, skaters, hippies, metallers and skinheads and for the most part we all got along. There was nothing going on in Wisbech, so we had to create our own entertainment. We used to travel about to gigs anyway, but forming Combat Shock meant we had even more excuses to get about and make a noise…"

As well as Mel and Sonny, the first Combat Shock line-up was completed by 'the Peterborough contingent', namely second vocalist Matty 'Splatty' Humphries, guitarist Simon 'Shithead' Cottingham and bassist Dave. Naturally enough, the band made their first live appearances at the Bowling Green.

"Yeah, our first gig was there in December 1994," recalls Sonny, "with Suicidal Supermarket Trolleys, Decadent Few and PMT. We played a last-minute impromptu set without a bassist, but it was great to just get onstage and make some noise with some bands we respected. Our first gig with a *full* line-up was also at the Bowling Green [15 April 1995] supporting Red Flag 77 and the Shrinking Violets from London…funnily enough, we ended up playing our very last gig with Red Flag 77 too! Anyway, it was a great night and a really good turnout; Mel wore a tutu and fairy wings and Dave wore a stocking over his face for some reason…"

"The first few dates were very scary for myself," admits Mel. "I had not been in a band before and didn't really know how I was gonna cope…for all my mouth, I can be quite a shy person at times! I think the dressing-up bit was partly something to hide behind, but I soon ditched doing that as, in all honesty, I looked like a complete prat. Although I did wear one last hideous outfit, which was two Santa hats turned into a stuffed and very, very pointy bra… worn over a T-shirt of course!"

On something of a roll, Combat Shock rushed into Boston (Lincolnshire, not Massachusetts!) studio, Gem's, to record their eight-track 'Born To Booze' demo; their first and last recording to feature dual male/female vocals, it was shoddily produced and played, but a feisty debut effort nonetheless. "I'm not sure it's aged too well either, but it was definitely of the moment," comments Sonny.

"The sound was crusty in feel and the lyrics were mostly political; there were a few animal rights songs on there too ['Bloody Butcher' and 'Bricks To Brightlingsea', the latter about the Essex port that saw heated protests in the Nineties for allowing live exports of veal calves to Europe], mainly because half of the band were full-on hunt sabs at the time. I also remember we were really pleased by the cheering we recorded at the beginning of 'Housewrecker', our obligatory song about drinking, a pastime we all enjoyed no end. One of our friends once alarmingly said that the production was on a par with NOFX at the time…it's amazing what alcohol and drugs do to the brain!"

To help sell the demo (although at the time anything as calculated as actually 'promoting a release' would have been the furthest thing from their minds; they just wanted to hit the road…because they could!), Combat Shock undertook a 10-date UK tour with Birmingham's Police Bastard. This was both the best and worst of times, with ill-feeling between Dave and Mel leading to the band splitting in two upon their return to Wisbech; the Peterborough guys deciding to quit (Shithead ending up in 7 Foot Monster alongside members of the Monks Of Science), leaving Mel and Sonny to pick up the pieces.

"The tour with Police Bastard was pretty early on in our so-called 'career'," laughs Sonny.

"We hadn't played that many gigs before then, so on reflection we were probably a bit premature in taking it on. We haven't really spoken that much about the split within the ranks that followed, but basically Mel and Dave were not getting along which caused some friction and after a bit of stirring from various parties, the Peterborough half of the band went their separate ways, but Mel and I decided to plough on…"

"It was a great and exciting time," agrees Mel, "but it turned out badly and the resulting split came about at around 4.30am. We'd just been towed back from Nottingham and were outside Jon from Doom's house with Dave waving an empty cooking sherry bottle above my head, shouting 'Sack me, sack me!' We thought it was a joke at first, but it wasn't, so we did! We did however play the last date in Birmingham the following evening and I seem to recall it was the best date of the tour in the sense that we were actually quite tight and together – but none of us were speaking to each other!"

Two young Wisbech skaters were recruited for Combat Shock MK II, namely 16-year-old guitarist Simon 'Mooner' Cribbett and bassist Lee Richmond and the new line-up made its public debut at the second Edinburgh punks' picnic supporting 2000 DS. The gig was a great success and the band resumed gigging all over the country before releasing a split demo, 'In Cider We Trust', with the Bus Station Loonies. This tape brought them to the attention of the newly-founded Bomb Factory Records, who in 1998 released Combat Shock's only album, 'Wishful Drinking'. Featuring a staggering 21 tracks of honest, pissed-off and occasionally tuneful, punk rock, recorded at Meadowside Studios in Wisbech by Riko Burrows, it remains the band's defining moment. And with songs like 'Eat A Nazi', 'Bullshit Manifesto' and 'PC Scum' it was very obvious that Combat Shock had plenty to say for themselves and that no-one was safe from the band's ire. Armed with anger…? For sure.

"We recorded and mixed it in two days," recalls Sonny. "An old friend and occasional stand-in bassist, Rob Mardle, designed the cover and Dave from Riot/Clone designed the layout. We're still really happy with how it turned out, to be honest and it holds many happy memories for us. It also featured 'I Love My Liver', which turned into a bit of an anthem for us in the end and was probably us at our most productive…"

"We were so excited about getting offered the chance to do an album, we crammed far too much on it," laughs Mel, of that epic track-listing. "A mistake in hindsight, yes, but still, in some ways I'm glad we did it, as we never got offered anything else again album-wise. Which was a shame 'cos none of us could afford to do it ourselves; everyone was in really low-income jobs and I was a dole waller at the time. But it was great fun recording it… maybe we *should* have taken a bit longer to get a louder, clearer sound, but we could only afford the two days. And as for the cover? I do like Rob's drawing – except for one detail: for some reason he gave me the most humongous sticky-out chin ever! I look like I have no teeth in it and for that I will never forgive him…"

A UK tour was undertaken with Chesterfield's W.O.R.M. and a French tour with Red Flag 77, during which the band had ample opportunity for drunken shenanigans themselves and also to see the unfortunate effect alcohol can have on the punk scene's more susceptible characters…

"Hmmm, yes, on the W.O.R.M tour, there was a 'Punk Points Cup' up for grabs," begins Sonny sheepishly. "It was a mug painted silver (!), which was to be given to the individual that racked up the highest quota of obnoxious punk-rock behaviour…childish I know, but good fun all the same! On the motorway, heading to a gig in Hackney, I mentioned that I would

Combat Shock

Combat Shock, live 2003

need the toilet very soon – and not the kind you can deposit very easily in a bush or up a tree, if you get my meaning? After realising there were no service stations on the horizon, I decided to sleep my way through the trauma, but when we got to the venue I rushed to the loo, only to discover I'd had an unfortunate trouser-soiling accident while asleep. It didn't make that night very comfortable, but it clinched me enough points to win the Punk Points Cup!

"And once we were booked to play the South London punk's picnic at the Goldsmiths Tavern," he adds, of an infinitely more unpleasant incident (if such a thing is possible?). "Mel and I had spent the morning at my god son's christening so we were pretty mellowed out, but when we got to the venue, the police had already turned up and were hassling the punks for sitting and drinking on the pavement outside. They were threatening to close the venue and, as we turned up, a copper was explaining that they would give us an escort to make sure we parked away from the pub. "Meanwhile, the Ozric Tentacles bassist was toying with the idea of putting his guitar through the policeman in question's car headlights; they had also built a lager-can barricade in front of his car, which was quite novel!

"As you can imagine, the gig was volatile; we had Joe Dunton standing in on bass on this night and at one point he locked himself in the pub's toilet cubicle, waiting for a mass brawl to stop, which was nice. We were supposed to play early on, but bands kept hi-jacking the stage – to get their set out of the way, no doubt – and, much to our surprise and horror, we ended up as the headline act! That was interesting because Instant Agony from Liverpool had played before us and were dismantling the drum kit around me as they needed to get home – I don't blame them! – so, with minimal equipment to play with and a rabid crowd to play to, we ploughed through our set as best we could.

"This effort was met with a few cans flying past our heads, ending up with a pint glass barely missing Mel and shattering against my tiny drum kit. Phil from PAIN calmed the audience down, bless him, and we managed to play through to the end of our set unscathed. Some of the crowd truly were wankers that day; we certainly wished we'd stayed at home!"

"Actually the glass *did* hit me," corrects Mel. "It hit my shin and broke, but I was wearing jeans so it didn't cut me. I hated that gig though; I remember standing outside talking with Richie from MDM and I felt sick at the thought of going on as the gig was so hostile. That's the one and only time I could quite easily have walked away and not played at all; I think that one pretty much put us off playing at the Goldsmiths Tavern ever again…"

As well as recording an excellent version of Omega Tribe's 'Is There A Future?' for a Crass Records tribute put together by Ruptured Ambitions (and entitled 'Angry Songs'), Combat Shock released the five-track 'Hospital Food' 7-inch on Weird in 2000, which was dedicated to Mel's younger sister, Abbie, who had sadly died of meningitis two years previous and featured Sonny's only ever turn on vocals, on the track 'Punchbag'. Soon after its release, Lee left to become a father and Mel and Sonny relocated to Brighton.

"We just fancied a change and felt we'd got everything we could out of living in Wisbech," explains Sonny. "We'd basically reached a bit of a dead end and needed to get the fuck out of Dodge! We'd visited friends from Brighton quite a bit previously and thought that it seemed quite an open-minded place, which unfortunately Wisbech was not. We have a lot of good friends in Wisbech, but we just needed a change and the band wasn't strong enough to keep us there. It could have spelled the beginning of the end for Combat Shock, I suppose, but Mooner said he was happy to commute to gigs and, together with our new look Brighton line-up (Bemble from the delightfully named Anal Beard on bass and Garth on guitar), we managed to hold things together for a further seven years. I must admit, gigs did start to dry up when we moved to the south for some reason; it seemed really hard to break out once you were rooted there…like some strange force field had been set up to keep us there – called the M25! We still played some top gigs, though, with the likes of Discharge, Sham 69, Disorder, Hard Skin and Deadline, to name a few…"

Beat Bedsit Records, ran by Paul from Anal Beard, released 'Celebrity Hitlist', a split EP between Anal Beard and Combat Shock, in 2002 and 2003 saw the band self-releasing the five-song 'TWAT' (short for 'The War Against Tony') EP. With a furiously fast title track inspired by the then-Prime Minister Tony Blair, it was the band's finest release, well played and perfectly produced. It proved to be the band's swansong. Mooner's work commitments made it harder for him to honour gigs, so Malc from Joyce McKinney Experience and Identity joined to share guitar duties and brought a new element to the band's live shows with his wacky stage costumes. But eventually Sonny joined Constant State Of Terror (alongside ex-members of MTA and Substandard) and Mel decided to fold Combat Shock once and for all. One last mini-tour of the UK culminated with the band's final gig at the Prince Albert in Brighton on 7 October 2006, with Red Flag 77, Terminal City Ricochet and Constant State Of Terror.

"I really don't know how we would like to be remembered, to be honest," admits Sonny, who sometimes drums for Anal Beard now as well as Constant State Of Terror. "We just got our heads down, made some noise, sang about the things we believed in and plunged head-first into the DIY scene. In a way, organising gigs was as important as being in a band and it was great to be involved in such an active scene. To be remembered is very nice, but that's not what we were thinking about at the time…it was just great to be a part of it all."

"It *would* be nice to be thought of occasionally and remembered as a sometimes ramshackle but mostly good band," adds Mel wistfully. "And one that worked very hard putting as much as possible into the scene; I would like to think that we made a lot of good friends all over the country and helped give a few people a good laugh and some memorable times."

Nowadays Mel still resides in Brighton with Sonny, where she is a health and safety manager in her place of work. Mooner works as a transport logistics manager in Wisbech and is planning on joining recently-reformed fenland punks Anti Patriots; Garth lives in Wales, where he makes underwear out of metal at his 'Fetish Forge' (he has even made outfits for Toyah Willcox!); Bemble teaches English over in Spain, where he also plays with Tres Y El Ingles and Malc's also in Brighton playing with the Lovely Brothers and the Cravats.

"I really enjoyed the Nineties scene," concludes Sonny, now a warehouse supervisor. "It was all about the DIY way of doing things…whether that be writing a zine, organising a gig or playing in a band. Punks' picnics were always a highlight of every year and there were plenty of benefit gigs to get involved in. Another good thing was that a lot of the gigs had very varied line-ups; you could have an anarcho band playing with a street-punk band playing with a pop-punk band and so on…it really helped to unify the many different factions within the scene. And, of course, punk was still quite politicised at the time, which I think has fell by the way side lately. It wasn't just about getting a support slot with your favourite re-formed band from the Eighties! I shall look back on it all with fond memories…and a shrunken liver."

SELECT DISCOGRAPHY:

7-inch:
'Hospital Food' (Weird, 2000)

CDEPs:
'Celebrity Hitlist' (Beat Bedsit, 2002) – *split with Anal Beard*
'TWAT' (Combat Shock, 2003)

CD:
'Wishful Drinking' (Bomb Factory, 1998)

AT A GLANCE:
Beat Bedsit's 36-track 'Forgotten But Not Gone' CD features not only the 'Wishful Drinking' LP but also the 'Hospital Food' single, the first demo, the Omega Tribe cover from the Crass tribute compilation and various live and unreleased material.

URKO

Named after the infamous gorilla general in the classic Seventies TV series *Planet Of The Apes*, Boston's **Urko** formed from the ashes of Middle Finger sometime around Christmas 1995 and were just as brutal as their namesake primate. That first line-up comprised vocalist Daz Rivet, guitarist Craig McKenzie, bassist Jason 'Jas' Toomer and drummer Lee Winter and would terrorise the punk scene with their ultra-raw thrash for the rest of the Nineties.

"Urko was Daz's first band," explains Martin 'Marv' Jolly, author of long-running fanzine *Gadgie* and close friend of the band. "But Lee had played in a metal band, Jade Serpent, as well as Outpatients, Sickbus, Neurophobic, Latch, Freaky Friday, Tobogan, Furious Dripping Urchins, the Pissed Offs and Faceache. All were relatively unknown local bands except Faceache, who were a power-violence trio and played places like the 1 In 12 and recorded a couple of demo tapes.

"Craig played in Chud, a local pop-punk band – the less said, the better – and he also had a short-lived band with Darryl from Poindexter (who went on to be in the Leif Erikssen] that only had one practice at the Fenside Community Centre, which the caretaker cut short halfway through their first song (Black Flag's 'Wasted') 'cos it was too loud! Jas, meanwhile, had a punk CV as long as your arm from the early Eighties onwards…his band Fatal Conflict even supported Subhumans at a local scout hut! He also played in 'Fenpunk legends' Piss Tank Twat, among many others."

Urko, live at the Warzone fest, Belfast

Urko, Lee, pic by Brian Sayle

Urko on the streets of Belfast

"I was originally gonna play bass," adds Craig. "But Lee and Daz knew Jas, who was from Spalding, and they got him in as I really wasn't very good. We practiced in Lee and Daz's town centre flat in Silver Street and then started rehearsing at the [much-loved Boston pub] Indian Queen when Derek and Teresa moved in as the landlords there…

"There were lots of pop-punk bands around," he continues, of the Lincolnshire scene that spawned them, "and emo bands from [nearby] Holbeach like Tribute. Jas wrote to loads of people, bands and zine writers, so he kept us in touch with other bands and scenes. We all read *Maximum Rock'n'Roll*, but there were no local zines until Marv started *Gadgie*. There had been a half-decent scene previously that had died off a bit as all the original folk (like Aston from Boss Tuneage Records, Estelle and Vehicle Derek) had all moved away and we wanted to get that Indian Queen scene started again; it was the only venue in Boston and all the punk bands played there…and continued to do so for over 20 years."

"Urko managed to upset the local emo fraternity with the anti-emo song, 'Emotional Blackmail', " adds Marv. "Oh and probably because Craig had 'ANTI EMO' painted on his guitar strap too…"

Craig: "Yeah, but we just wanted to take the piss and have a laugh really."

Taking their early cues from Discharge, Urko predictably made their live debut at the Indian Queen ("All I remember about it is fly-posting loads of posters around town with a picture of a skinhead and the line-up for the gig in a speech bubble," laughs Craig) before moving into more extreme (much, much faster) musical waters.

"Japanese hardcore was a big influence too," reveals Craig. "Especially Deathside, as they were so 'over the top'. At our very first practice, I ripped off a Deathside riff for our first song. Over-produced Swedish crust stuff was also a favourite and UK bands like Doom as well… their 'Rush Hour Of The Gods' and 'Fuck Peaceville' LPs were very influential. I was also into US hardcore like Bad Brains and Lee was really into raw, thrashy stuff and power violence bands. Then there was Daz, who was into everything and bought records all the time and Jas, who was into garage stuff, punk rock and all sorts of hardcore bands."

The first Urko demo was an eight-track self-titled affair, recorded at Meadowside Studios in nearby Wisbech on 23 March 1996. While not reaching the insane velocities the band would soon become renowned for, it was still a solid offering in the vein of Hellkrusher or the aforementioned Doom.

"Well, it's part of our story and it's always good to look back at your early tapes," considers Craig. "Given the chance, I would have turned the guitar up and downtuned a bit more, but it was just good to get something recorded and be part of the crust scene that was really strong back then – before Luke Hall ruined it!"

With a demo tape to flog at gigs, Urko started gigging whenever they could, including their first out-of-town gigs and once the (wrecking) ball was rolling the Urko juggernaut took some stopping!

"We played the Birds in Spalding a lot," recalls Craig, "but the first one I can remember which was right out of the area was supporting Drop Dead and (I think) Scalplock at the Red Eye in London. Doom were there too, although I can't remember if they played as well and after our set they asked us to tour with them. We went to Ireland with them later on.

"I also remember playing with Freebase early on, who were like Madball at that point, in Wisbech; that was mental…we played a lot of the Wisbech all-dayers that Sonny and Mel from Combat Shock put on. It was in the days when you had to actually write to people to get gigs and it took ages to set one up; there were no mobiles or internet, but Jas was in touch with loads of people all the time, just to get us gigs and reviews..."

"In a review of the Drop Dead gig a writer for [metal mag] *Terrorizer* wrote that the London crust set stayed at the bar for Urko and were 'unimpressed' (or words to that effect)...it was actually members of Doom they were talking about and they were so 'unimpressed' that they invited Urko to tour with them!"

"I remember a gig at the Bristol Skate Park, where I tried to do a star jump at the start of the set and smashed my guitar into my face," admits Craig. "Blood went everywhere and I had to go to the toilets and clean my mouth up. After that I broke a string and borrowed Bjorn from Imbalance's shiny white guitar and he said, 'Don't bleed on it!', as I was covered in blood. Cowboy Killers were there too and Jas asked one of them if they were cowboys that killed or did they actually kill cowboys? The bloke just said, 'I don't fucking know!' Jas was always saying daft things to people."

The first demo brought them to the attention of Mike Clarke from Inflammable Material Records, who booked them into Rubber Biscuit Studios, Nottingham, for half a day to record four songs – not dissimilar to Septic Death in places – for a split 7-inch with Chineapple Punx. The two bands played loads of gigs together to support the release, which quickly sold out and soon (10 August 1997) Urko were in recording their 'Pissing Blood' demo. Early 1998 then saw them recording the 'Prepared For Helter Skelter' demo, which paved the way perfectly for the truly savage split 7-inch on Enslaved, that Urko shared with Suffer, that saw the band riffing on their apish moniker with the track 'Prime-Hate' and covering Youth Of Today's 'I Have Faith' as 'I Have *No* Faith'. Recorded at the Stables, "by Graham", on 7 June 1998, the single confirmed that Urko had expanded and tormented their humble D-beat (inspired by Discharge) origins into whole new areas of unadulterated extremity and the inner sleeve featured yet more emo-core baiting with the statements 'Fuck Fugazi' and 'Anti Emo Rock'.

"We knew Sned [from Suffer] from playing with Drop Dead and Doom and we knew Nick Loring from going to gigs and playing with bands like Health Hazard, Suffer and Ebola. It was actually a split release between their labels, [Sned's] Flat Earth and [Nick's] Enslaved... that was a brutal record."

Inflammable Material then released Urko's 'Thrash It Up' 7-inch in late '98, a three-track affair, complete with a lovably cheesy *Nosferatu* sleeve, that saw the frantic aural assault continuing unabated. It was however the last release to feature Daz's vocals, as he and the band parted ways soon after its release and not altogether amicably.

"How can I put this?" sighs Craig. "During our UK tour with [US crust punks] Detestation, Daz had to pull out of the dates due to 'unforeseen circumstances', but we decided that we would do the rest of the tour as a three-piece anyway, as we didn't all want to drop out. It worked well and a lot of people liked us as a three-piece. When Daz then moved to Nottingham, it became difficult to practice and meet for gigs as he didn't drive and seeing as Daz couldn't get back that often we decided to go on without him. We told him at a festival at the 1 In 12 and he wasn't too happy. It meant I moved to lead vocals and Jas went to back-ups; my vocals were more screaming than gruff and we started playing faster around then too."

While Daz went on to play with Nottingham-based Helvis, Urko entered what many consider their best period, the stripped-down three-piece line-up now sounding more like

Drop Dead than Doom and more dangerous and chaotic than ever before. Three songs (including the deliriously fast '(I Wanna) Fuck You Up') were contributed to a split 7-inch with Scarborough's Active Minds, which was pressed on both clear and green vinyl by Mel Hughes' Direct Hit Records – the clear a limited run of 105 copies and the green given away free with the first issue of Mel's *Direct Hit* fanzine – before Urko unleashed the aptly-titled 'Fast3chordhardcoremotherfuckingthrashcrustpunkshit' 7-inch on Disintegration Records in September 2000.

"That was a result of Jas's friendship, through the simple wonder of writing to people around the world, with Jay Unidos of *Urban Guerrilla* fanzine in Berkeley, California," recalls Marv. "Jas would contribute to the zine, which covered the US's brutal crust and thrash scene. It was strange to see that zine, which would be all stark black-and-white bullet belts and patches…then a handwritten Jas page would pop up about crashing fork lift trucks at work or something!

"Anyway, Jay put out a compilation CD with his zine, with both Urko and Los Cano's Electricas on it [Urko contributed 'You're A Cunt', while Los Cano's Electricas, an Urko side-project, contributed 'Piss Stain' and 'Lunacy In L'Orcy'] and then he did the 7-inch single on his label, Disintegration. Jas's flier for it said something like, '£2 post paid, or free to Wayne Kramer and members of AC/DC…'!"

The best Urko release though was unfortunately the band's last. A split LP with Southampton's Minute Manifesto had been recorded back in April 1999 and in true DIY punk fashion took two years to appear on Enslaved, but just before it was released Jas was tragically killed in a car accident on Sunday 24 March 2001.

"Craig didn't really want to go into this too much," says Marv, sadly, "but suffice to say it was devastating and the end of Urko. Jas was the driving force behind the band and they didn't want to go on without him; there could be no replacement for Jas in terms of personality and what he brought to the band and scene.

"The final Urko gig was with Sawn Off and Imbalance, one that I booked as the Ape City Collective at the Indian Queen on 27 January 2001. However, Jas played with SuperEagle [Jas, Lee and Craig's Seventies rock band with two other Boston lads] on 10 February and then with Shot To Fuck, a very short-lived, stripped-down Eighties hardcore band with Gords from Hard To Swallow and Nick Loring, not unlike DS13, on a bill with [Danish thrashers] Amdi Petersens Arme at the IQ on 16 February and his last ever gig with anyone was a Tuesday 'Alternative Night' set at the Axe And Cleaver with SuperEagle on 6 March 2001. We obviously didn't know at the time that these were his final gigs, but what I do remember is that Jas had taken to bleaching his hair and wearing an old British Army jacket like the ones out of *Zulu* – he looked very strange!"

Jas's untimely death sent shockwaves through the local – and international – punk scene and a memorial gig was held that September that saw the likes of Imbalance, Sawn Off and even Endstand (from Finland) eager to pay their respects. And while Urko may well have died with Jas, the memory of both band and bassist live on with those lucky enough to have encountered either.

"Lee didn't play in any more bands after Urko," concludes Craig, who nowadays runs Voodoo Tattoo And Piercing in the Boston town centre. "He is now married with kids and still in Boston. We did keep SuperEagle going for a bit, with Sam Jarvis on bass, but it faded away. I didn't play in bands for a long time after we lost Jas, but am now back and in Wolfbeast

Destroyer with people who were in Boston bands Burning The Prospect, Patient Zero and the Phuck Ups. We've just had a 10-inch released ['Far From Grace' on Underground Movement] and play brutal crust…"

But what else, of course?

"We [Urko] were just a bunch of alright lads who you could have a laugh and a drink with," he adds wistfully, before admitting, "we probably did ruin a few nights for some people!"

SELECT DISCOGRAPHY:

7-inch:

'Split' (Inflammable Material, 1997) – *split with Chineapple Punx*

'Split' (Enslaved/Flat Earth, 1998) – *split with Suffer*

'Thrash It Up' (Inflammable Material, 1998)

'Split' (Direct Hit, 1999) – *split with Active Minds*

'Fast3chordhardcoremotherfuckingthrashcrustpunkshit' (Disintegration, 2000)

LP:

'Split' (Enslaved/Boy Useless, 2001) – *split with Minute Manifesto*

AT A GLANCE:

Here's a band crying out for a proper CD retrospective, but until then, try blagging Marv to run you off a complete discography: mrgadgie@hotmail.com

SHREDS

Hailing from Cranwell, Lincolnshire, the **Shreds** were a trashy pop punk/power pop band in the vein of Senseless Things and Mega City Four; fuelled by youthful enthusiasm and teenage angst, they only released one 7-inch during their four-year existence but demoed enough songs for about four albums.

"We formed in 1993," begins bassist Austin Rocket. "Me and Russ [Holland] had been mates since we were kids and had grown up together, going to the same schools. And I met Martin [Bell] while working a crappy evening job cleaning offices when we were both seventeen; we hit it off straight away 'cos he was wearing a Mega City Four T-shirt and I'd just discovered them and bought their first LP. I'd also just bought a bass off a schoolmate and, as Martin could play the guitar, he suggested we form a band…only problem being that we didn't know any drummers, so Martin said he'd play drums, basically 'cos he had a job and could afford a cheap kit and he'd teach Russ how to play the guitar. Despite the fact that we could barely play, we practised all afternoon every Saturday and Sunday in the local youth club; it was way too hard to even consider learning anyone else's songs so Martin started frantically writing his own. After about a year, Bruce joined on lead guitar, but was replaced by Matt [Chapman] a few months later, who stayed until the end.

"Due to the fact that we were driving round the country to watch the Senseless Things play live as much as possible, it wasn't much of a surprise that we were heavily influenced both lyrically and musically by them and all the other bands they played with, in particular Snuff and the Hard-Ons. Our lyrics usually revolved around our poor luck with girls, with titles like 'Tracy's The One', 'All Over Now', 'You Make Me Wonder Why' etc. We used to watch any bands we could for tips of how they played and I remember spending ages at Senseless Things gigs stood against the barrier in front of Morgan, watching everything he did and then trying to remember it when I got home in the early hours to try it out on my bass!"

Being in the middle of rural Lincolnshire, the Shreds had no real choice but to travel to nearby Nottingham to be schooled in the ways of hardcore punk, in venues such as the Old Angel and the Narrowboat and record shops like Selectadisc. Their real education came by way of the humble fanzine, a genuine lifeline for any scenester stuck out in the sticks and a sure-fire way of tapping into the national network, regardless of your local connections. Soon they were playing their first gig – with one of their favourite bands, no less (after all, punk rock encouraged bringing the mountain to Mohammed...) – and recording their first demo.

"We recorded that sometime in 1993 at Bandwagon Studios in Mansfield, with one of the guys that played in a band called Slaughterhouse 5, though I can't remember his name. The place had been recommended by another band we'd played with and they let you record cheap if you were students, which me and Russ were at the time. I hadn't realised just how bad my cheap Rickenbacker copy bass was until we tried to record and it sounded absolutely dreadful, so thankfully the studio took pity on me and let me use one of theirs instead. We did six songs: recorded them all on the first day and then mixed the following. When asked what kind of mix we wanted, we all shrugged our shoulders, having no idea what the engineer even meant, so his response of, 'Okay, I'll give ya the standard Senseless Things mix!' was perfect. We all loved it; it was pretty rough around the edges and far from perfect, but the songs sounded good and we got a great response from some fanzines and managed to get gigs with other bands around the country off the back of it.

"Our first gig was at the Narrowboat in Nottingham with Lovejunk. We'd seen them supporting MC4 in London and, being huge fans of Wolfie's previous bands Perfect Daze and the Stupids, we desperately wanted to play with them. So, figuring if we paid them they'd come, we asked them to play a couple of gigs with us, one in Nottingham and one in Lincoln (the first shows we'd ever booked ourselves). The Nottingham one was a disaster; even though we'd been flyering after gigs over there and managed to get the odd poster up around town, I think we had about 10 paying punters! Lovejunk all looked pretty pissed off, having dragged themselves over from Ipswich, but were cool about it and just said, 'Well maybe Lincoln will be better?' Thankfully all the hard work we'd done promoting it around Lincoln did pay off and our first gig at the Duke Of Wellington pulled about 120 people in, so nobody lost any money..."

The Shreds started booking gigs at the Duke on a regular basis and started their own local fanzine, *Arsehole*. After playing several gigs with the Revs from London, the band hooked up with Detour Records for their only official release in their own right, the 'Brutally You' 7-inch. Recorded at Stable Studios in Lincolnshire, it featured three tracks of exuberant bubblegum

Shreds, Austin, Martin, Russ

Shreds

punk rock…although nowadays it's often listed as a 'mod revival record'!

"As a nod to Snuff, who were using a lot of mod-influenced pics on their record sleeves, our demo at the time had Jimmy from *Quadrophenia* on the front. Dizzy from Detour liked the tape and offered to do the 7-inch for us and we obviously jumped at the opportunity. Due to the sleeve and pics of Martin and Russ at the time having real short hair and wearing Fred Perry shirts, I think he probably thought we were more of a mod band but, after the single was released and he'd seen us live, he soon realised we were far from it…

"After a few years of trying desperately to find someone to release something for us, it was the best thing ever to have our very own 7-inch in our hands. Dizzy did an amazing job with a full colour glossy sleeve and even did a limited run on white vinyl as well as the standard black copies. As usual with us, it was pretty rough around the edges and sloppy in places, as we were never the most polished band out there, but energy-wise it still holds up pretty well, as does most of the stuff we recorded…"

The 7-inch was to be the only stand-alone release by the Shreds who, despite making several compilation appearances (on the 'Tinpot Island' four-way split 7-inch on Potential Ashtray and the third and fourth volumes of Bluefire's 'Snakebite City' compilation albums), would only go on to release a slew of demos before splitting, leaving several albums' worth of material virtually unreleased.

"I think we recorded 45 songs in total over the years," reckons Austin, "that all came out as demo tapes. We'd go in the studio for a weekend and record and mix at least five or six songs, always more concerned with getting them down on tape than whether they were played absolutely perfectly. The order they [the demos] came out was 'All Over Now', 'Imaginary Friend', 'Brutally You', 'Maim And Shred', 'The Shreds Have Left The Building', 'No-one Likes Us', 'Anthems For The Kids' and 'More Songs, Less Style'. I'd struggle to pick a favourite as they all have songs I like on and, as much as I like the charm of the early ones when the three of us were getting better all the time, I also like the later ones when it was me, Russ and Matt [Martin left after the single and rather than find a new drummer, Russ swapped to drums], as it was like a different side to the band.

"The fact we only released the one single always frustrated all of us and, even though we were on those other compilations, it's never the same as having your own releases. I still have a pile of reviews from fanzines at the time, though, that all contain lines like, 'Why is nobody releasing this stuff?' or, 'If these guys were from the States they'd have been snapped up by now…' but hey, that's the way it goes, I guess and it never stopped us recording and selling the stuff ourselves."

Eventually getting demoralised by all their positive reviews never snaring any serious label interest, the Shreds split in 1997, playing their last ever gig at the Grafton House Labour Club in Lincoln with Scarper from Hull.

"The dizzying heights of success, eh?" laughs Austin. "After we split up, me and Russ got back together with Martin as the Headchecks, wrote some songs and then very quickly recorded a five-track demo. This was picked up by Speedowax Records, who released three of the tracks as a split 7-inch with Travis Cut and then used the remaining two tracks on 'Volume One' and 'Two' of the 'Punk Rock Disc' compilation 7-inchs. Martin then left again, Russ went back on drums and we got Will [Burchell] in on guitar; then, some time after that, Luke [Moss] also joined on second guitar. We gigged quite a bit and played with Panic, One Car Pile-Up, Bradworthy, Vanilla Pod and Goober Patrol etc and then knocked it on the head when Will joined Consumed. Luke went on to play with Army Of Flying Robots from Nottingham…

"Out of the Shreds, I'm the only one that has continued to be in active bands ever since.

I joined [Nottingham garage/rock band] God's Chosen Dealers with Coop from the X-Rays and Steve Charlesworth from Heresy [and the X-Rays]; we gigged for a couple of years before we split and nowadays (since 2007) I'm with the Hip Priests, who are continually playing and releasing records.

"For me I'd just like the Shreds to be remembered for having good tunes," he offers, "and the energy we used to play with. We always put everything into playing live and, while not always being the tightest band out there, we were always all about playing with as much passion and angst as possible, something that a lot of bands have often been missing. Why just stand there looking at the floor when you can be leaping around like an idiot?"

SELECT DISCOGRAPHY:

7-inch:
'Brutally You' (Detour, 1995)

AT A GLANCE:
Crappily-named Japanese label Fixing A Hole recently released the Shreds' 'Maim And Shred' discography CD…all 30 tracks of it!

SICK ON THE BUS

Playing raucous two-fingers-in-the-air street punk since late 1990, welcome Bedford's **Sick On The Bus**. Formed from the ashes of the Varukers, the band's hard-drinking/hard-rocking approach has made them a hit with audiences and a terror for promoters ever since, although the lads' involvement with punk rock can be traced right back to the late Seventies.

"My first band was called the Drop Outs," recalls guitarist/vocalist Ian 'Biff' Smith. "We made badges by peeling other bands' badges open and cutting out letters from the newspaper and stuff. We didn't have any guitars or anything, but we still got everybody wearing the badges – even though we didn't really exist. Then we *got* some guitars and started a band called Uproar, but found out there was another band called Uproar… So we started Death Sentence – and a couple of years later we found out there was another Death Sentence as well, but we were too far down the line anyway, so we just carried on with it.

"Then I joined the Varukers in 1985; Brian [Ansell, who would become the Sick On The Bus bassist] had joined Death Sentence too, but we were kinda falling apart; the singer had left, John wanted to do different things and no-one seemed interested. I saw the Varukers in

Sick On The Bus, British Invasion tour,
Biff and Brian

Sick On The Bus, drummer Skum

Peterborough one night and they were really going for it, so I joined them and then, when the bass player left, Brian joined as well.

"I first met Brian as I was leaving school and we were looking for a bassist," adds Biff. "He turned up to try out, opened his case and he had a Rickenbacker and that was basically the first time we'd seen a *proper* guitar, so he was in the band before he'd played a note. But Brian's a fantastic musician, he can do anything he wants…and we've been together since I was 15 or 16, one way or another.

"And then Kev [Frost] joined the Varukers as well and he ended up as the original drummer of Sick On The Bus. SOTB were basically the Varukers without [vocalist] Rat… The Varukers ground to a [temporary] halt, because we were doing gigs where we'd drive halfway across the country and there'd be no posters, no PA, no microphones, nothing; we didn't have any money anyway but it was costing us to play gigs. So it ground to a halt and I did various other bits and pieces, played in a local funk band, a metal band, but it paid…although I really wanted to just play noisy rock'n'roll punk…"

Which is where Sick On The Bus came into the equation, their name belying the power and tunefulness of their take on punk rock, their first gig – the band being rounded out by vocalist Doug Eales – descending into absolute chaos and setting the scene for many more over the years.

"I was at work and the site agent (at the building site I was working on)'s son was starting a band," explains Biff, of *that* name, "and his dad said, 'Why don't you call your band Sick On The Bus? 'cos everyone's been sick on a bus!' And his son said, 'I fucking hate it…' but I was like, 'Don't you want it? I'll have it!' So I said to Brian and Kevin, 'Let's call ourselves Sick On The Bus!' and the name gave us a focal point to do something.

"That first gig was at the Vine in Newark; we'd only been together eight weeks and we had about eight of our own songs and about the same number of covers, by bands like the Damned and UK Subs. But Kev's a pretty loud drummer and you have to play to the volume of the drums; we started off with 'New Rose' and 'Neat Neat Neat' and they told us to turn it down, to which we said, 'Fuck off!' So after four songs, they switched the PA off and got us off stage and it kicked off a bit. We were really drunk, we pulled a radiator off the wall and then some water pipe in the toilet and steam was blasting everywhere, so the police got called and the landlady was crying. Years later I bumped into her daughter over in Nottingham and she was like, 'That was my mum's pub! It was you lot, was it?' Yeah, sorry, it was…"

Just a few weeks after the gig, in late 1990, Sick On The Bus recorded their 'Get Sick!' demo, at Far Heath Studios near Northampton, which they released themselves in early '91. After many local gigs to promote it, Doug left and the band went through a slew of singers, including Graham (then bassist with the Varukers), before deciding it was easiest for all concerned if Biff sang as well as played guitar, as he was writing all the lyrics anyway. A second guitarist was added to the line-up, in the shape of Tony Evans and Paul Blaber replaced Kev on drums, before the band recorded their first single, 'Scary In The Dark', in 1995, a stomping Ruts-like anthem.

"Kev lived in Newark and it was a long haul for him and we really weren't a band that was getting offered shitloads of gigs and making loads of money," explains Biff of the line-up changes. "We were all local and he had to drive 75 miles to rehearsal, so he started missing them and when it got to a monotonous point, we said, 'Fuck this…'

"And we met this guy Paul in Bedford, who had really long, dead straight, hair and worked in a record shop. He didn't look like he'd fit in with us, but from the first time we met him we felt like we'd known him for ages, he was just a really nice guy. And that's the thing with SOTB, we're just a bunch of mates at the end of the day.

"So, anyway, Paul was in the band and I took over singing…and I'd known Tony since school. He was a few years younger than me, but we were going to do this other band – me, Tony, Brian and a few other lads we knew. We had a couple of rehearsals, but that didn't pan out and Tony was so up for doing it, me and Brian felt a little bit sorry for him! So we said, 'Oh, come and join us!' It wasn't as if we were ever looking for another guitarist, it was just 'cos he was our mate and he wanted to be in the band."

The single was recorded at Premier Studios in Corby and released by BIP Records, as a direct result of Sick On The Bus entering a local Battle Of The Bands contest. They only came fourth, but Premier's owner was so impressed by the snotty attitude of their spirited performance, he offered to do the single.

"But that record never really got out there," sighs Biff, "because they [BIP] were so far detached from the punk scene, they didn't really know what to do with it; I forget how many they pressed, you can't buy it for love nor money now, but I heard they chucked four or five hundred copies in a skip because they couldn't get rid of them. They just had no decent outlets for it…"

The band's self-titled debut album followed in March 1996 on Bus Pop Records and saw them combining the hard melodies of early Damned with the filthy bottom end of Motörhead and the frenzied energy of Wakey-fronted English Dogs. 'Just Sex' is even reminiscent of prime-time Dead Kennedys (think 'Too Drunk To Fuck') and by rights it should have seen the band taking on all comers on the international punk scene. But tragically Paul died of leukaemia before the album was even mixed, although his family encouraged the lads not to disband as a result.

"He seemed perfectly fine the last time we saw him," Biff recalls sadly. "It was at a nightclub in Bedford called Winkles and the Varukers were off on a two-week tour of Europe, so we all got hammered the night before we left and were out in the car park, all drunk, waving goodbye…

"Then we were out in Germany somewhere, when our mate Mad Andy's ex-missus got hold of us – tracked us down on tour, which was more or less impossible back then! – and told us he'd died. And we were devastated, because he was a good mate. So that night we did the Varukers set and then a couple of SOTB songs for Paul.

"His funeral was packed out – he was a popular bloke – and there was a bit of humour there. He had some songs playing: Ramones, Hard Ons and then some SOTB, a song called 'Law And Order'. And the vicar was walking out just as the song goes, 'Right up your fucking arsehole, copper!' And this vicar stops mid-step, closes his eyes, composes himself and carries on and the whole place erupted. That was really funny and Paul would have loved that. And I spoke to his brother afterwards about what to do and he said, 'Just carry on, make it a success and have a drink for Paul along the way…' We didn't make it a success, but we still have a drink for Paul, still raise our glasses to him now and again…

"The other disaster related to Paul's death was the Bedford River Festival," smiles Biff. "We decided that – as a tribute to him – we'd make a raft, set his drum kit up on it, stuff it with straw, douse it with petrol and set fire to it. The plan was to float it past the river festival and everybody would stop what they were doing and go, 'What the fuck's that?' But we got it in the river – me and Tony were waist deep in this quagmire of mud – and set fire to it; the petrol got in the water so there was fire all around us and the raft went about three fucking yards and sank. I'm sure if Paul had been looking down, he'd have been pissing himself laughing! About nine months later, there was a thing in the paper about what the Bedford council had pulled out of the river: bicycles, cars…and a whole drum kit! I wonder how that got there?"

The band recruited new drummer, Simon 'Wag' Wagstaff, from Bedford-based anarcho-thrashers Legion Of Parasites and headed off to Europe in support of the album, a two-week stint with Contempt that was predictably enough complete chaos from start to finish.

"That *was* funny," agrees Biff. "The first gig we ever did outside the UK was in Groningen and I introduced us with, 'Right then, you foreign fuckers, cop a load of this!' And all the guys from Fleas And Lice were there and we just hit it off; they just went berserk for us, it was the perfect first gig in Europe and we're still good friends today. It was a great night and we went back to where we were staying and we had a day off the next day and it got a bit out of hand…! We had this weirdo cross-dresser with us, [the aforementioned] Mad Andy and we'd used one of his stockings when the fan belt broke on our van, so he had a top hat on, one stocking, a basque and a colostomy bag strapped to his leg. He didn't get the nickname 'Mad' Andy for nothing; he's like Spike Milligan, highly intelligent but right on the cusp of insanity…and he used to get us in a lot of trouble.

"Anyway, Tony climbed up a tree, totally drunk and he obviously fell out, then pissed and puked on the floor before passing out. And I'm stripped to the waist in a pair of fisherman's trousers, chopping firewood, 'cos I used to be a tree surgeon. Anyway, I'm chopping these logs, but I start messing around, tossing some of them like a caber onto what I thought was a wrecked car, but it wasn't, it just had a flat tyre. But by the time I'd finished with it, the roof went in and the windows popped out…

"Meanwhile Andy started rolling around on his back, turning the tap on his colostomy bag on, tapping it and spraying piss into his mouth. And Stumpy Steve, from Mad Cow Disease, said that whatever Andy did, he would do, so he started drinking Andy's piss as well – it was fucking horrible, you know I mean? And this went on and on, until Andy found all these maggots under an old water barrel and put one down the end of his cock…and Steve was like, 'No fucking way!' And Andy reckons he's been pissing bluebottles ever since! And it went on like that, with stuff getting broken in the house and all sorts…

"In the morning we were sheepishly trying to clear up our mess and the promoter came downstairs and we were like, 'Alright, mate?' And he was like, 'No, I think you have to go home!' He was really pissed off, but Keith from Contempt talked him into letting us stay on the tour, telling him we weren't normally that bad…!"

Wag made his recording debut with the band on the eight-track 'Suck On Sick Of The Bus Fuck Heads' 12-inch, another high-energy slice of catchy cock-sure punk rock which the band issued on their own Get Sick label during June 1997.

"We just have a laugh when we record," offers Biff, when pondering how Sick On The Bus capture their live vibe in the studio, "and we record pretty fast, basically do it all live… If anyone makes a mistake we do the whole thing again. We'll go back and fix the odd mistake here and there, but really we want to keep the energy of recording it together, by keeping it as live as possible and standing up when we record – the headphones usually fall off 'cos we're all moving around as we play! Obviously we've had a few awful gigs along the way, but normally we sound pretty good, especially if we've got our own backline with us: we sound very close to the records…

"We're pretty heavy drinkers," he adds, quantifying his reference to a 'few awful gigs along the way', "but we're used to operating when we're drunk so we normally play alright regardless…only occasionally we overdo it! We played the Astoria once, one of them all-dayers and I'd been out for three days; my mate Adam had to take me home to get my guitar and my ex was spitting bullets when I turned up, grabbed my guitar and left. Anyway, we got down the Astoria and apparently I was swaying about and mumbling incoherently in-between the songs, but when we were actually playing I was fine. We did one in Rushden and it's a bit embarrassing 'cos Brian comes from there and I didn't even know what song we were doing; I thought Brian was going to kill me! I sucked really badly – probably one of the worst performances ever."

The 'Punk Police' 12-inch followed in April 1999 on Data Records, another strong eight-track 12-inch that opened with the superb 'Never Enough', highly reminiscent of GBH at the peak of their powers and complete with riotous backing vocals from Wakey of the English Dogs. Wakey also provided lyrics and lead vocals on 'All Over Again' and played the penny whistle and, er, a pencil sharpener on several other numbers. Sick On The Bus undertook their first US tour – up the East Coast with Molotov Cocktail and Distraught – before re-mixing and re-packaging their sold-out self-titled debut for Data, who reissued it as the 'Set Fire To Someone In Authority' CD. A headline tour of Europe followed, before the band played main support to the Damned around the UK in November and December 2000 and signed to US label Go Kart in early 2001.

"We did a lot of good tours, but the most memorable ones aren't memorable 'cos of the gigs but 'cos of the things that we got up to," laughs Biff, remembering that hectic period of non-stop touring. "Some of the stuff Mad Andy did…some of it's really, 'Oh my fucking God…!' I remember once in Sweden, we went into a petrol station late at night and this spotty 18 year-old kid serves us through the hatch. Andy asks if he can see this copy of *Arse Destroyer*, so this lad gets this porno for him and holds it up to the window, turning the pages and Andy immediately drops his trousers and starts wanking – on the forecourt of this fucking garage while we're all sat in the van waiting to go! I mean, fuckin' hell…things like that are hard to forget.

"I remember getting hit in the face with a bottle in Ladronka [Prague]. We'd travelled god knows how many hours to get there, playing the seventh day of a seven-day festival and we got there and got given every substance under the sun…so we did all that and then I was bubbling for a shit before we went on. And I went to the bog, but there was a pyramid of shit piled up in the toilet, so I went outside in the woods and fell in a bramble bush with my bare arse and had to explain all the scratches up my back when I got home! Anyway, we went onstage and smash: three-quarters of the way through the set, I got a full bottle of beer in my face; smashed all my crowns, fucking blood everywhere… I was like, 'If you've got the bottle to throw it, come up here and have a go!' And they were like, 'No, you come down here…' so I threw my guitar over my head and jumped offstage. But my guitar hit Wag in his head – he was just undoing a cymbal at the time! – and all hell broke loose. I don't think we were playing our best, but I don't think we were *that* bad!"

2001 was another busy year, with tours of France and Japan and a well-received slot at the Holidays In The Sun festival in Morecambe, although Wag broke his foot running out to the van to get his drum bag five minutes before they went on, so bravely played the set in complete agony. Another album, 'Go To Hell', was recorded for Go Kart – albeit over a six-month period due to the label double-booking some of the studio sessions – and a planned US tour with Conflict was cancelled, with the dates rescheduled for the following summer, only this time supporting GBH. As usual with Sick On The Bus, Biff called on the many weird and wonderful experiences had on these tours to inspire his latest lyrics.

"We're just a punk-rock band," he states matter-of-factly. "I mean, everyone in the band has got their own political views, but we've never felt the need to ram it down people's throats. I don't like to sing about things I don't know about…and what do I know about multi-national corporations? I know about stuff like when my ex-missus broke up with me; I can sing about that with some authority, y'know? But I can't sing about McDonald's…I just know the food's 'orrible. That would be a short song: 'McDonald's – the food's 'orrible! Tastes like cardboard!' [laughs] But do you know what I mean? I sing about stuff I know and a lot of it is autobiographical…because there's nothing funnier than life.

"There's a song called 'No Regrets' [on 'Go To Hell'], that goes, '6,000 miles away, what could I do?' The Varukers were on tour in Japan and we were in Kobi, staying God knows how many floors up in this guy's flat. He put his wife in the cupboard – one of those cupboards with a sliding door – to make room for everyone, stuffed her in there sat on this sewing machine or something…and his mate comes around and we're all crammed in this fucking flat, trying to sleep, but there was an earthquake going on as well and things rattling off the fucking shelves. And we could hear this noise in the kitchen, in the bit where everyone takes their shoes off. Anyway, I know a little bit of Japanese and I heard the word for 'arse' and then I heard the word for 'dick' and I thought 'What the fuck?' So I look around the corner and he's bumming his mate over his missus's shoes in the kitchen. So I looked at Iggy and said, 'Fucking hell, Iggy, he's bumming his mate over her fucking boots!' We got these little knuckleduster things out and put them on and zipped up our sleeping bags real tight and thought, 'They ain't coming anywhere near me…' Anyway, they went out on the veranda next, in case they woke his missus up in the cupboard, I suppose and they were bumming out there…

"And in the middle of all this, I had this feeling, 'I've got to phone home!' So I went all the way down the skyscraper and up and down the street, found an international payphone and tried to phone the ex up. Her sister answered, 'Oh, uh, she's not here, she's round at mum's…' 'Well, have you got your mum's number?' And then her mum tells me she's gone to the doctor's…at 6.30 in the morning? And that's when I realised that my missus was having an affair, but I'm 6,000 miles away in the middle of an earthquake with people bumming each other over fucking footwear…and that's what I wrote 'No Regrets' about.

"Then we played in Baltimore with Oi Polloi and had a bit of a to-do with Deek Allen. We'd played Gissen with them on our first European tour and they'd turned up and jumped on our gig and ended up headlining it! And then took the lion's share of the money, if I remember rightly. And they had their whole backline with them in the van but wanted to borrow all our stuff…including our guitars! I mean, c'mon, fuck off! Deek had a big Coca-Cola sign with him and I said, 'What's that for?' And he said, 'I'm going to smash it up onstage, of course!' So when we went on I cracked open a can of Coke and said, 'Coca-Cola – symbol of the free West!' And I think that was the start of the friction between us…

"But also we've got this song called 'Punk Police'. Punk is all about doing what you want, thinking for yourself, it doesn't all have to be the fucking same. When I got into punk rock it was for any kind of fucking weirdo. And I hated the fact that punk had got so regimented and you *had* to be a vegetarian or a vegan, you *had* to think and act and dress in a certain way…that was so *not* punk rock. Punk rock was whatever you wanted it to be, not defined by rules and guidelines. Some of the squats we played were ran by a committee and you had to be voted in and everything…yet they call themselves anarchists? Then go form a mini-government, with their own little hierarchy, all wanting to control their own little bit? Everything they claim to be against they end up being, but on a smaller scale. So I thought, 'Fuck all this lot!' and that's what 'Punk Police' is about. But when Oi Polloi got on after us, they said, 'Sick On The Bus sing about punk police…we sing about real police!'

"Anyway, we're in America, in Wisconsin, playing the Old Barn Fest and I admit I got fucking messy, firing bottle rockets out my arse and all sorts. And Oi Polloi played and onstage Deek's going on about fighting the police and direct action and stuff. Then later on, it all kicked off and the police turned up and kids are throwing stuff at them and Deek's sat there by the fire, so I went over and said, 'Well, aren't you going to go and help them out?' But he just looked back at the fire and didn't want to know and I think that was wrong. You shouldn't encourage kids to do something you won't do yourself; don't tell people to throw bricks at coppers if you ain't gonna back it up, know what I mean? It's okay for me to tell people to get drunk and snort coke and shag some fucking whore because I've done it! I mean, I'm married and wouldn't act like that now… Well, I still get drunk and get loaded, but…I don't say anything that I wouldn't do, especially if some kid could end up in prison for it, 'cos that could set off a chain of events that could ruin their fucking life! Don't be a fucking general sat at the back of the army! And that's what I wrote '(Don't Be A) Freak' about."

Things have been a bit quiet on the SOTB front since 'Go To Hell' (with Biff and Brian keeping themselves busy touring with Varukers), although in recent years they've contributed three songs to the 'Tormentum Insomniae' split MCD with the Destructors on Rowdy Farrago, new drummer, Chris 'Skum' Furphy, taking over from Wag in 2005. And a brand new full-length, 'If It Ain't Broke…Break It!', was finally released in 2011, songs like 'It Won't Suck Itself' and 'Whores Not Wars' proving there's plenty of life left yet in the band's riotous drunken depravity.

"We've never been popular enough to have that continuity of doing an album, then touring, then doing another album," admits Biff. "We're too lazy for starters and it's never flowed for us, we've always had problems…the wheels always come off the bus! But we don't write for anybody else apart from ourselves. Every label we've had has fucked us over anyway, so we certainly don't write for them and we've never had a reputation for just one style of music either. If you're a 'hardcore band' you can't turn round and play something that isn't hardcore, because everyone's like, 'What the fuck's this?' But we've always played anything we want – if a riff makes us smile, we'll use it. It's more for us than anyone else. I'd hate to write songs that everyone else liked that we hated playing…

"We just do what we do," he adds, in closing. "We're not out there to impress anybody, not out there to change the world, not out there to spread a message… We just play decent punk rock and if you like it, you like it, but we're not bothered if you don't! The important thing is *we* fucking love it! We're a bunch of mates, having a laugh – me, Tony and Brian have known each other for 30 years. We're not out there to achieve anything, but when we're on form, there's not many people that can hold a candle to us; we play good music and we mean it. It's not contrived, we're not just saying something because we think we should… we could've been taken a lot more seriously if we'd changed our name, changed our attitude, but that's not us – this is Sick On The Bus and what you see is what you get. We may be going nowhere, but we've *had a laugh* going nowhere…"

SELECT DISCOGRAPHY:

7-inch:
'Scary In The Dark' (BIP, 1995)

12-inch:
'Suck On Sick Of The Bus Fuck Heads' (Get Sick, 1997)
'Punk Police' (Data, 1999)

LPs:
'Sick On The Bus' (Bus Pop, 1996)
'Go To Hell' (Go Kart, 2002)
'If It Ain't Broke… Break It!' (Anti-Acoustic League, 2011)

AT A GLANCE:
'Suck On Sick Of The Bus Fuck Heads' and 'Punk Police' have recently been reissued on one disc in a very nice Digipak by Mass Productions/Brain Damage. A 'greatest hits' album, 'Piss'n'Vinegar' was also released by Sick Bus Records in 2010. That new album kicks ass too.

CHAPTER SIX:
THE SOUTH EAST

ABOVE ALL

After a stunning debut 7-inch, Southend's **Above All** really should have taken the hardcore world by storm, but despite signing to metal giants Roadrunner they fizzled out after an unsatisfying debut album, yet another naive victim of the music industry's voracious appetite.

Formed from the ashes of Stand Off, an old-school hardcore band who issued the much-sought-after 'Worthless Is The Unity Bought At The Expense Of Truth' 7-inch on legendary German label Crucial Response in 1993, Above All were instantly heavier and more metallic than their musical predecessors.

"[Bassist] Hallam Foster and myself formed Stand Off," begins vocalist Tony Maddocks. "We did the 7-inch and played a few local shows here and there… even did a mini UK tour… but soon disbanded as I had managed to get myself a place in a US university on a swimming scholarship. Hallam and [guitarist] Ben [Doyle] became friends while I was away in my Speedos, watching local friends' band Understand, but over time I came back during the holidays and we talked about getting together our own, much more metal-edged, hardcore band. That's basically how we formed; we added drummer Mark Harpley and as soon as I came back permanently from the US, we hit the rehearsal studio and started jamming…

"Then, after only about a month, we managed to talk Roadrunner Records into letting us support Life Of Agony! Looking back, we were nowhere near ready to start gigging with a band of that level, but we just thought we'd go for it in a big way. Many thanks has to go out to our good friends in Understand and also Louise, Miles and co at Roadrunner who showed such a lot of support in the beginning – when we really probably didn't deserve it!"

But before the Life Of Agony gig, they cut their live teeth playing Southend dive, Sak's Basement Bar, capturing the imagination of the small but enthusiastic local scene with their wide-boy take on the whole vegan SXE sound and ethos expounded by the likes of Earth Crisis and Snapcase. Given that the vegan SXE scene was so select in the mid Nineties, it was only a matter of time before Above All came to the attention of Nick Royles and Sure Hand Records, who released the aforementioned 'stunning 7-inch', 'Blood Of Ages', in 1995.

"Our early influences definitely had us likened to Earth Crisis and Snapcase," agrees Tony. "Also Resurrection and Sick Of It All and pretty much every other metal-edged US hardcore band around at the time. Integrity were a huge influence on me personally as well… I still

Above All, Ben Doyle

Above All

Above All, Tony Maddocks, 1995, by Vique

listen to all their records to this day. Ben and Hallam came out with most of the riffs and I did most of the lyrics. I tended to follow the SXE formula lyrically and I think it's fair to say that Ben definitely came from more of a varied metal background and Hallam probably did as well. Obviously, back then, the new metal sound we were hearing from the US was exactly the direction we wanted to hear and more importantly play. Mark was basically into loads of different music styles so he just went with the flow.

"I met Nick Royles through getting hold of *How We Rock*, a monthly hardcore newsletter that he was producing up in the lovely sunny town of Bradford. He was like my hardcore guru, along with Rob from Understand. Nick was basically running loads of shows at the 1 In 12 Club; I think he saw some promise in our early enthusiasm and I'm still pretty proud of that 7-inch, it's very raw and there's no messing about..."

A minor classic in the vegan metalcore canon, 'Blood Of Ages' is reminiscent of the 'All Out War' EP by Earth Crisis, resonating with emotional power despite its basic production values, its profound message of compassion delivered via a brutally simple medium. However the band wouldn't remain true to their SXE ideals for long...

"Yes, we were all SXE at the start, but I think that I was the only one left walking the 'path of resistance' at the end," laughs Tony. "It was never an issue, though, as we were all good friends and people change, as did our music as the years flew by. I think it *was* an issue for a few scenesters... I did hear a few funny rumours about how I was this intense SXE guy who had to have a separate dressing room from the others and demanded my own tour bus! We couldn't even afford a Transit van and our dressing rooms mostly consisted of a smelly toilet. But that was all part of the fun, I guess..."

"I don't think it was a major deal, us stopping being SXE, to be honest," reckons Ben. "We had done a bunch of touring by then and I guess we were more into our music than our morals. I don't think it caused a backlash or anything like that either, although we had starting playing with more metal bands as opposed to SXE bands by then anyway..."

Indeed, things moved incredibly quickly for Above All following the 7-inch, partly because it was a great record that rightly garnered them a lot of attention, but also because they knew some influential people in the music industry. No sooner had they had their song, 'Saviour', given away as a free flexi with issue 14 of *How We Rock*, they were signed to Roadrunner and recording their debut album with Fudgetunnel's Alex Newport. They were also gigging with the likes of Korn and Fear Factory and threatening to cross over to the metal market in a big way.

"We hooked up with Roadrunner through friends of Understand," explains Tony, "mainly their manager and friend, Tank, who also became our manager and an A&R guy who was looking at Understand at the time. We were very lucky; I think we showed a lot of ambition for a very young band, but we also happened to be in the right place at the right time. But, as a consequence, we did a lot of maturing and morphing on a very public level and should maybe have showed a little more patience developing our sound. We still managed to clinch the deal, though, which at the time I thought would be a good idea, but hindsight is a great thing and personally, looking back, I think it was probably one of the contributing factors for us to later disband.

"Sure I feel lucky to be able to say we released a record on such a well-known label, but ultimately the support we received from the main players there was non-existent. I still can't get my head round the fact that we were signed, but there seemed to be no collective notion that we were a band they wouldn't be able to market on a national level, let alone worldwide; in fact, we seemed to be thought of as a band that would release one record and then be forgotten about. It's sad for me personally, reflecting back; I think we had a lot of positive momentum at the time and we just thought things would naturally take care of themselves and we would be touring the world with both hardcore *and* metal bands. Unfortunately the reality was far from this ideal. And, as far as people accepting us from different scenes went, although we knew we would alienate ourselves from a small minority by signing to such a big label, we genuinely thought that we could release a debut album which would appeal to the majority of fans of a very infant crossover scene…"

Despite some great reviews (Avi Pitchon from *Terrorizer* magazine still rates the album as his all-time favourite metalcore record!), 'Domain' didn't strike the same chord as the EP; being both over-produced and under-realised, it seemed just a little polite and one-dimensional compared to the band's underground hardcore flailings.

"Personally I don't think 'Domain' reflects Above All in the slightest," says Ben scathingly. "We had quite a bit of pressure on us for that record to tone it all down and take it from pure vocal venom to something with melody. Alex was cool, but we were all pretty fresh to the business and we kinda struggled to make it all happen, to be honest. At the time, Tony was being pressured into injecting more melody into the songs and I think Roadrunner wanted us to be more… er… marketable. So my fave Above All stuff would have to be either the original 7-inch or one of the killer demos we did way after 'Domain'… those and the live show really showed how metal we were! 'Domain' is too clean and slow-paced; also we were in a rush to fill a record with songs and in hindsight I think that shows too. Live, we had a much faster, more aggressive vibe, with loads of energy; the album totally failed to capture that…"

"The writing went well, but I personally hate that record with a passion as well," agrees Tony. "It did not sound like the real Above All. Alex was a great guy, but everything transpired against us, from me having a throat infection to our label basically saying, 'Change your sound!' I felt very unhappy during my vocal sessions and regret putting ourselves under that pressure; we produced a bad album that was quite rightly rejected by many people. That was not the record we intended to release; it bore no resemblance to the hard-hitting, gritty sound we had developed earlier.

"I'm not attacking any of the other guys' performances; I just think collectively it didn't come together on many levels. We should've stuck to our guns and produced the record we were capable of, but we were like a rabbit in the headlights and definitely got hit full-on! For me, the final nail in the coffin regarding our position with Roadrunner was the fact that we got talked into going on tour with Pitchshifter. They were great guys, but it was totally the wrong tour for us; we were turning up at the regional offices of Roadrunner, at most major cities across Europe and none of them even knew we were touring… We had no press, no support and most of them hadn't even heard of us. It was a complete waste of time and money for both us and them; it actually became embarrassing walking into the various European Roadrunner offices and introducing ourselves. It came as no surprise to either us or our management when we were dropped soon after, as our record sales had been poor across Europe…no surprise there then, as it was a bad record that had little or no support…"

In 1997, Hallam was asked to leave the band, right after the Pitchshifter tour ("We just found it harder and harder to relate and cracks started to appear," sighs Tony) and was replaced by Daniel P Carter. Rob Coleman joined on second guitar as well, kick-starting the band's creative juices for several more demos, but nothing came of the recordings and, after a brief period with Dan Stewart on second guitar, Above All decided to call it a day.

"We just felt that the band had run its course," admits Tony. "We all became very negative and jaded anyway, but I do regret it in the sense that maybe if we had kept it together a bit longer we could have found ourselves getting things back on track, as it seems that a lot of bands who followed us went on to bigger and better things, especially with the definite growth of the metallic hardcore scene all around the world. But everything happens for a reason and we have all moved on to be very successful people in different avenues of life."

"We played our last ever gig in Southend-on-Sea, of course," says Ben, who became a guitar tech after Above All, working with bands such as Incubus and Reef, "at the Esplanade. It was a great show; we even did a cover of 'South Of Heaven' as well! I also joined Hundred Reasons after Above All; me, Colin [Doran] from Hundred Reasons and Dan [Carter] also did a band called the Lucky Nine [who released 'True Crown Foundation Songs' on the Hassle label in 2005]."

Prior to the Lucky Nine, Daniel Carter played with A, but nowadays is best known for doing the Radio One Rock Show. Rob Coleman is an in-demand lighting guy, who has worked with the likes of Iron Maiden, Mark Harpley restores furniture, Hallam is a graphic designer and Tony fronted Light Of The Morning before working himself up to be a director of a gas utility company.

"I'd just like us to be remembered as one of the early pioneers of English metallic hardcore," he states proudly, before admitting, "who could've done a lot better a few years later on! The really frustrating thing for me though is that, just as we perfected our sound, we split up. We got some great songs demoed that no one's ever heard, that I think would probably still hold their own with bands today. I think I'm going to dig 'em out sooner rather than later and do a stadium reunion tour!"

SELECT DISCOGRAPHY:

7-inch:
'Blood Of Ages' (Sure Hand, 1995)
'Saviour' (1996) – *one-sided flexi, given away free with* How We Rock *fanzine*

LP:
'Domain' (Roadrunner, 1996)

AT A GLANCE:
Some sort of timely re-issue of 'Domain', with lots of early and latter-period bonus tracks would be most welcome.

UNDERSTAND

Southend's **Understand** also burned very briefly and very brightly, signing to major label East West and releasing the wonderful post-hardcore/proto-emo album, 'Burning Bushes And Burning Bridges' before imploding and leaving a good-looking corpse.

"It's funny you should say that, because when they asked me to join [at the end of 1990], I thought they were the four best-looking boys I had ever seen and I was reluctant to join at first, because I didn't want to be the 'Sporty Spice' of the band," laughs guitarist Rob Coleman, who had previously played with Cynical Smile during the late Eighties (with Hallam Foster, who went on to form Stand Off and Above All).

"We weren't *really* a hardcore band," continues Rob. "Our combined influences were fairly varied and, on reflection, there wasn't a huge amount of quality control. It's hard to answer this honestly and I would love to pretend to be cool and say it was all Dischord, Revelation, Sub Pop, Amrep [Amphetamine Reptile] or Touch And Go, but we were also listening to other things at that point that haven't aged so well and I'm going to say it anyway…'funk metal'! Yep, Faith No More, Fishbone, Urban Dance Squad, 24-7 Spyz…personally I blame Token Entry. And it seemed okay at the time. For me, though, my biggest influence was always Verbal Assault; I was obsessed with the 'On' record. I couldn't say for the others…but a mixture of bands from the above labels, I suppose.

"We kind of fell into the hardcore scene via Dave Potato, who we first encountered at a NOFX show, giving out flyers; at that time he organised shows in the Kent/Sussex area, for bands like Strength Alone, Angus Bagpipe and his own band, the Couch Potatoes. He let us play a show in Eastbourne with them and from there on we played fairly regularly in that part of the world.

We never used the word 'hardcore' to describe ourselves; we didn't sound like Heresy or the Cro-Mags, but as hardcore became less hard we found ourselves more comfortable in the UKHC scene. I personally really liked the term 'emo'; I wouldn't use it now, but back then it could mean anything from Articles Of Faith to Verbal Assault… and there is nothing wrong with being associated with bands like that!"

Those aforementioned 'other members' were vocalist Dominic Anderson, guitarist John Hannon, bassist Stuart Quinell and drummer Andrew Shepherd, who all went to the same school in Southend and had tried out several other band names before arriving at Understand. They started their musical career fairly incongruously, playing around Essex with very non-hardcore bands like Revolver and Stereolab, although there was already a potent scene bubbling up in Southend.

"The gradual way that Understand came about means that I couldn't really say what the first show was," admits Rob, "But it was a big jump at the time to start playing with bands like Strength Alone and Couch Potatoes; that was the most fun time for me, it was all pretty innocent and geeky. By this point, there was a dozen or so people into the hardcore scene in Southend and I can't describe how much fun it was on a Friday night, driving in a mini-convoy to go to somewhere in Kent to see someone like Jailcell Recipes or Sleep and meeting people like Tony Sylvester and Vique Martin for the first time… and basically just getting involved with something outside Southend.

"It was, like all towns I suppose, pretty bleak there culturally in the early Nineties; there

Understand

really wasn't much to do if your life didn't revolve around alcohol, so just being able to get to shows in another town was pretty incredible. By the time Stand Off had formed, though, there was a pretty decent scene developing in the Southeast…"

As the band began to move in more hardcore circles, they came to the attention of Richard Corbridge, who had just started his Armed With Anger label and included the fiercely jagged 'Poll' on his 1992 'Consolidation' compilation 7-inch, where Understand appeared as part of a very hardcore line-up alongside Voorhees, Nailbomb, Stand Off, Kito, Ironside and Submission.

"I heard that song for the first time in years the other day and I have no idea what we were thinking of when we wrote it. I saw the Belgian band Blindfold once and the singer was onstage banging these two metal pipes together; he then told me later that he had the idea from the Understand song on that 7-inch… the sound he was referring to was actually a pencil on a milk bottle! I remember recording it thinking, 'This is going to be a hit…it just needs more milk bottle!'"

The compilation EP helped pave the way for gigs further and further north and then, during December 1992, the band recorded their own three-track 7-inch that was released by Armed With Anger early the following year.

"We couldn't really tour back then, it was just mainly one-off shows," recalls Rob. "The high point was definitely playing one weekend in August '92 in Durham, Bradford and Middlesbrough with Stand Off. We stayed at Lecky's house and it was the first time we had met him; we had heard all these crazy stories about him being some kind of straightedge maniac – I can remember we were all a bit nervous about staying there – but he was incredibly nice and the whole thing was just great. "Simon Kelly, from *Punch In The Face* fanzine, came over; we met Ian and Helene from Subjugation… Nick Royles and Richard Corbridge were there too. This might sound silly now, but just getting to meet all these people that held the scene together was amazing; we really felt included in something that went beyond the tiny area we lived in. Another high point was playing in Leeds with Farside and Fabric in December '92; that was another really good show. I remember we did a cover of Steadfast's 'I Hope You Die Real Soon'… we assumed Lecky would sing it, but he just looked really embarrassed, so Tony Leathers sang; I thought he had broken the mic, but it turns out he always sounds like Norman Collier!"

With the likes of Fugazi and Quicksand bursting from the underground hardcore scene and the band starting to make real waves with their own take on the rhythmic post-hardcore sound, it was only a matter of time before a major label came sniffing and East West snapped up Understand in time to release their one and only full-length album, as well as the 'Bored Games' EP and two 7-inchs lifted from the album session. Signing to a major obviously opened many (too many perhaps?) doors for the band and for a short time the world seemed their oyster as regards perfect support slots and recording with childhood heroes, but the move was predictably accompanied by the inevitable backlash from the DIY hardcore scene. They also went rather rapidly from being big fish in a small homely pond to tiny minnows in a vast unwelcoming ocean.

"We were playing a show with Fabric and Onefold at the George Robey in Finsbury Park," explains Rob. "The East West A&R man, Nathan McGough, actually came to see Fabric, but ended up seeing Understand and we just thought he was some Care In The Community patient – especially in that area of London – because he was talking about how he used to manage the Happy Mondays and now worked for East West. He kept going on about one particular song in the set that he thought was amazing; we found out some time later that this song was the cover of 'Pet Tricks' by Swiz we did that night… which I suppose to his credit *was* actually the best song in the set!

"Anyway he came to a few other shows and offered us a deal and we soon discovered how unimaginative the major-label world is, when other labels started offering us deals or showing some kind of interest just because of the interest from Nathan; he was something of celebrity in those circles…

"It all appeared to start off well; nobody from the label interfered in any way: we recorded whatever songs we wanted, with whoever we wanted and we did all our own artwork… however it soon transpired that what we thought was some kind of respect for the artist was actually a total disinterest in us. And yes, we now had bands like Simply Red to 'compete' with and when you walked into the reception of your record label and saw that their album 'Stars' had gone platinum 10 times over, just in the UK, you soon realised just how insignificant you were.

"Surprisingly, though, there wasn't too much of a 'backlash', as you put it; I thought it would have been worse, but I think the personal relationships that we all had as individuals with the people in the scene helped over-ride it. What I mean is that my involvement with the hardcore scene went beyond Understand, so it didn't personally effect my relationship with people like Nick Royles or Richard. The day we signed, I called Helene to tell her… then bought a 'Still Life' 12-inch from her! It didn't seem that important in the big scheme of things. I also remember someone telling me that Simon Kelly was happy to see me wearing a Punch In The Face T-shirt in *Kerrang!*

"After signing to East West, we still continued to play with Above All, Fabric, Tribute, Dead Wrong and Schema, among others; Bob Tilton were the only band to not want to play shows with us any more, but even they were still very civil about it all.

"I guess the whole of the backlash was probably one interview in *How We Rock* [fanzine] with Rob and Seth from Baby Harp Seal; they made the accusation that we had deliberately used Armed With Anger as a stepping stone to 'major-label stardom', which was entirely untrue. And that was about it.

I also remember that a lot of people seemed to think us signing to a major was 'inevitable'; I never saw that myself and if that's what we *had* intended, we never would have chosen that type of music. Recording another record for Richard would have been much better for Understand undoubtedly; however, I don't regret signing to East West – somebody had to do it! It got me out of the situation I was in; I had a good job in the city, which is okay when you are young, but if I had stayed there I probably would have gone nuts. So being 20 and not having to work for a living was a pretty privileged position to be in.

"The best thing to come from that time was definitely meeting Steve Reddy from Equal Vision. We were recording ['Bored Games'] in New York with Don Fury and he dropped in the studio; we got talking and he ended up releasing that record in America for us. He had the coolest set-up I had ever seen: a Hare Krishna temple and a hardcore record label in the same apartment in New York… I was pretty much in awe of him and it was a great honour to have a record released by him."

Apart from the rampant old-school hardcore influences at work on 'The Rudeness We Encounter' (a very nice touch on a major-label release, it has to be said), the 'Burning

Bushes…' album lilts compellingly along like Tool jamming on Rites Of Spring. And if that sounds pretty fucking awesome, it's because it is.

"The producer, Chris Sheldon, was great and the whole thing was fairly relaxed although also, much like a lot of Understand's experiences, totally uneventful; I don't know if that's because we were mostly straightedge and didn't take drugs, but we never really invited anything crazy. Everything we did always seemed so matter-of-fact and rational; that's not a complaint, but it doesn't make for good stories 15 years later…

"The record received a lot of good reviews, especially in some of the indie press, which was a surprise. I don't think it has aged well; the recording sounds a bit too much of that era for me and I think the whole thing could have been a bit…er, ballsier? We got the production we wanted, but I think at the time we were so conscious of *not* being 'too rock' that we sucked some of the life out of it. There are some live tapes from the time that I would be far happier people remembering Understand by…

"The touring side was definitely better and we could now afford to stay in hotels instead of sleeping on people's floors; floors are okay in the short term, but I couldn't take a month of it. We toured a lot in the UK, with all the obvious bands – Quicksand, Jawbox, Shelter, Sensefield and Civ – and we toured in Europe with Helmet, which was a high point for me; much like a lot of UKHC people, I had developed what was probably an unhealthy interest in all things American, so it was a valuable experience to discover there was more to the world than New York and DC.

"The low point was probably touring with Sick Of It All at the end of '95; we had played with them previously in '93 in London and '94 in New York and the shows had been great, but back then they still had a fairly broad-minded hardcore audience… By the time they played in '95, it seemed they had attracted more people from the Biohazard side of things and we didn't go down well at all… I even remember someone shouting, 'Fuck off, REM!' at us!"

A split CDEP with Jetpak (whose guitarist went on to form Hundred Reasons) from Kingston-on-Thames followed on Gravitate Records, but proved to be Understand's last release before they split…in typically unspectacular fashion.

"Well, we didn't really split up, we just played less frequently and kind of fizzled out, so I guess we are *still* going," laughs Rob. "The last gig was in Bedford and was probably one of the reasons we stopped playing; it was with some awful punk band. Time passes differently when you are younger and I can just remember playing songs that were a few years old and feeling the whole thing seemed pointless. The thing that excited me about Understand and that whole scene was the feeling of optimism; for me, everything I did was driven by it. But by 1997, that had all gone and we were just left with the music and that didn't make much sense by itself.

"We forget sometimes that what made hardcore exciting was how quickly it changed and evolved; bands had a pretty short shelf-life then, things just moved at a different pace. Look how much things changed between '89 and '92. And from then on, everything just became so stale and I don't think that just applies to hardcore but all forms of music… Did anything new or exciting really emerge after that time?"

After Understand, Rob played with Light Of The Morning (alongside Tony Maddocks from Above All), who released the 'All Else Is Error' MCD on Blackfish Records in 1999; John went on to do Woe (now Liberez) and make a name for himself as an in-demand producer, while Stuart joined the Wonder Stuff! Yes, really.

"I have since met people from bands like Biffy Clyro and Funeral For A Friend, who have been very complimentary about us, saying that we inspired them in some way, which is always surprising to hear," concludes Rob, who is now a concert lighting designer living in Berlin. "I thought we had only ever played shows where we were on first-name terms with the entire audience! I'm not particularly proud of Understand, but I am proud to have been a part of a scene that was so exciting. I remember the first time I saw Bob Tilton and literally being covered in goosebumps for the whole set, they were that incredible; I loved watching Fabric and how no two shows were ever the same and there was the whole excitement of watching Tony talk in-between songs, wondering what he was going to come out with. And they could go through a whole style change from one week to the next. I loved Dead Wrong too, I still think their 7-inch on Armed With Anger sounds incredible; if it came out tomorrow, it would still sound relevant. I realise now how lucky I was to be able to go see bands I truly loved in such intimate environments and to have been friends with some of them.

"I had the misfortune of seeing Fallout Boy a little while ago and remember just feeling *so* sorry for the audience; the show was horrendous and bland, the polar opposite of the kind of shows that I went to. But this is what kids have to put up with now. And, as for what set *us* apart from our peers, I guess it has to be that I'm – and I'm not sure what the word is, but it's somewhere between 'proud' and 'slightly amused' – that we were the only UK hardcore band to sign to a major… Like I said, somebody had to do it!"

SELECT DISCOGRAPHY:

7-inch:
'Forgot' (Armed With Anger, 1993)
'Bored Games' (East West/Equal Vision, 1994) – *also released on 12-inch and CDEP*
'Around For Nothing' (East West, 1995)
'Southend' (East West, 1995)

CDEP:
'Screwtop Milkshake' (Gravitate, 1997) – *split with Jetpak*

CD album:
'Burning Bushes And Burning Bridges' (East West, 1995)

AT A GLANCE:
The album still stands up to repeated listens even today.

FABRIC

London's **Fabric** were the original prototype emo post-hardcore band…and all at a time when hardcore was dead on its arse in the capital. Their 'Body Of Water' LP remains a powerful introspective classic to this day and members of the band went on to form or join some of the most influential underground bands of the late Nineties. It's also safe to say that their influence lives on through bands like Gallows.

"Basically I just wanted to do a band," begins bassist Tony Sylvester. "I'd never been in one before and I was trying to pull different people that I knew together to try and do it. This was 1991 or 1992 and I'd been going to shows since '87 or '88. I was really good friends with Long Cold Stare, who effectively *were* the London SXE scene, along with maybe John from Insight… I was 18 or 19 and travelling a lot to shows, but I was getting kinda tired of 'Youth Crew' hardcore and Jamie [Tilley] and Barry from Long Cold Stare were getting me into all sorts of stuff. They were the first two post-hardcore guys I ever met; in the sense that they were hardcore kids who had moved on and were now listening to pretty much everything they could get their hands on and were being very enthusiastic about old music, new music and dressing slightly differently…

"They *always* looked different anyway – when everyone else was in combats and trainers, they were wearing Converse and Chinos and Polos… They were always very smart, very savvy…and they were feeding me lots of new stuff and encouraging me to check out lots of old stuff at the same time. And Barry was from the mid-Eighties tape-trading days and he would do these legendary tapes, with like Morbid Angel on one side and the Byrds on the other – mind-blowing!

"Anyway, I really wanted to do this band and I wanted Jamie and Barry to be in it and we just needed some other people. Originally I was going to sing; I'd never sung before, but I was a mouthy little fucker, so I thought I'd be alright. Barry was going to play bass and Jamie was going to play guitar… At the same time, I knew Chris Turner, who was from the Midlands originally but had moved down for university…he tells this story better than me, but apparently I never used to talk to him because I didn't think he was cool – which is probably true! But we started up a friendship because he worked at Slam City Skates and he was one of those guys that could play anything, so immediately I thought, 'Drummer!'"

The concept of Fabric was ultimately conceived during mid 1992 at a Shudder To Think show at the Islington Pied Piper, quite an apt birthplace as the band set out to subvert genre expectations from the off ("We knew what we *didn't* want to be – we didn't wanna be a run-of-the-mill hardcore band…"). They took their lead from the likes of Revelation Records' more avant-garde roster such as Iceburn and Statue while acknowledging the vast importance of the traditional DC sound and taking heed of exciting new rock bands like Soundgarden and Screaming Trees. However Barry decided it wasn't for him after just a few rehearsals, so Tony moved to bass and was replaced behind the mic by Andy Hartwell, a young skater from Bedford band Ordinary Eye. But no sooner had he joined, he vanished off to America for three months, leaving the band to write a set without him and start making some plans.

"Yeah, we had a couple of months to work some material up while he was away and when he came back we pretty much went straight in and recorded the first demo," recalls Tony.

"But there wasn't really a scene for us; we were caught in this weird vacuum… there was only really a hardcore scene in the north and wasn't really anything going on in the south – I was travelling up to Leeds, Durham, Liverpool and Nottingham for gigs, following all the touring bands like Gorilla Biscuits and Slapshot around. I became good friends with all the Northern Wolfpack kids.

"Understand started coming to shows in London about then; we called *them* the Woodworm Kids, because they just appeared out of the woodwork, literally out of nowhere, one day. We had no idea who they were, but we'd see them at Quicksand and Transcend shows and we got chatting to them and they told us they had a band. They'd just recorded as well and done a few shows; they were definitely like our 'big brother' band, y'know? We played our first show with them at Colchester Arts Centre, in December 1992 and it was nerve-racking and terrible, but we built on it from there.

"We gave the demo out to a lot of people and they seemed to be into it. Subjugation liked it… I gave one to Walter from Quicksand and he gave a copy to Doghouse and Dirk there was talking to us about doing something by about early '93. We did a few shows up north; the first one was at Leeds University with Ironside and a bunch of other bands… because there wasn't a scene as such, we'd play with anyone…"

March 1993 saw the band in Adelaide Studios with Grant Matthews, financing their own recording for a planned release on Subjugation. But when they took the masters to the label, they didn't like the more metallic direction of the new material and Fabric were left £300 out of pocket with no release to show for it.

"But the strangest thing was that the person who stepped into the breach was Gary Walker from Wiiija, who were the last label that we thought would sign us up because there'd been a lot of bad blood previously when a band that had stayed at my house had *allegedly* shop-lifted from Slam City Skates and Wiiija had close ties to Slam City. But Gary didn't want to sign us to Wiiija, because he didn't think we were really a 'Wiiija band' – at the time they were doing Therapy? and all that noisy kind of stuff – so he suggested setting up an imprint label just to do Fabric. At the time we were just like, 'Sure!' but looking back it was a ridiculously gallant thing to do. There really wasn't much going on at the time and he obviously saw something in us… despite journalists really not knowing what to make of us.

"We were getting compared to everybody from the Levellers to the Clash to Faith No More; there was such a gulf between the DIY punk scene and the Northern Wolfpack hardcore thing – neither of which we were really a part of anyway – and what the mainstream media was writing about, they couldn't make the connection. But we weren't paying attention to all that; we were literally record collection rock, just trying to put together all the disparate elements of the bands we loved: DC hardcore, old rock records and angular post-hardcore stuff… We were really searching for something and it wasn't helping that one day we'd be playing with the New Bomb Turks, the next we'd play with Biohazard…"

Managing to make two singles from that first session ('Colossus' and 'Dislocation'), Fabric busied themselves playing around the UK, but, deciding that something was still missing from their sound, they then added Kevin Williams, who had played with Andy in Ordinary Eye, on second guitar.

"Our first show with him was at the 1 In 12 in October '93," recalls Tony. "We'd just recorded a Peel session, so we were feeling pretty buoyant on the way up and I can remember we decided to all play in navy blue T-shirts and brown trousers! It seemed a really important

Fabric, Tony Sylvester

Fabric, Chris Turner, 1996, by Vique Simba

Fabric, pic by Vique Simba

Fabric, by Vique

thing to be conceptually right…it was me and Jamie, really, who had this innate drive to really cover the details. To the point where I'd made stickers and logos before we'd even practised as a band. Plus we were on the dole, living together, with no money and lots of time on our hands, stuck in a flat obsessing all day about getting it right.

"Anyway, I think it was the 'Subjugation Fest', an all-dayer and we got up there mid-day Sunday to discover that we were headlining and everyone was using our gear. But on the bill were two bands we knew nothing about: Bob Tilton and Dead Wrong and it was a scales-falling-from-the-eyes moment. Dead Wrong did this bizarre, lurching, heavy – but not metal – droning, with this fucking aggressive hippy guy singing and spitting on the audience; it was really something, very controlled but total attitude…

"And then Bob Tilton were genuinely in a league of their own and already seemed fully formed despite not having been going that long. I loved them, but they slavishly aped all those bands they were influenced by, like Heroin and Moss Icon… but no-one else was doing that and they really had the moves down! But they were as fragile in real life as they were as a band. We struck up a good rapport with both of them and, pretty much from then on, we played around with those two bands more than anyone else; we felt a total kinship with them."

"I literally saw them twice before joining them and I thought they were messy but had something unique about them," reckons Kevin, of his joining the band and what he brought to the table for them. "I think me joining altered their sound dramatically. Jamie had this real metal style to his playing; I think he was trying to do a cross between Pantera and Swiz. I was definitely a lot looser and I loved discordant structures and sounds. In 1992 I'd been to DC and stayed with the folks at Positive Force for about three weeks; that trip was so inspiring and the bands and the people I met totally changed the way I wanted to play… to say I was a fan was an understatement. The first song I wrote with them, 'Quilt', showcased that pretty well; the sound pretty much went from melodic post-hardcore to that screamy DC/Gravity style overnight…"

And Fabric really embraced the 'Gravity' sound, that whole angular post-hardcore thing with their debut album, 'Body Of Water', Kev's chuggy Dag Nasty style of playing really tempering Jamie's more proggy leanings, to create something that was both choppy and surging yet also emotional and release-based, a sound not dissimilar to early Clutch that they arrived at quite organically by virtue of fortuitous line-up changes.

"Organically, sure, but not very successfully," laughs Tony. "I don't think we were ever *that* successful at achieving what we were after – mainly because I'm not sure even we knew what we were trying to fucking achieve! There were moments in that band when it really worked – a handful of shows that seemed like the music was happening on its own and we were just involved rather than us actually pushing and playing it. I listen back to our records now and a lot of them sound clunky and really not that good, but on the other hand, we were really operating in a very strange place and we were almost scrabbling in the dark; there wasn't a scene to latch onto when we started, so at least when post-hardcore came along we had a direction to explore…

"We recorded the album with Pat Collier at Greenhouse and the sonic template we took in with us was 'Gish' by Smashing Pumpkins. That was the record we took in for actual sounds, to master to, because I still think it's an astonishing record; it's so heavy but with no fat on it…that great Butch Vig production.

"Anyway, that record ['Body Of Water'] came out and got loads of really good press... we probably got more press than anyone apart from Understand, but that was mainly due to us being in London. We were still only playing these pissant gigs at the Bull And Gate and the Laurel Tree, but, of course, that was where the journalists were drinking, so we always got reviewed."

"Pat Collier looked like *Dr Who*-era Tom Baker," smiles Kevin, "but was a well respected producer who had recorded albums for the Wonder Stuff and Ned's Atomic Dustbin and he was wanting to work with bands trying to do something different, so he offered us a long weekend's recording for free. If we liked what he did, he hoped we'd go back...and what he did sounded incredible. Back then UK hardcore bands couldn't afford big plush studios with great producers, so nearly all UKHC records seemed to be let down by poor production. "

That first session would become the first four tracks for 'Body Of Water'; we went back two more times and we had our first full-length. If you listen to it now, it still holds its own in my opinion, partly due to the production and partly due to the fact we were writing stuff at the time that was completely different to most bands around in the UK. I still can't think of one UK band that sounded – or *has* sounded – like us since. Bob Tilton were probably our closest musical allies. And it did garner some really strong reviews, from *NME* and *Melody Maker* etc. I think it even got '9/10' in one of them, but it probably sold very little. The UK wasn't really a great place for hardcore at that time; the last 'big' UKHC band would have been Snuff or the Stupids and that was because they had crossover appeal. We were playing this noisy, arty shit, not covers of popular adverts..."

Once the album was recorded, Fabric paid their only visit to Europe, to play a handful of shows over a long weekend, and one can but only wonder how the fortunes of the band might have been different if they'd only undertaken a *full* tour of the mainland.

"At this point, the European kids – well, certainly the Belgians – started hearing about us," recalls Tony, "We did a few shows over there, one of them in Ieper; we played the Vort'n'Vis with Refused and Acme during the summer of '94. We weren't SXE by that point, so we were very drunk and excited and this was when SXE was really breaking in Europe. I was dating Hazel who was in Rise Above and Shortsight and I'd already looked after Hans from Liar's flat for him for a summer while he went to the States, so I knew all those guys really well. I remember Jamie setting up on stage with a cigarette hanging out his mouth and he was having problems with his amp, so he said, 'Can someone help me with my amp, please?' And someone told him, 'I think you'll find you'll get more help if you weren't smoking!'

"I can remember it was so hot in there, I played in my underpants! And I think we really struck a chord with some people at that show, because we were doing something different... then Acme played and fucking destroyed the place."

After a self-titled 7-inch on Belgian label Machination and a split single with New Jersey post-hardcore band Greyhouse for Simba, Fabric found themselves increasingly leaning towards the stoner rock and doom-metal scenes, a far rockier style that manifested itself on their final release, the 'Lightbringer' 12-inch.

"We became very jaded and very cynical in a very short time," sighs Tony, "because we couldn't realise what we wanted to do, both musically and otherwise... We didn't know what we were chasing. We were in the same trench as the Gravity bands, but also listening to Danzig...and soon we were listening to St Vitus and Kyuss and the Obsessed and Monster Magnet and that really started infiltrating the writing; by the time we did 'Lightbringer', we were opening with [King Crimson's] '21st Century Schizoid Man'... We had beards and Aerosmith shirts!"

"When we came to write 'Lightbringer', the songs seemed to take longer, because they weren't these noisy little firecrackers any more," elaborates Kevin. "We seemed to all be listening to more classic rock, especially Kyuss and Soundgarden, and this was coming through quite prominently in our sound. Just listen to the track 'Lightbringer'; it reeks of Kyuss – who no-one gave a fuck about back then! The songs were also better constructed, which I think made them more commercial-sounding. Maybe it was us subconsciously trying to get signed to a major? Anyhow, it's a much different beast than 'Body...' It was the sound of a bunch of guys who were hungry for all kinds of music from jazz, Sixties, Seventies, metal, hardcore...right through to the bands of the time like the Verve, My Bloody Valentine and, yes, we even quite liked this band called Oasis! I think I prefer the energy of 'Body...' but really liked the songwriting of 'Lightbringer'..."

"We were breaking up by the time we did that last record," admits Tony. "We didn't really know what we wanted; some of us wanted to be more metallic, some of us more noisy, some of us wanted the band to have much more exposure, some of us didn't...and Andy's lyrics became very, very pessimistic. Just before that last record, his long-term relationship broke up; he was very deflated and his lyrics were pretty harsh.

"We got offered some shows with the Offspring, a tour that was booked just before they broke really big and we found ourselves in really small venues and that was crazy, with twice as many people who couldn't get in as who had tickets. Like all our UK tours it seemed to be the 'three Ls' – London, Leeds and Leicester – but they were a good time band having the worse time of their lives; they were just so grumpy, it was untrue...

"After that tour we went on tour with SNFU and we had big arguments the whole time, to the point we were throwing beer bottles at each other onstage because someone played the ending of a song too slow...it was definitely all over. Then we got booked to play our last show ever, with Quicksand at the Garage, which was May 1995, a sold-out show with them and Understand... We were looking out at a sea of 500 kids all dressing the same, a new generation of hardcore kids just getting into it and there we were, in our twenties but already growing out of it, all jaded and hateful and sick of scene conventions... That was inadvertently our last show, because we were meant to get together soon after to practise, but James decided to go to Glastonbury instead – and that said it all really..."

After Fabric, Chris Turner joined Terminal Cheesecake for a few years before ending up in the UK's biggest stoner metal band, Orange Goblin.

"I remember falling off my seat laughing at such a ridiculous name for a band...but they were great!" says Tony, who then joined Chris alongside ex-members of Iron Monkey and Ironside in the Dukes Of Nothing. "Jamie Tilley did a new band afterwards too and then went into picture framing...but he's playing music again now, doing weird 'proggy' one-man-band stuff, which is probably what he should have done all along. Then Andy Hartwell, the singer, went into advertising and started a really successful clothing line. Me and him started Aurora Borealis, the record label, which he's done solidly ever since...

"But being a hardcore kid was a really important part of my life," adds the bassist, who has worked for Southern Records since 1995, recently setting up his own PR company as well. "Everything I do and am now goes through that filter of me being in the hardcore scene. Most of my time now is still spent with old hardcore kids who've grown up and gone on to other things and I still listen to Breakdown, Outburst and Raw Deal…all that hardcore stuff from '87 to '90 is still a huge influence, even though I'm a northern soul DJ and have a huge collection of English folk records and everything else. But hardcore will always be the era I grew up in. It's a very strange genre; you can wax lyrical all you like, but the most important thing might be two songs off a band's first demo.

"Take a band like Underdog, or Bold; I love those bands, but only five or six of their songs are any good and those songs became totemic, despite being badly recorded and sloppily played. And a lot of that is to do with the social aspect, all the ritual surrounding the music… and friendships, of course. I'm so glad I spent several years of my life, travelling the country and jumping on kids' heads and grabbing the mike off singers! Instead of popping pills, which is what all of my friends were doing, 'cos the rave scene was getting huge at that time."

"When Fabric started out, the UKHC scene was pretty much dead," reckons Kev, who went on to play in Desman Diabolo alongside ex-members of Dead Wrong, Capricorns alongside ex-members of The Dukes Of Nothing (all very incestuous!) and then Alabaster Suns (he currently plays in the "totally DC" Trieste with James Sherry from Done Lying Down). "After the little boom at the end of the Eighties, when bands like Napalm Death, Stupids and Snuff were all getting front covers of the *NME*, there was nothing in terms of good strong UKHC. In fact, Leatherface were about the only UK band that could kinda hold its own against the quality of the US acts that were bombarding our shores and those guys had been round the block a few times.

"But by '92 or '93, there started to be a lot of new faces starting bands. Kids that had started listening to hardcore at the end of the Eighties and were now wanting to be in bands themselves. It was funny 'cos the north had always had a strong scene, but hated southern bands 'cos they thought we were all rich kids on major labels; it really was that rubbish. But suddenly there seemed to be something happening. It became clear that we weren't on our own when we played with Bob Tilton and Dead Wrong at the 1 In 12; they both blew me away, two totally different styles and quite unique. I still think they are without doubt two of the best post-hardcore bands this country has ever produced.

"Also, Understand, who were good friends of ours were playing a more commercial Quicksand style of hardcore that managed to get them signed to Warners. Between the four of us I think we kickstarted a flagging scene and I even think the *NME* or someone like that tried to call us bands the 'New Wave of British Hardcore', but it didn't really catch on. In the end, I think Fabric stood out purely because we were trying to do something fresh; we weren't the best musicians, but we were definitely asking questions musically that most UK bands weren't."

"It's really funny," adds Tony, who nowadays fronts not only 33, an exciting hardcore band featuring ex-members of Strength Alone and Iron Clad, but also legendary Norwegian punk band Turbo Negro. "A lot of people — people like Jake Bannon [from Converge] and Aaron Turner [from Isis] — during my first conversations with them, when I've worked with them on press for their labels or whatever, they often say that Fabric were a really important band for them, because we were one of the first post-hardcore bands. Which is sorta gratifying to hear, because I don't feel there's any direct legacy, any one band directly influenced by us… so I'm always pleasantly surprised if someone remembers anything about us at all!

"But the idea of trying to cultivate that legacy, by reforming or something, is not something I'm into, because I don't think anyone would actually be that interested. The fact that we were being written about by certain people and there was a fair amount of scrutiny of us, didn't amount to anything at the time; it was just there, but I can see that it may have looked like we were bigger than we were from the outside, but I can tell you, we weren't! Just by how many people were coming to see us…

"If we played to more than two hundred people, it was because we were playing with another band that was a draw. We sold a few thousand records, but that was a time when bands sold a lot more records than they do now. We never made any money off any of them…but we didn't expect to; you don't make money off being a hardcore band. And being in Fabric, being involved with hardcore, has totally shaped my appreciation, not just of that music, but of the form, the format…just seeing a DIY band in a small room. You can't beat that."

SELECT DISCOGRAPHY:

7-inch:
'Colossus' (Whole Car, 1993)
'Dislocation' (Whole Car, 1994)
'Saturnalia' (Doghouse, 1994)
'Fabric' (Machination, 1994)
'Split' (Simba, 1994) – *split with Greyhouse*

12-inch EP:
'Lightbringer' (Whole Car, 1995)

LPs:
'Body Of Water' (Whole Car, 1994)
'Stella Maris' (Simba, 1997) – *posthumous release of the pre-production demos for 'Body Of Water'*

AT A GLANCE:
If you can track down the CD version of 'Body Of Water' on Doghouse, it includes the first three 7-inchs as bonus tracks.

BLAGGERS ITA

Blaggers ITA actually started life as the Blaggers in the late Eighties, a straight-up, but strongly anti-fascist, street punk/Oi! band; they rapidly evolved into something far more interesting though: a defiantly political dance-punk act, on a major label no less, who unfortunately fell foul of the fickle music industry and its myriad trappings, before they had chance to ever realise their full potential.

The original Blaggers line-up was Matty Blag and Tim 'Bilko' Wells on vocals, Steve Serious on guitar, Matt Vinyl on bass and Jez 'The Jester' on drums. Matty and Tim had both fronted Complete Control, a left-wing Oi! combo who were the first band released by Roddy Moreno from the Oppressed's Oi! label in 1985 with their 'Bricks, Blood'n'Guts' LP, while Tim had been in the reggae band Anti Social Workers, who released the 'Punky Reggae Party' on Ariwa in 1983. Although it wouldn't manifest itself for another few years, a similar radical collision of influences would shape the eventual sound, style and approach of Blaggers ITA.

"I had wanted to get a band together for some time and convinced Vinyl that it would be good idea for him to play bass; the fact he couldn't play at the time didn't matter at all," laughs Steve. "We all kind of learned our instruments as the band progressed. True punk rock stylee! A few mates joined in on vocals for a while (a nod to Cliché Ray and Dave), but they were far too musically sophisticated for us at the time. Anyway, I had also been talking to Tim about the band we were trying to form (as I remember, we had given it the name of Peasant Army) and he turned up to a rehearsal with Matty, whose involvement with the band was all quite coincidental. He just happened to be calling around at Tim's house as Tim was leaving to come along to the practice and decided to join him; he'd been in bands before and I suppose he thought it would be a laugh, a good way to spend the afternoon. And the rest, as they say, is a cliché!"

"I knew Steve from going to see bands like the Redskins and Newtown Neurotics," explains Vinyl, "and through being involved in AFA [Anti-Fascist Action] and Red Action. He was trying to get a band together in 1987 and needed a bass-player so, although I'd never played bass before, I'd done a bit of keyboards at school and said I'd give it a go. We spent months rehearsing with Steve's mate Jez on drums and various different mates on vocals until Matty and Tim came along to that rehearsal in early '88; with their experience of having played in previous bands, the first line-up was complete and we were able to seriously start looking for gigs. It was Bilko's suggestion that we be called the Blaggers.

"My own personal reason for the band forming was to promote AFA and militant left-wing/ anti-fascist politics. At the time, Blood & Honour [the white power organisation established by Skrewdriver vocalist Ian Stuart Donaldson] were having a big influence on the skinhead scene, especially in London and it was important to counter this influence. AFA's propaganda was always aimed more at the potential recruits of fascism, the white working class, so it made perfect sense for us to initially go for the skinhead/Oi! scene and put across AFA's view that fascism had nothing to offer the working class…and was in fact *anti*-working class…"

Playing a mix of Complete Control numbers and brand new songs, plus covers of the 4-Skins, Ramones and Oppressed, the Blaggers made their predictably raw live debut on 28 May 1988 at the London Midland And Scottish, a pub in Hendon, North London, supporting Two Dead Pigeons.

Then, as a cultural alternative to Blood & Honour, the band helped set up Cable Street Beat, which became the musical wing of AFA and July 1988 saw the first CSB promotion, the first of many, when the Blaggers played with The Neurotics and The Price at the Old White Horse in Brixton.

Just seven months after their first gig, the band released their first LP, 'On Yer Toez', on Oi! Records, which coincided with a major support slot to the Angelic Upstarts.

"The CSB gig at the [George] Robey in January 1989 with the Upstarts was one of the most important we ever played," reckons Vinyl. "In May '88, the Upstarts had played at the Astoria and Blood & Honour had smashed the gig up and said the Upstarts would never play in London again, but the Upstarts, with CSB's support, wanted to show that they would not be stopped from playing by a bunch of Nazis. It was also a direct challenge to Blood & Honour's view that they could dictate who could or couldn't play in London. During the day a picket was organised in Carnaby Street to stop the sale of Nazi propaganda, much of which was supplied by Blood & Honour, at shops; the picket was attended by over 400 people and, along with the gig in the evening, was a great success. Blood & Honour made no attempt to attack either the picket or the gig and, as one AFA member commented at the time, 'the fascists were conspicuous by their absence...' In other words, they bottled it!

"Then, the following week in Telford, some local boneheads attacked our gig at the Cultural Centre. It kicked off during the third song when a small mob attempted to enter through a side door by the stage armed with bricks and bottles; basically our roadies battered them and put three of them in hospital. Most of the band were arrested, with the police saying we'd all get 10 years for inciting a riot! In the end, Matty, myself and one of our roadies got charged with violent disorder, but eventually the case was dropped due to lack of evidence. This gig did, however, bring it home to everyone what being a militant anti-fascist band was all about but, apart from Jez, our original drummer, who quit the band soon after, none of us ever considered taking a different tack. It's also important to mention that during the months when the three of us were on bail, we received fantastic support from AFA and, had the case gone to trial, would not have been left to 'face the music' alone..."

"The Telford gig hit the front page of the local paper the following week," adds Serious. "The *Telford Star*, I think? With the headline 'Punk Band in Chapel Clash!' We never considered taking a different course as a result of it though and I think it's well worth noting that, considering our militant anti-fascist stance and that we were a prolific gigging band, this was the only time we were attacked during a gig. The only other time the fascists even got close was when we played the Venue in New Cross in 1993, a warm-up gig the night before we joined the Manic Street Preachers' 'Gold Against The Soul' tour [as main support]. A group of C18 had assembled in a nearby pub and made an attempt to attack, but were thwarted by anti-fascist stewards who beat them back from the entrance door and the gig went ahead with no trouble."

Replacing Jez on drums was Jason from Trenchfever and Bad Dress Sense, who brought some US hardcore influences to the table, but these were tempered somewhat when Brendan joined on trumpet, who came from a heavy dance background. Trenchfever's Paul 'The Pig' also joined on second guitar and he added some nasty discordant solos to the band's growing arsenal of tricks.

"Yeah, I brought dance music to the Blaggers," admits Brendan. "I was heavily into 'On U Sound', acid house and US hip-hop at the time and I was soon dragging Vinyl, Steve

Blaggers, Christy, Camden
Underworld, 1993, pic by Steve Hall

Blaggers, Matty Blag, Steve Serious
Newport 1993, pic by Steve Hall

Blaggers, Matty Blag, London 1993, pic by Steve Hall

and Matty out to On U Sound raves. Jason was also open to more dance-oriented rhythms and, at the time, I don't really think there were any other punk bands incorporating such disparate influences. Matty Blag was mainly influenced by US hardcore and, later on, hip-hop, especially Ice T, but lyrically he was into writers such as Iceberg Slim and Hubert Selby Jnr and political writers like Malcolm X and George Orwell…"

"I didn't really know how to play Oi!" adds Jason. "I was more into American hardcore and always played the songs too fast. I can remember after a few gigs, Matty saying that maybe they should get rid of me because I played too fast and he couldn't keep up! But they stuck with me and the songs got faster…"

After a whistle-stop mini-tour of Europe in June 1989, this line-up changed the name to Blaggers ITA and recorded the 1990 7-inch, 'It's Up To You' for Network 90. Limited to 1,000 copies, the EP served as a fine introduction to the band's inspirational energy and outspoken political agenda (the title track a weighty voice-over about the insidious nature of fascism over a jangly upbeat tune) and brought the Blaggers to the attention of Newport label Words Of Warning, who included one of the band's early tracks, 'New York', on their 'Mind Pollution' compilation.

"That first trip to Europe was with Belgian Oi! band Comrade," explains Vinyl, of their continental debut. "Klaas, their singer, got in touch with Matty and invited us over to play in West Berlin, Frankfurt and Antwerp. Berlin was definitely the best; it was at the Ex Club on a Friday night and was packed. I remember there were lots of skinheads there and all of them were red skins; it made a welcome change to what we were used to in London, with left-wing politics having a real influence among skinheads in Germany. The atmosphere was fantastic and when reports came through of boneheads approaching the venue the skins all charged out to confront them and chase them off. This was easily the best gig we'd played up to that point and was to be the first of many around Germany and other parts of Europe.

"The next day we played in Frankfurt and this was when we met Olaf for the first time. Olaf became our main contact in Europe and helped organise many tours for us… Later, in 1992, he moved to London and joined the band for a while on sax and then formed the Stage Bottles, an excellent anti-fascist Oi! band, the following year. Then, when the Blaggers reformed in 2002, Olaf became frontman and vocalist…"

"The gig at the Ex does stand out as being a great gig," agrees Serious. "Musically, upon reflection, we were probably a bit rubbish at that time, but the atmosphere was electric and we went down really well. We were always well received in Germany and met a lot of good people. There were many memorable tours and gigs in Europe; it still amazes me how many people and how much equipment you can get into a Transit van! Not always the most comfortable of travelling experiences – crammed in like sardines, lying across the backline, travelling through the night on to the next gig and being woken up by condensation dripping on you ["Or worse, if you were lying next to Jason," interjects Brendan] – but we had a great time and there are some enduring memories."

German label Knock Out released the 1991 single 'Beirut' where the band betrayed their Oi! roots with a stirring cover of the 4-Skins' 'Wonderful World' and it was during another German tour in February 1991 that Christy, one of Brendan's DJ friends, brought his hip-hop vocals and acid- house influences to the Blaggers line-up.

"I knew Brendan from the clubbing scene and we were involved in AFA activities on a virtually weekly basis at this time, as the Blood & Honour issue was coming to a head," recalls Christy, of his accidental induction into the band. "After a severe exchange of views with Nicky Crane, the head of Skrewdriver security, three AFA members were jailed, one of those being my girlfriend at the time's brother and this – and our degrees of involvement in the incident – certainly gave me an extra impetus in involving myself in helping the prisoners. The Blaggers were due to tour Germany and it was partly to act as a fundraiser and publiciser for both the jailings and the recent poll-tax riots; they asked if I would like to come along to help with the publicity work and act as a roadie. I thought this was a great idea as I was working on the buildings at the time and DJ-ing at night…little did I know the effect this would have on my physical and mental well-being over the next 20 years!

"I'd sort of developed this demented, crap Geordie rapper persona, going to raves, dancing on speakers and it always being fun. Anyway, having no idea what being a roadie actually involved, apart from crouching on the side of the stage and pushing people off, I got rather over-excited by the reaction of a packed crowd of Berlin punks and skins. Matty Blag sort of pulled me on and off it all went, a rant of politics morphing into spontaneous rapping nicked from Wham! and Schoolly D – and dancing that would make Bez [the Happy Mondays' dancing 'mascot'] cringe!

"Apart from Brendan the band were very unaware of youth culture at the time," continues Christy, on how he helped further the Blaggers' very organic musical evolution. "They were completely immersed in the punk and skin lifestyle but really wanted to know what else was going on (apart from Vinyl, who has always been stuck in some 'Groundhog Day' re-run of 1981!); conversely I knew all about dance music and had always loved punk since my pre-teens but was very ignorant about it and also eager to learn. Matty was constantly asking questions; I think he felt that an outside view would help the band change in the way he knew it had to to survive.

"After latching onto a brief discussion of Bez, he reappeared from the next service station with a selection of maracas and tambourines and informed me they would be my props for the gigs from now on. We would be immersed in music and politics, crammed in the back of a camper van, then playing gigs that lurched between regular violence and E-like euphoria. There was a constant threat of attack from Nazis around the gigs, but there was an effort from the band to foster a sense of togetherness with the audience. We'd begin gigs at the back of the audience, chanting as I'd carry the rider and props to the stage, handing out drinks as we'd pass. Some nights would end with old school German skins chanting, 'Rave on!', while waving maracas!

"We were primarily playing squats and community venues and the commitment of the people to their lifestyle and politics really hit me, so when the band offered me the chance to participate regularly I knew that I wanted it all – and more. We'd try all sorts of things: samples and scratching on [Clash cover] 'Guns Of Brixton' (on a household record player), megaphones on stage, turning up to venues with my decks to play intros to songs where the sound men wouldn't even know how to connect them… There were no samplers back then, so 'Blaggamuffin' [the band's 1991 MLP] was spliced together with a razor blade and bits of tape!"

Recorded at Southern Studios, the six-track 'Blaggamuffin' was the perfect introduction to the band's sassy-smooth, street-wise sound and their fanbase began to increase exponentially as each new member brought an extra facet to their overall style.

"Yeah, I think that generally the audience reacted positively," confirms Brendan, whose tasteful brass added a classy extra dimension to songs like 'Bastard Chillin'. "The scene was changing anyway, particularly in London, where we were playing squat gigs alongside techno DJs. We also made a conscious decision to organise gigs with non-punk bands such as rapper Blade and Fun-Da-Mental; the audience crossover was immense and benefited all sides…"

1992's 'United Colors Of Blaggers ITA' is widely regarded by hardcore fans of the band as their strongest release and not without reason, the Harvey Birrell/Paul Harding production capturing the band's irrepressible live energy to a tee and songs like 'It's Up To You, Part 2 – Battle Of Waterloo' reminiscent of the Mighty Mighty Bosstones at their gleeful best. Two tracks, 'Here's Johnny' and 'Before I Hang', were lifted from the LP and re-mixed for the 'Here's Johnny' 7-inch, which came in a picture sleeve depicting the then-Prime Minister John Major with a gun to his head. Controversy and mainstream appeal don't usually make comfortable bedfellows, but the Blaggers walked this tightrope with aplomb, signing to Parlophone/EMI in 1993, following a well-received support to Hyperhead in Islington. Of course, elements of the anti-corporate punk scene never forgave them, but they had their reasons for signing and, as was always the way with the Blaggers, they involved more than just music.

"I think there were other labels there too, although I never spoke to any of them," reckons Serious. "Paul, who also played guitar for us at the time, decided to leave the band as a result, as he really did not want to sign with EMI; he left during a rehearsal by saying he was just going to the chip shop and never returned!"

"But we thought long and hard about signing to them," qualifies Brendan, "and felt that it would enable us to get our message across to a wider audience (which it did). We pissed a few people off (we even had a small number of gigs picketed) but never regretted the decision. The band's politics were not compromised at all and we now had the money and support to promote various causes. Importantly, we were also able to record at some of the best studios in the UK… the only regret I have was that, with all the resources available to EMI, I don't think we ever really found the right producer…"

"The thing about signing to a major is that none of the big indies wanted to touch us," reckons Christy. "Small indie labels like Words Of Warning and Fluffy Bunny had always treated us really well and we had a lot of mutual respect for each other; however by the time we signed we were getting too popular for them to deal with and a whole load of ancillary crap came as a package with us. From my personal experience, the large indies were even more up their own arses and cliquey than the majors; as Nicky Wire put it, we were a bit too much 'for real' for their Camden/*NME* sensibilities. The reality of your latest signing having kicked a bonehead across Waterloo station in a non-postmodern ironic style didn't sit easily in the [trendy Camden pub] Good Mixer! It was a complex that has been faced by several other political bands, but at the time EMI couldn't care what we did as long as we made money and that money enabled us to spread our political message to the max. Full-page adverts of politics, billboard posters, radio interviews… they funded it all and we took it all. We went in with our eyes open, knowing the corporate morals we dealt with and even now I think we did the best out of it for our own political stance.

"What many people don't get is that most folk at major record companies are a) absolute music lovers and b) very good at their jobs. When it all went off with the *Melody Maker* [more on this in a minute!], we were totally shunned by virtually every record company, promoter, journalist and band in the country, but the day-to-day staff at Parlophone kept plugging away and believing in us and I have a lot of respect for them for doing that. The bands that didn't listen to rumours and innuendo, such as EMF, Carter and PWEI, proved to be lifelong friends well after the band had folded and the dust settled..."

The first release for Parlophone was the quite sublime 'Abandon Ship' single, which fell somewhere between the Clash and Faith No More and suggested that the band really were destined to be 'the next big thing'. 'Oxygen' followed and then the hard-hitting ram-raid anthem, 'Stresss', which proved that signing to a major label hadn't dulled their urban edge. However, trouble was around the corner in the shape of the aforementioned '*Melody Maker* incident', when Matty Blag got into a fight with journalist Dave Simpson at an after-show party on the first night of the Manic Street Preachers tour mentioned previously, where Blaggers ITA were main support.

"Dave spent most of the night after the gig with the Blaggers and was pressing Matty on his earlier – brief – involvement with the British Movement during his youth," explains Brendan. "Simpson had previously written articles in *Melody Maker* which implied that 'the leopard can't change its spots' and had even argued that the band's physical opposition to fascism and Matty's in particular, was itself akin to fascism..."

"I think it's worth putting all this into context, to try to understand where Matty was coming from," elaborates Serious. "He was completely open about the dodgy political viewpoints he had once held as a disaffected white working-class youth, when he had right-wing tendencies without really any understanding of what that actually meant. He had found it difficult to relate to the middle-class left and instead identified himself with those on the right. But he was also very open about how he was subsequently influenced and politically educated by someone he met in prison, a Marxist who gave Matty books by George Orwell and basically got him thinking. When Matty came out of prison, he then became actively involved in left-wing anti-fascist politics.

"Dave Simpson may not have agreed with Matty's stance on a physical confrontation with fascists as well as an ideological one and I am not saying that Dave Simpson intended to call Matty a fascist, but that is how Matty perceived it. Since Matty frequently put his life and liberty on the line by selflessly and actively confronting fascists, he naturally took offence at Simpson's remarks. He felt angry, misunderstood and quite saddened by what Dave had written and that led to the incident.

"The case eventually got thrown out of court on a technicality and it is probably more appropriate to talk about the repercussions of the incident between Matty and Dave Simpson rather than what exactly happened..."

Indeed, it was blown out of all proportion by the music press and the band were snubbed by all the major publications of the time; they were removed from the bill of that year's Reading Festival and even snubbed by many of their musical peers. EMI were obviously perturbed by this chain of events and although Blaggers hit back with one of their best albums, 1994's 'Bad Karma', the effect on their career and, indirectly, the personal effect on Matty was profound; blaming himself for the band's worsening relationship with EMI, his inherent self-destructive tendencies came to the fore and both his drug habit and his behaviour started spiralling out of control until eventually he left Blaggers ITA. He died of a drug overdose on 22 February 2000, aged 36.

"Contrary to what has often been said in various band biogs, Matty was *not* sacked by the band," corrects Serious. "He made a conscious decision to leave which I don't believe he took lightly. We had parted company with EMI by then and Matty felt responsible for this. He basically thought we would stand a better chance of getting another deal without him; he believed he was holding the band back and that, while he was in the band, Blaggers ITA did not have a future."

"The last time we went to Germany was pretty hard work," reveals Christy sadly. "We'd reached the stage where we were bringing someone along just to hang round with Matty. On this occasion it was Ricky, a long-term smack addict with a lot of baggage of his own; I really liked Ricky and he stayed with me for a while later on… He actually seemed very knowing that he was trapped in a life that wasn't going to end well [he overdosed and died shortly after Matty], but him and Matty together weren't a good combination. We struggled through the tour with everyone just doing their own thing, apart from at the gigs.

"It all went tits-up when I got woken up one night with someone saying Matty had attacked the promoter and that he and Ricky were in jail. Given that we were being really well looked after by these people and that we were staying in his house, this was all bad. We had to drive to the police station the next morning, load them directly into the van and get out of town, but when stuff like this started happening the atmosphere began to go sour; a lot of the people we dealt with were more like friends than business associates and we needed to treat them as such…"

Brendan had already left, following an inevitable disagreement with Matty and, although the band soldiered on, landing a new deal with Disinformation Records and Christy handling lead vocals, the best they could manage was the very disappointing 'Rumblefish' single in 1995. Jason also left and Blaggers ITA played their 'last' gig at the New Cross Venue in 1996… 'last' because they reformed in 2002, primarily to raise money for the IWCA (Independent Working Class Association), and still play infrequently to this day.

"I was involved in dance music and DJ-ing after the band and ran various club nights, but that was always more as a hobby," says Christy. "Nothing can ever capture the sheer effort and energy that the band contains even now. I recorded vocals for a couple of projects but it never felt natural; Blaggers were always a particularly dysfunctional, but nonetheless very close, family.

"Nowadays of course we just want it to be fun, a reunion, no hassle. The message is just as important now, but I'd like to think someone a bit younger and more relevant is putting it across somewhere else anyway. We haven't rehearsed since the Nineties and it can show sometimes, but when it comes together and you can see the enjoyment and sense of unity in the audience, it's all still worthwhile.

"I think the whole experience has affected us all deeply," he concludes. "We always punched above our weight in musical ability through sheer belief, passion and hard work and none of us have ever matched those times yet… we were like nothing else and we were never scared."

Just prior to leaving Blaggers, Brendan formed DSC-GB (Demolish Serious Culture) with writer/artist Stewart Home and then, once Blaggers was over, he formed Rautam with Carlos Coutinho, the band's latter-period keyboard player and sampler. Jason meanwhile joined Neck for two years, before relocating to America where he played for his sister's band, Reno, who were signed to country label Curb. Nowadays he plays with Bristol ska/punk band Spanner, as well as with Hi Class Joe, 'an early Sixties British-style beat and rhythm'n'blues band'!

"Matty was a great frontman," he offers in closing. "He was so enthusiastic about music and, although he wasn't very well educated, he was always reading books. He could have been a poet if it weren't for music. We were good friends in the early days, but unfortunately he beat me up before one gig in Germany and after that our friendship began to wane. I think the pressure of being on drugs and signed to a major label got to him at times and he would threaten members of the band. I was in the States touring with my sister when I found out he was dead, so I couldn't come to the funeral and pay my final respects, but I miss him. We had some great times together and he was an inspiration both on stage and off."

SELECT DISCOGRAPHY:

7-inch:
'It's Up To You' (Network 90, 1990)
'Beirut' (Knockout, 1991)
'The Way We Operate' (Fluffy Bunny, 1992)
'Here's Johnny' (Words Of Warning, 1992)
'Abandon Ship' (Parlophone, 1993)
'Oxygen' (Parlophone, 1993)
'Stresss' (Parlophone, 1993)
'Mantrap' (Parlophone, 1994)
'Guns Of Brixton' (Disinformation, 1995)
'Thrill Her With A Gun' (Damaged Goods, 1995)
'Session' (Disinformation, 1995)
'Rumblefish' (Disinformation, 1995)

LPs:
'On Yer Toez' (Oi!, 1989)
'Blaggamuffin' (Words Of Warning, 1991)
'United Colors of Blaggers ITA' (Words Of Warning, 1993)
'Bad Karma' (Parlophone, 1994)

AT A GLANCE:
In 2010, 'United Colors…' and 'Blaggamuffin' were re-released by German label Mad Butcher as a single CD edition, with additional bonus tracks.

COITUS

London band **Coitus** really did fight on the front line of the punk wars so you didn't have to get your hands bloody. Formed from the messy remains of Blower and Sons Of Bad Breath by guitarist Martin and drummer Alien, they were originally called Eternal Diarrhoea, but thankfully changed their name to the infinitely more tasteful Coitus in February 1989 when Skinny (ex-Paranoid Visions and DT Warriors) joined on bass. Martin only played two gigs with the band, though, before he left and was replaced by Pato.

"Our first gig was in our mate Mad Maggs' garage in Radstock in late '89," recalls Alien. "There was enough room for the band and about four barrels of cider; the crowd were outside, dancing in the wind and the rain and constantly walking through the band to get more cider. Also, Benny, one of our mates, injured his arse when he fell on the leg of an upturned floor tom…painful! Maggs was a great character, a real madman, who died about 10 years ago – RIP Maggs.

"The first gig with Pato was at another mate Amelia's birthday party in Portobello Road, in late 1990. Amelia was friends with loads of the Hackney punks and yes, she was a stripper; she used to ply her trade onstage with the UK Subs. Coitus were playing in a small room where the crowd had to take turns to peer round a door at us; it was quite strange. It was a bondage party, so there were some crazy outfits; one of our mates Harry Callaghan was so encased in PVC no-one knew it was him…"

After gigging around London's then-numerous squats for a year, five tracks were recorded by Scratchy at Hornsey's La Rocka Studio in North London during March 1991. A further five numbers were recorded by Albert, the then-drummer of Paranoid Visions at Sonic Studios in Dublin during May '91 and all 10 tracks were released as the 'In Two Minutes You'll Be Smoking In Hell' demo, which neatly showcased the band's rough'n'ready'n'raw heavy punk style. However Pato stayed in Dublin after the recording and Coitus returned to London without him, where they recruited Mik as their new guitarist.

"Alien and Skinny asked me to join Coitus after Pato left," explains Mik. "So I jammed with Skinny in his bedroom beforehand; he lived not far from me and we had a coupla practices to learn the set for my first gig at the Hellhouse [a Blackfriars Road squat]. I was pretty nervous, it being my first gig and all, but it was a good buzz; a fairly big crowd was there, we played okay and I remember enjoying myself. It weren't long after we finished the set though before the cops burst in, all shields and helmets and began truncheoning anyone in their way… male or female, they didn't care. It was sickening to see, pumped-up riot cops hitting people just for being there; lots of people got nicked or bashed or both, including some mates.

"Me and Alien ended up outside while these chippys [carpenters] boarded up the place in their slippers; the cops must've got 'em out of bed. I remember Alien going up to one of 'em boarding the windows with plywood and saying, 'Let me back in, mate, I left me socks in there!' It cracked me up; even the cops laughed. After a while the cops and the builders left, so we just ripped the plywood off and got back in to crash out.

"This was not an uncommon event back then; my third gig with Coitus at Peckham Barclays Bank squat ended in the same way, only worse. After a great night, all the bands had finished playing, the riot cops broke in at about four in the morning; most people were crashing out or had left when they decided to raid the squat. Same scenario, all boots and truncheons;

Coitus

Skinny sitting by a lake in
Wood Green

I'd just bought a top Chappie Dog Food guitar off Martin, the old Coitus guitarist and didn't want it trashed, so me and loads of other people had to leap over two garden walls to get away from these thugs in riot gear – only to find the whole High Street crawling with riot vans and police dogs…nightmare, nightmare! A police dog bit my guitar and ripped the strings off; my mate Snail got his crotch bitten by a dog, good thing his spray-ons were baggy… The dog-handlers were nasty bastards, it was absolute chaos. We managed to get away without getting nicked, but many didn't; it was horrendous seeing the police behave so aggressively over people just enjoying themselves. To witness police brutality on that scale is something I'll never forget; they really trashed us that night…"

"The squat scene in London was proper active, even though its intensity was nearing its end by the early Nineties," adds Alien. "You have to realise this was before the property boom really kicked off, so there were loads of empty gaffs everywhere and the laws on squatting weren't as tight as they are now; there were squatted communities all over the country. Thousands of squats that would've otherwise been left empty…and there were squatted venues all over London. It was nigh-on impossible for a single bloke to be housed by the council, so squatting was a viable option back then. It seems mad now, but there were boarded-up houses and buildings in London areas that are now gentrified for the very wealthy…

"Coitus hung about in Wood Green, Tottenham and Hackney and there were squats in all those places… A lot of sessions and gigs were at squatted houses or buildings; the usual set-up was live bands upstairs, a techno rave/disco downstairs and a blazing fire in the garden…and this could be in a boarded-up factory, a school, a library, or just a house. You'd find out from word of mouth or fliers (no mobile phones or internet back then!) and it's brilliant to have been a part of all that; they were good times. Back then, you would get evicted, then just break another squat; we didn't know it at the time, but the powers that be were planning measures to bring it all to an end, which is why the squat scene doesn't exist on that scale any more, at least not in this country. They came down hard in the mid to late Nineties with draconian laws like the Criminal Justice Bill to get squatters out quick and break up raves and festivals. And the police were totally heavy-handed when it came to implementing these laws; we saw them do it, it was brutal…"

Coitus returned to Dublin to record their next two DIY releases, 1992's 'Submission/ Domination' cassette-only album and 1993's 'When We Depart… Let The Earth Tremble' cassette-only EP. Both captured the band at their sweating, grunting Celtic Frost-worshipping best!

"Blimey! 'Cassette-only' just sounds Victorian nowadays," laughs Mik. "We did try to get it out as a bigger release, but no labels seemed interested – or we just asked the wrong ones! I'm gutted now we never pushed harder to secure a vinyl release for either of those recordings; in my opinion it was the best stuff we ever did. We recorded them at Sonic Studios, in Dublin ['Submission/Domination' during February '92 and 'When We Depart…' that December]… Deko from Paranoid Visions helped us out a lot; we were skint, but Skinny was old mates with him and the guys at Sonic were bang on. Joe Wearan and Albert, who was also in PV, did the mixing for us and pretty much got the best sound Coitus ever had in a studio. We also did some gigs in Dublin to coincide with the recording, to help finance it; Deko sorted them and we played with some great Irish bands: Brinskill Bomb Beat, Indecent Exposure and, of course, Paranoid Visions and they were storming nights."

In between the sessions at Sonic, the band headed out on an eventful two-month tour of Northern Spain, the first of three visits they would pay the region over the next few years.

"The first tour of the Basque country was great," smiles Alien. "I'd advise any up-and-coming bands to go there. The good thing about Basque people is they are really hands-on about squatting venues; sometimes they'd have to fight a siege with the Spanish cops to stay in there and keep them running until they got licensed through the local council who would sometimes give them a subsidy to maintain the buildings. That way they pay the rent, keep the venue going, do the repairs and maintain the building; the police generally don't want to mess with them if they don't have to, 'cos they're a right handful, they fight back and usually riot! They have their own Basque identity and are very militant about it; they don't look to England or America for any influence and least of all Spain; not so many of them dress punk, but they drink and maybe get a bit high and they're always ready to group up and have a go at authority!"

"A guy called JC who was a soundman for a lot of gigs at squats and pubs back then asked us if we wanted to go out there with him on tour," explains Mik, of how the tour came about. "I didn't believe it would ever happen; I hadn't travelled much at that time so to tour north Spain seemed unbelievable and when it *did* happen I was over the moon. I went with Alien to buy our tour van, a white Transit with a small red demon painted on the side; it ended up being our tour van that Alien whizzed about in right 'til we broke up, it took us everywhere, that van.

"We took everyone with us on the tour: girlfriends, mates, children! Skinny's first child Jade was nine months old and Alien's daughter Jodee came, who was three; looking back we must have been off our rockers, but we were just buzzing off the fact we were going on tour, so we thought, 'The more the merrier!' JC had a coach with all his sound gear on it, there was Alien's Transit packed to the roof with all our gear and we were followed by our friends Bob and Niamh on a motorbike; it was great. The tour itself was mental; we camped in forests and fields, played all the Basque squats, drank ridiculous amounts of Kalimutxo (the Basque tipple, red wine and cola) and partied the night away at the fiestas that go on during the summer. I was shocked and stunned at how well we were treated; we got fed lush food, all the booze was pretty much free for the bands, we'd get a place to crash *and* we got paid at the end of the night; all that was unheard-of in England and it was my first taste of the respect Europeans show to travelling bands and how organised they are.

"As time went on, people eventually went home or travelled elsewhere, until only a handful of us were left. There were times when the hangovers took their toll and we had moments when we wanted to kill each other, but that happens on tour; I suppose it's inevitable with getting wrecked, enjoying the highs and suffering the lows, it can be gruelling. Fair play to JC for putting up with us for two months; I bet he had moments of regret dragging us boozy lot to the Basque country, so cheers, mate – respect! "The tour ended with us doing a gig with Sociedad Alkoholika [Society of Alcoholics], the local Basque thrash heroes; fuck, they're a superb band and it was an honour sharing a stage with them. For me the whole tour was one of them life-changing things and everyone I know who came with us still talks about it to this day; after we got back to England, all I wanted to do was gig and tour!"

"One day, we were on the beach at Gros, San Sebastian," continues Alien, "and me, Mik and Skinny were having a dip, as you do; the three of us swam out a bit, oblivious of the very dangerous cross currents and winds from the Bay of Biscay that were quickly churning up the sea and we got caught in the currents but didn't notice 'til it was too late. We tried to swim back to shore but it was no good, swimming against a strong tide…we were getting nowhere! I panicked at this, as I was the furthest one out, I really thought I was gonna drown! Mik was quite a strong swimmer and so was Skinny, so they managed to get back to the shore; I swam to the sea wall and somehow got out up that way, although I got myself cut up on all the barnacles. It taught us a lesson, though, the whole band could have drowned…"

After contributing the track 'Unknown' to a split 7-inch on Fluffy Bunny with The Losers from Nottingham, Coitus toured Europe with them to promote it and – in true Coitus fashion – trouble seemed to follow them everywhere they went.

"Apart from that first tour of the Basque when we were there for two months, we only ever went away for two weeks at a time," explains Alien. "We'd be dead by the end of a fortnight! Anyway, the first gig of the Losers tour was in Arnhem, Holland and there was some incident outside the gig between these German punks and some Dutch police. The cops came back in full force and battered their way in; I'd just woke up and was having a piss when I got clubbed round the head and about three coppers chased Mik into the same bogs. They knocked Mik about a bit, then he fell over me and I ended up on the floor by the urinals, a foot away from my own piss; it would have been comical if they weren't trying to do us in. They were trying to knock me out with their clubs and Mik was copping all the blows; his head was pissing blood, they really hurt us and all the while they were screaming away in Dutch, it was very bizarre and very painful.

"Steve Loser was attacked by a police dog, his leg was badly bitten and they whisked us off in a van and chucked us in the cells. We were there all day and what was really comical about the whole episode was that Skinny had crashed out drunk in the back of Alien's van earlier that night and slept through the whole thing; he woke up later that morning and wondered where everyone had got to, oblivious that anything had happened! They eventually deported the Germans and let us go and we had to drive to Eindhoven for the next gig, bruised and battered but not beaten. There was some talk of trying to do the Arnhem cops for brutality, some people from Hotel Bosch (the squat where it all happened) were gonna help us out, but in the end we didn't bother."

Alex from Tribal War (now of Leech Woman) produced the band's 1994 'Darkness On Streets…' 7-inch, which captured the band at their most metallic and driving, a sound not dissimilar to Amebix or Antisect in their prime. The violently insistent title track remains not only one of the band's heaviest moments but also one of their catchiest. That's 'catchy' as in 'a meathook in the earhole', of course. A second album was recorded, which would have been entitled 'Failure To Communicate' if it had ever been released ("We were too busy gigging and drinking to find a label," sighs Alien) and further tours of Ireland and Europe were undertaken, before Coitus recorded the 'Real Cold Fear' 7-inch with Pete Lippy (from the aforementioned Antisect) during August 1995. It wasn't released until the following year though (through Inflammable Material) by which time Skinny had left the band, returning to Ireland with his family; he was replaced on bass by Keith from Dread Messiah and the band made an impromptu appearance outside the Sex Pistols' Finsbury Park reunion show.

"I can't remember what prompted the gig outside the Pistols gig," admits Alien. "It probably sounds like a [Malcolm] McLaren-inspired publicity stunt, but it was all word of mouth. Anyone who was there will remember it as a bit of a laugh but that was it and it remains but a memory now. We knew this couple, skinhead Joe and his missus Karen, who were squatting a little building tucked away behind some trees in Finsbury Park; nobody knew they were there, but they'd been there for years. That's where we got the electricity to do the gig; we set up on the grass and then some official-looking bloke comes over asking what we thought we were doing. I told him we were playing a free concert and he said we weren't allowed, but I told him we got permission from the park's planning department and then we started playing before he'd even walked off. Luckily he never came back, so we finished our set and later on some of us climbed into the gig to watch the Pistols…"

However, after further tours of Ireland and Spain, Coitus split, playing their 'last' gig in the Basque capital of Vitoria in October 1996. "We were all fucked up after a brilliant two-week tour of the Basque country and we missed our ferry at Ostend," recalls Mik. "So everyone was pissed off 'cos we had to wait 24 hours 'til the next one. We were skint and hanging and then a row started over fuck knows what and that was that; the journey home was horrible, all hangovers and bad feelings. In hindsight, a lot was going on in our lives, a lot of change, not all good either, so the band wasn't a priority for any of us any more. It felt to me like we were flogging a dead horse; the fun had been replaced with an 'It's all a bit of a drag' feeling… I thought it was the end of Coitus, for sure – but fate had other plans!"

Indeed, because although Skinny became the bassist/vocalist in Cold War, Mik formed the Restarts, Keith went on to work with the Reknaw sound system and form Mush with Alien, who himself also played with Screamer and Dirty Love alongside original Coitus member, Martin, Coitus itself kept rearing its ugly head every few years. In 2000, Gamp Records released an anthology CD, the brilliantly-titled 'Necrocomical' and the band sporadically reformed every few years for various gigs in London and Ireland, most notably the Across The Decades festival in Milton Keynes, Holidays In The Sun in Dublin and the 2009 Scumfest in Brixton. Unfortunately that was the last time the classic line-up of Coitus played together, as Skinny sadly passed away later that year.

"Skinny was a dear friend, regardless of me being in a band with him," offers Mik, by way of tribute, "and losing him is still a very hard thing to deal with. Along the way we have all lost friends, but losing Skinny hit us all badly; his funeral was utterly heartbreaking, his good nature reached a lot of people's hearts. Thinking of all the chats and laughs I had with Skin and the noise we belted out together often makes me very sad. He was one of the best people I ever met; it makes you think when you lose a good mate that friends and family are not always gonna be there, we should all appreciate our time together 'cos you never know when it's all over for good. As far as the band went, playing with Skinny was so easy it was a pleasure, we really connected. Skinny was the best bass man I ever jammed with; I could show him a riff and he'd get it first time.

"We had a lot in common as far as musical tastes went…all three of us did. We could all hammer through our set blindfold, so it didn't matter how drunk we got (our audiences might disagree on that one); even doing the practices for the reunion gigs, it felt like we'd only jammed the week before when it would actually have been years. I'm proud to have made a racket with Skinny and to have been his friend and I like thinking that somehow I'll laugh, chat and booze with him again, when I cop it myself; I deffo ain't religious and I dunno if that's the truth, but I like to believe it…"

"What else can I say about Skinny?" adds Alien. "He was one of the best mates I ever had, with or without the band. I met him in the mid Eighties with the rest of the Dublin lot, who'd all moved over to London. My god, when they got together with our lot, we lit up all of North

London! There wasn't a dull moment…or a sober one. The punk scene in London was never the same again.

"Skinny was a great character; he liked a drink and loved to roar his arse off, but he was also a sensitive soul, who loved his mates and would defend them to the hilt. He never hated anyone, but he'd no time for anyone who wanted to control or harm others, or play mind games to get their way. He'd do all he could to help anyone less fortunate and would get really upset if there was nothing he could do; he had his problems, like we all do, it's the way of the world, I suppose. He left behind Michelle, the love of his life and two of the greatest kids you could wish for and I know that to anyone and everyone who ever knew him, he'll never be forgotten… The booming voice and blasting bass can still be heard!"

After a pause to remember their old friend, Mik concludes defiantly: "The UK punk scene of the Nineties was great; easily as good as it was in the Seventies or Eighties. Nothing hacks me off more than some miserable, nostalgic, ageing punk twat that starts waffling on about '*back in the day, when punk was real…*' That's all bollocks, it's as real now as it was then; just 'cos a band or a person was around in '77 or '82 don't make 'em any better or any more 'real' than any other time. People like to brag about their youth as though punk (or whatever scene they were into) mattered more then than it does now, when the reality is probably the opposite. To me the DIY scene will always be around, as long as people want to take the stage, make a noise and create something of their own; it will change to suit the generations and yes, punk is a mainstream commodity these days, but in defiance of all that's corporate and how shit this world is run, there will always be people who keep the DIY spirit alive. That's what it's all about: get off your arse, travel, see the world, go mental, make a racket, have a laugh!

"Music is controlled by corporations now more than ever, so that DIY ethic is vital in today's more sinister times; it's the spirit of resistance against a world of absurdity. With hideous banality like the *X-Factor* conveyor belt churning out boy/girl band shite, free speech under attack, brutal wars without end, lying bastard corporate politicians, global recession and fuckwit toff royal weddings going on, people with a bit of intelligence will not accept the shit that's fed to us; they'll break free from the apathy of the herd and recreate the energy anew… The best times are yet to come, DIY forever! Up the fucking punks! Blah! Blah! Blah!"

SELECT DISCOGRAPHY:

Cassette LP:
'Submission/Domination' (Hate Tapes, 1992)

7-inch:
'Split' (Fluffy Bunny, 1993) – *split with the Losers*
'Darkness On Streets…' (Tribal War, 1994)
'Real Cold Fear' (Inflammable Material, 1996)

AT A GLANCE:
Underground Movement's (2009) 40-track double-CD retrospective, 'Fucked Into Oblivion', compiles everything the band recorded apart from the very first 'In Two Minutes You'll Be Smoking In Hell' demo.

SUICIDAL SUPERMARKET TROLLEYS

The **Suicidal Supermarket Trolleys** may not have released that much music on vinyl given that they were together almost 10 years, but what they did was fantastically punk rock in its snotty delivery. They remain semi-legendary as part of the triumvirate of bands – alongside Dread Messiah and Coitus – at the heart of the tight-knit Stoke Newington, Hackney, squat community of the early Nineties.

"Well, much has happened since those admittedly aged and substance abuse-filled days, so I have to think long and hard about this," begins guitarist Chris. "But I guess the band was conceived in 1987, at an all-dayer at the Cardboard Box in Wood Green. [Drummer] Oz, [vocalist] John Marshall and I decided that we would get up on the stage for some reason and make a fuckin' racket but, somewhat unsurprisingly, none of the other bands playing that day – Mulch and Rubella Ballet both come to mind – wanted to lend three drunken kids their instruments... Actually, only two of us were drunk, because Oz didn't drink, but I remember we went to the supermarket down the road from the gig especially to steal supermarket trolleys for stage props... Gwar watch out!

"Anyway, that sowed the seeds in our mind that we wanted to start a band and gave us an idea what to call it too. We were all music fans more than anything; I got some money off my old man for a guitar, then bought one using only half the money he gave me so I could spend the rest on records and we were all set..."

The band didn't play out for several years, taking their time to learn to play their instruments, write songs and generally arrive at a competent line-up, Oz moving from drums to bass and then out of the band altogether (but Chris is quick to point out, "There were no hard feelings, though, we were all mates after all..."), with Ben joining on bass and Simon Trolley joining on drums.

"I always remember seeing Simon around at gigs," recalls Chris. "I remember seeing him on a crutch in the pit at a show – it was either Bad Brains or Conflict – and he always used to chat to John. I don't know how the subject of drums came up, but the next thing I knew was he was going to show up to play for us. I seem to recall this was sorted out at a Toxic Reasons gig down at the 100 Club?

"Anyway, we met at a rehearsal studio one day; Simon was late (nothing new there, as I was to discover!) but inside the studio, lo and behold, he could actually keep a beat! This was something new for us and we soon wrote enough songs for a demo..."

Said demo being something a bit special, seeing as it was recorded by none other than Dave Goodman (1951-2005, RIP), famous as the Sex Pistols' live sound engineer, who also recorded three of the early Pistols demos.

"I knew Dave from hanging out with Andy Blade from Eater and Ray Stevenson, the photographer employed by Malcolm McLaren to photograph the Pistols and brother to Nils Stevenson, the Pistols' road manager," explains Simon. "Dave and Ray were wonderful people and regular chats about whether Sid actually stabbed Nancy, whether punk was dead 'cos it was created by a bunch of fuckin' binbag-wearing art students with stupid swastika armbands and, most importantly, 'Whose round is it anyway?', prompted me into asking Dave to give us some studio time. He kindly did us a deal for very little money and we all got to spend some time recording with his magical punk rock/hippy ears. None of the first line-up

Suicidal Supermarket Trolleys, Debbie

Suicidal Supermarket Trolleys, Chris at the George Robey

Suicidal Supermarket Trolleys,
Simon

of the Trolleys had been in a recording studio before (none of us had been in a bloody band before either!) and there we were, being regaled with stories about his days with the Pistols, as we had a couple of pints with him before we started, at his local, round the corner from his studio…"

"I think the real reason for us taking him straight to the pub was that we were so nervous we needed a couple of drinks beforehand to 'help' things along a bit," adds Chris.

"I think we had six hours to mix and record four songs," continues Simon. "He put up with the inevitable band squabbles and I remember his head being in his hands over the mixing desk console as we all were arguing over what the backing vocals should be, for a song called 'Radioactive Jelly Baby'. Sadly I later changed the lyrics to 'Poor Man's Genocide' when John left the band. John very graciously gave me permission to use the lyrics that he had written, which was very cool of him, but I felt I wanted to do my own thing, which is something I regret, because those 'Radioactive Jelly Baby' lyrics were brilliant and I wish I had just kept them as they were. Anyway, I think Chris Trolley has the only copy of that Dave Goodman recording, which was never released."

As intimated by Simon, John Marshall left the band after the demo and seeing as Simon had demonstrated a decent set of pipes while messing around at rehearsals, he moved to vocals and Keith Milne was recruited behind the kit. Ben also left and was replaced on bass by John from Mulch and finally the Trolleys had arrived at their gigging line-up, making their live debut at the Lady Owen Arms with Trench Fever and Designer Fear.

"All our friends came out and filled this very narrow pub stuck down an alleyway opposite the Angel tube station," recalls Simon. "I think we were well rehearsed, so we banged 'em out, while our friends drank and took the piss… Nobody went bonkers, there were no circle pits or stage diving and no, *Maximum Rock'n'Roll* wasn't there, nor did they review the gig! But I still have the flyer and I managed to go home wearing the same trousers I arrived in. I honestly didn't expect that many people to show up, but all our friends made the effort and made our first gig a great night out. The Angel looks completely different now and I have a hard time recognising anything in that entire neighbourhood… I think the land where the pub was got bulldozed and turned into a shopping mall. Real shame, 'cos I miss that place: good times with good people."

Once they started, they didn't want to stop, gigging wherever/whenever they could and recording several more demos, one of them being released as the 'Greetings From London' 7-inch by Swiss label Resistance Productions. It ably set out their stall as natural successors to the Eighties chaos punks like Exploited and English Dogs, their defiantly non-metallic punk delivered with maximum bollocks and attitude.

"When I was introduced to Jello Biafra last year, he said, 'I always thought you were a Swiss punk band 'cos your first single was pressed in Switzerland…'," laughs Simon. "I paused on hearing this and replied, 'But Jello, the 7-inch *was* called "Greetings From London"…'

"Anyway, we all had decent record collections that helped define the style of punk that we wanted to play, even though originally we didn't really know how to play our instruments… but in a DIY anarcho-punk scene, that isn't really what it's about. I sometimes think of that phrase from the Notting Hill carnival, 'Don't spectate – participate', so I guess we just wanted to do *something*. We practiced and drank and swapped records every Sunday for the first two years and never did a gig, until Keith joined the band and made us play out. Bastard.

"In the beginning, during the late Eighties, Wood Green, Bounds Green and Manor House had very large punk rock communities, squatting in abandoned council houses. Getting the tube back from gigs was always a laugh, due to the number of punks all piling onto the train at the end of the night. In the end, during the early/mid Nineties, Stoke Newington in Hackney was the neighbourhood where we eventually ended up living, alongside Coitus, Dread Messiah and a slew of other bands too long to mention. There was a real sense of punk rock community in Stokey, based around the DIY ethic of creating something out of nothing and just making things happen.

"The crust thing was raging when we formed and bands like Antisect, Concrete Sox, Napalm Death and ENT were all around us. The Trolleys got to play with all those bands and were at those early hardcore gigs; that's what I remember it was called back then, though the term seems to have been dropped for some reason. I have always hated metal and never liked Slayer and their ilk, or the rock-star pretensions that seem to accompany so many metal bands. I suppose that is one thing that separated the Trolley style and the way we played, from others at that time…

"Every time Slayer played the Hammersmith Odeon, all the crust bands would come to London to see the gig, but for me, personally, I did not want to play in a band that sang about Satan, played guitar solos or even had a double kick-drum pedal for that matter. So, as far as I was concerned, the Trolleys were always gonna play that early UK style of punk that we all grew up with and loved. Back then, I remember being in the White Horse pub in Brixton at an Instigators and Detonators (from Canada) gig and seeing someone flogging the Sore Throat 7-inch with 76 songs on it. I mean that was it for me; how on earth could you play any faster, or even put any more songs on a 7-inch, for fuck's sake? Fuck DRI thrash, as far as speed went, this was it. Done, sorted and, I might add, fuckin' hilarious. The Antisect LP was also genius. Chris used to regularly wear an Electro Hippies shirt, though, so he was officially crusty-friendly!"

A storming split 7-inch with Public Nuisance from New York City was released by US label Squat Or Rot in 1994 and the band continued the 'Drunken Rampage' of its title across the UK, Ireland, Europe and even America (the 1994 New York Beer Olympics Punk Fest!).

"Dublin was one of the best places we ever played," smiles Simon. "Deko from Paranoid Visions and all the Dublin punks hooked us right up. We played a pub called Mulligans and had been warned by Chaos UK that opposite the pub was quite a rough housing estate, so to keep an eye on our van. We got to Dublin and after being told numerous times that we had 'a very nice van', we parked up outside the pub, took the spark plugs out so the van wouldn't be nicked and carried our equipment in. First thing we saw was a bunch of old men watching Man United on the telly and the landlord cleaning up this large pool of blood on the wood floor. He looked up at us, smiled and asked if we were the band and then directed us upstairs to the venue and a laughing Deko. We played two gigs there, the first was supporting the Tofu Love Frogs [from London] and the second we headlined, with local Dublin bands, Paranoid Visions and Indecent Exposure. Chris got into a fight with a Tofu Love Frog on our first night there. I think the Indecent Exposure boys put us up; a great bunch of lads.

"It was at a Spermbirds gig I was bottled across the back of the head during the first fuckin' song and there was lots'n'lots of blood due to my blood being so thin from all the booze I'd drank at the pub beforehand. Luckily the hospital was only walking distance round the corner from the venue. And it was at Broken Bones at the Marquee where my head was impaled with a stiletto heel. A crazy psycho bitch mistook me for someone else; I really shouldn't have given her her shoe back after she impaled my head with it, I am far too nice.

"Manchester was also amazing. They are so fuckin' punk up there; during our soundcheck we were asked if we minded one of the Manchester punks doing some vocals when we played 'Beer'. I said I had no problem with it, but when we played it that night, the fella who jumped up to sing had no tongue! It was one of the best, if not *the* most memorable version, of 'Beer' we have ever played…

"I used to squat at the Dole House in Peckham, South London, along with Keith from Dread Messiah and about 10 other people. The squat was a huge, abandoned, two-storey unemployment benefit office which Keith and one of our friends, Bev, had broken open. We had regular gigs every fortnight, complete with a vegan cafe, two DJ rooms, one live gig room, two bars and even a chill-out room for when you just wanted to give up and have your shoes stolen after you fell asleep. I have very fond memories of an infamous Coitus, Dread Messiah and Trolleys gig there, which ended up with a mini-riot outside with the local Peckham constabulary.

"We also played the Dole House on the night of the Poll Tax Riots, which is another favourite; the atmosphere after the riots that night was carnival-esque, 'cos everyone had worked out all their aggro that afternoon at the riots and so that night everyone was friendly and just wanted to have a drink and a laugh. I seem to remember the Levellers headlined and finished their set with 'I Fought The Law'…"

While in Dublin (April 1993), the Trolleys recorded what would eventually become side A of their 'Shut Up And Drink' LP with Albert Cowan at Sonic Studios (including a kick-ass cover of 'When The Shit Hits The Fan' by Circle Jerks), but they wouldn't record the six songs that would appear as the B-side for another two years. By this time the band would have undergone a drastic line-up change, Chris and John leaving, to be replaced respectively by Debbie (from Dirge) and Ned.

"I got restless," reveals Chris. "I had also met a lady from New York, who was to become my first wife, so when the opportunity to move to the US came about, I grabbed it. Also at that time, John was thinking seriously about moving to Australia with his Australian girlfriend, so it looked like the end of the Trolleys was imminent. Keith and Simon asked me would I mind if they carried on, though, which was something I didn't have any problem with and I wished them all the best with it. The LP came out quite a while later and all but two of the tracks ('John Tyndall' and 'Shut Up And Drink') had been written by the original band anyway, although John and I only played on the one side of the LP. I didn't realise at the time of the recording that the side I played on was going to end up on a record; as far as I was concerned, we were just recording another demo… I would have tried a little harder if I had known!"

However, the LP wasn't released until after the Trolleys had long split up, because Simon also upped and moved to New York just a few months after recording the B-side tracks at London's Boundary Row Studios in August '95. It remains a fine epitaph for the band though; an essential listen for lovers of rabid UK82-style punk, it fetches silly prices on eBay. The last ever Suicidal Supermarket Trolleys gig was at Chat's Palace in Hackney and unfortunately it wasn't the auspicious farewell everyone hoped it would be.

"For me, that was the worst gig we ever played," says Simon sadly. "John and Chris had already left the band and I had decided to move to New York. We decided to do one last gig at Chats with Dread Messiah and some other band whose name escapes me; it rained, it was cold and nobody came out. I think the words '*very* empty' spring to mind. Dread Messiah were due to go on before us, but Harry, their vocalist, had failed to turn up for soundcheck and so their drummer Russell was dispatched to see if he was still at home. Fifteen minutes before they were meant to go on, Keith from Dread Messiah walked up to me and said he was really sorry but they didn't know where Harry was and they couldn't play without him…

"I think Coitus, Dread Messiah and the Trolleys had all formed in the same year and broke up the same year; I'm not 100% on that, but we all played a lot of gigs together, lived in the same neighbourhood and were all good friends, so I was obviously looking forward to playing with and having a session with, Dread Messiah one last time before I left for NYC. Anyway, the first band finished and we got up and played and it was all very anti-climatic, empty and not at all the way I hoped our last gig would be. And we packed up our gear and all went our separate ways.

"It wasn't until the next day we were told that when Russ went to Harry's flat, he discovered Harry had died. Horrible, horrible day and that was the Trolleys' last gig; I guess I will always associate it with Harry's death. It was obviously the end of Dread Messiah as well; they were an awesome punk band and Harry was such a good man and a great friend – he is greatly missed."

In New York, Simon was invited to join Brooklyn's Distraught, with whom the Trolleys had been good friends and who then morphed into Thought Crime and released the 'It's All In Yer Head' LP on Profane Existence, which featured guest vocals from Steve Ignorant (albeit appearing under the pseudonym Alfie Elkins). Thought Crime split up in 2008, allowing Simon to concentrate on his career of the last 20-plus years, self-employed freelance video editor. He even made a short film about the Stoke Newington punk scene, entitled *Stokey* (look it up on YouTube).

"All in all, it was a great outlet," summarises Chris, "a great escape from the humdrum existence of work, girlfriends and just life in general. I have been in a few bands since, here in the US, but nothing compares to being in the Trolleys; we were first and foremost friends… I guess that's over-romanticising it a bit, but there's nothing wrong with that, is there?"

"I agree with Chris," concurs Simon. "I didn't really think anyone would care, let alone remember us; the LP and 7-inch records were made in such small numbers that I am amazed people have found them. We were nothing special, just another punk band out having a laugh with their mates. That is what the Trolleys were in my eyes; nothing more, nothing less. It's just nice to be remembered."

SELECT DISCOGRAPHY:

7-inch:
'Greetings From London' (Resistance Productions, 1991)
'Drunken Rampage' (Squat Or Rot, 1994) – *split with Public Nuisance*

LP:
'Shut Up And Drink' (Profane Existence, 1996)

AT A GLANCE:
Maybe Profane Existence will release the SST discography they have been threatening for years one day soon?

THROW BRICKS AT COPPERS

Although London band **Throw Bricks At Coppers** were together for the best part of seven years and played nigh on a hundred gigs, they only released one demo tape, 'How Many More Brutal Fucking Police Murders?' The original cassette version sold a modest 500 copies upon release, but since then has been downloaded 10 times that amount in just the first year of being made available online and *Terrorizer* magazine even voted it into their Top Fifty all-time punk chart in 2002, demonstrating how influential their police-baiting thrashy punk was proving to be.

The band was started back in 1997 by bassist Sergeant Seamus (of metal/stoner band Blood Island Raiders), with Vice Officer Ben on lead guitar and Rookie Cadet Stu Thumper on drums (both from death metal band Epitome). After a few rehearsals, the line-up was completed by second guitarist DI Poshi, from Fatal Error and Method Of Murder and vocalist Commissioner Rob Filth, formerly of Lethal Bedpan and Ostracised, who had just endured a lengthy and well-publicised blasphemy trial for wearing one of Cradle Of Filth's 'Jesus Is A Cunt' T-shirts in public.

"Basically all of the band members used to frequent a London underground metal club called the Devil's Church," says Rob. "And one of the earliest and more notable bands that played there was Cradle Of Filth, who were gaining in popularity incredibly fast at the time, but whom I would say were still pretty much 'underground' at that point. *Terrorizer* had only just taken to championing them, but the larger metal mags such as *Metal Hammer* and *Kerrang!* were certainly not plugging them to any great extent. Cradle's 'Jesus Is A Cunt' T-shirt had been doing the rounds on the underground circuit for about six months or so by then and I thought it was a fantastically eye-catching design which really appealed to the punk in me, in much the same way many of the more outrageous Vivienne Westwood/Seditionaries designs also did. I think it was in March of 1996 when I bought one.

"Then in June or July, I got nicked by Bow Street cops on my way back from the Devil's Church one night. They stole my shirt off me and proceeded to charge me with 'offering a profane representation' under the 1829 blasphemy law! A law which no-one had successfully been convicted under for over 100 years! Basically the real reason why I suspect they arrested me was because of my hardcore punk haircut; the West End pigs have always persecuted punks on trumped-up charges because they know the biased magistrate will take one look at them and immediately think it's a shut and closed case of 'guilty'.

The charge was tailored in order to fit my appearance; the original wording of the law was defined to specify street hawking of profane material and was so ridiculously out of date that it was nestled between laws to do with not throwing dirty hay out in the street and the tethering of horses in a public area... However, the cops proposed that my pink spiked hair was 'exhibiting' and 'selling' the image of the T-shirt in a public place and the judge found me guilty. The whole thing felt very much like a witch trial and a persecution of my libertarian freedom of expression.

"As for the effect it had on the band," he ponders carefully, "I was quite embittered and angry by what I felt was unfair treatment by the police and the judicial system and because I was given no opportunity to appeal against the original judgement of the court case, my legal aid having been taken away. I had also previously often experienced prejudicial treatment from

Throw Bricks At Coppers live

Throw Bricks At Coppers, vocalist Rob, pic by Naki

the police due to my extreme alternative appearance (once getting stopped and searched in the street over 20 times in one weekend!), so to be suddenly given the opportunity to vent all that frustration from those events was what probably led to every subsequent song I wrote for the band being an anti-police statement.

"This unfortunately got misinterpreted by *Terrorizer*, who assumed our whole set was purely sour grapes over the T-shirt trial. This led to us being kind of dismissed from their pages, when in fact our songs were to do with things such as the deaths of Ibrahima Sey (the first guy in the UK killed with the CS spray then newly introduced into police arsenals) and increased surveillance laws with the rapid growth of CCTV, as well as highlighting various forms of religious indoctrination and systematic suppression and censorship…all the things which any other anarcho hardcore punk band would sing about, but perhaps less po-faced and with more humour and aggression. In fact, only one of the songs in the entire setlist was actually specifically about my T-shirt trial, which was 'Jesus Is A Cunt'…"

After two gigs, making their live debut at the very first Uxfest in 1997, drummer Stu Thumper left, later to join black-metal band Thus Defiled; he was replaced by WPC Monkey Martin, from Carnis and Ignoramus. This line-up lasted over 60 gigs and was occasionally supplemented by Rookie Cadet Steve, from Beatdown Fury, on second guitar, who recorded the aforementioned 'How Many More Brutal Fucking Police Murders?' with the band. Featuring seven songs tracked at Survival Studios, Kingston, during late August 1998 and four live tracks (including covers of ENT's 'Murder' and Discharge's 'Protest And Survive'), the tape sold out of its initial run within two weeks and landed the band some glowing fanzine reviews, not to mention gigs around the country with the likes of Conflict, Vice Squad, Subhumans, Doom, Labrat and Assert.

It was a raging collection of raw punk tunes that boded well for the future of TBAC, but one can only wonder what a full album might have turned out like. Athough they continued in one form or another for another six years, the band never wrote or recorded any more material and eventually their live appearances dried up as well. DI Poshi left in 2004 and with relations between Rob and the other members becoming increasingly strained, he left the band on New Year's Day 2005, leaving the other guys free to join Leo from 17 Stitches in his new project, Defcon Zero.

"The very last gig was the night before I left, at the Harp Club in Croydon with the Vibrators; as usual the band had no soundcheck and, despite my constant requests beforehand, they all decided that they didn't need any prior warm-up rehearsals, so my vocals were not broken in sufficiently for the gig. We were gigging fairly infrequently by that point and in order not to over-exert when doing vocals in an extreme shouty manner, my larynx needed to be regularly 'broken in' first. Because of this and my inability to make anything out in the mud of distortion from the piss-poor monitors, my vocals were seriously out of time with the others; subsequently it was a particularly bad performance on my part.

"If I were a guitarist instead, it would have been like the rest of the band deliberately cutting the strings of my instrument with scissors, taking away my distortion pedal before the gig and then turning around and saying, 'You're shit!' afterwards. I felt completely undermined as regards my position and role within the band, to the point where there was literally no place left to go other than to reluctantly turn my whole back on the thing and leave. To be brutally honest, the last gig was total and utter shit."

Possibly as a result of this acrimonious split, Rob hasn't played in a band since and nowadays works full-time as a school keeper for an art college, nurturing a healthy disillusionment with all things 'scene-based'. DI Poshi is now with When Gods Burn, while Monkey Martin, Ben and Seamus are still with Defcon Zero.

"Most of the punk bands these days seem to be pretty retro, rather than progressive," bemoans Rob, "singing about the same old tired subjects, usually how much alcohol and drugs they've consumed and what 'hilarious' sexual disasters they've experienced as a result. Either that or ranting out the same generic protest slogans from the Eighties which are well past their sell-by date and devoid of any satirical humour or observance. Salacious gossip on the punk scene is like something from *The Jerry Springer Show* or indeed *EastEnders*; it's so facile and the scene is far more homophobic than 20 years ago, stylistically backwards-looking and in a complete rut. I find that the ability to question all things including oneself and the political intelligentsia as well as to experiment with various musical styles and original artwork forms to achieve something new has all but been eradicated within the punk scene by an unquestioning acceptance of uniformity and peer-group conformity.

"There doesn't seem to be any constructive focussed anarchism within punk any more, the over-riding purpose of the scene seems to be to look like a London postcard from 1984 and consume as much alcohol as possible, to the point of acting a total arsehole and that is defined as 'anarchy' – it's fucking moronically naive. Personally I am more into listening to gothic orchestral doom metal nowadays, because I find a cookie monster singing next to a high-pitched soprano, accompanied by a string orchestra with blastbeats, musically far more funny, interesting and progressive to hear than stuff I was listening to 20-odd years ago, even if the genre is lyrically as unchallenging as most hardcore punk currently is...

"I'm not sure we ever will be remembered, to be honest," he adds, in closing, on the mark left by Throw Bricks At Coppers, "although when there have been over 1,000 deaths in police custody since 1969 in the UK – and only one officer has ever been convicted as a result – I think the band's music is just as relevant today as it was while we were going. I suppose the best epitaph is that TBAC were by far the most obsessively anti-police punk/metal thrash band there ever was and they were to the British Cuntstabulary what Discharge were to nuclear war!"

AT A GLANCE:
Go track down that one and only demo recording because it's a fucking beaut.

SINK

Truth be known, London's **Sink** should probably have appeared in the last book of this series, seeing as they lurched into life in 1988, rising from the ashes of the overlooked Bad Dress Sense. But rather than dismiss them with a few paragraphs at the end of that previous chapter, their wildly eclectic and wonderfully listenable work certainly merits proper examination in this volume…and besides, they released most of their material in the (very early) Nineties anyway.

"I was writing some new songs with the intention of carrying on Bad Dress Sense," begins vocalist/guitarist Ed 'Shred' Wenn (once described by Understand's John Hannon as 'the grandfather of UK emo!'), "But it never really happened. This was the summer of '87 and I was still doing the Stupids as well and they listened to a lot of rock music, like AC/DC and Aerosmith and it's not a big leap from that to something a bit more rootsy, like, maybe, um, the Byrds, the Stones, Dylan… I really got into the Woodstock movie as well, which was a big turning point for me…

"Anyway, there was all this indecision going on about Bad Dress Sense and I'd written these songs, when John Walters from the BBC called and asked if we could do another Bad Dress Sense session for John Peel. He used to call me up on spec when bands cancelled their sessions, 'cos he knew I was in loads of different bands and he used to say to me, 'As long as it's the same old racket…!' I knew he wouldn't mind if it was a totally different band… and you couldn't pass up a Peel session, could you? It was £80 each!"

So, after just one rehearsal, Ed recruited bassist Paul Duncan and drummer Pete Whitehouse and Sink were born, recording a John Peel session as their opening gambit to boot; the name was left to the last minute as well…

"I was really into AC/DC and they had this song called 'Sink The Pink'," Ed explains, "which actually wasn't a very good song, just transparently stupid, but Tommy [Stupid] thought it would be a good name for the band, although he would never have called his own band Sink The Pink! I knew it wasn't the right name, but I was quite happy to shorten it to Sink… Ian MacKaye [of Minor Threat and Dischord Records fame] was in town and trying to get me to put on some shows for his brother's band Ignition and I ran this past him. He really liked AC/DC as well but he was like, 'It sounds funny now, but if you call your band Sink The Pink, you're going to regret it…' He was totally relieved we shortened it to Sink…anything but Sink The Pink, basically! And that's where we got the name from, just two days before the session…"

Ed also used and abused his Stupids connections to land Sink some pretty choice support slots, their first gig supporting the Hard-Ons and Space Maggots at the George Robey.

"It was a much smaller scene back then and I knew virtually everyone," he concedes, before adding, on the wide mixture of influences that contributed to the unique Sink sound. "I had had nothing to do with the Stupids musically, whereas Bad Dress Sense was my own band and, although I wrote most of the songs, I was with three people who knew hardcore inside out, probably better than me. From that, I went into this three-piece [Sink] with two people who knew nothing about hardcore, but had loads of other influences… So, the sound was always going to be noisy and punk, but with other influences too and we quickly found some common ground, like the Black Flag instrumental stuff…and Pete was obsessed with Frank Zappa…"

"And that's why one song was like this and another like that – and then there would be a hillbilly song!" laughs Paul. "But that was because it was fun! Right from the start, Sink was a band that did a completely fucked-up mixture of stuff; there was never any thought given to trying to make a living off what we were doing, so we did exactly what we pleased."

Come July 1988 and Ed had left the Stupids to concentrate on Sink anyway ("Ironically, my musical career was pretty much downhill from there, at least in terms of popularity and funding!") and the band had been joined by a dedicated lead vocalist, Laurence Bell, of Ipswich's bubblegum pop-punkers Perfect Daze, who made his recording debut on their second Peel session during September of that year.

"I've never really wanted to be the singer in any of the bands I've been in," confesses Ed, "but I always end up doing it, mainly because I don't trust anyone else to do it – plus, if I wasn't the singer, it usually meant I couldn't write the lyrics, which is a bit of an issue for me! So anyway, Laurence joined Sink and that actually worked out pretty good, although it changed the style a lot…we got less dark. He loved one of our songs called 'Baby', a bit of a 'Dag Nasty number' which we'd recorded on the first Peel session, and we basically started to do more of that kind of thing."

And the Dave Smalley influence on Laurence's vocals were in full effect on the first Sink single, 1989's five-track 'Mama Sink's Ugly Firstborn', which was recorded, mixed and mastered in just one day at RMS in Croydon by Andrew Fryer and released by Vinyl Solution on their Poontang imprint. It pleasingly suggested that the band could be the UK's answer to the edgily melodic punk rock of Virginia's Scream.

"Another strange thing was that we never used to put the title of the records on the sleeves," says Ed, "and so most people thought that first single was actually called 'God Loves You' because that's what's written on the sign the guy's holding up on the cover. The real story is that, Link Wray, one of Paul's big heroes, had released this swamp/country album, this totally acoustic album he'd recorded in his shack; it was a big influence on us – we even used to cover one of the songs, 'Fire And Brimstone'. On the album credits he thanked his mum for the 'hot coffee and good chilli' and he called her 'Mama Wray', so that's what started us off with the whole 'Mama Sink' thing.

"Laurence was well into his country, too; he was a big Hank Williams fan, so there was this whole collision of ideas in the band at that time and that first single had three punk songs on it, an acoustic song and this jokey country thing… And that was important, because right from the start we were doing what we wanted to do with Sink: taking it away from only playing hardcore. The sound on that single is pretty weird, though, pretty wobbly. Pete was still in the band at that point and he wasn't the most solid of drummers…"

"So I guess that hearing that recording back was when we knew that Pete had to go," adds Paul. "You can't be a great band with a bad drummer and, as a bassist, he was really awkward to play along with."

"Punk rock is all about dynamics," claims Ed, "and keeping it interesting and the drummer is vital to signposting those changes. By then we'd got the first year out of the way and realised that Pete wasn't the drummer for us. He was a lovely bloke, we just weren't the right band for him. So Paul phoned him up and told him not to bother turning up for the next gig…"

Said gig was supporting Fugazi at their first ever UK show (at the George Robey, of course!) and the drum stool was temporarily filled by Tommy Stupid. "We'd only had one practice with

Sink, live Bristol 1989,
by Andrew Testa

Sink, Newport TJs 1989
(Lawrence's first gig),
by Steven Ad

Sink, in Kensington Gardens 1989

Tommy," recalls Paul, "and even though he didn't know the songs, they already sounded so much better than with Pete and Tommy did the show and it sounded great; although he fucked up this Creedence [Clearwater Revival] song we did that night…"

"It was a defining moment for us too," claims Ed. "We'd started wearing strange clothes onstage, kaftans and pyjamas and playing Creedence songs was just part of that. Some reviewer called us 'hippy hardcore' after the show, in *Fear And Loathing* fanzine or something, which was funny, seeing as Creedence weren't a hippy band at all; they were blue-collar and bluesy, but it was a fair comment, I guess. The majority of the set was still pretty full-on punk rock. But hardcore is such a narrow church, you only have to do something slightly different from the formula and that's what you get known for – if we'd sounded like DRI, but worn kaftans, we'd still have been labelled as hippies, you know?"

But Tommy was only killing time and Sink had to find a permanent drummer to maintain their momentum. He appeared in the shape of John Howie, a talented sticksman from North Carolina who was staying with his sister in England. However, Laurence left to start his own label (he now runs the well-respected Domino Records), playing his last show with Sink in Brixton and contributing just backing vocals to the band's second single, 'On The Tracks, Feeling Blue'. Recorded by Iain Burgess at Von's in February 1989 ("Which was fucking great," says Ed, proudly, "because he recorded 'All Rise' and 'Vanilla Blue' by Naked Raygun, which are two of my all-time favourite records…"), it was a much more rounded and confident Sink than displayed on the first single, with 'Blue Noodles' even sounding like prime-time Ruts (no small compliment).

"Lyrically we were always trying to treat the audience intelligently," reckons Ed. "We figured we were clever people and they were too and we didn't want to beat them over the head with stuff…so we had songs like 'Blue Noodles', which was absolutely a song against racism, which in itself was nothing new, but it was nice to present it in a slightly different way. Looking back, though, I can't believe how arrogant I was about stuff and how little I knew about life either."

Paul: "Like all young bands…"

Ed: "Yeah, but I wasn't that young by then!"

The single was promoted by a six-week European tour supporting the Instigators, whose popularity by then was thoroughly in decline in the UK, but they were still drawing the best part of a thousand people on the continent. Ed maintains it was a turning point for the band, if only because they were "totally focused on Europe from that moment on and didn't really give a shit about the UK!

"It was a very liberating experience for us, whereas the Instigators had some new stuff, but were mainly playing this kind of 'greatest hits' set-list by then… But they were fucking huge over there and so good to us and introduced us to so many great people including Toddy, who booked all of our subsequent European tours and – inevitably – took a lot of shit from us; not all of which was deserved. I can't underline enough how much we owe to Andy Turner for taking us on that first tour and I'd like to thank both him and Toddy for their support.

"Touring Europe was amazing and a total education, but sometimes it was hard. Like in Italy, we played in Florence, in this squat and there was no toilet for hundreds of people and everyone was shitting in the river…we dragged our mattresses out of the van and slept on the roof that night! So it was hard work, in an 'us against the world' sorta way, but we didn't pay for anything and it really bonded us together as a band and was a great time. It was an interesting tour – gigs were getting cancelled and re-booked and changed as we were going around and the Instigators booked it all themselves. We learnt so much from them on that trip."

Paul: "And they did it all by letter or phone, or the occasional fax; there was no internet or mobile phones back then…and we used to tell all the border guards that we were a country band not a punk band, so we didn't get strip-searched…"

"I bought a carpet in Poland on that first tour," smiles Ed, "because we had so much money from the gigs there; we would get paid in literally inches of notes every night, but because it was still a communist state you couldn't bring it out of the country, so you had to spend it there… Only there was nothing to spend it on – so I bought a carpet!"

"I tried to pay for everyone's shopping in this queue in this supermarket, just to get rid of all this money we had," remembers Paul. "But no-one knew what I was on about and they wouldn't accept it. We stayed at this house after one gig and they treated us really well, but wouldn't take any money off us, so we went round the house hiding money for them to find after we'd left…!"

Upon their return, Sink wasted little time recording their debut album, 1990's 'Another Love Triangle', for Decoy Records (who were basically Poontang but with a less offensive name). Drummer, John Howie played on the album, but he had to return to the States and left the band before it was released, playing his last gig at the Tufnell Park Dome supporting Nomeansno.

"I always wanted to be as creative as possible in the studio," says Ed, on the Sink recording philosophy. "It didn't matter if we couldn't reproduce it perfectly when we played live… they're two different things, playing in the studio and playing live, so why not be as creative as you can with both? So we went up there [Huddersfield] armed with a ton of guitars and amplifiers and acoustic guitars; it was the start of us trying to really layer stuff on top of other stuff. By then, I was very much into the mythology of rock and there were a lot of influences coming to bear and you can hear some of them on that first album. Listening back, it's quite a thin-sounding album, not enough bottom end. We always had this philosophy in Sink along the lines of, 'The reach always exceeds the grasp' or something like that. The point being that we were growing up in public and always trying to do something we couldn't quite pull off! But it's really important to shoot for something that's exceptional – if you only get halfway there, you've still achieved something great…"

Despite all their efforts, the album got a scathing write-up in *Sounds*, the reviewer pouring scorn on both Ed's voice and his lyrics, but the band were too busy breaking in a new drummer, James Kermack, to really care. "He was a very different drummer to John Howie," says Ed. "Howie was all about feel and going with the song…very easy to play along with…"

Paul: "Whereas Kermack was basically, 'Let's hit as many things as I can as hard as I can as fast as I can! Until it's time to stop!'"

Ed: "But he was also, in his own way, very precise: amazing timing, very 'on the money'. He made us sound tighter without either of us having to do anything different. People used to come to gigs just to watch him!"

Paul: "Yes, they loved his showmanship; he'd be twirling his sticks, standing up on his chair… A very big presence when we played live, very loud and brash, but there was nothing malicious or calculated and everyone loved him."

Ed: "He was a legendary character and no-one we'd ever met had prepared us for

Kermack… He came from a totally different background – Paul and I were both from nice middle-class backgrounds, our parents were teachers, we had university degrees, all that kind of stuff…and Kermack was a classic East End kid, who'd got into all sorts of trouble when he was younger and the way he told it was that drums kept him out of prison. He lived in a tower block in Leytonstone and all his mates were wrong 'uns…"

But enough about Kermack and back to Sink. An EP, entitled 'Don't Burn The Hook', was recorded and released at the same time as the album, so with two records cooling in the racks and not only a new drummer but a new lead guitarist as well, in the shape of Perfect Daze's John Ruscoe, Sink finally arrived at the line-up that would see them out to the end of their days. Two lengthy European tours were undertaken in 1990, the first that spring with Vernon Walters from Holland and Ugly Food from Germany, the second much later in the year, to promote the 'Old Man Snake And The Fat Black Pig' MLP, co-headlining with (Washington DC post hardcore legends) Shudder To Think, a tour Paul dubbed 'Shudder To Sink'!

"And it was fucking great," remembers Ed happily. "Loads of people at all the gigs and I got to see one of my favourite bands, at their peak, every night for like nine weeks… 53 shows, I think… Then after the tour they went straight to Southern and recorded [their 1991 album for Dischord] 'Funeral At The Movies' – with all our gear… And did they fucking thank us on the record? No they didn't!

"Anyway, we recorded 'Old Man Snake…' at the House In The Woods down in Surrey, which was very nice – you couldn't ask for better hospitality and catering – but not exactly state-of-the-art equipment-wise. The gear wasn't up to much, but the setting was amazing. They didn't have enough compressors to put on the vocals and the drums at the same time, so the drums sounded shit; the toms were especially ropey, but Kermack did a good job on the playing side of things. It was basically a demo studio and the guy who owned it used to record these jingles there and everything.

"It was the first record that both John and Kermack played on," he adds. "It's a shame it doesn't sound better, but there were some good songs and it was quite creative… but I hate the cover. And seeing as I'm obsessed with album art, that does still hurt! Thinking about it, we failed miserably to come up with one decent album cover in Sink…"

1991 saw Sink recording their final album, 'Vega-Tables', while the 'first' Gulf War was in full catastrophic swing. It was a lengthy session they had to fund themselves because they had parted ways with Decoy/Vinyl Solution. Perhaps it was the troubled times that spawned it, or perhaps because they were free agents for the first time in their career, but whatever the reasons behind it Sink unfurled a slightly delirious but nonetheless majestic sprawling rock album, capable of going from quiet introspection to rousing chest-beating choruses to quirky self-indulgence at the drop of a plectrum.

"One of the other bands on the label had beaten up a friend of ours," sighs Ed, regretfully, of their falling-out with Vinyl Solution. " I had a chat with them [the label], but they weren't prepared to kick this band off the books; they actually said they weren't the police and they basically resented the fact I'd even approached them about it…to which I replied, 'If you're going to have bands on your roster who go round beating people up, fuck this!' Which was a shame because we had Dale Griffin booked to produce the next album and everything…"

"And when we left Vinyl Solution, we didn't have enough money to pay him," Paul picks up the story, "so we had to tell him we couldn't do it and then we raised enough money ourselves for just the studio. We had to sleep in the studio for three weeks – Ed slept in the vocal booth! – and we didn't have anything decent to eat; we lived on Pot Noodles, I don't think we had any vegetables or vitamin C the whole time…"

Thankfully German label City Slang was more than pleased to pick the band up and seeing as they were one of the bigger independent labels in Europe at the time, things were looking up again for the industrious quartet – but the December 1991 tour of Europe, in support of the new album, was to be the last they would undertake as Sink.

"We'd already booked a European tour before striking the deal with City Slang, with about 20 gigs in Germany, because I guess we knew we'd always get someone to release it over there for us… The last ever Sink show was at the Fabrik in Hamburg, in December 1991, with the Frogs Of War, who were lovely people despite the dodgy name and a band that Andy Turner had talked us into taking out with us…"

So things had come full circle; quite literally in fact, with Andy Turner releasing the track 'Drainpipe Jane' as a single on his own – yes, you guessed it – Full Circle label to also coincide with the tour.

"It was a really good tour too," reminisces Ed. "I have some videos of some of the shows and we were rocking by then, playing really well together, an hour and a half every night, for 30 or 40 shows… We had our own sound engineer, Chris Yap and Dave Turner was our roadie and tuning all our guitars for us…we were like a machine…

"A really good friend of ours, Graham, came out for the first few weeks, to sell T-shirts and stuff. He was a massive Green Day fan and they were on tour at the same time, playing the same circuit. Graham was really excited that we might play with them, if our paths crossed, but we didn't…until a week after he went home, when we played with them in Poland!"

"We didn't just play with them – they were our support band," laughs Paul, incredulously. "But I'd contracted food poisoning in Switzerland a week earlier and ended up in hospital in southern Germany…"

Ed: "So we did Hungary and Poland with roadie Dave playing bass – it was lucky he was a bassist, he'd been playing for years – and we just did a stripped-down set, rather than cancel four or five shows. We chose the easiest 12 or 13 songs for him to learn and he spent hours on the drive from Germany to Budapest listening to them in the back of his van on his Walkman…

"And we did four or five shows with him and then this gig with Green Day arrived and, for whatever reason, it became very clear during the course of the day that they hated our guts! I went over to them at their merch stall after they played and said, 'That was great!' and told them all about Graham being a huge fan and having to fly home a week before we finally played with them and they completely blanked me. Then later, when we were loading out, they were really arsey and even their tour manager had a go at us. It was all really weird and left us totally nonplussed.

"Years later this book came out in Ireland, which was in part a history of this gig collective that we'd done a tour with over there. In it, this guy Niall's talking about how Green Day stayed at his house and pointedly took all the Sink stickers off his bass before they'd use it… so we didn't dream this all up and I have no idea what happened in Poland or why they would even be the slightest bit concerned about us, but we obviously did something to piss them off. Of course it wouldn't even be a story if they hadn't gone on to become so huge…"

The single for Full Circle was the final piece of Sink vinyl, although the band did record a third and final Peel session before they morphed into Big Ray, Christof Ellinghaus from City

Slang persuading the band to record a full-blown acoustic album ('Naked') which they all thought would be too much of a departure to go out as Sink, so the band changed their name before the album was released.

"He thought that would be a short cut to getting us out of the squats and onto the college circuit," admits Ed. "I guess we felt we'd taken Sink as far as we could and were open to a change, so we went ahead and did it, but it was probably a mistake looking back. Aside from anything else, it wasn't the kind of acoustic album Christof wanted and his distributors weren't behind it either. He was expecting a quirky, lightweight, pretend-country record, but we wrote a proper album, full of proper songs…"

"It was a punk-rock record but with acoustic guitars," offers Paul, proudly.

"What's even more frustrating is that I met up with Christof years later at a huge gig celebrating 20 years of City Slang, or something like that," remembers Ed. "He referred to 'Naked' as 'an undiscovered masterpiece', which was a bitter-sweet moment considering he was the guy who dropped us after we recorded it." So, Sink, uh, sank and from the ashes rose Big Ray, who after 'Naked' would go on to quietly garner an appreciative cult following and release 'You Get What You Deserve' in 1999 and 'Business Class' in 2001. Drummer John Howie moved back to Raleigh, NC and joined the very influential rock band Finger, before switching to guitar and vocals and fronting the seminal alt-country outfit, Two Dollar Pistols. He's currently back behind the kit playing for new Raleigh punk band the P-90s and simultaneously fronting a new alt-country band, John Howie Jr And The Rosewood Bluff.

Sadly, John's replacement, the irrepressible James Kermack, by then a father of two, died of a brain tumour in June 1992 after a long illness during which the tumour went undiagnosed for almost a year. After the demise of Sink, Ed Wenn formed 'a sloppy punk band', Chocolate, in 1993 with ex-Stupid, Wolfie Retard and John Ruscoe, who toured Europe and recorded several singles and an album for Out Of Step. After moving back to London in 1999, he formed K-Line who recorded three singles and an album for Boss Tuneage before splitting up in 2004. Since then he's played in You Disgust Me and Liquidman, before joining his old friend, Duncan Redmonds, in Billy No Mates in 2008. He's also been playing solo acoustic gigs since 2003 and continues to record and tour sporadically as Big Ray.

John Ruscoe played on the first two Big Ray albums then switched to drums for his stint in Chocolate. After moving back to London, he joined Indie popsters Mover, who signed to a major and did reasonably well, getting BBC Radio 1 daytime plays and tours of Japan, without breaking into the mainstream. He can usually be found in Cass McComb's touring band whenever he's in the UK, but mainly makes a living playing guitar in jazz pubs around the City.

Bassist Paul Duncan stayed with Ed through all of the subsequent Big Ray albums, as well as recording a solo album under the name, Iodine and joining a hardcore outfit, Rated R, for a couple of tours. He also played bass on the final Chocolate album before joining Ed in K-Line in 2000. Paul's country/rockabilly alter ego, Chicken Willie, can also be found playing chickenbilly songs at parties and Bar Mitzvahs…

"The Sink legacy as regards other bands and/or the punk scene in general is probably very small, because we were hardly million-sellers" admits Ed. "For whatever reason, though, there does seem to be a significantly larger crossover these days between punk and other forms of music, especially roots music. Back in 1988, I don't think there were too many punk/hardcore bands that included full-on country and blues numbers in their regular set list. We

Sink, Peel session, May 1990, by Neil Emery

probably bridged that small gap between DC hardcore and bands like the Replacements in that respect. Music seems to be less ghettoised these days and more open…that's probably a natural progression, but it would be nice to think that Sink had something to do with pushing that progression along a bit!"

SELECT DISCOGRAPHY:

7-inch:
'Mama Sink's Ugly Firstborn' (Poontang, 1989)
'On The Tracks, Feeling Blue' (Poontang, 1989)
'Don't Burn The Hook' (Decoy, 1990)
'Drainpipe Jane' (Full Circle, 1991)

MLPs:
'Old Man Snake And The Fat Black Pig' (Decoy, 1990)
'Mama Sink: The First Eighteen Years' (Decoy, 1990)

LPs:
'Another Love Triangle' (Decoy, 1990)
'Vega-Tables' (City Slang, 1991)

AT A GLANCE:
http://edwenn.com

WAT TYLER

Completely disposable yet strangely collectable and even quite good – on occasion – **Wat Tyler** could really have been in any of my first three books, having been in existence since the early Eighties, but the majority of their actual releases were in the Nineties, so here they are.

"Our first ever name was Malcolm And The Nasal Sprays," begins Sean Forbes, who would eventually become the drummer/vocalist of Wat Tyler. "But that was really early on. After that we became Four Minute Warning and the first gig was in my dad's garage in Cheddington and it was a Rock Against Rock gig! And whenever anyone new turned up, we started the whole set over again, so we ended up playing for about 10 hours… Smithy turned up and said he could play guitar, but we said, 'Just play bass for now…', so he played bass for 10 hours, having never heard any of the songs before – and 30 years later, we probably sound quite similar; we haven't got any better.

"That would have been 1979 and we did loads of demos…we were really righteous…and we changed into Wat Tyler about 1982 or 1983, when the Four Minute Warning drummer Wimp decided he was going to live in Spain, so Smithy went over to guitar and Tuck went from guitar to bass. I ended up playing drums…but we were still really righteous! We always said that if we got too good on our instruments, we'd swap around again, but we never did…

"Wimp had been learning about Wat Tyler at school, so we changed the name to that; he led a peasants' revolt in 1381 and he got beheaded – he was rubbish! Which is why it was such an apt name for us, because he had all this potential to do something but in the end he was no good at it!

And then I don't know quite what happened, but we went from being angry and righteous and turned into a raving comedy band! I think it was 'cos no-one liked us and we started mucking around a bit and people used to laugh and feel a bit sorry for us and eventually no-one still liked us, but at least they knew who we were…"

"I went to school with [bassist] Tuck, at the Wing Secondary School," recalls guitarist Smithy of those early years. "Sean is a year or two younger and went to Aylesbury Grammar School; I met him and Wimp [the band's first drummer] through Tuck. Before I knew Tuck, my primary school played his primary school at football and we stuffed them; Tuck says he remembers me having a broken arm and being smarmy, but I don't remember that! Me and Tuck were in the same French class when we arrived at secondary school; he was written down on all the registers as Martin Tucker, even though his name is Simon – he had got mixed up with Martin Shillingford! – and in all of the classes, he said 'Simon, actually…' to all of the teachers. I called him Simon Actually for the whole of the first year…

"Anyway, I formed a dreadful heavy-metal/prog-rock band called Heathen's Arch (yes, I know!) and asked Tuck and Wimp to play bass and drums. Heathen's Arch, Four Minute Warning and Asmodeus used to gig a lot in the village halls in Buckinghamshire, all around Cheddington and Stewkley where we lived. I thought Four Minute Warning were a bit shit and that Heathen's Arch were much better…but both were shit in retrospect. Since Tuck and Wimp were in both Four Minute Warning and Heathen's Arch, we had a lot of overlap. When Mole, the bass player, left Four Minute Warning, I joined on bass; we continued to gig as the two separate bands, but I spent more time playing with Four Minute Warning."

Soon after moving to London, the band played their first gig as Wat Tyler ("I can't remember anything about it," smirks Sean. "But it was almost certainly bad…!"), before recording several demos and eventually releasing their 'Contemporary Farming Issues' single in 1989. Featuring five tracks of lo-fi tomfoolery, 'No ID' is actually a decent Oi! song and 'We Pledge Our Allegiance To Satan' a throwaway but amusing heavy metal pastiche, but it's 'Hops And Barley' that makes this single, a genuine little classic that has been covered countless times since by the likes of Leatherface and UK Subs.

"We were playing a few regular thankless gigs in London," recalls Smithy. "At one afternoon gig, in Islington, I think, very few people turned up so we just mucked about and played loads of terrible cover versions of rock songs (as per Heathen's Arch)…and people found it funny. That gave us the confidence to fuck about and make jokes when we played and I think that was the first real Wat Tyler gig in the sense that we found our niche that day. It made up for our pretty poor musical skill…we could now get away with it by trying to make people laugh.

"I had always regarded bands that had recorded their music and released it on vinyl with awe," he adds, on the subject of the first EP. "So it felt amazing to make our own single and I still think that 'Hops And Barley' and 'We Pledge Our Allegiance to Satan' are two of our best songs. The other feeling I got was one of anti-climax… When I realised that cunts like us could make a record, it demystified the process a bit and I remember thinking, after that, that making a record was no big deal and a band was not necessarily good just because they had made a record…"

The single was promoted by a UK tour with Snuff and by the time they returned home two weeks later, there wasn't a single copy left of the first pressing. "We just jumped in a car," says Sean. "We didn't have any gear…we never owned any gear, in fact; I've never even owned a pair of drumsticks in my life. It's a bit embarrassing really, going up to another band's drummer and saying, 'Mind if I borrow your drums?' and they're like, 'Yeah, that's alright…' 'And your cymbals?' And they're like, 'Uh, okay, that's cool…' 'You haven't got any drumsticks, have you?' But I never thought of myself as a drummer, which was a bit stupid, because some years we'd play 50 gigs, so I suppose it was incredibly rude to keep asking to borrow everything, but you don't really think about it like that when you're young… We were sometimes the touring headline band, borrowing off the local supports – which made it even more embarrassing!"

The band's first LP, 'Bavarian Drinking Songs', was actually recorded in two halves, side A recorded during September '88 and originally intended for a split LP on Wetspots Records with Idiot Strength and side B recorded during July '89, when it was realised the split was never going to happen and Meantime Records suggested they record some more material and make it a full album. It was promoted with the first of many European tours.

"We've been to Germany so many times, I can virtually speak German," reckons Sean. "But the first ever gig we did abroad was in Bavaria; just 'cos our album was called 'Bavarian Drinking Songs', someone actually thought it *was* Bavarian drinking songs! So we got taken to this big beer festival in Passau and we played with this German clown called Jango Edwards; he was making all these jokes in German and his drummer would actually do a little roll after each punchline! Anyway, they hated our fucking guts…it was raining and Smithy and Tuck were so drunk, they were fighting each other in the mud… It was horrible."

Wat Tyler rehearsal

Wat Tyler

Wat Tyler... not the most serious band in this book

The 'Appetite For Axl' 10-inch followed next, another demented 12-song effort, pitched somewhere between Rudimentary Peni and Altered Images (!), complete with an adult-rated cover of 'The Smurf Song' and a brilliant neo-thrash anthem in the shape of 'Violent Precinct'; not only does it feature some of the most hilarious cover art you're ever likely to see (depicting the Guns'n'Roses frontman, Axl Rose, being triple penetrated by the members of Wat Tyler!), but there was a limited version of 100 copies that, thanks to a mis-press at the Czech pressing plant, came with an additional 10-inch featuring the wrong songs (all of them already released on the first single and LP). Rather than bin them, Wat Tyler decided to use the erroneous records to create a pointless limited edition for the hell of it.

Smithy still rates it as his favourite Wat Tyler release: "There's tons of tracks, some of them funny – all of them a fucking shambles. It was great fun to record [over one weekend in Yeovil at the Ice House] and was at a time when we were gigging a lot and able to play the songs live. A lot of the songs were actually made up onstage during gigs…usually when we were taking the piss out of other bands ('Why?') or the annoying pop songs of the day ('Brostitute'). It also has songs by all of us on it; it's nice to have a mix of different styles on the same album, so we always go with each other's ideas and everybody adds a bit to each. Sean's indie songs are largely pap; my metal ones are definitely better…and Tuck's beer/ football/love songs are different again. Occasionally I would make up a poppy one and Sean or Tuck would write a more metally one, but the common thing is that none of us are really competent enough to make them sound good. It would be nice to hear some of them done by a proper band!"

After a split double 7-inch with the mighty Leatherface for Clawfist (the fifteenth in their 'Singles Club' series, where Smithy's above wish came true and each band covered two songs from the other, Wat Tyler choosing 'Discipline' and 'Not Superstitious' and Leatherface opting for 'Hops And Barley' and 'A Public House'), 1993 saw the release of 'Sexless' on Damaged Goods, a ruthless spoof of Madonna's *Sex* book that would become the band's best-selling release by far…for all the wrong reasons!

"We're not the most handsome of men," laughs Sean, "and the three of us together is quite gruesome – but we got our cocks out and the record sold 10,000 copies! Which was a lot of records at the time… But no-one actually listened to it, they were all too busy laughing at the pictures…

"And when that came out there was a full page in the *Sunday Sport* about it. All the national papers offered to do pieces, all the really tacky ones anyway, but in the end we decided to go with the worst one. They asked if we wanted to be interviewed for it, but we were like, 'What's the point? You'll just write what you want…so go ahead, write whatever you want!' To which they said, 'Okay, we will!' And they did: that Madonna was really angry about it and her lawyers were going to get in touch… They printed three or four of the pictures, so we had a full page out of 'em. So, as you can see, I'm probably too famous for your book…er, where do I send the invoice for my time?"

A split single with Muck Giovanett for Gold Und Rosen that featured four tracks recorded live at the Hamburg Fabrik was released in late 1993, entitled 'There's People On The Pitch, They Think It's Over…It Is Now!'

"It's weird," ponders Sean. "We were really popular in Germany and the Germans aren't known for their sense of humour. But although we headlined the Fabrik, we didn't fill it – I want you to know that! And the guy that booked us there, Jens, loved us so much he asked us to fly out and play at his dog's funeral… apparently his dog was a massive, massive Wat Tyler fan!"

"I have always found the Germans I know very witty and with a great sense of humour," retorts Smithy. "There are no taboos with the jokes… Second World War jokes are surprisingly a favourite. I think we did okay in Germany because the German government used to put loads of money into the arts and into youth clubs and that money was accessible by well-organised youth groups. This meant that punks in different towns could use some of the 'arts' money allocated to the town to put on gigs – so it was always easy to tour in Germany. The other thing that might have helped us is that German bands at the time (*most* punk bands, in fact) were very serious, technically gifted and with a political message. We were a fucking shambles and I guess some people found that refreshing…!"

After the 'Operation Ivy And Don Brennan' single for Sean's own Rugger Bugger Records in 1994 (inspired by UK soap opera *Coronation Street* and backed by the hilarious 'Rude Girl'), Wat Tyler signed to Lookout! in the US, who released the 'I Wanna Be Billie Joe' 7-inch and the 'Tummy' LP, which, Sean states proudly, was "the third worst selling release on the label!" Despite all that, an American tour was a resounding success – even if that *was* because of the bands they were playing with actually having a fanbase there.

"America was a fantastic experience," declares Smithy, sounding somewhat surprised himself. "Again we were amazed that people would pay for us to go there to play, because, apart from a few in-the-know punkers, America didn't really know what to make of us. They were used to punk bands being pretty good and were a bit bemused by us being so shit and just arsing about on stage instead of playing songs. They were probably as surprised that anyone would pay us to go over there as we were! The way gigs were run was also odd: you either played 'all-age' gigs which were alcohol-free and only kids turned up, or adult gigs where very few punks turned up and you played to a bunch of pissed-up rockers, so it was all a very different experience. We toured with J-Church who had a good West Coast following, so the gigs were fairly well attended. We played in San Diego with Tanner and J-Church at a venue that Supergrass had played the week before to only nine people! So it was a funny old time…"

"Well, we were friends with Green Day," adds Sean, of the inspiration behind their '… Billie Joe' single, about the Green Day vocalist. "We played with them quite a few times; they even spent half of one Christmas with me in Gipsy Hill…then they went to Bath in the afternoon. That would have been 1991. And we played their first ever London gig at Rails, in Euston Station, with Jailcell Recipes opening up. Green Day were a good band…they still *are* a good band, but they were a good band back then as well; you could always see they were going to be massive. And they weren't little American whingers; they just got on with it. I was actually the Easter Bunny in their nativity play up in Wigan [when Green Day held a spoof nativity before their 21 December 1991 show at the Wigan Den, which the band themselves rate in their Top 10 Green Day shows]… See, told you I was famous! *Kerrang!* keep e-mailing me to get a quote about that – and I never give one… I mean, who cares?"

A dizzying slew of throwaway vinyl releases followed during the mid Nineties, including splits with J-Church, Thatcher On Acid and Mambo Taxi, most of them limited pressings and all inspired by things the band found amusing.

"I mean we've known each other since we were kids," explains Sean. "I've been mates with Smithy since I was eight years old and we don't speak for years, but it doesn't matter because there's this connection there. And that's what it was like in the band too... You know when you make a joke in the pub about doing something, but it shouldn't really ever happen? We were the kind of band that made those things happen! We were the people that followed it through! 'Wouldn't it be funny if...?'

"There were loads of things we didn't do as well... We wanted to do 'Who Is Wat Tyler?' We were going to do three separate solo singles to sell, with a form inside, asking 'Who is your favourite member of Wat Tyler?' To prove who really was Wat Tyler once and for all! And we wanted to do a single with all our dads playing, called 'The Fathers Of Wat Tyler', but Tuck's dad died before we could get to do it. And we had all these other stupid ideas; it was never-ending! Smithy is one of the funniest men you'll ever meet...

"But yeah, Wat Tyler was all about other people's stuff and our response to it. Like we did a single under the name of the Brothers Wat, a Gary Glitter song... 'Do you wanna be in my gang? No, fuck off, you're a paedo...!' [laughs] It got reviewed in the *NME* where they said, 'This will be funny, IF he's found guilty...' So when he *was* found guilty, we sent them a letter saying, 'It's now funny!'

We got 0/10 in the *NME* for one of our albums; they said it was 'pompous, badly-played pub rock...' And Smithy wrote them a letter saying we'd be angry if it wasn't so true! But getting 0 out of 10 was brilliant, a career high! Two days later, we did a gig and read the review out before we started and everyone was cheering every time they slagged us off..."

Only 86 copies were pressed – *with a little sleeve*, no less! – of 'The Little People' 7-inch, an EP that compiled all of the band's 'Little People' songs (another creation of Smithy's demented imagination...) onto one single; the 'Ability Stinks: Shit Series' was a five-LP box set featuring all the band's worse out-takes (limited to just 40 copies!) and then the 'Tour Only' EP which was released by Suspect Device to coincide with a UK tour alongside J-Church boasted, ahem, individual handmade covers...

"Well, Suspect Device ran out of money," laughs Sean, "and the pressing plant had given him the records in these old sleeves, so he thought, 'Fuck it!' and put them out like that and we sold them all on tour. Most of the sleeves were from Menswear singles... I mean, our standards are low, so anything went and we just stuck stickers over them! All sorts of chaos went on with Wat Tyler... But that's how I am about music – I care enough...but not too much. And I always want it all available...complete transparency, with all the mistakes... put it all out there.

"People just kept asking us to do things and we had this never-ending ability to record absolute bullshit!" he explains, of their seemingly inhuman prolificacy. "We'd go in the studio to rehearse one day before we were recording and we'd have a list of things we needed to do: Damaged Goods single, Boss Tuneage compilation, random Czech compilation...and we'd just work our way through it all. Actually we've just had a song released on some compilation, a cover we recorded of this Slovenian band, CZD, we'd never even heard of...! We were asked to go on this tribute album and thought, 'Brilliant!' so Smithy learnt a bit of Slovenian and we chose a random song and actually recorded it about 10 years ago. But that shows we were just up for anything and the more inappropriate it was, the more we wanted to do it."

Hence songs like 'Teletubbies', 'Spice Girls' and 'Michael Bolton's Hair' on 1999's brilliant (yes, really, if you check your sense of propriety at the door) 'Fat Of The Band' CD. In fact, it's full of well-observed comedy and wonderfully quirky tunes – be assured you won't hear another album quite like it.

"But my favourite Wat Tyler record was when we did a joke band that was all of us with Julie from Dan and Blyth Power singing and we did a fake indie pop record under the name Eggplant," reckons Sean. "We got £2,000 to record that, but did it in two days and kept the change for spending money in America. Smithy hated indie music; we'd had an argument about who wrote better songs... I said I wrote better indie songs and he said he wrote better heavy-metal songs, so we had a challenge where we'd make up fake names and send our songs away to labels to see who could get signed first.

"I had three offers from labels wanting to release my indie songs with this girl singing and he didn't get any response at all...I don't think he actually sent anything away in the first place! But even if he had done, it wouldn't have happened; his songs are rubbish! He loves heavy metal so much he's the only man I know who bemoaned Reading turning from a heavy-metal festival to a punk-rock festival...

"I remember a kid came up to him in America and asked him what record he'd just bought and he took this Wishbone Ash album out of the bag, saying he'd been looking for it for years. This kid was crushed 'cos he didn't know who they were!"

A Slovenian festival, 'No Border Jam', with anarcho-punks Cress inspired the bonkers 'Mr Crust' 7-inch in 2000, but it was to be the final proper release for the band, although Sean insists they never officially split so can still be termed 'active'.

"We recorded a Cress song to the tune of Mr Funny from the Mr Men series," says Smithy. "My kids were very young at the time and listened to all this music and story tapes of the Mr Men and I thought, 'What would be the least appropriate soundtrack for the Cress lyrics: 'If you want to eat meat then eat it – it's your decision and you must live with it'?' And the Mr Funny tune seemed to fit the bill, so we made a Cress song around a Mr Funny tune and Mr Crust was born. And I think Jamie Hince [now Kate Moss's fiancé] drew the picture for the single cover...

"No, we never split, but our last CD was released in 2000 and we haven't recorded any new material since then – and only played gigs every couple of years – so 'active band' is a bit of a bold statement. Wat Tyler is not dead – just in an advanced state of near-hibernation! We might do a few more gigs, if the time and location seems right (the Snuff/Leatherface/ Sofahead/Wat Tyler gig at Camden Underworld in 2006 was fantastic fun), but I can't see us doing a retrospective of European folk songs or a new concept album any time soon..."

Nowadays Sean still plays with the immensely popular Hard Skin, the spoof Oi! band he started in the mid-Nineties (read on for more details!) and when not touring the world with them he still plots the downfall of the mainstream music industry from his secret lair behind the Rough Trade shops.

"It begins with 'S' and ends with 'it!'," he chuckles, when asked to comment on the Wat Tyler legacy. "But seriously, everywhere I go in Germany with Hard Skin, people tell me a Wat Tyler story, about something we did at some gig or other and I'm always like, 'Wow, did we *really* do that?' There isn't a legacy as such, but we seemed to touch a lot of people... in improper places perhaps! I don't think anyone cares that much and we definitely don't care, but it's been an absolute pleasure anyway..."

"I would just like us to be remembered as a band that didn't take itself too seriously, that hopefully provided people with some giggles," offers Smithy, by way of conclusion. "We couldn't play, but we tried to turn that to our advantage and it might have even influenced a few other hardcore bands to lighten up a bit too... But of course we will never know if that would have happened anyway.

"I am now a posh Professor working in climate change at the University of Aberdeen, a real pillar of society! I had never considered that playing with Wat Tyler had any bearing on my real life, but thinking about it, the fun I had with Wat Tyler allows me to be myself at work. We laugh a lot every day and I am very aware of my own limitations (as I was with Wat Tyler musically). I still like to try and make people laugh and this is equally helpful socially in science as it is in punk rock. So thanks for asking that question – I hadn't really thought about it but I think Wat Tyler has allowed me to become a better scientist!"

SELECT DISCOGRAPHY:

7-inch:
'Contemporary Farming Issues' (Rugger Bugger, 1989)
'Split' (Clawfist, 1992) – *split with Leatherface*
'Sexless' (Damaged Goods, 1993)
'They Call It Puppy Love' (Incognito, 1993)
'Operation Ivy And Don Brennan' (Rugger Bugger, 1994)
'I Wanna Be Billie Joe' (Lookout, 1994)
'Extra Shite Poos Explosion' (Suspect Device, 1994) – *split with J-Church*
'The Little People' (Rugger Bugger, 1996)
'Tour Only' (Suspect Device, 1997) – *split with J-Church*
'The Vicar And I' (Boss Tuneage, 1999)
'Mr Crust' (Rugger Bugger, 2000)

10-inch:
'Appetite For Axl' (Rugger Bugger, 1990)

LPs:
'Bavarian Drinking Songs' (Meantime, 1989)
'Yurp Thing' (Allied, 1994) – *split with Thatcher On Acid*
'Ability Stinks: The Shit Series' (Rugger Bugger, 2000) – *five-LP box-set, limited to 40 copies!*

CDs:
'I'm Forever Blowing Bubbles' (Rugger Bugger, 1992)
'Tummy' (Lookout, 1995)
'The Fat Of The Band' (Rugger Bugger, 1999)

AT A GLANCE:
If you want something you'll actually listen to over and over again, search out 'The Fat Of The Band'… If you want something that will just make you laugh, any of it/all of it.

HARD SKIN

And talking of laughing, one of the most enjoyable Oi! bands to emerge from the UK in the last 20 years, **Hard Skin** had their tongues firmly in their collective cheeks when they released 'Hard Nuts And Hard Cunts' on Helen Of Oi in 1996. Ironically for an album that satirised skinhead culture, it became acknowledged as a classic of the genre – the band proudly proclaiming themselves and rightly so, 'the new wave of close shave'! – and was subsequently licensed successfully around the world. "Hard Skin formed 'cos there was fuck all happening and we wanted to get birds, booze and beer," reckons bassist Fat Bob. "The three B's, know what I mean? It all started a long time ago…maybe 1993 or maybe some other year…It's all a bit vague, to tell you the truth, but our main inspiration for music is the Cockney Rejects and our main inspiration for lyrics is the Cockney Rejects. We don't try to look like them, though, as they are fat and old.

"We all knew each other from the pub, know what I mean? Fucking old school, mate. [Guitarist] Johnny Takeaway was a semi-professional darts player, Nipper was in Oi Polloi – but then every Jock has been in them – and I was in Arthur Lager, a semi-legendary Oi! band from Millwall from 1983, who released one single on No Secret records…"

If truth be known, Hard Skin feature ex-members of Wat Tyler and Thatcher On Acid who not only love Oi! music but have a wicked sense of humour. The resulting parody was so perfect it was embraced by street punks, skins and herberts everywhere and the band have been around the world several times on the back of what was a very clever, well-timed and brilliantly executed gag, their interviews to promote their various releases always convincingly conducted in character. And, all joking aside, often used to great effect to denounce the negative influence of right-wing politics in Oi! music.

"Clever? Fuck off!" scoffs Bob. "None of us have got an O-level between us…but Nipper is close to being a millionaire from his car-valeting business, Johnny works on the market selling spuds and beans and I'm fat for a living. Anyway, we *are* the best modern skinhead band and all the skins know that and just accept it!"

For all the talk of Nipper, the first Hard Skin drummer (who played on 'Hard Nuts…') was Nosher. "And the first Hard Skin gig was at the Cock Well Inn, Millwall," smirks Fat Bob. "It was recorded by Damaged Goods to release as a 'Live And Loud' album… was it any good? Are you 'aving a bubble ['bubble bath', having a laugh]? We woz fuckin' top banana, mate. It's true; shit always sinks and stinks and the cream goes to the top and we are the fuckin' cream."

With opener 'Oi Not Jobs' – and every other song on the album, to be honest – ably channelling the singalong aggro charm of classic Rejects and Sparrer and tracks like 'Beer And Fags' and 'Me And The Boys' so knowingly hilarious, 'Hard Nuts And Hard Cunts' *is* a skinhead classic. *Carry On Oi!* indeed. And rather similar in concept to Chumbawamba masquerading as Skin Disease with the track 'I'm Thick' for Garry Bushell's 'Back On The Streets' EP in 1982… but one hundred times better musically.

However it would be another eight years before a second album would materialise, but it was well worth the wait, because 'Same Meat, Different Gravy' – released by Household Name's one-off imprint Oi Sold Name in 2004 – was the most listenable Oi! album released in years. It had genuine crossover appeal for punks because all the violent posturing was for

Hard Skin... likely lads!

Hard Skin

Hard Skin, givin' it some

fun, ridiculously over-the-top anti-police songs like 'Copper Cunt' and 'Law And Order (Up Yer Arse)' gleefully rubbing shoulders with the sort of naive sexism ('Make My Tea' and 'She's A Right Sort') and directionless nihilism (the centre-spread of the CD booklet proclaiming 'At the end of the day, it's all bollocks!') that epitomised the original Oi! scene. Again the album was a runaway success and prompted international touring and several follow-up singles.

"The best gig we ever did was on a boat in Texas," reckons Bob. "We played bare-chested with our tats on full show and all the birds were dressed in bullet belts and bikinis…the rest really is unimportant, although Johnny Takeaway had to make a swift exit on a speedboat. The worst gig…? To tell you the truth, there's never been one; we've always been 100% on top of our game at every gig we play. We guarantee quality, every time.

"Captain Oi! does sad reissues," is the response when asked why Hard Skin can't get themselves a deal with a proper Oi! label. "We are new and we are the new breed and I don't think Captain Oi! can deal with that. We released a record on No Future, though: a gig-only 7-inch with [Canadian hardcore band] Fucked Up… the first bands in 22 years to do anything on that label, so stick that in your hippy pipe and smoke it."

While displaying the No Future logo and catalogue numbers, it's safe to say that said 7-inch wasn't an official No Future release, certainly not as far as anyone who used to be involved with No Future is aware of anyway. But that's the beauty of Hard Skin: totally irreverent and not afraid to make beefburgers of Holy Cows…while having a right ol' knees-up at the same time.

"Someone asked me what class Hard Skin were," concludes Fat Bob. "I answered, 'We *are* class!' I think that says everything you need to know, don't you? We still tour the world and elsewhere and 'Hard Nuts And Hard Cunts' has become *the* must-have album for those who love to glue sniff, fight, fuck and play the game of darts. We recently signed to Hellcat Records, too, so the only way for Hard Skin is… sideways."

SELECT DISCOGRAPHY:

7-inch:
'The Christmas Fisting EP' (Household Name, 2001) – *split with Southport and Capdown*
'We Are The Wankers' (Rudeness, 2006)
'Make My Tea' (Feral Ward, 2007)
'Split' (No Future, 2007) – *split with Fucked Up*
'These Are My People' (Snuffy Smile, 2010) – *split with Blotto*

LPs:
'Hard Nuts And Hard Cunts' (Helen Of Oi, 1996)
'Live And Loud! And Skinhead!' (Damaged Goods, 2002)
'Same Meat Different Gravy' (Oi Sold Name, 2004)
'Where The Fuckin Mic' (Fat Punk, 2009)

AT A GLANCE:
Just get the albums. Fucking brilliant.

KNUCKLEDUST

One of the few combos in the hardcore scene (and probably the general music scene as a whole) to have kept exactly the same line-up from their moment of inception right through to the present day, London's **Knuckledust** are one of the hardest/harshest sounding of all the UKHC bands, yet also some of the most likeable, down-to-earth geezers imaginable. Their ill-deserved reputation as a 'tuff-guy' hardcore act can only be attributed to their ferocious musical beat-downs, because they have been nothing but a positive influence on most of the people they've encountered over their 15-plus year existence.

That said, an image of vocalist Pierre Mendivil graces the cover of this very book because of all the bands contained herein, few are as armed with anger as Knuckledust.

"Anger drives us, definitely," agrees the quietly-spoken frontman. "And our music is the perfect vehicle for us to express our anger and frustration in a positive way. Our writing has always been kinda dark, but always trying to express something positive... We never set out to be political; we've just always written about what's in front of us."

"People don't realise that," agrees drummer Ray Bussey. "We always get lumped in with that tuff-guy scene, but we've never once written a song about beating people up! The majority of our songs are positive; Pierre writes about trying to improve things for the youth and we talk a lot about how fucked-up society is and how things could maybe move forward...

"The one thing we all have in common is that we grew up poor. We couldn't even afford our instruments, to be honest; I wanted a cymbal for Christmas and I couldn't have one, because my family couldn't afford stuff like that."

"My parents were always arguing," continues Pierre, with obvious regret. "All I really remember is them arguing, arguing, arguing...and then my old man killed himself. But I was making music by then and obviously there *was* a lot of anger there, waiting to come out."

The musical origins of the band are less intense, though, with Ray's first band being Hidden Reality, a youth-club band based in Beckton that also featured Knuckledust guitarist Wema Maduhu.

"It was a soul and funk covers band," he laughs. "We did James Brown songs and all sorts; it was the first time we'd picked up instruments and there were youth workers there all the time, encouraging kids to come off the street and play music. Wema was a bassist in that band – there were two bass-players, 13 singers, two keyboard-players, three guitarists and two drummers...but in the end that all whittled down to just me and Wema! And we'd got into metal about then anyway and thought, 'This is crap!' So we started doing Metallica and Slayer stuff instead.

"[Bassist] Nic [Baxter] was your average school metaller, a typical weirdo, this freak with long hair and a biker jacket; when we asked him if he could play anything, he said, 'Yeah, I'm a guitarist!' But he wasn't, he was rubbish. We knew him anyway from school and we got together at his mum and dad's house and started jamming. We eventually formed Uphold, with Danny Evans, who lived round our way but couldn't sing in time...and then we saw an advert in Selectadisc in London that said, 'Hardcore vocalist seeks band...' And that was how we met Pierre [in early 1996]."

"I was trying to start something with a couple of guys, one of them based in Reading," Pierre picks up the story. "But they wanted me to sing like Ray Cappo [from Youth Of Today and Shelter] and I wasn't really feeling that, you know? But I'd seen these [Uphold] guys at gigs; I distinctly remember seeing them at a Biohazard gig at the Forum and stuff. I kept seeing them at shows, but didn't know who they were, so it was kind of weird when they got in touch with me but it worked out well. They had all their shit together, having grown up with each other, so twice a week I started travelling down to east London for practices..."

Pierre brought with him the new band name (apparently so-called because he hadn't been in a fight for so long his knuckles were at last collecting dust...) and Knuckledust made their live debut during October 1996 supporting Stampin' Ground at the Laurel Tree in Camden (Vehemence and FLS were also on the bill), their aggressive energy onstage instantly aligning them with the then-emerging new London hardcore scene.

"I was going to shows that were billed as 'London Hardcore', where bands like the Couch Potatoes were playing, but I was expecting something a bit harder and maybe more New York-influenced," admits Pierre. "I found it a bit depressing sometimes, sitting through all these gigs and none of the bands were doing it for me or representing me. Over the years, we got to know some of the people in some of those bands; they were all good kids and some of them did end up playing some harder stuff."

"Mmmm, there *was* a London hardcore scene," offers Ray, carefully. "But nobody knew each other at the time. We didn't even know what we really liked then either. We knew we liked SOIA and Madball and stuff, but from our own country, we had no idea what we liked at that stage. We respected the likes of Exploited and Discharge and that style of hardcore, but when we saw Stampin' Ground on the Crossover tour and Consumed playing with Downset, we thought, 'This is it, this is where we fit in!' Every big show you went to then, there would be Above All or Understand opening up as well..."

"It was also a dancing thing for us," adds Pierre, "'cos when we were young we were all about dancing crazy and causing havoc and shit...not hurting people or anything, but just getting buck wild, that was all part of the fun for us. And we thought, 'Let's write some songs to set it off like this!' You know?"

"And it did seem like everyone was an outcast then as well," continues Ray. "It might sound corny, but it didn't matter what you looked like or what you wore, everybody at those shows hated everyone that was outside of those shows. There wasn't an internet; you could only hear these bands if you went to the gigs or went to the specialist music shops.

"Me and Nic would sometimes go up the Ruskin Arms on a Friday night, but we wouldn't get too drunk because we'd have to be up early the following morning to get up Rough Trade before everyone bought all the hardcore CDs! That was the magic of it all, hunting out stuff you liked. We'd buy stuff by bands we'd never heard of just because they were thanked on some other CD that we liked. Sometimes you'd buy a pile of crap, but because you'd spent all your money on it you'd get into that band anyway; you had no choice, you now owned the CD and you couldn't afford any more for a bit, so you'd play it over and over."

Soon hooking up with Liverpool label Days Of Fury, once they started trading gigs with other UKHC bands and getting out of London regularly, Knuckledust issued the seven-track 'London Hardcore' MCD in 1997, a rampant debut that gave a huge nod to the NYHC scene of the late Eighties while maintaining a distinctly gnarly UK edge to proceedings. The band looked unique as well, at least for a UKHC band anyway, a multi-racial line-up that not only featured a seven-foot-tall black guy on guitar but a mohawked punk-rocker on bass. With their aggrocore beatdowns complemented by plenty of street-wise anthems, it was obvious

Knuckledust, by Naki

Knuckledust, Nick and Wema, by Naki

Knuckledust, outside the
Red Eye, by Naki

even then that Knuckledust had potential to crossover.

"We didn't have a clue about nothing," laughs Pierre. "We had *no* idea about recording; it was the first time we went in a proper studio with a proper engineer…"

"We used to sit in a room and play music," says Ray. "That's how we did it. That whole MCD was recorded live, all of us in one room together. Everything else, we were so green about it all…but I remember doing it and when I listen to it, I remember the fun of it, the excitement and I can still hear that energy. The songs are faster than they should be, there's mistakes… All our mates came down from the pub to do backing vocals…it's all in there."

A split 7-inch with Manchester band Area Effect was released by Black Up, which was Tom Brandon from Ninebar's label that eventually evolved into Rucktion, a hardcore label ran by Tom and Pierre that is still going strong today, with over 40 releases to its name. And loosely based around Knuckledust, Ninebar and Rucktion, the LBU crew emerged, as did London's grossly-exaggerated reputation for violence at hardcore shows.

"Thing is, when these people came down to London, it was for bigger bands," sighs Pierre. "And those shows attracted a lot of people that weren't normally at the underground London hardcore shows. So when something did erupt, it was usually caused by someone who we'd never even seen at a regular hardcore show before, but people would still say, 'Oh, it's just London! Thirty people beating up one guy…' And those people who did that were not involved in the London hardcore scene in any positive meaningful way.

"There was a gig in Northampton once," recalls Ray ruefully, "and a kid came in and sprayed 'LBU' on the wall; the venue went mental at me and basically banned Knuckledust from there forever…and none of us had ever seen that kid before in our lives! He got thrown out of the venue, but he never spoke to me after, before, or during that gig! I've never seen him since either… Yet that incident was blamed on us and it had absolutely nothing to do with us or anyone we knew."

"Before the LBU, there was the Northern Wolfpack, the 151 Crew, the H8000 crew and they had more of that shit going on than us," reasons Pierre. "But no-one hated on them! There was a couple of fights at their shows, as there was at ours and a couple of people got hurt… but then the internet came about and it got blown out of all proportion. Next thing we knew, we were apparently driving around London pulling guns on kids and stuff! And obviously we didn't say, 'No, we don't do that'; we just sat back and laughed at them all."

Ray: "You'd get 400 posts about someone getting a slap at a gig! In the old days, people got slapped at gigs all the time… if someone goes to a gig and gets drunk and starts acting like an idiot, they're gonna get a slap – whether you're 'LBU' or not, anyone would get a slap, even at a regular music show. But Pierre used to get the blame for all sorts of stuff.. He even got blamed for smashing a wall at a venue in Wolverhampton when he wasn't even there – it was Stu from Public Disturbance!

But everyone who knows us and knows Ninebar, they know that's not what we're about. And it started out as these guys booking shows for bands who no-one else would book a show for and putting out CDs for bands that no-one else would put out CDs by… Now that all the hype and the crap has died down, that's what it still is. Now everybody has left, the crux of it is still there – that's what it is and that's what it always was…but they'll be back, I'm sure, a new bunch of idiots for us to contend with for the next 10 years. But that is the internet, I'm afraidand in the end, I stopped going on there… The message boards were a waste of time, just people trying to get a rise out of everybody."

"As for Rucktion, they've still got the same ethic they always had: making bands, not taking bands…they won't release anyone who's already signed. They'll help a band out with their first release…and a lot of the bands like Six Foot Ditch and TRC have gone onto bigger labels, doing bigger things. But Rucktion would never approach a band on, say, Goodlife and ask to put their next record out; it's always about a band's first release and sometimes their second as well…there's no re-releases, no moneyspinners…"

After a mini-tour of France in '97 courtesy of Herve from Gundog, Knuckledust appeared at 1998's Evilfest, an ambitious hardcore all-dayer at the London LA2 that also featured Stampin' Ground, Liar, Congress and Stormcore and was organised by scene stalwart Lil from Household Name Records. A rough-as-assholes live Knuckledust 7-inch was issued by HHN soon after the event and paved the way for a split MCD with Brooklyn's hard-working Indecision. A split MCD followed with Stampin' Ground for Blackfish Records and then Blackfish released the band's first album, 'Time Won't Heal This'. While an undeniably potent full length, literally dripping with intensity, much like the previous KD recordings before it, 'Time Won't Heal This' didn't enjoy the best production and it wasn't until 2004's 'Universal Struggle' for Dutch label GSR that Knuckledust finally captured the primal power of their live assault.

"Every detail of that record got picked on," remembers Ray, of the album, recorded with Tue Madsen at Antfarm Studios in Denmark. "Every vocal got pulled apart, every guitar riff got scrutinised… It was agony to make, but I thought the end result was the best album we've done. The songs aren't the best, but the recording and the energy is – because we'd learnt a lot from all our previous fuck-ups. It only took us seven years to get our shit together! And we took a lot of time to do everything right…a day to set up the drums, a day to record them…"

"Tue was a big help," adds Pierre. "He approached things very differently to how we'd recorded before and he was almost like a fifth member of the band. He had a lot of new ideas about how we could do stuff…that was our first album for Theo and GSR and we'd put out a lot of crap, so it was important we got it right. And GSR put up a lot of money for us, so we didn't want to let them down."

Since joining forces with Theo, Knuckledust have grown immensely in popularity in Europe, especially France where they first toured under their own steam in '97 and GSR released their 'Promises Comfort Fools' album in 2007. At the time of writing, the band's fourth album is finally due out on the label, tentatively entitled 'Bluffs, Lies And Alibis'.

"We've stayed with Theo for so long because it works so well," explains Ray. "He manages us as well now and if it wasn't for Theo, we wouldn't still be doing it… I wouldn't be doing it all like I used to anyway. When we go on tour in Europe now, we'll drive to Calais in a car and he'll meet us in the van, with all the merch…he drives us and manages us and his wife sells the merch… He takes 15% of everything and we're happy with that. We put our full trust in him and he keeps us updated with everything every month… So for the new album, there was no question who we were going to do it with…straightaway it was, 'Let's speak to Theo!'"

"We don't want to push it in any major direction or anything," agrees Pierre. "We just wanna play music and have this outlet for our stuff. You don't make money off CDs these days anyway and we just want to work with someone who knows us inside out. We're not interested in fishing around for another label who'll put more money into us or anything…

"But yeah, France is always great for us; every time we tour Europe, we go through France, whereas most bands just go straight to Germany and back. We always, *always* get stopped by the police in France and there's never just one or two of them, it's always 10 of them, with guns and everything. But I remember we got stopped and searched in Calais once and they were taking all the bags out…taking our jackets off… Then this cop finds a Blood For Blood CD in the door and he was like, 'Ah, Blood For Blood, these guys are my favourite band!' And then he saw all the Knuckledust stickers on our stuff and he was like, 'Ah, you like these guys?' And we all looked at each other and went, 'We *are* these guys!' And he called the whole thing off, put all the stuff back in the car and went! I'd never seen anything like it… I thought, 'We've got a song on one of our CDs about killing policemen…and this guy likes the band?'"

With the time between their releases now reaching near-epic Metallica/Guns N'Roses lengths, one could be forgiven for thinking that Knuckledust were easing off the gas pedal but the truth of it is, they're still booking DIY shows and running Rucktion, while Ray also plays with popular Oi! band Argy Bargy and Pierre moonlights in Maldito and both Pierre and Wema have recently become fathers. They also like to take their sweet time to write their material.

But, as Ray points out, "So many bands rush out albums just so they can go and play all the European festivals and you can sense it, there's no feeling in the music; the releases have been thrown together so they can hit the road. Mind you, I think there was a bit of that with our last album, 'Promises Comfort Fools'; it had a release date before we'd even finished writing it and we were writing lyrics the night before we were recording some songs. But I hated working like that and won't ever work like that again; that's why there's been five years since that record came out.

"We've had all the arguments that other bands have, but we work through it all," he ponders, as to just why their line-up is so stable. "Because we never had a plan, never had a goal. Some bands set their sights way too high…and then good bands break up because they don't achieve their goal. We played with a band recently who were really pissed off because there was no pit… I told them, 'When we started playing, there were no *kids!*' And they were talking about no pit! We played gigs in front of a crusty with a dog, who stood there sticking his fingers up at us…and these kids were moaning because the place wasn't going off to them? Fair play to them if they manage to skip all that shit – sleeping in the back of vans and stuff – but for me, that was what gave it all character. I hated it at the time, but when you think back on it, it was the time of our lives. I won't sleep on floors these days; I'm 35 years old and my back will play up! Besides, I've got credit now, so I'd just book into a hotel!"

"Just London hardcore, through and through, mate," concludes Pierre, when asked how he would like Knuckledust to be remembered in years to come. "This band is a part of me; I can't remember a time when I wasn't in Knuckledust, y'know? I look back at what we've done and yeah, I've got a kid and a wife and everything, but it's me, it's a part of me and I can't ever stop doing it. I wouldn't know how to."

Ray: "And I'd like us remembered as a band that had the same ethic from the day we started 'til the day we died…there's no plans to die just yet, of course, but you know what I mean. No matter what other people read into it, no matter what agendas other people tried to attach to it, the four people who were in it knew what it was about."

SELECT DISCOGRAPHY:

7-inch:
'Split' (Black Up, 1997) – *split with Area Effect*
'In Yer Boat!' (Household Name, 1998)

MCDs:
'London Hardcore' (Days Of Fury, 1997)
'Smash Tradition' (Household Name', 1998) – *split with Indecision*
'The Dark Side vs The East Side' (Blackfish, 1999) – *split with Stampin' Ground*
'Together We Stand, Divided We Brawl' (Blackfish, 2001) – *split with Unite*

LPs:
'Time Won't Heal This' (Blackfish, 2000)
'Universal Struggle' (GSR, 2004)
'Promises Comfort Fools' (GSR, 2007)

AT A GLANCE:
2007's 'Dustography' double-CD compilation features 50 songs from the band's pre-GSR period. Essential.

CHINEAPPLE PUNX

As the name might suggest, the **Chineapple Punx** weren't the most serious punk band to emerge from the UK during the Nineties… In fact, they were downright daft, fuelled by mischief and juvenile humour, most of their gigs ending in some form of good-natured chaos. That said, they penned several great tunes, released some undeniably energetic records and for every comedy cover song they played there was a serious song about genetically modified foods, racist boneheads and, er, drinking.

Formed one drunken Saturday afternoon during 1994 in the Iron Horse pub, Amersham, the first line-up of the Punx featured Alan 'Growbag' Marshall on vocals, Graham 'Frankie Slapcabbage' Badcock on guitar, Chris 'Flurpy Bumpickle' on bass and Paul 'Uncle Creaky' Bayes on drums.

"I think we were all a bit bored of hearing the same type of bands," reckons Alan. "Although we certainly shared a lot of the politics of bands we grew up listening to, they all seemed a bit too serious. As with our previous bands we wanted to have a laugh as well – involve our anarchist beliefs but take the piss a bit and entertain ourselves really. Paul thought of the name and our senses of humour did the rest…"

"The first time any of us met was at the local Polish Club when Alan's band of the time, Suck Not Blow, ["A sadly regrettable load of bollocks," interjects Alan] didn't have a drummer," claims Paul. "Someone said I'd been in bands before [DIY Lobotomy and Tea Bag Alley] and introduced us; I played a child's drumkit that our mate had to sit on top of to stop it falling off the stage. And if it wasn't for that chance meeting, the rest might never have happened…"

"Me and Graham shared a flat at the time with a crazy heavy-metal dude called Steve," continues Alan. "It was total chaos like 'The Young Ones', but Graham played guitar and shared a love of punk and poo jokes, so he was a natural choice. We all knocked about together and had been in any number of bands with transient line-ups and questionable talent, mostly late-Eighties thrash and noise stuff: Taddish McRadish, WANK, Happy Cow, Lump Hammer, Having A Baby, etc. Chineapple Punx was just the first time we were all in the same space at the same time!"

"You know, I'm not exactly sure how we all met," ponders Chris. "I just know that there had been many moments of hilarity between us before the band was formed. The Wycombe and Amersham music/drinking scenes crossed paths regularly, so we all got to see each other's bands and basically enjoy ourselves. I'd see them on Wycombe piss'ead coach trips to the seaside and at gigs down the Irish Club in Wycombe and discos at the Iron Horse in Amersham. I'd recently finished a long stint with a band called Blossom [including ex-members of Chainsaw Enema], who played this spooky fairground ska/punk while dressed as clowns and I'd spent a short time in an industrial band called Overdog."

"I guess there were lots of bands about but no-one big," continues Alan, of the Amersham/High Wycombe scene that spawned them. "We had a great local scene of drunken youth-club noise; Social Dandruff, Anal Yam, Rabid Cat Flaps and Chainsaw Enema all just made an unholy racket to piss off the neighbours. Chineapple Punx sort of developed this weird mix of Oi!, anarcho and thrash, a healthy dose of both the Riot City and Manic Ears type stuff. We all just liked punk in general, I think; there was no conscious musical direction.

"Lyrically I was really inspired by Doctor And The Crippens, Stupids, Half Man Half Biscuit… I couldn't write serious stuff, it was too hard, so abstract surreal stuff started to creep in to fill the gaps. I've always thought that making jokes about serious issues is the best way of disarming people. You can't hit someone who's saying you are a wanker if they are brandishing a rubber chicken at the same time. It just makes you look like an even bigger wanker!"

The Punx were soon playing their first gig, at the Roundabout Pub in High Wycombe and it was a suitably manic affair. Doog Tidswell, who would become the band's bassist from 1996 onwards, remembers it well. "I was in the crowd and it was vaguely organised mayhem; the audience were truly an essential part of the gig – this bloke was stripping off and chucking his clothes at the band – but in addition the band were actively involving the crowd. I had a TV shell on my head and had to impersonate a TV gardener to win a prize (I did Percy Thrower crying over the *Blue Peter* garden, in case you're wondering…) and you could even win a fiver… although this would have involved pissing yourself onstage. Our mate Pus tried it, but was gutted to find he'd just been to the loo and had nothing left to give. I'd never seen such an entertaining band before and I was hooked from that point, never missing a Chineapples gig…"

"That gig gave us the best review I have personally ever had," laughs Chris. "The local paper wrote, 'Worst band I have ever seen!' We were all very pleased and immediately placed the review in our scrapbook for posterity."

The Chineapple Punx wasted no time recording their first demo "In a studio in a bloke's garden in Marlow," the seven-track 'Green Suede Head', which pitched itself stylistically somewhere between GBH, the Test Tube Babies and Conflict, although a puerile rendition of 'The Wheels On The Bus' and a misguided-but-fun cover of the Osmonds' 'Crazy Horses' left the listener in no doubt that this was a band that weren't out to change the world.

The following year (1996) saw the band return to the same studio to record three songs for a split 7-inch with Ciderfex, which they released on their own Duel Cabbageway Records. Blessed with a raw, distorted sound, it saw the Punx leaning more towards the 'UK82' sound of Chaos UK and Disorder. And again, politics and idiocy went hand-in-hand, with 'Dig For Freedom', about growing your own food, rubbing shoulders with the woefully dim-witted 'Our Friend Arthur'.

"We all agree that that 7-inch is the best thing we did for sheer noisiness," says Alan. "How Graham got that guitar sound we still don't know; it's got a real crust-type edge to it. And yes, I suppose in hindsight that 'Our Friend Arthur' is indefensible. Arthur was the owner of the local Chinese takeaway, who really did go off on one in a spiel of breakneck Cantonese when he got stressed out [the song features impersonations of these outbursts]. He was a great guy and we gave him a test pressing of the single which he hung on the wall…"

Having some vinyl out there, getting reviewed in fanzines around the country, led to the Punx playing further and further afield and befriending such like-minded bands as the Bus Station Loonies, Combat Shock and Urko. However Chris left for university and was replaced by the aforementioned Doog Tidswell, whom the band had met when he was standing in on guitar for Ciderfex.

"Doog definitely brought some organisation to the band," says Paul. "He was proactive and got us out of the pub and away from Wycombe. He also set up our website, which rather bizarrely won us an award for the best punk website – beaten only by the Clash and Sex Pistols!"

"Soundwise, Doog was a heavy-metal fan into Maiden, Metallica and Slayer," reckons Alan, "hairy nonsense like that anyway, so his fingerpicking style made us move from that sloppy Disorder thing towards a more clear punk sound."

A tighter style that was in evidence on the band's next release, another split 7-inch, this time with Urko for Inflammable Material. Recorded at RA Sound in Wantage and released in 1997, it was entitled 'A Right Royal Knees-up' and, as well as the Urko tracks, featured two new Chineapple numbers, 'Braindead' and the brilliant 'Parasite', that saw a little SoCal influence creeping into the band's sound, with Alan sounding for all the world like a young Davey Havok from AFI.

A cracking cover of Chumbawamba's 'That's How Grateful We Are' never made it onto the anti-Chumbawamba EP, 'Bare-Faced Hypocrisy…Sells Records', released in 1998 by Chris Willsher's Ruptured Ambition Records, because EMI intervened and threatened to sue Chris if the record featured any actual Chumba covers.

"Given that the whole single was to highlight how they had sold out to a major label, I think that was kind of ironic!" scoffs Alan. "Anyway it eventually got sorted [the Chineapple and Wat Tyler tracks were given away under the radar on cassette and the EP only featured original material from Oi Polloi, Riot/Clone and Bus Station Loonies] and we were all spared going to jail.

Chineapple Punx, Hazels, Aylesbury, Feb 97, pic by Ian Jenk

Chineapple Punx, at Hazels

"We enlisted a friend called Elspeth to play accordion and violin for that session too; she was heavily pregnant at the time and did a cracking job recording while being kicked about from within! She's a highly respected medieval music academic now, so I'm sure it wasn't the pinnacle of her career, but we had a laugh all the same."

1998 also saw the release of the 10-track 'Brainspotting' cassette, by which time, Graham had left and been replaced by James 'Pies' Paterson from Rumpleteaser, who brought even more of a US hardcore influence to bear on the band's sound.

"When I first started listening to music, in Lincolnshire, there wasn't really a local music scene," explains James. "My first band in 1987 was a thrashy DRI/Anthrax-type crossover band called We Are Shit. We played at a pub called the Union and we managed two songs before they threw us off and we were ejected from the pub. That's not bad going! After that I was in Corruption and a band called Ringburner. After moving to High Wycombe, I joined Rumpleteaser, a band formed from the remnants of an Oi!/skinhead band; we obviously crossed paths with Ciderfex and Chineapples and when Graham left, they were doing faster punk stuff – so I forced myself on them!"

James joined just as the Punx were gigging prolifically, not only the length and breadth of the UK, but also making several inebriated trips to Belgium with Ciderfex. While their recorded output is nothing to be ashamed of, it's probably for their off-the-cuff live performances that they will be best remembered.

"I generally carried as much stuff to our gigs as the guys playing instruments," laughs Alan. "I had this newspaper delivery bag full of plastic toys, giant pineapple masks, rubber severed heads, foam rubber bricks etc which all came out at various points to torment the audience and illustrate the songs. On top of this we used to think up these stupid games for the crowd to get involved with, like taping bowls of custard or mashed potato to their heads and having a pogo competition. It was hardly high art, but fantastic fun; no-one seemed to mind that it was all for our own entertainment and they always suffered more than us.

"We seemed to have a thing about vegetables for some reason, so there were always Brussels sprouts and runner beans flying at high velocity all over the place. A well-launched Brussel fucking hurts when it hits you too, so we often had bruises the following day. One time I emptied an entire sack of them on the audience and you could hear them pinging off the cymbals and whistling past your head for the rest of the set; it was like *Saving Private Ryan*!

"I think a lot of the stage antics were more influenced by people like Tommy Cooper and Spike Milligan than other bands, although Chi Pig from SNFU used stage props to good effect too. I remember being impressed by the frenetic energy of this dreadlocked loon hitting people with a rubber ham!"

"The Wisbech show supporting PAIN and Combat Shock was a highlight for me," offers Doog. "It was in an incredibly hot back room but everyone just went ballistic. For our song 'Riot Cop Diet Cop', Alan used to dress as a policeman and encourage people to throw foam bricks at him and that night there was excellent deployment of the riot bricks and it was just thoroughly good fun. We cooled everyone down by spraying them with beer from inside a stuffed toy cat…"

"One night at the Indian Queen, Boston, we played with Urko and arranged a game of Russian Roulette with donuts," recalls Alan. "We had four jam donuts, but one was filled with Dave's Insanity Chilli Sauce. This goth guy drew the short straw, ate the donut and it nearly killed him! He was puking and generally not feeling well at all; he asked me afterwards if we had fed him acid as he thought he was going to have a heart attack… I have to say I felt a little pang of guilt over that one…! "

I also remember we got asked to play a biker club Christmas party one year; it was out in the middle of the woods in a couple of marquees and they were all fucking nuts! Most of them were into blues rather than punk and we were a little concerned as to how we were going to go down and if we would actually make it out alive. In our infinite wisdom we decided that taking the piss out of them was the way forward, so we learned a cover of 'Born To Be Wild' and I came onstage on a child's tricycle dressed as Santa with a long wig and Viking helmet! You could have cut the atmosphere with a Hell's Angels' hatchet, but eventually – in the middle of our 30-second-long cover of 'Freebird'! – I think they realised that we had to be harmless, retarded or both and started to join in."

The band's final release was a CD-album for Greased Pig, 1999's 'It's Good But It's Not Right', a decently-recorded (especially seeing as it was done in one day, at Absolute Studios in Hayes) collection of 18 songs that still stands up to repeated listens today. A final EP, to have been entitled 'Pants People', never saw the light of day because the Chineapple Punx split up in 2000. They played their last gig at the Roundabout that July, with Anal Beard and the Blue Meenies supporting.

Alan: "We really wanted to go out with a bang so, for no apparent reason, we all dressed as wrestlers and challenged the audience to a fight in a paddling pool we'd filled with jelly and hops. By the end of the set there was jelly and beer dripping from the ceiling and everything was completely fucked. I think keeping one eye on the beer sales was the only reason we didn't get our arses kicked by the landlord!" An appropriately deranged end to a madcap band.

"Straight after Chineapple Punx we started Thingy," explains Doog, who nowadays plays alongside James in 'High Wycombe's premier Bad Religion tribute band', Bald Religion! "Indeed Thingy's first gig was the day following Chineapple's last, in the same pub. Thingy brought in Simon Beard and Pete from Ciderfex alongside Alan, James and myself. We recorded one single ['Sausages And Plants And Goldfish', self-released on an unnamed label] which if anything was even more stupid than Chineapple Punx and then Alan left to go to university in Winchester."

Since then Alan has been playing bass in the thrash/D-beat outfit Whole In The Head, with Nath from Haywire and Jamie from Minute Manifesto, but he recalls his time with the Chineapple Punx very fondly: "I'm glad that we walked a line between chaos and actually having something to say. We often teetered off the edge of right-on PC-ness, but never meant any ill to anyone. I think people understood it was all just a joke made within our safety net of friends. When all is said and done, we were keen to support numerous good causes and played a lot of animal rights, anti-fascist and Class War benefits, while being as daft as a box of frogs!"

"Stupidity of a very high level," is how Doog sums it all up very neatly. "We were cabaret anarcho-punk rock… politics with a smile!"

SELECT DISCOGRAPHY:

7-inch:
'Chunk And Disorderly' (Duel Cabbageway, 1996) – *split with Ciderfex*
'A Right Royal Knees-up' (Inflammable material, 1997) – *split with Urko*
LPs: 'It's Good But It's Not Right' (Greased Pig, 1999) – *CD only*

AT A GLANCE:
The band would dearly love to see the Greased Pig album remastered and repackaged as a vinyl LP, but until then the CD version is as good a place as any to begin exploring the weird and wonderful world of the Chineapple Punx.

STRENGTH ALONE

Hailing from the rural idyll of Sussex, **Strength Alone** were one of the UK's earliest SXE hardcore bands, but remain a mysterious entity for most due to them only releasing one 7-inch and imploding before they ever had chance to reach their full potential. They emerged from the vibrant hardcore scene centred somewhat disarmingly around the Shelley Arms in the tiny village of Nutley – a country pub that became notorious for its storming hardcore gigs – and with their melodic brand of posicore could easily have made significant waves internationally if they'd enjoyed more longevity.

"Nutley's perhaps most famous for Jailcell Recipes naming it the 'hardcore centre of the universe' on one of their records' thanks lists," smiles vocalist Barry Thirlway. "Yep, its name is legion alright! The Sussexian CBGB's! We'd play there most regularly with bands from both near and afar: the aforementioned Jailcells, the BBMFs, Understand, Couch Potatoes, Stand Off, Crossbow, Fabric, Angus Bagpipe, Go!, Close Call, Joeyfat, MTA and loads more. We had the more established venues in [nearby] Brighton as well, such as the Zap, the Richmond and the Basement and then there were also shows in Eastbourne and Tunbridge Wells and the occasional show in London…

"But we were just four school friends from the wrong side of the country lanes," he adds jokingly, of the rural environment that spawned the band. "Asking one of the local skaters what the 'Agent Orange' graffiti I'd seen in the village was led me to hearing punk and hardcore for the first time. Guys three to five years older than us were already playing in hardcore bands, most notably the BBMFs (Big Bastard Motherfuckers) and seeing *them* play led a number of us to form our own bands. We loved the music; it looked like great fun to be up onstage and you didn't need to be able to sing (which was a big plus for me) or be a virtuoso musician.

"Rather than live the music we loved from the other side of the Atlantic vicariously through records and zines, the key motivation was trying to create something for ourselves and eventually, the three or four bands our immediate circle of friends had put together condensed into one, with what I can only assume was the supposed best players all coming together. The notable exception here was me as vocalist, as I had no discernible talent other than probably being the most enthusiastic… I never did get round to finding out just why they asked me to take care of vocal duties…"

As Barry points out, Strength Alone took very little influence, either musically or lyrically, from their immediate locale, preferring the sublime sounds and responsible messages of American hardcore to the boozed-up, nihilistic punk rock that was so the rage in the UK at the time. "We were basically a group of kids who lived locally and skated," reckons guitarist Simon Goodrick.

"And through the skateboarding fraternity and magazines like *Thrasher* and *Transworld* just ended up getting into hardcore – it seemed to go hand in hand. We got heavily into bands like Suicidal Tendencies, Dead Kennedys, Minor Threat, Descendents, Misfits, Stupids, Ripcord…pretty much whatever we could get our hands on… After that we got much more into bands like 7 Seconds, Uniform Choice and Dag Nasty, which ultimately led to finding bands like Gorilla Biscuits, Youth Of Today [both of whom had just toured the UK to rabid sold-out venues] and No For An Answer – basically all the early Revelation releases, then the New Age Records stuff…you sort of went by label and record covers…

"Meeting people like [scenesters] Tony Sylvester and Vique Martin helped; they always had the latest stuff…this was the days before the internet, so there were lots of tapes going round… Everyone was hungry to get their hands on new stuff and there was a huge amount of bands coming out of the States at that time, so we spent all our time writing to people and trading records and shirts. I used to travel up to London and go to Vinyl Solution and Rough Trade and just look through the 7-inchs and LPs and buy anything that looked cool; you learned to check out their shirts and what bands they thanked… I also used to buy loads of stuff from Alan's in Lancashire – he always had cool stuff – but once we discovered Revelation, that was pretty much the way forward for us…"

With their line-up completed by bassist Phil Secretan and drummer Jamie Donbroski, Strength Alone played their first show at Barcombe Village Hall, in East Sussex, with Blockmania, MBTF and the Raggers during the summer of 1989. Although a "strictly non-hardcore event", it went well enough for the band to want to play again as soon and as often as possible and they racked up plenty of support slots on the south coast before recording their 'Reflections' demo the following year, which Barry maintains he actually prefers to the EP they would eventually release.

"We recorded it at Wilbury Road Studios in Hove," recalls Simon. "We were so naive as regards what the hell we were doing, but some other local bands like Sleep and the BBMFs had recorded there so it seemed the logical option. I remember taking in a cassette of the Release EP and saying, 'We want to sound like this…'

"Basically we recorded it live; I think we did each song in one take and then laid the vocals down after and the whole thing was done and mixed in a day. At the time we thought it was great, but when you listen to it now I can't believe no-one said, 'Maybe we should record that one again' or 'Let's tune up first,' 'cos it's all over the place! But we just went in and played like we were doing a gig; I guess that's what it came out like too…it was sloppy as hell, but at least we had something out there and it got us a lot of gigs and made us some good friends;

we generally got good feedback from it."

'Sloppy as hell' it may have been, but forged from youthful enthusiasm, there was no denying its insistent raw energy. Its chaotic Insted feel soon brought them to the attention of Ian Simpson and Helene Keller who were about to start their own label, Subjugation. Returning to Wilbury Road in early 1991, they recorded four songs for a self-titled EP that became Subjugation's very first release and, although not the best produced example of the genre out there, it was manic enough to be a potent slice of old-school hardcore.

"Has the single stood the test of time?" ponders Simon. "Well, I'm not really sure about that… On the one hand, it's a great document of what we were doing at the time and for posterity of course it's a great memento, but it is very much of an era; what really let it down though was the mix – it sounds like it was recorded through mud in the next room! Again, just going into a studio and recording live is never going to get the best results; you need to have someone else there who knows what they're doing to pick up on things and to push you and that's why there's so many little mistakes (mostly with my guitar playing), but we were just excited to be recording.

"It *is* a weird mix of material, though, as 'Best Of Times' and 'Opinions Voiced' were older songs compared with 'Where To Turn' and 'Never Enough' which were written well after the others; I remember we only had the two newer songs when we went in to record. I can't remember if it was well received upon release, but I know there were only a couple of hundred pressed and I think we just gave our copies to family and friends… I don't recall reading any reviews either, but I don't think we were inundated with requests for a follow-up!"

Strength Alone had to pull out of a planned UK tour with Understand and Stand Off because of illness and – apart from an all-dayer at Leeds University during February '92 – they didn't really get very far afield to promote the single, although playing support to Sick Of It All at Happy Jacks, London, was one of their higher profile gigs. In early '93, Phil moved to second guitar to give the band more musical scope, with Macca [aka Mark Wilkinson] from the BBMFs joining on bass and the band started to lean more in the direction of the introspective melodies of New Jersey's Turning Point. But they never got to record any of the new material, as they split up in late 1993, playing their final gig at the 1 In 12 Club, Bradford, that December.

"Personally I think coming from a small village in Sussex didn't help," pontificates Simon on the reason for their premature demise. "There really wasn't much of a scene any more and there were no new bands coming up; our scene consisted of a bunch of people who had grown up together but were slowly drifting apart. Remember, we were very young when we started – all 13 to 15 years old – and hardcore as a unifying element was only a factor for so long…and you need to have that in a band. You need to push each other and dedicate your time to it, you need to inspire each other or you just stagnate and that's what happened to us. A shame really, because I think we had our best to come, but circumstances meant that we couldn't realistically carry on and the older you get the harder it is to dedicate your time to being in a band…maybe it's time for that Strength Alone 20-year reunion?"

"I honestly wish we'd put more time into rehearsing and playing out, particularly outside of the southeast, but being as young as we were, getting around the country to play was easier said than done," adds Barry. "I know that Harry from *Hate Edge* fanzine was dying to sing along with the hits at least! Some lyrics about our struggle to unite the tough village streets wouldn't have gone amiss either: 'Don't forget the struggle, don't forget the streams!'"

Strength Alone, Barry Thirlway,
by Vique Simba

Strength Alone

"We actually had an offer to record an LP from Mike Warden of Conquer the World Records, who I'd met at the first More Than Music festival in Dayton, Ohio, in 1992. Unfortunately, we fizzled out later that year so we never got to record again. Perhaps we should have stuck it out for another year or two, 'cos looking back we split up just as we were finally starting to find our own sound – as opposed to appropriating the records we happened to like at a particular time; best put that down to youthful exuberance and total immersion in the records and photos we'd pore over for hours upon hours. However, the drive wasn't there at the time, so it's pointless to mull over what might have been…

"In true youth crew lyric tradition however and I appreciate it might come as a shock to learn this, we pretty much exclusively ripped off bad straightedge lyrics," laughs Barry (who nowadays plays guitar, alongside members of Cardiff's Ironclad, for the nihilistic hardcore troupe, 33, who issued a split 7-inch with Kill Life in 2010). "The best thing of all about Strength Alone would be the friendships made during that time, that have now lasted for more than 20 years. Now we really *can* talk about those halcyon days, as opposed to what must have been the very strange spectre of four kids in their early teens reminiscing about the 'good ol' times'…"

SELECT DISCOGRAPHY:

7-inch:
'Strength Alone' (Subjugation, 1991)

AT A GLANCE:
Nope, sorry, but you could always e-mail Barry for a CDR: bthirlwayjnr@yahoo.co.uk

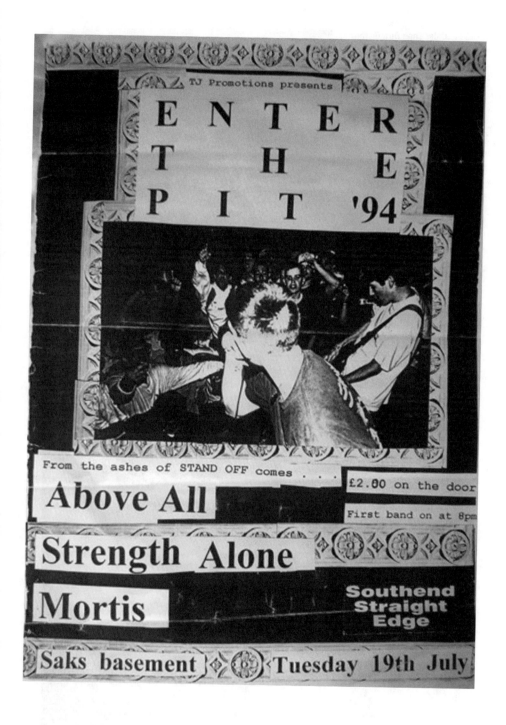

Older Than Dirt, on tour in Ireland

Older Than Dirt, live at the Joiners

CHAPTER SEVEN: THE SOUTHWEST

OLDER THAN DIRT

Southampton's **Older Than Dirt** were one of the best hardcore bands to come from the south coast; very heavy, very powerful and very sincere, they should have been way bigger than they were, but their popularity was unfortunately confined to their local scene where they established a strong and loyal following.

Formed in 1990, when guitarist Stuart Woodward (formerly of Society's Victims and Riot Assembly), bassist Paul Vary and drummer Andy Malloch (the latter two of Time To Kill), hooked up with vocalist Mike Fox, the band almost ended up being called Semtex.

"I kept on joking that I would go on stage and scream, 'We are Semtex and we are going to blow you away!'" laughs Mike. "I always loved the cheesy rock talk! Thankfully Semtex was dropped as a name and we went with Older Than Dirt, which was from a Hell's Kitchen LP… Stu had a list of about 50 names and OTD just jumped out as being our name – it chose us really.

"I remember I got a call from Paul asking if I wanted to try out as vocalist," he adds. "Paul picked me up as I didn't drive back then… I didn't want anything to interfere with the opportunity to drink! At the practice room they played a song which didn't have any words, so I wrote 'All Or Nothing' in a couple of minutes and shouted along. It seemed to go pretty well and I was asked if I minded going along next week… I don't think they ever told me if I passed the audition or not, but Paul kept on turning up and taking me to practise with them…and I took that as a good sign!"

"Our first gig was an open-air all-dayer in Winchester [at the Rugby Club] on 30 June 1990," recalls Paul. "We had only changed our name a couple of days before that from Semtex. Mega City 4 were the headliners and we did a cover of one of their songs… well, it was actually a Capricorn song – the band that became MC4. I was good mates with them at the time and was disappointed that they didn't watch our set; they were sat in their van listening to the World Cup on the radio, if I remember rightly."

The band wasted no time before recording the 'Harder Than Nails' demo in Southsea's Crystal Rooms studio, a four-track offering that demonstrated that OTD were more than just a basic hardcore band, ably turning their hands to some uptempo ska-punk as well as intense ragers like 'We Still Care', that fused old-school hardcore to metallic chug sections with impressive results.

"I can still remember being really excited to get in the studio and record," reckons Stuart. "I love recording and all that kind of related stuff. All I had was a 30-watt Marshall combo, which sounded a bit thin, but hey, it was us at the time and, apart from the massive amounts of reverb used, I think it kinda turned out pretty good…"

"I remember reading a Leatherface review in the *NME*," adds Paul, "and the interviewer said their sound was 'as hard as nails,' so I thought, 'If their sound is as 'hard as nails' then we are '*harder* than nails!' And that's where the name of the demo came from."

The demo landed the band some deservedly positive reviews from the underground fanzine press and offers to play gigs further afield started rolling in, although Older Than Dirt were by then right at the centre of a thriving south coast scene that revolved around the tireless efforts of the local STE (Southampton, Totton and Eastleigh) collective.

"We were pretty lucky having the likes of Rich, Rob and PJ doing regular gigs," agrees Mike. "I think it encouraged others… like the Ooops collective and Oomf and Brighton's Just One Life…not to mention the other good bands from all over the soutHCoast [sic]; from Weymouth to Brighton, stuff was happening in its own right. There was nothing organised as a movement or anything, but stuff came together in a nice way… Looking back, it was a very special time and place, I enjoyed it. Not saying it was better than anywhere else or any other time, but it *was* a great place to be."

"It just felt great to belong to a group of people really into the DIY ethic, who were putting on shows and really into the scene," adds Stu. "I remember we always wanted to play the West Indian Club, but when we had a chance it ended up being double-booked; All and Samiam played and as there were so many bands and we were the local band, we decided to step down. I can still remember to this day Bill Stevenson helping me and Paul with our gear back into our cars… I mean I was the biggest Black Flag fan in the world!"

"In those days touring bands used to do 20 or so dates in each country and a lot of bands would say that Southampton was the best – or one of the best – gigs of the tour," says Paul. "The Joiners Arms *was* a great venue; the STE used to put on the gigs, we had Suspect Device fanzine and Older Than Dirt were the local hardcore punk band who would support all the touring American bands…has Mike told you about when Green Day stayed at his house yet?

"So, anyway, it was a really good set-up, but even though it was a cool scene, not many good bands came out of Southampton at that time. The band I used to really like was Pogrom who did a sort of post-punk Killing Joke-type thing. They used to practise in the room next to us, which was a community hall right by the train tracks. The local kids would be running riot outside, trains used to go by every five minutes and you had two bands practising at 110 decibels; it was a crazy situation, but great fun."

Summer 1991 saw the band back in the Crystal Rooms recording four tracks that they released as a flexi-disc single – cheaper than a regular vinyl record, but usually inferior in sound quality, the Older Than Dirt flexi sounded exceptionally good, a flurry of metallic riffs and double bass drumming a la latter period DRI making it a veritable wet dream for lovers of UK crossover. The band headed over to Ireland to promote it, but the tour didn't go to plan… do they ever?

"It was an absolute disaster from start to finish," laughs Paul. "We hired a Transit van from [Southampton punk band] Strange The Butcher, which was in a bad way; there were more diesel fumes coming in the back of the van than going out through the exhaust pipe. The bloody thing wouldn't do more than 50mph and it finally broke down somewhere near Stoke; we had to crash [sleep] in the van and hire another in the morning to drive up to Holyhead to get the ferry.

"The first gig was in the back room of a really rough pub in Belfast; we got there at about 6pm and the main bar was packed and everyone was totally pissed already. The promoter had told us he was expecting about 200 people at each gig... I think there were about 10 in Belfast! The next night we played at a Republican pub in Downpatrick; I thought we were going to get a load of aggro in the pub, but the people couldn't have been more friendly to us. That was a much better gig as well, with about 50 or so people there and they seemed to like us.

"The next gig was in Dublin, but for some reason it was cancelled and they couldn't find another venue for us; we were supposed to be playing in Cork the following day, but that was cancelled as well. It certainly was an eye-opener driving across the border with watch-towers and soldiers with SLRs questioning you! I don't think it helped our case that we all had grade one haircuts and were wearing flight jackets – so basically looked liked squaddies... probably not a wise move in Northern Ireland in 1992...

"We got the ferry back to Holyhead and then the hire van broke down as well, so we had to wait for the tow truck to drive us back to Stoke and wait there for my mate's brother to drive up from the south coast to collect us. Our friends Matt and Chris had printed 100 T-shirts for the tour... I think they sold three!"

Upon their return home, Lee Wagstaffe joined as second guitarist but, due to the band not gelling properly with the expanded line-up, had departed before the band released their 'New Age Of Rage' 7-inch in 1993, on Andy's own FNG Records (short for 'Fucking New Guy' apparently). Recorded in April of that year with Martin Nicholls at the Whitehouse Studio in Weston-super-Mare, it saw the band developing their exciting style to incorporate some angular post-hardcore rhythms and even a jazzy intro or two, into their high velocity hardcore, with Mike wearing his Minor Threat influences proudly on his sleeve in the vocal delivery department.

"I loved the Whitehouse recording sessions," enthuses Stu. "Martin managed to get a great sound, although funnily enough I wanted an even heavier sound on the guitars, but just didn't have the gear! I was really happy with it anyway and for me personally it was the best OTD release...not sure the others would agree, though."

"The Whitehouse *was* a better studio than the Crystal Rooms," concedes Paul, "and the engineer definitely didn't let us get away with any sloppy playing or anything, whereas the bloke who ran the Crystal Rooms was a lot more laid-back. Personally, I hated recording there as me and Andy weren't even talking at that point and we had to stay the night there, so it was a bad time. I actually prefer the flexi – the sound is a lot more powerful than the EP, where the guitars are too low in the mix and, even though it's a really clear sound, the whole thing lacks bollocks."

Unsurprisingly given the above statement, Paul left soon after the EP's release and was replaced by Rik Godfrey. "Me and Andy hadn't been getting on for a long time," he sighs, by way of explanation, "and it got ridiculous in the end; he wouldn't even talk to me at rehearsals and refused to play any new ideas I came up with, saying he didn't like them. Something had to give so I rang him and arranged to meet him for a 'clear the air' meeting. I thought we would have a chat or row for half an hour and sort things out, but he had other ideas; he told me he didn't want me in the band any more and was setting up his own record company to release OTD's music and take control of the band.

"What you have to realise is that, up to this point, apart from playing the drums he had done nothing for the band. It was me, Mike and Stu that did all the work; Andy had always been totally negative towards everything. John Peel had played us a few times and wanted to do a session with us (I still have the letter from him) but Andy didn't think we were good enough so we couldn't do it. Meantime Records wanted to do an LP with us but again it never happened, because *Andy* didn't think we were ready. I arranged three gigs in Bournemouth but in each case Andy decided (for reasons only known to him) he wouldn't do them…

"He regularly used to turn up over an hour late for band practices and for gigs as well, which caused us all sorts of problems with the other bands that were on the bill. At one stage, I remember me, Mike and Stu were outside a phonebox in Southampton and we had all had enough of his attitude and wanted to call him to sack him, but I persuaded Mike and Stu to give him another chance. So it was ironic that, a few months later, I was the one being forced out of the band by the person who I had kept in the band. Maybe if I had spoken to Mike and Stu about it we could have found a new drummer and things would have turned out different, but, to be honest, I was sick of the whole thing by then. Even though I was gutted, 'cos OTD had been a big part of my life for three years, I was glad to get away from all the bullshit that came with it…"

"I think everything Paul has said is probably fair comment," adds Andy bravely. "In a nutshell, I wasn't acting rationally; I certainly wasn't being very mature. By that time our musical tastes (mine and Paul's anyway) had changed to the point where there was no common ground, which really didn't help matters. The only other thing I can say is that I was always hard on myself with regard to drumming; I never thought I was that good and I was always worried about being the weak link in the band. With hindsight it probably would have been better for OTD, at that stage, if they had've kicked me out."

"It might sound big-headed but after I left, that band wasn't really Older Than Dirt and they should have changed their name," continues Paul. "Stu and I wrote the music and Mike wrote the lyrics and we all bought something different to the table, which reflected our different influences and musical tastes; it was that chemistry that made OTD different from other UK hardcore bands. If you listen to anything recorded after 'New Age of Rage', it is basically a different band…"

To make matters worse, vocalist Mike also departed, possibly frustrated by the band's complete failure to get over to Europe to play and was replaced by 'Big' Stewart Watt, so Older Than Dirt really *were* a different band, their new style starting to lean more towards the hard alternative rock sound of the Rollins Band, Prong and Helmet than the UKHC sound of the late Eighties.

"Actually, when I think about it now, I understand that I was scared that we were about to do something pretty amazing," admits Mike. "It was looking more and more likely that we would get a level of success that was more than I was able to deal with… I may have been kidding myself, but I freaked a bit and decided I would leave while they had time to get a new singer and not leave the band in the lurch if and when something happened. It was a pretty hard decision to make and after I told the band I went home pretty gutted, feeling really sad; it was really hard."

"It was a big question for us at the time," recalls Stu. "Shall we change the name from

Older Than Dirt or not? We spent a lot of time discussing it and we very nearly called ourselves Tongue; in hindsight we should have changed it, as it was a very different band. We downtuned, we got heavy and we wanted to go to the next level. Obviously there was always going to be elements of the old hardcore/punk Older Than Dirt in there, as I wrote most of the old and new music anyway…"

Mike Barrow briefly joined on second guitar to add more bite to the band's sound, but again, like Lee before him, he didn't quite fit into the OTD dynamic and the band's 'No More Excuses' CD was recorded as a four-piece.

"We recorded the album at Von's in London, just outside Camden, off the Holloway Road somewhere," says Stu, of what was a fantastically heavy and ambitious release, but lacking the spark of intensity that made Mike-era OTD so memorable. "We recorded during the night as it was cheaper; I think it was recorded over two weeks, which was an amazing experience. The guy who recorded us was called Lee Rumble and he did a great job; he played in a band called Suck Henry, if I remember rightly?

"I was a bit overawed being in such a big studio; Von's was used mainly for bands signed to big labels to demo stuff. We hired a load of gear to get the best sound we could and I think we had our guitars sampled for a rap album after I recorded them…the name of it escapes me. At the time of recording, Whitehouse had just been in and we shared the studio with Spiritualized; I still have the rough demos they left. One of the strangest experiences was seeing Malcolm McLaren in reception, the first evening we arrived, and also Tommy Stupid was in recording with two friends in some kind of country-punk band; they seemed pretty stoned all the time to me and I don't remember that band's name either, but needless to say it was quite an experience for all of us.

"The album really stands on its own as it's not really what I would call an OTD release… it's still hardcore in places…but far more adventurous in other aspects and it kinda took us to a new audience…"

Two tracks from 'No More Excuses' – 'Too Late' and 'Dig Your Own Hole' – were used on a split 7-inch with Japanese band Volume Dealers released by HG Fact Records in 1996, but, in true Older Than Dirt fashion, the guys failed to take advantage of a golden opportunity to play in the Far East and split later that year, playing their final gig at the Portsmouth Wedgewood Rooms with Outshined and Fat Babe.

"All I can remember is me, Rik and Big Stew turning up to a rehearsal one night and Andy not turning up again and that was it, all over!" explains Stu of the band's decision to call it a day. "Though fairly recently Andy did admit it was a big mistake it ended that way and he wished he hadn't done some of the things he did. I really didn't want it to end, but I reckon if we had given it another year or two things would have been very different. With the invention of house/acid/dance, or whatever you want to call it, taking such a hold of people in the Nineties, myself included, it seemed like a bad time for hardcore-influenced music in the UK, really dark days…"

Indeed Stu, who is still involved with graphic design, tried his hand at techno music until 1999, when he returned to the hardcore fold to do Parade Of Enemies and since then he's played with Half Life, Ficus, Bloodshed, Dissentient Revolt and is now in Hummune with Rik from OTD and Mike (Barrow) from Killjoy. Andy went on to do the London circuit, playing session drums for various bands, before returning to Southampton to play in Killjoy and the Winchester band But Me No Buts alongside Lee Wagstaffe. Big Stew ended up fronting Intent, among others.

"A year after leaving OTD, I moved to Spain, where I still live," adds Paul. "I stopped playing for ages but was still going to loads of gigs and still into the scene; I recently came out of retirement and have started a new project called This Is Brainwash with Stu, Jaime Cerebros from the legendary Spanish band Cerebros Exprimidos, Toni Maltraste from Bad Taste and Pablo X. Mike Fox sings on three of the songs as well, so that makes it three-quarters of Older Than Dirt on those three songs…"

"At the end of the day," reckons Andy, "bands are judged mainly on their recordings. I think OTD wrote some good songs and I think we held our own against most other bands – although there were some classic bands from that period which we could only hope to aspire to. We just played what we wanted to play and what we thought sounded good and – most of the time – we had good fun doing it. Nothing more, nothing less."

In recent years, Older Than Dirt have been considering reissuing their Nineties output as a double-CD set, should interest be high enough. Meanwhile, Stu would like the band to be remembered "as a UK hardcore band not afraid to change and try out new things. I don't think we ever intentionally tried to sound or be like anyone really, we just played what we liked and didn't get restricted to any one scene; that was definitely truer of the last phase of Older Than Dirt anyway. For me it was always about the music and the feeling we created as four people on stage raging together. I really believe we could have achieved so much more than we did, but I hope that people remember us fondly and that maybe, just maybe, someone got something out of what we did musically and lyrically at some point along the line."

SELECT DISCOGRAPHY:

7-inch:
'Flexi' (Older Than Dirt, 1991) – *flexi-disc*
'New Age Of Rage' (FNG, 1993)
'Split' (HG Fact Records, 1996) – *split with Volume Dealers*

MCD:
'No More Excuses' (FNG, 1995)

AT A GLANCE:
Until the aforementioned reissues do/don't appear, readers needing a fix of progressive UKHC can contact Stu for an OTD discography: stuartwoodward@itsascream.com

MINUTE MANIFESTO

Formed in Southampton in early 1997, **Minute Manifesto** were so-called because all their songs were less than a minute long and most contained a serious message. In true DIY punk fashion, they only did split releases and burnt themselves out in just a few years, but during their short existence they made a lot of people smile with their stupidly fast politico-thrash and most of these guys are still making hardcore noises even today.

"When Minute Manifesto first started practicing I had been listening to bands such as JFA, BGK, Heresy, Larm, Chaos UK, Stupids, Scream, Minor Threat, early Hüsker Dü, DRI, Verbal Abuse, Black Sabbath, Born Against…oh and the Deep Wund 7-inch!" begins guitarist Matthew 'Dingo' Valaitis. "The list is endless! I had been getting into the anarcho-punk movement at the same time, though, so I was also listening to bands like Crass, Antisect, Icons Of Filth and Rudimentary Peni."

"I was listening to a lot of US hardcore too," reckons vocalist Jamie 'Festo' Goddard, "like Jerry's Kids, Negative FX, Void and Citizen's Arrest, but lyrically I was really influenced by the political nature of UK bands like Health Hazard and Oi Polloi and just by what was going on around me. A lot of the lyrics were honest and heartfelt, but it has to be said they were quite of the time. The BNP were recruiting and getting votes on estates like where my parents lived. I became a vegetarian during my short spell as a not-so-dirty squatter; I was going to some of the Reclaim The Streets stuff and it felt like the Zapatistas in Mexico had opened the gateway for the downfall of capitalism…"

Joining Jamie and Matt were drummer Mat Sweet and bassist Rob 'GG' Callen, formerly of Thirst; they were prolific writers from the offset and played their first gig – for the STE collective, of course! – at the Joiners Arms on 28 May 1997, supporting Konstrukt from Germany and Rydell from Tunbridge Wells.

"We started off as we meant to continue," laughs Jamie. "A shambolic, out-of-tune, out-of-time mess, where I was so nervous I couldn't even face the audience…"

"But the local scene was really cool when we started," adds Rob. "There were lots of local bands and many gigs put on by the STE and then other people got into it too and started putting on their own gigs; there was always something happening. I could talk about the STE for ages as I was involved with Rich Levene from the start and a whole lot of others who helped out too, but to summarise I think it created a focal point, which people could relate to and gave a medium in which a tiny bit of freedom existed: to put on different bands, meet friends, play music, listen, talk and have fun, all under a DIY ethic. It gave those who were involved a little bit of control, as well as making us lose money when people didn't turn up, but it was a fun time.

"The Joiners Arms was one of the main venues the STE used at the beginning and for a few years that worked well, until they started putting the prices up and eventually decided to put on gigs themselves. So other venues in small pubs around Southampton were used for a while, until the King Alfred ended up being the venue which was used the most at the end. There's still the occasional gig there even now and Rich still puts on a few all-dayers under the name of 'Almost The STE'…"

A 14-song demo tape was recorded with John Stephens at Chukalumba studios – deep in the New Forest – on 14 June 1997, a "typical rites of passage, rough-as-fuck demo tape," which the band started selling for a pittance at gigs in Southampton, Portsmouth and Brighton. One of the Southampton gigs was with Month Of Birthdays and Imbiss from Leeds, with whom Minute Manifesto struck up a strong friendship that led to their first gigs in the north and then January 1998 saw Jonathon 'Lobster' Shaw, ex-Ebola vocalist, joining the band on second guitar.

"I still think the best gig we ever did was when we played up in Leeds for the first time – in our friend's cellar!" declares Dingo. "I remember going up in Rob's beaten-up Vauxhall Cavalier – the 'Minute Mobile' – and every time we stopped at services the bonnet of the car had to be opened to start the car, but somehow we made it for the afternoon. This was my first time in Leeds; I remember the cellar being packed – no room to swing a cat – and I didn't have a guitar plectrum so I used a 10p piece. Someone lent me their distortion pedal and I had no idea how to use such a thing, but someone turned it up for me, full volume and I was like, 'Yeah, that'll do!' We started playing to the drunken crowd; I couldn't move as it was too packed. I remember Jamie crouching on the floor to shout and when he looked up someone's crotch was staring him in the face. People were having fun and the atmosphere was great; I liked what the Leeds people were doing at the time, they had the same ethics as the STE…"

"That gig was with Hari Kari and loads of other bands," adds Jamie. "The venue was the size of a toilet and we played really late when everyone was crazy drunk. They attacked us 'til we played more songs and then when we played more songs they attacked us again – great stuff. I remember equipment going everywhere, Lobster fighting to keep hold of his guitar, Dingo crowd-surfing while still trying to play and me crawling around on the floor trying to find the microphone…amazing stuff."

The new line-up returned to Chukalumba to record six songs for a split 7-inch with Manchester band Grover, which Dingo released on his own Boy Useless label in June 1998, Minute Manifesto's side of the disc throbbing with an urgent intensity pleasingly reminiscent of Italy's Raw Power (before they went all heavy metal). The single was launched at a two-day STE festival, where Minute Manifesto played one day and Grover the next and the two bands spent the rest of that summer gigging up and down the country with the likes of Scatha, His Hero Is Gone, Unhinged, Sawn Off, Logical Nonsense, Unslug and Avail.

Eight more songs were recorded, including a "pretty rubbish" cover of 'Wipe Out' by the Stupids, during September '98 for a split 7-inch with Scotland's Shank that was released as a joint effort between Boy Useless and Enslaved Records. Tighter, faster and harder than the first single, this split got great reviews upon its release in early '99 and Minute Manifesto played gigs in support of it with Asshole Parade, Urko, Drop Dead and John Holmes. But things were quietly coming unglued in the Minute Manifesto camp, with band members spending more time in various side projects than they did jamming with each other.

"About the time of the split with Shank," explains Jamie, "Lobster, Nath from Haywire and Gonzo from local hardcore band I Confess got a short lived Discharge/Skitsystem-inspired band together [White Finger] and did a couple of gigs in Portugal, plus one gig with Uncurbed and Hard To Swallow in Southampton in September 1999. Also, Rob and Mat, a local zinester called Clive Henry and Tom got an instrumental Slint/Leeds 6-influenced band together called Trophy Girls. They mainly did gigs in Bristol, Brighton and Southampton and struck up friendships with similar edgy progressive math rock-type bands…"

So Trophy Girls played with the likes of Month Of Birthdays and Bluetip and recorded

Minute Manifesto, live at 121 Centre, Brixton, pic by Nath

Minute Manifesto, Dingo, 1 In 12 Club

an interesting enough demo of angular post hardcore, but – despite a planned release on Rosewood Union – never really realised their full potential.

"Trophy Girls were all about playing difficult songs with crazy time changes," offers Rob. "It was common for Clive to start screaming into his guitar pickups at random times during most of their shows. Tom eventually left to go travelling and the band split up to do other things after that, but not before one last STE all-dayer, for which they wrote a brand new 30-minute song by practising every day for a week and then played it for the first and last time at the gig…original to the end!

"Then in late '99 Mat, Lobster, Clive and a local metalhead called Chris got another criminally short-lived Iron Monkey/Eye Hate God-influenced stoner metal band together called Green Hearse. I can only remember them playing two Southampton gigs, one with the Sorts and the other with Victory At Sea. Both gigs were great and they even recorded an amazing album that unfortunately never got released…"

In amidst all the moonlighting, Minute Manifesto found time to write 16 songs for a split 12-inch with Boston's Urko, which they recorded at Chukalumba during January 2000, although the record didn't appear until July of the following year, long after the band had decided to call it a day. But the final recording, which sounds for all the world like a demented fusion of early Napalm Death and 'Animosity'-era COC, with a few jazzy interludes for good measure, remains a wonderfully potent epitaph.

"By the diversity and song structure, it may technically have been our best release," ponders Rob, "but there was always a large amount of sarcasm and fun mixed in there too; the most obvious example being the locked run-off track, which has Dingo screaming back-up lyrics of 'It never ends…' to one of the songs. Lobster recorded it with a Dictaphone while Dingo was doing backing vocals in the studio and it was just put on the end of the album by itself and he didn't know anything about it until the record came out! There was a bit of interest from [the influential American label] Slap A Ham after this release, but unknowingly we played our last gig in a small pub in Southampton on Thursday 13 January 2000, at STE gig No 174."

"It was at a shithole called Copperfields," recalls Jamie, "with Sarah from Brittany and a local band called Aside. I remember the only way you could watch the bands was in front of them or behind them. I watched Sarah from behind; the drummer had this weird drumkit and it was great to watch him play. I'd bought this guitar for fifty quid a week earlier, that gig being the first time I used it, but one of the tuning pegs snapped off the fat E-string, so I couldn't tune up properly and I had to borrow someone else's."

"For the last few songs, first Lobster and then everyone else apart from Mat ended up on the floor collapsed on top of each other while still trying to play," adds Rob. "I think it was fun for the crowd and it was a lot of fun for us too. But we didn't know it was our last gig at the time, we just packed up, got home late and then went to work the next day as usual; there wasn't any big speeches or sad farewells or anything…"

Later that year Lobster moved back to Newcastle to be with his family while Jamie started a band called Parade Of Enemies with Dingo on bass for a short period, before the latter moved up to Leeds the following year, where he stills resides and plays bass for War All The Time.

"And before that, I played guitar with Boxed In and even joined Sawn Off for about five gigs," Dingo says proudly. "I've toured all over Southeast Asia, Australia and Europe; this is what I always wanted to do in a band and for me it's a dream come true. Where are we touring next? I haven't grown up at all! I still squat a house with my mates and live the punk-rock lifestyle…"

"Sned once described us as, 'The five biggest geeks in Southampton all in one band!'," laughs Mat, who nowadays lives in America, trying to define what set Minute Manifesto apart from their peers at the time. "I think if we'd actually known what we were doing and been more competent at achieving what we had in mind, then we would have sucked. Victory through failure then, or something?"

"Victory through failure…', that's fucking brilliant!" adds Jamie, who left Parade Of Enemies in 2002 and currently screams for Whole In The Head – when he's not working on an organic farm in Devon. "I highly doubt we'll be remembered, I've forgotten most of it myself. Nothing set us apart from anybody else either, other than the fact that there was no way you could have guessed we were a thrash band by *looking* at us. I always liked that."

"No, we won't be remembered for anything," agrees Rob, who went on to play with Disoma, Wreck Of Old '98 and Strands and who is still a rocket scientist. "Apart from being a bunch of innocent weirdo noise freaks who had some fast songs. Our friends might remember us, I suppose, so that's the main thing and *we'll* certainly remember it as being lots of fun. Anyway, there's been a lot more bands who were better than us, who are more worthy of remembering, but for me that's not the point; the important thing was to have just done what we did and play our music. In that respect, we were very similar to many of our peers, both bands and friends, who were doing something and being part of something and changing something for the better – even if it was only ourselves…" Sadly Lobster, who had also played guitar with Sawn Off, died of cancer in 2007, leaving behind a wife and young family.

"I have many fond memories of him," says Rob, "from the first time I ever met him at some rubbish night club in Southampton, with him collapsed over a table, too drunk to talk, to leaving the squat I stayed at (for just a week); saying goodbye to him and Chikage [his wife] and him putting on his gold 'Elvis Presley' sunglasses, strumming an acoustic guitar and singing an Elvis song (it may have been 'Love Me Tender', but I can't quite remember!), in his deep low voice, with me and Chikage in hysterics. He was pretty unique, to say the least, but as far as Minute Manifesto was concerned, he added definition, power and intensity to our sound and was an integral member of the band. Everyone kept in contact with him after MM finished and I made a regular yearly visit up to see him and Chikage in Newcastle on New Year's Eve for ages. When he sadly passed away, a whole vanload of people from Southampton went up to Newcastle for his funeral, which says more than I ever could of his influence on those around him…"

SELECT DISCOGRAPHY:

7-inch:
'Split' (Boy Useless, 1998) – *split with Grover*
'Split' (Boy Useless/Enslaved, 1999) – *split with Shank*

12-inch:
'Split' (Boy Useless, 2001) – *split with Urko*

AT A GLANCE:
Nothing official, but if you e-mail Jamiefesto@hotmail.com he'll burn you a CDR of the band's output and he might even have a few copies of the split 7-inch with Shank he can spare.

DEMONIC UPCHUCKS

The **Demonic Upchucks**, their name affectionately inspired by the Angelic Upstarts, are probably one of the more obscure bands in this book, but since when has 'popular' necessarily equalled 'worthwhile'? And the UK punk scene is littered with the remains of bands that, although they supported the scene as enthusiastically as the next man, never got the breaks they deserved.

Formed in Bournemouth during the summer of 1997, the Upchucks were Alex Upchuck (aka Ayling) on bass and vocals (formerly of Benosi Kill), Matt 'Upchuck' Webb on guitar and vocals, Smash Adams (aka Adam Linfoot) on second guitar and Matt's younger brother Dom on drums. Taking their lead from such Bournemouth punk luminaries as Self Abuse and Poze, they played their first gig at the Gardening Club (now the Sound Circus) on the 27th of that July and it was a suitably deranged affair that will no doubt horrify the vegetarians reading this book...

"It was at a 'Teenage Rampage' (no alcohol) night," recalls Alex. "We had only just recruited Dom on drums and hadn't yet practised with him, Smash only had two strings on his guitar and we had spent the day drinking and smoking. We turned up – blind drunk – to play with a sorry collection of indie bands...two of which cancelled and the other two didn't show anyway, so we played to a small group of indie kids wanting to hear duff Oasis covers. Which is not what they got... We had just got into the third song when, from a plastic bag side of stage, we produced a collection of pigs' trotters to throw at the less-than-impressed indie kids. A small pork-based battle commenced, the electricity was turned off and we were given 10 minutes to get ourselves and our equipment out of the venue before the police were called!"

A gig or two later, we pulled a similar stunt with some ducks' heads," adds Matt. "Alex's dad's missus got given some ducks from someone she worked with and after the ducks were eaten, Alex cut the heads off and put them in a carrier bag in his guitar case. Three weeks later, at the gig in question, they were pretty manky... "Animal rights? I don't think we had really heard of it; we were more interested in upsetting the pathetic and sedate status quo of the Bournemouth music scene. Matt *has* been a vegetarian for over 10 years now..."

Smash soon left and moved to Mallorca and the band continued as a three-piece. After a few more local gigs, they were taken under the wing of Roger 'Jarvis Presley' Smale of Self Abuse, who booked them into Poole's Active Studios in October 1998 to record an eight-song demo, four tracks from which ('Aborted', 'Cultural Dictatorship', 'I'm An Upchuck' and 'All Ravers Are Wankers') ended up on Helen Of Oi's 'Punks, Skins And Herberts, Volume Five' compilation, released early the following year. "Roger taught us how to play our instruments a little bit," adds Alex gratefully, "And bought us equipment, cider, beer, smokes and anything else we said we needed! The Active recording perfectly captured the spirit in which it was played, as well as the incompetence and chaos that was inherent in the band! 'All Ravers Are Wankers' was in response to an evening some track-suited little shits confronted Matt while on his own in Springbourne... Nowadays people might call them 'chavs', but 'ravers' was the best – and only – label to use at that time..."

Matt then explains the Helen Of Oi release: "It was actually Alan of Dig That Groove Clothes who came to a show and said that his friend might be interested in putting some stuff out for

Demonic Upchucks, by Roger Smale

Demonic Upchucks

449

us, so we gave him a CD and he took it to Helen Of Oi! That release had a massive effect on the band as it had worldwide distribution and, all of a sudden, people in London, Scotland, San Francisco…even Japan…all knew who we were and wanted to book us for gigs. Our young age and empty pockets meant that we couldn't do many of them unfortunately, including the shows we were booked to play in California with Clit 45 and Poxy, but that release was a real boost for us…

"And we were fine with the whole 'Oi!' thing," he adds, when pondering whether or not their affiliation with such a brazenly-named label might stereotype them forever more. "We loved the Angelic Upstarts, of course and the Bournemouth skinheads were a really good bunch who always looked out for us. Other bands on the comp, like Dick Spikie, Age Of Chaos and the Bollocks were not traditional Oi! bands either, so it didn't bother us at all; there was no real distinction as far as we were concerned."

Unfortunately it was to be the only official Demonic Upchucks release, but the band did some great shows to promote it – and a fair few that were memorable for all the wrong reasons.

"Worst gig?" sighs Alex. "Somerford in Christchurch could be a contender. It was the opening for a skate park in the middle of a council estate; some of the buck-toothed locals heard that the circus was coming to town and came out in their droves to assert their authority over 'their patch'. A series of fights broke out with the Bournemouth punks and the police came onstage and told us we couldn't play – but we played anyway. 'All Ravers Are Wankers' went down a storm as torn tracksuits and baseball caps littered the surrounding streets! By the end it had become a siege and we were boxed in; we just couldn't leave, the place was surrounded. The police made some crass and racist remarks to a young punk girl which enflamed things further, but we eventually got away, literally being chased in our van with angry chavvy fists belting on the side of it all the way down the road… I hope we ran over a foot or two! But those early Upchuck gigs were all about getting banned from wherever we went and once we ran out of places to get banned from in Bournemouth, we set about getting banned from everywhere in Salisbury too – which we did with honours!"

Further recordings were made in October 2004 and May 2006 (the former turning up two minor classics in the making: the poundingly powerful 'An American Werewolf In London' and the Meteors-tinged 'TSO Zombie') but the proposed album for Pumpkin Records these sessions should have furnished never happened, although a successful visit to Sicily was undertaken anyway.

"Ah, Sicily…," remembers Alex fondly. "Matt, completely by accident, when looking for the song 'How Much Is That Doggy In The Window?', came across a band from there called Dog A Dog. After having heard only one song, he asked them to come to Bournemouth, which they did for the 2006 Bournemouth Punks Picnic [with Disorder, Spitroast, Extinguishers, the Taxidermists and Self Abuse]. The next year we went over there and it was a real culture shock. Everyone was really friendly and the beer – and absinthe! – was laughably cheap. There were millions of Demonic Upchucks posters all over the streets in Catania. The first gig was in a huge disused print works which was being squatted, overlooked by a nunnery. I hope they enjoyed the gig as much as we did. We also played a really messy gig with a free bar which the *carabinieri* [armed police] broke up. Dom was asleep on the floor doing an impression of a rug, Alex was asleep with a glass of Limoncello in his hand and God only knows what Matt was doing, but rest assured it was not why the armed police turned up…"

Although they occasionally galvanise themselves into action infrequently, the Upchucks, *possibly* because of the non-appearance of their album, *probably* because they're so busy with other projects, find themselves in a state of hiatus right now. Dom drums for both the reformed Self Abuse and also the C30s (alongside Andy Nazer from Self Abuse), Matt plays guitar with grunge-punks the Subatomics and Alex is with Blandford-based Thunderdump ("We only play seven or eight times a year in strange West Country villages…!") and new 'thrash-punk' band Double Cross.

"And Smash was last seen living in Bournemouth pier toilets! No-one has heard from him since," laughs Matt, before adding on the band's fairly localised legacy. "When we started the Upchucks, we wanted to have fun and try to kickstart something which was different to the awful piss-poor indie scene of the mid/late Nineties, so, in that sense, we achieved everything we wanted to. It was always about engaging kids into doing their own thing, forming their own bands and their own scene and we are pretty convinced we did that. People needed that choice, away from sorrowful indie shit, rave or Bon Jovi and if we gave them that…then mission accomplished!

"We started out as nihilistic youngsters fuelled by our hatred of popular music and conservative tastes and although little changed in that respect, we also set our sights on bigger issues like private security, right-wing tabloids and devious political agendas. The message has remained the same: there is always a choice, don't believe what you are told…and the biggest crowds are never the best!"

SELECT DISCOGRAPHY:

LP:
'Punks, Skins And Herberts, Volume Five' (Helen Of Oi, 1999) – *four-band compilation*

AT A GLANCE:
It's a shame the planned album never made it into the racks, because the Upchucks have some great unreleased material just waiting for a label that believes in it.

BUS STATION LOONIES

While not quite an out-and-out comedy band, Plymouth's **Bus Station Loonies** have certainly had their tongues in their collective cheeks most of their 'career' and are also the only band in this book to have made it into the *Guinness Book Of Records*! Yes, really, but more on that later; for now, let's start at the beginning and discover exactly what shapes such a bizarre anomaly as a band that can only be described as half Splodgenessabounds/ half Crass…!

"The Bus Station Loonies were a band name long before we were a band proper," admits vocalist Chris 'Wheelchair' Willsher. "It was New Year, 1995 and I'd not long got home from a 38-date tour, as drum monkey with Edinburgh anarcho-punks Oi Polloi. When you play out for that length of time, you lose a certain sense of reality; for me, once I'd returned to real life (and by that, I mean, not touring), I found myself craving a return to gigging all the more. My previous band [CDS] had split as well, so I was feeling slightly at a loss. I had always been a drummer and sometimes (not including the bands already mentioned) it had been with bands I felt took themselves way too seriously. I also felt those not penned-in by a drum kit didn't take advantage of their legs and the space around them…in other words, I felt an overwhelming urge to go bonkers on stage.

"With that desire to inject a hefty dose of humour back into punkdom (while still attempting to convey a serious message…but more of that later), I contacted various people I knew from other bands, who all possessed a temperament likely to be interested and the ability to humour me for the next six months, while I got it out of my system. In a wonderfully short space of time, my fellow Loonies were recruited: Tony Popkids (drums), his previous bands Wyrmturf and Bikini Atoll having recently dissolved; The World-Famous Nuf (bass), with whom I drummed in his (also none-too serious) band Hooray! We're Dead; Dancin' Dave Worth (Flying V guitar and matching moustache), also from HWD and Paul Tax (guitar), who I'd also drummed with in his band Valium Ten.

"Of note, to anyone who may have the patience and anorak-ish inclination to create rock family trees, the previous drummer with Valium 10 was Andy Hoare (original drummer with Amebix) and Hawkwind's Martin Griffin was Hooray! We're Dead's first sticksman. So, the Loonies have connections, vague and loose though they may be…

"Our first practice was in an electronics workshop, in the middle of Dartmoor, during a snowstorm. I was still playing with Oi Polloi and would latterly join Disorder and Eastfield for tours and recordings, but the Bus Station Loonies would continue to rattle on regardless and against our better judgements. During our 'life' as a band, we've managed to ruin the careers of at least a dozen guitarists and seven bassists, as well as several 'guest appearances' (including Dick Lucas, Josef Porta and Taf Disorder) who've all soiled their reputations on our behalf. Tony Popkids and I are resigned to the fact that we're lumbered with each other by now."

After making their live debut at the Plymouth Cooperage during July 1995 (with local band, Our Fate) ("It was a shambles," laughs Chris. "More a fancy-dress puppet show than a gig…"), the Loonies self-recorded their desperately-ropey-but-charming-in-a-very-strange-sorta-way 'Dodgy Cider Fix' demo, before venturing into the local home studio of 'Wild' Johnny Clipboard to record their 'A Thin Veneer Of Stage Paint Rebellion' demo.

With its intriguing title lifted straight from a letter criticising the Loonies that had been published in the Plymouth arts and entertainment magazine *Scene*, it included a reggae version of 'Temple Of Love' by the Sisters Of Mercy, which was either genius or sacrilege depending upon which side of the goth/punk fence you tended to hang out. Four tracks, including their cover of 'Hops And Barley' by Wat Tyler, were used on the 'Squiffy On A Small Amount' 7-inch, released by German label Campary early in 1996, which was promoted by an eventful UK tour with PMT and the Filth, as well as a multitude of one-off gigs around the country with everyone from the UK Subs and Citizen Fish to X-Ray Spex and Bad Manners.

"We're very fortunate to rarely experience a bland gig," claims Chris. "We've had entire

Bus Station Loonies, live in
Exeter, Chris Wheelie

Bus Station Loonies, 1995

audiences leaving the venue, entire audiences taking over the stage (while we all leave… well, apart from Tony…you see, drummers are prisoners!), trapped antics beneath a stage, tear gas incidents, laxatives fed to us disguised as locally produced wine before a gig, policemen encouraged to join us in an open-air conga, public head shavings and last-minute (literally just before the gig) drumming volunteers, very much in a sorta poor person's Play-Doh version of the Who.

"One gig – an engagement party – resulted in my breaking an ankle, when guitarist Paul Tax landed on top of me, somewhat unexpectedly… In fact, that set the trend for quite a number of gigs; I suffered a broken nose three times, twice due to my new-found over-excitement at being able to leap off stage into the audience (the novelty of not being hemmed-in behind a drum kit still being very much in its prime) and once due to my lying on the floor in the path of a rather inebriated reveller, whose dance path included my face. Two broken ribs too, due simply to a sudden urge to fall forward onto the floor, without putting my arms out to cushion the obvious (in retrospect) impact of a hard wooden floor.

"Miraculously we've only had the plug pulled on us twice; the first being a gig which was on some kinda minstrel's gallery and there was a staircase which ran down to where we were playing. It seemed like a fun idea to hurl myself down the staircase during one of the band's obligatory guitar solos…the first time was done a la professional stuntman, all floppy and pain-free; the second tumble was slightly more hurty. And didn't go down well with the management.

"The manager at another venue was, for some reason, offended by the fact that we had people dancing – such debauchery! – and when she expressed her distaste, we got everyone to sit on the floor. That didn't go down well either…you can't win sometimes. A further venue wasn't happy with all the shaving foam on their delightful carpet after our set. Punkers, eh? You give 'em a free carpet shampoo and that's the thanks you get. I nearly had a set-to with an enraged PA engineer once after getting shaving foam in his £80 microphone. The final song we played then somehow involved my singing the entire thing with a whole jam doughnut crammed in my mouth; when he stormed the stage, demanding the full price for his microphone, I tried to apologise with the doughnut still making coherence somewhat tricky and he stormed off just as quickly, leaving me with my £80 intact.

"Oh yeah, we played in Falmouth [Cornwall], with our new bassist [their old recording engineer, Wild Johnny] clad in a life-jacket and ski-mask and, no sooner had we finished the set with 'Temple Of Love', than we were berated by a – quite literally – weeping audience member who managed to choke, between sobs, 'You bastards! You've ruined my favourite song!' Actually, memorable gig experiences could be a whole chapter by itself for us and I could easily write a book entitled *You've Ruined My Favourite Song!*"

After split cassettes with Fungi Gone West and Combat Shock and countless contributions to DIY punk compilations around the world (including a version of 'The Sideboard Song' by Chas'n'Dave for 'The New Wave Of Chas'n'Dave' LP released by Spanking Herman), the Loonies finally recorded their debut album, 'Mad Frank's Zonal Disco', which Chris released on his own label, Ruptured Ambitions in 1999.

"Ruptured Ambitions actually started life as a compilation tape label in 1989," he explains. "It was also a fanzine and eventually the two were married, with each issue having an accompanying cassette featuring many of the bands being written about. This helped my passion for promoting the unknown, the new and the underdog and I still find discovering hitherto-unheard punk bands far more exciting than a new release or gig by an established and well-known group.

"Anyway, the first compilation was a 95-minute (yup, just being bloody awkward…) tape entitled 'Fish Out Of Water'. Released with a massive booklet in the summer of '89 as a fund-raiser for the Dr Hadwen Trust for Humane Research, it included everyone from Oi Polloi and Conflict to lesser-known bands like Family Bastardo, Groovy Trash and Hooray! We're Dead. It was this tape which enabled me to first come into contact with such wonderful and helpful people as Dick Lucas, Charlie Harper and Dean Beddis, as well as fuelling my interest in helping arrange benefit all-dayers with local bands.

"With the fund-raising aspect of releases still in mind, 1993 saw the release of the first vinyl from Ruptured Ambitions, 'You've Heard It All Before', a double album of Crass covers, sold in aid of Rape Crisis Centres in the UK. Because it was the first release, it has a special place in my heart; the wonderful interpretations of Crass songs from the likes of Blyth Power, Decadence Within, Wat Tyler, Oi Polloi, PMT, the Apostles and Maggot Slayer Overdrive were all a breath of fresh air. There were elements of reggae, metal, techno (Influx was Col from Flux of Pink Indians dabbling with the genre) and folk, as well as inventive forms of punk.

"The Levellers were due to contribute 'Big A Little A', but their management wouldn't let them and Alice from Chumbawamba simply blurted, 'We no longer want to be seen as "a Crass band"!' Get away! But we had the Spinners (three punk women from Turkey), Ten Naked Fish (a Citizen Fish/Naked Aggression collaboration) and Roddy (editor of Manchester's *Shit, Not Another Fucking Fanzine*) drinking lager and quoting Crass lyrics in his kitchen, so I was more than happy. Most importantly, we had Ernie, my dad, guesting on trombone on the CDS track 'You've Got Big Hands'; that makes that album priceless. It really is about time it was re-issued on CD, as it's a gem…

"Ten years later, a 'sequel' entitled 'Angry Songs And Bitter Words' came out on RA, another Rape Crisis benefit that featured cover versions of songs by the Mob, Conflict and Rudimentary Peni, etc performed by UK Subs, English Dogs, the Varukers, Fleas and Lice, Subhumans, Terminus and Chineapple Punx. If anything, it was better than 'You've Heard It All Before' and needs a proper re-release too. The Bus Station Loonies recorded a version of Zounds' 'Can't Cheat Karma' which, for me, ranks among our better covers…

"But no, Ruptured Ambitions has not been overly prolific in the vinyl, tape or CD stakes, although, looking back, there have been a few: EPs by Police Bastard, Sensa Yuma, the Dangerfields and the infamous Anti-Chumbawamba EP, 'Bare Faced Hypocrisy Sells Records', plus albums by Eastfield and the Loonies. I suppose the Loonies are probably the best seller on the label, but in a steady and constant kinda trickle rather than any sort of hysterical boom. The link between both the band and the label is that both are an expensive hobby and have an awkward charm which is a bit tatty and tinpot. Plus, both are a childhood dream come true, so I've little to complain about…"

A superb collection of great tunes – from the strident folk rock of 'Kill That Nazi (In My Head)' to 'Bloody Drunkards', which sounds like an uptempo fusion of the Test Tube Babies and X-Ray Spex! – all linked together with an assortment of silly interludes, 'Mad Frank's Zonal Disco' is undeniably one of the most fun punk albums of the Nineties. Your author defies anyone to listen to 'Have You Any Idea Who We Are?' (which is pure early Antz filtered through the Toy Dolls and the Rezillos…yes, really!) without a smile on their face.

"What I can recall most about that album is that it took a bloody long time," laughs Chris.

"A ridiculously long time, in fact; something like 18 months… I mean, who did we think we were? Yes or something? I'm not wishing to sound ungrateful, 'cos I am very happy with the album and still enjoy listening to it 12 years on, but it's the problem with having an ambitious bassist in the band who also happens to be an incredibly talented sound engineer. He wants it to be better than anything else and so goes somewhat over-the-top. That said, we are something of an over-the-top band anyway, so I think, as a debut album, it's quite fitting. Some people say they don't listen to it, as with the plethora of overdubs and silliness, it's far removed from what we sound like live, which they prefer and I can very much see their point. I still have the 'live' in-studio recordings on tape, complete with 'guide vocals' and us just playing the songs all together, with no additional overdubs or anything and, for many of the songs, it makes for a far better recording. The Loonies may be larger-than-life and theatrical, but it's also that stripped-down rawness which is more in keeping with our sound.

"It's very easy to get a bit carried away when in a studio, but I suppose, why not? Have some whizzy effects because you can! Some inserts between tracks I find irritating and I think there are far too many of them, but that was Wild Johnny for you and you couldn't knock the fella for enthusiasm. He loved the Loonies, quite passionately and unhealthily; I ruined his life by replacing him and, despite only living in a recording studio on the other end of the city, haven't seen him in 10 years. That is definitely another story which could take up an entire chapter in my own book. And will one day…

"As for the title, you can put it all down to the mind of Loony Tony Popkids. When we were in Nottingham during the 1996 tour, Tony noticed posters advertising 'Mad Frank's Disco', boasting Fifties, Sixties, Seventies, Eighties and Nineties music; Tony became obsessed by the concept, having decided that Mad Frank played all these eras simultaneously, surrounded by a booth containing five separate turntables. Each played to its allocated 'zone' (separated by a rope fence, if memory serves correctly) and, having paid only to dance to Eighties music, for example, punters were not allowed to stray into another zone, on pain of ejection. This notion became a fixation for 'Rambling' Tony Popkids, who would engage everyone he met during the rest of the tour, with tales of Mad Frank's 'Zonal' Disco, much to their bemused smiles as they reassuringly backed away from the gibbering eejit. Again, it's a title which intrigues…couldn't have been called anything else, could it?

The oddest aspect of 'Mad Frank's…' for me is that there are singers and other musicians Johnny recruited who, despite my singing along with 'em on record, I've never met. Not sure I like that somehow, but when all is said and done, I still like the album; it makes me smile…"

Unfortunately it would take the Loonies 10 more years to record another full album, but they kept busy with various compilation appearances and the organising of the annual Plymouth punks' picnic – which led to a Channel 4 documentary about them, entitled 'Punk's Picnic' funnily enough, which aired in 2000 as part of 4's 'Other Side' series and re-ran in 2001 and 2002.

"Matt Tiller, the bloke who produced the documentary, used to play guitar in a local band we gigged with," explains Chris. "He started working for Channel 4 and, having made a documentary about naturists, decided a feature on Bus Station Loonies was the natural progression. When he spoke to me about it, I replied that I thought it would make for extremely boring viewing and that a film about the Plymouth punks' picnic would be much more interesting; the event was coming up and would involve a variety of intriguing folk he could interview. Having experienced punks' picnics in the early Nineties, playing with CDS and Oi Polloi in Nottingham, Birmingham, Southampton and London, I was aghast when I discovered Plymouth had never held one.

"So, in 1997, I cobbled together the first of what was to become an annual event, the first one being a bit of a scoop, as it was very much a key part in the reformation of the Cult Maniax, along with lots of other wonderful bands from all over the place: PMT, Chineapple Punx, Red Letter Day, One Chord Wonders, Combat Shock, Kreosote, who all helped make it a dazzling debut. It was a somewhat ambitious start, being a three-day weekend affair, but it seemed to work; a surprising amount of people travelled especially for it (and we *are* out on a limb down 'ere) and it even got a double-page spread in *The Big Issue*! I carried on as (dis) organiser of the Plymouth picnic for several years, knocking it on the head after 2004, but the baton was passed on, I'm delighted to say, to local legends Taz, Spud and Dave 'Mister' Jones (himself a part-time Loony, whenever Popkids injures himself doing his daredevil stunts), with involvement from Mark McCann (a character who, nationwide, wherever you go, if you mention you're from Plymouth, people say, 'Oh, you must know Mark McCann!') So the picnic is now in its sixteenth year and I came out of 'retirement' to put it on again in 2011.

"The TV documentary was from the 2000 picnic and features interviews with No Comply, Spudgun, Dr Gruff and Charlie Casey, from the band Menace, who is now very much a part of the Plymouth punk scene. Despite way too much on the Loonies (in particular, some buffoon with a mohican and massive eyebrows) and a notorious look at the Plymouth Morris Dancers, it's finally been posted on YouTube, should anyone fancy being tickled? I was amazed at the amount of people who watched the original broadcast – it was on a Friday night, around 2:30am, back in the days when pubs and clubs still chucked out long before then – but would've loved more on other individuals and bands. Mysteriously, there was nothing of Citizen Fish – perhaps Dick scared him? – but it sure did us Plymouth punkers proud…and it was great being on the telly!"

The next milestone in the Loonies' relentless quest for global domination was an inclusion in the *Guinness Book Of Records* for playing an incredible 25 gigs at 25 different venues in just 12 hours…! "I often ask myself now how the hell we managed it! And, in all honesty, I've not actually been quite the same since this madcap escapade, but I'll elaborate further about that in the next part.

"Basically, our then-bassist Wild Johnny Clipboard was (and probably still is) a workaholic and it was all his idea and, to his credit, organized brilliantly. 25 gigs in 12 hours…? I need a lie-down just thinking about it! So, it was Wild Johnny's whim, his pet project and the rest of us just let him do all the spade work. All the gigs were in and around Plymouth, each set was 20 minutes long and it was filmed again by Matt who'd made the *Punk's Picnic* documentary, but has never seen the light of day, as far as I know. And it did raise a few thousand quid for a special-needs music school in Devon, so it wasn't all for puff and pomp. We managed it, quite simply, thanks to Johnny's meticulous planning (which wasn't quite faultless; one gig in particular was right out in the sticks and nearly cost us the whole thing, having spent way too much time going up rickety lanes and being chased by irate locals with flaming torches) and, especially, by the six-man crew we had, who were working in three pairs, setting-up all the amps, drums and PA as needed. So, as one gig was being played, another was being dismantled and a third set-up ready; those fellas deserve the true credit.

"It got the band a mention in the 2002 and 2003 *Guinness Book Of Records*, which was another childhood dream come true – and without having to wear a beard of bees or anything! Somewhat amazingly, the record has since been beaten by another Plymouth band (and also mates of ours), Black Friday, who made it up to a staggering 30 gigs. There must be something of the masochist in groups around these parts. Angus Old, the present Loonies guitarist, has often spoken of our attempting to gain the record back… he's welcome to try, but I'm staying in bed that day!"

Although they toured the UK in 2001 and 2006 and Ireland in 2003, the band were somewhat restricted by Chris contracting ME (Chronic Fatigue Syndrome) and it wasn't until 2010 that their sophomore album, 'Midget Gems', which pretty much picked up the baton of choppy, quirky pop-ska-punk handed down from 'Mad Frank's Zonal Disco', was released by Ruptured Ambitions. Apparently there's enough unreleased material from the last decade for a third album ("But it didn't seem fair to inflict that on folk just yet," laughs Chris) and plans are afoot for a return to Europe sometime soon.

"I don't think anything really does set us apart from our peers," he offers, far too modestly, of the impact the band has had over the years despite their frugal back catalogue. "Like a lot of punk bands, we're a bunch of geeks when it boils down to it. Only Popkids is tattooed, only Angus is pierced and I'm the only one with the vague remnants of a mohawk. The Bus Station Loonies are just another punk band…unusually, perhaps, getting angrier with age.

"It has been remarked upon that 'Midget Gems' veers more into protest and politics, while 'Mad Frank's…' is more comedic tomfoolery, but that's no bad thing. We're still into social commentary and we're still very much about daft entertainment and if we can somehow still include elements of the two in whatever we do, I'll be a happy chap. We ain't ever gonna change the world and would never be seen as anything remotely representing revolution, but I do know of at least one right-wing skinhead in Essex who dropped his fascist mates and radically changed his views after he'd written, asking me for a copy of the lyrics to 'Kill That Nazi (In My Head)'. I'm forever humbled by that and suppose that's some kinda difference we've made right there; small-scale, I know, but pretty major nevertheless. If we are remembered for anything, though, I just hope we helped brighten up a day…"

SELECT DISCOGRAPHY:

7-inch:
'Squiffy On A Small Amount' EP (Campary Records, 1996)
'Ensure Your Needle Is Clean And Free From Dust' EP (Ruptured Ambitions, 1998) – *split with Anal Beard*

LPs:
'Mad Frank's Zonal Disco' (Ruptured Ambitions, 1999)
'Midget Gems' (Ruptured Ambitions, 2010)

AT A GLANCE:
Chase Chris up for one of the albums – the most fun you'll ever have getting politically indignant! chris_willsher@btinternet.com

ANNALISE

The strangely-named **Annalise** are a quietly influential band from Exeter, utterly integral to the development of an ethical punk rock scene in the Southwest, who are still making their painfully personal melodic hardcore noises even today. They came into existence as Annalise during 1995, basically an extension of another well respected band, Wordbug, who themselves were a fusion of two bands featured in previous books in this series, Dorset's Hate That Smile and Exeter's Mad At The Sun.

"Myself and Paul Chambers from Hate That Smile had heard Ed [aka vocalist Martin Edmunds] in Mad At The Sun and really liked what he was doing," explains original guitarist Alex Vann. "We didn't know him but we got in touch anyway and asked him if he wanted to form a band. I didn't have a plan; I just needed to express myself through music and I still do.

"My first band Atrox was definitely a punk band and I'd say Hate That Smile was too, whereas I definitely saw Wordbug as hardcore, us being much more influenced by American bands. I would say the album that influenced me and Ed the most at that time was Television's 'Marquee Moon' but I admit I was totally obsessed with the first two Dag Nasty albums. Also Hüsker Dü, Minutemen, Firehose, Minor Threat, Black Flag... all the usual suspects really, but also Seventies punk and anarcho punk – not to mention all sorts of other music that I dare not mention here...!"

After recording a three-track demo at PIJ Studios in Bristol, Wordbug, who after Paul's departure comprised of Alex and Ed with guitarist Dave Bibby, bassist Dan Schwalm and drummer Nigel Coleman, entered Weston-super-Mare's Whitehouse Studios to record a second demo, quickly followed by the 'Losing It All' LP, a debut album that saw the above-mentioned Dag Nasty influences in full effect and the band enthusiastically hitting the road in support of it.

"I really enjoyed the sessions for that album," remembers Alex. "We were very haphazard and under-rehearsed, with cheap, badly set-up instruments and amps, but somehow despite those adverse conditions – or maybe because of them – we came out with a good album.

"I remember touring being a bit farcical, though," he admits. "We'd forget to bring plectrums, leads or drumsticks, we couldn't tune up properly, we'd break strings and not have spares; Ed would lose his voice, occasionally the band would be happily playing one song – except for one member who would be doggedly persevering with a different one. I remember a gig at the 1 In 12 where all the above happened to such a degree that it must have seemed to the audience like a very challenging piece of performance art! Also etched into my memory is us all sitting in a motorway service station cafe in the middle of the night, starving hungry with no food and absolutely no money between us. I remember asking myself what the fuck I was doing there....having said all that, we did also play some great gigs".

After taking a year off to travel the world ("It must have seemed like a walk in the park after touring with the band," laughs Alex) Ed, alongside Alex and Nigel, recruited new guitarist Steve Craig and bassist Dave Goodchild, the latter of whom was another ex-member of Mad At The Sun.

"After Mad At The Sun, I joined a band called Soundhouse [with Wayne Maskell who later went on to drum for the Heads]," explains Dave. "That was about 1990; then when Ed got

Annalise, Bri and Dave,
by Russel Remains

Annalise, Ed and Jo, by Dave

back from his travels, he set up the second incarnation of Wordbug and I joined as bass-player shortly afterwards. About that time, we were full steam ahead putting on punk and hardcore shows at various Exeter venues under our banner, Hometown Atrocities; stuff like Fugazi, Victim's Family, Snuff, Senseless Things and the like. My club, the Cavern, had its first show on St Valentines Day, 1991, with Quicksand and a Dutch hardcore band called Nations On Fire."

A second album, 'Nothing Clear Remains' was recorded but never saw the light of day while the band were together due to the demise of their then-label, SMR Before the label folded, though, the band toured the UK twice to promote the album.

"We did one tour with Blaggers ITA," recalls Alex, "and about a week before our gig in Blackpool, Ian Stuart, prominent National Front member and lead singer of [notorious right-wing skinhead band] Skrewdriver, rang up the venue and told them to cancel the gig or he'd come down with his NF mates and smash it up. The Blaggers called a meeting with members of Anti Fascist Action to organise for them to bring lots of its members along to protect the gig and after a week of backroom meetings and subterfuge and secret rendezvous, we played in a room full of hundreds of AFA skins all tooled up and ready for action. Everyone had one eye on the door and you could have cut the atmosphere with a knife; the gig was good but very weird and thankfully the Nazis didn't show…"

After 1993's 'Zero' 7-inch, Alex left and then Nigel also departed, to join Dead Inside and was replaced on drums by Adrian Stroud in time for the 'Locked In' and 'Die' 7-inchs (1993 and 1994, respectively); the latter single featured guest vocals from Pippa Wragg and remains the band's most powerful, poignant moment. "Yeah, I think that was our best song too," offers Dave. "It seemed to sum up the mixture of politics, emotion and alienation that I feel Wordbug was all about.

"But my best Wordbug memories come from the shows we did in Belgium and Holland at the time. We hooked up with a band called Byetail, because their drummer [Stefaan DeKonick] organised shows in Belgium; we played some great shows in venues like the Pitz in Kortrijkt. I loved the squat scene in Europe… I loved all that stuff with huge distros laid out, cool posters, big bowls of vegan slurry made by members of whatever collective were running the shows…that's why I loved punk venues like the Pitz and TJ's in Newport, both of which actually informed what I try to do with the Cavern.

"If I could make the punk scene today play out like that scene from the early days by touching it with a magic wand, believe me I would… Anyway, the band at that time was complete chaos. Our driver was a young kid called Bobby, who had just passed his test and had a sense of direction so bad that it took us an hour to get from Eddy's house to Adrian's – even though it was only half a mile away in Exeter! It was amazing that we made any shows in the days before satnav – but we did.

"Then there was our guitarist Steve, who lived with that road protester Swampy and was so hooked on weed that he'd often merrily play a completely different song to the rest of us with his baseball hat slung on backwards and his eyes closed into heavy slits, thrashing away with a contented grin on his face while the rest of us were fuming at what a shambles it all was!

"I remember on one trip, which started off in Holland, he necked back a bag of mushrooms just before we got on the ferry, then was trying to get out of the car as soon as he saw a sign that read 'Amsterdam'. He was literally opening the car door as Bobby turned onto the eight-lane autobahn into the city. He'd heard that dope was legal in Amsterdam and thought that you could buy it over the counter anywhere – even in the motorway service stations! He said, 'Just drop me off here and I'll find my own way to the gig…' That was an hour outside Dam Square; eventually we convinced him to wait until we'd got to the Grasshopper Café, where he spent all his money on a massive bag of super skunk and wandered off loving life!" Steve's heavy use of dope eventually came to a head when Wordbug returned to the Whitehouse to record a new album, a situation that inadvertently perpetuated their metamorphosis into Annalise.

"He always was a pretty edgy guy," concedes Ed, "but he was getting more difficult to deal with as time went on. He was basically doing our heads in and I'm sure the feeling was mutual, but, despite this, his musical contribution to the band was at its peak around the time of the planned album; his melodic guitar style was pushing the band in a certain direction and he was writing some great stuff. His behaviour though was getting more unpredictable; getting out of your head is one thing, but doing it all the time is just boring for the people around you.

"He was doing daft stuff like demanding to be let out of the van on the way back from a show to take a lie-down in the middle of the road. We had to stop and let him out and he was just lying there in the middle of nowhere. Dave and Ade were saying, 'Let's go, just leave him!' And I was saying we couldn't 'cos he'd obviously get run over and then Steve would pipe up from on the road, 'It's okay, I'll be fine, just go!' as some car swerved past him…! He had just become too much of an effort to be in a band with, but we still thought we could at least make a cool album before things imploded. Turns out we were wrong!

"When it came to recording his extra guitar parts in the studio, he just froze completely; he had no idea what he was going to do. He just flipped out, slammed his guitar down and let out this stream-of-consciousness tirade about anything and everything, before letting everyone know that he wanted to go back home to Exeter. He didn't say a word to anyone then until a friend came to pick him up and get him out of the studio…

"Unsurprisingly upset and annoyed at their friend for letting them down at such a crucial moment, Dave and Ed called upon old friends Paul Symes from Speed Urchin and Darren Johns, who had been in Mad At The Sun with them, to learn Steve's guitar parts and a few weeks later the recordings were complete, albeit sounding far harder than originally intended. "Dave wanted harder guitars," explains Ed. "Paul and Darren's guitars were much thicker with a more distorted sound than what Steve recorded. This was totally deliberate on Dave's part and it was him who convinced me at least that we should start a new band in this vein. I think Adrian wanted to continue as well, but I remember thinking at the Whitehouse that I'd had enough and wanted to stop; it was basically Dave's determination that made Annalise happen…

"Once the recording was over, John Tripe joined on guitar (he had previously played in Blenderhead with Paul Symes) and Wordbug headed out to Europe one last time to fulfil dates they already had booked, before changing their name to Annalise ("John actually came up with the name in fact and we all liked it because it just isn't your typical punk name…"). They were soon planning a return to Europe with the new moniker and the 'Fettered' EP (for Out Of Order/Snuffy Smile) was lifted from the turbulent recordings with Paul and Darren so they had something 'new' to hawk on the road.

"Well, Mad At The Sun, Wordbug and Annalise always had volatile relationships with guitarists," admits Dave, "mostly I think because of our lack of aspiration to 'make it'.

Often our guitarists have gone onto more successful bands – like Paul Symes to Dead Inside, Brian Read to Kids Near Water and Darren Johns to Crazy Arm. When I say 'lack of aspiration to make it', I mean that quite literally too – not because we're lazy but because of what I think our bands are about: small-town hopes and dreams. The big difference in my mind between Wordbug and Annalise is our exact realisation of what kind of band we are; we're folklorists talking about small-time DIY culture, punk on a basic level of how it affects working-class kids and just hanging out in nowhere towns like Exeter. I've always thought most band people aren't really musicians, but with us I know it. We're all about narratives, the scene and cultural influences.

"We were spawned – like most DIY scenes by definition actually – by a lack of an existing scene. We knew that the only way we were going to make Exeter a better place was to terraform it! A lot of younger scenesters wouldn't know that punk in the Nineties – pre-Green Day selling out, I guess – was a completely niche market; there was no TV vehicle for it like Scuzz or *Kerrang!* TV. The only punk 'technology' that existed was 7-inch vinyl and cassettes, so you really had to make an effort to get hold of interesting stuff. I think that's a big problem today and is why the scene now is in some ways a simulation; one can not only buy an identity (including badges, T-shirts, music, books and zines) online, but a search engine will point you in the right direction of what other cool people like yourselves might identify with! I hate this. Do you know that a top seller in guitar shops now is the 'pre-worn' guitar? A new instrument that looks like it's been gigged hard! What a joke!"

Two demos recorded with John on guitar led to Pigdog Records approaching the band to release two MCDs, 1997's 'Always 18' and '98's 'Something's Got To Give', both of which also featured Adrian's brother Martyn on second guitar, tastefully thickening up the sound and helping put some 'oomph' behind Annalise's sublime melodies. After a slew of split singles with Astream, the Tone, Snatcher and Meanderthal, Annalise recorded their beautifully catchy 'Our Story Goes Like This' CDLP for Pigdog, another likeably raw record that revels in its simplistic transparency; there's no slick production, no trendy gimmicks, just good tunes…and plenty of them. Opener 'Signposts And Alleyways' and 'Selling Sand To The Arabs' instantly snare the listener with their huge, good-natured hooks. Just prior to the album, John left to go to university, so Ed and Dave wrote most of the record with Alex Vann from the old Wordbug line-up and although his full-time recruitment was seriously discussed, Brian 'Maiden' Read from Terminal Youth (themselves named after an Annalise song) ended up joining in time to finish the album.

"That debut album drew heavily on the mod revival sounds of '79," reckons Ed. "It opens with a Secret Affair sample and includes a cover of the Crooks' 'All The Time In The World', while another tune from the same sessions, that ended up as a B-side, includes a Purple Hearts rip. And the lyrics for the most part are about growing up around that period – a concept album of sorts…"

"I think that first album was the first time Ed totally understood that we had to sing about real-life people and places and be content to be a bunch of nobodies from a small town," adds Dave. "I love any songs that mention things that remind me of good times we had before real life concerns kicked in and some of the songs on 'Our Story…' are some of the best we ever wrote…" The album was also released by AGE Records in Malaysia and Annalise became the first UK punk band to ever play there in 2000, their ambitious Pacific Rim tour also taking in Australia and Japan.

"Travelling overseas was always the whole pay-off for being in a band for me," explains Dave. "The people you meet, the bands you see in different countries, the way the DIY scene is so similar across all sorts of other boundaries… I always remember when we played a punk gig in Kuantan in Malaysia; it was a lunchtime show and the massive mosque over the road was doing a call to prayer. The Malay scene seemed pretty into hardcore like Napalm Death, but one thing that stuck in my mind was how a load of girls came in with their faces covered, but wearing T-shirts from bands like the Exploited, with UK coppers giving the 'V's up' on them, that sort of thing. Halfway through our set at this bar called Lips Boom Boom, mothers were coming in and pulling their kids out – which was just like the shows we used to do in Exeter early on! The massive realisation for me was how identical the DIY punk scenes were in all the countries we played: Japan, Malaysia, Germany, Holland, Belgium…England. It's all the same people into the same things.

"That was probably the best time I've ever had in any band, when we toured the Far East. A great guy, Joe Kidd, set up the Malaysian shows; he has been in the hardcore scene since the early days and used to write a column for *Maximum Rock'n'Roll*, which is how we got to hear about him. It's interesting that we were the very first English alternative band ever to play in Malaysia; the negative exchange rate for the ringgit meant that most bands bypassed fabulous cities like Kuala Lumpur for Singapore. So we were the first… just before Napalm Death became the second.

"Japan was obviously a dream tour; such a fantastic place, with awesome bands playing with us every night like Screaming Fat Rat, 8-Roof and Pear Of The West. That tour was organised by Yoichi Eimori who is a bastion of the punk scene over there and runs Snuffy Smile, our Japanese label; he took us to some fantastic places such as Tokyo and Nagoya…

" More split singles followed (a mainstay concept in the DIY ethic of networking with like-minded bands) – Annalise sharing vinyl with the likes of J Church, Navel, Gunmoll and Three Minute Movie – with Brian leaving to concentrate on his other band, Kids Near Water, after the second album (2001's 'Versus Everything', where the mod vibe continued unabated with a cover of the Chords' 'Now It's Gone').

"When we played in Malaysia and Japan, I think we experienced a collective reminder of how amazing punk-rock culture can be, which sort of affirmed the route we were taking at that point," reckons Ed. "But on the downside, that tour was also the first sign that Brian wasn't 100% on the same wavelength as the rest of us. He wanted to tour constantly and make the band a full-time thing, which at that point we could have done; we had been talking to Vagrant Records in the States and were turning down so many tours (we said no to US, Brazilian and a couple of European tours around about then) that he just got frustrated with the whole thing.

"We didn't want it to be our jobs; we picked and chose exactly what we wanted to do, to fit in with the other things happening in our lives. Brian saw that we could do a lot more and when it was obvious no-one else wanted what he wanted, he began to concentrate on Kids Near Water. I remember when we got back from Japan, we played some shows with Discount and the Tone and he was pretty down and when I asked him what was up, he said, 'This is what we should be doing all the time…' He recorded 'Versus Everything' and then moved on to do his own thing."

Brian's departure paved the way for the brief return of Paul Symes, but by the time Annalise recorded their third album, 'Here's To Hope', for No Idea in 2005, Paul had been replaced by Jon 'Shoe' Curtis. Pippa Wragg, who had sang on the final Wordbug single, also provided some vocals for the album, which was essentially a continuation of the tried and tested Annalise formula: good, rocking tunes and heart-felt unpretentious lyrics.

"Touring abroad did have an influence on us," says Ed. "Playing with all those Japanese punk bands in 2000 definitely had an impact on the sound of 'Versus Everything'; the energy and intensity of the likes of Screaming Fat Rat and the Urchin helped shape that album. The song tempos are faster and the guitar sound is rawer and more upfront compared to 'Our Story…' and that's mainly down to being exposed to those Japanese bands live – the best of whom were mind-blowing – and wanting to bring that to our own music. That's the album that got No Idea into us; Var at the label was really into that one and eventually reissued it, as well as releasing 'Here's To Hope'.

"It's funny because no matter what influences I bring to the table I already know what our songs will end up sounding like and that album is a prime example of that. I was referencing a lot of acid folk and psychedelic stuff on those songs, which meant nothing to the others but they'd still just turn the oddest ideas into your typical Annalise tune. On the flip-side of that, when I do bring what I think is an obvious punk-rock number to the table, they don't get it at all! I did this song called 'One Final Chance', that came out on a 7" as a catchy punk thing and everyone was looking at me in complete bemusement. Jon said, 'I can't do this; it's like you've written it to be played on a lute!' But bring an idea based on some 15-minute Tibetan chant and within seconds it's turned into a two-minute Annalise classic! I don't get it but it works!"

"I don't think our 'sound' developed at all over the three albums," confirms Dave proudly. "And I really hope we never move on or change either. The only difference between the records is what Ed is singing about… The first one was about the DIY punk scene in our small town, the second was about some of the places we visited overseas and the last one was about how Eddy's dad died and shortly afterwards his son was born and how growing up fits into a punk/alternative person's life. We're writing a new record right now and I think Ed will want to move onto deeper relationships etc, but I want more stuff about the things we've done, the books we've read, the places we've played, the records we've listened to… More of the same, in other words!"

"I don't think anything sets us apart from anyone else," continues Dave, pondering on their apparently uncalculated and effortless, longevity. "I love the fact that we've never had an agent, never had a manager, never had a roadie, never had a rider… I don't even want to get paid for doing gigs any more and I even hope we don't get our expenses covered when we put out the next record. We're not that kind of band; we're just a bunch of disparate individuals that somehow, reluctantly most of the time, wrote the same song 30 times and got away with it!"

So, although the band went into a long hiatus after a gig in Cardiff in 2005 (at the Newest Industry Records all-dayer with No Choice), they never split up as such; they just carried on living, laughing, dreaming, crying…all those things that inspired them to make great music together in the first place…until they were ready to do it again. Since then, Adrian and Martyn have also become fathers, Jon has got married and has his own band, The Cut Ups and Dave still runs the Cavern Club – "24/7!" – with Pippa. In 2011, Ed also had a solo album, 'Here Come The Intrepids', released by Fixing A Hole Records in Japan and Unsane Asylum in the US.

"We haven't really stopped gigging," reckons Dave, of Annalise. "In fact we played with Dillinger Four a short while ago and are playing with the Bomb in Newport this weekend! I never wanted to officially split up my band for one major reason: nobody gives a shit! I talked about this to Eddy, about how people post all this, 'After much thought and sadness, we've decided to go our separate ways…' bullshit – like they've split up with their girlfriend or something…

"Mate, your lousy band has finished – please realise that it's only you staggering round town thinking the world has ended. Get over it! So, we will never actually split up, just to save this sort of embarrassment; 'Mum, I've got some awful, awful news…' 'What, you've been fired again?' 'No, worse that that!' 'What…you've got MS?' 'No, even worse than that, mum: tragically and due to irreconcilable differences, me and Ed won't be writing any more shit songs about Exeter EVER AGAIN!'"

SELECT DISCOGRAPHY:

7-inch:
'Zero' (1993) – *as Wordbug*
'Locked In' (1993) – *as Wordbug*
'Die' (1994) – *as Wordbug*
'Split' (Mother Stoat, 1998) – split with Astream 'Signposts And Alleyways' (Boss Tuneage,1999)
'Split' (Suspect Device, 1999) – split with the Tone
'Split' (Snuffy Smile, 1999) – split with Snatcher
'Split' (Deplorable/Squirrel Records, 2000) – split with Meanderthal
'Too Much Music And Too Many Bands' (Boss Tuneage, 2001) – CD single
'Split' (Beat Bedsit, 2001) – split with J Church
'Split' (Waterslide, 2001) – split with Navel
'Split' (No Idea, 2004) – split with Gunmoll
'Split' (Snuffy Smile, 2005) – split with Three Minute Movie

EPs:
'Fettered' (Out Of Order/Snuffy Smile, 1995) MCDs:
'Always 18' (Pigdog, 1997) 'Something's Got To Give' (Pigdog, 1998)

LP/CDs:
'Losing It All' (1991) – *as Wordbug* 'Our Story Goes Like This' (Pigdog/AGE, 1999/2000)
'Versus Everything' (Pigdog/Boss Tuneage/Snuffy Smile/ No Idea Records, 2001)
'Here's To Hope' (No Idea, 2005)

AT A GLANCE:
The 'You Can Dye Your Hair But Not Your Heart' CD on Canadian label KYMF compiles the 'Fettered' and 'Always 18' EPs, while the 'Tour Issue' CD (on Boss Tuneage in the UK and Ding Dong Ditch in America) compiles various Annalise singles. Also on Boss Tuneage, the CD version of 'Losing It All' compiles all of the best Wordbug recordings onto one disc if you want to check out the guys' earlier efforts.

CITIZEN FISH

The wonderfully invigorating (both musically and intellectually) **Citizen Fish** rose from the ashes of Culture Shock, the 'festival favourite' reggae/ska band featuring Subhumans vocalist Dick Lucas, A-Heads guitarist Nige and Organised Chaos drummer Bill. When they split in 1989, after three rather good albums, Dick and the band's last bassist, Jasper from the Rhythmites, formed Citizen Fish with ex-Subhumans drummer Trotsky and ex-Myriad Lifeform guitarist Larry.

"We got the name from [old friend] Pete The Roadie," begins Dick. "I wanted the word 'fish' in the name 'cos I like fish; I used to have pet fish when I was a kid and I like the way they calm you down when you look at them…just the way they swim around. And in theory – and everyone can make their own theories up, so I did – they don't fight wars, they don't pollute the earth, they don't kill each other…well, except that some of them *do*! But everyone knows what fish are and there are all sorts of varieties; there's no racism among fish…

"But anyway a shoal of fish moves as one, like birds do; it's the whole power of numbers thing and I like numbers too. Anyway, Pete was into his *Judge Dredd* comics at the time and he said, 'How about Citizen Fish?' Because there was a lot of 'citizen' names in Judge Dredd or something? So I thought, 'Yeah, alright!' Possibly not the best name ever, but it'd do; it was easy enough to spell, easy enough to pronounce…and it's a mixture of what we are instinctively. We're *all* a bit fish-like, aren't we? We have to co-exist with other people and get on with life and in reality we're all part of civilisation to some degree. And it was all about the contradictions inherent in that and how civilised people could be more unified if only they could take on board some more of their natural instincts and behave along those lines rather than blindly following the rules and the laws and the deadlines and the wage packets and all the structured stuff… So it was a mixture of structure and a free-form lack of it…

"Of course, we were in the shadows of the previous bands, which was an advantage because people would come along to the gigs just because it said 'ex-Subhumans' and 'ex-Culture Shock' on the posters, but also a disadvantage because of people's expectations and them wanting us to sound like one, or the other, which didn't quite work out. And whereas there's some people that say Citizen Fish is the best of all three bands, there's equally a lot that say we're actually the third best, or second best, or whatever. That's a pain in the ass, but that's the way it goes; the thing you do first will always stand out in people's memories most…"

Actually, Citizen Fish weren't/aren't a million miles away from Subhumans and Culture Shock and certainly not enough to cause fans of either band any consternation if they were hoping for a continuation of the stylistic arc began by them. Although it's safe to say they were faster and punkier than Culture Shock and slower, more ska-driven, than Subhumans, but with the same energy as both of those bands and of course Dick's provocative lyrics a welcome constant throughout.

"My lyrics reside in lyric books," he explains. "So there are old songs I originally wrote for Subhumans that might finally get used in Citizen Fish 10 years later… just because they haven't fitted with anything else yet. I don't write for any particular band or style of music – although I've got a beat in my head when I'm writing it – so it's whichever lyrics best fit the tune being played at me at the time. Though sometimes the guys have written a song and it's *this* long – any longer and it wouldn't be musically correct for them… They're getting a bit theoretical with their music, so age and wisdom are coming to bear on song structure…and I'll be like, 'Well, can we add one more verse? Because I've got a final verse here that sums it all up…' And they're like, 'No, sorry, it's long enough! Any longer and it just wouldn't sound right!' So sometimes I have to cut a verse out and my songs aren't just random reflections with a chorus shoved in here and there; they go in some sort of order and a story's being told and there are consequences to the verses as they go down…and to cut it short is very tricky – but it's three against one at this point, ha! It's give and take."

After playing their first gig upstairs at the Weymouth Arms in Warminster ("Everyone came along to see what the lack of fuss was about!"), Citizen Fish wasted no time getting back out on the underground live circuit and were soon in the Refuge, Reading, recording their first album, 'Free Souls In A Trapped Environment'. The album was remixed at Southern Studios, London, during the summer of 1990 and released soon after on Dick's own Bluurg label. However, by the time Citizen Fish recorded their second album, 1991's 'Wider Than A Postcard', Larry had been replaced on guitar by ex-Subhumans bassist Phil.

"Well, the vibe in the band just deteriorated with Larry, for some reason," reckons Dick. "So we said all this to him and he was okay about it, 'cos he wanted to go off to India anyway; in fact, he was so nice about it, we felt completely guilty! It's a horrible thing to have to do, to tell someone you don't want them in the band any more, but at that point it had to be done. It had all got a bit tense and odd, to be honest…

"And then we got Phil in, which upped the number of 'ex-Subhumans' to three and it was interesting hearing Phil play full-on ska music for the first time, but he was very good at it. 'Sink Or Swim' was the first song he wrote…a bit of a classic. Of course, the 'ex-Subhumans' thing on posters then intensified – and even more people were shouting for Subhumans songs…but then we [Subhumans] reformed in '98, which at least stopped people shouting for Subhumans songs, because they could go and see the Subhumans play them instead. So that took one little niggle away…"

'Wider Than A Postcard' was recorded by Harvey Birrell at Southern Studios during late November 1991 and as well as the aforementioned 'Sink Or Swim' featured the wonderfully quirky 'Give Me Beethoven…', complete with a fuzzed-out intro refrain from Beethoven's celebrated 'Fifth'.

"Talk about writing about what you know," laughs Dick. "That was written on an aeroplane, listening to Beethoven on the headphones they give you, thinking, 'This is excellent, what a way to go, if this plane crashes…' Because every plane flight you take, you think for at least five minutes, 'What happens if…?' And Beethoven would be very good music to die to… in a plane crash."

You see? Mad as a fish! But along with the manic 'Chili Pain', the plaintively moody 'Smells Like Home' and the insistent thump of 'Language Barrier', 'Wider Than A Postcard' remains a strong collection of cerebral tunes and established the band as a force to be reckoned with in their own right and definitely not reliant upon past glories.

After two singles – 'Disposable Dream' (b/w 'Flesh And Blood) and a split EP with AOS3 – Citizen Fish were soon taking their high-energy live set around Europe and the 'Live Fish: Alive In Germany' album was released in late 1992, a split release between Bluurg and German label Red Rossetten.

By this time, the band had supplemented their sound with a fledgling brass section, namely

Citizen Fish, Matt, by Joe Short

Citizen Fish, by Joe Short

Alex and Jim from Bender playing occasional trumpet. However, with the benefit of hindsight, Dick doesn't rate their recording debut – 1993's 'Flinch' – particularly highly.

"It's got great songs, but I think it's a weak recording," he ponders. "It was before Phil had discovered the best sound for his guitar – which was roundabout 'Lifesize'…when suddenly and I don't know whether it was the make of guitar or his pedals or what, but it started to sound more like the Sex Pistols as opposed to the Vibrators! He just had this massive guitar sound and it was really punchy and powerful…if he'd had that on 'Flinch', it would have changed the entire record, so I wish that had happened. It's not a regret, though; it's a good record with some good songs on it…it just doesn't sound that great. But the brass section was good too; having an extra instrument, with all those extra notes going on, it really brightened it all up…"

1993 also saw Citizen Fish undertaking the first of many tours of America, where they have cultivated a large – and encouragingly youthful – following through persistent gigging over the last two decades.

"Comparatively large, I suppose," says Dick, modestly. "We get between 50 and 850 people, depending upon where we're playing and what day of the week it is and what the weather's doing – all the usual restraints! We *do* average a larger crowd over there than over here, but there's more people over there and more venues…and there was, until lately at least, more money over there, going into people's pockets…probably still is actually. *And* there's more rabid fanaticism over there, which is scary, but definitely helps with people turning up to the gigs and buying the records and stuff.

"There are bits in the middle that are quite a long haul with a few half-empty shows in between, of course… I mean to get to Florida from, say, New York or Texas, which are the nearest large scenes, you have to traverse the Carolinas and Arkansas and Kansas… the Bible Belt basically…where on a weekday you'll be lucky to get 100 people at a gig. You can be driving along the roads there and see vast crucifixes sitting in the fields… 'Jesus died for your sins…' and now he's in real estate or whatever…

"I remember we played Oklahoma and there was this young kid who pulled out a pocket Bible and said, 'Can you sign it?' And I was like 'No!' 'Why not?' 'It's a Bible, I don't believe in all that…' 'Oh, go on!' 'No! Look, it's ridiculous, it's full of rubbish….' So I grabbed it off him and started flicking through the pages and told him to tell me when to stop, so he did; then I moved my finger around and he told me when to stop again and then I read that bit out loud and it was something along the lines of, 'Women shall take second place in the home…' So I said, 'There you go! Suppression of women – right there…picked out at random…this is the sort of stuff that's in the Bible! Treat women like shit, kill your enemies, believe in God or suffer; it's all about suffering and mindless belief…' Then his mate says, 'Yeah, but it was written a long time ago!' And I said, 'Well, stop reading it *now* then!'

"But it's always fun touring there and yeah, the more new people you play to, the less likely you are to give it up, I suppose. We have a lot of 40-plus year-olds over here; at least 50% of any given crowd are our own age…whereas in the States, the 40-year-olds can be counted on one hand in a crowd of 300 people, so there's a lot more younger kids over there. And it's not as if they are out to compare Citizen Fish to Subhumans and one's better and one's worse; they'll come and see both…they're just quite happy to see it played live at all, really. And they're not all bible-bashing rabid fanatics! There's plenty of completely sorted, fantastic, DIY people who are battling against a government many times worse than the one we're fighting against here; they're in the heart of the beast really, with a lot more things going against them: the whole structure of the government over there, the police system, the prison system, the state of poverty, the cost of medical protection…it's really bad right now."

By the time of 1995's 'Millennia Madness (Selected Notes From The Late 20th Century)', Alex's trumpet was firmly ensconced in the writing process and Citizen Fish were evolving into a big happy-but-angry, noisy-but-mellow, punk-rock-ska explosion of irresistible foot-tapping rhythms and synapse-stretching lyrical wordplay. Take the anti-consumerism rant 'Panic In The Supermarket' and convincing album opener 'PC Musical Chairs'.

"I wrote that because of all the political correctness going on, which – at the time – was just getting stupid. Certain words could no longer be said and actresses were now 'actors' and there were no chair*men* any more, just chair*persons*! When it started affecting the language, I got quite irate because I like language and it shouldn't be fucked around by people trying to be politically correct all the time. It was nothing to do with politics in the strictest sense anyway, it was more about politeness and not wanting to offend anyone, but sometimes you have to offend people to get a reaction and get things out in the open and discussed a bit. Political correctness was good initially, because it tackled things like racism and sexism and bigotry of all sorts, but then it went further and further and eventually got ridiculous…"

'Millennia Madness' was co-released between Bluurg in Europe and Berkeley label Lookout in the US, as was the band's next album, 'Thirst'. Recorded at River Studio, London, during early May '96, it was more of the same Fishy magic, the band subtly managing to find new ways to challenge the listener's preconceptions about life, love, work and…er…crying babies ('Scene 496: Cafe In Melksham').

"Yeah, I really like 'Thirst' too," agrees Dick. "It's got a very good sound and a great cover – which really shouldn't have much to do with it, but somehow it does! Great title too and lots of really eclectic songs on it, a real mixture of everything. There's odd bits, funny bits, heavy bits…

"'City On A River' was written after walking back home from a Bath pub," he adds, of one of the album's many stand-out tracks. "Through the streets and over the river and I came in and wrote that. It's about Bath really and watching buildings being knocked down and more buildings going up in their place, all along the river, with the river representing nature; it's just about structures and all the homeless people and housing being unaffordable… 'Wet Cement' [on 'Flinch'] was written along the same lines…there's too much concrete. Not enough greenery."

1997 saw the band touring Australia, with the 'Habit' 7-inch coming out on Lookout the following year and then the 'Active Ingredients' album in 1999. "We recorded that at Phil's house, on his own equipment," recalls Dick fondly. "It was a very DIY recording…a bit rough and ready, but I like that!

"Punk got very poppy in the Nineties," he adds, of that turbulent decade and the alternative music it spawned. "Rancid… Bad Religion… Green Day… Very Americanised versions of punk rock, with lots of close-harmony singing; well, certain scales of singing that a lot of bands do…and that took over a lot of the scene, at least to the idle listener. I heard Blink 182 the other day, for the very first time, on the radio in a shop and I thought, 'How can anyone call that punk rock?' It all got very commercialised, didn't it?

"But then you had bands like Eastfield, carrying on all through the Nineties, singing songs about the system and railways and having fun doing it – completely off most people's radar, but carrying on regardless, providing for the scene…admittedly a lot smaller than those American bands, but just as genuine, if not more so and the fact that corporations had caught on to the fact that punk rock was a saleable product – again! – didn't really change their approach. Underground punk rock has remained on a constant level all the way through since the early Eighties when it first went self-sufficient. Ever since Crass demonstrated we can do it without *their* help, any reversal of punk rock into the corporate coffers is despicable really."

The millennium came and went, without too much fanfare, to be perfectly honest and by the time of 2001's 'Life Size' album, the band had hooked up with San Francisco label Honest Don's. Another corker (seriously, these guys have always been *reliable*), with plenty of hard-rocking tunes like 'Internal Release' and 'Lose The Instructions', it also featured the song 'Autographs', an impassioned plea for common sense and dignity primarily inspired by their extensive touring in America.

"That song just had to be written, it really did! 'Read this and stop asking me to sign stuff!' Americans ask for a lot of autographs…the British ask for about 2% of what the Americans ask for…and mainland Europeans don't ask for them at all! And that's a whole statement about the nature of culture between America and Europe, right there…and even though celebrity culture is massive over here and horrible, it's all seeped over from America. Particularly Hollywood, of course. Hence all the shit Saturday-night TV, thrusting the public against one another to become celebrities…

"And it's seeped through to the punk scene, just like it's seeped through to everything else and you're up against google-eyed young kids, who can't believe they're stood next to you and say so, because they're very forthright with their opinions… 'Oh, I can't believe I'm stood next to Dick Lucas!' Well, do believe it, because I have to be somewhere on the planet and I'm right here at the moment…

"Part of me wants to get them into conversation about anything other than me, the band, the music…talk about the weather or something, anything on a level playing field with them…but it's hard in a gig situation. As for autographs, I used to write a slogan or draw pictures, anything but just writing my name; I used to be quite uptight about it and wouldn't do it at all and I used to give people lectures about why I wouldn't do it, until one day I lectured this kid who was about 13 in Tucson, Arizona and he burst into tears and I was like, 'Oh my God, I've made someone cry, this is bad!' So I signed it about eight fucking times… and realised I'd gone too far the other way then; there's some middle ground somewhere, where you can *not* sign things and get away with it, leaving people as happy as if they didn't even want you to sign it in the first place…but I've not found it yet.

"I thought I'd write a song about it anyway, to pre-empt it happening again, 'cos punk rock is a scene where we're all meant to be on a level, all meant to be equal…we're all oppressed, all miserable, all fucked-up in some way or other, but the basic unity in punk rock comes from us all being angry that we're not given enough respect in society and that things could be better. A mixture of those two things anyway; a basic awareness of bad things that are out there or inside yourself and being able to express those feelings. And in that sense, no-one should be asking for autographs, because there shouldn't be any heroes in punk rock… respect is a nice thing, but hero-worship is a horrible anomaly to the whole scene. And if you do or you don't sign them, you're either a rock star or an asshole; you can't win."

After the 'Deadline' split LP with New Yorkers, Leftover Crack, that enjoyed a vinyl issue through Alternative Tentacles and a CD issue through Fat Wreck Chords, Citizen Fish released the 'What Time We On?' live compilation on Bluurg in 2008, before losing long-time drummer Trotsky to the ravages of fatherhood and international relocation; he became a dad and moved to Germany. He still drums for Subhumans, but has been replaced in the Fish by the rather talented Silas, who has already made his recording debut (alongside new trombonist Matt) on 2011's 'Goods' album for Alternative Tentacles. Another bass- and brass-driven skankfest, it also boasts the band's best production to date and, now with well over 1,200 gigs under their belt, Citizen Fish show no signs of slowing up, despite both Dick and Jasper having just turned 50.

"Ha, yes, not so long ago I was thinking, 'I'm twice as old as most of the people here...' 'cos the average age of people at gigs is probably 20-something, but soon I'll be *three* times older," laughs Dick philosophically. "There's one review of the last album which said, 'The singer looks like your granddad!' Which was a bit extreme, I thought – but at least he liked the record. Getting older isn't a problem; I'm just grateful that I'm still doing this and haven't lost my marbles yet...

"If it reaches a point where I'm stood stock-still on stage and having to have lyric reminders for all the songs, then it's time to quit – when you physically or mentally can't do it, or just haven't got the same energy...'cos it's all about energy at the end of the day. Once the excitement's gone, then forget it, because you know it when a band's not excited by playing; they're just stood there, going through the motions...

"So, yeah, just to be remembered would be quite nice!" he concludes, when probed for his thoughts on the legacy the band will one day leave behind. "'They were fun and they made sense!' Not all heavy politics and not all dancy-dancy...but somewhere inbetween. You *can* have fun while you're being serious. I'd like to be remembered as a band that didn't fuck up along the way; it would be nice if no-one had anything really bad to say about us...as long as there's no negatives hanging about for our tombstones, 'They were a good band *but*...'! And if we inspired another band to form, or inspired someone to do something off their own backs, that would be the best achievement: 'Citizen Fish were great, they inspired me to – *fill in the gap here*!'"

SELECT DISCOGRAPHY:

7-inch:

'Disposable Dream' (Bluurg/Lookout, 1992)
'Split' (Bluurg, 1993) – *split with AOS3.*
'Habit' (Lookout, 1999)
'Split' (Thick, 2001) – *split with the Tossers*
'Split' (Fat Wreck Chords, 2006) – *split with Leftover Crack*

LPs:

'Free Souls In A Trapped Environment' (Bluurg, 1990)
'Wider Than A Postcard' (Bluurg, 1991)
'Live Fish' (Bluurg/Red Rossetten, 1992)
'Flinch' (Bluurg, 1993)

'Millennia Madness (Selected Notes From The Late 20th Century)' (Bluurg/Lookout, 1995)

'Thirst' (Lookout, 1996)

'Active Ingredients' (Bluurg/Lookout, 1999)

'Life Size' (Honest Don's, 2001)

'What Time We On?' (Bluurg, 2008)

'Goods' (Alternative Tentacles, 2011)

AT A GLANCE:

That's not as easy as it sounds when a band's this prolific and this consistent. Why not start with 'Goods' and work backwards? Incidentally, Active have recently reissued the three Culture Shock albums on CD as well.

SPITE

The origins of Bristol's **Spite** can be traced back to when drummer John Millier, formerly of Ripcord and Can't Decide and guitarist Pete Rose teamed up with bassist Mike and vocalist Bleeker, from the Institute Of Grinding Technology, as Dishcloth, a jokey Discharge covers band. They played a couple of local gigs – mates' parties and the like – before splitting, with a view to Pete, Mike and John doing a 'proper' band, Pete handling both guitar and vocals.

"But it was absolutely appalling," laughs Pete. "How the hell people can sing *and* play guitar is beyond me, because I certainly couldn't do it! As was very evident at those first few practices. No wonder then that Mike very quickly thought, 'Sod this!' and buggered off. I was going out with Beckie, who had played bass for Chaos UK, at the time and she said she'd have a go and John got Steve, who had been in Ripcord with him, in on vocals…"

This was late 1994 and with a fully functional line-up to break in, Spite spent the next six months practising up a set before playing their first gig at the Porter Butt in Bath on Friday 21 July 1995, supporting Meanwhile (who had previously been known as Dischange), Doom, Extinction Of Mankind and Haywire.

"We all had common ground, of course," says Pete, of Spite's influences when they started, "like Discharge, One Way System and Rudimentary Peni, who we all really, really liked, but we all had other influences as well. John was very into the Boston hardcore scene, Steve and Beckie were into early British punk and the UK82 thing like Partisans and I was into the anarcho-punk stuff. I'd been living in squats up in London, like the Peace Centre, where we put on bands like the Mob and Subhumans, so that was *my* background.

"We basically wanted to keep the band really varied…there were too many bands from that period who were just trying to outplay each other, forgetting about substance and tunes, playing faster and faster rather than working on their songs a bit: you know, trying to slow this part down, or putting a different part in here or there, or trying to have the bass playing something different to the guitar for once. That was what we were *trying* to do anyway and I hope it's evident from the two records we made. We wanted to make our songs layered and interesting, so people would keep hearing new things when they listened to them more than once, you know what I mean?

"A good band should be the sum of four equal and different parts. If everyone in a band just says, 'Well, I really like Antisect…', what's the band going to sound like? Antisect! And it's all been done before – by Antisect! There didn't seem much point in going down that route. So everyone brought something a bit different and we all had an influence on the songs, regardless of which instrument we were playing – we were all open to ideas from everyone else… there wasn't just one person taking the creative role. And if anyone thought that an idea wasn't any good, or had been done before, they would say and we wouldn't use it. It wasn't like we didn't care and would just use any old riff…"

So, armed with a good work ethic, some strong quality control and a clear vision of what they wanted to achieve with the band, Spite started gigging in earnest: places like Southampton, Nottingham, Birmingham and, of course, Bristol greeting them with open arms as they played out with the likes of Aus Rotten, Substandard, PMT and Masskontroll. And January 1996 saw them in Whitehouse Studios in Weston-super-Mare with engineer Martin Nicholls, recording the 'Last Orders' 7-inch, which Pete released on his own label, Blind Destruction (named after his favourite Crucifix song).

"I started the label literally because we'd recorded these tracks and we all thought they were good enough to be released, but nothing was really forthcoming. And I was doing alright out of my body piercing shop and – without wanting to incriminate myself too much! – sometimes it's better to spend the money you make rather than give it to the taxman. So I put the single out myself. But that was never a plan we had, to do our own records; we sent the demo round to a few people, but nothing was really happening on that front. I didn't really want to do it, I was totally out of my depth, but I had a lot of help from Marianne at DS4A, who had done a few releases and she gave me loads of contacts for distros and fanzines…it got pretty good reviews and we sold 2,000 copies of it in the end."

Not bad numbers for a self-released 7-inch and deservedly so, the EP being an exceptionally strong debut that demonstrated the musical diversity that Spite were striving for; the title track a tuneful mid-tempo number with some catchy guitar harmonies, the eponymous 'Spite' a raging thrasher of the highest order that would surely give the Varukers a run for their money and 'Crucifixation' a pounding anti-religious powerhouse, solid meat'n'potatoes punk riffing memorably underpinned by John's cascading drum fills. The band promoted the single with a 10-date UK tour with Cardiff's Four Letter Word during April 1996, before heading out to Europe the following month.

"It was brilliant," recalls Pete, of the UK dates. "We bought a van just before that and had it all boarded out by a mate and stuff; we contacted all these people up and down the country and booked nine or 10 gigs. Everyone told us we were mad, that we were going to lose money, that no-one would come and see us after just one single, but we did alright – we broke even and covered our costs anyway and we sold a fair bit of merchandise and stuff as well. The starter motor on that van caused us all sorts of problems; I remember it broke down once at this truck-stop where we met the Wurzels, who were also stopped there and we got talking to them – and the fucking Wurzels ended up pushing us down the road while we bump-started our van!

"As for the European dates, we just did a three-date tour, over a long weekend. I've got mates in Bremen; I used to go there quite a lot and there's this thing called the BOB Festival, which is Bremen Oakland Bath, so we used to go over there quite often. A friend there set us up a gig in Bremen and one in Hamburg and we knew the Fleas And Lice lot in Groningen, so they got us a gig there at the Glasfabrik. The Bremen gig was really good, then we went on to Hamburg, where the promoter, who was about six fot six with wild eyes and hands like shovels…he had that kind of look in his eyes where you thought he was going to kick off at any minute! He got more and more drunk and started insisting that we go with him to the police station to break out his friends who had been arrested! And we were like, 'Well, actually, we'd rather not, we'd like to get some sleep because we have another gig tomorrow!' And he was like, 'No, we *must* do it!' And we had to keep changing the subject to stop him dragging us down there…

"Then in Groningen, we somehow ended up on the door – don't ask me why; we knew nothing about Dutch money and couldn't speak the language! – and all these guys asked if they could come in on the guest-list. We said we needed every penny we could get so we could get home and they went, 'No problem!' And off they all went…they came back about 10 minutes later with this big canister of stolen diesel and said, 'Can we come in now?' 'Yeah, alright then!'"

Moving at something of a frightening rate (too fast for their own good, as it turned out), Spite were back in the Whitehouse recording their second EP in July '96 before returning to Holland for several more gigs in September, including an appearance at the North Sea Punk Fest in Den Haag.

"We *wanted* to put out three singles a year," reveals Pete. "So things remained relevant and we could keep things topical; also you could trace our development literally as it happened. I think I was trying to be too ambitious; it was my first real experience in a band and I was trying too hard to make it all happen… I was a frustrated guitarist, who'd always had these ideas that I couldn't do and then all of a sudden I *could* do them! I was finally in a band – so I naturally wanted to go on tour and record all the time! But Steve, John and Beckie had done it all before and it wasn't such a big deal for them…plus different people have different ways they like to unwind and going on tour and making records isn't necessarily it for everyone!"

'A Threat To Society?', as the second single was entitled, boasted a meatier, more 'upfront' production than 'Last Orders' and remains one of the more powerful, listenable punk EPs of the Nineties, songs like 'Don't Bother Me' filtering the spirit of early Exploited through the band's anarcho-punk and USHC fixations. The song 'Junkies…' – and indeed the cover image of Sid Vicious jacking up – were all inspired by personal experiences of the detrimental effect that hard drugs could have on the punk scene.

"Basically, at that time, a lot of my friends were starting to get into heroin," sighs Pete. "When I first started squatting in London in1983, it was at the Peace Centre in Roseberry Avenue and I came from a council estate – and heroin was not a drug that people took on council estates… I know it is now; it's prolific, but it wasn't then. It was something that rich kids who'd explored the hippy trail through Turkey, Afghanistan and India during their gap year did, so I didn't really understand what it could do to people. Anyway, we had a brilliant squat: gigs in the basement, a cafe and a bookshop on the ground floor, a big meeting room on the next floor and some bedrooms and a printing press on the top floor and everything, it was brilliant. We were these punks who had grown up listening to Crass and dreaming of

Spite, guitarist Pete Rose

Spite, live, Pete, Steve, John and Beckie

these autonomous zones and there we were, making it happen; we really had it going, a big building right in the middle of London. Then a couple of junkies moved in and things started going missing and all of a sudden people were moving out and the junkies were moving more of their mates in and soon everyone moved out.

"We squatted that building in September 1983 and by March 1984 they were stripping the pipework out and the place was fucked. So that was my initial experience with heroin and then when I moved to Bristol a couple of people I knew died from smack…but then it dissipated a bit. The people taking it either died, or got off it…but it seemed to come up again in the mid-Nineties and that was what the whole 'A Threat To Society?' concept was about. The song 'Junkies…' actually started life as a song about people in seaside towns such as Weston-super-Mare, where John and Steve are from; it was about people that live empty, meaningless lives, where getting hammered is the be all and end all of everything. We added the heroin 'dynamic' afterwards, because it was affecting the punk scene, at least here in Bristol.

"Punk could be such a positive force, all about building a better society; my opinion was always that those in authority were hypocrites and that we could do better than they could ever dream of, simply because they were too influenced by money and greed…but when all your mates are on smack, you know it's never going to happen. I can kind of understand why people were getting into smack, though; you've got all these ideas about change and equality and a better life for everybody and all we seem to be doing is banging our heads against a wall – and maybe some people thought it's sometimes easier to just stick a needle in your arm and forget about the outside world…"

The band continued gigging, including what Pete considers their best ever performance, supporting Battalion Of Saints in Newport, but soon started to pull in different directions and sadly split up rather prematurely in late '96, following a disastrous German tour.

"Personally I wanted to gig all the time, play here, there and everywhere, but John and Steve wanted to slow down a bit," explains Pete. "I can see now that not everybody wants to spend their whole life on the road, but back then I started to get resentful that they weren't 'pulling their weight', as I saw it, seeing as I'd bought the van and Beckie and I were doing all the driving…and *they* were getting resentful because they didn't want to play every night! So we were all pulling in different directions.

"Then Beckie got really ill with Crohn's Disease and was actually in hospital, right when we had this two-and-a-half week tour of Germany booked. I have no reason why I didn't just put it all on hold – I guess I didn't want to let the promoters over there down – but I got this guy called Rob in on bass from [Bristol band] Cripes. Steve and John didn't really get on very well with him though and they said they weren't doing the tour either, so I was like, 'Fine, see ya later!' We were all so stubborn and headstrong back then and we should have just sat down and talked about it, but we didn't and I ended up getting Jay and Phil from Chaos UK in. Rob ended up singing, because he used to sing in Cripes as well and Jay was a great bassist, but Phil just couldn't drum like John and so it didn't sound like Spite really. He was very powerful and could keep a good beat, but he was also very basic and really flattened the songs that John had made so dynamic. It didn't work anyway and with hindsight, we really shouldn't have gone over as Spite, so in the end I felt like we let the promoters over there down more by going over the way we did – it would actually have been better if we'd stayed at home. But hindsight's a wonderful thing and who knows?

The band might have survived if I hadn't done what I did."

After a final Spite gig at the Pack Horse in Bristol, Pete went on to play with In The Shit for several years, before joining the reformed Icons Of Filth, narrowly missing out on playing on their excellent comeback album, 'Nostradamnedus'; he also continued to run Blind Destruction, who, among other projects, issued the first two EPs by the Restarts, who would go on to issue three superb albums on other labels in 2002, 2003 and 2007. Meanwhile John did Dumbstruck, who released their 'If It Ain't Broke, Don't Fix It' 7-inch on Blind Destruction in 1999, before he and Steve started Violent Arrest, where they've since given full vent to their love of 'all things Boston' on several releases for Boss Tuneage.

"It was a shame that such a good band finished so quickly," concludes Pete. "We just about had enough songs for an album, but we never got round to recording them…we'd just about got to the point where we were really gelling together as musicians too; we were really starting to understand each other musically.

"But there were tons of gigs in Bristol during the Nineties; loads of squat gigs, loads of gigs in pubs and stuff and there were loads of good bands. Bristol always had strong links with Nottingham and with London, so there was a lot of travelling and visiting going on between those places and there were all these amazing gigs over in Newport at TJ's. I know punk was supposed to be lean in the Nineties, but I reckon there was tons happening and loads of great bands, so I don't know why people think like this. Maybe people understate what was happening at that time because, by its very nature, punk can be very cynical and sometimes very negative? But people shouldn't forget that it's actually about getting off your arse and making things happen which, without a shadow of doubt, loads of us did and still do."

SELECT DISCOGRAPHY:

7-inch:
'Last Orders' (Blind Destruction, 1996)
'A Threat To Society?' (Blind Destruction, 1996)

AT A GLANCE:
Both 7-inchs were also released by the Polish label Nikt Nic Nie Wie as a cassette; otherwise you'll just have to scour the internet for a download link.

MAGGOT SLAYER OVERDRIVE

On a slightly less serious note than Spite, the brilliantly-named **Maggot Slayer Overdrive** featured ex-members of popular Eighties Bristol bands Lunatic Fringe and Rancid and with song titles like 'Dial B For Bernard' and 'I Spit On Your Llama' could easily have been misconstrued – and subsequently dismissed – as some sort of joke band. But despite those scattershot lyrics and their manic live shows, their often ambitious punky crossover was more than hefty enough to encourage discerning investigation.

"The band officially formed early in 1989 when [guitarist] Pig [ex-Rancid] and I were joined by [vocalist] Alan O' Gallon and Mike Burton on bass guitar," begins 'other' guitarist John Finch. "The line-up was completed by Jules [also ex-Rancid] on drums. I don't want to destroy the mystique surrounding the birth of the name, but I *can* say that we had been considering 'Molequeen' and 'Combat Maggot' too, so you'll see that it was probably best that we went with Maggot Slayer Overdrive in the end. In terms of content, both musically and lyrically, almost all of the songs were written by either myself or Pig, roughly 50/50 I'd say, although the early set also contained a few songs Mike had written in previous bands, as well as a couple of 'humorous' covers, such as the *Flashing Blade* theme song…"

With John's material leaning towards an older punk style and Pig's more towards metal, the crossover element of the band's sound was well established early on, but few were prepared for the slightly surreal subject-matter of some of the songs and the chaotic live shows.

Admits John: "I suspect that, in the early days at least, the onstage gimmickry, which usually included some carelessly prepared and at times near-hospitalising pyrotechnics, coupled with the sometimes obscure song subject-matter, may have defined us as something of a joke band. I do recall that most of the band were a bit bored with how deadly serious parts of the UK underground punk and hardcore scene had seemingly become and so some elements of how the band presented itself were a bit of a reaction against that. In addition, it is fair to say that MSO members generally tended to verge towards the eccentric and this approach to life and music would usually be coupled with an extraordinary enthusiasm for alcohol consumption…"

"The first gig was in Hulme at Manchester punks picnic," recalls Pig. "I think we may have managed one song – probably that theme tune to *The Flashing Blade* – and were rubbish, but enjoyed it immensely. I remember on the way up the night before, John wouldn't stop the van for us to sleep until we found somewhere suitably haunted enough. We ended up next to that massive cemetery in Manchester and chased each other around the gravestones, dressed in sheets and sleeping bags…oh, the twatness of youth!"

However, Mike left after four or five gigs and was replaced by Luke 'Leathershredder', formerly of Night Terror Syndrome and Nessun Dorma ("His rather hyper approach to playing fitted in well with the band," laughs John) and the band settled down to some concerted writing and gigging. This line-up was responsible for the suitably manic 'Maggot Saki Nightmare', an 11-track cassette-only release, which they recorded under cover of darkness at a BBC studio in Bristol where a friend of Jules worked without his friend's bosses ever knowing they were even there. Until now. If they read this book.

More line-up changes were imminent though and by the end of 1992 both Luke and Jules had left, with the bass vacancy eventually being filled by Rude-Part The Bath (yes, his name

Maggot Slayer Overdrive, at Blaise Folly

Maggot Slayer Overdrive, on tour in the Land Of Nod

was Rupert and he came from Bath) and the drum stool by – and these are John's words, not mine – "the lunatic and unpredictable German drummer Fybs.

"Although the split with Luke and Jules was amicable," adds John, "it was perhaps then that the remaining members felt most isolated, as we struggled to find anyone prepared to replace them. There were always people involved in the Bristol punk scene who were prepared to work hard to put on gigs and organise other events during the low-key years of the late Eighties and early Nineties (most notably the Kronstadt Club and the *Skate Muties* [fanzine] guys); however, no-one could deny that there was also a cliquey aspect to parts of the scene, as well as deliberate uncooperativeness between some Bristol bands.

"It became clear that MSO would never really be accepted by some people and could therefore not come to expect any help or favours from certain quarters. But Pig, Alan and I still believed in our songs (and in our mission to spread the mayhem) enough to sustain the band until replacements were finally found. We had also by now built up something of an identity through our gig posters and somewhat humorous publicity hand-outs, which had helped to strengthen the band…"

The new look MSO made their live debut at the Sion Hill College in Bath with, among others, Citizen Fish and Knucklehead. As well as their friends in Bath, the band also enjoyed close ties with Corpus Vile, with whom they then shared a split LP on MCR (UK).

"We'd been friends with Corpus Vile for years," explains Pig. "I used to live with most of them, then they moved to a large semi-detached house opposite the HTV studios, complete with a practice room in the front room, which later featured in a TV programme where they used it as an example of a house left in the worst kind of condition and rebuilt it.

"We used to play together a lot and when Mike from MCR said he'd put a record out on his label, we decided to do a split. The recording was paid for by Fybs, who also painted the [awful] front cover – by looking at himself in the mirror when he had hepatitis! We both recorded our individual sides at the Whitehouse in Weston, where the bloke would always make everything sound too clean; he still does even now and you can instantly tell something recorded there by its lack of 'oomph!' I'd also say that, apart from being too clean, our side – in my opinion, at least – is too *slow*, but that was just how Fybs played. One good thing about the split though was that Corpus Vile got offered a tour and, due to having done the split with them, plus our new drummer had a big Mercedes van, we were asked to go as well, which then led to a tour at least once a year from then 'til we split up…"

Despite looking pretty bad due to the garish cover art, the split LP was a cracking example of the crusty punk/metal crossover thing that has reared its ill-tempered head in the UK on several occasions over the last three decades, both bands contributing suitably intense material delivered with a compelling urgency, the Maggots sounding not unlike the English Dogs at the height of their powers, while Corpus Vile leant more towards the Varukers – but with dual male/female vocals.

Inspired by its release, MSO played their first gigs in Germany and Holland, instantly taking to the squat culture that dominated the European punk scene and although not technically a 'Bath band', they also became involved in the BOB (Bremen/Oakland/Bath) collective, which opened more doors for them, not only on the continent but also across the Atlantic as well. Disaster was never far away though and in 1995 Fybs was replaced by – another resident of Bath – David 'Dimblebrain'.

"I suppose those were the 'glory days' of the band," John suggests, "with regular touring, many memorable gigs and more studio recordings and releases, but to some outsiders, the band still looked like it would implode (or explode) at any minute, with people secretly making bets on how many days into a tour it would be before we would split up or kill each other! I think one had to be of a certain mind-set to really understand the Maggot universe and, during those years, the band was fortunate enough to consist of five people who were somehow able to make sense out of it all..."

The impressively tight, but undeniably deranged, 'The Angry Buzzing Of A Million Flies' EP was released by Hamburg label Epistrophy in 1995; four tracks of super-fast, super-tight and extremely quirky and technical hardcore punk, it remains the definitive MSO release and was promoted by tireless gigging across the UK and Europe with the likes of Police Bastard, Corpus Vile, Muckspreader and Extinction of Mankind...

"Each trip producing a hundred and one tales of joy and terror, in equal parts!" laughs John. "It all culminated in September 1996 with a month-long tour of Europe, which we christened 'The Angry Touring of Five Maggots'. The good fortune of the last year or two ran out on this tour, which rapidly turned into an ongoing ordeal. The first of many mishaps occurred on the way to the first gig in Stendal [Germany] when the van's engine blew up on a busy stretch of motorway. There are so many stories surrounding this tour – 11 days of which were spent marooned in Leipzig! – that it would take a book of its own to cover it all; however, one certainty was that Dave would be leaving the band at the end of it, as he had planned to relocate to Lancaster. It is fair to say that Dave's drumming had become rather irregular by then anyway and towards the end of the tour he became progressively more erratic in his behaviour as well, which climaxed with a return ferry journey of outright insanity and drummer-instigated violence, as various band members had to keep fleeing and hiding from Dave until he became sedated!"

Despite relations being strained to near breaking point by the constant touring – and the boredom and madness that forms a large part of it – MSO weren't ready to quit just yet and recruited new drummer, Badger from Frome, who had previously kept time for Far-Que and Kill Van Helsing. New material was written, with a view to releasing an album on Epistrophy and a tour of the US west coast was undertaken in 1998, a string of gigs built around that year's BOB Fest in Oakland. However, apart from one final gig in Bath upon their return, that tour *did* spell the end of Maggot Slayer Overdrive.

"Needless to say, the US tour was another incident-laden affair," sighs John, "with riot police closing down one gig and the final gig seeing the band not only having to dodge the by-now customary end-of-tour custard pies, but also whole potatoes, propelled over our heads at high velocity with a home-made potato cannon! As fun as it all was, this time round, the internal strains and tensions generated by being in such constant close proximity to each other, had become too great to overcome and the band finally ground to a halt on its return to the UK..."

"The way I remember it, I'd been disillusioned with the whole thing for a while," adds Pig. "People couldn't be bothered to practice and would rather just go to the pub, no-one wanted to do new songs etc. We'd just come back from America, which was great fun, but some of the others had really started getting on my nerves…there's only so long you can spend in a van with others before they start to bug you! We'd sold merchandise and made enough money to cover what I was owed for the T-shirts I'd made and I'd just had a kid so couldn't spend as much time touring, so for me it was time to call it a day…and the others decided not to carry on either.

"But I have no regrets about quitting. I'm glad we did what we did and played where we did; it was great fun and a great way to see the world… I thoroughly recommend it to anyone."

With Pig going on to form Gurkha, who released the ominously-titled 'Drinking From The Skulls Of Dead Gods' in 2006, a split CD with Czech band Malignant Tumour, Badger continued with his various bands and Alan played in Keine Ahnung with ex-Corpus Vile member Chaps. He was also in Bad Blood and, since having relocated to Germany, is currently with the Aftermath.

"To try and sum it all up, I can only say from my own perspective that my time with Maggot Slayer Overdrive included some of the best times of my life to date," opines John. "I thought that our combination of styles produced something unique and because of the nature of the band, I never felt constrained by any boundaries when it came to songwriting, which to a degree I *had* done with my previous band. And it may sound odd, but I take great satisfaction from knowing that, in the whole history of civilisation, there will almost certainly only ever have been one song written from the perspective of a vengeful giant cephalopod ['I, Nautilus'], or indeed about sustaining oneself with homely thoughts of Yate llamas in times of adversity ['I Spit on Your Llama'!]

"Being in the Maggots sometimes felt like being caught up in a whirlwind – entirely unable to control the madness unleashed by it, at times a torment, but never ever dull, bland, unexciting or monotonous. I can only speculate as to what our audiences really made of us, but if nothing else, I feel sure that most who saw us will at least remember us, even if for the wrong reasons…and I can live with that.

"I would guess that this whole book is in many ways a tribute to all of those people who kept the underground scene going in those lean times, whether it be organising gigs, releasing cassettes, playing in bands or producing fanzines, so I would like to thank everyone who was doing all of that back then, particularly those that had to put up with us in our more unmanageable times. The likes of Nicole from Bremen and *all* the many BOB people, Mike MCR, Frank Epistrophy, Corpus Vile, Muckspreader, Knucklehead, Korrupt, Alesh, Uli, the Biel crew, Maus and Dystopia, the Stokey punks, the good people of the 'Evil Triangle' (Hamburg, Groningen and Bremen). The list could go on and on…so many great people and even greater stories."

"For me, just to be remembered is good enough," states Pig. "Whether we were liked or not isn't that important, but it obviously gives us a good feeling if we were. A couple of years back this American bloke got in touch through MySpace just to say thanks; after he'd seen us play in LA, it inspired him to play guitar and form a band of his own and just to hear that once is such an unbelievable feeling. I wouldn't swap it – or the memories – for the world."

SELECT DISCOGRAPHY:

7-inch:
'The Angry Buzzing Of A Million Flies' (Epistrophy, 1995)

LPs:
'Soggy' (MCR, 1993) – split with Corpus Vile

AT A GLANCE:

Nothing official is out there on CD, but you could try contacting John and begging for a CDR burn of the MSO discography: stobor@hotmail.co.uk

STATEMENT

Credible one-man bands are few and far between, but in the context of the UK punk scene, they are an even more unique phenomenon. In fact, there was only one and that was **Statement**, the militant vegan straightedge vehicle that was/is Pat 'Rat' Poole.

"I remember the day I bought my first punk record," he recalls fondly. "Well, I almost remember! It was 'Pretty Vacant' by the Pistols… I guess I was 12 or 13 at the time and I was staying at my nan's as my mum and dad had gone away somewhere. I remember putting it on, on my nan's record player, one of those mono 'box things' and hearing, 'We're va-cunt…' Well, that's how I was hearing it anyway! After that, I started getting all the usual suspects: the Clash, Stranglers, Damned and Dickies. My cousin, who was five or six years older than me, asked my dad if I could go to see a band at the Marshall Rooms in [our town] Stroud and he obviously said it was okay if I was with her…it turned out to be Crass! My first ever gig was Crass, how fuckin' punk rock is that? Poison Girls also played and I'm not too sure who else.

"I was young, not even political in any way at that point and very naive too. I remember these punks and skins rolling coins onto the dancefloor before the bands went on, shouting 'Go!', then all fighting to get the money. I was pretty scared, unaware that it was just a macho game. I also remember people started fighting and Crass stopped playing and went into the crowd to stop them; it was pretty amazing – I realised that this band Crass were serious! I got to see them twice at that venue and, by the second time, I was actually starting to think things through a bit… I think I was even vegetarian by then.

"The Stroud scene was pretty good; in fact, I think, back in the early Eighties, there were scenes of some description in most towns. Gloucester was only 10 miles away and that scene was huge! I remember seeing Demob in Stonehouse, with punks and skins brawling again, albeit in a play manner; it confused me… me and my mates were stood at the back, real youngsters; I was wearing some bright yellow bondage pants with black zips! I had to store these at my aunt's house, 'cos my dad didn't like me wearing stuff like that; he was concerned what people would think of us!"

Because he had a drum kit – and could almost play it! – it was only a matter of time before he was in a punk band of his own and after doing a short stint with La Masque, which saw his animal-rights sensibilities coming to real fruition (they had a song, 'Meateaters, Die!'), he formed Muted Existence with Gary Cooke and Al Strudwick, he and Gary also doing Arrogance with Johnny Reynolds and Sean Mundy. Both bands played a handful of local shows and did a demo each, the Muted Existence tape being a split release with Rat's one-man-band side-project, the aforementioned Statement, following which Rat made the decision to devote the majority of his energies to the latter.

"Initially the one-man-band set-up appealed because I couldn't find people who shared exactly the same ideas and ideals, as me. They not only had to be vegans, but vegans who wanted to play certain stuff. I also found it easier to do it all myself, as I could write and record whenever I felt like it. I guess it was an accident really; I bought myself a four-track [portable studio] and just fucked about with it really…recorded 10 or so songs and thought I'd release it as a [cassette] demo. I recorded more and more music and released 10 or more demos, of very varied music, from basic punk to metal, interspersed with all sorts of bizarre stuff, even a bad attempt at some Smiths-inspired material!

"The pros of keeping Statement as just me were obviously that I could do what I wanted, when I wanted. And the cons? Well, were there any? I've never been a big fan of playing live anyway, so the only possible drawback of not being able to play gigs, wasn't a problem…"

So, when he wasn't out hunt-sabbing and attending animal rights demonstrations ("Too many vegan SXE people just wore the T-shirt," he sighs. "But coming from the anarcho-punk scene, this was real to me, not just a fad…"), the Eighties saw Rat experimenting with the medium of home recording and slowly developing, through a process of trial and error, a definitive Statement sound. There were two vinyl releases as well as the multitude of cassette demos, a split 7-inch and a split LP, both of them shared with the confrontational anarcho band the Apostles, but Statement didn't really 'arrive' at the sound for which they will forever be remembered until 1990 and the 'Prepare For Battle' 7-inch which was released by Sean Muttaqi from Vegan Reich's Hardline label and showcased a much more metallic, thrashy direction.

"I became very friendly with the Apostles over a pretty short space of time," recalls Rat, of his Eighties output. "I was lucky enough to drum on their first album [1985's 'Punk Obituary'] and then we did the split 7-inch and LP on my own Active Sounds label. I wasn't happy with them, though; the 7-inch was okay, but the LP got fucked up in mastering. The test pressings arrived and my side was awful, but stupidly I didn't want to prolong the release any longer and went ahead with the press. A big mistake in hindsight, but to be honest, my stuff was bad anyway and better mastering would have made very little difference.

"The Apostles were a tremendous influence; musically, as they dared to challenge the traditional punk sound and as individuals, because Andy [Martin] and Dave [Fanning] were such great people, always challenging the things around them and never bowing down to 'the norm' of punk rock.

"But yeah, those splits with the Apostles were *so* different to 'Prepare For Battle'," he agrees. "In fact, it was like two completely different bands. I'd discovered Slayer and that really was a turning point… The whole Slayer-style death/thrash-metal thing was the musical influence I had been looking for. [Third Slayer album] 'Reign In Blood' really did change my musical direction. 'Prepare For Battle' was/is probably the best Statement stuff I've done, in terms of music and production; the irony is that, while I was recording that, the engineer was smoking weed and eating bacon sarnies! Lyrically too it was probably the turning point for me; I hadn't got mellower with age – in fact I'd become way more pissed off – and after meeting Sean a few years previous to doing the 7-inch for Hardline, my attitude had become way more, well, 'militant', tho' I hate that term…"

Statement, Rat recording 'Vegan Inquisition'

Statement, Rat with Scott Anorexia

Indeed, the Hardline movement, while admittedly promoting many positive ideals, outraged the libertarian punk scene with its fundamentalist condemnation of abortion and homosexuality and Rat got caught in the crossfire to an extent. "It was assumed that I totally agreed with and aligned myself to Hardline, but I didn't; I had many discussions with Sean about it all and nearly didn't do the record. I agreed with much of what Hardline had to say, but by no means all of it. I'm not sure anybody knew just how controversial it would become… As with any new thing, it attracted the dickheads and maybe that was a big part of the problem – it got a bad name from the way certain people who claimed to follow it acted.

"I'd known Sean for a good few years prior to 'Prepare For Battle'; I'd even had a track on his first release, an ALF benefit featuring all sorts of well-known bands like Oi Polloi and Chumbawamba, so I knew a lot about him and the direction Vegan Reich would be taking. I think the positives of Hardline far outweighed the negatives, because it really *did* help many people to see the contradictions in consuming dairy products while claiming to care about animal rights. It bought veganism to the forefront of the hardcore scene…even Earth Crisis were inspired by it all and look what they've gone on to achieve, in terms of spreading the message. Without Vegan Reich there probably would never have been Earth Crisis and the thousands of vegans that have come since then…"

The success of the single led to Statement almost becoming a live entity to perform at the first 'Hardline Gathering' in Memphis in 1991. "Yeah, we practised with Chad from Raid on guitar, Mark from Raid on bass, Ray from Vegan Reich on drums and me doing vocals. Initially it was supposed to be Steve from Raid on drums as well, but he couldn't do the beats! I've no idea why, as it's all just standard 4/4 timing, but he couldn't do it, so Ray stood in and we practiced in the 'Hardline House', as it was known. Events changed leading up to the night of the gig though; Sean was pissed off that people seemed more interested in seeing Vegan Reich, Raid and Statement than taking part in the gathering itself, with its various workshops and stuff. He decided he didn't want to play because of all this and asked how I felt; I was happy to not bother either, so we headed back to California just as the show was about to start! As I've said previously, it was all a bit weird, people I didn't know playing Statement!

"But that whole trip to Memphis was crazy; there were six of us driving from Southern California to Memphis…it was a fun road trip, I always enjoy them. Then, when we got to Memphis, there were about 20 or so people staying at the Hardline House, but on this one evening, there was only about 10 of us there. We were just about to leave the house and go somewhere, but when we got out onto the porch, all I could see was about 30 kids walking around the corner, holding baseball bats and chains…and it was obvious they were coming to the house where we were. A shouting match developed; they were after someone who lived in the house, who had had a run-in with one of their friends and basically they wanted a fight. Mark, the Raid bassist, tried to calm things down, he was very level-headed, but the redneck gang kept saying they had come for the 'vay-guns'!

"As we were stood on the porch debating with them, all of a sudden over my shoulder, a gun appeared! I won't say who was on the other end of the gun, but I just told them not to do anything stupid and they said, 'Well you better take the gun off me then…' so I went back inside the house, got a coat and took the gun off the person holding it. I went back in the house and asked if anybody knew how to disarm it, as I had no clue! Later that evening the gun would be completely stripped down, cleaned off piece by piece and the next day thrown in the Mississippi!

"Eventually the rednecks walked off, thanks to Mark, but not too long later they returned and one of them said, 'Our mate here, his grandad died few days ago and he's really pissed off, so he wants a fight!' Chad, the Raid guitarist, a 16-year-old, said he'd happily do it, so this two-minute fight started, with Chad blocking the other guy's punches and hitting him back. It literally didn't last two minutes before the other guy said, 'Okay, that's enough, you win…damn, I need to quit smoking!' So, 10 of us, 30 of them, one of them beaten. I'm thinking, 'Now we're in trouble…' but no, they just walked off! I couldn't believe it; I'm sure that would never happen here in the UK!"

After Rat spent a year or two playing guitar with Birmingham punks Anorexia (as well as gigging with them, he played on a six-track demo that never saw the light of day), Statement went on to record a split 7-inch with American band Dim Mak for Italian label Surrounded and release the hard-hitting 'Genocidal Justice' CD on French label Green Fight. The CD included tracks originally recorded for a second Hardline EP that was never released that would have been entitled 'The Vegan Inquisition'. Another track, 'Flight Of The Halberd', also appeared on the 'Animal Truth' compilation CD released in 1998 by Sober Mind Records (the label ran by Hans from Belgian SXE band Liar) and another, 'Anguish', appeared much later, in 2005, on a three-band compilation EP released by New Eden.

"But that was the last Statement release, with Rat choosing instead to concentrate on his other myriad projects – in particular Cracked Cop Skulls and Unborn – both alongside his old friend Nick Royles and Krat, with his wife Kat on vocals. He also spent a year in the reformed anarcho band Riot/Clone playing guitar on their 2004 'Mad Sheep Disease' 7-inch for US label Alternative.

"But Statement will always exist, purely because Statement is me," he adds. "Okay, okay, it will exist until I die, which I'm hoping will be when I'm around 60; I don't want to live any longer than that – I've already made a big enough footprint on this earth, I really shouldn't make it any worse! In fact, I often feel really egotistical wanting to stay around 'til I'm 60… actually, no, I don't *want* to stay around until I'm 60, I just don't want to be here after that. I don't want to be just another burden on this planet, existing purely to exist, sucking more and more out of the earth for no reason. Do I sound like a hippy? Tough shit!"

And, in closing, he ponders how he would like Statement remembered: "As the band that made somebody see the light and respect veganism for what it is – a fight to end suffering…

"It's a bit weird, really, but the Japanese seem fascinated by the UK's vegan SXE scene of the Nineties at the moment. I'm getting a lot of interest from there… The irony is, that the vast majority of these people that contact me about Statement aren't vegan! Shame so many of the people from those bands sold out on veganism too; that really pisses me off, it's like they were just playing music, it's taking the piss out of the millions of animals that get smashed to fuck just to end up on someone's plate. Being vegan isn't a personal decision; it's a necessity!"

SELECT DISCOGRAPHY:

7-inch:
'Who Won The Human Race?' (Active Sounds, 1989) – *split with the Apostles*
'Prepare For Battle' (Hardline, 1990)
'Split EP' (Surrounded, 1998) – *split with Dim Mak*
'Three Way Split EP' (New Eden, 2005) – *split with Tears Of Gaia and Extinguish*

LP:
'The Other Operation' (Active Sounds, 1988) – *split with the Apostles*

AT A GLANCE:
The 'Genocidal Justice' CD on Green Fight would be the best place to start
(seeing as all the vinyl is rarer than rocking-horse shit).

MEDULLA NOCTE

When one thinks of intense live bands from the UK metalcore scene of the Nineties, Ross-on-Wye's **Medulla Nocte** are usually near the top of the list. Fronted by iron-lunged madman Paul Catten and propelled by miniature man mountain Jammer behind the kit, they terrorized the underground circuit – and each other – for most of the decade and left behind some deliciously difficult material.

"Medulla started in 1992, I think," begins Paul. "That was me, [guitarist] Neal [Jenkins], [bassist] Bones [aka Chris Jones] and [first drummer] Dave [Morgan]. We were still learning to play really, doing a mixture of our own songs, but we chucked in a Faith No More cover or a Rage Against The Machine cover, just to keep us going. It was our first band after all; the only musical background any of us had was me being a roadie for Decadence Within for years and years. So I knew what the tour game was like and knew that was what I wanted to do. I knew it was fucking tough, a thankless task, but I just wanted to get out and play.

"Mike Patton *was* a big influence," he adds, of one of his more obvious inspirations. "But I was diving on the floor and shocking people when he was still a long-haired goon in Faith No More. He's made a career out of stealing my ideas and moves! But my main inspirations were people like Colin from Conflict; I was an angry young man with a lot to get off my chest… Discovering Johnny Rotten changed my life as a kid, but I developed my own character eventually and was soon getting props for being a frontman on my own merits, so I gained some confidence and didn't need to rip people off…the only person I behaved like was me."

Medulla Nocte played their first gig in 1992 at the Cinderford Dean Centre "with a bunch of fucking hippy bands…" and recorded two shoddy formative demos in local studios the following year, before parting ways with drummer Dave in late 1994, who was replaced by the aforementioned Jamie 'Jammer' Airns.

"Dave wasn't great," admits Paul. "So we did the ever-so-brave thing of advertising for a new drummer before we fired him – as you do! At least we didn't split and then reform without him…but it was the next worst thing, you know what I mean? And this great big fat guy turned up [Jammer!] and we thought, 'Yeah, he'll do!' And he could actually play; he was perfect for the band really and gave us the ability to play the songs how we'd always wanted. We just didn't let him book us too many gigs, though, not after he sorted us a gig somewhere in mid Wales and we got run out of town because they were expecting a rock covers band… There was a couple of kids there in Pantera shirts and a load of bouncers – most of them chasing us down the fucking road! So he was exempt from getting us any more gigs after that, but we were still learning a trade; we'd play virtually anywhere…"

The last demo with Dave, entitled 'The Grudge Remains', had included their ferocious anti-police song, 'ACA', which became a staple in their live set for many years, but the true Medulla Nocte sound didn't really start to emerge until Jammer took over on the drums, bringing an incredibly chaotic, super-heavy rhythmic foundation to proceedings, which allowed guitarist Neal to truly blossom as the innovative attacking player he was always meant to be and Paul to rant and rave like the demented sociopath that everyone remembers fronting the band.

Another demo was recorded, this time at the Whitehouse in Weston-super-Mare and two more were tracked at Rich Bitch in Birmingham, the latter of which, 'Drastic Measures', garnered the band good reviews from the likes of *Terrorizer* and *Kerrang!* and landed them some high-profile gigs in London, eventually bringing them to the attention of London label Household Name.

"Yeah, we finally blagged onto a decent gig in London, where we met Paco from Conflict – which was great, because, like I said, I was a big Conflict fan. And through him we met Lil [Household Name's head honcho] and started going up to London a bit more and playing with bands like Knuckledust and getting involved in that scene, y'know? I've always been around punk and hardcore and Bones was into his hardcore as well, but Jam and Neal were more metal orientated…actually Neal was never really that bothered, as long as it was good – and brutal!

"Anyway, we'd end up playing some metal club on a Saturday night with a load of black-metal bands and then the next day we'd be doing an all-dayer in Walthamstow with Knuckledust and Public Disturbance. We didn't really care, to be honest, it was just about playing – and being decent and honest about it.

"Then Household Name said they'd put a single out [1997's 'All Our Friends Are Dead'], so we did that, in some studio by Oxford, I think? And we got 'Single Of The Week' in *Kerrang!*, but it wasn't like any of us were chasing a golden egg or anything. We started getting loads of metal shows then and it was never a case of, 'Oh, we've arrived…' We just did it! And again, we'd play some underground hardcore show in Cardiff and the next night we'd be doing a big metal support in London…"

The single, particularly the frenzied title track, fused the hostile grooves of Pantera with a filthy UK punk vibe and, although they were never going to be 'the next big thing', Medulla Nocte certainly captured the imaginations of the British press and won over anyone unfortunate enough to be confronted by them on a stage. Tours of the UK were undertaken,

Medulla Nocte, by Naki

Medulla Nocte live, by Naki

first with Strapping Young Lad and then with Logical Nonsense, before Medulla Nocte took the plunge and recorded their debut album.

"But a classic Medulla moment was when we played with Rock Bitch," laughs Paul. "It was ridiculous really; we just played to a bunch of dudes…every song would finish and there'd be silence. But afterwards, we were backstage and there was a knock on the door and it was their road manager or someone, saying, 'If any of you guys want to fuck any of the girls, just let me know!' Ha ha! And it was their full-on stage show that night and we had a perfect view from the side of the stage, of this lesbian orgy basically…so that was a crazy night. But there wasn't a lot of fun times with Medulla, to be honest, it was all very serious…"

First album 'A Conversation Alone', released by Household Name in 1998, was recorded in Tewkesbury by none other than Steve Grimmett of Grim Reaper, Onslaught and Lionsheart fame. "Jammer knew him and we thought it was fucking great having him on board… We even wanted him to do some backing vocals, just so we could say the Grim was on there, but he clued on. It was about then that the *Beavis And Butthead* episode was on [where the cartoon metalheads were making fun of the 1984 Grim Reaper video, 'See You In Hell'] and we were all ripping the piss out of him! But we knew fuck all about the recording process even then… I don't actually think that first album even got mastered; it was just mixed and went to press. All good tracks, though; the hardcore kids seemed to like it and the metal kids seemed to like it…"

Despite the overwhelmingly positive critical response to the album, Medulla Nocte still hadn't found their niche in the UK's music scene of the time – "It's a cliché, but we were too metal for the hardcore kids and too hardcore for the metal kids," reflects Paul – and touring to promote the record was still a hard slog. About a year after its release, disillusioned bassist Bones left and was replaced by Mark Seddon from "Norwich oiks" Subvert.

"Yeah, Bones always found the touring thing a bit difficult; he had work commitments and he got himself a new bird and let's face it, you're either cut out for touring or you ain't. Medulla used to play a lot and it was always tour and work and tour and work…and if you're not tough to that, you won't last. You have to be a bit of a selfish bastard really and put everything else aside for the band – and Bones was too nice! But he did the honourable thing and fulfilled all his commitments with us; I think his last gig was some big *Terrorizer* bash.

"We'd already found Mark by then and he was a great musician, really young; I couldn't fucking stand him, to be honest with ya, but we've since become best mates, you know? He was a fucking buffoon when he joined, whereas Bones had been really organised and that was how I liked the band to run, like a well-oiled machine…

"We got nominated for a *Kerrang!* award and that was a fucking joke – 'Best Newcomer'?" scoffs Paul. "We'd been going eight fucking years and were working on our second album! We had no chance at winning, but they obviously wanted to make the numbers up and took pity on us…but typically we had a fucking bust-up on the way there. Mark was the only one in a suit, 'cos we'd wound him up saying it was a suit-and-tie do and he'd borrowed this car, 'cos we'd elected him to drive and the tyres were bald, so he had to change the tyres at this garage in his suit and he was covered in oil…even before we got there we were fucking arguing! It was a total farce; one of the guys from Raging Speedhorn had to stop me and the singer from Reef having a punch-up… I've no idea how it started, 'cos I don't give a fuck about Reef. Actually *that* was probably how it started: I told him I didn't give a fuck about Reef!"

2000 saw the band signing to Copro Records (a move that Paul describes as "like signing our own death warrant...") and recording their 'Dying From The Inside' sophomore album with Dave Chang in Henley-on-Thames at Philia Studios, another experience he doesn't care to remember.

"The songs were great," he concedes. "But I blew my voice during the second day of doing vocals and didn't get any support from the band or label – and I've never listened to that album in its entirety since. I just can't listen to the vocals, y'know? I wanted to record them again, because they sound like...well, like someone's who just blown their voice and it's pretty shocking!

"I hate the second album, I really do; I'd take the first album over the second any day. It just reminds me of a very miserable time, the four of us stuck in one room at a B&B; I can't think of anything worse or more intense. And the sound of a man screaming his fucking lungs out until his voice bleeds is exactly how I felt – but at least it's honest. And lyrically it's the best thing I've ever done, I've not come close to it since; if I could have only re-recorded the vocals, it would have been our best release, but Copro wouldn't cough up for me to re-do it.

"And it's a shame, because the songs *were* great and we were at our peak live around that time too. I wanted to hold the mike when I was doing the vocals and Dave Chang was having none of it and – a little bit of inexperience, I think – I didn't want to rock the boat so I toed the line...stupid thing is, about six months later I went down there to do some guest vocals on the Matter album and he was like, 'Do you want to hold the mike?' To which I obviously replied, 'Why the fucking hell couldn't I do this last time?' But I learnt from it and I've dug my heels in for every recording since, to do it the way I want..."

Paul's claim that the songs were great isn't a false one, with tracks like 'Twice The Trauma' and the pounding 'Outcast' so belligerent it almost beggars belief and the thraped vocal chords just add to the vibe of excruciating edginess. But the band's unwillingness to back him up in the studio drove yet another divisive issue through the heart of Medulla Nocte.

"No, it was never the same again," he confirms. "I hated Mark and Neal hated Jammer and even me and Neal were frosty...it really wasn't great and when the record came out, we still had all this stuff to do! So, we were back out on the road, playing all these gigs and we were playing some of our best gigs too, but it got to a point where the van would be quiet, or we'd go separately in our own cars, just so we didn't have to talk to each other. At the gig we'd be in four different corners of the room, but then we'd get onstage and it would be fucking great, because of all this pent-up aggression. And afterwards we'd be alright then – 'Cool gig...' and everything – but just for an hour or two and you can't really function like that, can you?"

No, you can't, especially when all your gear gets stolen while on tour with Crowbar, just a week before you're heading out to Europe with Strapping Young Lad again. But the show must go on.

"We'd actually started finding a bit of momentum too, writing a few new songs and even getting along a bit better," recalls Paul. "And then we got offered some dates with Crowbar, which we were really excited about. The first date was in Bradford, so we called in to see our T-shirt girl and have a cup of tea, right in the middle of the day...then went back out and there's no fucking van there! It was gone – with all our gear in it! I can remember stood there thinking, 'Oh shit, we're never going to recover from this...'

"And this really was like a week before we were due to go to Europe with Strapping [2001], so everyone got their credit cards out and we bought new guitars, hired some other gear... and borrowed the rest off Strapping and it was great. There were no drugs involved, the gigs were good and we had a great time...but as soon as we got back, it went right back to how it had been. We did another UK tour and borrowed this backline that had belonged to Venom and that was fucking great 'cos it still had all their logos sprayed all over it and kids were just coming up to it at the gigs and touching it in awe...!"

Inevitably Medulla Nocte endured one blazing argument too many and finally self-destructed in 2001, with Paul, Jammer and Mark forming Murder One with various members of Raging Speedhorn (vocalist John Laughlin), Pulkas (bassist Jules McBride) and Iron Monkey (namely vocalist Johnny Morrow, who tragically died of heart failure in 2002).

"We were still playing a lot and to be fair, we were fucking untouchable live at one stage, really intense, but we started playing with bands – like a young Raging Speedhorn – and admittedly we were different people and not at the top of our game by then and all of a sudden we were getting our asses kicked. And it seemed the only way we could rise to our best again was to have a fucking good dust-up just before we played!

"So typically we did a few more metal shows and then Conflict reformed for a big show in London and asked us to support them and I can remember walking onstage at that gig and thinking, 'You couldn't write this...our final gig is with a band that inspired me to want to be in a band in the first place!' And I knew it was the last time I'd be stood onstage with that band and deep down I'm sure everyone else in the band knew that as well. And we had one rehearsal after that, where we switched a guitar amp on and nothing happened and that turned into an argument, which escalated into a war, a four-way slanging match and we never got back together as Medulla again. It all ended over a blown fuse...although admittedly that was just the straw that broke the camel's back!"

As well as Murder One, Paul went on to do time with Lazarus Blackstar, Co-Exist, Stunt Cock and the Sontaran Experiment and nowadays splits his time between teaching and tour managing, while – until recently – Jammer drummed for the ultra-heavy Anger Management.

"I'm still proud of those years and it's helped me work with good musicians," concludes Paul, who himself had a near-death experience, shortly after the release of Murder One's only album, 'Some Things Are Better Left Unsaid' (Grind That Axe Records, 2006), when he had an allergic reaction to anaesthetic during routine appendix surgery that left him in a coma. "I've never had to start slogging from total scratch in a band since. If things had panned out a bit better, it would have been different, but you make your own luck in this game, you know? And we'd have still fucking hated each other even if it had. But we weren't doing it to make friends, you know?

"There was recently talk of us doing some sort of 'Greatest Hits' retrospective, but I could never willingly be involved in anything like that. And besides, it would be a one-sided 7-inch with 'All Our Friends Are Dead' on it! But it's only now that we've realised that we were quite influential, people talking about us, 'Oh man, they were fucking brutal...' Unfortunately we didn't get that support at the time; no matter what we were doing, we were always second best. If you put it in football terms, we were a Championship team...that never quite cut the Premier League, but would get to the play-offs a couple of times – and blow it! A good result now and again, but going nowhere fast.

"We were just a brutally honest, hard-working band, I suppose. We weren't rock stars, we had to get up and go to work the next morning, but we helped people realise what you could achieve even with very limited talent…and there's no harm in ripping off Slayer! You see bands like Devil Sold His Soul, saying they started off by jamming Medulla Nocte songs in their early rehearsals and that's pretty cool. Whenever there's an internet forum about the most intense live bands of the Nineties, we're usually mentioned somewhere in there… it's not much of a legacy, but it'll do."

SELECT DISCOGRAPHY:

7-inch:
'All Our Friends Are Dead' (Household Name, 1997)

CD albums:
'A Conversation Alone' (Household Name, 1998)
'Dying From The Inside' (Copra, 2000)

AT A GLANCE:
Shame you can't see 'em live and feel the full force of their wrath for real, but you'll have to content yourself with the first album, if you can find it.

SHUTDOWN

Hailing from the Three Counties of Herefordshire, Gloucestershire and Worcestershire, **Shutdown** were one of the UK's best-kept melodic hardcore secrets. Given the right breaks, they could/should have made a far greater impact than they did and they pre-empted the whole melodic emo scene that sprang up several years after they split with their unorthodox fusion of catchy tunes and jarring noise.

The band formed in early 1990, when bassist Christian Burton, formerly of Terrorain (see *Trapped In A Scene*) and Detriment (who were basically Terrorain with a different vocalist anyway and issued two demos, 'Deception' and 'Values Misplaced'), teamed up with guitarist Robert Chumbley and drummer Stephen 'Danny' Daniels. Rob and Danny had previously played together in thrash-metal band No Compassion and the much more hardcore New Blood, who issued just the one demo, 'Elephant'.

"No Compassion had played gigs with Terrorain and we'd become friends over the years," begins Chris. "And we started practising with Kev Brookes [ex-Decadence Within] and Gem [aka Jeremy Wood, also from Detriment], so we had two singers and John Collier [the New Blood vocalist] on second guitar as well; yeah, we were a six-piece to begin with."

"But we only played one gig as a six-piece," adds Rob, "at the Star in Upton [12 July 1990], with Can't Decide, Decadence Within, Prophecy Of Doom and Tall Man…"

Chris: "Actually our first gig was at the Talbot [in Upton again] and we didn't even have a name then and just called ourselves Headbutt; we did two of our own songs and 'Glue' by SSD…"

"That's right," recalls Rob, "We did the whole set twice because it was so short! Everything about it was spontaneous – 15 minutes of sheer chaos… Collier had smashed his head on the ceiling and was rolling around on the floor with blood all over him…"

The band's choice of cover song for that first gig was very indicative of their influences at the time and their brutal 'Boston' (as in the city, not the AOR band) sound won them much favour with the burgeoning SXE scene that was gathering momentum in the north of England at the time. They travelled up to Bradford and Durham to play with Steadfast and No Way Out. Gem and John had left the band by this point, both of them relocating to London (the latter becoming a studio engineer) and Kev followed suit soon after, leaving Chris, Rob and Danny to recruit Tall Man's Neil Cox as their new vocalist.

"When I joined, Danny told me I'd never be as good as Kev," laughs Neil incredulously, who played his first gig with Shutdown at the Riverside in Tewkesbury on 27 December 1990, alongside Decadence Within and Prophecy Of Doom. "And I spent the next six years with that hanging over my head…he kept wheeling that quote out of the woodwork!"

Neil brought a more melodic edge to the vocals – and, by extension, to the band – and by the time they recorded their first demo in December 1990 (at the Whitehouse in Weston-super-Mare), they were starting to incorporate some seriously tuneful, slightly rockier influences into the old-school hardcore mayhem. This was evidenced by sublime opening track, 'Self', that recalls second album Uniform Choice, although the other five songs were more representative of the band's generic hardcore roots and even incorporated some of the UKHC feel embodied by the likes of Heresy and Ripcord.

"One of my biggest ever regrets is not seeing Heresy play live!" exclaims Chris. "The closest I came was when they were playing with Rose Rose, but they turned up late and didn't get to play because they let Rose Rose play instead. And then I had chance to go see them in Coventry as well, but the van left without me; I was 10 minutes late turning up! But yeah, Heresy – and Ripcord – were definitely an influence…"

"There were two sides to the band," offers Rob. "Me and Danny came from metal and Neal and Chris from hardcore and punk."

Chris: "When I was at school with Jarrod (his band-mate from Detriment and Terrorain, who also served time in Prophecy Of Doom), we listened to a lot of stuff like Attitude Adjustment and Septic Death and from that we got into anything to do with Pushead basically, including the 'Cleanse The Bacteria' compilation – and the best band on there for me was Siege. And from there I thought, 'What else is from Boston…?' We used to get into bands by looking at the thanks lists on their records…"

"And what T-shirts they were wearing in their photos," adds Neil. "So in a funny sort of way bands like Anthrax and SOD and Nuclear Assault had the biggest influence because of those huge montages of photos they did, wearing all those different T-shirts of obscure hardcore bands! The Jam were always my favourite band, though, so I bought a bit of a mod influence as well. Bbut the best compliment I ever had for that first demo was when someone said it reminded them of the first Scream album…that'll do for me!"

Three of the songs from the demo were meant to be released as a 7-inch (which would have been entitled 'The Ben Dover Sessions') by American SXE label Outback, which never materialised ("We never knew whether the guy was just flaky and ran out of money, or didn't get our sense of humour and was offended by the title," laughs Chris). Wigan label First Strike also expressed an interest, but never followed through with an actual release and it was eventually Swiss label Off The Disk that picked them up for their self-titled MLP.

"Some kid who saw us play got our demo and sent it to them," explains Neil, "and it was quite flattering when they contacted us – out of the blue – because they had released the Infest 12-inch, which was quite legendary and the guy that ran it was in an influential grind band, Fear Of God. Anyway, the guy who sent it off to them eventually came up to me and introduced himself at a gig, someone called Simon from Portsmouth, so we owe him a debt of gratitude! And they paid for us to go and record the 12-inch…"

Which didn't come out until 1992, despite being recorded – at the Whitehouse again – during the summer of '91 and featured eight tracks, all of them far more abrasive than the first demo. The band's style was rapidly evolving into something that US hardcore labels like Revelation or Dischord might put out, fusing the traditional aggressive vibe associated with the genre with a little melody, some angular post-hardcore sections and plenty of UK grit.

A defining moment was when Neil decided to play second guitar as well as sing, a decision based on the power of Leatherface's live performances and one that gave the band so much more depth and texture.

"I'd always liked Leatherface," he confirms, "And we'd played with them up at Planet X and they had two Marshall stacks, two blokes playing Gordon Smith guitars…they were fucking brilliant! And I went home and thought, 'Right, I'm going to play second guitar in the band…' And the sound got more melodic from then, it went to a different level, it was a much fuller sound…"

Chris: "We realised there was a lot more scope with two guitars; we could build a melody out of it, or go into a complete wall of noise. We had three guitars really, with my bass as well and we soon realised we could all play different things – and usually did – but then crash into the same riff for a chorus and it was much more dynamic."

Neil debuted in his new dual role on a five-track demo recorded during May 1992 that would eventually lead to them signing with Golf Records for three studio albums, but not before they'd toured Europe with Decadence Within in 1993 and released the 'Sheltered Homes' EP for High Wycombe label Potential Ashtray in 1994. Their awesome cover version of 'Mirror In The Bathroom' by the Beat even landed them some airplay on Radio 1.

"It was one of the funniest times and we got treated so well," remembers Chris fondly, of the European trek. "We were put up in disused railway cars after the Dusseldorf gig, which sounds awful but was really comfortable, because they'd put all this bedding in there and left their tape recorders and all these tapes for us to listen to…nothing was too much trouble for them.

"The next day we played Wuppertal, with Intricate and they'd made a big vegetarian stew and I just dunked a big pint glass into it and was walking around with a pint of stew in my hand! Then we played Arnheim and got given the strongest coffee ever, it was like treacle. And someone threw a slice of processed cheese at Mobs [the Decadence Within drummer], which stuck to his face and he flipped out because he has a fear of cheese – he can eat it but can't touch it with his hands! And we did the Star Club in Dresden, somewhere in Heidelberg

Shutdown, bassist Chris and drummer Danny

Shutdown

and Erfurt, which was the worse attended gig we ever did – there was more people at the soundcheck than at the actual gig…after one song we stood onstage and clapped ourselves! Then we did Austria and that was awesome, really unbridled, really raucous; we headlined and all the guys from Off The Disk were there. And finally we did this all-dayer in Ieper, with Jughead's Revenge and 18th Dye. Active Minds played as well – they were on a 350-date tour of Europe or something…in a little car!"

1995's 'Emits A Real Bronx Cheer' album was recorded at the Whitehouse again, where it also earned its unusual title as the band were playing with a whoopee cushion, "and that's what it says under the cartoon on a whoopee cushion; it was nothing to do with NYHC or anything!" Despite the vocals having to be re-recorded at an unplanned-for follow-up session – or maybe because of it – the album was a sonic triumph and although the band never made a concerted effort to promote it, they wandered around the countryside at weekends playing gigs wherever and whenever they were invited to do so.

"Yeah, we were pretty fucking unprofessional compared to a lot of the bands of the time," admits Rob. "Although we were very serious about the music we were writing, we never planned anything…"

Neil: "I never had a guitar lead that worked the whole time I was in the band!"

Chris: "You used to use it to tie the bonnet of your car down! But it was all about getting up there and being as energetic as we could and playing through any old gear, it didn't matter…"

"We were very raw when we played live," confirms Rob. "We let our adrenaline carry us away and we'd really go off…and you'd either see a really bad gig or the best gig we'd ever played! It was either one extreme or the other…"

Chris: "Like seeing Wat Tyler at their worst or At The Drive In at their best!"

When asked for a prime example of 'a really bad gig', the whole band are unanimous in nominating one in Blackpool, when Neil was paying far too much attention to his theatrical muse…

"It's one of my favourite anecdotes ever," chuckles Chris. "Neal was going through a phase of wearing masks and everything onstage, because he'd seen Chi Pig from SNFU doing it. Anyway, we started off with this instrumental intro we used to do at the start of our set and then Neal ran on wearing these big, baggy MC Hammer pants, furry slippers that were meant to be warthogs smoking cigars, a joke Big Foot hand, a Viking helmet, a fake beard and these joke glasses with eyes on springs dangling out on his cheeks…and no-one in the crowd batted an eyelid; they just stared at him as if he'd walked on and said, 'Hello!'"

"One of the most embarrassing gigs for me was the White Horse in High Wycombe," adds Rob, warming to the topic of memorable lows. "And we started with a song where I start playing and everyone else crashes in, but it was all out of tune…so we stopped and did it again and we were out of tune *again*! And just before we started, Danny had karate-kicked Neal off the stage while he had his guitar on and he knocked Chris's bass over as well, so everyone was blaming Danny… 'Fuckin' hell, Danny, you've knackered my guitar up with your stupid fucking karate kick!' So anyway, we did it again and there was quite a few people there and we were out of tune again and it was really embarrassing, with everyone arguing onstage with each other; it looked really bad… and it was only then I realised I was playing the wrong chord! I didn't admit to it until we were halfway home in the van, but I had a hot flush for the rest of the set!"

Chris: "We also played a terrible gig in Ipswich with Cradle Of Filth, who were really shit. It was their first gig and they were fucking arseholes – they wanted to go on after us and wanted to use all our gear; we mocked them all night, they were so shit. Then the promoter ran away so we didn't get paid and we had to sleep in some side street in the van. We were in the van looking out the window, about one o'clock in the morning and there's this person just stood in the window of an old house opposite us, staring down at us. We thought they were casing out the van and were going to come and nick the equipment when we fell asleep! Every time we looked up, they were still there and it was quite frightening really, because it looked like this weird old woman…and it went on all night, so we didn't get much sleep, we were so scared. But in the morning we looked up and in the daylight could see it was a cardboard cut-out of Alice Cooper!"

The band's second – and final – album, 'Icarus', was released by Golf in 1996. This time recorded at Rhythm in Bidford-on-Avon, it perfectly captured the band at the height of their not inconsiderable powers and, with their DC influences in full effect, it remains an unsung classic of that whole post-hardcore scene made so popular by the likes of Quicksand and Fugazi. Sadly Shutdown's relationship with Golf was growing increasingly strained and despite gigs with the now-legendary (in emo circles, at least) Texas Is The Reason and a UK tour with Shelter and Understand, they split in late 1996.

"Unfortunately I had a drunken 'handbags at dawn' moment with Steve Beatty, who runs Plastic Head [and Golf]," admits Neil. "There had been a lot of tension between the band and Golf, especially between Steve and myself; we just didn't get on very well and it all culminated in this argument at the LA2 at our last ever gig, with No Fun At All, Millencolin, Samiam…"

"They [Golf] never really got us any good gigs of note," complains Chris. "Yet they knew what we were into, knew what bands it would be good for us to play with and they were putting out all this stuff by bands like Offspring, so we *could* have played some really good gigs. We were always bigged up as a priority for Golf, but it never felt that way…"

Rob: "The Shelter tour was just after 'Icarus' came out and that was quite memorable – for all the wrong reasons though! Shall we just say that there was a clash of cultures?"

Chris: "We were just looked upon as the naughty schoolkids – on holiday for a week!"

Like so many of their peers in the UK scene at the time, Shutdown eventually got fed up of the continual slog to keep the band moving for little or no return and they really were a classic case of, 'Right band, wrong time…' Factor in college and work commitments and a general disillusionment with the hardcore scene and it was almost inevitable they would grind to a halt when they did.

"Yeah, we were a couple of years too late – or three years too early," agrees Neil. "You probably get loads of hard-luck stories like this, but it's true; we were basically doing what subsequently became – and I hate to use the term – 'emo'. You know, where it moved away from the shouty kind of emo and more towards some melody, when bands like Hundred Reasons came along with a few more good tunes…"

Chris: "People used to come up to us at gigs and say, 'You guys were really good. If only you were American…'"

Neal: "…it would have been even better!' Ha ha! It was such a cliché, 'If you were American, you'd be on Revelation!' But, whatever, the primary reason for the band was always to have fun with our friends; it was all about the doss and the music was almost of secondary importance really…"

"The *writing* of it was very important and playing the songs at gigs was great," reckons Rob. "But the gigs were mainly great because you were with your mates. I mean, if anyone says to me now, 'Describe being in a band...' I always say, 'Sat in the back of a van, having a laugh!' And because some of the gigs were poorly attended and you'd travelled for hours and hours to get there, straight from work, the only thing you could depend on was having fun..."

Eight years later, the four members of Shutdown were back together, albeit briefly, as The Great Leap Forward, playing just four gigs and recording a three-track demo with Understand's John Hannon at his Mushroom Studios.

"We always knew we'd play music together again at some point," says Chris. "We teamed up with a keyboard player as well [Guy Bartell] and the whole thing had a bit more of an electronic influence. It still had very obvious influences from Shutdown, of course, except with none of the restrictions we felt in the hardcore scene...but again, it was more about getting together as friends than making music."

"We were never in it for financial gain," adds Neil, who nowadays plays guitar – alongside ex-members of Burnside and Stampin' Ground – in ultra-melodic hardcore band Thirty Six Strategies. "But we wanted to be respected and appreciated for our music...although we weren't up our own arses about it and could always laugh at ourselves when it all went wrong."

"The band was always greater than the sum of its parts," concludes Chris. "There was something special there and it was because of who we were not what we did. We were always brutally honest with each other and we respected each other because of that. Any arguments we had weren't about the band; it was about trivial stuff, usually because someone overstepped the mark when taking the piss out of someone else..."

"Hopefully someone came to one of our gigs and had a great night; just knowing that makes me happy," offers Rob, when asked if he thinks the band will be remembered, before adding with typical Shutdown sarcasm: "but if they had a bad night, that makes me happy as well!"

SELECT DISCOGRAPHY:

7-inch:
'Sheltered Homes' (Potential Ashtray, 1994)

12-inch:
'Shutdown' (Off The Disk, 1992)

CD albums:
'Emits A Real Bronx Cheer' (Golf, 1995)
'Icarus' (Golf, 1996)

AT A GLANCE:
Boss Tuneage's 'Shutdown 1990-1995' collects the demos, 7-inch and 12-inch onto one disc and seems a good place to start, but be sure to check out 'Icarus' as well. Plans are also afoot for Boss Tuneage to possibly release The Great Leap Forward's demo.

STAMPIN GROUND

Stampin' Ground were one of the second wave of UKHC bands that really managed to crossover to a more mainstream metal audience, eventually signing to Germany's Century Media Records, receiving various 'Album Of The Week/Month' accolades from the glossy metal press and even appearing on the main stage at Castle Donington for the 2003 Download festival. Yet their humble beginnings were just as DIY-orientated as any of the other bands in this book and they slogged around the same circuit in the same way.

Formed in late 1994 by guitarist Antony 'Mobs' Mowbray and bassist Ian Glasper, who had just disbanded their previous act, Decadence Within and were then also playing with Burnside, the very first line-up of Stampin' Ground also featured guitarist Martin Spencer, drummer Richard White (who had previously sang for Decadence Within and was also fronting Burnside) and vocalist Paul Catten, from Medulla Nocte. Martin was soon replaced by Scott Atkins, who the band poached from Cheltenham thrash-metallers Cambodian Holiday, basically because he had the nastiest guitar tone they had ever heard locally and the band set about writing their first set of material, an uncompromisingly slow fusion of Earth Crisis and Crowbar.

"Our other bands just weren't heavy enough and we had this yearning to do some *seriously* heavy shit," explains Mobs. "We wanted to be utterly focused, completely to the point musically – no intricacies, no complexities, just straight down the line, totally brutal hardcore…no solos, nothing. It was a release for us really; we were running Burnside alongside Stampin' Ground for a while, but before we knew it, we had a few labels interested before we'd even played live and it started to get too busy to do the two bands."

After tracking a six-song demo at Rich Bitch in Birmingham during February 1995, which was well received despite being 20 turgid minutes of anti-social detuned chugging ("Fuck me," laughs Mobs, "that first demo is such hard going; I couldn't listen to it now, no chance!"), Richard was replaced on the drums by Adrian Stokes, also from Cambodian Holiday, who brought a whole new dynamic to the band's rhythm section.

A second demo was recorded during May '95 at the Whitehouse in Weston-super-Mare, that much better captured the power and intensity of the band, but vocalist Paul left to concentrate on Medulla Nocte and heal his throat which was developing nodules on his vocal chords, him abusing his voice so hard in two such extreme bands. He was replaced by Heath Crosby, from Bradford SXE band, Neckbrace.

"When the whole straightedge scene began up North, I actually started vocals in a straightedge band called Intouch," begins Heath, of his musical endeavours pre-SG, "who then changed their name to No Way Out; that band included Nick Royles on the drums, who went on to do Sure Hand Records and play in Ironside. We played shows with a lot of other bands, such as Goober Patrol and Steadfast, and around this time there were a lot of us hanging around together who were straightedge and so the famous Northern Wolfpack was formed! We played a couple of shows with Gorilla Biscuits when they toured the first time and recorded a couple of demo tapes – all this was around 1989 – and then I went on to do vocals for Nailbomb, who included Rich Militia of Sore Throat and Soulstice.

"While in Nailbomb I played shows with bands like Slapshot, Sick Of It All and Biohazard, to name but a few and we released a split 7-inch [the first release on Armed With Anger

Records, sharing vinyl space with War Torn] and a demo tape and were featured on a couple of compilations. Nailbomb also had Richard Corbridge on bass who went on to do Armed With Anger Records and Stoney on drums, who currently plays in Lowlife UK. I then went on to form another straightedge band called Neckbrace, who released a 7-inch on a German label [No Cruelty] and we played a couple of festivals in Belgium and Holland…all this before I even joined Stampin' Ground!

"Anyway, while I was in Neckbrace, both Richard Corbridge and Nick Royles lived with me; Neckbrace was on its last legs and Nick informed me that he knew a band that were looking for a vocalist…at this time I hadn't heard of Stampin' Ground, but I knew that Nick was in touch with Ian and he told me they just had parted company with their first vocalist, Paul. I was given a demo tape and asked to go down to Cheltenham for a rehearsal and we seemed to gel straight away…"

Stampin' Ground made their live debut at the 1 In 12 Club, Bradford, on Sunday 2 July 1995, on the second day of a weekend hardcore festival, with Above All headlining. Their next two shows were also at the Club as well, one in October, supporting 108 and Abhinanda and one in November, with Manfat. Early September 1995 also saw them in Whitehouse Studios, Weston-super-Mare, recording six songs, three of which became the 'Dawn Of Night' 7-inch for Days Of Fury (with the slogan 'Hardcore Not Emo-core' etched around the label!) and three of which became the 'Starved' 7-inch for US label Too Damn Hype. To promote the releases, the band began playing around the UK, hitting London so many times some people eventually thought they *were* 'a London band'; they also made their first trip to Europe during November 1996, touring as support to Ignite and Straight Faced, getting signed by German label We Bite in the process, who released the band's debut album, 'Demons Run Amok', the following year. It was promoted by tireless gigging, the band over in Europe almost every month, hitting most of the regular hardcore festivals and when in England opening for the likes of Sick Of It All, Vision Of Disorder, Agnostic Front, Napalm Death and Madball.

"The best UK towns to play in were probably and this is in no particular order, Bradford, Manchester, Cardiff and London," reckons Heath. "I guess that's based on the amount of people that used to turn out to see us. But I remember one show in Kidderminster that we played, at the back of some old cattle market; just before we went on stage there were probably no more than five or six people and we felt a little deflated, to say the least, but we all agreed before we went onstage that we would play at 150% and really go for it – we went *mental* and I gotta say I really enjoyed that show! At the opposite end of the scale, I also remember walking out onto the stage at the Brixton Academy when we played the Fuck Reading festival and thinking, 'Fuck, this is one big stage!'"

However, Heath's final European tour with the band was during August 1997, two weeks in support of Despair, with things coming to something of a head between he and the rest of the band in Hamburg.

"Hard work and very tiring, but fun!" is how Heath recalls the band paying their dues across Europe. "I remember spending a lot of time travelling around in the van. The Belgium shows were the stand-out ones for me; they had such an incredible scene back then, with bands like Liar and Congress and the whole H8000 thing going on. The leper fest was always great to play and the people and the crowd were always good, but we played with some great bands all over Europe and met a lot of cool people. There was one show in Belgium with around 1,500 people there, which was a definite highlight, with hundreds of kids up the front, singing our songs. But the show that really sticks in my mind is the one in Rennes supporting Fury Of Five and Integrity; that was a great show, not just because I love Integrity but because of the response we got from the crowd: I remember crowd-surfing and being passed around the whole place for most of our set – great fun.

"My worse show was probably in Hamburg, which was when things went wrong for me and SG. I remember giving the crowd some grief because it appeared that some of the kids were taking the piss out of the band and in particular my SXE stance of wearing 'X's onstage. Me and some of the other band members had disagreements about how I had handled the crowd, but my trouble was that I always had that attitude; when I was in Neckbrace we played the 1 In 12 once and nearly got banned from playing there, due to me being overly vocal with my opinions about certain things!

"In hindsight, I think the split was probably a mixture of things, one of which could have been musical direction. I hated leaving SG and it was a bitter pill to swallow, as I felt that I had put a lot into the band, but shit happens! Time has moved on now; it took me a little while to speak to some of the guys, but that's all in the past now and I was – and still am – proud to be associated with those early days of the band…"

While Heath went on to front the short-lived Silent Season (he's now happily married and living in Herefordshire and recently contributed guest vocals to the Rot In Hell album on Deathwish), Stampin' Ground recruited new vocalist Adam Frakes-Sime, from Southend band Blood Oath.

"I actually think Ian wanted this guy, Andy, the singer from a Southend band called Outbreak to join," laughs Adam. "But he wasn't interested, so Stuart Clapp from Outbreak suggested me. I wasn't in any other bands of note, only really Blood Oath, but that was totally different to SG; there was zero focus…and zero ability!

"The scene in Southend wasn't really a scene either; it was just two bands: Above All and Understand, but when those two bands played, the place would be rammed! Then, if those bands weren't on the bill, it would be 40 people max! But I suppose those bands eventually inspired a hardcore scene there and then you had bands like Unite and Special Move coming through."

Adam's first gig for the band was 31 January 1998, at the Wheatsheaf in Stoke-on-Trent, with Imbalance and Shallow ("It was…alright!" he deadpans) and soon the band were back to their default setting of non-stop gigging, some of the highlights of '98 being the Evilfest at London's LA2 on 13 June and playing the Dour Festival in Belgium with Sheer Terror, Snapcase and Suicidal Tendencies the following month. During the first half of '98, the band also negotiated themselves out of their contract with We Bite and into a three-album deal with Century Media, their second album, the Dave Chang-produced, 'An Expression Of Repressed Violence', coming out on that label's hardcore imprint, Kingfisher, that October to much critical acclaim. It saw some decidedly faster tunes coming through and boasted both a savage, raw mix and some definite Slayer influences; it was promoted by an eventful two-week tour of Europe in support of Cause For Alarm and many more gigs around the UK upon their return.

"We were one of the only UKHC bands that were prepared to *really* tour back then," says Scott. "We were playing almost every night and still going to work at the same time; it was ridiculous…"

"And some of those early European tours were so bleak," adds Adam. "All of us sleeping

Stampin Ground, Heath, by Naki

Stampin' Ground 1996, Ian, Scott, Mobs, Ade and Heath, pic by Dave Thomas

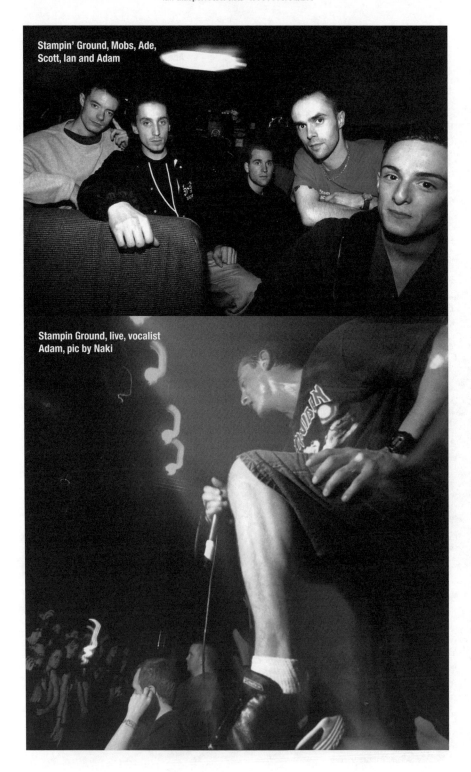

Stampin' Ground, Mobs, Ade,
Scott, Ian and Adam

Stampin Ground, live, vocalist
Adam, pic by Naki

in the back of a Transit in the middle of winter…with candles gaffer-taped to the side of the van just to give an illusion of heat! We really suffered for our art!"

After a split CDEP with Knuckledust on Ian's own Blackfish Records, the road-work continued unabated in 1999: a UK tour with One Minute Silence and Breed 77, then the 13-date UKHC Tour with Knuckledust, Freebase and Unite, a 15-date UK tour with Tribute To Nothing and Lockdown, plus lengthy stints across Ireland and Europe and headline gigs in their own right every weekend in-between. Sales of the second album were strong enough to merit Century Media moving the band from the Kingfisher imprint to the main metal label itself for 2000's 'Carved From Empty Words' album, which is widely agreed – even by the band themselves – to be the definitive Stampin' Ground recording. It certainly garnered them their best reviews, which in turn helped land them some outstanding tours with the likes of Hatebreed, Earthtone 9 and the Lostprophets.

"You can't rely on the press to sell records," stresses Scott. "You have to capitalise on that interest and get out there and sell your band yourselves. We never sat on our laurels, we were always looking for the next gig or the next tour. I listen back to 'Carved From Empty Words' now and it still sounds amazing; it really has got a life of its own. It was a moment in time, I think; it totally captured what the band was about."

The album spawned the band's best-loved song, 'Officer Down', that saw Ian's punk background coming through in the lyrics, it being a rant against police brutality that also questioned realistic alternatives to the police force; after all, it's easy to point out what's wrong, but a lot harder to define what's right. But the lyrics definitely played second fiddle to the music with Stampin' Ground and 'Carved From Empty Words' saw the band ruthlessly hone their hardcore/thrash crossover sound to a near inhuman efficiency, Ade's drumming being singled out for special praise in virtually every review.

"It was a monolith of a hardcore record," claims Ade, proudly. "The vibe, the songs, the energy and the passion…we captured it perfectly on that album; every song a killer with something so unique to offer within it. I loved writing the drums for 'Carved…'; I always write my most fluid and groove dominant drum parts in my head, or through vocalising them, then make them physical writings and I found an endless well of ideas and inspiration at that point in time. The drums were faster, more aggressive and with some very subtle technical difficulties, but without distraction. And it's still a beautifully constructed masterpiece in my opinion…"

Also in support of the album, Stampin' Ground headed out to the States for two east coast tours (the record being licensed through Thorp Records to coincide with the dates), the first with Cause For Alarm (that also hooked up shows with Blood For Blood, Voice Of Reason and Disciple) and the second with God Forbid, an exchange tour in true DIY fashion as SG brought God Forbid to the UK for 11 sold-out dates (with 'Blackfish recording artists' Decimate opening) six months earlier.

Unfortunately the hectic schedule was starting to take its toll and the band parted ways with Ade immediately after pre-production on their Andy Sneap-produced fourth album, 'A New Darkness Upon Us' ("I just needed some space in my life and time to regroup," explains Ade, "so it was a natural process for me to depart and start a new journey…"). He was replaced by the talented Birmingham-based Benediction drummer Neil Hutton, who learnt the set of new songs in record time and put in a sterling display on the actual album before hitting the road in support of Biohazard. Again, the new record was incredibly well-received, but probably over-produced to an extent where some of the classic 'SG grit' was lost in the exhaustive recording process.

"The last album was the most professional and the songwriting was probably the best," agrees Adam. "But it didn't capture the magic of 'Carved...'. They're both really good albums, just that one has better songs and one has a better vibe..."

"There are some amazing songs on there," offers Mobs. "But Neil didn't really have enough time to put his own stamp on that last album; it was frustrating for him, because within a couple of weeks of joining the band he was in the studio recording!"

Scott: "Which is a shame, because those songs sounded more exciting live and in rehearsal, once he wrote some of his own stuff to them."

By the time the album came out, Ian had also left, to spend more time with his wife and young daughter, his last tour being a successful headlining stint around Greece and his last show being the Download appearance mentioned in the introduction to this section, in front of 50,000 hyped-up metalheads. Ben Frost from Unite then joined, slotting into the role with consummate ease, having previously stood in for Ian at several gigs when mounting personal commitments meant the bassist had been unable to make it to a show.

Stampin' Ground were never ones to turn down a good gig and often called on mates for cover, some of the other stand-ins being guitarists Wes from Underule and Alex from Decimate, bassist Adam Sagir from Labrat and drummer Colin Baker from Sanity Reigns. However, after another hard year touring, with the likes of Anthrax and Arch Enemy, Mobs also left the band and with the band's two main songwriters gone (Mobs having done the majority of the music and Ian almost all the lyrics), the writing was finally on the wall for Stampin' Ground.

"Castle Donington was fucking insane," Mobs remembers fondly. "Having two huge circle pits, at the same time on opposite sides of the field and two massive walls of death...it was madness. We then had a brilliant year after Donington too and played some of the best gigs we'd ever done, but everything went a bit Pete Tong soon after. I wasn't feeling the same about the band by then and there was no real motivation there to write another record..."

The final Stampin' Ground show was at the London Underworld, with No Turning Back, Cinders Fall and (Ade and Ian's new band) Suicide Watch in support, on 10 December 2006. Adam also introduced his and Ben's new band, Romeo Must Die, from the stage at that show; they have continued the hard-gigging tradition of SG and in 2011 released the 'Hardships In Season' album. After two albums with Suicide Watch (2004's 'Global Warning' and 2008's 'Figurehead Of Pain'), Ian and Ade reunited with Mobs (and Jim Saunders from Seventh Cross) for the short-lived Betrayed By Many (themselves named after an early SG song) and at the time of writing, Ade plays drums for Anger Management, while Ian and Mobs have joined forces with Rid White from Burnside and Neil Cox from Shutdown in the speedy melodic hardcore band, Thirty Six Strategies. Scott, meanwhile, has hung up his axe and made quite a name for himself as a sought-after metal producer.

"I would like SG remembered as one of the first UK hardcore bands to have pioneered that 'Earth Crisis sound' over here," concludes Heath. "And we helped kick-start the UK hardcore scene back into life and triggered a whole new set of upcoming bands at that time. We were a band with solid beliefs embedded in the lyrics and the majority of the members held – and hold – some of the beliefs that are still so important to me as a person today..."

"I look back on the SG years with so many fond memories of experiences I will remember forever," adds Ade. "I feel the success of the band was never really justly met, but we believed in ourselves, we made our mark, we took it to the front line and we kicked fucking ass like no other band around at the time. Our success was mainly attributed to the fact that we had a fantastic chemistry in our writing and live performances and each member took pride in excelling and bettering each milestone we erected…we pissed on Hatebreed, for fucking sure! Ha ha!"

"Not sure about *that*," laughs Mobs, "but we had a really good work ethic and we would tour with anybody, which is why we turned into a good live band…but we were always a great support band and we never quite took it to the next level of being a great headlining band. I'm just pleased we made an impact on the UKHC scene; it was an amazing time and we were honoured to be there…we were nothing special, just in the right place at the right time."

SELECT DISCOGRAPHY:

7-inch:
'Dawn Of Night' (Days Of Fury, 1995)
'Starved' (Too Damn Hype, 1996)

CDEP:
'The Dark Side Versus The East Side' (Blackfish, 1999) – *split with Knuckledust*

MCD:
'Self-Titled' (We Bite, 1997) – *first two 7-inchs released on one MCD*

10-inch:
'Trapped In The Teeth Of Demons' (Vacation House, 2003) – *limited edition live picture disc*

LPs:
'Demons Run Amok' (We Bite, 1997)
'An Expression Of Repressed Violence' (Kingfisher/Century Media, 1999)
'Carved From Empty Words' (Century Media, 2000)
'A New Darkness Upon Us' (Century Media, 2003)

AT A GLANCE:
'Carved From Empty Words' was the band's watershed release and remains their finest hour.

WHIPPASNAPPA

Cheltenham's **Whippasnappa** wrote one of the most ludicrously catchy pop-punk albums to ever come out of the UK and by rights should have been huge, but the road to stardom is littered with the dried-out husks of thousands of defunct bands that *should* have been huge and Whippasnappa's is one of them. What? You were holding out for a happy ending? Sorry, wrong book, my friend, this one is full of losers and wannabes!

The band formed in early 1998, when vocalist Rid from Burnside (and previously Decadence Within) teamed up with guitarist Jeff Baehr from the Droids, bassist Simon Bayliss from Spunge, guitarist Matt Earl from Dangerous Babies and drummer Tim Dutton. Both Jeff and Matt had also briefly served time in Burnside and Simon in the Droids, just prior to Whippasnappa forming, so it was no surprise that the early set of Whippasnappa mainly comprised Droids and Burnside numbers.

"I'd loved playing with the Droids, but Burnside was a bit too raw for me," reckons Simon. "So when Whippasnappa came along, it was the perfect blend of the two: the Droids songs we did now sounded fuller and more vibrant and the Burnside songs felt more polished and clean. Throw into the mix the Bear [Jeff]'s ability to write the catchiest pop-punk songs in the world and what could you do but love it?"

"One thing that benefited the band greatly was having three songwriters," adds Tim. "So there was rarely a time when we didn't have 'a new one' to play. Jeff would tend to bring complete songs; he was like, 'I've got a new song – it goes like this,' and we'd all have a go and within the same practice, we'd all have it nailed. I think Beaver [Simon] was similar, although not as frequent; I'm fairly sure most of his songs we did ended up pretty much the same as he'd intended. Matt brought ideas that we all joined in on and formed collectively, as far as I remember.

"There was also a bit of style variation between the three writers. Jeff would come up with 'pop' songs; you could sing along with every word and they always had an upbeat/fun feel to them, even though the subject matter was sometimes quite dark. The rest of us then roughed them up a bit! Matt was a bit heavier, so provided the harder-sounding elements and Beaver was somewhere in the middle I'd say. So, as a result, the new songs we were jamming were always varied, which kept us all on our toes and enthusiastic to play each one."

"Musically we fit like a glove," continues Simon. "For me, playing with Tim was great because I need a good drummer to 'key off' and I loved what he did. Jeff and Matt were both spot-on too and made the perfect sandwich for me to fit into. And Rid's energy and vocals were like nothing I had seen before. I've often thought that, as a singer, it's as much about the showmanship as it is about the voice and seeing Rid rolling around the floor and donning his Mickey Mouse glove still sits in my head and makes me chuckle."

After playing their first show at the Cheltenham Axiom Centre, Whippasnappa gigged enthusiastically around the UK and contributed a convincing cover of 'Religious Wars' to the Subhumans tribute CD on Blackfish. They recorded – and released – their own 'Indestructible' CD at Planet Rock and FFG Studios, with the final mix coming courtesy of Dave Chang at Backstage in Ripley.

"The goon at Planet Rock talked the talk but didn't walk the walk!" explains Rid, of why they called on Dave Chang to find the "missing middle" from the recording, with Jeff confirming,

"The guy was a bellend, who thought he knew everything but was never there."

Despite the trials and tribulations of recording it, though, the album is an overlooked classic of the melodicore/pop punk genre, sounding something akin to Good Riddance crossed with Snuff; in other words, California-style punk rock, all dripping harmonies and songs about unrequited love done with some proper Brit-grit, with 'Most Popular Man In The World' even nodding towards early Antz with Rid's clipped vocal delivery. In fact, the Antz influence was worn on the band's sleeve with a fine cover of 'Beat My Guest' appearing as a hidden bonus track and being a staple in their live set.

"I still listen to the album and play along to it with the acoustic," reckons Simon. "I like the sound we got…could it have been better? Yes. Could it have been worse? Yes. We had a limited budget and I think we made a great album; 12 years on and I think it has stood the test of time admirably – apart from too many soundbites, but hey ho, I guess we got excited! What we did was true to ourselves and at least we didn't disappear up our own arses like so many bands do and that's what keeps it fresh for me."

In support of the CD, Whippasnappa rushed round the UK with Cardiff's Four Letter Word, a tour that had its share of good and bad gigs, of course, one of them even seeing the band leave their drummer behind when they headed home.

"I was indeed left behind after we played Southampton at the Joiners Arms," laughs Tim. "Matt's roll-call wasn't the *best* thought out… 'Everyone in?' 'Yep'! 'Okay, let's go!' Perhaps a more 'person-specific' check would have worked better! I walked back to someone else's house (in the days before mobile phones) not knowing who I was with or where the others had gone. I think we walked past Brum-based punks Rotunda on the way there as well, who had played with us that night; there were the four band members, plus a mate, all trying to sleep sat upright in their Ford Fiesta as none of them had decided who would be driving home and as a result had all got pissed!"

"I only left Tim because we had no light in the van," counters Matt, "and there were about 12 peeps in the back and all the gear, so I couldn't see shit! Everyone was pissed except me, so I do remember it being a right kerfuffle trying to check, but it was a genuine mistake and totally pissed me off as I would never have left Tim…Beaver maybe, but not Tim!"

"One gig that will haunt us for the rest of our days is when we played Norwich," sighs Rid, "which was good apart from the journey back, which took about 10 hours. The van decided to develop a wiring fault which meant everything died after travelling about 20 miles; then the side window decided to just fall out! Now this gig just happened to be in the middle of winter, so we were going nowhere fast and were freezing to death. Not only that, the fuel bill for the whole journey was around £100. We got back to Gloucester just in time for Tim to walk straight into work…"

Tim: "And didn't we push the van to that venue in Norwich as well? After running out of petrol again just round the corner? Another classic moment."

However, after self-releasing a live album, recorded at the Gloucester Guild Hall during December 1999, and despite having some strong material written for a *second* album, Whippasnappa called it a day prematurely, after Jeff and Tim came to blows over a girlfriend and Jeff left soon after, the band playing their last ever gig at the Indian Queen in Boston.

"A gig that also featured a hideous stripper," chuckles Jeff, who admits to not having touched an instrument "apart from his man-flute" since the band's demise. "And there was someone there who looked suspiciously like the son of Trigger from *Only Fools And Horses*!

Whippasnappa live at the Axiom, Cheltenham

Whippasnappa, in the rain!

And me and Tim sat at the bar until God knows when and got locked out from the lock-in."

After Whippasnappa, Matt continued tour-managing for bands like Stampin' Ground, Atreyu and Shadows Fall, while playing in the Screamin' 88s and nowadays he plays with the melodic thrash metal band, Reign Of Fury. Simon Bayliss also plays in a thrash metal band, the old school revivalists, Suicide Watch, while Tim plays with alt-rock band, JC's Revenge.

"Although Whippasnappa didn't last long, I personally had a blast and thought we had some really strong material which I still listen to today," says Rid who, after Whippasnappa, went back into Burnside before fronting Suicide Watch for two albums and nowadays sings for classic-rock covers band Jibbafish. "There have been a few attempts to resurrect the band over the years, but I just don't think it will ever happen; a shame really because I think the songs were timeless and would still work now."

SELECT DISCOGRAPHY:

CDs:
'Indestructible' (Snappa, 1999)
'Live' (Snappa, 2000)

AT A GLANCE:
If ultra-catchy pop-punk is your bag, hit Rid up for a copy of 'Indestructible' or 'Live': rodhandler@hotmail.com

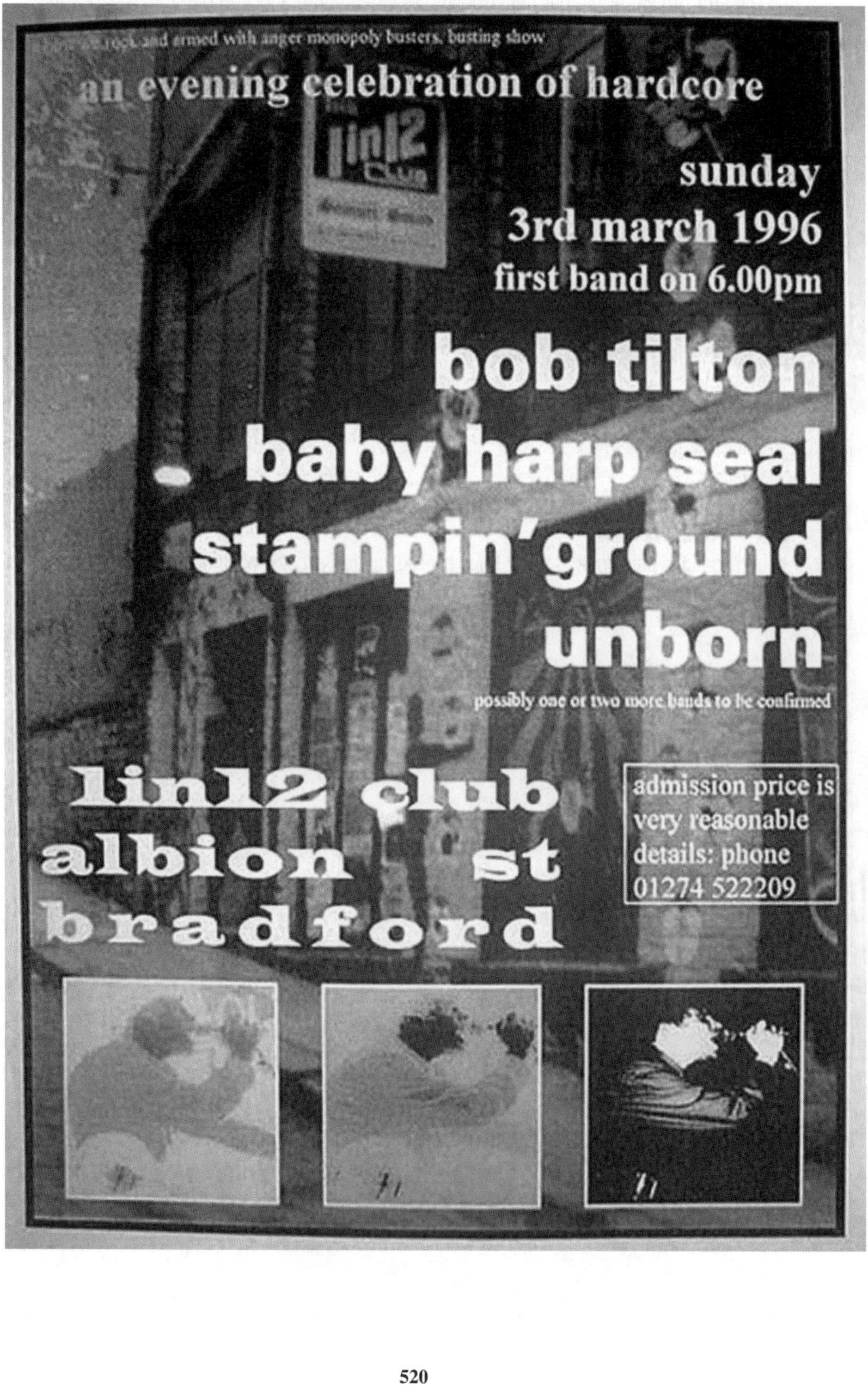

CHAPTER EIGHT: WALES

FOUR LETTER WORD

During their 20-year existence, Cardiff's cerebral melodic hardcore punkers **Four Letter Word** dropped four fine albums, undertook two huge US tours and endured one hard-fought major lawsuit, so it's hardly surprising they wore out 25 members along the way, with only vocalist Welly (aka Gary Welton) hanging in there 'til the bitter end during early 2011.

"The Cardiff scene that spawned us in 1991 was non-existent," he remembers, casting his mind *waaay* back to the very beginning. "We'd all been pretty much involved in the local scene of the mid-to-late Eighties here, which revolved around going to gigs at Stow Hill Labour Club and then the ones at TJ's in Newport, put on by Simon and the Rockaway/Cheap Sweaty Fun lot and going to our mate Marvin [later of Chaos UK and Varukers fame]'s Anti-Cash gigs in Cardiff, that moved around between places like the Mars Bar, the Venue and the Bristol Hotel. Marv also had a record stall circa '88 called Autonomy, in a flea market, which is where a lot of people met, as well as at Spillers Records [officially the world's oldest record shop, founded in 1894!] and, of course, at gigs.

"I'd known Kip [Jenkins], the original drummer, since school and later when I started my zine [the meticulously constructed and utterly readable *Artcore*] in '86 when he was in the Heretics and then the Cowboy Killers. We'd always talked about doing a band and it was his getting booted out of the Killers that saw us actually do it. Thinking about it, I first got on stage in, like, 1987 to do the vocals for the Heretics' cover of 'MTV, Get Off the Air' because their singer didn't know the words. But yeah, anyway, we started looking around for people. This was spring or summer '91; I was in art college doing graphic design, right at the end of my course and I was in a shared house with some students.

"One of those guys was Jake Keeler, who was this long-haired Nirvana and RHCP fan; he was a guitarist and we got on well, so he said he'd play guitar. We also got Chris Davies, who was a kid we knew from the valleys, who was into the straightedge style of hardcore and played bass; we met him at Marv's shop and we'd had a few jams with various people, including Marv, which never got past one practice. This was the genesis of the band, but when Jake's course finished he moved to London for a career after only a few practices and we met Jon [Butler] via mutual friends and he said he was interested in playing, so we started writing our own material; we didn't really hope to achieve anything, we just wanted to play in a band and write some songs.

Four Letter Word, Cardiff 1997

Four Letter Word, pic by Dave Goodchild

"Back to the local scene though and it cannot be understated how bleak it was in the early Nineties. We'd gone from an active scene in the late Eighties that gradually became more and more obsessed with metal and then the rave scene came along and literally took a scythe to everything. A lot of the people we'd known locally just dropped out and went to raves. Most of the old anarcho guard, in fact, pretty much everyone apart from a small minority who hated it, which I'm proud to say I was part of..."

Although taking some inspiration from the UK's traditional and anarcho-punk scenes, Four Letter Word looked primarily to the US for their influences and right from the off their style was informed by the likes of Bad Religion, SNFU and the Dischord Records roster, although their own early efforts took a while to evolve into the rough-hewn melodic anthems most will associate with the band. After making their live debut at the Cardiff Student Union bar, Finistré, on 5 May 1992, supporting Slowjam, two demos were recorded, 1992's 'Eden' and "A disastrous unreleased recording in '93", but it wasn't until 1995's 'Burning A Better Britain' (named after the Tory party's '*Building* a Better Britain' election slogan of the time) that Four Letter Word found their sonic identity.

"We recorded the first two tapes at the studio upstairs from where we practiced," explains Welly. "Soundspace was down these back streets just outside of Cardiff city centre. It's all been bulldozed now and replaced by gleaming new towers, but that was part of the dirty old side of town, between the city and the docks; it was full of old buildings that housed stuff like the legendary venue Bogiez and the [punk venue] Bristol Hotel next door. We used to practice in the room next to the Manic Street Preachers when they were fairly new; I just remember them being really small in stature, hearing this wailing coming through the wall and putting a note on our door saying, 'For the sake of the whole music world, split up – please!' So we stuck the note on the back of our first album! Both of those demos were engineered by Alex Silva, who we'd known since his old mod-band days in Street 66, but who went on to produce the Manics' 'M*A*S*H*' cover and is now a well-known producer based in Germany.

"The problem, apart from our turgid, confused music, was that engineers back then didn't really know what to do with punk rock. It was at the start of the Nineties, punk had gone underground a long time ago and people who worked in studios were fairly conservative, or only knew how to mix general rock and pop, but with all these new technologies that were emerging. The outcome was pretty weird. We put out the first six-song tape 'Eden' with a printed sleeve and probably sold over 100 copies around the world. The second one, was only, like, three songs; we didn't like the outcome, so got it remixed and it was still so bad we never released it. No-one's even heard it. It has the earliest version of 'Rich White Ghetto' on it, but it's pretty strange... awful in fact.

"After Chris disappeared under dubious circumstances in 1994, we got Dog on bass [aka Steve James], this older '77 punk who we knew through Marv and going to gigs. We decided at this point that everything we'd done so far wasn't working and we started from scratch and dropped everything we'd written up 'til then – apart from 'Rich White Ghetto', which we used as a starting point. We stripped all our music down and everything we wrote from then on, we purposely kept it simple. Since then, everything we write is like this; we write songs inside an hour, keep the structures simple and if anything becomes laboured when we are writing, we just dump it. Most bands start out simple and get more complex, but we did it back to front; I think the overly complex nature of what we started out with so disgusted us, we never wanted to go there again..."

'Burning A Better Britain' was recorded at the Whitehouse in Weston-super-Mare, with Martin Nicholls, an engineer who definitely *did* know what to do with punk rock, having recorded everyone who was anyone in the Eighties hardcore punk scene – and a few more besides – and the results were undeniably impressive. Soon Welly had Andy Higgins from Blackpool label JSNTGM (Just Say No To Government Music) offering to split-finance a Four Letter Word single and the 'Words That Burn' EP was the result. 500 copies were pressed and soon sold, thanks in no small part to a UK tour undertaken with Bristol's Spite.

"My main memory of that tour was the first night," reveals Welly. "I'd contracted a stomach bug from my friend Paul, who was doing a stall called Forbidden Beat with my girlfriend Tina in the same flea market that Marv's stall had been in six years prior, who'd just had what he described as 'gastric flu'. So the first night of the tour, we're in this squat in London and we get served this curry, which turned out to be dodgy vegetables from a skip. We did the gig, getting heckled constantly for being Welsh, which happened a lot back then and on the way back to Bristol I felt ill and we stopped somewhere so I could vomit like I'd never vomited before in this car park.

"We did the rest of the tour with me making foul smells from the stage, which was a constant source of both revulsion and amusement; I remember having to run to the gents' [toilet] in Birmingham just before we played, which thankfully was right next to the stage. We played the art college in Glasgow and the big punk pub in Hackney and we had covers of Toxic Reasons ('No Pity') and the Ruts ('Something That I Said') in the set for that tour, as well as a Billy Bragg song. The Ruts went down the best if I remember rightly. Spite were great every night and every day we'd sit on these benches that Pete had made to convert the back of his van; we got talking to John and Steve, who we knew were in Ripcord and found out that we all listened to all these old US hardcore bands."

And it was Shawn Stern from one of those old US hardcore bands, Youth Brigade, who offered Four Letter Word a deal with his BYO label and released the band's first Frankie Stubbs-produced album, 'A Nasty Piece Of Work', in early 1998. Taking the Californian blueprint for punk rock but injecting it with some working-class Brit grit, it was full of raucous, well-observed socially aware anthems like 'Sleight Of Hand' ('Am I fair in my assumption that we're all merited by our consumption?') and 'The Gunpowder Plot' ('The best-laid plans of mice and men are tucked away inside Number 10...').

"I'd been in touch with Shawn for years, as BYO was pretty much my favourite label as a kid," reckons Welly. "Alongside Dischord, SST and Alternative Tentacles, they had a whole ethos that I really believed in; I wrote to BYO for an interview for my zine sometime around 1990 and got back a tape, where Shawn had got Becca at BYO to read the questions out and he answered them. So I kept in touch via letter and after about a year of the 7-inch being out, I had a few copies left and thought, 'Why not send one to Shawn, just to see what he makes of our band?' The thought of them wanting to do anything with us didn't even enter my mind; we had no idea if we were going to even do another record.

"A few weeks later, though, I got a letter from a guy called John who was working at BYO and had his own label called Devil Doll and he said he was interested in doing something with us. Before I could even reply however, I got a phone call from Shawn and he's talking about us doing a record and I'm thinking he's referring to Devil Doll; the conversation gets a little confusing and I ask, 'What do you mean?' and he's like, 'I'm talking about you guys doing a record on BYO!' At this point I think the room was spinning and I don't think he got much more than mono-syllables out of me after that," he laughs.

A track from the album was also released as a limited 7-inch (b/w 'Access Denied') on red-and-black vinyl to promote the band's first US tour, an ambitious eight-week, 36-date trek across North America and Canada.

"I look back on it now and it's absolutely crazy," smiles Welly. "I was so immersed in organising everything and making sure everyone got in the van and we made all the gigs, even though we were driving 10 or 12 hours a day, that I don't think I really appreciated it for what it was at the time. I mean, it was incredible; I just wish I could've relaxed and enjoyed the ride, but if I had, then I don't know if we'd have made all those dates! We got to Los Angeles and stayed at Shawn's down on Venice Beach. We took our friend Graham Sleightholme [Crime Scene Records] to drive, 'cos I don't think any of us drove at that time and BYO sent Rory Rogers out with us to help out.

"The very first gig we played, we drove all day through the desert to Phoenix, Arizona and this weird warehouse, that was all in darkness with people sleeping in various rooms. One of the guys showed us the venue, saying, 'The stage has a fence in front of it and the red circle in the pit is so the blood don't show up...' It was baking desert heat and we met up with fellow BYO band Jon Cougar Concentration Camp, who were also playing. When we went on, I said something about America in relation to 'Rich White Ghetto' and it didn't go down well and as soon as we finished, the guy running the place, who looked like an ex-marine with a jarhead cut, shouted, 'Who called my country a ghetto?' and proceeded to come towards the stage with a few angry counterparts.

"I legged it and this guy went to hit our then 17 year-old year drummer, Will. BYO's Rory put himself in the way and got hit instead; we then spent the next couple of hours sat on this beat-up sofa in this fenced-off compound outside where we'd played, while in the parking lot outside, these redneck guys were circling in their pick-up trucks, throwing up all this dust as the sun went down, shouting, 'Get the English, fuck the English!' Of course, the fact we were from Wales was lost on them...

"A few sympathetic punk kids hung out with us and hatched a plan to open the gate so we could just drive out as fast as we could, which we did and drove all night back to Los Angeles. The next night we played a club called Bollocks, which was down in east LA somewhere. People would go outside to cool off, looking out at this railway track on the other side of a fence and we could see and hear gunfire across the street. It was pretty scary. We played the Whiskey-A-Go-Go the following night, it was all very surreal. From here we went up the West Coast on our own, into Canada, where we had to leave Rory on the side of the road at the border as he had no paperwork, across Canada with the Swingin' Utters, Brand New Unit and 22 Jacks, as far as Winnipeg. Then down to Minneapolis and southwest to Utah via Denver, where we hooked up with Pinhead Circus.

"From there it was northwest via Montana and Wyoming, back into Canada, where we met up with Youth Brigade and played Vancouver, Vancouver Island and Whistler. Then it was all the way back down the West Coast with Youth Brigade and Pinhead Circus, culminating with three dates in Los Angeles, with those guys and 7 Seconds, finishing at the Troubadour in Hollywood.

"It was absolutely insane, especially considering we didn't play very well. Just before recording the first album, we'd enlisted a guy called Hairy [Gareth Jones] on bass, after Dog had left and things didn't go too smoothly. There were personality clashes from the start and two months on the road will test the most resilient of bands and people. He left after the tour and the rest of us didn't go into the outside world for about three months… That kind of touring does strange things to your head, especially leaving your girlfriend with your two-and-a-half-year-old son at home for two months. That was the hardest part of all for me, but it was the chance of a lifetime, so you just have to go for it."

Hairy was replaced by Tim O'Donovan and, come April 1999, Four Letter Word were back in the Whitehouse with Frankie Stubbs recording their second album, 'Zero Visibility (Experiments With Truth)'. A superb collection of gruff but eminently memorable tunes (not to mention some bona-fide ragers like 'Remote Control' and the jaunty upbeat folkiness of 'Your Gods Won't Save You Now'), it was their best album, but ironically received next to no promotion and virtually vanished without trace. A love-sick Tim left the band just before a scheduled European tour, taking best friend Will with him, meaning the tour got cancelled and a disgusted BYO withdrew their support of the release. To top it all off, BYO then had proceedings started against them by the biggest law firm in LA who were representing MCA Records and their newest signing, Minneapolis boy band 4 Letr Word; they promptly dropped *our* Four Letter Word and, in the wake of all this turmoil, Jon left the band as well.

"It was a 'cease and desist' letter sent to BYO," explains Welly, "saying that they had the US Trade Mark for the name (and all phonetic variants); this mega corporation were basically clearing the global decks for another cookie-cutter boy band and in the process had bought the US and UK trademarks. The thing with Trade Mark law is, you're supposed to check that no-one else is using the name and therefore has 'prior usage', which they did and had heard of us…so they bought the name illegally basically. I know this because a punk journalist contacted the law firm after the fact and they went on the record and basically said that they knew about us, but what was some tiny band going to do against this corporation? I was pretty bitter about it at the time, but what was BYO going to do? They had no choice basically and we were consigned to the dustbin of history. I decided I had to do something, so we booked a tour of the UK (originally with the Cro-Mags, but they cancelled) to try and raise funds and draw attention to our plight.

"I put a totally new band together: Neil Cox on guitar [formerly of Shutdown], Tom Stanleigh on bass [formerly of Aspirin Kid and the Surfin' Turnips] and Wedge [Mark Wedgbury, formerly of Rectify and Classified Protest] and we went out and played. It was amazing, as people were literally coming up to us and giving us £10 and £20 notes. People were paying for merch and leaving the merch on the table. Cov John in Southampton turned our gig into an all-dayer and all the bands played for free and gave us all the money. *Suspect Device* did a special issue of their zine just on our case and Andy JSNTGM re-released the first EP as a 12-inch with extra tracks ['The Band That Time Forgot'] to promote the cause.

"We came away with about £500 and I spent this on speaking to a TM lawyer and having him write some letters, which is an expensive business. The lawyer discovered, that for some reason, the boy band's legal representatives in London had forgotten to buy the 'live performance' aspect of their UK TM (you have to buy a TM for each part of the marketplace, so a band would usually buy three 'classes' of TM: records/CDs, merchandise and live). I'd run out of money, but the lawyer was sympathetic as he said he'd listened to the Buzzcocks in his youth, so he told me what to do next, rather than do it for me and have to charge me. I went away and did a crash course in TM law and filed my own Trade Mark in the UK for live performance, including TV, radio and internet. This meant, if the boy band ever tried to launch in the UK, I'd be able to stop them performing live.

"A few years later, I would occasionally check the TM government sites and discovered that the boy-band company had recently abandoned their full US Trade Mark, covering all the bases and the project had collapsed. I had just got a bonus in work and bought the US Trade Mark. I paid for all this out of my own pocket; both TMs must've cost me about £1,000…and then I got people saying I was as bad as them for buying the Trade Marks and putting it on our website and releases. You can't win! This all basically got us to the point where we could operate internationally again. I told BYO and they reinstated us on their website and can sell our music once more; I figured it was the least I could do. It was a point of principle really; I didn't give a shit how big this major record label was, they were in the wrong and we were somehow going to continue. By the way, some footage of the boy band recently surfaced on YouTube and it's jaw-droppingly bad…!"

After recording the five-track CDEP 'Cold Day In Hell', which was released in 2001 by Suspect Device and a UK tour with Falkirk's Turtlehead, Neil left rather abruptly due to some personal problems and was replaced by Matt Proom, formerly of The Spartans. The 'Four Ninety Four Tour', with Joe Ninety and Fig. 4.0 was a great success, but by the end of 2001 both Tom and Wedge had left, the latter relocating briefly to Scotland.

More line-up changes followed and it seems that the only constant in the Four Letter Word camp, apart from Welly, of course, who has picked up an undeserved reputation as someone it's 'difficult' to be in a band with, is change, although original member and co-songwriter Jon rejoined in 2005 and did much to get the band back on an even keel. Even with the turbulent personnel problems, the Noughties saw two more EPs (2004's 'Crimewave' and 2007's 'Staring Down The Barrel') and two more Stubbs-produced albums (2005's 'Like Moths To A Flame' and 2010's 'Follow As The Crow Flies') and another US tour in 2007.

"Even less people knew who we were, if that's possible," scoffs Welly self-deprecatingly, of the last American trek. "A whole generation had come and gone and we were slap in the middle of this new scene full of beards and black jeans that didn't really warm to us. I don't think we went down too well. We have a punk name, I still have spiky hair, we're old and we have a kind of Nineties feel to us, which couldn't be any less 'hip' right now. Jon couldn't do that tour either, so that didn't help with our overall performance…it's always good to go on a punk holiday though!"

The final Four Letter Word line-up included guitarists Jon and Nick (Morgan), with Gavin Gates on bass and Glenn Tew on drums, but they unfortunately – for those who like a bit of belligerent honesty to keep the punk rock scene anchored firmly in the underground – called it a day in early 2011.

"Twenty years seemed like a good place to stop and no-one else seemed to notice that we were still releasing records anyway," laughs Welly, before adding, "we never really had it said that we sounded like any other specific bands. People never easily pigeonholed us, at least not in reviews and we're a pretty straightforward punk band. I always thought that we must've been doing something right because of that. If there was one thing, we never set out to fit into a specific sub-genre of punk. This worked against us right the way through. Unless you sound or look a certain way at a specific time, then people tend to switch off.

"We always joked that we were too pop for the punks and too punk for the pop punks. As a band, not taking the path of least resistance is pretty much commercial suicide, but we do what we do, regardless of what's 'in' this year; that's what we were always about.

"Will we be remembered? I'm not going to sit here and pretend like we broke any new ground, mattered in some way, or changed anything. I'm not going to spew any misguided 'listen-here-sonny' nonsense about how back in our day we had to load in our own gear, book our own tours and never got paid, as I know that's how it still is and that's all we've ever done. We're just another band in a sea of thousands. Sure, it was all very important to us when we put out new music, but I'm also aware that it wasn't to other people.

"I'm happy with our achievements; I've fulfilled any ambitions I might've had for the band many times over. We wrote some songs to the best of our ability and those songs luckily enabled us to travel and have a few hundred laughs with friends. We met some great people along the way, mostly for a few hours, that we'll never ever see again. We saw some incredible sights, like driving through Oregon at night or in the early morning down the Sea To Sky Highway from Whistler to Vancouver; that stuff is priceless…standing in the desert looking at the night sky with your friends, realising you will never replicate those moments. Punk rock is nothing without the people involved. The people who will put up strangers in their house even though they only have a few records in common and feed them and trust them. Ultimately, it's not about how many lives a band's music might have touched, but how many lives touched the band along the way…"

SELECT DISCOGRAPHY:

7-inch:
'Words That Burn' EP (JSNTGM, 1995)
'Do You Feel Lucky, Punk?' (BYO, 1998)
'Crimewave' (Newest Industry, 2004)
'Staring Down The Barrel' (Newest Industry, 2007)

CDEP:
'Cold Day In Hell' (Suspect Device, 2001)

LPs:
'A Nasty Piece Of Work' (BYO, 1998)
'Zero Visibility (Experiments With Truth)' (BYO, 1999)
'Like Moths To A Flame' (Newest Industry, 2005)
'Follow As The Crow Flies' (Newest Industry, 2010)

AT A GLANCE:
It's gotta be 'Zero Visibility', if you can find it, but 'Follow As The Crow Flies' was a formidable parting shot, both musically and lyrically.

PUBLIC DISTURBANCE

Cardiff's **Public Disturbance** are probably most 'famous' as one of the bands that 'launched' the musical careers of Ian Watkins and Mike Lewis, now with the massively popular Lostprophets, but the ultra-heavy and aggressive New York-style hardcore they played back then had little in common with the hugely popular alternative rock music they put their names to now.

"The first talk of forming the band happened back when we were still at sixth form college," recalls bassist Sean McKee. "There was a rock night coming up and [vocalist] Stu [Butcher] and I were pretty envious that some of our mates would be up onstage cranking out some noise and we weren't involved. We didn't have a band ready for it, but it did spur us on to get something together ourselves. The very first PD line-up – long before we even had a band name or a clue what we were doing – was Chris Andrews on drums, me on bass, Justin Taylor [aka 'Speedo'] on guitar and Stu on vocals. We didn't even get as far as a proper practice, although Chris's parents' garden shed was 'modified' with a lump hammer and some graffiti to give us a rehearsal space…

"Meanwhile we were regulars at [the dingy Cardiff club] Metros; our mate Andy Kelly put on a hardcore night in there and we would turn up and stand hard in our finest NYHC T-shirts. One night some kid called Ian approached Stu saying, 'Hey, you're wearing a Sick Of It All shirt; you might like our band, Fleshbind…' and handed over a copy of the demo. Stu took it home, duplicated it a bunch of times and it quickly became essential listening for our whole crew. Stu had already also met Chris West and the chaps from Disco Assassins, who similarly had demo tapes out and were playing live.

"It was experiencing both these bands, realising they were a disorganised bunch of chancers just like us yet they had managed to pull together to create something awesome, that provided the real boot up the backsides we needed. We booked into a proper practice room, added a second vocalist called Jeff and wrote some very terrible songs that sounded so basic and simple they made the first Agnostic Front 7-inch sound like Dillinger Escape Plan! Somewhere along the way we lost Chris in a drumming capacity, although he was always at practice and will always be the sixth member of PD in my eyes. We also lost Jeff as he quickly proved surplus to requirements and we jammed without drums for a few months until Ian Watkins – then the Fleshbind drummer and the chap that gave Stu the Fleshbind demo that fateful night – felt sorry for us and offered to come and drum for us.

"He also brought Mike Lewis with him, who joined on second guitar and hearing our songs with drums for the first time and with the thickness of two guitars, was amazing; we were all grinning at each other like idiots as we jammed through them. Obviously with a full and proper line-up, we were able to ditch the previous material and start again from scratch."

Armed with this new material, Public Disturbance – albeit billed as 'IDC' ("Just don't ask what it stands for," scoffs Sean, "because it's super rubbish and I'm still trying to erase it from my memory!") – played their first gig on 13 March 1996, at the Four Bars Inn, Cardiff, with Fleshbind and Disco Assassins.

"It was the same day as the Dunblane massacre [when Thomas Hamilton tragically killed 16 children, one teacher and then himself at Dunblane Primary School in Scotland], so I will always remember it," says Sean. "A ton of people from mine and Stu's sixth form college

Public Disturbance live, by Naki

Public Disturbance, Stu and Sean, by Naki

Public Disturbance, by Naki

came down, as well as the FBFC – the 'Fleshbind Fighting Crew', complete with T-shirts to prove it – and the full Disco Assassins entourage. There is a VHS video of it somewhere: Mike with a bright orange guitar, Stu chewing his cheeks on speed, me with a bass around my knees…and one too many dodgy basketball vests. Tremendous. I have no idea if we were good or not, it seemed to be irrelevant; there we were, playing alongside the two bands that got us kick-started, to a room full of our mates. Not a bad start.

"Our goals when we started PD really were: 1) to play on a bill opening for Disco Assassins and Fleshbind and 2) to hear some Agnostic Front tunes jammed in Cardiff. The first we obviously achieved immediately; the second one was a case of knowing that the buck stopped with us as other 'heavy' bands were covering Pantera or whatever and AF themselves were on one of their hiatuses, so it was unlikely to see the real deal on home turf any time soon. Subsequently we loyally did two Agnostic Front covers every gig we played for the first year of our existence, 'Last Warning' and 'Friend Or Foe'. The first time we ever met Tim [*Mass Movement* fanzine] and his buddy Ian was at a Bogiez gig [*another* dingy Cardiff club] and they came up to me and said, 'Bloody hell, 19 year-old kids covering Agnostic Front!'"

Spring '96 saw the band in Grassroots Studio, Cardiff, recording the 'Lash Out' demo with engineer Paul Durrant ("He was so disgusted with the condition of my bass guitar that he banned me from recording with it," laughs Sean, "and got some plush Ibanez down off the wall and let me use that instead – result!") Although undeniably mushy in sound and with very little attention paid to detail, the viciously raw demo tape captured the rough'n'tumble Public Disturbance style to a tee and got the band a decent write-up – and their first national publicity – in *Terrorizer* magazine.

"I must have had 50-odd letters over the next few months," recalls Sean, "and I replied to every single one, sending out demos, getting other bands' demos in return, exchanging fliers and basically finding out about a bunch of other bands around the UK doing exactly what we were trying to do. That *Terrorizer* feature put us directly in touch with Pierre from Knuckledust, who then put us on in London where we met even more hardcore bands in the same boat as us and who also produced the *Time For Some Action* newsletter which itself gave PD a bunch more exposure.

"It seems too hard to articulate this, 15 years later in the age of the internet, Facebook invites and other sterile digital promotional methods, but there was this unspoken feeling of benevolence. Any time another band hooked us up with a gig, we'd try to return the favour; any time someone wanted a demo, they could have it free – although most people would force money into our hands anyway, because, after all, it funded the next stack of blank TDK cassettes…"

Buoyed by the enthusiasm of the scene they'd tapped into, Public Disturbance played wherever and whenever they could ("Once we got across the Severn Bridge, we found Above All and Stampin' Ground, as well as Knuckledust, to be on a very similar journey as ourselves") and became mosh pit favourites at seedy UKHC dives like the Red Eye in London and the Star'n'Garter in Manchester. Eventually they hooked up with fledgling Liverpool label Days Of Fury for their first MCD, 'Victim Of Circumstance', a seven-song onslaught of violent primitive metalcore with hateful, revenge-fuelled lyrics that perfectly suited the bludgeoning riffs. However Ian Watkins was increasingly occupied with his and Mike's other band, Lostprophets and was replaced behind the kit by Paul Bailey.

"Yeah, Ian always had designs on moving out from behind the drums and becoming a singer," explains Sean. "He'd tested the ground a couple of years earlier by getting up front and covering a Deftones song with Fleshbind at Bogiez and I think everyone who saw that realised that's where his heart really was. Lostprophets started in '97 and Ian did another two years on the PD drum stool, but it became obvious it was a chore for him. We made it easy for him in the end, by lining up another guy in the background and having a jam with him; it felt right and so Mike told Ian the news. As it happens, the new guy was someone whose family had been friends with my family since we were kids, so he fitted right in."

Paul's studio debut was the 'Possessed To Hate' MCD for Retribute Records, the label ran by Chris Meadows from Withdrawn and Slavearc, an even more savage affair than 'Victims Of Circumstance', the band really honing their metallic chops. The cover of 'No One' by Integrity, not to mention the hilariously entitled '18 Stones Of Pure Fucking Death', hinted that the band were certainly moving away from their old-school hardcore roots and delving into deeper, darker waters for inspiration, verging on 'hatecore' in places.

"I was penpals with Chris," says Sean. "He always seemed very sharp, with his eye on the ball and the timing came together perfectly in that he seemed to know exactly what to do with us at a time when we were evolving away from that straight-up NYHC sound and getting heavier and more metallic. Our new drummer was probably also a pivotal point as he brought a much more metallic style of drumming to the band and allowed us to really let rip.

"We also covered that One Life Crew song, which seemed to get a few people's goat, but I think it was more of a telling-off for being young and blindly echoing the sentiments of a band just because we liked the music, which is completely understandable. Were we ever a hatecore band too? Maybe…we did listen to a few of them. And we had shirts with 'Pure Hate Style' on them, so I guess we qualify on a technicality! There wasn't much going on in the way of positivity in our lyrics anyway, but them's the breaks. We were from Ely, Pontypridd and Barry, after all; to sing about high-fives and stage-dives like we had nothing more urgent to get off our chests would have been a complete cop-out. But I still love 'Possessed To Hate'; I dig it out every couple of years and kind of re-discover it; it's by far my favourite PD recording…"

It was unfortunately also the last, the band playing their final show at Cardiff's Clwb Ifor Bach in 2000. "It was an all-dayer, I believe," says Sean. "I don't remember much about the line-up, but I think we went down well and I definitely remember some serious mosh…

"It's not like we ever spoke about it," he adds, of the split, "but my view at the time was that it was just going to be a 'cooling off' period, but it ended up becoming a permanent hiatus. Mike had already left because Lostprophets was getting more and more serious and the band was getting pulled in all different ways at once. Stu worked as a doorman too, meaning we had to turn down any gigs offered on certain nights of the week and there was friction in other places of the band as well. Although this actually resulted in some of our best songwriting, I think there had been a serious shift in the band's chemistry.

"Originally we were just five guys that would have been hanging out anyway, choosing to use that time to do something constructive; at the end it was like we had other things to do and it was difficult to put them on hold just to make the band continue. If it wasn't going to happen through inertia or the previous momentum, then it wasn't something that could be forced. In hindsight, it was the perfect time to put it to sleep…"

Mike and Sean joined forces with Neil from Disco Assassins and Nick from Losing Sun to form "a Bird Of Ill Omen-style band" called New Born Lord, but when Lostprophets and Losing Sun both took off, Sean and Neil recruited Jimbob from Taint and Chris West from

Diabolo and the sound turned far sludgier. Nothing was ever recorded though and when Sean moved to London he joined SXE band Seventh Judgement, who played on some strong hardcore bills alongside the likes of Hatebreed, Unearth and Terror. When that band folded ("It had just run its course…and much edge-breaking was going on!"), vocalist Troy and Sean hooked up with Ignoramus guitarist Chico and BDF drummer Ali as Deny Everything.

They eventually released a storming 7-inch, but not before Sean had left to move back to Cardiff where he joined both Routine Check and (alongside original PD drummer Chris Davies and guitarist Speedo) Twist The Knife (who would later morph into Chains Of Hate and record for Rucktion Records). Nowadays Sean plays in Inherit alongside vocalist Adam Malik from Pain Runs Deep, guitarist Rich Shiner from xCanaanx and the Break In, guitarist Rob Moss from Dirty Money and drummer Dave Mayes from Age Of Kali and Lightbringer.

"I can't answer for the other guys, but I think Public Disturbance got a lot of very simple things right in terms of how to go from a humble first practice to being a regularly gigging band," he offers, when asked what set PD apart from their peers. "I've jammed with several other bands in other parts of the UK since then and I've often been baffled by how much of a rigmarole they make out of writing the most basic music. I realised this when jamming with some kids in Cardiff in a band called Soul Reversal, who were completely on the same page as me about this.

"We wrote six great tracks in two, maybe three, practices, then we had a change of bassist and thought nothing of ditching the lot and starting again from scratch; we wrote another three in a week and recorded them that weekend. And then, on the flipside, I've been in the jam room with bands who spend three hours trying to teach their drummer one single drum part. Unless you're in Tool or Bloodlet, I don't see the point of making the songwriting process such a time-suck!

"I don't think we were actually worth remembering, though," he concludes modestly. "There was a bunch of other bands doing the same thing around the same time. I'd like to say we left some kind of ugly scar on the Cardiff music scene, but that's not the case. We had a few memorable hometown shows but we basically went down a lot better when we played out of town. What set us apart? I think we had a frontman rather than a singer and that makes a world of difference. I've seen enough bands that have some guy up front who can hold the stuff down vocally but who lacks any stage presence or conviction whatsoever and just mumbles into his shoes between songs. That's fine if your music is indirect and timid, but if you're gonna have aggressive and confrontational lyrics you need someone up front that can back it up. That's a bugbear I've often had with bands that play that toughened-up style of hardcore. In the words of Gunnery Sergeant Hartman, 'You don't scare me…work on it!'"

SELECT DISCOGRAPHY:

MCDs:
'Victim Of Circumstance' (Days Of Fury, 1997)
'Possessed To Hate' (Retribution, 1999)

AT A GLANCE:
No plans for any sort of retrospective, so you're gonna have to mail Sean for some sounds if you can't track down the two MCDs: sean@deadheroesclothing.com

DISCO ASSASSINS

As detailed earlier, Cardiff's **Disco Assassins** might only have released two demos, but they played an important part in the development of the Welsh hardcore scene, inspiring the likes of Public Disturbance and Fleshbind (and, by extension, the Lostprophets) in their formative years and their members went on to play in pivotal bands such as Diabolo and Taint.

Originally a three-piece with a drum machine, Disco Assassins were formed in late 1993 by guitarist Ryan Heeger, vocalist Gary Rowlands and bassist/vocalist Christian 'Sinky' Sinclair, who had played together in various low-key punk, metal and grunge bands, namely Angel Dust, the Sewer Youth and Sweet Sick, mainly playing covers and a few derivative originals. They were soon joined by two friends from college – Chris West, who became bassist, allowing Sinky to concentrate on vocals alongside Gary ("He could never play the fucking bass anyway," laughs Ryan) and Neil Smith, who became second guitarist.

"Disco Assassins was mine and Neil's first band," explains Chris. "We had grown up playing in a few cover bands, just jamming around with mates of mine from school. He was a bit older than me, so had a good few years more experience shredding compared to me and the other boys, but we were best mates, always played well together and always wanted to do something a bit more 'real'. We grew up sharing a love of bands like the Misfits and Danzig, along with all kinds of thrash, punk and crossover bands. We had been introduced to hardcore via some gigs in Cardiff and immediately 'got it'; the speed, the anger, the rebellion and the unity it conveyed, totally clicked with me and Neil and we knew we wanted to be doing that kind of thing stylistically.

"Unfortunately, the scene here was still quite glam rock; we had one real rock club called Bogiez, which me and the guys would frequent. It was full of glammed-up rock chicks and ageing rockers and would usually have gigs on there from no-name bands and cover acts, but suddenly, out of nowhere, it started getting better for gigs; I remember we had Sick Of It All, Clutch, Biohazard and a load of others, all around the same time, all playing this relatively small club. It brought a lot of people from all over South Wales together for the first time in one place, where they could get to know each other. We had always had it rough here as no bands would come to Wales on their UK tours, which I think was maybe why Wales seemed so stuck in a time warp when it came to heavy music. The only place you could see a good band was at St David's Hall or the Leisure Centre in Newport and although they were great gigs, there was no chance of local support slots as they were always big headline-act shows like Metallica, Pantera, Slayer or Megadeth.

"We didn't really know of a hardcore scene at the time; that's not to say there wasn't one, but we certainly weren't part of it if there was. The only other South Wales punk bands I knew of back then were Cowboy Killers and Four Letter Word and we didn't get to know those guys 'til a bit later on. So when we started, it felt like we were the only ones doing this kind of thing and people started catching on by seeing us at gigs and spreading the word, I guess. The guys who went on to form Public Disturbance were big fans of ours and when we met them for the first time we were most surprised that there were other guys around even into hardcore! Another local haunt of ours was the alternative club, Metro's...basically a stinking underground tunnel-shaped club, where it seemed we practically lived for several years. This was to be the venue for our first ever show."

Disco Assassins, left to right, Chris West, Ryan Heeger, Jon Timney, Gary Rowlands, Neil Smith

Disco Assassins

That show happened on 14 July 1994 ("The buzz afterwards was immense," remembers Ryan, happily, "a real feeling of starting something exciting musically...") and Disco Assassins recorded their first demo, 'There's No Justice...Just Us', soon afterwards. Six tracks of brutal simplistic hardcore, with ultra-fast, ultra-aggressive tracks like 'Scum' and 'Fuck The Filth' clocking in between one and two minutes in length, it was recorded at the Grassroots Youth Project by Paul Durrant.

A second date at Metro's was riddled with drum machine-related technical problems, but was thankfully witnessed by a talented *human* drummer, Jon Timney, who Gary had played with in metal band Split Infinity several years earlier and who joined Disco Assassins two weeks later. At about the same time, Sinky was asked to leave and Disco Assassins arrived at their short-lived definitive line-up, which gigged regularly around South Wales with the likes of Cowboy Killers, Channel 9 and the aforementioned Fleshbind.

"Jon had a huge effect on us when he joined," Chris enthuses. "It suddenly became much more 'real', y'know? There's nothing like having a solid drummer playing behind you, especially for myself as a bass player, so I was immediately much more happy and I definitely think it made me step up my game as a bass player and made me a better musician. Jon's a great guy, with an enthusiastic personality and a shit-hot drummer, so dynamically it gave us all a huge boost and the kick up the arse we needed to become more of a proper band...

"Meanwhile, Sinky was always a strange character. I think he was a bit paranoid about the whole world and was hard to get on with or get close to...but fundamentally he really wasn't that good! He had absolutely no sense of time or rhythm, which may not necessarily be important in punk rock, but I had to physically conduct him when it came to recording etc. It all came to a head when we discovered he was talking shit about us behind our backs, so I had the job of telling him we had to part ways. This, along with Jon joining the ranks, made the atmosphere much more fun and allowed us to record our second demo in a much more enjoyable fashion."

That second demo was recorded at Grassroots again, during spring 1995 and entitled 'Same Genius, Different Species'. A tighter, heavier and all-round more cohesive effort than '...Just Us', it saw the band starting to experiment with their material and push impatiently at the perceived boundaries of their chosen genre. Sadly it would also see Disco Assassins start to fall apart at the seams before ever realising their true potential. "The last track, 'Into Insanity', was written by Chris," explains Ryan, "and was doomier than anything we'd done before; it actually showed signs of what he'd go on to do next in Diabolo.

"However, Gary was moving towards a more traditional punk sound that also had influences of Brit-pop in it and as our two main songwriters – and both of them equally strong-willed – Chris and Gary were starting to clash in terms of direction. I vividly recall one practice when Chris brought along a crusty dreadlocked guy called Mike with his didgeridoo; Gary just stood in the corner watching, as the rest of us smoked weed and jammed instrumentally and then walked out...!"

"This was the start of us all slowly moving in different directions musically," sighs Chris. "I wanted us to become heavier and tune lower and mix that with the nastier hardcore stuff, but Gary had other ideas and really didn't like the way I wanted things to progress. Looking back now I totally understand how he must have felt, but at the time it seemed to me that – out of nowhere – he started loving bands like Oasis and Stone Roses and the tunes he was writing were very influenced by them and to say I hated playing them was an understatement! I guess he felt the same way about the tunes that I was contributing though and looking back I can see that maybe I was being a bit selfish and blinkered. I'd even just sing them on my own, while Gary would be at the side of the stage until we played one of his songs or an old tune.

"It was an altogether weird and uncomfortable situation and one that had to come to a head sooner or later…which it finally did towards the end of 1996. Jon had to call it a day not long before then, as he had to move away from Cardiff to Birmingham and couldn't commit any more and when he left it was the beginning of the end for me, although it took me a while to pluck up the courage to leave myself. I loved the times I had with DA, especially as me and Neil were so close and had always said we'd play together, but I was writing more and more at home and the style was getting further and further away from DA and more into the territory I'd go on to explore in my next band Diabolo…"

As well as Diabolo, Chris then joined the critically-acclaimed Taint on bass, as well as playing drums for the Cull and Black Cesar and is presently playing drums in Spider Kitten. He also did a stint as bassist and singer with Bristol stoner-rock outfit Gonga and played bass on an EP with Nukebirds. Meanwhile, Jon was replaced in Disco Assassins by Adam Powell (who would leave to join Chris in Diabolo), then Matthew 'Moley' Stowell for a period in 1997 and finally by Mark Watson, who was with them until they finally called it a day in 1998. Second guitarist Ryan stepped into the bass role vacated by Chris.

"There was never a really a moment when any of us said, 'Right, that's it…'" reckons Ryan. "The last DA gig was in the upstairs hall of the Star Leisure Centre, Splott, on a Sunday night during October 1998; I remember we were headlining and the two or three considerably younger bands before us all played US pop-punk in Green Day style. Then, as we played, they were all packing up their gear with their backs to us, congratulating each other before fucking off, taking their supporters with them.

"By our last song, almost everyone had left; I remember how pissed off the few friends who had come along with us were, but we just laughed about it and still do. As Neil recalls, Will introduced us by saying, 'Right ladies and gentlemen, it's the band you've all been waiting for, clap your hands, stamp your feet, for…Disco Assassins!' After that night, we took a hiatus from jamming that we never came back from…"

Neil briefly joined Public Disturbance before forming Dead Man's Hand with Jon; he eventually moved to Australia with his girlfriend, while Jon moved to southwest England and nowadays plays with Chains Of Hate (with several ex-members of Public Disturbance). Chris, Gary and Ryan have all become fathers in recent years, with the latter now a successful journalist who is working on his first novel.

"It would be nice to be remembered for helping kick-start the scene in South Wales a bit," concludes Chris, "although I'm not really sure if we'll ever be thought of as being part of any bigger picture. We were an important underground band around here, but I'm not sure how widely we spread that feeling, although I'll always be very proud of what we achieved and the doors it opened for me afterwards. I know we directly inspired some people to start up bands of their own and were a huge influence on bands like Public Disturbance, for example. I guess what set us apart was us just doing what we wanted and never bowing down to trends or scene politics and having a very traditional British – nay, *Welsh* – punk sound. At the end of the day, and all that matters when it comes to punk rock, is that we kicked ass, pure and simple!"

AT A GLANCE:

What are you waiting for? Go hunt those demos down online.

IN THE SHIT

Newport's **In The Shit** was formed by ex-members of Disarm, Four Letter Word and Cowboy Killers, but managed to be heavier than any of those bands with their very metallic take on crusty hardcore punk. Strangely enough, they were far 'bigger' in France than they were in the UK, but France's gain was definitely our loss because the band turned in some top-quality raging tunes.

"I got into punk in 1979, mainly because my older brother was into it," admits guitarist Paul 'Payney' Payne. "He had all the records by UK Subs and Sham 69 and I, being a typical nine year-old boy, was fascinated with the swearing and angry music. I actually ended up nicking *my* first 7-inch, because I waited for hours at the counter in Smiths and no-one would serve me…probably because they didn't see me, being short'n'all. Anyway, it was by the Members, 'Sound Of The Suburbs'; a true classic, still have it to this day…

"Mind you, being a kid I still got excited back then because there was an aeroplane on the cover and a TV with a few circles, similar to what you got to see on the *Banana Splits*! Anyway, by the early Eighties every kid in the village was getting into punk; the main bands were SLF, Clash, Sex Pistols, Dead Kennedys, Exploited, Conflict and Subhumans. Some of my friends had a punk band called the Oddments, who played some youth-club gigs and started me off wanting to learn guitar – mainly because I couldn't sing! By the mid Eighties,

I had a few paper rounds and could afford to buy a shitty guitar; I used to learn round a friend's house, proper one-string wonders we were! When I could play a chord I was catapulted into the Oddments…big fame that was! And when that finished, me and Newt [aka Robert Newport] got Disarm together…"

Although Disarm never played outside South Wales, they did play with some very popular bands of the period – Blaggers, Chaos UK, Doom and HDQ, for example – and released three decent demos and really helped pave the way for ITS Disarm folded in '91, when Newt branched off with Rectify and Payney started DSM. In The Shit eventually started in 1996 and was basically Payney, vocalist Richard 'Flid' Bryant and bassist Rob Greenow, all ex-DSM – and a drum machine. However, Payney soon recruited a real drummer, Kip, who had just left Four Letter Word (he'd previously played with Cowboy Killers as well) and Rob was replaced by Martin 'Buffy' Harris on bass, completing the first proper ITS line-up.

"The first gig is a bit of a debate, I suppose," reckons Payney, "as it was an all-dayer at the Frog'n'Bucket [in Newport], with various bands of all different styles of music. Date-wise that was the first, though the first actual *punk* gig was the '96 Bristol punks' picnic at the Full Moon, with Varukers, Combat Shock, Excrement Of War, Police Bastard and a few others. It was amazing too; we played first, but it was completely packed out and probably even emptied a little bit after we played…. Saying that, being Bristol, between all the band members, we probably knew every bugger there as friends, so loads of 'em wanted to see our first attempt at a gig. So, that was really cool, that friends gave us the time and there was a lotta banter…the usual sort of stuff!"

Full of youthful enthusiasm, In The Shit released their 7-inch EP, 'Can't Take Anymore', on their own In The Shit Records during early '97, a strong debut that saw gig offers flooding in from around the country. "We immediately thought of the Whitehouse in Weston-super-Mare, which seemed to be the place to go back then and it was obviously a good choice for us as everything ITS ever recorded was done in there from then on. Anyway, we recorded seven tracks and were very happy with them, totally thrilled with the sound; it was originally to be our first demo, though I had never made a 7-inch before and had always liked the idea of starting a label, so I decided to release it myself.

"Welly from Four Letter Word helped me with the art and 960 EPs were pressed, with the first 280 on brown vinyl…we sarcastically put government toilet tissue in with the first ones we sold just for a laugh. It was actually the fastest selling release we did and more or less sold out in less than a year and half – 600 being sold in the first three months! Looking back at it now, it was definitely the best thing to do at that time, because so many more things started happening for us once it was out, with all the gigs we were being offered. I remember reading in *Ripping Thrash* [fanzine] once that 'In The Shit was appearing at every gig in the UK'…"

As well as one-off gigs with the likes of Varukers, Restarts and Coitus, In The Shit also toured the UK with Sheffield's Truth Decay and Mass Murderers from Rennes, France, which led to their inclusion on the six-band compilation 7-inch, 'A Tour Story', released by French label Mass Productions during November '98. This in turn led to a French tour with Truth Decay and the second ITS single, 'The Fall Of The Damned', being a joint release between Mass Productions and UK label Inflammable Material. Released in September 1999 and featuring five songs, including a cover of 'Americans Are Cool' by Spermbirds, the EP saw ITS adopting a much heavier but cleaner guitar tone than their first, more 'crusty', single; 'The Fall Of The Damned' even leaned towards more metallic territory, although the band's inherent punk attitude ensured this was purely a stylistic leaning, not a spiritual one.

"We first met Vincent from Mass Productions on the UK tour we helped organise for Mass Murderers," explains Payney. "They did four gigs over here and it was a really good tour and the 'Tour Story' compilation was all bands they played with on that tour [as well as ITS and Truth Decay, it also featured Throw Bricks At Coppers, The Rong 'Uns and Peer Pressure, plus Mass Murderers themselves]. Six months later we were over in France, just as they promised; we had our first gig in Paris after meeting Truth Decay in Dover.

"It took eight hours to get to the gig as we couldn't find the venue; we asked for directions for the Peniche Blues Café and were told several different places and it eventually turned out to be *a boat*, where we played with Tagada Jones. We all laughed at the name, but were in for a shock – they were a totally amazing band! I'm pretty sure it was their first gig in Paris and the place was rammed to the rafters; for those who don't follow the French music scene, Tagada Jones then went on to become one of the most well-known bands over there, with one of their albums topping sales of over 100,000 copies.

"It was a brilliant start to the tour; the gigs went really well and were full of humour…

In The Shit at rehearsal

In The Shit

on the travel side it was mainly us getting lost and then finding the venues by accident. The French customs took a fancy to us, I think and searched us about four times in six days; it was like something from Monty Python's *Life Of Brian*, where they were determined to find something! But we made some really good friends on that tour and soon after Mass Productions offered to put out our next single…"

However, after a second tour of France and Belgium in 1999, the band parted ways with Kip, who went on to drum for Da Capo and was replaced by Mike Chaney, an old friend of Flid's with whom he had previously played alongside in Goat Grinder. Within three months of joining, Mike was in Whitehouse Studios recording the 'A Cancerous Society' album, which was released by Mass Productions in Europe and Blind Destruction in the UK.

"'You Make Me Sick' was actually written in the studio while recording," chuckles Payney, of the spontaneity that lends that recording such undeniable energy. "And the solo thingy at the end of [crowd favourite] 'Screaming Beer' was a complete accident! I couldn't remember what I was supposed to play, so made a compromise…

"But 'A Cancerous Society' was probably our most popular release, or maybe that was just down to the timing of it? Whatever, it sold out on both CD and vinyl very fast; I never knew until a few years later, but it apparently helped Mass Productions out a lot, as they were struggling a bit at the time. I think it's aged pretty well too; the more polished sound on recording has helped towards that, plus the 'classic' 'Screaming Beer' went on many compilation CDs, which helped get the word out. I get asked more at gigs these days when I am doing a distro about 'A Cancerous Society' by people wanting copies of it than for any other release!"

A UK tour was undertaken with high-speed Boston (Massachusetts!) hardcore band Out Cold, before Spite's Pete Rose joined on second guitar. He lasted for several tours of France and the UK (not to mention a hundred and one punks' picnics all over the country!) before leaving to join the reformed Icons Of Filth; at which point Buffy left and was replaced by Craig 'Fletch' Jenkins. The album was then released on cassette in 2002 for Eastern Europe by Czech label Papagajuv Hlasatel Records, with the first two EPs added as bonus tracks and the band headed out on their first full European tour.

"All the European tours we did were very memorable, but that one that springs to mind – for all the wrong reasons! Our van broke down on the motorway when we were going to the first gig…a totally knackered piston had gone through the engine, so we sat on the roadside in Belgium deciding what to do. The recovery came and told us we had four weeks before we had to collect our gear, as the engine was completely gone, at which point we thought, 'Fuck it, let's get to Amsterdam on the train…!' So we took our guitars and breakables and off we went.

"We met up with Daniel from Schandmaul Records [from Berlin] who helped us organise the tour; he rang around friends and we played the gig and the next morning they took us to Germany, where we then jumped all the trains and made the whole tour – all except for one gig – without any transport! We got a lotta people at the gigs in Berlin and Leipzig too, because everyone was fascinated that a band would still continue to tour Europe after losing everything before they even got to the first gig! After such a bad start, they were all great gigs as well…

"Magdeburg was a bit creepy, though, to say the least, mainly due to meeting some mentalist who had cut his nose off, who later went on to slash the drum skins with a knife…

apparently he wasn't all there and had previously cut his penis off with a scalpel blade too! All a bit mental, but looking back we can laugh at it now… Anyway, the tour continued with some friends coming from Czechoslovakia to give us a lift to Prague, so we managed to play all the dates there and Slovakia…it was a real triumph in the face of adversity."

Unfortunately In The Shit then went on a temporary hiatus when Mike moved to Germany, but he moved back in early 2003 and the ferocious second album, 'A World Of…', was recorded at the Whitehouse and co-released by Blind Destruction, Mass Productions and Schandmaul. However, after another European tour and numerous dates around the UK, Flid left and bassist Fletch moved to vocals, allowing Mark Hirons from Smithgrind and Plastic Pigs to fill the vacant bass position. This line-up toured the UK with Italian hardcore legends, Raw Power and contributed tracks to 2004's 'Mizaru Kikazaru Iwazaru' six-band compilation and 2005's split CDEP with Brazilian band Acao Direta, both releases coming courtesy of Blind Destruction.

But Payney freely admits that Flid leaving signalled the beginning of the end for In The Shit, with Fletch unable to make their third European tour (Matt from the Viktims filled in at short notice) and Mike unable to make a final tour of Bretagne. The band played one final reunion show with Flid back on vocals at the Bristol Junction, with Pawns and Gurkha in support, which Payney remembers as "Business as usual, like we'd never been away, even though we hadn't rehearsed for 10 months!"

Mike moved to Sweden, where he still lives with his wife, Mark went back to Smithgrind and Fletch went on to play with the much more rock'n'roll Bag Of Bones. Payney meanwhile joined This System Kills, alongside Pig from Rectify, before playing with the Rejected, who released a split LP with Poundaflesh and a self-titled full length of their own before evolving into Bring To Ruin (with members of Threat Manifesto), who look set to drop their debut album in 2012.

"There were a lot of mishaps, for sure," admits the good-natured guitarist. "But generally speaking, the tours were really good and all the bad bits are more just memories to laugh at! France turned into our second home, because I think they are more open to music there, whereas the UK tends to be stuck in the past for punk rock; it's like here everybody only wants to see what happened yesterday and very few people care about the current DIY scene. Sure, there are some really cool people in the UK…but there's a lot who probably don't like the idea that a Welsh band can be good, because we don't live in a city or whatever.

"I never let it bother me, but just because we didn't have a record out before most kids were born doesn't make us a bad band and we worked hard for everything we did. Even today I get sick and tired of the elitest 'supergroups' asking a fortune to play and it's never the original line-up and usually the smaller bands go unpaid…is that really punk rock? Sounds more like 'Rock' to me! I still like some of the older stuff, of course, but it's *history* and, really speaking within any scene, if people don't move forward the whole thing becomes stagnant…

"But ITS was just a band of people who did something for the love of it," he concludes modestly. "I haven't got any ego to speak of, so I'm not really bothered how people remember the band; it was just 10 years of my life, lots of highs and lows but overall I was happy to be a part of it. And I'm pretty sure all the others would say the same thing: we made some really great friends and played with many great bands, old and new and never lost sight of the fact we were a *punk* band!"

SELECT DISCOGRAPHY:

7-inch:
'Can't Take Anymore' (ITS Records, 1997)
'A Tour Story' (Mass Productions, 1998) – *six-band split EP*
'The Fall Of The Damned' (Mass Productions/Inflammable Material, 1999)

CDEP:
'Split' (Blind Destruction, 2005) – *split with Acao Direta*

LPs:
'A Cancerous Society' (Mass Productions/Blind Destruction, 2000)
'A World Of…' (Mass Production/Blind Destruction/Schandmaul, 2003)

AT A GLANCE:
Until someone compiles a much-needed retrospective, track down either album for a thumping good selection of metallic punk rock.

100,000 BODY BAGS

Blackwood's **100,000 Body Bags** weren't, as the name might suggest, a bleak, depressing crusty thrash band, but instead a rather eclectic, unashamedly poppy melodic hardcore band. They were formed in 1994 by guitarist/vocalist Craig 'Brewer' Bruzas, who had previously played with Funeral In Berlin, a proto-goth band most famous for gigging regularly with Blackwood's biggest musical exports, the Manic Street Preachers, during their formative years. Original bassist Mickey Mills had also joined FIB in 1987 (albeit as a guitarist then) and after the band changed their name to Rape Of Lucretia and contributed two tracks to the 'Resurrection, A New Beginning' compilation on Tower Records (Nottingham) in 1992, they endured various line-up changes before changing their name *again*, this time to (the rather crap) Laura Is. Thankfully they eventually secured the services of drummer Simon Cullen from Xposed and became 100,000 Body Bags in late 1993.

"100,000 Body Bags was inspired by the fact that, when we were looking for a name for the band, the first Gulf War was happening in Iraq," Simon begins. "I remember watching the reports on the news and watching the night vision footage of the bombs smashing Baghdad into pieces and it being hailed as a 'clean' war with no casualties, ha! In that first war, 107,000 Iraqi civilians were killed – although estimates have now risen to more than 250,000 apparently – so the name was kind of a statement on that. It's a lot less relevant as a band name now, but I guess it kind of sticks out still.

"The stuff I was listening to when the Bags first got together was Nirvana, Public Enemy, Dead Kennedys and Cop Shoot Cop and it was a million miles from what I was playing in local metal bands. In the [Welsh] Valleys in the early Nineties, there were a *lot* of bands doing thrash metal, glam rock, that kind of stuff, but that wasn't what I was into any more. I knew Brewer was a cool guy and that his musical tastes were similar to mine at that time, so it worked really well. "Influences musically came from the music we were all listening to at the time, of course: a lot of old punk stuff, mixed with the explosion of the grunge scene in the early to mid Nineties.

"Locally, there were a lot of cool bands that we played with that influenced us too, such as Rectify, Cowboy Killers, No Choice and Sand. Lyrically, we just tried to write about what was going on around us; whether it was local communities being pulled apart by recession and unemployment, or empirical wars in the Middle East, or what was happening in American politics, I always thought that the songs had to say something of importance. But we didn't want to be a po-faced political band preaching to an uninterested audience either, so we liked to keep a sense of humour in the stuff where possible…"

Within a week of his joining, the Body Bags played their first gig at the Six Bells Workmen's Club in Abertillery ("I remember it being awesome and us rocking the hell out of the place," laughs Simon. "But the reality was probably that we were dreadful and three old men and a whippet booed us off…!") and the band soon worked up an interesting and diverse set of songs and built a loyal local following.

"The local scene at that time comprised lots of bands trying to be Mötley Crüe, from what I can remember," reckons Simon. "There were a few really good punk bands, but the biggest influence on us was TJ's in Newport: a venue where you could guarantee to go every single week and see an outstanding international band… I remember paying £3 to see NoMeansNo play! TJ's was where I first saw Fugazi, Cop Shoot Cop, Green Day, Grotus…this was a grotty little pub in a grotty area of Newport that was just totally owning the alternative/punk live music scene.

"The main promoter was [Simon from] Cheap Sweaty Fun and they had an ethic that they'd get the biggest bands possible to play there, put on local bands as support and charge as little as possible to get in. A hell of a lot of bands still touring now were born out of that TJ's scene and wouldn't be around if it wasn't for that place… and now, with [owner] John Sicolo's sad passing, I hear they're turning it into flats!

"I think one thing that's always made us different as a band is that we're not scared to put together a set of songs that have absolutely nothing in common with one another," he adds. "There were bands at the time that saw themselves as 'punk' or 'metal' and that's all that they would play; they couldn't get outside of that boundary. Whereas we just played whatever came to mind at the time; we had songs with rap parts and dub parts; songs that sounded metal, slow acoustic-styled songs, hardcore punk-type songs – and we'd cram them all into a live set wherever possible."

The band then landed themselves a deal with Damaged Goods off the back of what was little more than a rehearsal tape… albeit a rehearsal tape loaded with some unassuming punk-rock dynamite.

"The Damaged Goods thing was just a stroke of good luck, I suppose," says Simon, modestly. "We recorded a four-track demo in the room we rehearsed in at the time. We sent the demo around to the usual places for getting gigs and rather hopefully to one or two small record labels just out of curiosity. Ian from Damaged Goods loved '(We've Got A) Problem' and contacted us about releasing a 7-inch as soon as we sent it to him. We then recorded 'Problem' and the B-side, 'No Better', in Rockfield in Monmouth, with Richard Jackson [from 60ft Dolls and Novocaine] engineering for us. Damaged Goods pressed an initial 2,500 singles and sold out almost straight away, then re-pressed it on red vinyl…"

"I'm still really proud of that first 7-inch," adds Brewer. "It still sounds great to me even now and 'Problem' still seems fresh today, which tells me we did a good thing. The lyrics on 'No Better' are a bit dated, mind you, because of references to Rodney King etc, but both songs sound great to me. We started getting hand-written letters from weird places like Russia and the Philippines, telling us how they'd bought the single and loved it and we were on hundreds of playlists in America, sandwiched between the likes of NOFX and Fugazi etc. We even made *Maximum Rock'n'Roll*'s yearly 'Top Singles' list…"

Despite the critical acclaim heaped upon 'Problem', the band's next single – another driving tune managing to give nods to the Stooges and Damned without sounding hopelessly retro – wasn't so well-received, by either audience or record label…

"We went to record the follow-up single in a studio called Grass Roots in Cardiff," explains Simon. "We recorded three songs in that session, then – at a critical point during mixing – the main engineer decided he was going to go home and watch Ireland vs. Italy in the World Cup, leaving us with some dozy apprentice-type to finish mixing. If you listen to '… Stereotype' [that second single's A-side], you can actually hear where he turns the drums down halfway through the first verse… they then deleted the master tape the day after the recording and lost the DAT, so the single was actually mastered off an old TDK cassette tape! I don't think Ian was overly happy with it all, but he asked us up to London anyway, to play a label showcase with a bunch of other Damaged Goods bands. We took a minibus full of mates up; unfortunately, they spent the entire three-hour journey from the Valleys to London drinking Strongbow [cider], then went a bit mental during our set, slashed all the seats, smashed everything up and then smashed a chip shop's windows…"

"Lots of things were stripped off the walls and stuff," sighs Brewer. "Hell, it was a big day out for the boys in the van, some of them didn't even know London really existed 'til that gig; they thought it was a mythical place where fairy stories were based. Needless to say, we never heard from Damaged Goods again after that… There's an interesting quote on his website, though, proclaiming us to be 'The most obnoxious fuckers he ever worked with!'"

After the 'Love Is Dead'/'Last Of The New Wave' 7-inch for Nottingham label Weird (another edgy pop-punk gem, with some great choruses in the vein of Therapy?) and a compilation on Smokin' Troll entitled 'Schoolroom Politics', that collected all the singles onto one shiny digital disc, 100,000 Bodybags added Tony 'Mad Ant' Gingell to their line-up during 1999, although he had been lurking in the shadows for some years at that point.

"Yeah, he'd been a good friend of the band for a long time," confirms Simon. "Indeed, it was he who recorded the four-track demo that Damaged Goods loved so much and we'd played a load of gigs with his band at the time, Orange Free State. We loved those guys because more comical things happened to them than any band I've ever seen before or since and we used to steal songs that Ant had written for OFS and 'cover' them. He's a great songwriter and has a good ear for a nice chord progression or vocal melody, but he always favoured the slow, moody type of sound, so we'd take these songs that he'd written that sounded like REM and punk them up so they sounded like GBH!

100,000 Body Bags live at Slugfest

"'CAT' [the B-side of the second Damaged Goods 7-inch] was entirely written by Ant – lyrics, tune…everything – but we nicked it and made it our own. He never minded. And around the time that we were recording 'Left Wing, Right Wing, Ra! Ra! Ra!' he ended up hanging out with us more than his own band. Another of his songs, 'Father Of Lies', appears on that CD and he played a few guitar parts that sounded great, so we decided he'd be a pretty handy full-time member. As a three-piece, we had to keep things pretty simple, in order to allow Brew space to play guitar and sing, but Anthony joining changed all that and allowed us to write much more complex and interesting songs…"

Ant made his 'proper' recording debut on the 'Iconoclast' MCD that the band self-released in 2001, but it was to be the only release recorded as a four-piece, with Mickey leaving the following year, as the band busied themselves both writing a new CD and backing up ex-Rectify singer Pig as This System Kills.

"Mickey basically left the band because he became more interested in dance music," explains Simon. "He wanted us to play all electronic and stuff…he also got a bit obsessed with the internet and started missing rehearsals because he was too busy chatting online! The final straw came when he didn't turn up to a gig because…well, basically he couldn't be bothered. For a short while, my brother, Sean, replaced him on bass; he's an amazing bass player, but unfortunately, he lived in Oxford, so that was way too prohibitive and we were only rehearsing once a month. I have a recording of a gig we did in Cardiff at the Barfly with my bro' on bass and it sounds great. That was the last time we played anything as a four-piece though and, in the end, we decided to try as a three-piece again with Brewer switching to bass and Ant taking all the guitar parts.

"At the same time, Rectify had split up and Pig was looking for a band; I'd just worked with Pig on a track for the 'Barricades And Broken Dreams' compilation CD on Blackfish, which was a Conflict tribute. We did a cover of 'This Is The ALF', which sounded great, so we thought we could maybe do something with two singers in the Bags, to take the pressure off Brew a little bit. That was kind of the beginning of the end for Body Bags mark 1, though…and the beginning of the beginning for This System Kills! We originally formed TSK as a separate entity to the Body Bags and for a while we worked with both bands, but TSK eventually took over.

"We were using Body Bags songs and re-writing them slightly, but because of Pig's connections (and the fact that the band bloody rocked) we were getting a hell of a lot of gigs, so the Body Bags took an un-planned backseat…to the point where we were too busy with TSK to do anything with the Bags at all. But one Bags album *was* released during this time: 'There Are No Conspiracies But The One True Conspiracy', which was recorded entirely using drum and bass loops and samples with overdubbed guitar. It's a pretty interesting addition to the discography, with some great tunes on there; it's almost Nine Inch Nails-like in places…"

"The '… Conspiracy…' songs were never really finished, though," admits Brewer. "Drums still had to be added, the vocals were just the guide tracks and more guitar had to be done… but, due to time restrictions, we just put it out. I like the fact that it stands out so much from our other stuff; it kind of proves the point that we sound how we sound, without worrying about musical labels or what people think of us!"

The astute reader will have noted the use of the word '*sound*' in that last sentence, not 'sounded' – yes, the Bodybags are back together and they released a brand new, fragile yet catchy, six-song EP, 'Breaking Something Beautiful', in 2011.

"The new Body Bags don't differ hugely from the Nineties version really," claims Simon. "There are still a load of the same tunes in the set now as back then, although I think lyrically we're a lot more open now; not everything has to be so politicised. We can write more personal stuff without feeling odd about it… there are still politics and ideals in the lyrics, of course, but we don't feel like there *has* to be now. I think we have a better ear for a tune now too; instead of stretching a three-chord riff out for two-and-a-half minutes and shouting over the top of it, we try to throw in some melodies and maybe a catchy chorus or two. I hasten to use the words 'grown up', because I don't think that's true, but I *do* think our songwriting has matured."

"I remember the Nineties as being a pretty exciting time, to be honest," concludes Brewer. "The whole grunge thing brought back that feeling of DIY to the music scene. I guess the Nineties to us was what the mid-Seventies were to all the original punks: just the fact that, all of a sudden, you didn't have to be polished, over-produced and over-blown to make it. It was all about the music again, which is why I genuinely think Nirvana's 'Bleach' was one of the greatest punk albums ever. Locally there was a big explosion of Welsh bands becoming successful, mostly from around Newport, which goes back to the whole scene based around TJ's again. I suppose it's always a bit rosy looking 15 years back into the past, but I genuinely remember having a fucking blast for that entire decade…"

SELECT DISCOGRAPHY:

7-inch:
'Problem' (Damaged Goods, 1994)

'She's A Stereotype' (Damaged Goods, 1995)

'Last Of The New Wave' (Weird, 1996)

MCDs:
'Left Wing, Right Wing, Ra! Ra! Ra!' (Bodybag Records, 1999)

'Iconoclast' (Bodybag Records, 2001)

'There Are No Conspiracies (But The One True Conspiracy)' (Bodybag Records, 2003)

'Breaking Something Beautiful' (Bodybag Records, 2011)

AT A GLANCE:
The 'Schoolroom Politics' CD for Smokin' Troll compiled the first three singles and various obscure tracks from those sessions. It sold out long ago, but you can basically find the same tracks available for download online, with a title of 'Fuck The Famous Years'.

RECTIFY

Anarcho street-punk band Classified Protest were previously covered in *The Day The Country Died*, but in 1987 they morphed into the infinitely more focused and far more intense **Rectify**, who were a leading light of the Welsh hardcore punk scene throughout the Nineties and more than merit further investigation here.

"Classified Protest was more of a school punk thing," admits vocalist Wayne 'Pig' Cole. "We just wanted to play, so we wrote our own version of the punk music that was around at that time – the No Future and Riot City bands – and then a lot of the ideas built as we got older, as we were finding out more about what was going on in the world through other bands' lyrics and the whole movement at the time…!"

Indeed, Rectify were a much more socially aware and politically driven band than Classified Protest. Joining Pig in the new band were guitarist Rhys 'Ghandi' Martin, bassist Andrew 'Footy' Foot and drummer Mark 'Wedge' Wedgebury, who had all been in the final Classified Protest line-up, plus new guitarist Michael 'Mudgey' Mudge from Political Reform.

"We never attempted to write about vegetarianism, because we weren't all veggies," elaborates Pig. "But most of us were into the anti-hunting movement. The only song we used to get the animal rights/veggie issue over with was an instrumental called 'Decide' and even then we used *visuals* to get the point across. But our political ideas did vary and after the first six months, Ghandi decided to leave before we recorded the first EP after a few problems in the studio with the demo sessions… he went on to join the communist party and did many seminars along with the likes of [award-winning actress and political activist] Vanessa Redgrave!"

After cutting their teeth locally with the Welsh bands of the time, such as Shrapnel and Disarm (from Aberfan, with whom Pig also did a brief stint as vocalist), Rectify began gigging further afield, with the likes of Ad Nauseum and Conflict, before recording the '20th Century EP' at SAM Studios, Bristol, which they released on their own Taffcore Records. A strong four-track debut, despite the limited recording budget, the whole release was a comment on the stranglehold modern man has on the planet Earth.

"We released the first EP with money borrowed from my then-girlfriend Linda," reveals Pig. "We knew some of the Bristol bands that had recorded at SAM, so we thought we'd give it a go. In hindsight, if we'd had more money and a bit more experience, it could have been a stronger release, but we didn't and it is what it is, but that was punk for you – just do it! It seems people these days need things to be trendy, spot-on and more commercial than back when we did it all on a shoe string! The EP cover [drawn by Mudgey] depicts a fox in the countryside, with the urban concrete of the city engulfing the landscape with pollution and ever-increasing fast-food outlets: a man-made hell and basically 20th century Britain…"

After contributing their 'Piece By Piece' side to a split LP with Bazzy And The Budgies, on Blown To Bits Records (Bazzy did a long-running fanzine of the same name), that featured a guest appearance by John Donaldson on saxophone, adding yet another dimension to their rapidly evolving sound ("He was a Teepee Valley hippy guy, big into reggae and the Ruts…") and earning them a welcome rave review in *Metal Hammer* magazine, Rectify continued to gig wherever and whenever they could, taking their patented Taffcore to all corners of the UK.

Rectify, Pig and Wedge on tour

Rectify, early rehearsal

"Taffcore was an in-band joke," laughs Pig, "which did highlight the way some people perhaps viewed Welsh punk. We definitely found it difficult to get gigs outside of Wales; sadly punk was not totally free of trends and cliques, so if you didn't fit in, or at least know someone that did, the gigs never came your way. Having said that, we also got on a few gigs that then didn't happen due to circumstances beyond anyone's control, like when Marv from Cardiff was putting Nausea on in '90 or '91, but it never happened due to them cancelling the UK for visa reasons or something. The gig did go ahead with the new Antisect project, Kulturo.

"Previous to that, during the late Eighties, we once went all the way to London to play with Antisect at a squat in Brixton with only a phone contact for the gig,. When we got there it was shut down so it never happened and we ended up staying in the van and getting pissed. We had a veggie pie for food and I was cutting it into slices for everyone; Mudgey was in a right wind-up mood, so I blew my top. He jumped out of the van, I had the knife in my hand and just as the doors flew open there were two coppers standing there, so we nearly got arrested without even attending the squat gig!

"But we *did* do shows with Spermbirds, Blaggers ITA, Doom, Oi Polloi, Substandard, Agnostic Front, Econochrist, Pitchshifter and MDC, to name but a few, so it wasn't all bad and thanks should go to the Kronstadt Club, DS4A in Bristol, Marv and Pardy in Cardiff, the Inflammable Material and Nottingham Crew and the one and only Cheap Sweaty Fun from Newport, who always had time for us…"

One tour they were lucky to land, that most punk bands of the time would have given their left testicle to have been offered, was the six-week stint they did around Europe supporting Chaos UK during October and November 1991, arranged by former Lunatic Fringe frontman Bear. Needless to say, with touring partners like Chaos UK, it was a month-and-a-half of mischief and mayhem.

"Footy had left by then, so we had Chris Hughes on bass and I didn't think I would be able to do it after a knee cartilage operation I'd had following an injury from stage diving, but everything was okay after the op and the tour went ahead. We started off with a gig in Bristol and then took in Belgium, Holland, Germany, the Czech Republic, Poland, Austria and Switzerland. It was definitely eventful and there's only room to recall just a few incidents here, but I remember we were in a bar in the Czech Republic when some local right-wing guys thought that, because we were from the UK, for some reason we would sympathise with them; this ended up in a massive brawl, a full-on street fight and after being pepper-sprayed by bouncers, the police turned up, but luckily none of us were arrested.

"Another time in Poland, one punk guy took us back to where we were staying at his shared house; we arrived in the early hours, only to be asked to leave by his flatmate who was a semi-professional tennis player. We had nowhere to go and it was freezing outside, so [Chaos UK guitarist] Gabba decided to give him something to remember us by; he opened one of his drawers and pissed all over his tennis kit. Also in Poland, we turned up at a gig in Lodz a few hours late; as we drove into town, near the gig, there was a local police van overturned and when we got to the venue there was a gang of punks with facial injuries… Turns out we had missed the uninvited Nazi skinheads who had smashed the venue up. The organisers were obviously not happy as they lost a considerable amount of money…"

1992 saw Rectify recording the raging 10-track 'Ebullition' cassette-only release at Tudor Crescent Studios with Tony Williams, which they sold – complete with booklet, badge and sticker – for just £3.50 post paid. "We thought it was quite a tidy bargain for a tape pack, but of course some punks moaned about it costing the price of a pint and half of cider… what a crime on our part! It was costing us £15 a week to practice at the time, so work it out for yourselves…"

By 1994 and their next European tour with Korrupt from Bremen, the line-up had changed again, with Pig and Wedge now being accompanied by guitarist Greg Coomer and bassist Robert 'Newt' Newport. Mudgey had left the band on rather bad terms following a disagreement over the final mix of the track 'Order Of The Age' that Rectify contributed to the Squat Or Rot compilation EP 'Fukt Az Punx' the previous year.

In 1995, Mark 'Web' Webley and Kevin Bayliss, who had previously played together in the Swansea-based thrash bands Betrayer and State Of Confusion, joined the band on guitar and bass respectively. Rectify then recorded the six-track 'Virtual Reality' demo in Kidwelly studio Sonic One, with Tim Hamill of thrash-metal band Tortoise Corpse, during January '96. Two tracks, 'Scream' and 'No Future Now', ended up on a split single with Kuru, released by Inflammable Material Records, which the two bands promoted with a tour of the Spanish Basque region later that year and then two songs, 'Their Demise' and 'Virtual Reality', were also used on a split single with Scottish veterans External Menace on Suspect Device.

"That was a three week tour, organised by the REKNAW [read it backwards] crew from London," elaborates Pig. "It was with Flatpig, as well as Kuru, all round the Basque country in northern Spain; that was a real eye-opener playing gigs in the political heartland of ETA [the main organisation of the Basque National Liberation Movement], but what a brilliant time…"

"Then we carried on gigging around the UK throughout 1997," continues Web, of the band's gruelling schedule. "In 1998 we did another six-week tour of Europe in a Transit van; the first three weeks around Holland, Germany, Belgium, the Czech Republic and Slovakia and then the rest of the tour was down around northern Spain again, where we played with local bands and a metal/hardcore band from London called Hatred."

"Just to get something out there", seven songs were recorded at Sonic One during August 1999 and self-released as the 'Manmade' CDR and a stonking cover of 'Society' by the Subhumans was contributed to the 'Still Can't Hear The Words' compilation on Blackfish Records. Later that same year, four more tracks were recorded, two of them older songs from 'Ebullition' that were still deemed relevant enough to stay in the set and these latest recordings were added to the sessions from 'Manmade' and 'Virtual Reality' to make the 17-track 'Fall On Evil Days' CD, which was released by Polish label Pop Noise in 2000.

One listen to this definitive Rectify CD is all it will take to confirm their place right at the top of the metallic punk food chain, every song being a driving powerhouse of indignant, heavy-but-tuneful hardcore thrash. The band hit the road hard (the only way they knew how!) to promote it, slogging around Europe for another three weeks and trekking up and down the UK, but 2000 was to prove a particularly bad year for Rectify and they split during early 2001.

"Mudgey was still bothering with the guys in Ebbw Vale, where the rave scene and flat-out parties went hand in hand," begins Pig sadly, of one of the reasons that 2000 was a nadir for the band on a personal level. "Free Base was our local DIY dance crew; Mudgey started doing backdrops and flyers for them and started to get further and further away from the punk scene. His old school friends from Tredegar were also involved; they were all into the weed, as well as Es and whizz [speed]. Around '97 and '98, the Valleys also seemed to get flooded with heroin and ketamine etc. Lots of people dabbled with it, including Mudgey who previously didn't even smoke fags – but was now doing *everything*! After rehab and struggling with emotional problems, Mudgey stopped using as far as we know, but it had left him in a dark place and other people were dying from overdoses – the list was endless across the Valleys – and this truly affected him.

"He visited me at the end of July 2000 to get the lowdown on what was going on with the band; he even asked if he could rejoin when he got sorted. He came over the next day with all the tour posters from 1991 and a box full of Crass covers etc; he seemed to want me to have them, but I told him that I had them all, so off he went. He later called to reassure me he was okay and that he would return the £5 he'd borrowed for petrol…but we never saw him again. I got a call from his sister [on 7 August 2000] to tell me he had hung himself in his parents' house in Tredegar. He was 31 years old.

"Rectify had done a lot with Mudgey, so of course we were all very sad and depressed, but the bigger circle of friends in the punk community were also totally shocked. He had been a nutty character, full of fun and great company; he always made us laugh with his wild antics and we got up to way too much mischief to be covered in this book! He was a great friend of mine and is sorely missed and I'm sure that sentiment is shared by many others too."

As well as the tragic news about Mudgey, Web and Wedge were struggling to see eye to eye musically, making songwriting less and less enjoyable, so Rectify reluctantly played their last ever gig supporting Citizen Fish at TJ's in early 2001. As already detailed earlier in this chapter, Wedge went on to drum for Four Letter Word and Pig went on to form I Oppose Thee with members of 100,000 Body Bags, In The Shit and Mind Pollution. I Oppose Thee became This System Kills, who are still going to this day, although their current line-up comprises Craigy 'Two Tins' from Five Finger Discount, Newt from Disarm and Steve Riddle from Politrix.

Meanwhile Web and Kev returned to their metal roots as Sick Cell, with Web going on to form Lifer, who released their brutal debut album, 'Cursing Them Out', on House Of Doom Recordings in early 2011.

"Well, we always meant what we said," offers Pig, when asked how Rectify may have stood out from their peers in the Welsh punk scene. "We always tried to be more than 'just' a UK punk band, but that was also due to our many varied influences. People seem to remember the time we headlined above the Misfits in TJ's and ended up with them and Sub Zero onstage with us for an encore of 'Hard Times' by the Cro-Mags. A lot of people used to say we were too metal for the punks and too punk for the metallers, but, over the 15 years Rectify was going, it was a true journey of adventure and friendship…and tidy as fuck, butt!"

SELECT DISCOGRAPHY:

7-inch:
'20th Century E.P. (Taffcore, 1988)
'Split' (Inflammable Material, 1997) – *split with Kuru*
'Virtual Reality' (Suspect Device, 1997) – *split with External Menace*

LP:
'Piece By Piece' (Blown To Bits, 1990) – *split with Bazzy And The Budgies*

CDR:
'Manmade' (Self-released, 1999)

CD:
'Fall On Evil Days' (Pop Noise, 2000)

AT A GLANCE:
'Fall On Evil Days' is an essential purchase whether you're into punk, hardcore or intense articulate metal.

TAINT

From tiny acorns rock giants sometimes grow. And from their humble beginnings as a post-hardcore band in rowdy Swansea, **Taint** patiently transformed themselves into one of the UK's most overlooked alternative rock bands, crafting subtly epic modern classics that really should have seen them taking on the world instead of frustratingly imploding in late 2010.

"[Drummer] Alex [Harries] and I started jamming for fun when we were around 12 or 13 and picked it back up again at 16," recalls guitarist/vocalist James 'Jimbob' Isaac. "Taint was our first band. There were a couple of friends that tried out as vocalists and bassists, but they didn't last long which left me to handle the vocals as well as guitar…

"I was never really supposed to be a singer," he laughs. "But Taint *never* had a plan; we were just some regular kids that wanted to play and write music. The core bands that inspired us to form were Fudge Tunnel, Helmet, Quicksand, Eyehategod, Tool and Clutch. I grew up on classic rock and metal, but wasn't really able to play, or interested in playing such technical music at the time. It was those bands that made me think I was capable of actually writing and playing half-decent music. Alex was more into hip-hop and our first bassist Darren [Mason] was into anything from Joy Division to Slayer. Our tastes crossed over enough to record three demos over three years before Darren left. In the early days my lyrics were pretty abstract and were written in a more tonal capacity, rather than tackling particular themes…"

But first the band made their live debut with Cardiff death-metallers Parricide on 21 December 1994 at the Coach House pub, a 'salubrious' Swansea venue where many a UKHC band had their mettle tested by the chaotic (lack of) sound system and the incessant brawling in the street during load-out.

"There was an instinctive DIY approach to playing back then," recalls Jimbob fondly, of his wild local scene. "Swansea is pretty much at the end of the line in terms of accessibility for touring bands, so most bands in town had a really hands-on outlook to putting on gigs and mucking in together. Acrimony were kings to us and they brought down bands like Iron Monkey (who played their third gig there), Mourn, Consumed and Inextremis. They really cemented my obsession with underground music and doing things for yourself.

"The Coach House was a shitty biker's place that sold cheap booze and housed hash dealers. We mostly played with Acrimony, the Groundnuts And Independents, Parc Troli, the Milk And Cheese Experience and the Bundy Men. As well as Public Disturbance, Diabolo and Fleshbind from Cardiff. Acrimony and us were the only bands in Swansea that weren't explicitly punk in sound, but we all had the same attitude and the gigs used to get insane, with people hanging off the ceiling pipes, smashing glass and getting really drunk and rowdy… Swansea is a pretty drunk and rowdy town, full stop. I guess Taint offered a take on Sabbath-inspired music, in a different way to Acrimony and I think we had our own, albeit embryonic, sound from day one."

"I remember the inclusivity of the scene at the time," adds Alex. "Older bands like the Doctors always welcomed the new breed of young punks. I recall our first live review in local paper, *The Evening Post*, calling us 'a hardcore trio with undertones of 'Bleach'-era Nirvana and the pop of Hüsker Dü. That particular bill was completed by skate-punkers the Groundnuts, followed by folksy proggers the Purples, illustrating the diversity and the need to work together to get gigs organised and well attended."

Jamming at Alex's mum's house ("We'd often get kids loitering outside to listen to our loud, scruffy racket," laughs Jimbob, while Alex recalls "The hippy dad down the road would tip me off if anyone was threatening to call the police and *still* asks how the band's going when I see him…"), Taint patiently refined and defined their sound over the course of several home-recorded demos. With some bands, early demos are an incidental part of their development, but with Taint this was a crucial part of them making peace with their creative muse and they were careful not to rush it.

"[1995's five-track] 'Bellydown' was recorded with a local metal dude that had a home studio set up in his back lounge," says Jimbob. "It was pretty good quality for the time and affordable, even to us back then. It does sound like a young band when you listen back to it and my vocals are pretty cringeworthy in retrospect. The guitars were put through some kind of digital box, as the guy couldn't mic them up loud in his house. Something that I've never done since, but it was a reasonable solution at the time.

"I recorded 'Rough Recordings' [1996] and '10X Better' [1997] myself, on a friend's cassette four-track at Alex's mum's house. They're rough as shit, but a lot more real sounding than 'Bellydown'. I was also getting further into sludge, doom and hardcore, so was happy to go with a dirtier recording. I have some of the master tapes of these demos so am likely to put them online for people to check out sometime soon.

"We did take a long time getting to CD," he admits. "But, as I said earlier, Taint never had a plan. And I guess it never felt like an option to take music more seriously back then; in fact the whole idea felt so distant, which was possibly to do with our own self-perception, all the way down the road in Swansea. Dylan Thomas infamously described the city as 'the graveyard of ambition', which is why there have been plenty of bands who've never even made it out of the city limits.

"I love Swansea for lots of reasons, but there's something about it that cultivates a kind

Taint, Stophe live

Taint, promo shot 1994

of twisted loyalty to its own insular outlook. Also, the only bands that attempted to make a 'career' out of music there when we started were local cock-rock douchebags that had expensive gear and snobby attitudes. Funny, though, as I haven't heard about any of those old characters breaking out and touring. We were the antithesis to that, so were happy taking our time and had no real agenda other than having fun and expressing ourselves. And even though we spent a few years in the demo stages, I actually got those demo cassettes out to bands and zines all around the world. We did a few fanzine interviews that garnered interest from bands and tape-traders as far afield as Eastern Europe, America, Japan… even Colombia.

"This was pre-internet, of course, but, demos or not, I was hungry from day one to connect with people around the world and spread our music. That hunger has never left me and it's something that the local pub-rock 'heroes' of the time had no initiative about doing. It's funny how those types will accuse you of 'making it' when you do a 50/50 split deal with a DIY label and of 'sucking cock' to get gigs when really you're networking and doing gig swaps. Those types are simply too lazy to get off their arse and make things happen for themselves. Every single thing that Taint ever achieved was from me scraping away, communicating and backing up my belief in our music with hard work…"

Meanwhile the band scored their first gigs out of Wales in 1996, travelling to Bournemouth at the behest of Snub and to Nottingham with Acrimony to support Hard To Swallow ("HTS blew my mind and instantly became my favourite UKHC band, hands down," reveals Jimbob). Once they were a presence on the underground circuit it was then only a matter of time before a label would pick up on them for an official release, although oddly enough it was a full-blown hardcore punk label that decided to back them first. The seemingly unlikely union with Household Name, that gave the world the 'Die Die Truthspeaker' MCD [in 2000, after contributing the track 'Said And Done' to the 1998 'Fuck Off Household Name' compilation and 'Fatman Sedates Us Again' to the 1999 'Rumour, Ridicule And The Profit Motive' comp], only made perfect sense a few years later, when both parties proved themselves truly kindred spirits by bravely diversifying from their original core audiences.

"It was Sean McKee from Public Disturbance who recommended us to [Household Name head honcho] Lil," reckons Jimbob. "So I finally scraped our first London show in the hope that he'd come and check us out. Seamus added us to a bill at the Redeye, with Sally and Godzilla among others; we played well and Lil came straight up to us after the set and said, 'Welcome to the Household Name family!' We were really happy, as it was our first proper release and, at the time, Lil was already working with a more varied range of bands. We felt a kinship with Canvas, for example, as they weren't really pigeonholable and had a similarly diverse range of influences to us."

'Die Die Truthspeaker' was an awesome debut though and well worth the wait, the band demonstrating their fairly unique vision of uncompromising metallic noise, though they did wear their influences on their sleeves by closing out the disc with a hidden Clutch cover, buried in the outro feedback of climactic closer 'Release'.

"We were on our second bassist [Stophe Thomas] by then and he brought more cohesion to our sound. Our writing and playing had also got a lot better and I guess we were making steps towards sounding like a 'proper' band. We went up to Thumb Studios in Nottingham as we liked what Hard To Swallow had done there for their split with Canvas. It was affordable and we had also made friends with Chris Neary and Paul Inger who ran it, thanks to our

Nottingham connections. We recorded and mixed it in three days and were really happy with the results.

"Lyrically I felt like I really tapped into my own style of writing, with some pretty bleak imagery and wordplay. I remember the review in *Terrorizer* describing it as something like 'sludge-emo-core'. Not a bad description I guess, considering it pre-dated a lot of bands that came out with similar sounds later on. I think that we found our own sound even more with that release and it pointed strongly towards the direction we took for 'The Ruin Of Nova Roma' in 2004…

"We didn't really tour until just before '…Roma' came out either. We were all in university at the time of 'Die Die…' so we just gigged as much as possible, playing hardcore bills, all-dayers and support slots around the country. We learned a lot in those days and played with bands like Knuckledust and John Holmes, as well as our first slots with international bands like Converge, Karma To Burn and Unsane. They were all great experiences, whether it was playing to a packed room in London with KTB and having members of Eyehategod stageside while we were secretly shitting our pants (they played the next day), or playing in the depths of West Wales before being forced to sleep (or not!) overnight in a broken rental van, in sub-zero temperatures and with increasingly painful hangovers…!"

By the time 'The Ruin Of Nova Roma' came out on Lee Dorrian's Rise Above label, Chris West from Diabolo had joined on bass and Taint had finally arrived at *their* sound, a subtle yet incredibly dynamic sonic onslaught – fusing grinding discordant hardcore, doom metal and stoner rock – captured to perfection by Alex Newport from Jimbob's beloved Fudge Tunnel. Taint worked with both Alex and Rise Above again for 2007's 'Secrets And Lies' – another runaway train of complex layered arrangements and huge heaving grooves, reminiscent in places of the mighty Neurosis – before finally splitting in late 2010, just after the release of the sublime 'All Bees To The Sea' through Destructure.

"We actually made the decision to split in the autumn of 2010," Jimbob reveals. "It was a tough call, but it was really a case of me being dissatisfied with our part-time approach to playing. While I respect anyone that chooses to work a regular job, it got to the point where I wanted to play live more and more and no longer wanted to be restricted by other people's life choices. I love playing live and after creating art and music for so long, I'm more confident than ever that it is exactly what I'm supposed to do with my life. Taint was a really special band to me and the three of us are on great terms now.

"If we had stayed together any longer it would have been detrimental to our friendships. The stress that we put on ourselves by touring within the job constraints got too much; for example, there's only so many times that the guys can go straight back into work on a Monday morning after a 10-hour all-night drive from Holland. They're also starting families this year which would mean even less playing and touring…at which point I had to make the decision to disband, as I have no interest in being a studio musician.

"The live arena is where rock music lives and breathes and I feel like I have no choice but pursue that. To me art and music is a political statement in itself and if my life consisted of working a corporate job or a shitty nine-to-five, with a weekend of boozing as my only reward, I'd go fucking crazy. This is why I'm more driven than ever to keep playing and creating with little or no restraints…"

Although Chris and Alex are still full-time teachers and Jimbob a pretty awesome freelance illustrator and poster artist (visit jimbobisaac.com), the three guys still make music, with Chris

Taint, live Swansea 1995

currently drumming for Newport's Spider Kitten and the other two guys working on material with new projects as you read this. But whatever they create musically going forwards, it will have to be pretty special to eclipse the towering integrity of the Taint output.

"I'd like to think that we came across as a band that wrote honest and unique music," says Jimbob proudly. "With no attention paid to trends or scene politics. I don't believe that many bands have mixed influences in the way that Taint did and hope that our individuality will resonate long after our modest legacy…"

SELECT DISCOGRAPHY:

7-inch:

'Champion Boar Service' (SuperFi, 2005) – *split with Army Of Flying Robots*

CDEP:

'Split' (Black Phoenix, 2004) – *split with Black Eye Riot*

MCDs:

'Die Die Truthspeaker' (Household Name, 2000)
'All Bees To The Sea' (Destructure, 2010)

LPs:

'The Ruin Of Nova Roma' (Rise Above, 2004)
'Secrets And Lies' (Rise Above, 2007)

AT A GLANCE:

Taint really were one of the most intriguing UK rock bands of the last two decades. Start with 'All Bees To The Sea' and work back to their formative Nineties demos – when Jimbob finally posts them online…

VAFFAN COULO

Following in the footsteps of the quietly influential Anhrefn, Bangor's **Vaffan Coulo** mined a similar vein of defiantly noisy, darkly eclectic alternative rock. Although they weren't the most prolific band out there release-wise, they played virtually every week for several years and helped build a thriving scene in north Wales.

"I wouldn't admit it at the time," begins bassist Joe Shooman, "but I think the biggest influences on my playing style were [Iron Maiden's] Steve Harris and probably [the Stranglers'] JJ Burnel. At the time the Stranglers were kinda acceptable, but Maiden was a definite no-no. I was going through a 'I hate metal' phase and would only listen to the Pistols, Buzzcocks, Kennedys and other Cherry Red/Alternative Tentacles bands. Lyrically it was pure Jello Biafra, certainly at the start; [vocalist] Paul [Williams] even renamed himself 'Trifle Ethiopia' in a move where I can't work out whether he was having a laugh or actually being half-serious, but I think we kind of idolised Jello collectively. I also loved Motörhead, the Velvets and bizarrely, Donovan; there were moments when it *had* to be the hippy stuff.

"North Wales is a place that needs proper exploration and I was up for doing that… There were a lot of ways to mellow out, too; I smoked a fair bit in them days and it'd get quite psychedelic at other times. I know [drummer] Mikey [McMahon] was a major Metallica fan and Paul/Trifle would flit between REM, Pixies and the Reverend Al Green…"

Joining Joe, Paul and Mikey was guitarist Nick 'Bicko' Redfern, who had previously been in the Vinyl Erasers with Joe's older brother, Daniel; the band passed on the name 'Motoguzzi' and, quite bizarrely for a Welsh language band, opted for Vaffan Coulo, which is Italian for 'Fuck you!'

"Punk rock in Bangor was actually in a bit of a lull," reckons Joe, "but there was a definite alternative ambience that had been laid down not so many years previously by the mighty Anhrefn, Fflaps, Lungs, Cut Tunes, Paraletics and lots of other excellent, independent-minded, difficult buggers. So there was always a sense that if you wanted to do something, you could get it off the ground and do it yourselves – 'cos nobody else was going to hand it to you on a plate. When we started gigging, it was easy to get advice from these very supportive people who I think were pleased to see new young idiots getting involved in the whole music nonsense; we'd always see members of most of those bands at gigs and indeed played with loads of them.

"A very important band in Vaffan Coulo's story is Skinflick, which was mostly our mate Joskin and various satellite members. He was and still is, a massive fan of people like Foetus and later Ministry and people like that, so that brought a set of great new sounds to gigs. Industrial music, as it was known then I s'pose, was quite exciting as sampling technology was really just starting to become affordable. It was pretty cutting-edge and very noisy, and Joskin (and his usual cohort Jim) always had the maddest hair and best posters. We gigged loads together and experienced loads of silly adventures together, both on and off the pitch; it was a bit fucked-up at times…a lot fucked-up at others."

The band's first gig was an eventful one – of course – at the Ffridd student bar in Bangor. "We played last on a bill that was supposed to be three bands, but ended up with only two acts as the first were barred for being under age," recalls Bicko. "That started the evening on a bad note with the previously friendly bar manager and after Skinflick had played we ploughed through our set fairly successfully before we got to a song I'd written after getting annoyed in uni, called 'Shit Student Wankers'! That set off the end of our set and a stand-off with the bar staff, ending with animosity and aggression all round... I still haven't been back there."

"I had a ball though," laughs Joe. "I remember the build-up to it was a mixture of excitement and...beer. I don't *think* I was that nervous but I probably was shitting it. Bizarrely, too, my dad and uncle were there as I remember. I've got it all on tape; when we got kicked off stage you can clearly hear Matt the bar manager was really arsed off with the way it'd gone down as was his little four foot two karate mate who I can somehow still remember was called Warner. And there were the band that got kicked out, Nauzea, standing outside, their little faces pressed up against the window, cheering.

"The other thing I recall about it is Joskin being really hammered and somehow his Atari ST wasn't synching up properly either, so his set was a bit stuttery. It was the first time he played the genius track 'Barfly' live, too. Afterwards we just got our gear out, parked round the corner and cheered. I don't even think we had any beers, but I definitely knew we ought to do more of this kind of thing; it felt really naughty and cool...!"

A demo was rush-recorded with Graeme Rowlands at the Music Barn in 1992, which sold 500 copies and led to a session with Radio Cymru, which itself led to a deal with local jazz/folk label Madryn, who released the four-song 'Vaffan Coulo Yn Goch' 7-inch EP in 1994. An endearingly quirky release, it quickly sold out of its 1,000 print run and certainly showcased the band's eclecticism, with 'Cowbois Cymru' being equal parts Damned and Helmet, 'FMU' owing more to the grinding rhythms of Killing Joke and 'International Hitman' proffering a more laid-back, dub-heavy Fall vibe.

"I believe the first contact with Madryn came through *Sothach!*, a Welsh-language music magazine that I wrote for between '92 and '97 when it finally folded," explains Joe. "It was actually a really good mag that had also kind of grown out of the Anhrefn/Ffa Coffi Pawb atmosphere down in Bethesda. So I think I sent our first Radio Cymru session which we did in 1992 out to a couple of people and they got in touch. Two of the songs on the first EP were recorded in the middle of Anglesey with the incredibly talented Gorwel Owen, who had a great studio where most of the Welsh music scene recorded at one time or another, including Super Furry Animals a bit later down the line. There was another song, 'The High Street Side Eat All The Pies', which was a Bangor City [football club] song recorded with Graeme and we did 'International Hitman' virtually live with a guy called Mark Ferrari, down in a studio in Dyserth, then legged it immediately to the Radio Cymru studio where Ian Gill played it on his show about an hour later..."

The diverse sounds continued with the second 7-inch, 1995's 'Di Gymraeg Yng Nghymru', 'OJ Simpson' rolling along with a lo-fi psychobilly energy and the powerful title track being built around a disorienting twisty-turny riff. It soon became obvious that Vaffan Coulo weren't interested in just being superficial ear candy; their material was infinitely more challenging and didn't hand over its secrets without a fight. They seemed perched on the brink of real popularity, but unfortunately an album – that was to have been called 'Cowboys Cymru' – planned on Presteigne label Dragnet never materialised (likewise several other releases slated by the label for bands such as Decadence Within).

"It was fucking weird, that was," sighs Joe. "There was this bloke called Benny who ran Dragnet Records in mid-Wales somewhere; I think I started writing to him after trading some

Vaffan Coulo L to R Mikey,
Trifle, Kerz, Nick, 1991

Vaffan Coulo, live Benllech,
1991

tapes of ours with my mate Pete who ran a label/distro called Smokin' Troll in Bontnewydd, near Caernarfon. In them days the punk network communicated through tapes, zines, tape trades and even wrote letters to each other, a real proto-internet…so me and Benny batted back and forth for a bit. I think he'd sent me a Cowboy Killers tape, those magnificent Newport motherfuckers, so he was fuckin' alright with me. He wanted to put out what amounted to an album really; we talked about it being on vinyl and everything. We weren't that arsed about cash and things – just happy to get something out 'cos by then we had more than enough stuff to choose from…

"Then it turned into a tape project, so we knocked up the artwork (Joskin again) and got a master together, probably a DAT tape, sent it all off – and that was the last I heard of it. I have never seen a finalised version and nobody to my knowledge owns one. The only evidence of the whole thing is one mocked-up tape insert at an early draft stage that I have in storage somewhere. Shame, really; it would have been a good time to get out the first three EPs, the session stuff, a couple of unreleased bits and bobs and at least one really perverted remix. It would have been a cracking little album for us, shame it didn't work out."

The band's Spanish tour of 1996 was another mis-fire that they took bravely in their stride. Anyone who's toured with an underground punk band on the *real* DIY circuit will know, if you don't laugh about it, you'd cry! But this trip was doomed from the start…

"I'd been talking via letters to this guy, Miguel, for months, who was a very active punk guy based up in Cantabria that had big contacts in most of the major Spanish punk centres in Galicia, the Basque region and Madrid. We talked about a two-week tour and he said he'd set it up for us; it seems slightly ridiculous now, but the whole thing was done and dusted via post and we booked a ferry from Plymouth to Santander with a set of 12 gigs lined up across the top of Spain…

"We were due to head off on the Sunday and drive all day to get the Monday ferry. On the Saturday at literally 11.30 am I got a phonecall off my folks saying there was a letter in the post office I needed to pick up, so I got out of bed and legged it down there to find a very strange missive from Miguel saying that he wasn't going to come around with us as interpreter and that the tour had been curtailed to six or so gigs, giving us one phone number in Santander and basically saying he wasn't interested any more. These days we'd be able to e-mail – he wasn't a big phone type – and get it sorted out, but we had no choice but to head on down there. I think the whole thing was fucked from that point on. Needless to say, I didn't tell the other lads about this small-ish problem…so we drove through the night intending to stop off at my other brother's gaff in London (no chance, we ran out of time), got on the ferry and three of us drank ourselves into a stupor.

"So, 24 hours later we docked in Santander, got off the ferry, all excited…then realised we didn't know any Spanish, any Spanish people, or have anywhere to stay. Fuck, the feeling at that point…devastation. But eventually we tracked down the local contact who had been up all night at a festival and came to collect us from where we'd parked after driving around for about an hour in ever-more hysterical circles. He in fact took us to his mother's flat where his buddy Manuel turned up. Manuel was great: his English was really good and he hated the sun despite living in a city with 11 beaches…

"We went to Playa Sardinero and he hid under a tree while we sat, glowing with white-boy fat, knackered and bemused, on the sand. It was excellent. That night we found our accommodation…a *really* horrendous squat with rats and fucking all sorts of shit going on like mouldy ex-food in all the saucepans. It really was a cliché; the guy who lived there was young and didn't give much of a fuck. We spent the evening trying to sleep and me and him bonded over teaching each other the numbers one to 10 in Welsh and Spanish respectively!"

After a disastrous gig in Zaragoza, the band actually drove back to the ferry port and tossed a coin to see whether they should carry on in the face of adversity or cut their losses and run.

"It came up tails thankfully, which meant we stayed," laughs Joe, "because from then on in the gigs were mostly brilliant – one night we even got a hotel! – and we actually had one hell of a laugh for the whole of the next week, driving back and forth across the top of Spain and meeting some very cool people indeed. It wasn't heaven exactly, but at least it was *rock* purgatory! And it was a turning point for the band…it was all downhill from there anyway."

Upon their return from Europe, Vaffan Coulo cut another session for Radio Cymru before recording for 'Fast Multiplying In The Skin', a split 12-inch with German band Ultra Orange for French label Extune. Featuring a groovy remix of 'Maxwell', a new version of 'International Hitman' and two new songs, 'Bored' and 'Hwyl y Helynt', it caught the band at their creative peak, rocking out like a noisier Boomtown Rats or something, but unfortunately the spring was rapidly leaving their step and by the time of the 'Vaffan Coulo' LP, released by Slovenian label Crime Records in 1996, they had all but morphed into a new – shortlived – band altogether called Slater.

"It was a slow fizzle rather than a harsh bust-up," sighs Joe. "To be honest, by the time the 'Ultra Orange' 12-inch came out we were more or less ready to split; it was about five years since we started and I think we peaked just after the Spanish tour. The odd thing really was that the songs got more complicated but the playing was basically at a plateau, so things started stuttering. We should have called a halt there and then, but after a breather, me, Trifle and Mikey blahblahblah-ed for a while [Bicko leaving to concentrate on fatherhood]; Slater was a new band with Tom Kinkaid, a great keyboard player and a completely different sound and approach.

"But because there were three of us who had been in Vaffan Coulo, it was doomed from the start; there were some decent songs, a lot slower and more personal-political, I s'pose, a bit more of the storytelling-type stuff, but it really was flawed from the outset. It wasn't ever going to last long and the gigs and even rehearsals got less and less numerous until it was literally months – then years – since anything happened. I wish we'd done some proper recordings; there's some cool sketches on rehearsal tapes that might have ended up being a decent EP or album, but the impetus wasn't there.

"I don't regret the decision to call it a day; in fact I really think we should have looked at it earlier. I have plenty of subsequent regrets, though; we went through some really intense times together and I'm sorry to say I have lost touch with some people in a way I really never thought I ever would. I don't want to re-form the band or anything, but to feel that Vaffan Coulo feeling once more would be just unbelievable. To say I miss it is an understatement…"

Slater played their last gig in 1997, in Bangor with Cut Tunes and Skinflick, but it was an "entirely unremarkable" performance, that saw the band finally laid to rest. Joe moved to Liverpool in 2000 to do a degree in sound technology and has since established himself as a respected music journalist. He currently resides in the Caribbean, where his last live performance was as the bassist of the Cayman National Orchestra! Mikey is still playing as well, throughout North Wales and the UK with Seagull Kenevil (formerly Valleum), but Bicko and Trifle have nowadays retired from the money pit that is playing in a band for your own enjoyment.

"That's the whole shame about it," says Joe, in closing, "'cos when I unpick it, what I most regret about Vaffan Coulo was that there was so much misdirected energy. If we'd managed to take a half-step back I think we could have been much better – as musicians, but also as a much more powerful force toward what we wanted to do. I would say that the first 10 gigs – which were all about the fast, loud, angry, political songs, in the back rooms of pubs with an ever-increasing cast of mates, new bands and, above all, a unity and belief in the future that really wasn't misplaced – were the best. But time moves on and so do people, which is just how it shakes down.

"I don't think anything actually set us apart from our peers other than we just went for it 'cos we wanted to. We were fearless in those days; sadly that gets harder and harder as the years go by, but not impossible…hopefully. For me, personally, it was all about being active, creating things and not getting dragged down. I just wish I'd had a tiny bit more sense. Not much more, just enough to see that there were things I was railing against that really weren't enemies and that we maybe could have been a little bit more focused on making it sound a bit better sometimes…but on the other hand, fuck it.

"It was our band, we had a fucking good time and I certainly think the best times were so incredible that they really were worth all the boring and crap ones, of which there are many! 'Cos when you get older and further away, the bad bits even raise a chuckle and the good bits seem the most amazing thing ever. I sound like a right old bastard now, don't I? But fuck it: go for it and remember nobody has the right to dictate how you think, how you live and how you want to find your own art or whatever. Just don't be a cunt about it."

SELECT DISCOGRAPHY:

7-inch:
'Vaffan Coulo Yn Goch' (Madryn, 1994)
'Di Gymraeg Yng Nghymru' (Madryn, 1995)

12-inch:
'Fast Multiplying In The Skin' (Extune/Tontrager, 1996) – split with *Ultra Orange*

LP:
'Vaffan Coulo' (Crime, 1996)

AT A GLANCE:
Drop Joe an e-mail and ask him nicely to burn you a Vaffan Coulo 'Best Of'.
joeshooman@googlemail.com

WANTON THOUGHT

Being described as 'the best Instigators-sounding band in Wales' by some fanzine or other hardly qualifies as the greatest of accolades, but hardcore punk in the UK was never about what others thought of you; it was all about getting up and having a go, no matter where you lived and such humble ambition is what fueled Mold's **Wanton Thought**.

Formed during the summer of 1988, vocalist Craig Williams had previously drummed for anarcho-punk band, Blasphemy, who "never did anything other than crash their van on the way to play Hardcore Holocaust 2 in Birmingham!" Joining Craig on vocals was his long-time friend and "perpetual band partner" Mike Wright and 'behind' them there was guitarist Mike Foulkes, bassist Dave and drummer Chris.

"Musically we liked a variety of bands from Dead Kennedys, Snuff, Naked Raygun and Dag Nasty to Big Country, Housemartins and the Jam, but I think the band from that period that influenced us the most was HDQ. When the 'You Suck' album came out, with their take on the melodic American sound and just how frantic it all sounded, it seemed to grab our attention the most. "Lyrically Mike W and I were influenced by Dead Kennedys, Subhumans, Crass…basically bands that were more direct and actually had something to say. Mike had a bad habit of 'borrowing' lyrics from bands when we first started, though, so you felt like an MI5 code-breaker some days, trying to negotiate your way through all the blatant plagiarism thinking, 'Where have I heard that before?' I don't *think* anything got through our quality checks, though…

"Being from Mold in North Wales (not heard of it? You do surprise me!), there was no local hardcore scene in 1988. Bomb Disneyland lived just up the road in Buckley, where the Tivoli Ballroom did and still exists. There was a bit of a metal scene in the 'bustling metropolis' of Wrexham, but there were no zines or venues other than community halls and the back rooms of local pubs etc that would put hardcore gigs on. We mostly used to gate-crash other peoples' gigs… Welsh-speaking bands and indie bands, that kind of thing. In fact, we played a lot of gigs with Welsh-speaking bands, even though none of us could speak Welsh; we had a particular fondness for Anhrefn."

Although the band was soon to pare down to a four-piece – and then a three-piece – they recorded their first demo as a top-heavy five-piece. "I remember getting a phone call about 11 o'clock on a Saturday morning," remembers Craig, of the rushed live debut that preceded the demo, "asking if we wanted to play Planet X in Liverpool that evening. Now gigs at the Planet used to start at 5pm and finish about 10, with three or four bands playing and we were going on first, which would have been at about 5.30. Carcass were playing and I can't remember if Coroner played, or couldn't make it? So we decided to do the gig.

Some of us went there by train and some by car with the equipment, but Chris was working and said he would meet us at Lime Street station in Liverpool at 5 o'clock. Me and Mike went to wait for him, but he never turned up. 'Okay,' I thought, 'I can drum *and* sing and we can still play…' So that's what we did, but I underestimated just how hard it would be, with me not drumming for a year or so by then – it killed me! And we were shite personified (who I think also played that night!), but went down really well…strange how that happens sometimes!

"The first demo was very poor, though," he admits, "slipping in and out of hardcore and metal. The whole thing sounded like a band that didn't know what they wanted to sound like.

I listened to it a few months back; it embarrassed me… and I was in the room on my own – now that's quite a feat! We recorded all our stuff at Studio X in Holywell; it was a humble eight-track desk, but I always find if you go to the same studio more than once, you know what it can and can't do. The recordings after that were so much better, but we sent the first demo out to lost of labels and zines etc…with it generally getting a bad response from all of them!"

With Chris no longer in the band, Craig took over the drums permanently, Mike Wright became the band's only singer and Wanton Thought "tightened up overnight." Another – much better – demo was recorded in 1989, which was well received and definitely in heavy sonic debt to the aforementioned HDQ, although the next line-up change was also imminent…

"The second demo got us noticed," reckons Craig. "It was frantic, the guitars sounded better and so did Mike W's vocals; we got good feedback wherever we sent it. Meantime Records wanted 'Normal School Day' for the 'Spleurk 2' compilation and Looney Tunes wanted to do a 7-inch EP, so things really started moving after that demo. 'Normal School Day' *did* appear on the 'Spleurk 2' comp, but when Ian at Meantime asked for the mastered tape, we sent him the quarter-inch tape that was still in track form (we were very stupid!) and we were then surprised when the version on the comp had no lead guitar on it… After that, we realised you are supposed to master it onto DAT or something!

"But then Mike W rang me up one day and said he just didn't want to do the band any more, which was strange because we had been trying to do a band since we were kids in school; he was a little bit older than me and was always buying crappy guitars – which he couldn't play – so it was a bit of a shock because we were now finally in a band that *could* play and gig – and he wanted to leave! But there were no hard feelings; I remember we got together in the pub to talk about what to do and we decided that we'd all give it a go with the vocals… so now five had become three. Most of the positive feedback for the second demo had been for Mike's voice, too, so we were going to have to really go for it. We rehearsed with all three of us splitting the vocals; thankfully it worked, so that was it, we become a three-piece and we got even tighter again."

On the strength of the new demo, Looney Tunes offered to do a 7-inch with the band, but when that took a while to come to fruition, Boss Tuneage stepped into the breach and put out the four-track 'Mustard Mit' EP, a wonderfully raw yet tuneful slice of US-inspired UKHC. A proper tour was also booked to promote it, including some proposed European dates and Full Circle had offered the band an album deal, so things were looking up. How best to celebrate their success and really capitalise on the unexpected momentum they were generating? Why, split up, of course!

"The split did come out of the blue," sighs Craig. "There was a rehearsal on the Sunday before the tour was meant to start and it went really badly, no fire there at all. We'd been rehearsing less and less and I think energy in the band was waning and once you lose that spark, God knows, it's hard to get it back.

"So, anyway, this is how I remember it: we ran through the set a couple of times and it just wasn't happening; no matter how much we tried, it felt flat. I know you can have a bad rehearsal and it doesn't mean anything, but this just felt like our tanks were empty and after an awful Planet X gig a few weeks before (supporting Jailcell Recipes), we felt at an all-time low. We were outside the hall where we used to practise, all sitting on a five-bar gate and

Wanton Thought

Wanton Thought

it just felt like we couldn't do it justice any more. And we couldn't do it just for the sake of doing it, so we said, 'Let's call it a day…' We went back into the practice room, played the songs one more time for posterity and then that was it. I got home and rang Aston [from Boss Tuneage] to tell him we'd split; when I think of that now, it makes my toes curl, the amount of effort he'd put into organising the tour, but it must have been the right thing to do because continuing the band, or doing the tour, felt an even worse prospect…"

The three remaining Wanton Thought members all went their separate ways after the split. Craig drummed for All Too Human and then Rope and Mike Foulkes played in the Lolloping Donkeys.

"The timing of the split caused Aston a lot of hassle, so that was bad," admits Craig. "But, other than that, no regrets. We played with a lot of our favourite bands of that time, like Snuff, Spermbirds and HDQ and we had a bloody good laugh. I loved the feeling of being in a band with your mates and the band growing; you can't beat that. I even remember getting a buzz out of us gradually getting better equipment…going round to Dave's to see his new bass… going with Mike to get his new guitar. And shaving Mike's hair after a rehearsal and me and Dave were laughing so much we struggled to finish it. That's the stuff that's the fondest memories for me; we were kids in a band and it was fun, which is how it should be.

"Mmm…," he ponders, when asked how he would like Wanton Thought remembered. "Maybe as the best Welsh band to have their third release on Boss Tuneage? If that were a Venn diagram, we would be on our own and very lonely, though. There were so many bands at that time; it was 20 years ago and it feels like it all happened on another planet. But if there was a school report for us, it would say something like, 'Tried hard, but easily distracted…'"

SELECT DISCOGRAPHY:

EP:
'Mustard Mit' (Boss Tuneage, 1991)

AT A GLANCE:
2011's self-titled 10-track CD on Boss Tuneage collects all the band's recordings, bar the crappy first demo, and also demonstrates there were no hard feelings after the ill-timed split 20 years earlier.

Friday 1st March 1996

EX-CATHEDRA
SKA PUNK

SAD SOCIETY
77 to 80's STYLE PUNK

COMBAT SHOCK PUNK!

AT

The Old General

Radford Road

NOTTINGHAM

£3·00

£2·50 CONCESSIONS

CHAPTER NINE:
SCOTLAND

DISAFFECT

Glasgow's **Disaffect** not only rocked the punk world with their intelligent, thrashy hardcore during the early Nineties, but also the attitudes of various bigots within the scene with their outspoken statements against intolerance. They were formed in 1991 by vocalist Joe Deacons, from Systemised and Constant Fear, and bassist Andy Irvine, who recruited guitarist Brian Curran from the Psycho Flowers and drummer Ian Blue. After a few months, Lynne Entwistle from Vomithead joined as second vocalist and, towards the end of the band's existence, they were also joined by a second guitarist, Billy Steele from Sedition.

"Primary influences for me were pretty wide-ranging," admits Joe. "I got into punk in 1978 when I was 15 years old, which started out with the usual suspects of the time: Sex Pistols, Damned, Stranglers, Buzzcocks… Then a mate that I used to go to school with brought a copy of 'Feeding Of The 5,000' [by Crass, of course] for me to listen to; he didn't actually know what to make of them, but after listening to them and drinking four cans of Kestrel lager – ha ha! – I was hooked.

"He ended up leaving me the record, which was real nice 'cos it was the first pressing on Small Wonder Records. I think I just sat and read the lyrics and played that 12-inch over and over again and something just clicked with me. Then you had the whole anarcho scene, with Dirt and Conflict etc, that took off in the early Eighties and that was what influenced me both musically and lyrically… though looking back at some of the songs I wrote they were pretty simplistic!

"Anyway the scene in Glasgow in the late Seventies and early Eighties was, I imagine, the same as in every other town and city. We all tended to hang around outside the then-new Virgin megastore in Union Street in the city centre, before getting a carry-out and heading down to the Clydeside and getting pished on a half dozen cans and a bottle of El D [El Dorado, a fortified tonic wine]… I was gonna say 'cheap wine', but it wasn't! It was the big thing to drink here before Buckfast took over. All the gigs tended to be in big venues like the Glasgow Apollo, the Mayfair, or Tiffanys, with the usual bully-boy bouncers – especially at the Apollo. There was nowhere for any DIY gigs back then; even Conflict, when they first played Glasgow, played at the Mayfair…There were a few bands doing the rounds here as well: Last Rites, APG, Condemned, Practex, Toxic Ephex…"

After playing their first gig – for the Glasgow Music Collective – at the Bogglestone pub in the city's east end, Disaffect recorded their first demo at their rehearsal space in City Centre Sound. Although desperately under-produced, it captured enough of the band's intensity to sell well and get their name out there and of course it was defiantly DIY in its manufacture process.

"The tape turned out okay," offers Joe modestly, "although I've not listened to it for years now; in fact, I'm not even sure that I have a copy of it any more. It's amazing how when folk come to your house and see some Disaffect stuff and say something like, 'Wow, they were one of my favourite bands…' and the fucking things just disappear. Sticky-fingered punks!

"It was a nightmare copying them all tape-to-tape at home: a 20-minute demo, 50 times over…murder. Myself and Andy pulled together the cover and the lyric sheet, which I had the joy of typing out on an old typewriter; we then took the cover and the lyrics and went to a shop near Andy's place that did photocopying and copied about 100 sheets: all to be folded up and inserted inside the cassette cover, more fun. But folk seemed to really like the demo; we sold it, or gave it away, at gigs and it also got good reviews in zines worldwide, so we started doing trades with bands from all over the place…"

The demo also led to the band hooking up with Flat Earth Records in the UK and Nabate in Belgium for 1992's seven-track 'An Injury To One Is An Injury To All' 7-inch. Recorded in just one day again ("Most of us were on the dole, so money was tight…"), at Apollo Studios, with Richie Dempsey (drummer for manic Scottish noise-punks the Stretchheads) manning the mixing desk, it combined some melodic intros with plenty of tight, pacey punk-rock, not to mention some well-observed criticism of scene behaviour ('Fast Music Doesn't Mean Violent Dancing') and it landed the band great reviews in all the most-respected punk publications such as Maximum Rock'n'Roll and Profane Existence. It also landed Disaffect their first European tour.

"But it was a bit chaotic and not planned very well," admits Joe, "though that's usually the case with DIY tours! Billy offered to drive us, which he did for all three tours actually, which was really appreciated. He had one of those VW camper vans, which we filled with amps and drums and all our stuff, plus seven folk…and I think we'd only just got to Newcastle before the van nearly gave up the ghost. We were supposed to play the first gig of the tour at the 1 In 12 in Bradford, but there was no way we would have got there in time in that van – whenever we got above 30mph on the motorway – and only then when we were going downhill – it started swaying all over the place.

"So we went to friends in Newcastle who said we could borrow their Transit; this was Micky and Karen from One By One and, again, we appreciated the bailout, but the van needed a push-start every time. We stayed the next night in a squat in a block of flats in London and I was awake all fuckin' night because the light at the top of Canary Wharf was flashing and kept lighting up the clouds. I fell asleep on all the amps in the back of the van on the drive to Dover and that was when the rest of the band found out that I snored… I don't know how many times on tour I was dragged out of the room in my sleeping bag 'cos of it, waking up where I didn't go to sleep…

"Anyway we played Amsterdam and Groningen in Holland, Liege and Ieper in Belgium and somewhere in Germany, I think. The best gigs were in Liege and Ieper; the Vort'n'Vis in Ieper was just amazing, the place was mobbed for this all-day gig there and even though no-one had seen us before, everyone seemed to know who we were and it was just amazing. This

Disaffect, Lynne and Andy

Disaffect, Lynne and Joe

was the first Euro tour I'd ever done, so I was just blown away by the whole scene over there and how they couldn't do enough for you: they fed you, you got free booze, a bit of hash if you wanted it, you were always paid *and* would get a place to sleep! Compare that to over here where you don't get fed, there's no beer for the bands and you're called sell-outs if you even dare ask for money…"

"I have fond memories of all our tours," reckons Lynne. "We all got on really well and had a great laugh most of the time; Brian kept us all going with his madness and the odd singalong, or just singing loudly all together in the van, was not a rare occurrence. I usually took a fellow girl along with us on tour, to even things out a bit on that front…it wasn't like there was much discrimination, but I did experience a bit from some not-so-nice audiences now and again. Usually brainless blokes shouting, 'Get yer tits out!', for example. But I don't remember that kind of thing happening too often; organisers and promoters were always very respectful of me and I was treated as an equal."

"Things were quite elitist in the UK though," Joe adds. "There were folk here that didn't want to put us on, especially in London; they thought that the cover of the first single was clichéd [it featured some simplistic but well-intentioned anti-fascist symbolism] and didn't want to know us. Most of the places we played in Europe were squats; I remember the one we played in Groningen was an old squatted cinema-cum-dancehall, which was an amazing place. When we got there they had just had their first rainfall in months and everyone was out with the pails and buckets, getting the water as it came down the drainpipes so they could flush the toilets; *everyone* was helping and you just wouldn't see that here – most folk would just stand around, drinking their pish beer and slagging everyone else off!"

1993 saw Disaffect back in Apollo recording three tracks for a split 7-inch with Sedition, again produced by Richie Dempsey and co-released by Flat Earth and Nabate. The band then contributed three songs to a split EP with Bizarre Uproar, which was released as part of the ambitious (four 7-inch and one 5-inch) 'Pestilence' box-set issued by Wiggy Records, the US label ran by Bryan from Blownapart Bastards. But probably the best Disaffect release (and certainly the most vibrant) was the five-track 'Home Of The Slave' EP, originally released in 1994 on Andy's own Anonymous Records before being repressed by Uneasy Listening in Canada and then Maximum Voice Productions in Germany, its cover a loving homage to Discharge.

"Yeah, that's my favourite release of them all too," concedes Joe. "I just think that we were really starting to get our sound pretty tight and writing better tunes and songs by then. The cover was more of a piss-take than a homage, though, because at the time the D-beat clone thing was taking off and a lot of people who had never heard us before just saw the band's name and lumped us into the whole Discore scene…talk about judging a book by its cover, eh? I remember we played a gig at the 1 In 12 and the guys from Active Minds were there and even they were expecting us to sound like Discharge; they got a bit of a surprise when we played, ha! Just shows you how people are so eager to label you as something without actually hearing what you have to say…"

The 'Chained To Morality' LP was then recorded at Glasgow's Stuffhouse Studios (again with Richie Dempsey) and released by Nabate in 1994. It was the first and only Disaffect release to feature Billy Steele on second guitar, Sedition having just called it a day, and saw the band further refining their distinct take on punk rock (pulling it all into one cohesive whole on tracks like 'Internal Life', ominously heavy clean-picked passages rubbing shoulders with breakneck thrashy crust) and another self-booked European tour was undertaken to promote it.

"Actually I think we were in Spain *before* it was released, so folk had come along to the gigs to get the new LP and we didn't have any," says Joe. "This was my favourite tour we did; some of the gigs in France were just amazing. A couple were held in community centres and were mobbed; there were a few arseholes who thought they could just punch and smash into anyone they wanted, but the crowd soon put a stop to them. We also got to play with a lot of cool bands; we played with Rectify from Wales…you gotta go all the way to the Vort'n'Vis in Ieper to play with a band from the UK! We played with a French band called Tromatism too and those people put on a show and a half; they had scaffolding tubes that they set up and during their show they were up and down them, fire-eating, juggling…they were just manic, a superb band and you couldn't meet nicer people either.

"We also got to play in the El Paso squat in Italy… I mean this place was famous in the punk world, but hardly any fucker showed up for the gig. The folk in the squat didn't give a fuck about us either. We had heard so much about this place, that it was 'anarchy central' or whatever and it was just shit. I even fuckin' electrocuted myself putting a light out in the attic that they stuck us in. At this time I was starting to feel that things were changing in the band and I was thinking that this would probably be the last tour, which indeed it turned out to be…"

Because unfortunately and for whatever reason these sort of things happen (usually daily life getting in the way of that idyllic anarcho-punk existence we all had planned out to perfection in our heads when we were younger), Disaffect fizzled out after the release of the LP. Andy, Billy and Ian teamed up with Angus from Sedition and Jason from the Stretchheads to form Scatha, while Brian formed Quarantine and Joe eventually reformed Constant Fear with that band's original guitarist Watty.

"I was almost five months pregnant when we played our last gig," explains Lynne. "I knew I was going to be kept busy for quite some time after the arrival of my [eldest] son Eli, who is now 16 and, much as I enjoyed being in Disaffect, it felt right that it come to an end when it did.

"I eventually left Glasgow and moved to Liège in Belgium, where I still live today. I spent a few years being a mum and learning French, of course. I taught English for quite some time and now I'm studying to be a nurse, which is pretty mad as [our old bassist] Andy is too. I did a bit of guest singing for Unhinged here in Liège, but it was difficult finding arrangements for the kids during gigs and practices so that didn't continue. I still love listening to all sorts of music and although I'm not really involved in the punk scene any more. I'd like to get into doing music again, but I'm very busy with my studies and family. Never say never though!"

"Funny how you only recall all the good things that happen in a band – until you get back together and then you remember it's a bloody hard slog sometimes as well," laughs Joe, before adding, "the best thing for me though is when folk contact me and say that Disaffect were a big influence on their lives back in the Nineties; that's what makes me think that it really was worth doing. There were that many different scenes going on back then, but we just played the style of music we wanted to listen to, not to fit in with the hardcore crowd or the travellers or anyone else; if you didn't like us then you didn't go to our gigs. One thing we did do differently was that we stood up to all the macho dancing and posturing at gigs; we refused to be the soundtrack to some arsehole beating the shit out of other folk at the front. If they wanted to do that then there were plenty of 'tuff guy' bands playing gigs and they could fuck off there; it seems we're all about 'respect and unity' in the punk scene…until the music starts and then we start knocking the shite out of people.

"I think the Nineties was really the beginning of the end for punk, though, especially in the UK. I remember seeing folk in dreads at our gigs suddenly disappear and come back months later with their dreads cut off and their hair bleached blonde and doing all that fuckin' rave dancing with fuckin' dummies in their mouths…get to fuck, for fuck's sake. It totally fucked up the punk scene here. I remember asking one of them, 'Why?' and the answer was that there was no hassle at raves – even though they are full of wee 'ned' bastards (or 'chavs' for you folk down south); basically you didn't have to listen to the words, it was all about just dancing and everyone getting fucked up on E.

Then it was the 2000s and, apart from a few bands up here, the scene was dead. Oh, you still have that punk rip-off, 'Holidays In Wasted Rebellion' pish in Blackpool every year, where folk get their mohawks and studded leather jackets out of the cupboard for four days a year, but every year its just a wee bit harder to get into that old jacket…

"But the same divisive crap that was going on in the Nineties is still going on today. Would I do anything different though? I don't think so! Would I do it all again? Aye, of course I would! Punk as fuck!"

SELECT DISCOGRAPHY:

7-inch:
'An Injury To One…' (Flat Earth/Nabate, 1992)
'Split' (Flat Earth/Nabate, 1993) – *split with Sedition*
'Split' (Wiggy, 1994) – *split with Bizarre Uproar, part of the 'Pestilence' 'EP box-set'*
'Home Of The Slave' (Anonymous, 1994)

LP:
'Chained To Morality' (Nabate, 1994)

AT A GLANCE:
The 'Discography' CD issued by Anonymous/Panoptic Vision in 2000 compiles all of the band's vinyl releases. Track it down if you dare!

SHANK

Shank were a ferocious power-violence band from Glasgow, who razed the competition everywhere they went and even caused a bit of controversy en route... Let's face it, that's no bad thing if you want to shake up an apathetic scene, which is what Shank found themselves kicking against in the first place.

"Personally, it was the first real band that I was in that made it out of the rehearsal room," admits guitarist Jamie Thomson, "and the same goes for [vocalist] Wurzel [aka John Burridge]. [Bassist] Andrew [Nolan] was a founding member of Ebola, with whom he still played in the first half of Shank's existence and Jason [Boyce] had played drums in Scatha and the Stretchheads beforehand, so both of them were fairly inured to the rigours of touring as a DIY punk band. In terms of sound and approach, 'shorter, faster, louder' were our watchwords; that's not to say that Ebola or Scatha were not fearsome outfits in their own right, but I don't think there was any conscious desire to improve or augment on what Andrew or Jason had done with their previous bands; we just wanted to play loud, ugly, fast, pissed-off hardcore, stripped of all the posturing and pretence we saw in other bands of that era...

"By the time Shank started, I think the influence of the GMC (the Glasgow Music Collective, who were the folk responsible for me and Wurzel seeing the likes of Born Against, Nation Of Ulysses, Econochrist etc back in the day) was coming to an end and it seemed like the only bands coming through town were insipid third-generation emo bands, which pretty much summed up how stale the scene had become. Even when the rare hardcore show would take place, they were often such dull, turgid spectacles; the days when local bands such as Sedition and Disaffect would wipe the floor with the touring bands seemed a lifetime away. One particularly farcical gig – when Cause For Alarm and Freebase came through town – left such a bad taste in the mouth that myself and Wurzel vowed to start a band...in revenge? In defiance? In desperation? Probably all of the above!

"The aforementioned Sedition were definitely an influence on us," he adds, "but more in terms of us wanting to blow people away like they did than anything else. And, as a consequence of trying to boot the Glasgow scene up the arse, we ended up taking the reins in terms of putting on gigs, too. I would say that we were lucky in that we got to host – and play with – some truly great bands and as such re-cast the scene in the manner we saw fit. That was a fine time for the Glasgow scene, in my opinion and I think we can take some credit for that..."

Shank's first gig was actually south of the border, though, as part of the Bradford 1 In 12 Club's week-long Reclaim May Day event, during early May (of course!) 1998, alongside – among many others – John Holmes and Minute Manifesto.

"There's a video of Gords from Hard To Swallow shouting 'UKPV!' into the camera after we finished [UK power violence], which I took to be a ringing endorsement of our set," says Jamie proudly. "Personally, it was a total blur and the only clear memory I have of it is my fearing that I might fall of the side of the stage if I wasn't careful... As it turned out, my stage 'persona' never got much further than trying not to fall over! In all seriousness, we got a great response; I remember sitting in the cafe afterwards, beside Steve from Heresy, who was effusive in his praise for us – high cotton, indeed! – but we came crashing back to earth with our second, rather shambolic, gig supporting Refused and Ink And Dagger. It was these kind of 'boom-bust' inconsistencies that would characterise the vast majority of our 'career'…"

The first Shank recordings took place soon after, "In a basement in Leeds with the bloke from Bob Tilton…!" and the results were quickly released on two split 7-inchs, one shared with Minute Manifesto (for Enslaved Records) and one with Scalplock (for Retribution). The split for Enslaved stirred up a hornet's nest of disapproving controversy with its cover images of a baby's face with the word 'Parasite' written across the forehead and sketches of pushchairs with vultures snuggled in them…but what were people honestly expecting from an utterly misanthropic band that sounded like a more feral Napalm Death?

"There were no lyrics with the record," explains Jamie. "But I wrote an accompanying rant that railed against the folly of overpopulation and the peculiar and hypocritical consensus reality that stated 'Starting a family is the most important thing that you can do as a human being, unless you're poor – then you should be smart enough to resist the attention and affirmation that having kids will bring you because, let's face it, we don't need any more poor folks, right?'

"Obviously, being a punk band we took the most extreme position possible and said – and I paraphrase – 'Abortions! Yaay! Fuck the family unit!' Okay, it was hardly Swiftian (well, it wasn't like we said we should eat them or anything), but it was still very interesting seeing the reaction we received. From drunken idiots stumbling up to us at gigs asking, 'Why do you hate babies?', to a foam-specked rant in the UK punk scene's paper of record, *Fracture*, which basically – hilariously – accused us of being Skrewdriver – but against the precious innocents. Yeah, that never really stood up to analysis, but what made it all the more murkier was that this particular missive apparently came from someone involved in the distribution of that record… Presumably their heart broke into tiny pieces each time they packed up and sent off another one of our baby-hating opuses!

"Funny how the broad-brushstroke irony of 'Kill The Poor' [by the Dead Kennedys, of course] or 'White Minority' [by Black Flag] barely deserves comment, but as soon as you start raising issues a bit closer to home for the potato-sack-patch 'crust as fuck existence' herd, that might challenge their orthodoxy, you are suddenly a fascist. I have almost only entirely positive memories of my experiences with the DIY-or-die underground/squatter community, but I encountered far more knee-jerk dogma there than from the 'meat-head hardcore' circles they were apparently opposing. I think that's why we took such joy in baiting them with songs like 'Open Mouth, Shout Slogan', 'Kill Whitey', 'Pro-Militia' and 'No Logo? No Shit!'"

Musically both splits were heart-in-mouth intense, propelled by rage and booze and Infest worship, with the Scalplock single even featuring a song called 'I Love Power Violence'. Rather apt; Shank were definitely harsh on the ear and pulled absolutely zero punches with both their words and heavily abused instruments. Suitably incensed, the band toured the UK and Europe, recorded another frenzied split EP, this time with Japan's Unholy Grave for Sterilized Decay Records and then toured some more.

"The first time we went to Europe was with some friends from Glasgow, a (very good) post-rock band called Hernandez," recalls Jamie. "When we played with Hellnation in Germany, Spazz and Slapaham [label] supremo Chris Dodge was standing in on bass for them – he dug our crazy rock action and asked us to do an album for Slapaham a couple of months later. That was pretty much a lifetime's ambition achieved there and then. 'Where do we go from here?', I remember asking Andrew once the news had sunk in…taking so long to record the

Shank, first gig in Australia

Shank, live in LA

fucking album that the label goes out of business before we can submit it, that's where!

"But I digress. Personally, my favourite moment on tour in Europe was when – after a five-hour drive up through the Alps from Germany into Italy – our van's radiator gave out after being punished by the incessant climb. We had an unscheduled stop in Von Trapp country and had to find a mountain stream to replenish the radiator. Much fence-climbing, alpine gambolling and other larks followed. Then, as we were ready to set off again, Andrew noticed on the side of a roadside-rescue phone, right in the middle of fucking nowhere, a Ratos de Porao sticker. Someone else has always been there first, right?

"As for low points, that would have to have been on our second tour, when we hit Lodz in Poland. The scene was set by the massive amount of Nazi graffiti on every available concrete surface as we entered the city. By the end of the night, the massive hooligan skinheads clogging up the squat bar had taken exception to our dreadlocked driver ("Where are you, you Jew? We will kill you!"). Then , when we had taken refuge upstairs, protected by a massive iron gate, they started attacking our tour van. And when that didn't fight back, they just started hitting each other before walking off home, arm in arm.

"Two days later, in Poznan, we played to about six people as the support to a reggae disco…later that night I would take, as a pre-arranged 'guarantee', probably a week's wages off the hapless promoter as he apologised profusely to me. We had no option but to take the money, as we were broke and desperately needed the cash to fill up the van and get back to Germany. But seeing this man prostrating himself before me and emptying his pockets so we, a bunch of bourgeois hobbyists from the affluent West, could carry on our tour still makes me shudder to this day. Yeah, that was a fucking low point."

The album that was intended for release on Slapaham, entitled 'Coded Messages In Slowed Down Songs', was eventually released by 625 Thrash and Deep Six Records in 2002 and – as expected – it was a relentless barrage of anti-social diatribe set to insanely fast grindcore. Loaded with scathing sarcasm ('Kill Whitey', 'Future Wifebeater' and 'The Stupidity That You Embody', to name but a few), it paints a very bleak view of the world while smearing a nervous smile across your face.

After a tour of Australia with AVO, Shank flew out to the west coast of America to promote it…then promptly split upon their return. "Our California tour was set up around the Super Sabado Fest at Gilman St, a resurrection of the legendary Fiesta Grande gigs that showcased the cream of power violence and other extreme hardcore bands back in the day – that would have me crying/drooling when reading the line-ups while stuck thousands of miles away! We toured with Breakfast from Japan and there wasn't a night when we didn't play with some legendary, or on their way to being legendary, band in our milieu. It truly was the ultimate validation for us and more than an ample pay-off for all those nights playing to a bunch of disinterested nu-metal kids in Scarborough, or indeed, supporting a reggae disco in Poland.

"For us, headlining at Gilman St was the Motherlode: rubbing shoulders with the people that created our whole raison d'etre. We didn't actually headline it in the end, though, as we were supposed to follow Municipal Waste, who I'd seen utterly destroy for two consecutive nights in the run-up, so in a 'Hendrix/Who at Monterey' scenario, I said we'd be foolish to go on afterwards and did a bit of horse-trading. To be honest, we needn't have worried; we got an amazing response… 'The biggest circle pit I've seen at Gilman Street,' said Ken Prank afterwards.

"Funnily enough, it wasn't even the best gig of the tour. That came later at a community centre in LA; we played on the floor and the tidal wave of kids that kept pouring our way knocked over the drumkit numerous times and snapped the hi-hat stand. I had to play with my back to the crowd, braced against them, to stop them knocking over my gear. Oh and the best quote of the night/tour/our entire existence as a band was that night: 'You guys from Russia ROCK!' Ha ha!

"The last show of the tour – with Knife Fight at Headline Records in LA – was the last Shank show period, after which the band flew home, recorded a split 12-inch with Iron Lung and then split due to member dispersal around the globe. Andrew moved to Toronto to be with his girlfriend, where he started power-violence band the Endless Blockade, before playing with Slaughter Strike and Column Of Heaven. Wurzel moved to Sweden, although he recorded again with Jamie as Suburban Disease. Meanwhile Jamie moved to London, but still plays and records with Jason (who stayed in Glasgow) in the Process, alongside ex-members of In Decades Decline.

"I don't remember any great ceremony that ended our time as a band," admits Jamie, who also did a short-lived side-project with Andrew, Nation Of Finks, that featured Stiff from Fleas And Lice and Tommy from Atomgevitter. "We probably just finished recording the split and then went to the pub! The thing about Shank is that, rather than the hoary punk pursuit of changing the world, we only ever really wanted to change our own world, our own circumstances. And despite the missed opportunities, misfiring shows and generally hostile outlook, we managed that in as much as our lives would have been very different if we'd never got off our arses and did that and got to experience some pretty amazing things and meet some amazing people, as we did.

"Speaking purely for myself, as much as I would like to hark back to the nihilistic fuck-it-all stance we exuded all too easily back in the day, I can't help but feel that if I inspired the same kind of reaction in some disconnected fuck-up that I, as a disconnected fuck-up, felt when I heard the likes of Infest, Born Against or Citizen's Arrest, then that can't be regarded as time wasted. People have told me as much and I'm slowly letting myself believe them. But that's the thing about getting older – you become a sentimental cunt.

"It's hard to recall exactly why we were so ready to install ourselves as the opposition to whatever we felt was the prevailing mood of the day – whether it be UKHC muscle-flexing or some peace-punk squat-or-rot rhetoric – other than we were so fucking bored of posturing, whether it be politicised or just bone-headed. But I'm glad we were.

"What set us apart? When I think about the bands that we had the closest relationships with – Minute Manifesto, Scalplock, Hernandez, Catharsis, Iron Lung, Canvas, Shikari, AVO, John Holmes, Red Right Hand – people that I would regard as peers, we were all pretty bloody unique, except Shank were maybe drunker and grumpier when we turned up for gigs than anyone else. But if I were to make a grand pronouncement about my band and that loose-knit group of like-minded groups as a whole, we were the jaggy edges of hardcore that made the scene that much more interesting before the dread hand of internet homogenisation came into play and smoothed it all away."

SELECT DISCOGRAPHY:

7-inch:
'Split' (Enslaved, 1998) – *split with Minute Manifesto*
'Split' (Retribution, 1999) – *split with Scalplock*
'Split' (Sterilized Decay, 2000) – *split with Unholy Grave*
'Split' (Schizophrenic, 2008) – *split with the Endless Blockade*

12-inch:
'Split' (625 Thrashcore/Deep Six, 2005) – *split with Iron Lung*

LP:
'Coded Messages In Slowed Down Songs' (625 Thrashcore/Deep Six, 2002)

AT A GLANCE:
'The Curse Of Shank' CD on Out Of Limits (2003) – complete with very cool 'Scum' cover! – compiles the band's demos and early EPs onto one disc.

EX-CATHEDRA

On a totally different note, but also hailing from Glasgow, **Ex-Cathedra** were a buoyant ska punk band that mixed the exuberant chops of Operation Ivy and early Rancid with the more sardonic strains of the genre being cultivated this side of the pond by Citizen Fish and PAIN.

"After our old punk band, the God Squad, split up, me and drummer Brad [aka Alan Brady] met Issy Craig busking in town with her violin and asked her to join our new band on both violin *and* bass," begins guitarist Alex Aiken, of the band's inception in 1991. "After jamming and getting a few songs together, I placed an advert in the local paper for a singer; we had auditioned a few people but not found anyone suitable. Andi [aka Andrew Chalmers] answered that same day and got the job. Every other punk and hardcore band in those days played thrash and screamed like a banshee, but we wanted a more classic punk sound that incorporated all our favourite bands like SLF, Ruts, Specials, the Clash etc. I remember seeing all those bands and feeling this rush of excitement that I wanted to try and recreate with my own band; I wanted to write and play songs that made you want to sing and shout and *dance*. But we really didn't have many expectations other than playing a few gigs in town to our mates and maybe scraping enough cash together to record a demo…"

After several gigs as Défoncé (French for 'wasted'), including a Hallowe'en support to the UK Subs (then featuring a young Lars Frederiksen, later of Rancid fame, on guitar), Brad came

Ex-Cathedra second line-up

Ex-Cathedra, live at the Dublin Castle

up with the name Ex-Cathedra, but then left to become a fisherman soon after their first gig in December 1991 at the Glasgow Tech with Headstart and Disaffect. He was replaced by Jim Sewell from Dreadful and the band began some concerted gigging, before recording a seven-song demo in Glasgow's Rock Hard Studios. Although rougher than the proverbial badger's arse, it captured the band's manic energy to a tee and the track 'Hooligans In Suits' was included on the 1992 Looney Tunes compilation 'Screams From The Silence Volume Two'. After a high-profile support to Sham 69 at the Glasgow Mayfair, Ex-Cathedra landed themselves a dream show with SLF at the Barrowlands on St Patrick's Day, 1993.

"Aye, personally, it really was a dream come true," reckons Andi. "I'd been an avid fan since first hearing 'Inflammable Material' in 1979 – aged seven! I went through to my brother John's room, when I heard 'Johnny Was' playing and asked, 'Who's this?' I was already aware of the Clash, Ramones, Angelic Upstarts, Skids, Cockney Rejects, Elvis Costello, the Police and, of course, Blondie... I could go on and on about all the bands I heard through my older brother. Anyway, a lifelong (compulsive obsessive) love affair started right there.

"My brother got me a ticket for their 'last ever gig' in the Glasgow Apollo on Sunday 6 Febuary 1983, when I was 11 years old. I was so chuffed when they reformed and I lost count of how many times I saw them live, 200 or more... "Jake Burns actually offered me the support himself and if you had told me that would happen when I was aged 10, I would have thought you were mad! And it went well; the Glasgow Barrowlands is the best fuckin' venue in the universe and SLF are the best fucking band, so it was a good night."

"I'd seen SLF at the Apollo in '79 and it was one of the best gigs I'd ever been to,"adds Alex. "So to play at this big prestigious venue with some of my adolescent heroes was beyond belief. I just remember being incredibly nervous before going on stage and, as the doors had only just opened, it was totally empty to start with, but we played our hearts out and because you can't really see the audience we never noticed until halfway through the set. This great roar went up after a song and, as the lights briefly panned across the crowd, the place was bursting at the seams and the feeling was immense. We finished with a punked-up cover of the Pogues' 'Dirty Old Town' with our friend Matt coming on to play fiddle and 'cos it was Paddy's Day the crowd went absolutely bananas. That was definitely one of my high points with the band."

It was Andi's brother John who also helped finance the band's first single on their own Tartan Records, the 'Stick Together' EP which they recorded at Glasgow's Stuffhouse Studios in January 1994 with Richie Dempsey from the Stretchheads producing.

"It was a four-track 7-inch with white labels and these handmade cloth covers that had the Ex-Cathedra logo spray-painted on them with a stencil," says Alex proudly. "It took ages to assemble, sew and spray (my house stank of aerosol paint for weeks after); we got 1,000 copies pressed up and when they arrived we thought we'd never shift them all, but they soon sold out, thanks to the many DIY distros that were springing up in almost every town and the tour of Belgium and Holland [with Dutch band Anarcrust] that we did helped as well."

"Cannae recall that much about it," admits Andi, of their first excursion to Europe. "But personally I would like to thank Ritchie Scott, Billy Munn and Fin, who all came with us, but especially Angus ('Spam') Buchan who kept us on the road – best mechanic in the universe! Can't remember why, but after the gig in Groningen, where the infamous Mushroom Attack and Fleas And Lice all squatted, I was wide awake for a few days and left all me belongings there: sleeping bag, jacket, everything... So I ended up doing the rest of the tour wearing only my kilt and steel toe-cap willies, having to borrow Tizzy's stockings 'cos it was so cold. But I did eventually get my stuff back from a kind chap who brought them to our last gig – thanks mate! – and we did have a good time playing the Netherlands. Food, drink, a place to stay – as well as getting *paid*, wow! It was a far cry from the usual UK set-up and you could certainly say there were more highs than lows, though I do remember Ritchie the driver having to shit in a polythene bag on the tour bus, 'cos he couldn't get into the venue in the morning (sorry, mate, if you're reading this…!) But overall it was magic."

"That was an epiphany moment for me," concurs Alex. "To observe the Euro-punk squat scene with their DIY, well-organised network of venues, bands, distros, fanzines…and loads of beer! Every night was a party and meeting all these great likeminded people just consolidated our punk DIY ethic. I remember on the way to one of the gigs the radiator had a leak, so we tried to stem the flow with chewing gum. When the wipers broke, we tied string to each wiper and pulled them back and forward from the passenger seats through the side windows!"

The spirited 'Watch Out' EP was up next on Tartan, which saw the band supporting the likes of Bad Religion, NOFX and SLF again, before Ex-Cathedra signed with Ian Ballard's Damaged Goods label following a well-received London gig, the first fruits of this union being 1995's 'Trespass' 7-inch.

"Initially Ian wanted to do a one-off single with an option for an album if it worked out," explains Alex. "So we went back to Practise Pad with Richie and recorded 'Trespass' and [B-side] 'Sail Away'; 'Trespass' was an upbeat skanky riff and 'Sail Away' was a furious punk-rock song with a great bassline. When Ian suggested we do a cover song for our next single, we had been doing a silly punk version of Culture Club's 'Karma Chameleon' at gigs, probably inspired by Snuff who were doing really well at the time and were renowned for daft covers of TV adverts and classic pop songs. So we put that out but it turned out to be really naff and I have to hold my hands up and take the blame for it."

Undeterred, though, Damaged Goods put the band into Frankie Stubbs from Leather face's Bunker Studio in Sunderland to record their first album, 1996's 'Tartan Material'; both the title and cover being a respectful pastiche of SLF's 'Inflammable Material', it somehow failed to capture the band's irrepressible live verve, despite the songs being memorable enough to give Rankin's 'And Out Come The Wolves' a good run for its money and also marked the end of Missy's tenure with the band.

"We were big Leatherface fans so this was unbelievable," smiles Alex, of recording with Frankie, "*and* we were going to record it when it was warm and sunny for once; somehow all our previous recordings were done in the middle of winter, which plays havoc with your voice and circulation…well, have you ever tried to play guitar with hands like frozen fish fingers? Stiff [aka Stephen Maroon] had come down with us to play bass on a few tracks and he joined full-time not long after.

"Issy was having a few personal problems and was becoming a bit unreliable, especially with the booze. I think it was better for her to have some time out for her own good, because the touring environment is not conducive to good health at the best of times. She was a fantastic bass player, though, and an integral part of the band's early days. We also got Jenny Divers from Norwich punk band PMT to play sax on a few songs; Sue Spew, their guitarist, also came up with her and contributed to some backing vocals (and a lot of the booze chaos).

"I think the reason for the disappointing outcome of the album sessions was us not being on top form; also we seemed to spend more time in the pub than the studio. Every time there was a problem with, say, a vocal track or a drum part we would all bugger off to the boozer thinking that it would all be worked out when we came back. We also didn't have the studio knowledge to tell Frankie exactly what we wanted; being slightly in awe of him, we left it all up to him thinking he would know best. To me, the finished recording sounded flat and lacked the vibrancy of the first two EPs, but I don't blame Frankie at all; it was definitely down to our lack of professionalism ultimately. Frankie was great company and a lovely guy – and boy, can he drink!"

"We *were* a bit inexperienced, but I also had a nasty cold or flu," adds Andi, "so the singing was not going very well. Frankie suggested I needed some lubrication, so I took out my honey and spooned it down me throat, much to his disgust. 'Not that kind of lubrication,' he yelled at me…and after half a dozen pints and a few ports (Frankie knew port was good for the lubrication, bless him) we went back and recorded half of the songs that night. He let us all stay in his modest flat and was over generous with his table stash of Special Reserve miniatures; he also let me know that my pink mohican looked stupid and duly shaved my nut for me (at no extra charge!) He brought the punk-rock vibe with him, 'cos he *is* the real deal (whatever the fuck that means…) The recording was raw and took about a week to do, mixing included, as far as I can remember. Unfortunately something went wrong when it was pressed, as it did not turn out the way it should have…although there was a cassette bootleg done – that actually sounded better than the vinyl and CD release. It might have helped if we hadn't all been drinking so much as well, of course…"

To promote the album, the band did the only thing they knew how, which was to hit the road – and the bottle! – and this period of their 'career' saw them on tour with everyone from Rancid to Citizen Fish, although eventually the continuous gigging took its toll on drummer Jim, who was replaced by Ian Parker from Machine Gun Etiquette, who were by then one of the band's ubiquitous touring and drinking partners.

"All the constant touring honed us into a really tight unit, and when on form we could really rock the roof off a venue," says Alex, "but that's not to say we couldn't fuck up in spectacular style either. We played many a shit gig, usually down to boozing, like the time Andi was so drunk at a gig in Wisbech that he fell off the stage and had to be propped up for the duration of the set by two obliging skinheads, who held him up to the mic and danced around with him. Stiff played a few gigs lying flat on his back with punters pouring beer into his mouth and I once missed a gig in Norwich after I was attacked in Glasgow by two Nazi arseholes and ended up with 14 stitches in my head and hands like two balloons.

"My favourite place for touring was and still is Ireland; the Irish punk scene has the friendliest party-animal geezers on the planet, so much so that we have an annual GGI punk festival which rotates around Glasgow, Groningen in Holland and Ireland. Again, the Irish know how to drink and party and I always find that it's the party after the gig that you remember and the gig is just incidental. 'Do you remember that gig in Norway?' No… 'The one where Stiff found a staple gun and stapled his face all over?' Oh aye, *that* one!

"Another time, Stiff again, we had just completed a tour of Norway and were well pissed off at the continual strip searching at every border, so when the border control guards asked us to come with them, Stiff, in a drunken fit of petulance, decided to get it over with right there on the tarmac and proceeded to tear his clothes off, much to our merriment. Unfortunately the guards weren't so amused and promptly whisked him off to the cells; they told us that Glasgow police were coming to pick him up in connection with some other outstanding incident and we were to move on. They eventually dumped him, penniless, on the side of the A1 in Newcastle and said, 'North's that way!' Cunts."

After spending two years drinking, partying and playing (in that order probably), Ex-Cathedra recorded four tracks with Gavin Mearns at MT. Studios, Ibrox, Glasgow, which were 50/50 raging punk rock and sublimely melodic ska (all brought to life by Jenny's soulful sax playing) and released as the 'Anaesthetized' CDEP on Tartan in 1999. Further lengthy tours were undertaken of the UK and Europe with PAIN, Subhumans and King Prawn and eventually, after playing a blinding set at Holidays In The Sun (the annual punk festival currently known as Rebellion) in 1999, the band hooked up with Lol Pryor and Moon Ska Europe for their second album, 2000's brilliant 'Forced Knowledge'. Ironically enough, it took them 10 years to capture their magical live vibe and they split up soon after its release.

That skafest in Morecambe turned out to be Ian Parker's last gig with the band and although Ex-Cathedra soldiered on for several months with various stand-in drummers, they played their last gig at the Kentish Town Forum in late October 2000, supporting Prince Buster, the Selecter, the Pilfers, King Prawn, Mark Lamarr and Jerry Dammers of the Specials.

"I think that some of the members thought playing these big venues supporting the likes of Prince Buster wasn't DIY enough or something," offers Andi, who had moved down to his wife Niki's hometown of Southend six months earlier. "And there seemed to be an issue with being on Moon Ska Europe – maybe they were worrying that the band would end up sounding like all the other Moon Ska bands? It seemed to me that outside influences were really affecting people's opinions.

"I wanted to take the band as far as possible, from playing squats right through to playing the Forum, but somehow keep our morals and attitude and beliefs intact. I remember some friends who hung around the band suggesting we were selling out – I wish we had only got the chance. It just seemed to me that the group never knew what it wanted any more and we all ended up growing apart…well, 400 miles or so apart anyway!

"The Forum gig went okay though; it wasn't our best, but I was so chuffed to be on the bill with Jerry Dammers, who heavily inspired me and still does today – he is a fuckin' genius – and Prince Buster. The place was packed; we did a short set then watched the rest of the show, it was a brilliant night. Afterwards we went back to stay with our friend Boom Boom in New Cross; there was a bit of a funny atmosphere in the morning and Alex was kind of pissed off at me for moving south and we all left with a bit of a sour taste in our mouths…"

Alex, Jenny and Stiff started Scunnered (a Scottish phrase meaning 'pissed off'!), with Tommy Duffin from Los Destructos on drums and Rat (aka Kenny Cunningham) from Machine Gun Etiquette singing, who would go on to release two albums, while Andi and Niki started the Sicnotes with Simon, the drummer from the last Ex-Cathedra line-up and a guy known only as Dave on guitar; they played just one shambolic gig in a New Cross coffee shop before Andi was approached by Niki 'Nailbomb' Johnstone (of the Deathskulls) and Jonny One Lung (of the Filaments) and decided to relaunch Ex-Cathedra with new members. They played their first gig 'back together' at the Studio, Canterbury, on 11 September 2001 (the gig obviously overshadowed by horrific events on the American East Coast), Andi kept the band going for several more years with a constantly changing line-up, playing regularly in the southeast and touring Italy, Norway and Germany.

Although a few songs were recorded for compilations (including a souped-up version of 'Walking In A Winter Wonderland'), the ever-changing line-up prevented any real momentum being generated and Ex-Cathedra ground to a final halt late in 2003, Andi and his new cohorts then making music as Suicide Bid, who have since grown to a 17-strong collective and are working on their third album (the first two being 2005's 'This Is The Generation' and 2006's 'The Rot Stops Here').

"The last gig under the name of Ex-Cathedra was on 3 November 2003, a one-off in Belgium," explains Andi. "The van broke down twice – once in Essex and then again one hour away from the venue – so we got there really late and Niki the sax player's reed was really fucked, so her sax sounded like bad bagpipes. We had the multi-talented Niki 'Nailbomb', Dave from Nuclear Anarchy and Jonny [also of the Deathskulls] on guitar; it was not the best gig with that line-up and if I remember rightly, we had to use all the money paid to us to get the van home…and still had to push it on and off the ferry. After a whole decade or more, nothing had changed!

"In the end, I just decided to get on with a new project; the Sicnotes hadn't felt right, but the idea of doing a more dub/punk-style band really appealed to me; we were all fans of the Ruts and Clash etc and newer bands like Inner Terrestrials and PAIN, so as long as I was gonna carry on in that vein I was happy to drop the Ex-Cathedra 'brand'. To be honest, after the trip to Belgium and the van breaking down yet again and yet more new members…well, it was getting too much like Oi Polloi for my liking!"

"There were a few other reasons why we called it a day," adds Alex, who now plays with Glasgow street-punk mob Crossfire (whose recent album was entitled, 'Back Tae Auld Claes And Porridge'). "Although we were doing reasonably well, there were a few cracks starting to widen. On my part, although I loved touring, I had just become a father to a beautiful baby girl called Rudi and I was getting grief from my partner, understandably, who was stuck at home while I was out partying every night and coming home with fuck all money. But I found I didn't like being away from her and was drinking a lot on tour and behaving recklessly, I suppose, to block out the heartache. And me and Andi, who've always been like brothers, were starting to fight and argue over everything; Stiff was fed up with it and so was Jenny.

"Although I initially liked Andi's idea of moving south for the band, when I looked at things like house prices, jobs and nurseries, it just wasn't feasible. It was quite an acrimonious split to start with, but, to be honest , the band had reached its end and I'm immensely proud and grateful for all the good times and achievements we made. I'm also pleased to say that, 20 years on, me and Andi are friends again, meeting at places like the Rebellion Festival in Blackpool and still living the dream…"

As for the other members, Jen now studies naturopathy in Australia, Stiff resides in the Netherlands and plays bass for crust-punk legends Fleas And Lice, while Ian Parker sadly passed away in 2002, losing a long battle with cancer.

"One of my most enduring memories of Ian was actually outside of the band," says Andi fondly, "when me and Niki, my partner, along with Parker and Jenny were doing the best work in the world – if you're a hash-head, that is! We were cutting weed in Holland, so not only were we being paid, we had free beer, good food, a place to stay and, of course, all the *free* weed that you could consume in a fortnight. At first Parker was skinning up using tobacco, until I pointed out, 'Why waste yer tobacco? There's more than enough weed!'

"We had some crazy nights, mad apple fights, tripping from all the skunk and literally

Ex-Cathedra, Dublin Castle

rolling around in hysterics for hours and hours at all these crap Scottish jokes. Parker loved every minute of it and we seemed to share a very special time that fortnight. There were many special times, though; Parker was very passionate and deadly serious about the band, but he liked a good laugh too. We use to liberate large amounts of alcohol on the ferry from Newcastle to Norway; we also sussed that if you told the staff it was your birthday you would get a free bottle of champagne.

"Some of those times, especially when we had all agreed we would behave ourselves for once, within an hour or so a bottle would mysteriously appear and the drink would start to flow...and flow! So, anyway, this whole Ex-Cathedra story goes out to the spirit and memory of the best drummer and all-round good guy, Ian Parker, wherever you may be (I'm sure it's a better place than here). God bless ya, mate – and see you again one day, on the other side..."

SELECT DISCOGRAPHY:

7-inch:
'Stick Together' (Tartan, 1994)
'Watch Out' (Tartan, 1994)
'Trespass' (Damaged Goods, 1995)
'Karma Chameleon' (Damaged Goods, 1997)

LPs:
'Tartan Material' (Damaged Goods, 1996)
'Three Way Split' (Trapdoor, 1996) – *split with Machine Gun Etiquette and Nutcase*
'Forced Knowledge' (Moon Ska Europe, 2000)
'2 x 4 =' (Tartan, 2002)

AT A GLANCE:
Until someone comes up with a comprehensive retrospective, 'Forced Knowledge' remains the definitive Ex-Cathedra release.

CONFUSION CORPORATION

Definitely not as 'hardcore punk' as most of the bands in this book, Scottish grindcore band **Confusion Corporation** certainly moved in the same underground circles. They eventually mutated into Co-Exist and Man Must Die, two of the fiercest bands north of the border today, so they more than merit inclusion here.

"Back in the day I was in a real old-school death-metal band from Dumbarton called Cenotaph," begins drummer/vocalist Quzzy, "who were kinda like old Paradise Lost crossed with Voivod. As people left and in an effort to keep it going, I asked Alan [aka guitarist 'Fudgy'] if he wanted to join; he was in a thrash band called High Tensile and he got [vocalist] Malky and [guitarist] Charlie [Perratt], who he was at college with, involved. As the songs progressed, we changed the name to Confusion Corporation; at first we just wanted to play, record a demo and be part of the tape-trade scene, but we just thrashed away and it gradually turned into something as we got better.

"The Scottish scene was small, but well interconnected. We were all listening to thrash, hardcore and death metal, so it just seemed normal to see an extreme-metal band on the same bill as a hardcore band. And we were just a metal band who found kindred spirits with hardcore bands like Divide and Broken Oath... At the same time, we were playing with Churn, who were utter Napalm Death/Crowbar worship. So I think we got the best of both worlds...and that snowballed into our sound."

The first Confusion Corporation gig was in Clydebank and was predictably loud and chaotic and then the band recorded their first demo, 1994's 'Confusion Begins', in Glasgow's Ca Va Studios, which was, er, predictably loud and chaotic. "That first gig was with a whole load of local bands doing grunge covers," laughs Quzzy, at the memory of their public debut. "We were playing through rubbish amps, with everything as loud as we could get it; it probably sounded awful, but we were full of energy and just throwing ourselves about, playing in front of our mates...and there's nothing better when you're a kid starting out.

"As for the first demo, the songs on it were 'An Absence Of Colour', 'Confuse', 'Rust Coloured Skies', 'Intensified Tribulation' and 'Existence'. I am still fond of it, to be honest, even though there are definitely a few Suffocation riffs hidden on there!"

After playing locally to promote the recording, Confusion Corporation wasted little time in recording a follow-up, 1995's 'Purify', that saw them experimenting more and more with their vocal delivery and playing shows further and further afield.

"Yes, we were starting to develop a wider range of vocals by then and also just starting to find our own identity. It ['Purify'] was way more raw sound-wise, which Fudgy hated, but it was a good snapshot of where we were as a band, using death, thrash and hardcore influences to the best of our ability. And even with the benefit of hindsight, I think it was the best we could have done at the time.

"We did some great shows on the back of it too. Playing with Lock Up when they toured the first album was a great honour and getting a mini-tour with Raging Speedhorn was a riot. One of 'em got mugged outside the venue and we all went out looking for them...ha ha, minted! I've also got fond memories of playing shows with Iron Monkey and Medulla Nocte; that's how we got to know Paul Catten [who later briefly joined Quzzy in Co-Exist]. Playing the Braindead Club in London was a belter too... I think me and [Confusion Corporation bassist]

Confusion Corporation

Danny ended up fighting with a car alarm in the car park…just don't ask! I think Earthtone 9 were on that show too."

Some very positive reviews for the 'Purify' demo brought the band to the attention of Arctic Serenades Records, who were all set to issue the band's 'Decontrol' LP, until fate intervened, robbing the band of a full-length vinyl release.

"Arctic Serenades wanted to put out an album by us," explains Quzzy. "So, pretty much every week, I would meet up with Fudgy and we would write together, bouncing ideas off each other. We went into Ca Va again but, as we had no bass player, Jim from Break played on some of it. I think Fudgy did the rest – but it's a tad hazy, to say the least! That's about the time Danny joined us on bass too.

"Production-wise it's a bit lacking, but then again we had no cash and there was nobody recording stuff like that up here; I think the guy who did it was doing Wet Wet Wet in the next room too! But it was fun and I still really love the songs on 'Decontrol'. I would even love to re-record it now, just to hear the songs with a better production…

"And yeah, the title maybe related to Discharge, but that ain't a bad thing in my opinion. In the end the Arctic Serenades thing collapsed, but we must have still sold 500-plus copies of it, off our own backs and we gave away truckloads of the thing as well."

1998's 'IFF' demo saw the band continuing to refine and improve their increasingly unique sound (think a grindcore version of Fear Factory…), but although the band were drawing well locally, they were unable to secure any serious label interest and they were forced to self-release yet again.

"'IFF' was again another step up for us," agrees Quzzy. "When we finally got the clean vocals to gel. And the guitar-work, while still extreme, was catchy and uplifting; for all the anti-corporate/paranoid twist of the lyrics, we always tried to have a positive slant in there somewhere. Also, people in the local scene just loved that recording, so we *were* playing to bigger crowds. Everything just seemed to be coming right for us, but again, when you listen to it now, the production shows the lack of money that we had…

"And then Malcolm left; he just got fed up with being in a band. He had other interests in his life and, to be honest, the industry had little or no interest in what the scene was doing up here. So, when we went in to record 'As Described By Victims', I took over the main vocals, thinking that we would get another vocalist live. Dawson [later to be in Co-Exist] joined us on the back of that recording; he brought a more hardcore influence vocally and it all got more controlled and focused."

But, increasingly frustrated by lack of label interest, Confusion Corporation eventually buckled under the weight of their own expectations in 1999. "We just couldn't understand why we couldn't get signed and we started to second guess ourselves," sighs Quzzy. "And in-fighting started to be more common place over really petty stuff; when I look back now, with the benefit of age and hindsight, I think how foolish it all was, but at the time it just consumed us. Me, Danny and Charlie had Co-Exist on the go by then and Fudgy went on to form Godplayer [and later Man Must Die]. So we went our separate ways.

"Now we're all mates again and we look back and shake our heads at how it all collapsed, but at the time I think it just ran its course. "There was no last gig either," he adds. "It just couldn't be done at the time. We were *meant* to play with the Haunted in Glasgow that Hallowe'en, but I gave the gig to Madman Is Absolute for their first ever show. Actually, that's my only regret when I think about it: we never got to say goodbye to all the local crew with a final gig…"

Both Co-Exist and Man Must Die are still together and still releasing potent music ('Violent Intentions Begin With Slow Incisions' and 'No Tolerance For Imperfection' being their latest offerings, at the time of writing, respectively), the fiery intensity of Confusion Corporation now refined to the *nth* degree and gnarlier than ever.

"Both bands are still playing and recording because, at the end of the day, this is what we love and this is who we are," concludes Quzzy. "We were all down doing gang vocals on the new Man Must Die recording a few weeks back and Co-Exist have a new recording in the pipeline as well. Charlie has a few other projects on the go and I'm also in the stoner-rock outfit Bacchus Baracus, so we're all on the go music-wise. As long as we are all able to play...we will.

"And I know we are fondly remembered as one of the first extreme bands to open up the gig scene north of the border, along with Churn and a few others. The other day someone posted on Facebook that they were listening to our cover of the Subhumans song, 'Heroes' [from the 'Still Can't Hear The Words' compilation on Blackfish]; that may not be much in the grand scheme of things, but it made me smile and I think that's as much as you can ask."

AT A GLANCE:
The band did release a version of 'IFF' in 1999 which included the 'Decontrol' album as well.

TURTLEHEAD

Turtlehead were a quietly successful pop-punk band from Falkirk in Scotland's Forth Valley; the only UK band to sign to Sweden's respected Bad Taste Records, they released three albums of convincing melodicore and toured extensively in support of them.

"Although the band will forever be associated with Falkirk, I never actually lived there," begins drummer Robert Francis, "but the other guys did. The scene at the time in Falkirk was pretty dead musically...just the usual local live covers bands, I can't really remember any other bands around. We were kinda lucky geographically that we lived in-between Glasgow and Edinburgh and the Venue in Edinburgh was where I got most of my early punk fixes. Sunday night was punk night and I saw among others, NOFX with Guns And Wankers as support, Snuff with Leatherface as support (that gig would be a massive influence on me), Dee Dee Ramone And The Chinese Dragons and many others. Edinburgh always had – and still has – a good underground punk scene, thanks to the world-famous (and sadly long gone) Tap 'O' Lauriston and the Cas Rock; again in these venues I saw some classic gigs: the first Dropkick Murphys UK tour, Schwartzeneggar and, of course, all the great Edinburgh punk bands including Oi Polloi...

"Anyway, Turtlehead started out just as another band that we really liked, Green Day, were just about to go stratospheric; we had been into them long before 'Dookie' was about to come out; that pop-punk sound was what we were into big time, melody definitely played a big part in our musical listening. I think for [bassist] Paul [Bourne] and myself, we just wanted to be – musically – along the lines of our favourite bands at the time (and still, to this day): Descendents, Screeching Weasel, Black Flag, Dead Kennedys, Bad Religion, Snuff, Leatherface, Avail, Jawbreaker and Face To Face. 'Milo Goes To College' [Descendents] got played hell of a lot during those days, as did 'Boogada Boogada Boogada' by Screeching Weasel. We didn't want to be as heavy lyrically as, say, the Kennedys or Bad Religion, so we kinda went more along the lines of Snuff. The *Viz* comic also messed with our heads a lot... that humour was us to a tee!"

Robert and Paul had previously played together in Indian Angel, a sleazy glam-punk band in the vein of Hanoi Rocks and they were joined in Turtlehead by guitarist Gary 'Gazo' Cunningham. This line-up didn't actually play live, but did record 1994's 'High Flats' demo at the Riverside Studio in Busby (south Glasgow) with Duncan Cameron. Soon after, they were joined by vocalist, Brian Cooper and finally played their first gig at the Anchor Inn in nearby Denny during early 1995.

"Yes, it was quite a while after we had formed before we played live," concedes Robert. "But we wanted to record before we gigged, so that we had something to give out at the gig to anyone who might want it. Remember, this was before the days of MySpace and Facebook!"

Things then moved pretty quickly for the band, with 'High Flats' earning them a session on Scottish radio and – probably more importantly in the grand scheme of things – an interview in *Maximum Rock'n'Roll* No 151. Bad Taste Records contacted them soon after and the track 'Thought' was lifted from the demo and used on the 1996 Bad Taste compilation 'Quality Punk Rock'. April 1996 saw them back in Riverside recording the four-track 'Go' EP and by the end of the year they had released their debut album 'Back Slapping Praise From Back Stabbing Men' and played their first gig on European soil, at the Bad Taste Festival in Lund.

"We actually used the studio in Busby for all of our recordings," says Robert. "We really liked it in there, it had a great sound and, at the time anyway, everything was recorded onto tape through an analogue desk. The studio is run by two brothers, Duncan and John Cameron, and both recorded us at various times; they did all the button pushing and tweaking, but the whole band was always there during the recording/mixing process.

"I haven't listened to the EP in years; I think the last time I listened to it, I thought to myself, 'Yep, would have played that differently...that could do with a better middle-eight etc.' But at the time of recording, we all thought it was the dog's danglies! It was our first official record, so to speak; we had a release on a 'proper' label and, for us, that was awesome.

"As for the LP, we recorded that in seven days, then went back in a couple of weeks later to mix it. That was all the songs we had at the time; what got me was that the recording process got a lot harder. This was before the days of serious Pro-Tools and again everything was onto tape, so mistakes couldn't just be fixed on the PC. We never recorded with a click track either; this was for a few reasons: 1) I can't play to a click...couldn't then, still can't now. 2) The rest of the band never played to click track either! 3) John and Duncan both pretty much refused to put a click track on a punk band's recording; they both said that punk should ebb and flow – and how right they are!"

Click track or not, 'Back Slapping Praise...' is a fine debut album, full of understated hooks

Turtlehead, Dave, Paul, Brian and Rob

Turtlehead, Rob, Rich, Brian and Dave

and subtle poignancy and it was great to see four average guys from a small Scottish town giving the Americans a run for their money in the melodic hardcore stakes.

"The festival and just going to Sweden for the first time was also amazing," continues Robert. "The only thing that wasn't amazing (and we didn't know this at the time) was that Paul was afraid of flying…but more on that later!

"Meeting Bjorn and the Bad Taste guys was great. When we saw the boxes and boxes of demo tapes that were lying about, it made us realise how lucky we must have been to get pulled out of the bag and then for Bad Taste to actually like us, especially at the time when Millencolin and the Satanic Surfers were making such headway in Sweden and the rest of Europe, well…

"The festival was, at the time, the biggest gig we had ever played as a band or as individuals. The Satanic Surfers were the headline band and the crowd obviously went nuts for them, but we did okay too. I guess it was all Bad Taste bands, so people coming to the show would pretty much know all the bands playing, seeing as it was the label's hometown. It wasn't until we saw the reception that the Surfers got that we realised, for an unknown band, playing their first European gig for their European label, we went down okay. What probably made it even more special was that we had only really played a handful of gigs before that one; we signed to Bad Taste after only playing four gigs! I guess they liked us, though, as they put us out on several full tours of Europe after that…"

The first of those tours was the Flying High Across The Sky package tour in May 1997, with Millencolin, SNFU, Voodoo Glow Skulls, 3 Colours Red and Thumb. Turtlehead were a last-minute addition to the bill when DFL pulled out and only had two weeks to make the necessary arrangements – but were glad they jumped at the opportunity.

"We actually ended up only doing the German dates on that tour," explains Robert. "But it was our first taste of playing large venues, our first taste of stage times and being at the side ready to go on five minutes before our slot, our first time of having to play within our time limit and 'You do *not* go over!' We used Millencolin's gear for the whole tour, as well as their sound-guy who was kind enough to do us. We also shared their tour bus, so that was cool; those guys taught us a lot.

"It hit home about then the step-up that bands make when they get to the level that Millencolin were at; we were still 'back room of a pub' mentality and the transition was huge. We played first every night; again, possibly the hardest slot as most of the folk were there to see the other bands. Millencolin had, I think, went gold with their album 'Four Monkeys' and Thumb were a pretty big deal in their native Germany. Still, probably one of the nicest moments during that tour was when Millencolin's road manager came up to us and said, 'You guys are the most punk rock band on this tour…' I think our DIY approach was still very apparent to everyone!

"The only negative about that tour was that it kinda ruined us in a way, as we knew that it was never going to last, playing those kind of gigs; something we had tasted once, would forever spend the rest of our time chasing but never quite getting there again…"

A much longer (25 gigs across eight countries), albeit lower-key, European tour was undertaken during October 1997 with labelmates Pridebowl and as soon as they got home, Turtlehead were back in the studio recording their sophomore album. The brilliantly-entitled 'I Preferred Their Earlier Stuff' was released the following year and demonstrated that the band's extensive time on the road with some of the world's best melodic hardcore bands had certainly rubbed off on their songwriting. The band promoted it the only way they knew how, by hitting the road again, including a hefty 30-gig/10-country stint with the 1999 Bad Taste Tour, alongside the Almighty Trigger Happy from Canada, Misconduct and, for certain dates, Astream and Within Reach. However, chinks were starting to appear in the band's armour and Gary was replaced on guitar by Dave McIntosh, from Falkirk bands Godsend and Shatterhand, upon their return.

"Gary's leaving was a slow build-up in my eyes," sighs Robert. "It goes back to the point I made earlier about chasing but never getting there. The tour was okay, although some of the gigs were sparsely attended and I think this got to Gary; he maybe thought that we were bigger than we were. I also think that being cooped up on a bus with another band or two for five weeks didn't do him any favours. I can only speak for myself here, but I'm sure the others felt the same; we all knew (bar Gary, it seems) that what we had had on the Millencolin tour was unlikely to happen again anytime soon. We had lucked out big time with that; we knew that it was back to the van, or bus in this case and playing in pubs again – but these pubs were in Europe and that made it a hell of a lot better to our minds.

"During the tour, Gary even started travelling with Astream when they were on the bill, a sure sign that something was wrong... Paul also noticed that Brian and Gary hardly ever spoke to each other; we weren't hanging out like we used to and the gang mentality we had had was starting to fall apart. Brian, Paul and myself spoke at length about it and it was decided that, when we got back, Gary was out. But prior to that moment and probably quickening his exit, he then blew up during a gig and threw his guitar at me after a song, stating that we had played it too fast, even though we played it exactly the speed we always used to. Our label's head honcho was in attendance that night as well; I imagine it didn't look good."

The next line-up casualty was Paul, who left just two days before the band's Canadian tour during the summer of 2000, finally admitting that he was afraid of flying and unable to face the long journey over there. Despite having to teach the promoter's French-speaking friend the bass-lines the day before the first gig there, the two-week tour was still a great success, culminating in an appearance at the Revel'n'Ment festival in Quebec City in front of 5,000 paying punters.

"The Canadian tour was actually more a tour of Quebec," reckons Robert. "I think it was 10 dates in 14 days. The other bands were Leisure Sports and GFK; GFK were pretty big and very involved in the local scene, so it meant the turn-outs were pretty decent, while Leisure Sports were from California and were a great bunch of guys to share a tour with.

"We toured on a yellow school bus, complete with emergency axe in the front; it was just like the bus that Otto drives in *The Simpsons*... In fact, the driver was just a French-Canadian version of him, who didn't speak a word of English the whole tour. Some of the locals in the northern parts of Quebec *refuse* to speak English at all; even if you asked them a question in English, they would reply in French. It was kinda weird, as you always think of Canada as being an English-speaking country...

"Anyway, apart from the whole Paul scenario, it has to be said that Guttermouth were complete dicks. They were the headliners at the Revel'n'Ment festival; the bands' changing room/gear storage area was a communal one, for all the bands playing – except Guttermouth, who didn't want anyone in the same room as them when they were in there. As soon as they arrived, they kicked up a fuss and all the other bands had to leave. I should add that the changing room was a basketball court, as the festival was in the grounds of a college, so that gives you an idea of the size of the room and how big a bunch of dicks Guttermouth were. They were crap live as well."

Back in Scotland again, Turtlehead recruited new bassist Richard Bruce, whose fondness of playing chords allowed their 'til-then-simmering-under Face To Face influences to really come to the fore and soon the band were off on yet another European tour, this time for five weeks with US band, Digger. Work then began in earnest writing a new album to showcase their new, improved sound, but 'Burning Hearts And Burnouts', as it ended up being called, wouldn't see the light of day until March 2003, due to the band being dropped by Bad Taste. Instead Robert started his own Leatherback Records to release it, funding the entire thing himself, but unfortunately Turtlehead split soon after its release, before they even had chance to properly promote it. That is a crying shame as it was their best album by far – more urgent, more melodic and more mature than their Nineties output.

"The writing was on the wall for a while, to be honest and we were starting to flog a dead horse," admits Robert. "We played a gig in Kirriemuir, birthplace of Bon Scott, and I think three folk showed up… That was one of our last gigs; it seemed people had moved on and we needed to as well.

"However, with the release of the third album, I had booked a 10-day tour of the UK to promote it and try to shift some of the boxes of CDs in my house. We had been planning the tour for about six months; everything was in place and all systems were go for the first date… Dave then announced that he couldn't get time off his work. This was, I think, one week before the tour and rather than cancel the tour, I sacked him. We had another guy lined up, all ready to step in and learn the songs there and then, when Brian called and said he too was quitting, as he didn't want to lose his friends in Falkirk… I was kinda raging at this point; I had stuck a whole load of money into the album, spent hours booking a tour for us to go out on and then that happened. Rich and I decided that was it; Turtlehead was over."

Although they cancelled the UK tour, one final gig, too good to turn down, *was* undertaken and thankfully they laid the band to rest in a respectable fashion. "We had one last gig arranged, to support Leatherface and Handgun Bravado. After a meeting between Dave, Brian, Rich and myself, we all agreed to do it. It would be the last ever Turtlehead gig and yes, it seemed a fitting send-off, supporting one of the greatest British punk bands and one that had influenced me greatly.

"We had a couple of very tense rehearsals and the atmosphere wasn't great; the camp had split into Dave and Brian on one side, Rich and myself on the other. Still, we managed to get through them and the gig itself was great. It was in Bannermans, Edinburgh, so it was local to me and a lot of old faces showed up, including the guitarist from an early band I was in, whose comment was, 'I've never seen so much tension on a stage before!' It was a sell-out, we played pretty well and it was a relief to get through it; I was sad it was our last gig and sad that a load of new songs would never be recorded, but immensely proud of what we'd achieved in the lifetime of the band. It was also great to play with Handgun Bravado; Colin Sears of Dag Nasty fame was the drummer…star struck, ahoy! And Leatherface were just Leatherface: exceptional. It was also the last time I ever saw Brian; our paths have never crossed since and we've never kept in touch."

Robert and Richard formed one of Scotland's very few 'true' SXE bands, I Stand Alone, with Iain from Intake on guitar and tattoo artist Soap on vocals; they did a split 7-inch with Handgun Bravado in 2006 on Dent All Records and several self-released CDEPs before calling it a day, although Robert and Rich still play together to this day in Moonshine Docks.

"I would like to think that we played a part in the ever-expanding British punk sound and scene and helped keep the flag flying high for British punk," says Robert, of his time with Turtlehead. "Hopefully a few folk got inspired by what we did and gave it a shot themselves, but how folk really remember us, I'm unsure…we played at a time when I feel the UK scene had many great bands, like Consumed, Vanilla Pod, One Car Pileup, Beauty School Dropout and Four Letter Word, to name but a few. And all of them, in my eyes, were way better than Turtlehead! I think what set us apart was the fact we ended up on a European label and played in Europe more times than we played in the UK. I wouldn't change any of it, I had such a great time; there were many lows, but the highs always outnumbered them and I have memories and stories I'll remember for the rest of my life…"

SELECT DISCOGRAPHY:

CDEP:
'Go!' (Bad Taste, 1996)

CD albums:
'Back Slapping Praise From Back Stabbing Men' (Bad Taste, 1996)
'I Preferred Their Earlier Stuff' (Bad Taste, 1998)
'Bleeding Hearts And Burnouts' (Leatherback, 2003)

AT A GLANCE:
The third album is the best and I'm sure Robert is still keen to shift them. Contact him at: xsideshowx@hotmail.co.uk

BLOODSHOT

Aberdeen's **Bloodshot** were one of those – many – bands that never released anything on vinyl in their own right, yet through their sheer determination and belief in the DIY ethics that provide the unshakeable foundation upon which hardcore and punk rock have thrived, they not only brought some incredible bands to play in their remote corner of the world, but landed themselves several tours of the UK and Europe. These are the unsung bands that shaded the UK scene of the Nineties so many intriguing hues…

"We formed in Aberdeen around 1993, but myself and Fraser [MacDonald] had played in bands together on and off since 1987," explains Bloodshot's second vocalist, Mark Nelson, of his first band, ISM. "The first band we had together was Fischtanke, when we were living in the tiny Northeastern town of Ellon, where we happened upon a very talented American singer/guitarist called Dylan. We managed to make one demo [unofficially entitled 'FT'] in the hardcore/crossover vein and do one gig before Dylan moved to Bahrain, as his stepfather was in the US Navy.

"After that we started Grunge in 1988, quite an unfortunate name in hindsight but we were a grindcore band that played a few shows including a support to Napalm Death in Edinburgh when 'From Enslavement…' came out; we were all about 17 then. The Grunge bassist, Morag, left to join Oi Polloi [and appears on their 'Omnicide' 7-inch]; after that, I went and lived in Liverpool for a year or two. I was in an early incarnation of the death-metal band Devoid…and Carlos, who replaced me on guitar, ended up in Carcass. I also played with a squat-punk band called Lemon Baby Sick, with Rag from MDM and a few others; we did a few gigs and one demo… That would have been around 1989 or 1990."

Once relocated to Aberdeen, Mark and Fraser wanted to play fast, intense hardcore like Infest, Crossed Out and early Rupture, so, with Fraser drumming and Mark handling everything else, ISM was born. It was a studio-only project that recorded four demos of raging fastcore in local studio Fluxus, the best of which was probably 1994's 'Hostility Breeds' with its quite hilarious ode to Discharge, 'Mania For Sosmix'!

"The reason ISM never did any gigs is because we were like Dark Throne," laughs Mark. "We used to get offered gigs and did even consider doing some of them, but felt we just wouldn't go down too well. Power violence was not very popular in our neck of the woods at the time – everyone preferred more traditional punk bands like Toxik Ephex – and we kinda liked the freedom of just doing studio projects. After all, we make music for ourselves, not to impress our peers…although we used to like donating tracks to some of the many benefit compilation tapes around at the time."

Meanwhile, while ISM went on to record a demo each year until 1997 (Mark handling all the instruments on '95's 'Consumerism', because Fraser had moved to Hong Kong…), a band called Bloodshot were forming from the ashes of thrash-metal act Malevolence in the small town of Turriff to the Northeast. Comprising Kevin 'Maggots' Gray on guitar, Duane Ager on bass and Jake 'Skater' Thurlow on drums, they recorded a self-titled demo, that was rather pleasingly in the vein of Sheffield's Mau Maus, onto four-track tape in their rehearsal room and played a few local gigs before they asked Mark to join on vocals.

"I wasn't at the first **Bloodshot** gig because it was in Turriff, which is bloody miles away," he admits. "And it was with the Damned, so I wasn't really fussed. I know they had a good time though because they ate all of the Damned's sandwiches while they were soundchecking! They also played with the English Dogs up there, but I think the first time I saw them play was when I put them on with Citizen Fish, Bender and Diatribe at the Pelican Club in Aberdeen. They contacted me after Rags, who was then Duane's partner, bought an ISM tape and later asked me to sing…"

After playing a few gigs where he sang alongside the original Bloodshot vocalist (another Mark: Mark Wilson), Mark Nelson's first gig fronting the band on his own was opening up the 1995 Dunnichen Hill free festival, an infamously troublesome gathering that saw revellers clashing violently with police and was even mentioned in the House Of Lords during their Criminal Justice And Public Order Act debate. "Yeah, my joining was a gradual process, but as time went on I began to write songs and lyrics, as did Duane. I think I brought a more political angle to the band (a lot of people would've have called me an uptight PC vegan) as well as some more thrashy tunes into the mix. I would usually make a point about the subject

Bloodshot, somewhere in Germany

Bloodshot, live at the Edinburgh City Of Punk festival 1995

of songs when introducing them too, something often sadly lacking in today's scenes."

A second demo was recorded, again at Duane's cottage in Turriff; 'Who Writes The News?' contained six songs and was much faster, more metallic and opinionated, displaying a more USHC feel in many places and made the band's first recording sound rather pedestrian by comparison. The band really got behind it and sold – or more likely *traded* – literally hundreds of copies to all corners of the world. Polish cassette label Truja Falca bundled both demos together for an official release and Bloodshot headed out to Europe not once, but three times, to 'promote' it (at risk of making them sound like the corporate whores that pass for punk bands these days, which they weren't!)

"We were still one of the first UK bands to go to Poland," reckons Mark, "so it was amazing the reception we got; we were even in the papers and stuff. The second time we went over we toured Germany with PNET 95, but the third time was the total winner for me, playing in Switzerland, Czech Republic, Poland, Germany and Belgium. It was all done through the underground; we did a lot of reciprocal gigs for bands we played with, like a UK tour with the Berlin band HAF and two UK tours with Scatha. Along the way we got to play with many great bands like Homo Militia, Post Regiment and Aus Rotten…

"There are far too many highs and lows to try and remember them all; we played so many great places, like a squatted five-star hotel in Lucerne, Switzerland, marvelling at the view of the beautiful lake and mountains, or the shop they squatted for the night in Winterthur… all the gear was brought in by hand-pulled carts and passed through a window! Some of the kids that put that show on actually got jail time for their efforts! I remember playing the biggest gig we ever did, with Dezerter and during our set the organiser gets up on stage to announce, 'The Nazis are outside, everybody stay here and don't do anything!' Of course, all 1,000 punks in attendance went storming outside and there was a huge street fight between the punks, Nazis and police. And I'll never forget the time someone went for a shit in a very full chemical toilet at the 007 in Prague and, ahem, accidentally dipped their balls in the foul mess…naming no names!

"Or, a bit nearer to home, when we played the White Horse in High Wycombe, the landlord saw one of us drinking a beer in the back of the van – before the venue was even open! – so, at the end of the night, he refused to pay us the agreed amount. 'Somebody' happened to 'find' their dry ice machine and we made our money back and a band that *might* be called Cress got a real bargain as a result…!"

Two songs from the demo, 'Man Eats House' and 'Do I Not Bleed', appeared on the 1996 Looney Tunes compilation, 'A Scream From The Silence, Volume Four', but Bloodshot split up soon after their third trip to Europe, playing their last gig at the Zoro squat in Leipzig during September 1997.

"It was a great ending to the band, though," smiles Mark. "The place was getting evicted the next day, so there was a massive party and everyone smashed it up! I don't really know why we split up, to be honest; I think that, by the end of the last European tour, we'd all had enough. Enough of the songs and enough of each other! We were also onto our third guitarist by then [Paul 'Zoff' Ross, previously with Broccoli, who would later play with Engage] and maybe there were some personal tensions brewing…"

Mark and Jake had already collaborated on the fourth ISM demo, 'Number…Out Of 50' and with Bloodshot grinding to a halt in Autumn '97, they teamed up with Melanie Whittle from Aktifist for the bloodcurdlingly vicious Slain. This was a much noisier affair than Bloodshot, with the heavily distorted guitars and rampant blast beats providing a perfect backdrop for Melanie's brutal vocal attack. The 14-song '…In Blood' demo brought them to the attention of Andy at Smack In The Mouth Records, who released a 13-track EP split between Slain and Preston's State Of Filth in 1998.

"Musically and aesthetically it was worlds apart from Bloodshot," agrees Mark. "We were massively into stuff like Dystopia, His Hero Is Gone, Japanese hardcore and lots of metal. My fondest memories of Slain are some of the gigs though…the tour with Resisters was great fun and we always loved playing with Shank and Ebola etc. I suppose the real highlight for all of us was playing with His Hero Is Gone (and John Holmes) in Glasgow [at the 13th Note, on 13 June 1998].

"We also liked to make fun of how the scene had become so much about style over content, so, for instance, we would have a raging song called 'Nothing Left To Say' and just scream "Nothing! Nothing!' over and over again – and people would like it! We also did a one-off demo called 'Aggressive Swan Attack' and sent a few copies around; someone actually offered to release it! And that was when we decided to call it a day…"

Straight after Slain, Mark and Melanie hooked up with Lee Thompson, who had been the second Bloodshot guitarist (after Maggots and before Zoff!) and Tracey Fallon from Quarantine for Miles Apart (not to be confused with the many other hardcore bands of the same name from Europe, America and Australia!) who played half a dozen gigs and recorded one demo. Lee now drums for a popular indie act, Camera Obscura, while Melanie is a teacher and fronts folk band the Hermit Crabs.

Meanwhile, Jake went on to play with Ebola, as did Duane; the latter also did a stint with Eradicate and is now a professor of microbiology in Oxford ("Not bad for someone who used to sleep in a railway tunnel and eat dog food curry!" laughs Mark). As mentioned earlier, Fraser, the first ISM drummer, moved to Hong Kong and although he's back in Scotland now, is no longer a part of ISM, the drums on their brand new three-track 'Terminal Health' 7-inch for Problem? Records having been handled by Tommy from popular Glasgow thrashers Atomgevitter.

"I very much doubt that ISM, Bloodshot or Slain will ever really be remembered in the grand scheme of things," offers Mark, who has since also done time with Svartskit, Cobra The Enemy and Power Wolf (*not* the Hungarian metal band!) "However, I am very flattered and embarrassed when I go to a friend's house and they tell me, 'I still listen to Bloodshot every week; your lyrics changed my life!' I don't honestly know what I think about that, but I hope that some of the kids we played to in Poland where no foreign band had ever played before remembers the gig. I hope some of my lyrics inspired at least some thought for somebody, somewhere. I don't think anything really set us apart from our peers, though, but I hope through our hard work we inspired a few folk in our neck of the woods in some small way.

"If nothing else, it would be nice to be remembered for bringing awesome bands like Drop Dead, Los Crudos, Cress, Active Minds and Quarantine to old Aberdeen. It was all worth it, even fighting with jitters over microphones, stopping two people trying to steal a huge sofa from the venue 'for their van' and Headache somehow breaking the floor of Cellar 35, getting us banned. Anyway, there's always a new wave of punks coming through, doing it themselves; it's happening now and probably always will…"

SELECT DISCOGRAPHY:

7-inch:
'Split' (Smack In The Mouth, 1998) – *as Slain, split with State Of Filth*

AT A GLANCE:
No doubt Mark can be persuaded to copy you the best of ISM, Bloodshot and Slain, if you cover his costs: markaroonie@hotmail.com

CHAPTER TEN: IRELAND

THERAPY?

Oh, stop your bitchin' and moanin'; if you don't think **Therapy?** should be in this book you probably don't know enough about Therapy? And if that's not reason enough in itself to include them, I don't know what is. They went from making ambitious-yet-humble DIY noises in Larne, County Antrim, to being one of the biggest rock bands in the UK, selling over a million copies of their most successful album, 'Troublegum' – all without losing their self-deprecating sense of humour.

"I met [drummer] Fyfe [Ewing] at a charity gig at Jordanstown University," begins guitarist/vocalist Andy Cairns. "He was playing in a band called the League Of Decency and I was with a group called Crash Into June; I noticed them as soon as they started playing a cover of 'California Uber Alles' by the Dead Kennedys. I thought Fyfe was an amazing drummer and got chatting to him afterwards. The band I was in was a sort of Miracle Legion/garage rock-style troupe; we did a cover of 'Dead Set On Destruction' by Hüsker Dü and talking to Fyfe it soon became apparent that we both wanted to move more towards the kind of music we were currently listening to.

"We were very open-minded and I suppose we were looking for a freedom to experiment. When we eventually started getting together to try out ideas we would meet in Fyfe's house in Larne while his Dad was at work. We were both so obsessed with music, we were into so much stuff; off the top of my head, I remember we would listen to Big Black, The Membranes, Captain Beefheart, Sonic Youth, Minor Threat, Funkadelic, Die Kreuzen, Operation Ivy, Squirrel Bait, Snuff, James Brown, Minutemen, NWA, Public Enemy, Silverfish, Stretcheads, Stooges, MC5 and Ruts…also lots of early acid house and especially Belgian new beat, which we loved. The Irish punk scene was always present as well; my bag tended to be Rudi and the Outcasts and we both loved SLF and the Undertones. FUAL, Pink Turds In Space, LMS and Strontium Dogs were probably our faves from the then-current local scene…"

Recording their first demo, 'Thirty Seconds Of Silence', as just a two-piece, the band soon recruited Michael McKeegan from local metal band, Evil Priest, whom Fyfe knew from school. "Yeah, I was at school with Fyfe," confirms Michael. "And while we weren't *really* good friends at that stage, we knew of each other's bands and usually swapped or borrowed records and tapes from each other. I'd loan him 'Pleasure To Kill' [by German thrash-metallers Kreator] and he'd fire me 'Bedtime For Democracy' [Dead Kennedys] in return. Bizarrely our English

Therapy?, Leeds 1991

Therapy? drummer, Fyfe

Therapy?, Michael

Therapy? on the road

Therapy?, Andy Cairns

teacher, Mr Christe, was really into music and he would lend us Pere Ubu and Ramones records as well, so the pair of us got well schooled indeed.

"Anyway, Fyfe mentioned one day that he had started a new band with this guy from Ballyclare; the two of them were due to record a studio demo and he wondered if they could borrow my bass guitar to use on the session. I remember him bringing in a 'rough mix' of the demo and playing it to me on a cassette Walkman; it absolutely floored me how good it was…really well played, well recorded and really exciting, catchy songs. I was insanely jealous, as Evil Priest was still at the 'let's stick some riffs together and record them on a boom box' stage. Luckily they needed someone to play bass for a live show and I went up to meet Andy and practise with them; we all got on great and it sounded pretty good, so it was quite a simple, easy getting-together."

Therapy? made their live debut on 20 August 1989, supporting Decadence Within in the Conor Hall of Belfast Art College. "We were really nervous and watched Hüsker Dü and Minor Threat live videos before we headed to the gig," laughs Andy. "So we consequently tore through the set with more energy than we intended. The Decadence guys were really great; not just on stage, but after as well. I remember being made up when one of them told me my guitar sound was like Bill Nelson in Be Bop Deluxe; I don't know if they meant it as a compliment, but I certainly took it as one. Ah, the Boss chorus pedal – many a musical crime has been committed under your spell!

"At that point in time, Giros [the legendary Belfast punk venue] was the most important place in the world for us," he continues. "The only other places were the Limelight and the Rosetta Rock Bar. The Limelight was such an indie clique that you had no chance of getting in there without the right haircut, while the Rosetta liked our first demo tape and were going to offer us a gig supporting Candlemass, but when they found out we had short hair they withdrew the offer…I kid you not."

"I have mixed feelings about Giros," admits Michael. "Obviously it was a massively important part of the start of Therapy?; they embraced us as a band at a time when we were deemed 'too heavy' for the indie clubs and 'too weird' for the metal ones. Of course, with any kind of group that dedicated and insular in a way, a lot of petty jealousy and the like came about; I think in a way we were perceived as 'hicks from the sticks', which didn't sit too well with some of the more self-styled 'cool brigade' there and it did lead to some pretty ridiculous incidents. It was literally a case of, 'Oh my god, he's bought a guitar tuner; we'll have to have a meeting and discuss if he's still 'punk' enough for us…!'

"Ironically a lot of the more judgemental characters I still see around town and they all seem to be doing the 'suit and tie' thing these days – a long way away from their younger idealistic selves. However, the true hardcore heart of Giros and the Warzone collective are still there and I absolutely respect them for showing their support for us in the early days and for their dedication to local and international touring bands over the years.

"There were a ton of great bands around; Strontium Dog were a particular favourite, along with DFA, who were a bit more left of centre with a drum machine and Big Black-esque guitars. Then you had FUAL, Pink Turds In Space, Jobbycrust, Bleeding Rectum a bit later on, plus all the Irish bands who'd come up to play, like Not Our World, Pig Ignorance and Three Ring Psychosis."

Encouraged by the response to their early gigs (most people who saw them acknowledged they were destined for 'greater things' even then), Therapy? recorded a second demo, this time with Michael actually playing the bass guitar he had previously loaned them. This brought them to the attention of Words Of Warning Records in South Wales, who included the song 'Bloody Blue' on their 'Mind Pollution' compilation.

"Of the two, I'm still very fond of the first one," comments Andy, of the early demos. "Within seconds of the first tune starting, we'd referenced Motörhead, John Coltrane and early rockabilly and by the last track we were sampling Beefheart and Steve Albini. I remember it took about a day to record and an afternoon to mix; we did it on an eight-track in an attic on the Lisburn Road, Belfast…it was the, ahem, 'studio' of one Colin Muinzer, who used to be in a glam band called Cruella De Ville! "The second one was a wee bit more in thrall to Hüsker Dü and Fugazi, but there's a great 'Taxi Driver'-influenced tune on there called 'Here Is'. We pressed up the 'Thirty Seconds…' tape and passed it round the usual tape circles and sold it at gigs, of course. The cover had a xerox of Dennis Hopper in *Blue Velvet* on it. I think we may have actually tried to send him a copy too, tho' feck knows how we would have got his address…"

"Both of the demos got great feedback from anyone who heard them," reckons Michael, "and they opened the doors for a lot more gigging opportunities and even got us a bit of play on local radio. I'm a big fan of the first demo especially; I think it's a real statement of intent…all nine minutes of it! The second one is a bit cleaner-sounding, so some of the power of the songs is lacking. There's actually an early version of 'Screamager' on there too, which is definitely worth a listen; it's entitled 'SWT', which stands for 'spide with tache', which is how the more terrifying, aggressive 'casuals' were known in late Eighties Belfast… most had spider-web tattoos hence the 'spide' tag."

In true DIY fashion, Therapy? then issued their own 7-inch – the heaving, hypnotic 'Meat Abstract' b/w 'Punishment Kiss' – on their own Multifuckingnational label in 1990. "At the time, none of the record labels had any interest in bands from Northern Ireland," explains Michael. "And we always had a dream of our own 7-inch piece of vinyl nestling up on the racks in Caroline Music, which was the best record store in town. That was pretty much the ambition and seeing as no-one else wanted to release it, we formed Multifuckingnational, named after a song from the second demo ['Multi Fuck'] and saved up, recorded two tracks and then eventually got 1,000 copies pressed up.

"Everything was *total* DIY at that stage; there was no 'alternative music scene' at that time…bear in mind that, in Ireland about then, U2 ruled the world. There was no 'music industry' save for the remnants of the glorious Good Vibes days and most people's idea of aggressive guitar music was Guns N'Roses or Aerosmith. As a result, most bands we knew just did it themselves…recorded cheap, did the artwork cheap, got some tapes or a 7-inch printed up, mailed them out to fanzines and hoped to book some shows."

"We knew the only way to get a record out was to do it ourselves," affirms Andy. "We'd seen the way the Good Vibes bands had done it and especially the Crass lot. We all saved like mad, chipped in and pressed it up and then folded the sleeves in my mum's kitchen while having toast and coffee!"

The single was limited to 1,000 copies, but there was a definite buzz building around the band and their commanding live performances and soon they were signing to Wiiija (the uber-cool London label based out of Rough Trade in Notting Hill and named after the shop's postcode, W11 1JA) for 1991's 'Babyteeth' and 1992's 'Pleasure Death' MLPs.

"We weren't aware of a buzz as such," offers Andy, modestly. "But we did seem to stand out from a lot of other bands because we didn't look like *anyone's* idea of a band. A slightly chubby guy on guitar with face-fuzz, a taciturn bean-pole drummer and a bouncy bassist who looked about 12. Besides we were all from Larne and Ballyclare, which was definitely not cool at all, especially in Belfast.

"And not all the gigs were memorable for the right reasons! The worst was Magee College, Derry, where we'd been booked at a Gaelic Football night. There were about 50 lads in GAA tops and stonewashed jeans staring at the stage; we opened with 'Punishment Kiss' straight into 'Meat Abstract'. At the end of the second tune there was total silence until a bloke approached the stage, pint in hand, leant over the monitors and in a very country accent enquired, 'Do you know any ZZ Top?'"

"Another bad one was on our first UK tour," adds Michael, "when we played the Bradford 1 In 12, which was a big deal for us really, as it was pretty legendary in our eyes. Ironically, only 12 people turned up…

"But 'Babyteeth' was basically our live set at that time. We'd been working on the songs for a while and had a few of them on the earlier demos…from what I recall we were really excited to be recording the newer songs like 'Innocent X', 'Loser Cop' and 'Dancin' With Manson', as we'd had a few ideas for the sounds, samples and general production. Also we'd saved up, so we could use Northern Ireland's 'premier' studio, Homestead and that was a big deal…they were mostly known for country and western, but the owner/engineer Mudd Wallace was into what we were doing and had cut us a special rate if we recorded through the night when the studio wasn't being used.

"I'm not sure of the exact dates, but we did the single ['Meat Abstract'] in one session, then, a few months later, we did the other tracks between Christmas and New Year 1990-91. The sessions were great as Mudd was pretty much up for any idea – however silly – that we had. He even hooked up the studio telephone system so we could get a Bad Brains 'Sacred Love'-style vocal effect for 'Innocent X' and let us tear away with his amps, guitars and pianos for the overdubs on 'Loser Cop'. Talking of 'Loser Cop', the saxophonist Keith Thompson's nerves got the better of him so, after a bottle of tequila, he ended up passed out in the studio jacuzzi (which was empty, by the way!) on his alleged first day of tracking; the poor guy did his stuff the next morning horribly hung-over.

"But, as debuts go, I'm still really happy with it…we'd a lot of ambition musically and we really went for it, despite limited time, budget and experience. It's definitely one of my favourite Therapy? albums."

Early 1992 saw Nirvana's 'Nevermind' unexpectedly topping the *Billboard* charts in the US and guitar-driven alternative rock music, soon to be dubbed 'grunge', was suddenly very hot property and the subsequent major-label interest in what was previously a niche sub-genre opened even more doors for Therapy?, who signed to A&M for 1992's rather uncompromising 'Nurse' LP. Not that they owed their success to a scene exploding out of the Pacific Northwest; they'd also been touring their arses off with the likes of Silverfish, NoMeansNo, Babes In Toyland, Tad and Hole and proving their worth the old-fashioned way, on the road.

"We were a bit conflicted at first, having come from that DIY scene," admits Michael, of inking with a major, "but at the time we literally didn't have money to *eat,* let alone buy drum skins or guitar strings. Out of all the majors that approached us during that period, A&M seemed the most 'sane'; an A&R guy from another label trying to sign us once came to a gig in Hamburg and after the show suggested that he'd pay for some hookers on the condition we would shag them while he watched…true story! A&M were also the most into letting us choose our own path. In the end we went with them for a lot less money but a lot more artistic control, which worked to our benefit over the years.

"The best thing about the major deal was that we could finally get some new equipment and get the sonics of the band up to where we wanted them to be; reliable amps and guitars that stayed in tune were a luxury prior to that. Also, the fact people could actually buy the records in shops on the day of release was heartening and we made it out to America and a few other far-flung places where we had small but dedicated fanbases.

"Most people in the local scene were pretty supportive too, although obviously there was a lot of chat about 'selling out' and all that, but that was always going to happen. What did piss me off is that quite a few people had made their judgement even before 'Nurse' [the aforementioned major-label debut] had been recorded. Ironically it's probably one of our more abrasive, industrial-sounding records, with some quite weird-sounding songs on there [listen to 'Deep Sleep', if you don't believe him, folks!]"

Over the next three years, with singles like 'Nowhere' and 'Trigger Inside', EPs like 'Shortsharpshock' and 'Face The Strange' and albums like 1994's monumental 'Troublegum' (still one of the most *consistently* great rock albums to ever emerge from the UK, it has patiently racked up sales in excess of one million) and '95's sublime 'Infernal Love', Therapy? came into their own as being able to seamlessly blend metallic rock and dark gothic pop into ludicrously catchy, unpretentious anthems.

"In terms of sales and raising awareness of the band, it's definitely our biggest commercial success," says Michael, carefully, of 'Troublegum'. "But I certainly wouldn't say it's the definitive Therapy? album, although I do think it's the first one where the songwriting, the production and the musical climate all came together. At that stage, I feel people were ready for a record like that and we nailed it musically.

"I'm still really, really proud of that record too; I think it probably *is* a classic record and I can honestly say there is a constant stream of compliments on it from musicians, be they professional or amateur. The fact that it touched so many people around the world is amazing; as an artist that's the sort of thing you dream about…"

"And I was fine with being on *Top Of The Pops*," adds Andy, proudly. "It's where I'd seen the Buzzcocks, the Undertones, the Damned and Motörhead for the first time. We ended up being on the show quite a few times, but the awful reality was that recording it and miming to a bunch of bussed-in kids was not as glamourous a time as I'd imagined it to be when I saw Pete Shelley singing 'Ever Fallen In Love…' on the show! "But yeah, 'Troublegum' has a bunch of great songs on it and is probably the album that owes most to hearing Ulster punk as a kid. There's the Undertones in 'Screamager', SLF in 'Nowhere', the Outcasts in 'Die Laughing' and some Rudi-style riffing in 'Stop It, You're Killing Me'. People still love that record a lot and it *did* open doors for us worldwide; I suppose if we were going to be remembered for just one record, it could be a lot worse…"

The endless touring and promotional duties took their toll though and Fyfe left the band in 1996, being replaced behind the kit by Graham Hopkins. Guest cellist Martin McCarrick also joined as a permanent member, although it was to be several years before the band's next album, 'Semi-Detached', was ready and it was to be their last for A&M, it being decidedly more ominous than 'Infernal Love' and lacking the radio hits of 'Troublegum'. Moving outside the Nineties and the scope of this book, Therapy? remain a potent musical force to this day, not to mention thoroughly decent, hard-working approachable chaps who have never lost sight of their humble origins in the 'Norn Iron' post-punk scene.

"That's really hard," sighs Michael, when asked to sum up the band's career in just one word. "But looking back at the 17 years since 'Troublegum', I'd have to say *passion*. We could've made 'TG Parts 1, 2 & 3' since, or done the old 'split up/reform' routine, but at the end of the day we love playing, we love music and we love trying to evolve. Sometimes things click better than others on certain albums, but to be honest I'm pretty content with all the 'post-TG' stuff. 'Infernal Love', 'Suicide Pact – You First', 'Never Apologise Never Explain' and 'Crooked Timber' all rate pretty highly for me. 'One Cure Fits All' is maybe the one I'm not sure about... I think the actual production lets that down, though; the songs themselves are really good.

"We could easily have manufactured certain things to claw a bit more commercial potential, or jumped on the odd bandwagon here or there...maybe even rewrote history a bit like some bands do, but I feel we are way too honest and have too much integrity and respect for our band and fans. I think for better or worse we always did 'our' thing and that makes me very content at the end of the day..."

"I just think I'd like to be remembered as people who genuinely loved music for music's sake," exclaims Andy. "And without the noise/punk scene of the late Eighties and early Nineties, we wouldn't exist. Being inspired by the first wave of Ulster punk, doing Giros shows, meeting and staying in touch with other like-minded people and doing our own record because no other fecker out there would touch us – it all adds up."

SELECT DISCOGRAPHY:

7-inch:

'Meat Abstract' (Multifuckingnational, 1990)

'Teethgrinder' (A&M, 1992)

'Have A Merry Fucking Christmas' (A&M, 1992)

'Shortsharpshock' EP (A&M, 1993)

'Opal Mantra' (A&M, 1993)

'Face The Strange' EP (A&M, 1993)

'Screamager' (A&M, 1993)

'Perversonality' (A&M, 1993)

'Trigger Inside' (A&M, 1994)

'Nowhere' (A&M, 1994)

'Die Laughing' (A&M, 1994)

'Isolation' (A&M, 1994)

'Knives' (A&M, 1994)

'Stories' (A&M, 1995)

'Diane' (A&M, 1995)

'Bad Mother' (A&M, 1996)

'Church Of Noise' (A&M, 1998)

'Hate Kill Destroy' (Ark 21, 2000)

'Gimme Back My Brain' (Ark 21, 2001)

'If It Kills Me' (Spitfire, 2003)
'Rain Hits Concrete' (Spitfire, 2006)
'Crooked Timber' (DR2, 2009)

MLPs:
'Babyteeth' (Wiiija, 1991)
'Pleasure Death' (Wiiija, 1992)
'Born In A Crash' (A&M, 1993)

LPs:
'Nurse' (A&M, 1992)
'Troublegum' (A&M, 1994)
'Infernal Love' (A&M, 1995)
'Semi-Detached' (A&M, 1998)
'Suicide Pact – You First' (Ark 21, 1999)
'Shameless' (Ark 21, 2001)
'High Anxiety' (Spitfire, 2003)
'Never Apologise, Never Explain' (Spitfire, 2004)
'One Cure Fits All' (Spitfire, 2006)
'Crooked Timber' (DR2, 2009)

AT A GLANCE:
'So Much For The Ten Year Plan: A Retrospective, 1990-2000' (Ark 21) is just what you'd imagine from the title, although the 'Scopophobia' DVD (Eagle Rock, 2003) also has a great track-listing spanning the band's career highlights (but only up until 2003, of course).

JOBBYKRUST

Don't be put off by the crappy name, Belfast's **Jobbykrust** were a bitingly intense punk band, right up there with Toxic Waste or Pink Turds In Space, their turbulent sound unequivocally informed by the Northern Ireland Troubles that the band members grew up with. Formed in Rathcoole, a housing estate north of Belfast, during 1990 by guitarist Tim McAteer and bassist Craig McTaggart, Jobbykrust were most definitely a product of their environment.

"Rathcoole was very much dominated by 'spides', who were similar to but not exactly the same as neds in Scotland and chavs in England," begins Tim, by means of explanation. "Sectarianism and paramilitarism was rife and hard to avoid; these were things we both detested and desperately wanted to escape from. The whole punk subculture was ideal for this and we used to go into Belfast city centre for gigs, to share a bottle of cheap cider and then get the last bus home. We were really enthusiastic and decided to start a band, which seemed a really good idea even though we had pretty much no musical ability. I had been playing guitar for about one year, but Craig had never touched a bass in his life.

"We improvised with an acoustic guitar by amplifying the low E-string through a stereo until he was able to buy a bass sometime later; we played together for a while and then recruited other people we had met, to sing and play drums. Thankfully Rathcoole had a really good community group that had practice room facilities which we were able to use, as we had practically no equipment…"

Those 'other people' being vocalists Mark Walsh and Jennifer Brennan and drummer Chris Black, Jobbykrust played their first gig – a typically drunken affair – at Giros in February 1991, before making a concerted effort to revitalise their flagging local scene.

"Yeah, when we started the Belfast punk scene had gone into a bit of a lull," reckons Tim. "There had been some very good bands that had recently called it a day, such as Pink Turds In Space; however the local Warzone Centre was still going, better known locally as Giros, which was undoubtedly the focus of the scene. I think in 1991 that was pretty much the only venue, but it temporarily closed later that year while it moved to different premises. When it reopened it became probably the place we played the most; it was also the focus of everything – there was even a vegetarian café and eventually a recording studio. All our latter recordings were done there, by Marty [of Pink Turds In Space, Toxic Waste and Bleeding Rectum fame]. Giros eventually closed in 2004; however it is currently in the process of starting up again.

"Due to the absence of a decent venue in 1991 and 1992, we used to arrange gigs in a couple of local bars, particularly the Pennyfarthing, under the banner of 'No Name Productions'. It was a case of either organising your own gigs or not playing at all. We also tried playing outside Belfast, but those gigs tended to be really bizarre experiences and there were usually more people in the bands than actually watching the bands…

"Probably the best band that was going at that time was Bleeding Rectum, who were formed from the remnants of Pink Turds In Space and Toxic Waste. They started about the same time as us and we ultimately did a lot of gigs with them, including a European tour in 1994. There were a lot of other local bands, most of which didn't last very long; it was a very inbred scene with people in many different bands at once. The only local zine I can recall was *Uniform Hole*, written by a friend called Mac, which tended to be collections of his sometimes bizarre but very well-written short stories."

Unfortunately Mark soon left ("He decided there were other things he wanted to concentrate on, which was quite a blow, as he was a very close friend…") and another friend Bobby joined on bass, allowing Craig to move to vocals alongside girlfriend Jennifer for the band's first demo, 'Naivety Or Hope', a highly memorable anarcho-punk thrash-up very reminiscent of Dirt, mainly due to the intense male/female vocal delivery.

"Of the early releases, I think a few of the songs on 'Naivety Or Hope' mean the most to me, as they summed up the whole Northern Ireland thing really well and our frustration at it all," says Tim. "The political and social climate here in the early Nineties totally shaped the band, at least in the first few years. Craig and I started the band in part as a reaction to the sectarianism that was all around us in the estate in which we lived and a lot of our early songs were about that. It's actually hard to totally remember what it was like now, many years later, but starting the band and escaping from all that was such a breath of fresh air. All of our peers were sectarian and it would have been so easy to follow that path; Rathcoole is one of

Jobbykrust, vocalist Craig

Jobbykrust, live

Jobbykrust

those places that some people never leave or rarely stray far from.

"As the band went on over the years, I suppose we stopped concentrating so much on 'The Troubles', as we no longer lived in a polarised housing estate. Anytime we went to Europe however, the 'Northern Ireland situation' was all people wanted to know about and we were often appalled at the views of so-called 'left wing' people who felt that political violence and bombings were justified. These were people who had never lived in a society where such things were the norm, yet they strongly told us such things were necessary. I remember many occasions when people argued with us, believing they knew more about Northern Ireland than we did; it was a really frustrating situation…"

Bobby left – "After a drunken argument" – just weeks before the second demo (the only-slightly-less-memorable 'We Starve The Starving') was recorded during December 1992, leaving Craig to return to bass while continuing his vocal duties. Meanwhile three songs from the first demo were included on the Looney Tunes compilation, 'A Scream From The Silence, Volume Two', alongside various international hardcore acts, including Intestinal Disease from Belgium. After meeting with ID when touring Europe for the first time in 1994, by which time they had been joined by new vocalist Glyn, Jobbykrust were asked to appear on a split 7-inch with Blurred Vision by Grinding Madness Records, the label ran by one of ID.

"We first managed to make it over to Europe in September 1994, when we toured with Bleeding Rectum," explains Tim. "We played gigs in Belgium and Germany; it was a fantastic experience and so different to what we were used to. Undoubtedly the highlight was an all-day gig on a barge in Bruges. An interview on a local radio show called *The Horny Hour* after a tour of a local brewery was also a stand-out moment and really quite bizarre – there was no way anyone in Antwerp listening to it would have understood a word we said, with our already thick accents exaggerated by a day at a local brewery! The whole thing inspired us to get back to Europe as often as we could…"

Glyn also took on second guitar, as well as vocals, for the band in late 1994, bringing some extra dynamics to Jobbykrust's songwriting for their split LP with Swiss band, Viktors Hofnarren, for Maximum Voice Productions. Pitching in somewhere between Antisect and Varukers, JK's half of the release was a metallic punk attack of the highest order, both chugging and thrashing in equal measure.

"That was probably the best release we did overall," agrees Tim. "It was the first recording with two guitars and I think the songs were a good transition between the early one-guitar, more straightforward arrangements and the latter more hardcore, complex arrangements. The recording also captured the live sound well and wasn't over-produced…it helped that it was recorded by Marty from Bleeding Rectum, who was into the same sort of music and knew our songs inside out. There is no-one release we did that I don't like, but I do think a few of the songs we recorded were not up to scratch and should never really have seen the light of day.

"The bass player of Viktors Hofnarren and a few other people then arranged a European tour for us with his new band, Vide Psychique [March/April, 1996], which was easily the best one we did. There were so many things from that trip that I still remember so well: playing at this huge squat in Berlin with numerous police vans circling the place and bonfires lit outside (we left after the gig to drive into Poland and shortly after we departed it all kicked off).

"Being held at the Swiss border for 10 hours and strip-searched while Vide Psychique blasted disco music from their van and danced around…it turned out we were only strip-searched to allow the local customs officers there to teach trainee customs officers how to strip-search people! Oh and a gig in Leipzig where all the punks in the venue had bats and other implements ready as they were expecting the venue to be raided by local Nazis who had been attending a rally marking Hitler's birthday that day…thankfully that never came to anything."

The beginning of the end for Jobbykrust probably came in late 1996, when founding member Craig left the band ("He'd just had enough, I think," sighs Tim) and was replaced on bass by 'Trues' (aka Simon Truesdale).

After an Irish tour with Vide Psychique and another eventful European tour, this final line-up of Jobbykrust recorded back-to-back a split LP with Blofeld for Gotterwind Records and a full-lengther all their own entitled 'The Descent Of Man' for Funai Records.

"The 1997 European tour had many stressful moments, which tainted it somewhat; mainly that our driver (who was a friend of a friend and unknown to us pre-tour) lost his medication and became really agitated and angry. I remember vainly driving around Dijon with him, in the midst of an absolutely hectic rainstorm, calling at numerous chemists to try and get him his tablets. We failed and the remainder of the tour involved trying to keep him calm enough to drive us home without getting us killed.

"The writing and recording of the last two records was very time-consuming and involved Glyn, Trues and myself at it pretty much every day. The songs were quite a departure from what we had done before and were quite challenging; recording them was a nightmare as some of the songs were really long and we had not really practiced them that much with drums. Consequently there were a lot of mistakes made that meant it took a long time to get right.

"Overall I like the records, though. I think there are some really good stand-out songs on them and maybe only two weak ones. It is easy, from the LP especially, to see the direction the band was heading and the band that Trues, Glyn and I would later play in [the Dagda] was an evolution from that. In a way this record was the link between Jobbykrust and the Dagda; it represented a move from the more straightforward punk/hardcore riff-based songs to some much more complex, layered arrangements. Unfortunately we never really played those songs live, so had no idea what they would have sounded like in that context. I think the LP has stood the test of time well and doesn't sound particularly dated or anything."

Jobbykrust played their last ever gig at Giros during July 1997 with Ex-Cathedra and, as well as the aformentioned album and split LP, also had another post-humous release in the shape of a split LP with Wisigoth, utilising tracks from their first two demos.

"I just think we were exhausted and the enthusiasm had gone," offers Tim, when prompted as to what caused the split. "The opportunity came up to do another gig in Giros and we decided that was it. I don't recall there being a formal decision to end, just that we had had enough. I don't really see where it would have gone afterwards anyway and I think it was a good time to end. It was also really good that the last gig was in Giros and that we knew it was the last gig; I remember it being a good night and having no regrets afterwards that that was it. It was a typical Belfast gig – the usual faces that had seen us play far too many times before – but it was a nice atmosphere."

As mentioned earlier, Tim, Glyn and Trues went on to do the Dagda, who released the 'Blind King' 7-inch on Funai in 2000, the 'Threefold' CD on Enslaved in 2002 and a mightily heavy self-titled LP on Ruin Nation in 2006, but it was their time in Jobbykrust that paved the way.

"When we started, the whole social and political climate was a major factor in what we did and what we wrote songs about," concludes Tim. "It was a constant backdrop and unavoidable; 'The Troubles' were everywhere and dictated where we lived, where we played etc. In the years the band was together, the conflict carried on as it had done since the late Sixties; it's crazy thinking about it now, but it was all so normal and was what we were used to. I remember one time we were meeting in Belfast city centre to get a bus to a gig and there was a huge explosion; it turned out a couple of streets away some bloke threw a bomb onto the roof of a police Land Rover. This occurred and then, an hour later, it was all forgotten about and off we went to the gig…this was not unusual.

"The Northern Ireland peace process slowly emerged during the period the band was together; indeed we heard about the first IRA ceasefire in 1994 on a ferry to Calais, on our first European tour. The people we met at the gigs could not understand why we were so cynical and sceptical about it all. That ceasefire broke down, but another followed and eventually a peace process became firmly established, leading to the massive change that exists today. However the social problems, such as polarisation of different communities, still exist.

"To be honest, it doesn't really bother me if and how we are remembered," Tim states modestly. "To me, it was a great time that was shared with friends and a way of escaping the crap that was around us at the time. The whole DIY punk scene of the early Nineties was amazing and to be a part of that and all that it brought, was a privilege. I can see many flaws in the band now, both musically and lyrically and there are things I would certainly do differently, given the chance, but that's easy with hindsight. At the time, it was an absorbing and generally positive experience and I like to think we were honest, albeit a bit clichéd as well… I think there was a passion to the music that is so important and is unfortunately often lacking today."

SELECT DISCOGRAPHY:

7-inch:
'Songs About Shit Things' (Grinding Madness/Castafiore Vox, 1994) – *split with Blurred Vision*

LPs:
'Split' (Maximum Voice Productions, 1996) – *split with Viktors Hofnarren*
'Split' (Gotterwind, 1997) – *split with Blofeld*
'The Descent of Man' (Funai, 1997)
'Split' (Funai, 1999) – *split with Wisigoth*

AT A GLANCE:
The 45-track double-CD discography that was originally planned for release by Belfast Records is available for free download from Peace Not Profit.

BLEEDING RECTUM

Belfast's **Bleeding Rectum** formed in 1990 when guitarist Marty, bassist Dee and drummer Crispo, all from the well-respected Belfast band Pink Turds In Space (see *Trapped In A Scene* for more details) teamed up with vocalist Roy from Toxic Waste (see *The Day The Country Died*). Brian from Asylum also played lead guitar for a brief period, but it was only when he was replaced by Alan from FUAL that Bleeding Rectum arrived at their impressively slick yet gnarly take on metallic hardcore punk. They might sound like some trashy gore/grind band, but don't let the name fool you.

"For me personally, Bleeding Rectum just happened to come along at a desolate point in my life and I went along for the ride," begins Roy. "I don't think I had any real ambitions at the start of the band to do anything other than avoid the shitty life I was living in Belfast and Newtownabbey. The band practices initially allowed for some escapism, with a vague hope of travel and gigging. I don't think I took too much of it very seriously at the start, but that reflected my state of mind with the world around me. However, the rest of the band were fucking awesome musicians and somewhere in that little practice room at Merville House something clicked one day and things changed…

"The main difference as regards Bleeding Rectum and the other bands we were all involved in was that we had gone through the energy of the Belfast punk and anarcho-punk scenes and emerged with a collective band mentality of ironic self-debasement. There's no point trying to describe the awfulness of the political and social situation back then, other than to state that we tried to laugh at it and ourselves as people within it, because it was fucking bonkers!

"I never really asked the band what we were trying to achieve but I guess we all had some hope of changing our own situation and hoping to influence others to think about the shit that was going on, but basically we were just taking the piss with the whole thing, out of punk rock, metal and ourselves. Some of the songs reflected this approach, while others were quite dark, both musically and lyrically, mining the deep seams of meaning which we were all inhabiting as individuals…"

After playing their first gig at the Belfast Limelight and building a local following, Bleeding Rectum recorded a split LP with the legendary Californian power-violence band Man Is The Bastard, which Eric Woods from MITB released on his own label, DP.

"Roy, Dee and I were working at the same time as this was going on, trying to start up a PA hire company with help from the Rathcoole Self Help Group," explains Marty. "This brought us into contact with Dave Sinton, a local music-business 'entrepreneur' who had a small eight-track studio in Kirkcubbin. He also managed a local pop band called Ghost Of An American Airman who were signed to Hollywood Records. Their bassist, Alan Galbraith, recorded the split album with us in 1991…he later went on to be an A&R man for some major label in the states and 'created' the awful Evanescence!"

"It was quite a relaxed project for me," reckons Roy. "Marty and Dee did most of the work, with Alan engineering and producing, but it went swimmingly indeed! I remember we worked hard to get a good sound and polish the lyrics as best we could in the timescale. I think everyone was happy at the time, but there's no doubt the production could have been better with more time and resources. Still, I liked the whole vibe of that project and it was really

Bleeding Rectum, vocalist Roy Wallace

From top left clockwise: Crispo (sitting), Micky (finger in tongue) and Trues (playing bass)

quite a nice album to record – with some sick music too!"

Some sick music indeed, with breakneck-speed punk colliding headlong with tight, metallic riffing, a rabid vocal delivery and some evocative, amusing samples to usher in the songs. Although recorded in 1991, the LP wasn't released until early 1993, by which time Alan had left and Micky Death (aka Mick Tierney) was handling lead guitar for the band.

"Micky Death was playing for some wanky metal band in Belfast around that time," furthers Roy. "Marty and Dee kinda knew him already, he was around the Belfast scene and they were all from up the Falls [Road]. I'm not sure if he had yet formed Scald with Pete at that point, but he ended up coming along for a practice and he was such a cheeky fucker, as well as being a metaltastic guitar player, it all just clicked again."

The band continued gigging, including one especially memorable show with Neurosis at the Crescent Arts Centre, Belfast, which Roy still rates as a personal highlight. May 1994 saw Bleeding Rectum in Workshop Studios recording their 13-song 'Very Unpleasant Indeed' cassette release, which was even heavier and even more intense than the split with MITB and was promoted by the 'Daniel O'Donnell Must Die' tour with Jobbykrust.

"The last gig on that tour was probably the best gig I have ever done in my life," remembers Roy fondly. "It was on the outskirts of Dublin in a dodgy – but okay – bar where this crusty guy turned up with the infamous dog on a piece of rope, which helped define our tour humour. The rest of the band were fucking brilliant that night and I just tried to keep up with them; it was an amazing gig for lots of different reasons – but there wasn't many people there to watch the gig – then we went back to the 'Black North' to face the shit again!"

However, several months after the tour, the title they had given the string of dates came back to haunt the band, when Daniel O' Donnell [an Irish singer who has sold over 10 million records and is a household name in the UK] received a death threat from someone claiming to be with the Ulster Defence Association and when a newspaper mistakenly linked Bleeding Rectum to the threats it nearly landed the band in hot water with the paramilitaries.

"That was pretty serious!" exclaims Roy. "I had recently been to Donegal where I went to Daniel O'Donnell's hotel/bar; I'd been pissed up, with all the tourists paying homage to Ireland's favourite son, so I told them that I thought he was a right cunt and went on to elaborate for an hour or so which emptied the bar. The manager kept asking me to leave, so I told him to bring me Daniel or I would wreck the bar. Before the Gardai arrived, I decided to do a runner in my camper van and somehow lived to tell the tale, but I thought it would be funny to name our Irish tour after the incident.

"Then by chance Daniel announced he was due to do his own tour around Ireland and the press was hyping the fucking story on all fronts, especially on the local radio. So some spidery old grandad gets sick of his wife playing Daniel all the time and threatens to kill him to some local radio station and the next thing we know is that we're on the front cover of the shittiest Sunday toilet paper passing itself off as a newspaper, who are claiming that 'sick punk band threatens to kill Daniel!'

"Marty, Dee and myself were working within the confines of a loyalist-controlled area of north Belfast and, as they saw themselves as having cornered the market on threatening people, they then wanted to have a 'word' with us about the threats which were somehow linked to them by the fact that we shared the same geographical area on the planet. Lo and fucking behold, one of the local commanders decides to 'bring us in' to answer a few questions, which translates in Belfast as, 'You're now fucked'!

"I had the pleasure of that experience and I won't ever discuss what actually happened but will summarize in this way: I got the 'word' that they wanted a 'word', I went to *a place*, got shown into a room that didn't exist, was asked a load of stupid fucking questions about shit, some more people entered the room with '*things*', I shit a brick, but then nothing happened, they left the room and then I left the building…lucky bastard! Lucky band!"

The best nine songs from 'Very Unpleasant Indeed' (including the poundingly tuneful 'Sectarian Life' and the massive 'Filthy Blood Junkies', which was probably the band's best song and would have given Antisect a run for their money) were then released as one side of a split LP with crusty Dutch punks Fleas And Lice by German label Skuld during early 1995. Fleas And Lice had actually also recorded their side of the split in Ireland, at Dublin's Dungeon Studio during April '94.

The LP was promoted with a three-week tour of Europe, which Roy confesses to remembering very little about, and unfortunately that was effectively the end of Bleeding Rectum. With Dee no longer wanting to tour, several band members becoming fathers and Roy vanishing off to London ("As I usually did when I couldn't stand Belfast any longer…"), there was little alternative but to call it a day.

There was a brief reformation in 1997, with Petesy from Stalag 17 and FUAL replacing Dee (who went on to do live sound in a local venue) to tour Europe one last time, which Roy describes as "a good aul' laugh! I had got some resources to do an exchange tour between Belfast and Belgium, so we took the opportunity and all went on a 'beano' courtesy of the EU! The gigs were a great *craic*, with the Kontich gig being most memorable, especially the after-party because lots of old friends had made the effort to come up to see us all. We partied 'til dawn and beyond, then onwards into oblivion, with no real sense of purpose or rationale as regards the next gig.

"As part of the exchange we had to do some 'cultural' visits, so I arranged for everyone to visit the Stella Artois factory in Leuven for a tour etc. Afterwards we had the obligatory end-of-tour aperitif, which ended some hours later in debacle and disgrace, with all of us being asked to leave the bar as it had been ceremoniously emptied of all its contents. Nothing to be proud of, but a notable event in the history of the band and, of course, we had a gig that night which turned out to be slightly below par due to the alcohol consumed in the afternoon.

"I guess Belgian punks just thought we were a bunch of drunken paddies on tour, which couldn't have been further from the truth; as I was the designated driver I certainly was not drunk and nor would I refer to myself as a 'paddy' even when the police were insisting that we were just that!"

"I loved my time with all three bands – Toxic Waste, Pink Turds and Bleeding Rectum – and wouldn't change a thing," reckons Marty, who went on to work in Centre Studios. "Well, apart from one single regret; it's ironic, now that I record bands and teach sound engineering for a living, that the sound quality of all three bands' original recordings are so poor. We just never had the money at the time to do anything better and, although it does sort of capture the spirit of the time, it's pretty ropey in a lot of places! Maybe next time…"

Meanwhile, Micky Death still plays with the infamous Scald and Crispo still drums in various bands. "As one particularly cynical musical representation of a moment in time in Northern Ireland that was Very Unpleasant Indeed!" is how Roy, who nowadays makes independent films, would like the band remembered. "And with the slogan, 'Bleeding Rectum: working class, stuff the media up your arse'! Coming in your local parish hall, 2012 – ask any priest for details. Deadly band!"

SELECT DISCOGRAPHY:

LPs:
'Split' (DP, 1993) – *split with Man Is The Bastard*
'Split' (Skuld, 1995) – *split with Fleas And Lice*

AT A GLANCE:
The 'We Will Be Free' split CD on Rejected Records compiles all the Toxic Waste and Bleeding Rectum recordings onto one disc, all of which have aged remarkably well. Roy also has plans to release a Bleeding Rectum discography on vinyl on his new label, Camoccasie.

CONSUME

Consume were probably the biggest unknown band to come out of Ireland, holding the dubious distinction of being the only UKHC band to take lunch with Walt Disney in California… oh, the decadence! But seriously, they gleefully mashed up metal, hardcore and hip-hop and put on a seriously energetic live show and quite probably *should* have been destined for great things.

"We officially considered ourselves to be from Belfast which, was a pretty sexy town to be from if you were playing aggressive music, due to it always being on the news," begins vocalist Paul Clegg (the original line-up being rounded out by guitarist Justin Kyle, bassist Darren Stelle and drummer John O' Neill). "However the truth was a little more in line with sheepdogs than bomb dogs. Basically the drummer and I met in college in Belfast, but the band was really from a little idyllic fishing village on the north coast called Glenarm.

"None of us had really been in bands before, apart from John and I jamming with some friends on L7, Mudhoney, Pearl Jam and Rage Against The Machine covers with our friends for fun. Darren was also in a band called, I think, Emotion Of Fear, who were the big Megadeth and Metallica cover band that played all the local towns in Northern Ireland and had big stack amps. We used to watch them play and then get drunk and talk about how awesome Beastie Boys were, so he and I became friends. And Justin had the accolade of being in the band because he was the only guitar player in the village!

"From the offset, I always wanted to be in a band and had strategies in place from day one, the principal being that a straightedge, extremely talented, farmer's son was the best person in the world to be the backbone of a band. John was a kick-ass drummer, was used to driving places, had access to large vehicles and the farm was a perfect place to make a lot of noise without complaints."

As the band flailed about trying to arrive at their own sound, they unsurprisingly underwent several line-up changes. Justin was heavily into the pop-punk thing, while the rest of the band wanted to move in a heavier, more rhythmic post-hardcore direction, so he was replaced with not one but two new guitarists, Nigel and Stevie J. Then, when Darren also quit, he was replaced by Mark Haslett and what Paul considers the definitive line-up of the band finally coalesced.

"Consume consequently had a few 'first gigs'," he reasons. "Our first one was officially with Darren and Justin and was at a local bar in town; it was a fun show, but we were still very confused with our sound, so we jumped all over the place musically. Our next 'first' gig was when we got Justin out of the band and brought in Stevie and Nigel, again at a local bar, but our first *real* show – in my opinion anyway – was when Mark joined us, two days before we opened for Manhole in London. The show was sold out, people were going nuts and we played like champs; I remember thinking onstage at the time that we were going to be famous, 'cos it felt unstoppable – but obviously history records that this was a somewhat inaccurate prediction!"

'Their' sound, when they did arrive at it, was what haters might refer to as rap-metal, but was basically slowed-down metallic hardcore with rapid-fire, helium-key vocals, a style that was somewhat en vogue at the time with the rise of bands like Rage Against The Machine and Downset, the latter in particular helping Consume get a toe in the music industry's jealously guarded door.

"We came into the game in an exciting time when certain hardcore bands were evolving into – or had just become – new entities," agrees Paul. "Inside Out were becoming Rage Against The Machine, Youth Of Today were becoming Shelter, Burn became Orange 9mm and Gorilla Biscuits were becoming Quicksand. This was super-exciting to us and the concept for the band in its finest moment was to have a chugga-chugga old-school hardcore rhythm section with guitars that were coming from a Tool or Helmet perspective.

"Vocally, I was really into hip-hop at the time and loved the phrasing of people like Ad Rock and Zach [De La Rocha]. I also loved how Zoli from Ignite sang and this metal band called Warrior Soul were a huge influence, as were Prong. I thought I was being so deep and meaningful, but while I thought I was sounding like a cross between Chris Cornell and HR [from Bad Brains], everyone else was hearing way more House Of Pain than 'House Of Suffering'!

"Downset were by far our biggest influence. Without meeting those guys, Consume would probably have never left home and I probably wouldn't have a career today [Paul now works as a tour manager]; it really does run that deep."

Indeed, Downset took the band out on three tours, the first in 1995 with Shootyz Grooves also on the bill, trips that opened many, many doors for the band but also proved a sharp learning curve. "We got this major tour and we had no clue what to do," laughs Paul. "I can remember calling up James Morris from Downset and asking him flat out if we could use their cabs and drums, which is kind of *not* the done thing. He said that it would be okay though and we showed up to the Cathouse in Glasgow with [amp] heads and guitars, ready to rock.

"We had absolutely no idea how we were going to get around and the income was negligible, so we came up with a grand concept: we rented a super nice motor-home and, as all of our friends were really into music, we asked them how they would feel about coming on tour as their holiday that year. Some of them were super up for it, so we had up to 10 people at any one time on that RV, all paying us £100 a week for the privilege of being on tour with us… in the end, we actually made money on it!

Consume, by Naki

Consume live, by Naki

"Now, some bands are arrogant enough to make other bands pay large sums of money to open up for them, but how many bands were asshole-ish enough to charge their best friends a pretty considerable sum of money to carry their gear and then be made to sleep on top of an oven at 70mph? Consume were. Some might say we were visionary, but I think most will go for 'Dicks!'"

Over the course of the next three years, Consume recorded and self-released three EPs, all of them breathlessly exciting and earnest, had tracks on the 'Foundations' compilation released by Building Bridges and the 'UKHC' compilation from Household Name and played with everybody from Biohazard to EMF, some of the touring being especially eventful.

"Ferries were a big part of our tales, being from Ireland. One time we were on a boat with a young offenders soccer team. Young offenders are basically underage prisoners and these bad bastards were going nuts on the boat. Their group leaders could not control them and they were gambling, drinking and probably womanising, all while having a competition to see who could hang off the side of the boat the longest. It was pure pandemonium. The captain called ahead to the port police and warned that there was a minibus full of young offenders coming off the boat and to detain them while the staff could check that the boat had not been destroyed.

"Of course, being the band who realised that turning up early to a ferry on departure meant that you got off it first upon arrival at the other end, we drove off the boat in our white minibus to have the police pull us out of it and hold us against the sides of the van while telling us in no uncertain terms how much trouble we were in. While we were trying to explain that we were innocent, the young offenders drove off the ship (in *their* white minibus) all mooning out the window and shouting 'Wankers' at the police! We watched them drive off into the sunset and the safety of the Scottish coastline with wistful eyes.

"Also and while this may not be the most politically correct tale to relate, one form of expression that seems synonymous with rock'n'roll touring is sex. Consume's one foray into the world of groupies was in the terrifying climes of the Buckley Tivoli in Wales. We were playing there and these two girls came into our dressing room and told us in no uncertain terms that they were – and I quote – 'up for it'. They explained that they liked to 'hang out' with all of the bands and we diplomatically explained to them that we were not that type of band, which seemed to make them quite incensed and borderline hostile. After realising that we were not interested in them, they decided then that they would 'do' – again, their words, not mine – each other.

"Suffice to say, they lifted the bottle of Nutella that was on the table and did things that should have never been done with a delicious German chocolate treat. I wish that I could relay to you, dear reader, our enthusiasm for this Led Zep-style action, but I have to convey that we were never as scared of anything as before, during and after this traumatic experience. I have travelled all over the world with famous bands since then and the only continent that I have not been to on tour is Antarctica, yet the most rock'n'roll thing I have ever been privy to happened in North Wales. I peaked early, I guess!"

At the end of 1997, presumably by virtue of their concerted gigging and enthusiastic live performances, seeing as they actually pressed up relatively few of their EPs, Consume were voted into the Top 10 Unsigned Bands in *Kerrang!* magazine's annual readers' poll and it did seem as if the band were going places, especially when they were taken for the aforementioned lunch by Walt Disney Publishing.

"Oh, man!" chuckles Paul. "We were out in California with the Downset guys and 'took some meetings', which is apparently what you do over there; one was with a publisher from Disney and we had a lunch where we were told that Rage Against The Machine were the biggest band in the world and Disney wanted in on the 'hybrid thing' that was taking off. They thought that they could help 'get us to the next level' and would write a nominal check [or 'cheque', this side of the Atlantic] to retain us, pending further material there and then.

"One of the things that I realised early on was that lyrics were all about syllables and that when you needed an extra two to complete a line, the word 'fucking' was an easy insert to make a sentence fit into a bar of a song. Consequently nearly every song we had at that stage was littered with profanity and here was Disney enthusing over our songs…sweet lord!

"Anyway, the label people in general all seemed like morons to me. We met a few of them and, while we got some nice meals, pretty much everyone we met was a tool – unfortunately, by the time we were ready and set up for a potential deal, we were all tools also…"

And so the band split up, soon after a 1999 Irish tour with Stampin' Ground, pulled apart – inevitably – by the various personal pressures of all the opportunities opening up before them. "The thing about Consume was that we were a band not because we were super-tight as friends, but because we were all good players," reckons Paul.

"We were all determined and opinionated and none too diplomatic, so we all fought a lot. Towards the end, I am ashamed to say that ego was also creeping in for pretty much all of us. It was a good run, but the writing was on the wall. John was growing apart musically and wanted to do more traditional hardcore and I felt that if John didn't want to do the band then it was hopeless.

"Just as we had several 'first' gigs, we had a couple of 'last' ones too. John and Mark had formed another band and I was super-pissed that they were putting that before Consume as their priority and were using the momentum we had gained to forward their side project and I wanted to move on. I was also getting more into the business side of things, wanting to chase opportunities that were becoming evident from that; I wasn't content that the guys didn't want to do Consume shows, 'cos they were out with their other bands and I think I pissed them off when I went to America and wouldn't come home for a one-off show in Belfast opening for Refused. They ended up doing that show with a different singer and that basically marked the end of it. We played two more shows as Consume with different drummers and guitar players, with Mark and I being the core members, but while the music we wrote was my favorite ever and both shows were off the hook, it wasn't Consume as we knew it and it was time to either move on or change the name, so we moved on…"

John and Mark went on to do SXE hardcore band Breakfall; John then did Circle Again, another SXE band, with his wife, before moving to Canada where he now works with computers. Justin went on to live in Alaska, while Darren and Stevie settled into family life in Ireland and England, respectively. Mark also married and now lives in Glasgow, but did work on some more music with Paul and "A guy called Mark Hornby, who is a sensational musician…", which nothing ever came of. And, as mentioned earlier, Paul became a tour manager for bands like COC and the Voodoo Glow Skulls and now manages Gogol Bordello while running his own nine-vehicle tour-bus company, Crossland.

"My one regret probably belongs in the anecdote section, but here goes anyway," he concludes, with not one but two more irrepressible stories. "We made a lot of friends with many bands and a lot of crews and one of the guys who was teching for a tour we were on also worked for Rage Against The Machine. They were headlining the Reading festival and were doing a one-off warm-up in Dublin right before it; we got invited to the show, which you couldn't get into for neither love nor money and our friend told us we could watch the band soundcheck. Zach the singer wasn't there and to this day I remember [guitarist] Tom Morello speaking into the mic over the music as they soundchecked, asking, 'Who knows the words? Who knows the words? Mic check! Mic check!' Both John and our tech friend were looking at me, giving me the 'Go for it!' look, but I sat there like a scared rabbit. And it should have been, 'Tonight, Matthew, I am Zach De La Rocha…' *That's* my one regret!

"I did however get one life-altering recording experience through Consume, when Manhole asked me to sing on their record. Basically we went to Indigo Ranch Studios and recorded with Ross Robinson, who was *the* hot producer at the time for Korn and Limp Bizkit and had just done 'Roots' for Sepultura. It was my first time in a major 'pro' recording studio and we cut a version of 'Hard Times' by the Cro-Mags with Tairrie B, James from Downset, Lynn from Snot and little old me all trading lines. That was a lot of fun and incredibly scary, at the same time. But, with typical Consume luck however, Machine Head decided to release a cover of the very same song, so Manhole's label pulled the song from their record…oh well!"

SELECT DISCOGRAPHY:

CDEPs:
'Mouths To Feed' (Self-released,1996)
'In My View' (Self-released,1997)
'Truth Is Like' (Self-released,1999)

AT A GLANCE:
Look 'em up on YouTube.

GRISWOLD

Griswold were an under-achieving indie pop punk band from Belfast, but their story is an interesting one as it links into various other Northern Ireland bands of the time and their members have gone onto much bigger and better things.

"I was into metal first," explains drummer Andrew Johnston, of his initiation into punk rock. "Anthrax were my favourite band; I got into them through their 'I Am the Law' single, because I was a big 2000 AD fan. I used to go through the thanks lists on their LPs looking for other bands I might like; I got into loads of bands that way: Megadeth, Slayer, DRI, Suicidal Tendencies, Agnostic Front… I spent all my pocket money and lunch money on records. Then came the whole 'Britcore' thing: Doom, Napalm Death and so on. There were a lot of gigs by bands from that scene in Belfast in the late Eighties; contrary to what the BBC or Gary Lightbody might have you believe, we did actually get a lot of bands coming over here during the Troubles. So, Britcore became my entry into punk rock.

"Punk appealed to me because it seemed more 'open' than metal; you could talk to the bands at gigs, or write to them and they'd write back and there were no barriers or heavy-handed security, which all appealed to the teenage me. Also, there seemed to be very little violence, unlike at metal gigs… I remember my friend and I having our Slayer tickets stolen at knife-point in an alleyway beside the Ulster Hall in 1988! In hindsight, of course, punk was a clique like any other, but I probably have ENT's song 'Murder' to thank for me being veggie for 23 years and counting…

"I grew up in Antrim, about 15 miles from Belfast, but I went to school in north Belfast during some of the worst years of the Troubles: 1984 to 1991. One of our school bus drivers was shot dead by the IRA and we were evacuated many times due to bomb scares. But none of my bands ever wrote about politics. I'm not sure if that was a conscious thing; I think we were just too hung up on chasing girls and generally being teenagers. I also think perhaps we felt we weren't smart enough. Most of the bands who sang about the political situation here did so better than we ever could have.

"For the record, the two songs that for me best capture the experience of growing up in Northern Ireland during those years would be 'Each Dollar A Bullet' by SLF and '20 Years On' by FUAL. I'd love to write more substantial songs in future, if [Andy's most recent band] the Dangerfields ever come back and I definitely try to tackle big issues with my comedy [he's now a stand-up comedian]: religion, animal abuse, how much of a dick Jordan is…"

Andrew's first band was Adream, who played their first gig at Giros on 18 November 1989, a hunt saboteurs benefit supporting not only FUAL but also Pink Turds In Space and Sledgehammer, two other of the most influential Irish punk bands of the late Eighties.

"We were in the venue all day, pacing about with our guitars and drum sticks," he confesses. "We must have looked like silly kids to the older punks, but it was a huge deal to us, aged 14 or 15 or whatever. Adream styled ourselves as a cross between Napalm Death and Christian Death…'gothcore', I suppose. Basically because there were only two of us in the band to begin with, myself and the guitarist Marc McCourt and he was a goth and I was a punk. Later, we morphed into a fairly standard 'fraggle' band somehow – like a dopey, provincial version of Mega City Four. We'd been going since early '89 and we rehearsed almost every night, but at that first gig it just fell apart. We had drafted in a bass player whose name I can't even remember and two singers, Frank and Susie, who never came to practice and we were absolutely shite: out of time, out of tune and we had to get people up from the audience to help play some of the songs. Needless to say, it was the best night of my life!"

Adream blundered along for several years, recording a decent enough demo in 1991, but Andrew wasn't satisfied playing just one kind of music and started moonlighting in other bands, including Jobbykrust, eventually starting the short-lived Alumni Feedback in 1992 with Dan Tindall.

"Dan was a character and that's what I was drawn to in those days…still am, in fact. He was coming from a Doors or Velvet Underground-type place, but I tried to play everything at hardcore speed, so it was quite an unusual band. I still think Alumni Feedback could have 'made it', had we not been so completely disorganised. Dan's songwriting was first class and this was just as grunge was breaking.

Griswold, Leif, Ian, Andrew

Griswold, Andrew, Kes, Leif

"After Alumni Feedback, I got heavily into drink, which made holding a band together even more difficult. I was also promoting a lot of gigs around this time – or attempting to – and I went on tour to Europe as a roadie for Decadence Within, in the summer of '93… I say 'roadie', but mostly I just got drunk on whatever the straightedge guys didn't touch. Also in '93, I did a couple of gigs filling in on drums for a band called Confusion, who were peers of Ash from Downpatrick and whose guitarist, Leif Bodnarchuk, later became Tim Wheeler [from Ash]'s guitar tech – and still is, actually, to this day. He also worked for Leonard Cohen for a few years."

After Confusion fizzled out, Andrew and Leif formed Chopper and then Hangover in 1995, a two-piece band with pre-recorded bass, which soon mutated into Griswold, named after the dysfunctional family in Chevy Chase's *National Lampoon's Vacation* movies.

"It just seemed to fit our hopelessly good-time approach," laughs Andrew. "We wore Hawaiian shirts and pretended to smoke cigars and basically thought we were hilarious… most other people just seemed to think we were dicks.

"The scene that spawned Griswold was basically the post-grunge scene, the same scene Ash came from. The Warzone punk movement in Belfast had started to die out by '94 and there were far fewer punk gigs. Therapy? had broken big and most bands were trying to sound like either them or Nirvana. Griswold were rooted more in the indie-punk genre and when Green Day got big Leif started writing a lot of songs in that style. I honestly can't remember very many great local bands from around then. The one band I always thought should have been successful were Slight American Accent, from the Alumni Feedback gigging days; I remember them as a really interesting amalgamation of punk, rock, funk and soul, with an excellent lead singer…of course, if I heard them now I'd probably be appalled! There were also a few good bands hanging around from the Warzone days; Bleeding Rectum and Unsound spring to mind."

As well as Leif's love of Green Day, not to mention the Pixies and NoMeansNo, Andrew brought his AC/DC and Motörhead obsessions to the table and Griswold ended up sounding like none of them, but were a rocking melodic pop-punk band all the same. Completely out of context for such an inoffensive genre, they entitled their first demo, recorded as a two-piece, 'Piss Into My Tasty Wide Open Bum'!

"We recorded that in Leif's so-called home studio, which was basically a four-track in his bedsit in Belfast's Holylands area. I came up with the title – the most obnoxious statement I could think of – mainly because I was just fed up with all the 'safe' bands that had sprung up in Therapy? and Ash's wake, all desperately trying to tick the right boxes in order to to get signed. I suppose this was my cack-handed way of giving them the finger – even if it meant making a laughing stock out of my own band in the process. We did a joke song on that demo called 'Je Suis Le Capitaine', which Babes In Toyland heard when Ash toured with them in the US and they ended up doing a cover of it. It was basically just me beating a floor tom and us repeating, 'Je suis le capitaine' in stupid voices…it seemed rib-tickling at the time…"

Adding Cathy Mullin on bass and Denis Hunt on second guitar, Griswold made *their* live debut in May 1996, in a Belfast pub called Rock Bottom ("Which should have been a warning sign!" laughs Andrew). After recording the 'Can't Stop Dancing' demo (tracks from which ended up appearing on a split 7-inch with Edinburgh's Chi on Simpleton Records), Cathy was replaced by Kes Carew, who had played in Chopper and Confusion with Andrew and Leif. Denis then left and the remaining three became the best-known line-up of Griswold, releasing the 'Let's Pretend We're Gay' CDEP in 1998.

"We recorded the EP in the same studio that Snow Patrol used to rehearse in; we would often pass them coming and going. It was in an industrial complex in north Belfast, near a peace line, so there were often riots going on nearby. When we were recording the EP, it was the height of marching season; this was the year before the ceasefires, so Northern Ireland was still a pretty lively place for that kind of thing. I remember we were on the top floor of the complex, crouched down, watching the rioters up the road. There were helicopters overhead and we suddenly realised that, if the soldiers in the helicopter could see us, we would probably look like snipers and they might take us out. So we retreated back down to the studio and tried to keep recording – but the mics kept picking up the sound of the helicopters! It probably wasn't the most conducive atmosphere to be recording fun-loving pop-punk in, but we ended up with a pretty decent EP anyway…

"I just wasn't a fan of Leif's insistence on using click tracks; I thought it sapped some of the energy out of it. Lyrically, who knows? I actually to this day don't know what the title track was about and I found out several years later that the second track, 'Brand New Barcode', was written about me and what a dickhead I could be. I was a bit pissed off, but it was probably all justified. The third track was an Elvis cover, 'I'll Take Love', which was my idea, 'cos I was big into Fifties rock'n'roll by that point. And the final track, 'Learnin' The Hard Way', was about how we never learnt our lesson after behaving like drunken pricks…at least we were self-aware."

Due to Leif always being on tour teching for Ash, Griswold played very few gigs. After replacing Kes with James McCullough for one Scottish tour and adding Gavin Cole on second guitar for one rehearsal and one photo shoot ("He talked the talk, but no one's seen him since those photos were taken!"), they arrived at their final line-up when James was replaced by Ian Pearce.

"Some of the best gigs we did were in Scotland; we did three or four short tours there. We used to play a place in Edinburgh called Cas Rock and I remember we did one gig with an all-girl band called Pink Kross, whose drummer only used a floor tom and a snare – no cymbals or anything. This was a big influence on my own stripped-down kit in the Dangerfields a few years later. I also ended up going out with Pink Kross's bass player for a year and living with her in Glasgow, but that's another sorry, sordid story. We had such a good time on our Scottish tours, even though the gigs were tiny and we were only away for a few days at a time…but Griswold could pack weeks and weeks of drunken bullshit into just a few days."

Andrew, Leif and Ian recorded one unreleased single and did a week of gigs in London during November 1998, but Griswold ground to a complete halt in January 1999 when they played their last ever gig at Lavery's Back Bar in Belfast. Basically Andrew and Ian realised that Griswold could never compete with Leif's commitment to Ash. Andrew subsequently formed the Dangerfields in March 2000, a punk'n'roll band that released four EPs and one album (2005's 'Born To Rock') and played 850 shows across Europe with the likes of Zeke, the Dwarves and the Misfits. In recent years he has scratched his insatiable itch to get onstage by performing stand-up comedy.

"I never wanted to play pop-punk or indie music, but being a drummer and not much of a songwriter I just had to play with whoever was available and looking to start a band. Most of the time I was just happy to be gigging, but eventually I got sick of not playing the sort of music I loved and decided to take control. The Dangerfields was the answer – it would be *my* band and we'd do things *my* way, which meant only fast songs, screaming guitar solos and everything clocking in at under a minute. We stuck to that pretty much, apart from a few AC/DC-type things. Plus we would tour all the time and never turn down any gig; I was sick of bandmates trying to second-guess turnouts or PAs or what the other bands on the bill would be like. Leif was very fussy about all that kind of stuff. I've always just wanted to play and I really do believe that every gig is an adventure, no matter how far-flung or shittily organised or potentially fatal…

"As for the comedy, people had always been saying I should try it, based on my between-song banter with the Dangerfields. I thought you'd need to have two hours of material and be really good, but then I went to an open-mic night in Belfast and saw how low the bar is set. I've done about 60 gigs now. The Dangerfields ground to a halt in November 2010 – I haven't even played the drums since then – so this has replaced the band for me nicely. I just love touring and there is far less hassle with comedy: no drum kits to haul about, or other members to put up with.

"After 22 years in 'showbiz', with all the accompanying highs and lows (mostly lows, I hasten to add!), I have no fear of an audience. I don't think I've given up music for good, but it became so hard by the end of the Dangerfields just to get the band together for practices. I love doing the stand-up and I seem to be alright at it, but I would like to record another album with the Dangerfields at some point, if only for personal amusement…

"Leif went on working for Ash and Leonard Cohen as a guitar tech," he adds, on the other members' musical endeavours since Griswold. "Ian joined me on and off in the Dangerfields and now has a band called Comply Or Die. James and Leif are playing in a band together again, called Die Cherry. I don't think either Denis or Cathy have played a single other gig since Griswold – probably with good reason – and Kes is a black belt in various martial arts, so I won't be making any disparaging remarks about *him*. Pretty much all the ex-members are married with kids and settled down…except me – I'm still the same teenage dreamer I was in November '89…"

SELECT DISCOGRAPHY:

7-inch:
'Split' (Simpleton, 1996) – *split with Chi*

CDEP:
'Let's Pretend We're Gay' (Smile, 1998)

AT A GLANCE:
Andrew will sort you a free CDR of everything the band recorded if you ask him really, really nicely: a.johnston1973@gmail.com

STRIKNIEN DC

Dublin's **Striknien DC** flew the flag for real Irish punk throughout those lean years of the Nineties and in the process produced some real rabble-rousing anthems that neatly mixed up their hard-edged punk roots with some politically-charged ska and reggae. The band were formed in 1993 by vocalist Deko Dachau from Paranoid Visions and drummer Beano from Stigmatamartyr.

"When Paranoid Visions broke up at the end of 1991, having spent 10 years at the forefront of the Irish punk scene and having outlasted all the other bands and released a large volume of material on vinyl and cassette, I was a bit lost," admits Deko. "And the whole scene here was in the process of dying or becoming all Americanised and rock-orientated, devoid of the political elements and anarchist ideals which I'd long associated with punk.

"In fact, none of the bands we played with towards the end of Paranoid Visions were politically motivated at all and I, and a good deal of the older Dublin punk scene, were alienated by the new direction so-called punk bands were now embarking on. I spoke to Beano, who had been drummer and guitarist with Stigmatamartyr, a local Clash-influenced punk band that were now on their last legs as well, and we decided we would be interested in doing a new punk band primarily to put politics and aggression back into the dying scene in Dublin. Together we set the parameters for our new project and rule number one was that we were not going to repeat our previous bands' styles or reputations, but were to embark on a totally new style and sound. We loved reggae, the Ruts and Killing Joke, which was a far cry musically from what we were previously doing, and wanted to inject some lyrical politics into the mix.

"We didn't want to sound like our old bands and didn't want to be known as 'just another Irish band', so in the end we settled for a moniker which sounded as un-Irish as possible. We did go through a couple of other names first [Hellvision and Battery Humans] but finally settled on Striknien DC, which was deliberately spelled to sound German and incorporated an old Dublin punk band, DC Nien, into the mix – just to add to the confusion!

"Paranoid Visions had basically become bogged down in Ireland," he continues, "due to the total opposition to punk here from the Irish media, music industry, venue owners and the police and we were broke, unemployed, or now working and having families and, after 10 years of being shut out and denied and having no money to tour, we called it a day. I was not happy with this and was still completely immersed in the whole punk-rock lifestyle; I wanted a band that was young, free and ready to play anytime, anywhere, at the drop of a hat. And that became the number one priority for Striknien DC, which was a totally new departure for me; I had been shackled for 10 years in a band which at first could not get gigs and then later, when we did, could not tour because of work commitments and lack of finance. Striknien DC was going to be my vehicle to break out from the 'Emerald bile'"

After playing their first gig in the Roxy Bar on Hill Street, Dublin, during early 1993, while still under the moniker of Hellvision ("We had gone and sprayed it in huge letters all over the walls of the city and suburbs of Dublin in the weeks prior to the gig…but we changed the name very soon afterwards, so it was a complete waste of time!"), Striknien DC recorded their first demo, 'Welcome To The Gash Factory', a few weeks later at Sonic Studios. As well as Deko and Beano, the first line-up of the band also included guitarist Paddy Brady, who

Striknien DC, 1997

had previously played with the Subterranean and bassist Gipo, who had played alongside Beano in Stigmatamartyr and the demo demonstrated an edgy yet tuneful take on rootsy punk rock not dissimilar to New York's False Prophets. A raw, danceable track, 'Circus', was lifted from the demo for inclusion on Dublin label Rejected's first compilation EP, late-'93's 'Rejected, Volume One', that saw them appearing alongside Flexihead, Pincher Martin and Dr Shitface.

After a few local gigs, Gipo and Paddy were replaced by Greg 'Earring' O'Reilly and Donnchadha 'Batman' Grant respectively and the band began writing and gigging in earnest, including several trips to the UK to play with the likes of Dread Messiah, Coitus, Screamer and PAIN. However, Greg left "for family reasons" and was replaced on bass by Pete Townsend (no, not the one from the Who – and I'm sure this won't be the first time he's heard that!).

Steve Shannon also joined on second guitar, giving the band even more scope for their manic guitar harmonies and it was this line-up that recorded the 'Songs From The Smack Cradle' 7-inch for Rugger Bugger, which was a fast-seller for the label thanks to great songs like the irresistible 'Fear Of The Future' and the skanktastic 'Where Is He?' On the back of this four-track EP, Striknien DC built up a huge following in Ireland, as well as in mainland Britain, before recording the 'From The Dead Room' split CD with tuneful Belfast punks Monkhouse for Rejected. The following year saw the band issue their debut full-length, a release that Deko doesn't rate specially highly today.

"That was our worst release, in my opinion," he confides. "That album was recorded way too quickly, after some serious 'line-up surgery' and was recorded on a *very* tight budget in the middle of winter; both the sound and my vocals were grating and woeful. It was badly mixed and recorded in a rush. There was however an album recorded in between the split one and that, which *was* going to be our definitive release, but the poxy recording studio recorded over our masters before we got in to mix it and thus brought about the termination of the most prolific and potentially most skillful line-up in the history of the band…the bastards!"

During the rest of '97 and '98, Striknien DC contributed to several compilation LPs, including wearing their influences proudly on their sleeves with a superb cover of 'Jah War' for Rejected's 'A Tribute To The Ruts' CD and they played many gigs across Ireland, the UK and Europe, (almost) always leaving audiences impressed with their passion and fury.

"I think the most memorable show we played was the Hackney Homeless Festival," reckons Deko. "We played to a full marquee of anarcho punks and anti-Nazis with me in a Skrewdriver 'White Power' T-shirt…and nobody noticed 'til I took it off during the last song and burnt it on stage to rapturous applause. Other really notable gigs included an open air festival in Bilbao city square, in front of thousands, in the mid-afternoon sun, me dressed head-to-toe in heavy leathers and boots…idiot! And a tour of east Germany, which was hilarious – for non-musical reasons…

"The best Irish show was probably one supporting the UK Subs in the Da Club, Dublin. But I remember one trip to Bristol with Stagnation, where half of both bands were arrested in different parts of England all on the same night and we had to play at half-mast to punks who had heard we were really good, only to be confronted by drunken ineptness and stupidity. Sorry, boys and gals! Thankfully there weren't many of those and most gigs we did were stompers…"

By the time Striknien DC recorded their last album, 1999's 'Horses For Courses', Javi Garcia was on guitar and although it was undoubtedly their most cohesive album, they split the same year, which was a great loss to the Irish punk scene.

"I still love the songs," enthuses Deko, of their final recording, "and that was the first time we got to record a whole album together in one session. That line-up was also the best friendship and *craic* we'd ever had in the history of the band and we all remain friends to this day.

"But we parted company as Striknien DC in the autumn of 1999, right after coming back from a German tour with London band Zero Tolerance. We came home shattered, broke and disillusioned with all things punk, after spending two weeks on the floor of Zero Tolerance's van with no merchandise or CDs to sell, despite an overwhelming German reaction to the band. Our supposed record label at the time let us down in a big way after promises to back us and I suppose the enthusiasm for gigging and touring had by then vanished within us; we were tired and disillusioned and finally it became a bridge too far.

"This was just prior to the street-punk explosion which happened in the late Nineties and the internet explosion and we felt alienated by the whole process and tired. I was homeless, broke and manically depressed at that stage too. No regrets about the split, except that we didn't get the breaks we deserved for the hard work that we put in; we happened too early for the internet generation and too late for the '77 generation or the anarcho-punk one of the Eighties.

"I just want Striknien DC to be remembered thus: they came, they played, they drank and had a party everywhere they went and lived fast, died young, but left one hell of a mess! Up the punks! Revolt in style! Thanks to the following bands and mates, we won't ever forget you: Skint, Stagnation, Screamer, Dread Messiah, Reich and Shoen, the Steampig, PAIN, Coitus, Spite, Chaos UK, Monkhouse, Jack Leonard and all at the Old Chinaman. Oi! Oi!"

SELECT DISCOGRAPHY:

7-inch:
'Songs From The Smack Cradle' (Rugger Bugger, 1995)

CDs:
'From The Dead Room' (Rejected, 1996) – *split with Monkhouse*
'Ghetto Blast' (Rejected, 1997)
'Horses For Courses' (Rejected, 1999)

AT A GLANCE:
The 2002 'Playing With Fire' double-anthology CD on Rejected is an ideal place to start – if you can track down a copy.

"GEORGE, I WANT YOU TO GET TO **THE BIRDS** AT **SPALDING** ON **16TH AUGUST 1996**

-THERE'S A PUNK ROCK BLAG GOING DOWN WITH ALL THESE VILLAINS -

THE **X-rays**

URKO

Sufis

TIGER & X

PTT

"THAT'S RIGHT GUV-5 BANDS WITH FREE ADMISSION! THAT'S GOTTA BE DODGY..."

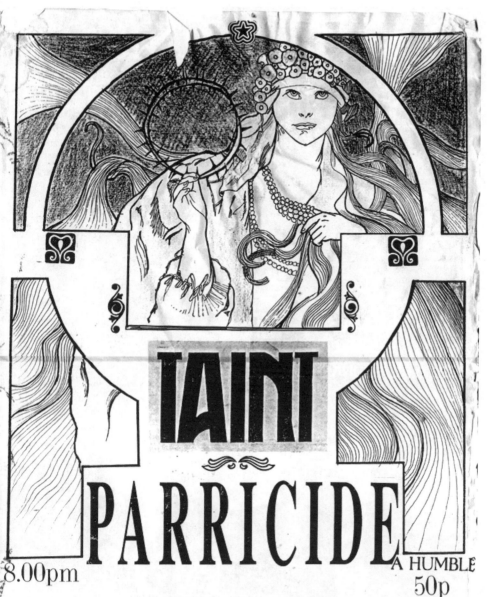

TAINT

PARRICIDE

8.00pm

A HUMBLE
50p

COACH HOUSE
THURS. 4th MAY

£1 a Pint

U.K.... RESIST

Issue 6

SMASH YOUR ILLUSIONS...

POISON IDEA
WAT TYLER
SOFAHEAD
GWAR
1 IN 12
BLITZ

LONDON GREENPEACE
VERSUS MCDONALDS

HOW TO BE A PUNK

TOURING

PATIENCE PLEASE...
A DRUG FREE AMERICA COMES FIRST!

ogie

...IT'S TIME FOR THE
DEATH OF COCK-ROCK!

released emotions flexi

KILL YOUR IDOLS

APPENDIX ONE: FANZINES

E very single band and indeed venue, label and political ideal, featured in this book was tirelessly supported and independently publicised by the underground fanzines that propped up the hardcore punk scene during the Nineties (and, of course, the Seventies and Eighties before them). Sadly zines seem increasingly a thing of the past, with the relentless rise of the internet, but here's a closer look – and it's by no means exhaustive, of course – at some of the people who, if you were there at the time, you may well have once met, hawking their DIY publication at some gig or other. The unsung heroes of the punk scene. We salute you!

ARTCORE

When and why did you decide to start your fanzine?
WELLY: I'd been looking at *Maximum Rock'n'Roll*, which was behind the counter at my local independent record shop. As it was at a distance I had to judge it on its covers and I thought it was just some political paper. One day I asked to look at it and flicked it open to see a Dead Kennedys advert; I quickly realised that it was a punk magazine and bought it. This was in December 1985, so I was quite late to the *MRR* party, as I'd been blindly finding my way into hardcore for a couple of years, basing new discoveries purely on cover art and thanks lists. I quickly soaked up this new world I was introduced to and when I got to the zine reviews, it was the moment where I realised that people were making their own magazines. I just decided there and then that I was going to make one and my first issue came out in January 1986. I'd been into doing my own art and making little booklets since I was a kid, so this was a natural progression.

I'd never actually seen a fanzine, though, apart from that copy of *MRR*, so my early issues were a right mess; even the content was weird, because I had no real template to base it on. The excitement I got from discovering how to make photocopies, do different things, create page layouts and print a zine was a strong thing for a young kid who knew no other people into punk rock. It served as a perfect way to meet like-minded people and from sending copies to some zines listed in *MRR*'s 'Between The Lions' that just mushroomed into trading records, tapes, zines, flyers and stickers. It was a really exciting time for me. It literally changed my life, gave me direction; it felt like I'd found what I'd been looking for with punk rock. Not only was the music the most intense, the lyrics speaking to you, but also your personal involvement wasn't limited to merely consumption.

Who and what were your main inspirations? And what did you hope to achieve with your zine? Like I said, *MRR* was the inspiration. I didn't really have any agenda for achievement; it was just mind-blowing to be involved in some small way in what I was interested in. It really cannot be understated how much of an impact hardcore had on kids like me back then. It was my education about the world. I went from being a young kid with no knowledge outside of my street, school and circle of friends, to having the entire world open up in front of me. I think this is why so many people of our age group are still involved in some way to this day – because it had a profound effect on the way we look at the world. People who have truly been involved in punk rock, have had it alter the way they live their lives, how they conduct themselves, it was a personal political revolution and fanzine production was at the centre of the conversation that punk had with itself.

What were the best – and worst – things about being a fanzine editor in the Nineties? I guess the best was that, by the Nineties, I got to reach further out and get to know other like-minded people. Photocopying, printing and desktop publishing moved forward in leaps and bounds, so it wasn't just a case of getting a typewriter any more. The worst aspect was the mass popularity that came out of the whole pop-punk thing, as it brought in all the money types and people only interested in commerce.

The landscape totally changed then and it never went back to how it was before. It went from writing a letter for an interview to queuing up outside a room with a PR person looking at their watch and pushing you in to interview these new punk-rock stars. I only did that once, as someone else set it up and I never did it again. I still conduct mainly written interviews and it's getting tougher to get bands to answer their questions these days, even though they initially agree. The internet has changed all that.

But back to the Nineties; the other big change in punk rock throughout the decade was the knock-on effect of all the money coming into the scene and that was that bands and people changed from co-operation to competition. Bands suddenly viewed each other as rivals. It was never spoken about, but we started a band in 1991 and by the end of the decade it had changed. To this day, you can get most bands a gig and you will never get the favour returned.

What has been your proudest moment publishing your zine? Your 'Wow, that makes it all worthwhile' moment? There's been quite a few of those, mainly ones that have come about from being around so long. A big one was securing a deal for Th'Inbred with Alternative Tentacles for their two LP/CD anthology set, designing the whole lot and writing all the liner notes…without even getting a tenner out of it! Putting out all the music projects I have with the zine, such as the 'Fuck Rock' ABC-No-Rio LP, America's Unknown LP, Beef People 7-inch and the international compilation LP I'm working on. It's been good fun and is very rewarding.

Another great one was having the opportunity to write some liner notes for bands' releases such as Offenders (which I also got to design), Gang Green, Moving Targets, MDC and the PEACE compilation. I've also been lucky via my graphic-design interests to be able to design

Artcore fanzine,
Welly circa 2009

quite a few releases for cool labels like Boss Tuneage and loads of other bands, which is something I wanted to do as an 11-year-old making fake record covers and like I always say, creativity is its own reward.

And, on the flipside, what about your lowest points? Ever feel like giving it all up?
The beauty of self-publishing is there's no big ongoing investment (although the record releases are pretty expensive); unlike when I had a record shop [Damaged Records], it's something you can just do when you feel like it. For quite a few years I was doing an issue once a year, as I try to sell all of each issue before making another, but lately I've been putting one out twice a year. It's getting tougher, though, especially if I don't put out a record with it. It's getting harder and harder to sell all of an issue. I've never felt like giving it up, though; it was the first thing I did and, after the band and shop, I still do it and it's something that has truly become part of my identity, so it's not something that would be that easy to switch off.

What else do you do for the scene as well as the fanzine? I started the zine in 1986 and from there I got involved in all sorts of letter writing and with it trading records, tapes, flyers, zines, which brought a total immersion in the international hardcore scene, or network of friends of the late Eighties. When friends who could actually play instruments finally became available, we started doing a band in 1991 called Four Letter Word, which was also the year I started Creator Graphics (an anagram of Artcore) as I finished college that year. I've put on quite a few gigs over the years, including a string in the Nineties and again for the last few years, but I've stopped doing them for now.

In the mid Nineties, I was loosely involved when my good lady was running a record stall in Cardiff (between '94 and '95) called Forbidden Beat. This led to a feeling of unfinished business and I waited years before getting the opportunity to open Damaged Records in 2005, which lasted until 2009, when a combination of recession and location saw me close. Four Letter Word decided to call it a day at the start of this year too so, after over 25 years of involvement, I'm now back to the safe old place of making a zine and designing record covers, which is good enough for me right now. It's actually quite nice to take a back seat for a change…y'know, turn up to a gig someone else has put on. The kids have a lot to say and you've got to know when it's time to move over and give them the space.

How would you like your zine to be remembered by those that regularly pick(ed) it up? What do you think sets it apart from 'the rest'? Blimey! I guess I'd just like it to be remembered. I think that would be good enough for me. As for what sets it apart? Well, I'd like to think it's different to other zines, otherwise what would be the point? I always try to make each issue better than the last, creating design and writing to the best of my abilities; I try to create a unique piece of work each time. Something people will hopefully want to keep. The most feedback I get is people saying they were inspired by something I wrote, or they got into a band because of reading the zine and that's great, y'know? Makes it all worthwhile.

Some people may read it and think I'm a miserable old sod and that's fair enough, even though it's largely written in character, but for me the whole point is about sharing the music. I come from a place where this music was hard to find out about or even hear; it had a real mystique about it, as opposed to the artifice you see a lot these days. So, sharing the music and spreading the word is what it's still about for me. I always think of rule #1 in graphic design: that it should clearly and correctly convey a specific message or meaning. And I think this is valid for a fanzine or anything else creative. Be distinct and concise with a specific message; take aim and when you're on target – BLAM!

www.artcorefanzine.co.uk

GADGIE

When and why did you decide to start your fanzine?

MARV 'GADGIE' JOLLY: I started writing *Gadgie* fanzine sometime in 1996 on an electric typewriter which I got from Argos for £50. All sophisticated, me! Issue 1 was released into the wild in March 1997 when a mate copied it up on his dad's photocopier. The print run was a grand total of 35 and they mainly stayed in Boston, where I sold them at local gigs.

I started writing the zine for a number of reasons: I had been reading fanzines for a good few years and, as I had recently moved to Boston and became involved in the local punk scene, I wanted to contribute something more than just attending gigs and buying records. I wanted to be more than just a consumer and, as the DIY scene is/was (!) built on everyone chipping in and doing their bit, I figured that writing a zine was 'doing *my* bit' and becoming active. As I have no musical ability whatsoever and I didn't really know enough folk to put a gig on yet, a zine was my best option.

There were some great and varied bands coming out of Boston and the surrounding area back then – Urko, Poindexter, Sirfis, Tribute, Fen Tiger, Faceache, to name but a few – and nobody knew of them outside of Lincolnshire…I wanted us to be on the punk map! I have always felt a need to document what is happening in our punk world. The things that we all do – bands, gigs, zines, art, fliers, political actions etc – will not be covered in the mainstream press, so it's not only up to us to do these things ourselves, it's also up to us to keep a record of it, to create an archive of it, so it isn't forgotten. Fanzines are punk's history books.

Who and what were your main inspirations when doing so? What did you hope to achieve with your zine?
As a relative newcomer I took my cues, with regards to content, from other zines when creating *Gadgie* – the cut'n'paste style, live, fanzine and record reviews, local scene news and the odd daft bit, or ranting and raving about animal rights, politics, religion, police oppression etc – but after a few issues I decided to put more of my own personality into the writing. I find humour in the mundane and everyday life and wanted *Gadgie* to be an outlet where I could write about such things. Childhood memories, messing about at school, misadventures on the way to a gig, you know…'a strange thing happened…'-type tales. I figured there were countless zines just interviewing and reviewing and telling us all what to think, so took a different approach.

Gadgie fanzine editor, Marv Gadgie

In terms of inspiration, it seems odd, but things like *Monty Python, The Young Ones, Fawlty Towers*, post-apocalyptic world B-movies, Hammer Horror, zombie films and generally just growing up and experiencing life in the Eighties were far more influential on my writing than any bands or records ever were! What did I hope to achieve? An outlet for my 'creative-cum-autobiographical' writing, I suppose. It was a means to connect with like-minded people; pre-internet, 'social networking' meant writing a letter, making a compilation tape, swapping zines…having a 'currency' to trade with, to contribute and add something to the scene. I wanted word on the local scene to be heard beyond the Fens.

I was determined that great bands like Urko and Faceache receive some coverage and I was driven to make the now-legendary Indian Queen a well-known venue that bands, initially from elsewhere in the UK, would come and play. Of course, things took off and bands from all over the world would come and play one day…

What were the best – and worst – things about being a fanzine editor in the Nineties? Without doubt the best part of being a zine writer in the Nineties was the enduring friendships that it led to. I now have friends all over the world who, although I have only ever met them in person a few times, I consider them old friends. Receiving a tape or zine or record or letter in the post from Leeds or London, Amsterdam or Australia, New York or Newcastle…it really was a network of friends. Some of the best times of my life have come from the humble fanzine I write! I still visit, write to, trade with, or am simply in touch with folk up and down the UK, in the Netherlands, Antigua, America, Canada, Australia…all over the place.

The worst? It wasn't as bad as it is nowadays, but the general apathy you would get at gigs when trying to sell them. Going to gigs and seeing some bloke wandering around with a carrier bag full of zines… 'Do you wanna buy a fanzine, mate?' It's now a thing of the past. I think most of the zines I sold were via the post, to be honest and still are with a bit of help from the worldwide web.

What has been your proudest moment publishing your zine…you know, your 'Wow, that makes it all worthwhile' moment? I must mention the wonderful Andrew Culture here, as it was he who published my book, *Now Then Gadgie…* Getting a box of zines back from the copy shop, the 'I did that' feeling is always something to be proud of, but getting a book published is easily my finest hour. I decided that all the autobiographical stories I write may have an audience outside of the punk scene. I figured tales of getting caught short without a toilet in sight, making dens in the woods, playground games, scraps with the school bully, alcohol-related buffoonery, holiday adventures, playing out on bikes… it's all pretty universal stuff that we can all relate to.

What if I were to take out all the punk content and compile all the tales of tomfoolery into a big omnibus zine? I would add in all the other stuff I'd written for other people's zines, the likes of *Scanner* and *Suspect Device* among others and I would pretty much have my life story placed in some sort of social/cultural context. The idea came when my wife's mother kept taking issues of *Gadgie* and reading them to *her* mother! I figured if the mother-in-law and her mother liked the zine, surely there'd be others! About this time Andrew became my biggest fan and offered to publish it as a book through his Corndog set-up. He did, at great personal cost to himself, and for that I am eternally in his debt! The day the books arrived and I looked at one thinking 'I'm a published author' is not just my proudest zine moment, but also one of my proudest moments full stop.

And, on the flipside, what about your lowest points? Ever feel like giving it all up? Every so often I think, 'Bloody hell, what am I gonna write about this time?' and as I sit listening to countless shit pop-punk, ska, metal, bog-standard meat-and-two-veg punk- rock CDs for review, I wonder why I bother. I figure occasionally it would be nice to listen to a new LP and just enjoy it without thinking of things to say in a review, but then I don't think I've ever thought of giving up either. Reviews have generally always been favourable and feedback is usually positive from folk. There's been the odd 'underwhelming' review, but never a real hatchet job slagging *Gadgie* off. Not yet anyway!

I've reduced the print-run over the years as less people buy zines these days – the internet has done its best to make paper zines obsolete, which is a whole other can of worms – and I often feel as if it's just me and other zine writers trading with each other, along with a few regular *Gadgie* readers. This can be quite disheartening, but I always manage to be inspired and, as an example, I wrote two-and-a-half issues in the six-week school holiday this summer just gone (2011) after only putting out one issue in the previous year! I love writing this stuff and I love punk rock, so I've no plans to throw in the towel yet…

What else do you do for the scene as well as the fanzine? I was and still am involved in booking gigs at the Indian Queen in Boston. It's a small pub in a small town in the arse end of nowhere that really had no right to punch above its weight as it did during the Nineties and 2000s. Under the 'Ape City' name and with various other locals, especially Jas, Lee and Craig of Urko, I booked over 100 gigs there for bands from all over the world… Sweden, Iceland, Denmark, Japan, Netherlands, US, Canada, Germany, Italy…crazy times. At one point there would be a bunch of crusty punks being fed and staying over at Gadgie Towers almost every weekend, being subjected to my young daughter's early morning wake-up call of a teddy bear attack. Not good for hung-over punks! There's always room at Hotel Gadgie for travelling punks to this day.

The Indian Queen became a world (in)famous venue and the legacy it has is something we are all very proud of. I also used my contacts to help out local bands and occasionally foreign touring bands, to keep the network going. Out of town, I would travel the length and breadth of Britain as Urko's roadie, usually trying to squeeze in my zine distro box wherever we headed. Nowadays I'm still writing *Gadgie* and contribute columns/reviews to *Mass Movement, Suspect Device* and *Lights Go Out* zines, as well as helping Eagle out with his Punk 4 The Homeless charity gigs in Boston. The Indian Queen is sadly currently closed down, due to a number of reasons, mainly Derrick and Teresa the landlord and lady retiring, but we live in hope that it will re-open and Ape City will rise again!

How would you like your zine to be remembered by those that regularly pick(ed) it up? What do you think sets it apart from 'the rest'? I would hope I have done what I set out to do, entertain the reader and ensure that as many people as possible know about the Boston punk scene. I have created an archive which ensures all the good work we have done is written down. It happened – *Gadgie* is the proof! Without wishing to sound arrogant, I hope and dare I say *believe*, that *Gadgie* has in some way been influential in the zine world.

I know of some zine writers who have started writing the sort of stuff *Gadgie* is infamous for – childhood misdemeanours and mishaps – and on a few occasions people have actually referenced *Gadgie* when listing zines that influenced them to put pen to paper, or finger to keyboard and do a zine themselves.

I think the universality of the content, as mentioned earlier, is why *Gadgie* still finds its audience and the fact it's not your typical punk zine sets it apart from the crowd. I once read a review that said there wasn't enough punk content in it (or words to that effect) as a criticism, which really missed the point. The fact it doesn't have all punk content is part of the appeal. The obsession with Blondie, *Planet Of The Apes* and all things sonically brutal, the nostalgia, the anecdotes… I like to think the zine is a look into my mind and an extension of my personality. Whether that's a good thing depends if you are interested in the inner workings of the mind of an immature 30-something PE-teaching, punk-rocking gadgie…

HOW WE ROCK

When and why did you decide to start your fanzine?
NICK ROYLES: I started *How We Rock* in 1991. The first issue was more of a fun thing to do: throw some text together, talk some crap and add a few photos. It eventually evolved into a larger newsletter and then into a full-on zine.

Why? Well, 1991 felt like a new era in the hardcore scene. Most of the people that were previously involved in hardcore had gone by 1990, particularly those that had crossed over from the metal scene from around 1987. There was an influx of new people and a mix of old faces creating new bands. I noticed an upswing after that 'sinking ship'/'dead duck' feeling of 1990 and I – as did others – felt inspired to create anew. It felt like time to pull your sleeves up and get involved and my newsletter was a beginning in this process pour moi. It was a time of new faces, new bands, new zines and new record labels; the scene was still tiny…miniscule but enthusiastic.

Who and what were your main inspirations when doing so? And what did you hope to achieve with your 'zine?
Hmmm, well there was always *Maximum Rock'n'Roll*. I used to write the occasional scene report in *MRR* and I guess that reporting buzz never left me. There was also the *Slug And Lettuce* newsletter, which was pretty damn amazing – great photos as well. When *HWR* was a newsletter, it was essentially a glorified UK scene report. In a sense I was aping back to previous European zines that attempted to cover the UK and elsewhere in that *MRR* format… Eighties zines such as *UK Resist* and *Feedback* were quite high in my estimation. Particularly *Feedback*, which just had scene reports from places you'd have thought didn't have a punk scene (at the time) – like the Canary Islands.

I hoped to cover most aspects of our European hardcore and punk scene fairly and evenhandedly. When it was more of a newsletter it evolved and expanded in size to cover some mainland European scenes, such as Norway, Holland, Belgium and Germany. I was also using it then as an advertising tool externally for this small island's hardcore punk scene; I would mail it out and deliver it to many record shops and other places where I thought people might come across it and decide to get involved. A bit missionary in some sense, but internally – through DIY distro networks and through the mail – I was hoping for a bit of connectivity on this island and some interest from the mainland as this island seemed quite isolated, an unknown. Though that's not to say I was the only source of scene information; it would be wrong to assume that.

Distribution-wise, I think it did get to quite a few places. It was getting up to around a 4,000 print run per issue. I'd mail them out to people on the mainland as well and touring bands would also take them away with them. I recall Sned of Flat Earth Records telling me that they lost 1,000 copies of one issue after a crash on the highway in Poland, but obviously I was more concerned about Sned having a crash than about copies of my newsletter splattered on a Polish road!

When Rich from Armed With Anger Records started the *Hardcore* mailout, *HWR* became an integral part of that. I think there were 700 people on that list. *HWR* was part of that mail-out for quite some time, but when it became a zine in a larger and costlier format I had to move on from that and focus on it becoming a 'proper' zine, which led up to the unfortunate issue of finances. I started selling advertising space to raise the funds to print it. Issue 13 had a print run of 500 copies and came with a Tribute flexidisc and the final issue came with another flexi and was 1,000 copies.

What were the best – and worst – things about being a fanzine editor in the Nineties? My struggles with computer technology, or lack of computer knowledge on my part! Which was mainly due to my inability to sit still for a long period of time and learn something; I've always been easily distracted.

What has been your proudest moment publishing your zine? The last two issues, I guess. While I'd been doing the 1 In 12 festivals with the Subjugation Records crew, I was able to work with them on something more concrete in the form of the flexis that came with the zines, particularly with Helene from Subjugation as that label funded the pressing of the flexis that came with the last issues. I thought those issues both had cool covers, while lacking a good layout inside and I loved the fact the flexis came with them, particularly the Tribute flexi; they were one of my faves, had released an amazing demo on Subjugation and were regulars at our festivals. Yeah, those two issues for sure!

And, on the flipside, what about your lowest points? The whole issue of No 13 being deleted on the computer two days before going to print; that was definitely the lowest point, but with huge help from Helene Subjugation, we did an overnighter locked in the 1 In 12 Club office. We were furiously laying out and printing the whole issue in time for the Juma Printers deadline; that was a huge low point as the new version was inferior to the original as the 1 In 12 computer and printer were not the greatest! But we needed the zine in time for the following weekend's three-day hardcore festival…it *was* ready in time, but not without a lot of anxiety.

How We Rock no. 13

When and why did you decide to stop doing the zine? I think I was just doing too many things and something had to go; the zine was one of them. Besides, it was keeping me indoors, when really I just wanted to be outside on my bike, riding on the hills, or hiking out into the Peak District.

What else do/did you do in/for the scene as well as the fanzine? Bands, a record label and arranging concerts.

How would you like your zine to be remembered by those that regularly picked it up? What do you think set it a part from 'the rest'? I'd like to think that people would see *HWR* as trying to cover small scenes in Europe in a fairly even-minded manner. Regarding the last few issues, I do hope people began to see it as a bona fide zine, as those issues took a lot of work. The last issue sold 1,000 copies, which I feel quite proud of, though not in an egotistical sense.

And, as someone involved in the UK punk scene for many, many years, how would you rate the Nineties? I preferred the Eighties – but the Nineties were really cool as well.

RIPPING THRASH

When and why did you decide to start your fanzine?
STEVE: *Ripping Thrash* started as an idea in early 1986 and the first issue came out June of that year. I had been into punk for a few years when I went to college in Liverpool and at that time was just getting into the more underground/international side of things, but I had no idea about zines other than *Maximum Rock'n'Roll* when I went away. Being in Liverpool opened me up to gigs and a whole host of DIY zines and records etc that were difficult to get connected with back in little ol' Burton-on-Trent! Being the person I am, I wanted to get involved and be active in the scene, contribute to it myself rather than be a passive consumer.

As I had few friends/contacts there at that time and no knowledge of playing in a band and those kind of things, doing a zine based on the plethora of DIY zines I'd come across seemed the logical step forward. I suppose, to begin with, my zine was a copy of all those around at the time, but I wanted to help support bands and people into the DIY political style of things and help promote bands etc from a wider geographical area who might not otherwise get any exposure.

Who and what were your main inspirations when doing so? And what did you hope to achieve with your zine? Main influences were *MRR*, smaller zines such as *Raising*

Hell, Problem Child etc (too many around at that time to name!) and the countless politically-charged anarcho and hardcore punk bands from the UK and from all over. What did I hope to achieve? I'm not sure really, I didn't have any specific aims (and still don't!) with the zine, other than what I stated above and let it just run and evolve in whatever way it can… I didn't really expect it to be going as long as this, one of the longest-running punk zines around!

What were the best – and worst – things about being a fanzine editor in the Nineties? The Eighties and Nineties weren't a lot different in terms of doing the zine, I feel…then again, I only started in the mid Eighties and was still feeling my way into zinedom when the Nineties arrived. I've got a shit memory anyway, so I don't remember…a lot of people said the UK scene was shit in the Nineties, though, with nothing happening etc but I don't really remember that being the case, to be honest. From my point of view there was still a lot of good stuff happening; I suppose all the old bands had stopped by then, or sold out and everything went more DIY and underground and that was okay by me, as I prefer it that way!

Best things: getting things done and new issues out (to keep the inspiration going!) and being a fanzine seller, which at times can be a pain in the ass but also meant that I got connected with lots of people. I made a lot of friends through selling zines at gigs and writing people through the mail etc; throughout the Nineties I think the DIY scene evolved a lot more and there became a better connected network of zines and distros, which as a fanzine seller certainly helped, so there became lots of places I could go to swap bulk copies of our zine or get them stocked for trade, or for sale/return etc. That was important as there became less and less record shops interested in selling DIY punk stuff, so I could get the zine sold in other parts of the country and abroad too. That's important if you want to get word out to more than a couple of hundred people.

Noughties…well, a lot changed…the internet came along, for starters: great for communicating and for instant responses etc. Ultimately not so good for zines, though, as more and more zines packed up and online zines came along. Much less demand for paper-based zines meant everything was done on a smaller scale. I'm not sure in the Noughties and in 2012, that there is enough interest in a resource-based punk zine like my own, as people prefer to search the net.

What has been your proudest moment publishing your zine? Not sure how to answer that one really! I suppose I am proud of my zine and the fact that I contributed something and did something hopefully worthwhile (for me personally, at least) for 20 years, but I can't particularly recall a defining moment in its history as I have mainly let it drift and follow its own course – to oblivion! I'm always proud to get a new issue finished and still get a satisfaction from that and inspiration to carry on with it when I can hold the zine in my hands and see what I have actually worked for. Getting to know people through the zine and keeping in touch with them for many years makes it worthwhile too and in 2008 finally meeting old pal Juantxo Franco, when he invited me to travel in Peru…that would never have happened without the zine and my being involved in the worldwide punk scene…hello, mate, if you're reading this!

And, on the flipside, what about your lowest points? Ever feel like giving it all up?
Lowest points: large gaps between issues when I have not had enough time or inspiration to get the zine done (usually the former) and lack of feedback from folk, which tends to make me think, 'What is the point?' There's not been many times I've felt like giving the zine up in truth, although I'm thinking along those lines at the moment due to lack of interest, feedback and poor sales for the two issues I did this year. I am thinking the next issue may be the last. Also, it's more and more difficult to fit it into my hectic lifestyle, which means I am keen to explore some different avenues and want to do more travelling, my allotment, move away somewhere different etc. We'll see. I just don't think my zine is as relevant today, in the world of the internet and revival bands etc.

What else do/did you do in/for the scene as well as the fanzine? For many years in the Eighties and Nineties I did a tape label, releasing many demos, split tapes, compilations, live tapes…often with nice glossy covers and info booklets etc. The tape format was a pain in the ass at times, but doing the tape label was great. Later on, I stopped that and ventured into records and CDs; the label (FCR) is not dead, but I haven't released anything since January 2010. I may release something occasionally if it's something I really want to do. Other than that, a lack of interest in the label and also my own lack of free time have all but killed that one off.

I also did and still do, a distro; again interest has waned in recent times, but I am still active with it. I will be trying to re-invent the distro in 2012, but on a much smaller scale and being much more fussy about what stuff I stock. For a time I also did a newsletter called *AKTSN* quite some years ago; it was meant as a resource/info guide to supplement the zine, which at the time was coming out pretty irregular, so the newsletter came out in between issues of the full zine. *AKTSN* stood for *Apathy Killed The Shitty Newsletter*…and in the end apathy did kill it! Actually I think the newsletter started out as *Ripping Thrash Ten-and-a-half* ! That's a recurring theme throughout my years; I always had tons of different names for my different activities… I think it got confusing at times and most things now are simply under the *Ripping Thrash* banner, as that's the name that's most familiar to folk. Zine-wise I've also been involved in the *Network Of Friends* omnibus zine; we might do something with that again in 2012…

How would you like your zine to be remembered by those that regularly pick(ed) it up? I just hope that they *do* remember my zine! There's lots of folk I bump into when I am selling the new issue that say, 'Oh, I haven't seen that zine for years…' and it's quite bizarre, 'cos I never stopped doing the zine and it seems a lot of people missed many issues of it throughout the years…but hopefully people remember picking up the zine and finding it worthwhile and were able to make contact with and discover new bands/people/scenes as a result. That was pretty much always the aim…

I am not so over-confident in myself, nor my zine, that I would say my zine stands out from the rest and I not going to presume such arrogance! But I try to make it different enough and, especially in the last few issues, I've tried to do two things: one is to interview a band or person who I know quite well and do a real long in-depth type interview… I've been pleased with how they've turned out. The second is: trying to feature bands and people from far away scenes and/or from places that don't get much exposure in the punk world…

Ripping Thrash editor, Steve, with Norr from Malaysia

SUSPECT DEVICE

When and why did you decide to start your fanzine?

TONY WHATLEY: Gaz and myself started the zine in 1984. We just wanted to get more involved; we'd both been into punk since the late Seventies and after spending the first few years just buying records and then going to the big 'concerts', a local scene had sprung up and we began to interact with all these new people who were our age and into the same stuff as us. New friendships sprung up and knowing that this was ours, we weren't just consumers and we were doing it ourselves, was a powerful feeling and we wanted to immerse ourselves in that DIY spirit.

I had actually wanted to do a zine the year before, but Gaz wasn't really into it then and, without the confidence or desire to do one on my own, I kind of lost the motivation. The second time I suggested it he was more receptive and we dug out old typewriters and started out on what has become a long and rewarding journey.

We already had the name; we were both into Stiff Little Fingers and had always talked about starting a band using the name Suspect Device, but that never ever got off the ground, despite the fact that between us we had a guitar, a bass and a drum kit. When we started the zine, Suspect Device was the obvious name.

Who and what were your main inspirations when doing so? And what did you hope to achieve with your zine?

GAZ: Getting into a local scene from the start really helped us for sure. In 1984, many of the bigger punk bands that Tony and I followed – plus the record labels and all the press coverage – were beginning to wane or had already gone. We never got the whole 'anarcho punk' or 'whatever punk' sub-division thing you wanted to be in. Punk is punk – no rules! I think I wanted it all to be joined up, to put the whole spectrum of punk in one fanzine and just live and let live. Hope to achieve? Yup! Communicate and show people that it was their scene made for them to be a part of…

What were the best – and worst – things about being a fanzine editor in the Nineties?

TONY: The best thing for me, was the feeling of community, not just locally but worldwide too. People I met back in the earliest days of the zine are still friends now. Even in my own area there are people I probably would never have met, if it hadn't been for the local scene, who became close friends; and with the zine that just expanded and people hundreds or thousands of miles away also became friends. One of my closest friends lives 300 miles away and we met because he decided one day to send off for a little zine from the south coast of England. That's what made – and still makes – it all worthwhile for me.

I'm struggling to think of anything too bad; it's been an interesting ride, but I think we've both regarded everything that's happened as just part of being a zine writer. It was a little disappointing when bands would write and declare their dedication to DIY punk rock and ask for coverage in the zine, when they were really just using the DIY scene as a stepping stone towards 'making it'.

What has been your proudest moment publishing your zine?

GAZ: Hard one, that! I once phoned Peter Test Tube and did an interview with him and sat and interviewed Steve

Suspect Device writers Gaz and Tony in 2011.
Right inset: Gaz and Tony in the Eighties.

Ignorant over a few beers (now there's diversity in punk for ya!) Seriously, though, the pride is that we have kept going and are still putting out a paper zine. The internet has done wonders for communicating and you can find punk as easily as you can find anything, but the 'wow' moment is giving them out at gigs these days and people still being interested enough to read a zine, or seeing the hits on our website…

And, on the flipside, what about your lowest points? Ever feel like giving it all up?
TONY: Probably the only time I came close to stopping was in the late Eighties when Gaz didn't contribute to a couple of issues, around issue numbers 7 or 8, I think. I thought long and hard about either stopping, or changing the name of the zine, because it didn't feel right doing *Suspect Device* without his involvement. But in the end I realised that I didn't really want to stop and I think even that early, doing a zine was something that I wanted to do and if I *was* doing a zine it should be called *Suspect Device*. As it turned out Gaz couldn't stay away long, thankfully.

What else do/did you do in/for the scene as well as the fanzine? TONY: As part of *Suspect Device* we did a tape label, putting out several compilations, then we started SD Records (our first release was in 1994, the first single for my then-band Thirst!) and on the back of that we did a distro, which meant we used to have a stall at most local gigs; something I was really into doing, as there were no independent record shops in town and I wanted to be able to provide locals with cheap punk releases at gigs, as well as a good old DIY punk rock mailorder. We wrote and published a couple of books too!

I have also played in several bands over the years, starting with Obvious Action in the late Eighties, then into the Nineties with Fusion, Thirst!, Portiswood and – as the decade came to an end – Chokeword. Over the last 10 years I've been in Pilger, Screwed Up Flyer and now the Shorts.

How would you like your zine to be remembered by those that regularly pick(ed) it up? GAZ: Well, we're still going, so it's hard to say! I have always wanted SD to be readable and full of variety and we started to achieve that more fully when people other than Tony or myself started to contribute. I've never thought *SD* has 'stood out' particularly' but we've always been ourselves and our only real rule has been 'No rules'. I have never wanted to be told, 'Oh, *SD* is this type of zine or that type of zine…' We are who we are and we're too old to care now anyway!

The nicest thing I like about the zine still going all these years on is just how much the battle lines between the different sub-sections of punk have blurred. Punk has history now, age and experience, which has made things so much more pleasant than when we were spotty, angry youth…we're now far more wise to the world and even less tolerant of the crap we're fed! Who knows how much longer we can go on, especially with the internet basically forcing us to fund a free *SD* giveaway of just a few hundred every issue? But we use that medium too and move with the times…long live DIY and long live punk rock!

www.suspectdevicezine.co.uk

The still-curious reader could do far worse than start further investigations into the UK's fanzine heritage here: **ukzinelibrary.blogspot.com** and **punksishippies.blogspot.com**

MAKING PUNK A TREAT AGAIN
Presents
bands at 9pm
£3/£2.50concs.
NOISY PUNK BASTARDS!
FRIDAY MAY 15
Eastfield
blistering anarcho-punk
POLICE BASTARD
FROM BIRMINGHAM
PEMBURY TAVERN
90 Amhurst Road, Hackney, E8
Hackney Downs, Hackney Central, Buses: 38, 22a, 22b, 106, 55 etc.

APPENDIX TWO:
LABELS

ARMED WITH ANGER

When, where and why did the label get started?

RICHARD CORBRIDGE: Armed With Anger Records started in Bradford, 1992. The original motivation was to release the Nailbomb/Wartorn split 7-inch. I was playing bass in Nailbomb around 1991-92 and we seemed ready to release something; of course, I thought I could do as good a job as anyone else at the time. So I tested the water with that first release, it worked and I sold 1,000 copies pretty quickly and gained a lot of confidence from that – especially since I was only 19 at the time!

What were you hoping to achieve when you set out? What labels inspired you to start your own?

The first year of the label really helped establish what I wanted to do, which was to document the new wave of UKHC which was really beginning to emerge at the time. I guess the UKHC scene sees a lot of new cycles and during the early Nineties, there was a lot of fresh, dynamic enthusiasm around, a relatively small but active scene – lots of co-operation and a great, positive atmosphere of something emerging with a lot of possibilities. There were plenty of established labels releasing slightly different genres, but barely anything that documented this new cycle of UKHC that I – and those around me – were part of.

So I really wanted to help support my friends in these bands and get them some international exposure. I can't say I really knew any other labels when I first started that well. I loved Dischord Records, who I'm sure had some influence, but generally I had a lot of encouragement from people I knew and had quite a strong DIY attitude, so before I knew it I had a label which took on a life and momentum of its own.

What was your first release – and how do you rate that release now, with the benefit of hindsight?

The Nailbomb/Wartorn split 7-inch. It suffered from a horrible production. I learnt a lot from that first attempt, though, about the whole process of releasing a record, designing covers, distribution and so on…since I was kind of making things up as I went along!

What were your best – and worst – releases? And why? Best? Well, I loved the early Voorhees material and was super-excited to release their first 7-inch and LP. In fact, I really took a lot from working with friends who genuinely appreciated the amount of time and effort it took to promote their releases…bands like Stalingrad and Imbalance. Funnily enough, the last couple of releases I did really said a lot about how the label had changed too. It was so UKHC-focused for so long, then I ended up doing a split EP with a couple of Swedish bands and a joint photo book. It felt like I had accomplished something to bring the label to a point where I didn't feel remotely guilty about not just documenting the UK scene, especially when there were eventually so many other labels doing something similar by that time.

Worst? I'm thinking the Nailbomb/Wartorn 7-inch says it all…!

What were the best – and worst – things about running a punk label in the Nineties? Best: being really motivated by the amount of enthusiasm and energy around the scene at the time and being able to really be part of that whole scene and help enable a lot of the recognition that some of those bands got.

Worst: despite running a pretty big distribution and mailorder service, as well as my own label, I found the day-to-day mailorder, filling of orders and taking bags of mail to the post office pretty dull and so very time-consuming, despite the help I had from some of my friends.

How did you strive to run your label that may have set you apart from other labels of the time? I didn't intentionally attempt to set the label apart, but wanted to run something with integrity, passion, honesty and drive. I also didn't particularly want to get stuck in a particular genre as most labels did. I have always had a pretty diverse taste, in a whole range of music, so I didn't have an issue with releasing fast, thrashy hardcore, right through to far more melodic, emo releases, since that diverse mix of bands tended to come together at the same festivals and shows pretty often anyway and I saw them at the time usually under the same umbrella. I don't think people outside the UK really understood that…or at times, even people *in* the UK for that matter.

What other 'fringe activities' did you get involved in alongside the label and why? I did a few issues of *Armed With Anger* zine, I did a lot of shows and festivals at the 1 In 12 Club in Bradford, a mailorder distro and wrote for other magazines like *Heartattack*. I also set up and was part of, the collective that produced *Reason To Believe* magazine, organised some European tours and so on…

When and why did you fold the label? Any regrets since? I spent most of my twenties fully consumed with the record label and all the other fringe-activities I was involved in, with barely any time off and eventually got a bit bored with a growing label that certainly broke even, despite there not being much other return. I just decided that I needed a change. It wasn't an easy choice; I'm sure I could have continued for many more years, but the scene around 2001-02 had changed a lot, for the better in some ways, though there were so many other labels just as capable as Armed With Anger at releasing and documenting what was going on within the scene. So I felt it was time to put the brakes on and hand over the reins to some of the others around. Plus I was still having to work a regular day job for at least part

Armed With Anger's Voorhees
vocalist Lecky, by Naki

Armed With Anger's
Richard Corbridge

of the time while running the label, which was a lot to carry.

   Ultimately, I decided to quit everything and go travelling around the world, which I proceeded to do, on and off, for the next four years or so. Absolutely no regrets since. I loved doing the label, took a lot from the experience and feel privileged to have had the opportunity to do Armed With Anger Records.

What was your last release and how was it, as epitaphs go? It was actually a book and absolutely the best way to end. It featured photos from live shows by a really talented photographer from Finland called Kristofer Pasanen. It was a joint release, making it easier to share the cost and distribute…the easiest release I ever did, in fact!

How would you like your label's contribution to be remembered in the grand scheme of things? For releasing some awesome UK hardcore punk bands during the Nineties and for helping to contribute towards a thriving scene.

DISCOGRAPHY:

All 7-inchs unless otherwise stated…

AWA01 Nailbomb/Wartorn 'Split' (1992)

AWA02 Various Artists 'Consolidation' (1992)

AWA03 Voorhees 'Violent' (1993)

AWA04 Understand 'Self-titled' (1993)

AWA05 Voorhees 'Everybody's Good At Something…' flexi (1994)

AWA05.5 Various Artists 'Nothing New' (1994)

AWA06 Kito 'Johnson, Mary: 188897764' (1994)

AWA07 Dead Wrong 'Self-titled' (1994)

AWA08 Voorhees 'Spilling Blood Without Reason' LP (1994)

AWA09 Stalingrad 'The Politics Of Ecstasy' picture disc 7-inch (1996)

AWA10 Various Artists 'A Means To An End' LP (1997)

AWA11 Schema 'Sooner Than You Think' CD (1997)

AWA12 Stalingrad 'Patty, We Kind Of Missed You On Your Birthday' LP and CD (1998)

AWA13 Voorhees '13' LP and CD (1999)

AWA14 Imbalance 'Wreaks Havoc With The Inner Ear' LP and CD (2001)

AWA15 The Get Up And Go'ers/Dead End 'Split' (2002)

AWA16 *Identity Parade* (A photobook by Kristofer Pasanen) (2002)

FLAT EARTH

When, where and why did the label get started?

SNED: The label started in the west end of Newcastle in March 1986 with the release of the first Generic EP, although on that release it said 'Flat Earth *Collective*' not 'Records', as that is what we were, my housemates Micky and Dave and myself; we had an 'office'/spare room in our house and were involved in producing leaflets and publications as well as some primitive screen-printing in the attic and putting on gigs. We had a PA and a collective van (called Boris…she was born in the Sixties and only got us to Sunderland and back once before conking out and dying); it was a hive of activity and we wanted it to work on many levels. This sounds pretty fancy, reading it back, but it was on as thin a shoe-string as it gets. Anarchy. Money was tight; the band had no amps or drums and practiced along with 20-plus other equipment-less bands at the Gateshead Music Collective's legendary venue, The Station. The music and the message was the thing and an extension of this was to release our own music; we wanted to propagate sounds and ideas – from ourselves and our friends – on our own terms, under our own control, without compromise.

Micky and I played in Generic; previously we'd played together in Blood Robots who had made a split flexi-disc with our friends Reality Control. This experience led us into the world of trading with other fledgling DIY punk labels around the country and internationally (opening my eyes to some incredible punk from Italy especially!) This was a small taste of how things could be done, so with help from some friends, we pooled our resources (borrowed, begged and stole) and made it happen – then had to get busy selling them to pay off the numerous debts we'd run up! The aim was to expand and help with other releases and projects we considered worthwhile and I'm pleased to say that particular objective was achieved over the course of the Nineties.

What were you hoping to achieve when you set out? What labels inspired you to start your own?

SNED: The collective's aims were a lot wider than that of the label – we wanted to change the world! Or at least become part of something that would do so by linking up with others and all that, locally and globally. Receiving the SAS EP in the post was a big thing, a genuine lost classic of UK hardcore; it was £1.00 postpaid and made by some geeks in Scarborough – and it absolutely rages! That made us want to step into the world of vinyl; flexis were pretty rubbish after all. The SAS guys went on to do Looney Tunes, of course and our third record was a collaboration with them and we remain good friends to this day.

Prior to that, the plethora of tape labels were very important to us and I'd say Fuck Off Records, run by Kif Kif from Here And Now was massively influential too: the Androids Of Mu LP and especially the 'Weird Noise' EP…20 minutes long and only 60p! Daft bands! I was fascinated with all that, the Swell Maps and their Rather Records, that was my first mail order. Micky had the Desperate Bicycles records and stuff as well…and the Apostles were a big influence. We hung about Listen Ear and Volume record shops, checking out whatever stuff was coming in, y'know? Stuff like Crass influenced our ideas with the band and in general, for sure, but not really with the activities of the label.

That early-Eighties era had massive quantities of independent releases being sold through the shops, but the times were changing and a new international DIY network of sorts was

Flat Earth band, Headache

Flat Earth's Sned, whilst drumming for Health Hazard

Flat Earth office, circa 1992

emerging; I can't overstate the importance of *Maximum Rock'n'Roll* magazine at this time and compilations such as the 'PEACE' double-LP. Children Of The Revolution (COR Records) from Bristol were putting out some great spirited releases around this time too.

When and what was your first release? And how do you rate that release now, with the benefit of hindsight? Generic's '…Free South Africa' 7-inch EP was released March '86. It was a struggle to get the cash together to release it, but it was an exercise of a collective in action. Anyway, after many delays, plus we couldn't afford to get the records delivered, our mate Slob went and picked them up from this outer London pressing plant as he had a free train pass; we met him at the station and carted them to 142 Brighton Grove and a mob of us sat round and folded all the covers, inserted all the inserts – and voila!

It was all very new and exciting and it sold well via gigs and us hawking it around, as well as dispatching bags of records – five here, 10 there – to friends who'd be going to gigs in other areas to go sell them for us; we put a load in Red Rhino (we were getting paid less from them per copy than it cost to produce…but it was all about getting the message out there somehow – this pre-dated the stalls and distros scene that dominated the Nineties…) and the other local record shops and obviously sold them at our own gigs.

It sounds pretty good for its time too, considering what fucking amateurs we were. I like the song 'Oldest Trick In The Book' the best, but plenty of it makes me cringe; we probably over-did it on the rhetoric, but we found it important to make those links clear between the high street and oppression. It was a call to boycott apartheid and attack those investing in it, an example of how fucked and sick capitalism is…making links to the bigger picture, if you like. The first pressing of 1,000 sold well and we did a second press of 1,000 copies, then the collective folded as people pursued other interests and I ended up holding the label baby. In time there was enough money, after paying off debts, to release the second and third records and so on; progress was very slow until around 1992, when Alec got involved, and that's when 'the golden era' kicked off!

What were your best – and worst – releases? And why? That's like choosing between friends and I'm proud of everything, even though some stand the test of time better than others. It doesn't matter about 'units sold' or anything; each release has a story and friendships and memories. I guess some stuff got delayed (like the Headache LP; they recorded it, it got to test-press, they went on tour…and decided to re-record! Argh!) or had a stupid idea for a cover print (like the Sedition LP – first thousand copies printed on hessian sack!), but it really doesn't matter in hindsight, does it?

What were the best – and worst! – things about running a punk label in the Nineties? I'd guess some people wouldn't consider the releases 'proper' punk, anyway; *Maximum Rock'n'Roll* wouldn't review the Witchknot record, for example, which seems bloody ludicrous, but it doesn't keep me awake at night how punk it all was. It was just how it was and some mates' bands fitted a certain style or genre of the time. Others were different; it's all relative – it was never about any of that anyway, ideas were what mattered. I enjoyed confounding expectation for sure – pretty punk, huh?

Shitting myself in case the dole found out what we were up to was something I didn't like; even though money was not being made, I wouldn't expect those fuckers to understand the concept of doing it for the love. And the idea of working a real job on top of the amount of time we were putting into this thing, terrifying…it was enjoyable but really, really fucking hard work! That is proper DIY: putting in the hours, folding up records in a freezing cold basement, hallucinating with tiredness behind the distro at some endless late-night gig, putting up with more shit than you should ever have to… I wouldn't change any of that for a moment!

The worst thing I would say is that my faith in human nature was shaken as people set up labels and distros, owed you money, then disappeared. I think my expectations were way optimistic and I'd always take that shit personally. For the best thing, I'd nominate the tireless enthusiasm and dedication of Active Distribution, who have helped on so many levels above and beyond the label and are a constant source of inspiration to this day. Plus the seeing through of a project and holding a new release in your hands and being proud of what can be achieved…all that sort of thing was pretty good too .

How did you strive to run your label that may have set you apart from other labels of the time? I can't think, really… In the Nineties there was a bit of a glut as labels took on trades and then all did distros at gigs, so you would see us alongside Armed With Anger, Subjugation, Looney Tunes, Enslaved and so on… I was and am friends with the people behind those labels and would consider us all part of a bigger whole; a good example of this would be 'the mail-out' initiated by Richard Corbridge and put together at the 1 In 12 Club. There was a large UK mailing list and the DIY distros would print up their lists and it all went out in a stuffed pre-internet envelope; it was fun to do. I guess the only thing setting Flat Earth apart was pre-dating most of the others.

What other 'fringe activities' did you get involved in alongside the label? And why? As I pointed out above, 'the mail-out' was that sort of fringe activity; we were involved in a lot of activity at the 1 In 12 Club in the Nineties and (for me) in the late-Eighties Leeds squat scene. We were playing in bands and touring around Europe a lot…and when the tours fell off, so did the distro; really the label and distro and bands and club was everything, it occupied almost all of our time .

When and why did you fold the label? Any regrets since? Somewhere around the end of the 20th century! I guess it all got a bit of a chore after so many years of intensive activity; Alec had moved on, so I was doing the label alone and the distro had become a bit cumbersome. Loads of people owed us loads of money and I just became disillusioned and burnt out, I guess. The shape of distribution had changed from placcy bags to distro boxes to giant distros and on to shops; the scene got more business-oriented and that left me cold… just so much bullshit I can't relate to… The time had come and my work was done.

Not all bad, though; many of the original objectives had been achieved and going into the '00s I spent ages (via dial-up!) putting MP3s on the website as a giveaway. And now that I've truly packed it all in, one day soon, by the time you're reading this, the whole lot will be ripped properly and freely available to all. Check the website address at the end. There were some releases in the '00s, but discographies and re-issues only. The distro lives on, but it's much smaller and select and a bit more fun. I probably should have packed it in earlier and cut the cord a little neater and got on with life…gone for the real goals in life instead of this bollocks – but there ya go! What can ya do?

What was your last release? And how was it, as epitaphs go? 200 copies of Martin Sorrendeguy's *Beyond The Screams* documentary on VHS – just in time for VHS to become a redundant format…that was about 2001, I think? I did the Cress, Sedition, Boxed In and PVC discography CDs in the '00s too and then the Doom and Health Hazard vinyl reissues in 2010, to cash in on the Lady GaGa crust revival!

To me, the last new and original release was the 'You're On Your Own' CD, which was a compilation of experimental stuff made by various pals from punk bands; I always wanted to release a song that was the boiling of a kettle, the flushing of a toilet and some distant drills provided by Yorkshire Water – that was the pinnacle of Flat Earth's achievements and, for me at least, a load more relevant and interesting than 98% of the dogshit in this book, no offence!

How would you like your label's contribution to be remembered in the grand scheme of things? Hindsight and nostalgia is a strange thing, so who knows how it'll go? I don't really care and I doubt many others do; it's time to move on. The people who were touched by what we did know what it was all about; the real DIY has moved onwards into different realms, as it should. *Flat Earth* was of its time and I'm proud of that, as part of a greater history/picture of resistance and creativity. Counterculture not subculture…stick that in yer fuckin' thesis.

DISCOGRAPHY:

All 7-inchs unless otherwise stated

FE001 Generic 'For A Free And Liberated South Africa' (1986)

FE002 Generic/Electro Hippies 'Play Loud Or Not At All' LP (1987)

FE003 Generic 'The Spark Inside (1987)

FE004 Generic 'Torched' (1989)

FE05 One By One 'World On Fire' (1991)

[FE 006 – 12 were joint releases with Nabate Records from Liège, Belgium]

FE06 Disaffect 'An Injury To One Is An Injury To All' (1992)

FE07 One By One 'Fight' (1992)

FE08 Sedition 'Earthbeat' LP (1993)

FE09 Hiatus/Doom 'Split' (1993)

FE10 Kitchener 'Price Of Progression' (1993) (co-release with Refusenik)

FE11 Unhinged 'Resisting The Murder Of Self' (1993)

FE12 Disaffect/Sedition 'Work As One' (1993)

FE12.5 Sedition/Pink Turds In Space 'Split' LP (a reissue of a self-release from 1991)

FE13 Health Hazard 'Self-titled' LP (1994)

FE13.666 Health Hazard 'Discography' LP (1996, later reissued 2010)

FE014 Witchknot 'Suck' (1994)

FE015 Headache/Recusant 'Split' (1994)

FE16 Drop Dead 'Discography' LP (1995)

FE17 Suffer 'Suffer' (1995)

FE17.5 VR 'Dreamstate' LP (1995) (co-release with Genet)

FE18 Scatha 'Respect, Protect, Reconnect' LP (1996)

FE19 Ebola 'Incubation' LP (1996)

FE21 Doom 'Rush Hour of the Gods' LP and CD (1996, vinyl later reissued 2010)

FE21.1 DDI 'Pazzi Da Asporto' 10-inch (1996)

FE22.5 Crudos 'Canciones Para Liberar Nuestras Fronteras' LP (1996) (co-release with Nabate)

FE23 Headache 'Headache' (1996)

FE24 Cress 'Monuments' (1997)

FE25 Ebola 'Imprecation' (1997) (co-release with Enslaved)

FE25.5 Manfat/Hard To Swallow 'Red Eye/Hard To Fucking Swallow' (1997) (co-release with Enslaved)

FE26 Health Hazard/Sawn Off 'Songs Of Praise/On A Path To No Tomorrow' (1997)

(co-release with Smack In The Face)

FE27 Doom/Cress 'Split' 10-inch (1998)

FE28 Solanki 'Buzz Or Howl, Under The Influence Of Leeds 6' 10-inch (1998)

FE29 Suffer 'Forest Of Spears' (1998)

FE30 Submission Hold 'Progress (As If Survival Mattered)' CD (1998) (co-release with Active)

FE31 Scatha 'Birth, Life And Death' LP (1998)

FE32 Kito 'Long Player' LP (1998)

FE32.5 Urko/Suffer 'Split' (1998) (co-release with Enslaved)

FE33 Headache 'Live In Slovenia' cassette (1998)

FE34 John Holmes 'El Louso Suavo' LP and CD (1999)

FE35 V/A 'You're On Your Own' CD (1999)

FE36 Cress 'From Violence To Consumerism' (1999) (reissue, originally on Worried Sheep)

FE37 Sawn Off 'Sawn Off' CD (2000)

FE38 *Beyond the Screams* VHS (2001)

FE-RE 001 Cress 'Propaganda And Lies' discography CD (2002)

FE-RE 002 Sedition 'End In The Beginning' discography CD (2003)

FE-RE 003 Pleasant Valley Children 'Welcome To Bedlam Valley' discography CD (2006)

FE-RE 004 Boxed In '2001-2005' discography CD (2006)

Those free downloads can be found here: www.flatearth.free-online.co.uk

HOUSEHOLD NAME

When, where and why did the label get started?
KAF: We started the label in London in 1996. We began with a compilation CD of bands which we mainly knew because we'd put on gigs for them; both of us were putting on independent DIY punk rock gigs, Lil in North London and Kafren in South London. Going to each other's gigs was how we met and came up with the crazy idea of starting a label. We hadn't really planned to put out anything beyond the first compilation, but then a couple of the bands asked us to put out their recordings and it carried on from there.

What were you hoping to achieve when you set out? What labels inspired you to start your own?
The objective of the first release was just to see if we could make it happen, have some fun and to get some more notice for the bands that we had asked to be on the CD. This was back when connecting to the internet happened through a modem and a phone line and you were lucky if a webpage with five lines of text on it loaded within a few minutes – and using MySpace and Facebook, Bandcamp and Twitter as tools for bands to get their name out there hadn't yet become a possibility.

We were inspired by labels in the US like Dischord and SST who were independent and released fantastic bands; also Epitaph, Fat Wreck and No Idea back when they were still a zine that put out compilation CDs on the cover. In the UK, we were inspired by labels like Words Of Warning, Armed With Anger and Subjugation and people like Active Distribution who released abrasive and energetic punk rock and were all about doing as much as you could yourselves and very much outside the major-label way of doing things.

When and what was your first release? And how do you rate that release now, with the benefit of hindsight?
As mentioned earlier, our first release was 'The Last House On The Left', a compilation CD featuring bands that we knew from putting on gigs. I still think that it is a good release; there are only a few tracks that, with the benefit of hindsight, we may have included someone else instead. But bands like King Prawn, Headbutt, the Flying Medallions and Pulkas were great bands and went on to gain many more fans as time went on. Also many of the people in the bands on that release are still in bands or involved in music today.

What were your best – and worst – releases? And why?
Well, we have always had a policy of never saying we liked one release more than another release... like anxious parents! But I think, again with hindsight, there are some I like more, that stand the test of time better... after all we've put out over 110 releases now. Definitely some of the releases that stand out are Medulla Nocte, the UKHC compilation, both Capdown albums, the Filaments and actually many more. No, I can't choose... we should really go back to that old policy!

What were the best – and worst – things about running a punk label in the Nineties?
Best things: that technology was on our side in that it wasn't so easy to upload/download and distribute music for free, which is a major challenge to any label these days. We were young and had a lot of enthusiasm and quite utopian ideas about what we were trying to do –

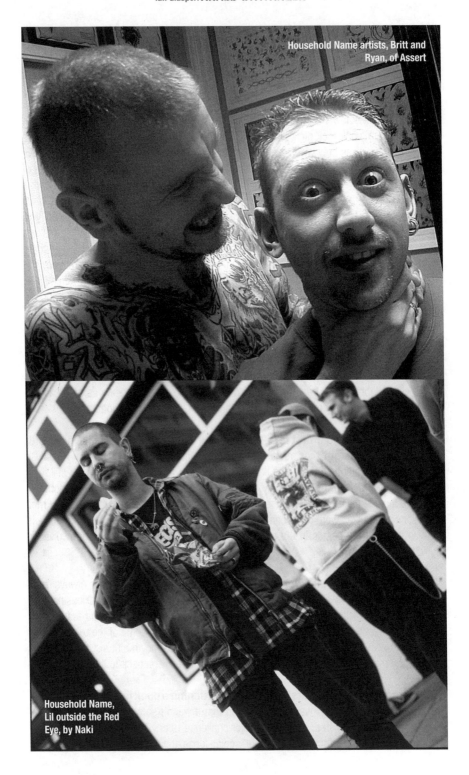

Household Name artists, Britt and Ryan, of Assert

Household Name, Lil outside the Red Eye, by Naki

anything seemed possible. We weren't daunted by the music industry and very much strove to operate outside of it, at least for the initial years until the success of some of the bands demanded that we get involved in it in some ways. It was great to meet other like-minded and talented and inspired people, both in the bands that we worked with and people running other labels, doing distros, putting on gigs and writing for zines. Worst things: probably the times when a band or release you really love and want loads of people to hear doesn't get out as far as you hoped. But other than that I don't think I can think of bad things from the Nineties; it was a pretty positive and inspiring time.

How did you strive to run your label that may have set you apart from other labels of the time? Our main aim, particularly in the Nineties, was always to merely be able to keep going from release to release. We did after a while start to get more organised and plan things in advance and do press and advertising as widely as we could afford. We have always been involved in putting on gigs for the bands that we release and we tended to try to do everything ourselves whenever it was sensible. We also used the internet a lot as it started to evolve and used to run a mail-order, listing both our releases and other labels that we traded with, which was really popular and we used to take our stall from gig to gig ourselves in big backpacks!

What other 'fringe activities' did you get involved in alongside the label? Well, as mentioned, we did put on an awful lot of gigs! We started at the George IV in Brixton and the Monarch in Camden, sadly both no longer venues. Over the years we've put on shows at the Underworld, the Garage, the Mean Fiddler, the Verge, the Windmill, the Rocket, the Barfly and several other venues around London. We ran quite a big distro for a while, selling lots of CDs, vinyl and T-shirts from – mainly hardcore – labels from all over the world.

One of the things we did for a few years was put on a festival called Evilfest, bringing hardcore bands from around the world and around the UK, to play a large gig in London. I [Kafren] also wrote articles and columns for various zines and we did our own zine – though that only managed one issue…! Later on, we were also involved in starting All Ages Records, a record shop in Camden that is exclusively punk and hardcore and all the genres in between. We also booked tours for bands from the UK, Europe, Canada and the US.

How have you had to change your approach to survive as a label since your involvement in the Nineties UKHC scene? We have continued putting out releases since the Nineties and the UKHC album we did. The style of music we put out changed over time to less hardcore bands and more melodic punk-rock bands. It wasn't that we were making a conscious decision to change our approach, but I think we were always affected by the bands that we put on gigs for, demos that we were sent or handed by friends and just interested in putting out what we thought to be good music. We still like and go out to gigs and see a whole range of genres of music.

What was your last release? And what's next for HHN? Our last releases were Chief, a hardcore band from Liverpool and Great Cynics, a punk band from London. Also this year [2011] we put out a 7-inch for Billy No Mates. We still go out regularly to check out new bands, so who knows what the future will bring? We aren't quite ready to quit yet! We're still open to new ideas and new ways of doing things and it's always inspirational to see some of the energy and enthusiasm and fun that the new bands are bringing to the punk and hardcore scenes.

How would you like your label's contribution to be remembered in the grand scheme of things? I'd like to think that we contributed to a very active independent scene and helped some bands by putting out their releases, setting up shows and distroing their records and that people enjoyed what we put out as Household Name Records. Hopefully people will remember what we achieved positively; it was a great time in our lives and long may it continue!

SELECT DISCOGRAPHY 1996-2001:

HAUS001 Various Artists 'The Last House On The Left' CD (1996)

HAUZ0GOD01 Spectreman 'Git a Relijiss Feeling' 10-inch (1996)

HAUZLP001 Scraper 'Built With Hate' 10-inch (1996)

HAUS002 Medulla Nocte 'All Our Friends Are Dead' 7-inch (1997)

HAUS004 Various Artists 'Four Way Tie Up' 7-inch (1997)

HAUS005 Griswalds/The Kenmores 'Legalize the Stupid/Potty Training' 7-inch (1997)

HAUS006 Loophole 'The Day The Monkey's Charm Wore Off' 7-inch (1997)

HAUS007 Various Artists 'UKHC: A Compilation' CD (1997)

HAUS008 Assert 'Thumb And Four Fingers…' 7-inch (1997)

HAUS009 Yeast 'Ten Second Memory' 7-inch (1997)

HAUS011 Breed 77 'The Message' CD Single (1998)

HAUS012 Lockdown 'The LDP' CDEP (1998)

HAUS013 Hard To Swallow 'Protected By The Ejaculation Of Serpents' LP (1998)

HAUS014 Knuckledust/Indecision 'Smash Tradition' CDEP (1998)

HAUS015 Assert 'More Than a Witness' CD (1998)

HAUS016 Imbalance 'March Of The Yes Men' 7-inch (1998)

HAUS017 Medulla Nocte 'A Conversation Alone' CD (1998)

HAUS018 Knuckledust 'In Yer Boat' 7-inch (1998)

HAUS019 Canvas 'Canvas' CD (1998)

HAUS020 Various Artists 'Evilfest '98' CD (1998)

HAUS021 Various Artists 'Fuck Off Household Name' CD (1999)

HAUS022 Snap-Her 'Nice Girls Don't Play Rock' 7-inch (1999)

HAUS023 Indecision 'To Starve And Steal In NYC' 7-inch (1999)

HAUS024 Capdown 'Time For Change' CDEP (1999)

HAUS025 Imbalance 'Spouting Rhetoric' CD (1999)

HAUS026 Withdrawn 'Seeds Of Inhumanity' CD (1999)

HAUS027 Not Waving But Drowning 'If It's Too Cute Set It On Fire' CD (1999)

HAUS028 Kafka 'Truths' CD (1999)

HAUS029 Assert 'Left Opposition' CD (1999)

HAUS030 Taint 'Die, Die Truthspeaker' CD (2000)

HAUS031 Silencer 7 'Directions On A Compass' CD (2000)

HAUS032 Capdown 'Civil Disobedients' CD (2000)

HAUS033 Canvas 'Lost In Rock' CD (2000)

HAUS034 Special Move 'Dark Overlord' CDEP (2000)

HAUS035 Yeast 'History = Fog' CD (2000)

HAUS036 HHH 'Making Changes' CD (2000)

HAUS038 Dead Inside/One Fine Day 'Split' 7-inch (2000)

HAUS039 Capdown/Link 80 'Split' 7-inch/CDEP (2000)

HAUS040 Various Artists 'Christmas Fisting' (Hard Skin, Capdown, Southport) 7-inch (2000)

HAUS041 Various Artists 'Rumours, Ridicule And The Profit Motive' CD (2001)

HAUS042 Five Knuckle 'All Ages' CDEP (2001)

HAUS043 Capdown 'Pound For The Sound' CD (2001)

HAUS044 Lightyear 'Call Of The Weasel Clan' CD (2001)

HAUS045 Red Lights Flash 'And Time Goes By' CD (2001)

HAUS046 Big D And The Kids Table/Five Knuckle 'Look What You've Done' CDEP (2001)

SIMBA

When, where and why did the label get started?
VIQUE MARTIN: *Simba* fanzine started in Brighton in the summer of 1992. I put out my first record early in 1995, as it just seemed like a logical leap. A lot of people I knew, like Dave from Indecision and Mike from Troubleman, in the US made that jump and I just thought it seemed like a good idea!

What were you hoping to achieve when you set out? What labels inspired you to start your own?
I would have to say that labels like Dischord, Artmonk and Revelation were probably the most inspirational. I was hoping to just release some great music by friends, make sure that they received a fair proportion of the press or profit and enjoy myself in the process. I had already set up relationships with distributors all over the world for the zine, so it was easy to sell the records too.

What was your first release? And how do you rate that release now, with the benefit of hindsight?
I still think it's great. I still love both bands and I still listen to them regularly, especially Greyhouse. Both bands were good friends of mine who did well in their respective scenes/countries – the split release helped both reach new people…

What were your best – and worst – releases? And why?
The worst would have to be the Hal Al Shedad 7-inch, as they ended up being total douchebags. So were Ink And Dagger though. So I'd say it's a toss-up between the two. The compilation wasn't that great, although I do like that Bob Tilton are on there.

What were the best – and worst – things about running a punk label in the Nineties?
The best was that anything sold really! You could press 1,000 of pretty much anything and people bought enough to cover the costs. That is totally not the case now. It gave a lot of freedom to release things you liked, rather than worrying if you would lose tons of money doing it. Worst was that there was no internet, so everything had to be dealt with by regular mail, which was a time-consuming and costly process.

How did you strive to run your label that may have set you apart from other labels of the time? I didn't really worry about that; I just put out things that I liked and didn't concern myself with trying to do too much. I also ran a distro and that took up a lot of my time.

What other 'fringe activities' did you get involved in alongside the label? And why? I ended up running a huge mail-order and booking tours and shows [in Leeds]. These included the Promise Ring, Refused, Ink And Dagger, Hal Al Shedad, Get Up Kids, Abhinanda, Starmarket, Sparkmarker, Rex, Sleepytime Trio, Four Hundred Years and probably a whole bunch more that I'm not remembering right now…

When and why did you fold the label? Any regrets since? I moved to California in 1998 and I guess I stopped putting things out around 2002. No regrets, just a crap load of debt from the last four releases that came out just as the CDEP became a dead format. So no regrets really…just glad not to have the debts and expense any more!

What was your last release and how was it, as epitaphs go? I released the last three CDs at once, so I suppose I went out with a bang! At the time I didn't realise they would be my last…and I guess it would have been nice to have made it to 20…

How would you like your label's contribution to be remembered in the grand scheme of things? I would say that I'd like it to be remembered as a small label run by someone who just released things she liked. They are the best labels to me…ones that don't release things because they think they'll sell, or because the people in the band are friends of theirs, but because they like the releases themselves.

Also tell us about your fanzine and how it interacted with the label… The zine started in 1992 and I think the last one came out in 2000, but I could be wrong about that and it could have been 1999. It's all a *long* time ago now. I did 13 issues and then just started writing for *HeartAttack*, *Fracture* and *Clamor*. At its peak I sold 3,000 of an issue, which is astonishing to me now, absolutely insane. People must struggle to sell 300 these days. I started it as a normal fanzine, but it quickly became more of a vehicle for my personal/ political writings and I devoted a huge amount of time to it. I still had interviews and band pictures in it, but they became less and less and the writings became the majority of each issue. I think it was a huge part of my identity and to some extent it still is; I'm *still* 'Vique Simba' rather than Vique Martin.

Just how important was the underground fanzine's role in the development of the Nineties hardcore punk scene in the UK? I think it had a hugely important influence in

Simba Records, Vique Martin

the scene…from reviews and interviews we found out about new bands and followed their progress and from the personal rantings and political dialogue we all grew as people within the scene. I think *Simba*'s place in all of that as a feminist, personal zine, was critical in providing some balance to the largely male demographic. And I am proud of the contribution that I made.

DISCOGRAPHY:

All 7-inch unless otherwise stated…

sim001 Fabric/Greyhouse 'Split' (1994)

sim002 Texas Is The Reason/Samuel 'Split' (1995)

sim003 Des Man DeAblo 'Missionary' (1995)

sim004 Rocket Science 'Well Known' (1995)

sim005 September 'Self-titled' 10-inch (1996)

sim006 Various Artists 'Love Is A Dog From Hell' CD (1996)

sim007 The Faint Sounds Of Shovelled Earth 'Self-titled' CD (1996)

sim008 Fabric 'Stella Maris' LP (1997)

sim009 Hal Al Sheded 'Yesterdays' (1997)

sim010 Ink And Dagger 'Experiments In Nocturnal Sound And Energy' (1997)

sim011 Kill Holiday 'Meant To Let You Down' (1998)

sim012 93 Million Miles From The Sun 'Self-titled' (1999)

sim013 Abhinanda 'Rumble' CD (2000)

sim014 Garrison/Hundred Reasons 'Split' CDEP (2001)

sim015 Halogens 'Resolution' CDEP (2001)

sim016 Garrison 'The Model' CDEP (2002)

sim017 93 Million Miles From the Sun 'Self-titled' (reissue) CDEP (2002)

sim018 Kristofer Astron And Hidden Truck 'Plastered Confessions' MCD (2002)

sim019 Marit Bergman 'It Would Have Been Good' CDEP (2002)

SUBJUGATION RECORDS

When, where and why did the label get started?

HELENE: The idea of starting a record label was one that was bouncing around for a while among friends during 1991-92. Ian and I finally brought the idea to life in summer 1992, releasing our first 7-inch. We were studying in Leeds at the time and moving around a lot so the label was based in terms of its postal address in Darlington (Co Durham), our home town. As to why we started the label…it's difficult to pinpoint something specific beyond youthful enthusiasm for the scene! But perhaps a motivation was that it seemed like most people were actively contributing to the hardcore scene at that time and you felt that you should do your bit too. The scene seemed small and tentative, as if it needed people to step-up and make stuff happen. With neither of us being musical in any way, doing a band was definitely not for us, so doing a record label seemed like a good option. I may be wrong, but I don't think there were too many labels active in the hardcore scene at that time and it seemed like a gap that could be usefully filled and so we started up. I think Sure Hand Records and Armed With Anger, also based up with us in Yorkshire, started in 1992 too.

What were you hoping to achieve when you set out? What labels inspired you to start your own? I don't think we had any particular goals for the label other than to do more than one release. Possibly we might have thought that we could make the music that surrounded us all the more real by making it tangible, fixed in time on vinyl. But, as I mentioned in the previous question, I think we were just keen to play a useful part in the scene and be part of the infrastructure that kept things going. Perhaps this was more amplified for me. Often there were negative perceptions of women in the hardcore scene, that we were on the sidelines of the scene, holding our boyfriends' coats while they rocked out… I think my youthful self was pretty determined for hardcore to be for girls and by girls, too!

I don't think we were inspired by any particular label. More likely we were inspired by all the hardcore/punk labels that we came across. They made you think that setting up your own label was indeed possible, even if you were only just past being a teenager! Ian was 19 and I was 20 when we started down this path and it was just exciting to think that we could actually be a record label. If you loved the feel of owning/playing vinyl, there was going to be no better feeling than putting the needle to a record that you have gone through the agony and joy (in equal parts) of manufacturing!.

When and what was your first release? And how do you rate that release now, with the benefit of hindsight? The Strength Alone 7-inch was our first release in summer 1992. The band had material recorded and had no record label to release it, but it was good stuff and so it was really just a case of being able to do something useful and get this UK band and a bit of our scene, out there to the wider world. I think this record still stands out against its UK peers of that time, I'm really proud of it. It was the start of an incredible time; the start of something I never imagined happening to me when I was a kid, kicking my heels around a north-eastern estate thinking life out there looked pretty uneventful.

What were your best – and worst – releases? And why? You may think I am side-stepping the question, but I like all our releases equally and I can back this up in a number of ways. Throughout the lifetime of the label we always released records by bands that we had pursued and nagged to let us release their stuff, rather than have bands approach us, so all our releases actually reflect what we were into at that time. Whatever I was releasing at that time was constantly played by me to the point that most of my copies of the vinyl are scratched and tapes of the bands' practice recordings destroyed. Pretty much everyone was a pleasure to work with and we seemed to all share in the excitement of putting the record out. Finally, each release invokes different periods in my life…you could say that the Subjugation discography is the soundtrack to my twenties…and what a brilliant time that was!

Subjugation Records, Helene, circa 1998

What were the best – and worst! – things about running a punk label in the Nineties? In the early part of the Nineties it seemed to me as if the hardcore scene was trying to get back on its feet after a lull in energy and activity. What there was left of the scene at that time seemed small, but everyone involved really seemed to be gearing up to give it another go. It is difficult to articulate a sense of this time, but there seemed to be a buzz and people had ideas and enthusiasm. New bands were starting, as were new zines, distros and labels. Up north people didn't seem to have much money or resources in the early Nineties, but that didn't seem to be stopping people trying to make something happen. I remember it as an exciting time and one where I was full of anticipation of what could happen next.

Another good thing was the amount of letter-writing that went on, as people tried to get connected (or re-connected in the case of the older folk) and as a record label we got quite a lot of letters. Those were the days before the era of mass communication through the internet and we eagerly sought out kindred spirits, often writing long letters filled with our ideas, politics, mix tapes and flyers. For me, looking back, one of the best things about it was the ease at which people – often almost strangers – would wear their hearts on their sleeves, keen to reveal what they thought and felt about the scene and this may sound cheesy, but also the world around them and what they thought was wrong with it. The radical politics of people in the scene was not something to be scoffed at and for many was a key part of the narrative of the scene and of its motivations. However the downside to not being able to e-mail people was the length of time it took to set up trades with other labels and distros. Waiting weeks to sort things out would now feel so frustrating, but I guess back then we had no other choice than to move at a snail's pace!

One of the other fab things about the scene was how it operated. The degree of trust and co-operation between us was pretty phenomenal. Although this trust could obviously be abused from time to time, on the whole it underpinned the scene. One of the finest examples of this for someone running a record label was the concept of the 'punk post'. Touring bands or people just travelling would deliver your trades half way across the world, passing them from one person to the next until they reached their intended destination. It was anarchic, uncoordinated, unregulated, but it was an underground network that delivered. You didn't bat an eyelid when, for example, someone from the US travelling with a French band turned up on your doorstep in Yorkshire with a package of records from a record label in Italy. Brilliant!

This brings me neatly onto one of the worst things about running a label in the Nineties, which both Ian and I would spontaneously point to and that is the ineptitude of the Royal Mail! I will always remember Ian receiving an LP through his letter box – clearly stamped 'Fragile! Do not bend!' – that had been folded in half. You can laugh about it now, but when you had like £30 a week to live on and a new record was a treasure, it was a catastrophe! Two other things also merit a mention: hardly anyone one had cars at this time, so getting around to gigs, taking your distro on the road and picking up stuff you needed for the label was pretty difficult…and also grappling with new technology as computers became more accessible and you felt under pressure to deliver better and better layouts and actually have a website. But that may just be me and my general and enduring ineptitude…

How did you strive to run your label that may have set you apart from other labels of the time? I don't think the label was ever set apart from the other hardcore labels around us in the early to mid Nineties. In fact, to me at least, it was very much *in step* with other hardcore/punk labels, particularly other labels I knew in the north: fiercely independent, a strong DIY ethos, a desire to make a difference (however small!), to sell records at near cost rather than make a profit, to get our community's 'soundtrack' and ideas out there and heard and trying to be fair to the bands on the label and wanting the best for them.

What other 'fringe activities' did you get involved in alongside the label? And why?
While running the label, which was a pretty much all-consuming activity in itself, Ian and I also put on gigs wherever we and our friends were based over the 10 years of the label: Leeds, Bradford, Darlington and, later on, in Sheffield when I moved there. Ian also booked tours for foreign bands from time to time. A 'fringe activity' I am particularly proud of is the two/three day hardcore festivals that we put on at the 1 In 12 Club from 1993 to 1997. We worked in the main with Nick from Sure Hand Records/*How We Rock* zine to pull these events off. We got permission from the club for a mass sleep-over, had 20-odd bands playing, both from the UK and abroad and lots of distro stalls from all around the country. More importantly we raised a not-insignificant amount of money for the Club, local support groups and social justice campaigns of the time, plus people had to donate a tin of veggie food for the Bradford Soup Run, a local charity for the homeless.

As well as releasing records, we also ran a mail-order, both for our own releases and those that we traded, as well as the plethora of music zines around at the time. I also did a fair stint as a columnist for *Fracture* fanzine and sometimes did record reviews for *How We Rock*. I tried as much as I could to be involved in the animal rights and environmental campaigns going on at the time and, on giving up the label, this is something that I have been able to dedicate more time to, which has been great. While running the label, I was also a volunteer for a pro-choice campaign group, going into local schools to talk to the kids, which was challenging but very rewarding.

When and why did you fold the label? Any regrets since? The label came to an end in 2002. You just naturally get to the end of the line with some things, when it feels like the right time to bow out. That year I remember standing in Out Of Step Records in Leeds with Nick from Sure Hand and Richard from Armed With Anger and we had this slightly poignant moment where we all shrugged our shoulders at the news that all of us had ended our labels; we kind of said, 'Well, that's that then...' and just started laughing.

But I don't really have any regrets about ending the label. There may be random moments where I get carried away with the idea of releasing records again, but it passes when I think of all the aches and pains that it would again involve. It was a brilliant time, but it became time to do other things and escape from being trapped in the house behind a computer with a never-ending 'to do list'. Now I have more time for my other passions namely travelling in my van, surfing, mountain biking and snowboarding – and other new forms of trouble causing! Most of which, if you notice, are based in the great outdoors...

What was your last release? And how was it, as epitaphs go? The last release was the Stapleton CD, but it was not planned as a final release. I think for me the epitaph is the full span of Subjugation releases. Ten years in music is a long time and the musical difference between our first and last release is clearly obvious. What may be less obvious to people in the scene now is that the evolution of the releases is more linear than you might at first think and it traces how parts of the UK hardcore scene changed and moved forward over the decade.

How would you like your label's contribution to be remembered in the grand scheme of things? As small, but nicely formed? As two cheeky kids from a small northeast town who made some stuff happen that little Britain would disapprove of? I guess I don't really have a sensible answer to this one!

DISCOGRAPHY

All 7-inch EPs unless otherwise stated

SUB 001 Strength Alone 'Self-titled' (1992)

SUB 002 Various Artists 'Realization' (1993)

SUB 003 Ironside 'Fragments Of The Last Judgement' (1993)

SUB 004 Bob Tilton 'Wake Me When it's Springtime Again' (1994)

SUB 005 Various Artists 'Autotomy' (1994)

SUB 006 Baby Harp Seal 'Self-titled' (1994)

SUB 007 Tribute 'Demo' cassette (1994)

SUB 008 Bob Tilton 'Songs Of Penknife And Pocket Watch' (1995)

SUB 009 Tribute 'Self-titled' (1995)

SUB 009.5 Tribute flexidisc (released with *How We Rock* fanzine) (1995)

SUB 010 Schema 'Self-titled' (1996)

SUB 011 Baby Harp Seal 'Self-titled' LP (1996)

SUB 012 Bob Tilton 'Crescent' 12-inch (1996)

SUB 013 Month Of Birthdays 'These Things That We Do Are Not Good For The Self' CD (1997)

SUB 014 Beacon 'Still Photographs From One Motion Picture' (1997)

SUB 015 Imbiss 'Self-titled' (1998)

SUB 016 Month Of Birthdays 'Heightened' (1998)

SUB 017 Unseen Friends 'Self-titled' (1999)

SUB 019 Spy Versus Spy 'Self-titled' CD '1999)

SUB 020 Month Of Birthdays 'Lost In The Translation' CD (1999)

SUB 021 Pylon 'Self-titled' CD (2000)

SUB 022 Spy Versus Spy 'Little Lights' LP and CD (2000)

SUB 023 Nathaniel Green 'Down To You Then, Super Girl' CD (2001)

SUB 024 Stapleton 'On The Enjoyment Of Unpleasant Places' CD (2001)

SURE HAND

When, where and why did the label get started?

NICK ROYLES: The label was originally started in Bradford, during the summer of 1992, for the sole reason of self-releasing the Ironside 'Neutered Innocence' cassingle. That was it. I came up with the label name, which I sort of stole and re-jigged from Ron Brotherhood's zine which was called *Open Hand*; I just liked the concept of hands and took it from there. After that release, it was dormant for some time and was then re-started in 1995 by me and the other guys in Unborn at the time, as a collective with the aim of supporting bands from the European scene.

What were you hoping to achieve when you set out? What labels inspired you to start your own?

Initially we just wanted to shift all the copies that we had pressed of the Ironside cassingle, so we had a really quick turnaround from recording to pressing, in time for us to sell them at the Ieper hardcore festival in August '92. I'm not even sure how many copies we pressed, but I think it was either 200 or 500 copies; the original inspiration was more from other bands doing their own releases, especially cassingles. There were no plans for any other releases on Sure Hand until it came back in '95; we came together to release an EP and had hopes to release another EP. That was it really.

How do you rate that first release now, with the benefit of hindsight?

It makes me cringe. I like the cover photo, which I took in the ruins of Fountains Abbey and that's the arm of Rich Corbridge from Armed With Anger on the front cover. The covers were kindly printed by a guy we knew called Dave, a hardcore scenester from Castleford, who has gone on to become a dance DJ. He did a great job, except for putting the track-listing and label logo on the front cover, which we never asked for. We had to take the covers to be cut ourselves, but the printing was only in black and white so we coloured the band logo in with felt tipped pens! The print cutters commented on the 'amazingly precise colour printing' on the covers; we chuckled at our amateurism taken as professionalism.

What were your best – and worst – releases? And why?

In some ways, I think the two best releases would have been the ones that were planned but never came out. The first of those releases was the H-Street demo on 7-inch vinyl: an amazing band from Wien, who I still rate as one of Europe's best ever hardcore bands…loved the people as well. I had the recordings and artwork ready, but I just sort of gave up running the label at that point; I do need to apologise to them for not putting it out.

I think the ultimate best release would have been our last, which would have been the Cracked Cop Skulls third EP we were planning. We had asked Karl Buechner [from Earth Crisis] to sing on that, which he was psyched about and had agreed to do, but we just didn't follow it up. I recall Karl went and did a punk demo after that, which they offered to Sure Hand…the CCS EP would have been the best though!

What were the best – and worst! – things about running a punk label in the Nineties?

It's so much easier to moan about the worst things and it's a fact that the good

Sure Hand Records, Nick Royles

far outweighed the bad, but here we go:

The Good: the independent network that spanned the globe was just awe-inspiring and all the connectivity that you felt communicating with people and other great labels all around the world. Just being in contact with so many like-minded people... I made so many friends – awesome times!

The Bad: parcels going missing, import tax duties, getting ripped off by distributors (too many to name), idiots putting their own addresses wrongly on their orders and then complaining that we'd ripped them off...and having to do all that crap record-label work when I'd rather be outside!

And the Ugly: one member of the SH collective getting mugged in Leeds while carrying 100 copies each of the second and third EPs...guess they got dumped in some bin after they looked inside the bags? Another collective member was also mugged of Sure Hand funds at a cash machine, losing several hundred pounds.

How did you strive to run your label that may have set you apart from other labels of the time? I think we were the opposite to your question really; we sought to be more *inclusive* with other labels. Particularly Subjugation and Armed With Anger, whom we'd organise shit together with; they were our partners in crime, particularly in running the festivals at the 1 In 12. We just saw our label as a part of the hardcore scene, nowt more, nowt less. And we operated in the way that we regarded as the norm within the hardcore scene...not all labels operated in this way, but we strived to be fair.

What other 'scene activities' did you get involved in alongside the label? I did a couple of bands, a zine and the Slender Means 1 In 12 benefit festivals. We always saw our scene as a community and thought there was something more than just the music, even if other people and bands didn't and we saw the festivals that we arranged at the 1 In 12 as our contribution to that communal ethos. We also managed to raise money for lots of causes that we were interested in and most importantly we were able to donate hundreds of pounds to the 1 In 12 Club when, at that time, it was in a dire financial situation. I'm really proud of the fact that the people from Subjugation and Armed With Anger made so much money for the club from the events that we arranged there. I should also mention all the bands that played those festivals for just petrol costs. Our festivals averaged out to about three events annually for quite a few years, from 1993 onwards and I just have to salute the bands that continually played for next to nothing. Ta.

How would you like your label's contribution to be remembered in the grand scheme of things? Hmmm... Well-intentioned but chaotically disorganised. Enthusiastic and passionate, but easily distracted...punk rock basically.

DISCOGRAPHY:

SH001c Ironside 'Neutered Innocence' cassingle (1992)
SH002 Above All 'Blood Of Ages' EP (1995)
SH002a Above All 'Saviour' flexi (1995)
SH003 Unborn 'Ancestral Pagan Roots' EP (1996)

SH003a Gatekeeper 'Demo' (European version) (1996)

SH004 Withdrawn 'A Certain Innate Suffering' MCD (1997)

SH006 Various Artists 'Justice For The Enslaved' compilation CD (1999)

SH007c In The Clear 'Demo' (1999)

SH008c Circle Again 'Demo' (1999)

SH0010 In The Clear 'Out Of Our Past' MCD (1999)

Some related discographies:

BLACKFISH

All CDs unless otherwise stated...

ORCA 001 Unite 'Playing With Fire' MCD (1998)

ORCA 002 Knuckledust/Stampin' Ground split CDEP 'The Dark Side Versus The East Side' (1998)

ORCA 003 Various Artists 'Still Can't Hear The Words: The Subhumans Covers Album' (1999)

ORCA 004 Light Of The Morning 'All Else Is Error' (1999)

ORCA 005 Freebase/Medulla Nocte 'From One Extreme To Another' split MCD (1999)

ORCA 006 POA 'The Fear Of War' (1999)

ORCA 007 Various Artists 'Ushering In A New Age Of Quarrel: A UKHC Tribute To The Cro-Mags' (1999)

ORCA 008 Spine/Primate 'Hope Versus Realisation' split MCD (2000)

ORCA 009 Unite/December 'The NATO Project' split MCD (2000)

ORCA 010 Out Cold/Voorhees 'Everything You Believed In Was A Lie' split MCD (2000)

ORCA 011 Knuckledust 'Time Won't Heal This' (2000) – *joint release with Rucktion*

ORCA 012 Underule 'Misfortune Comes By Means Of The Mouth' (2000)

ORCA 013 Various Artists 'Barricades And Broken Dreams: An International Tribute To Conflict' (2001)

ORCA 014 Decimate 'In The Name Of A God' MCD (2001)

ORCA 015 Knuckledust/Unite 'Together We Stand, Divided We Brawl' split MCD (2001)

ORCA 016 Various Artists 'UKHC' (2001)

ORCA 017 50 Caliber 'Internal Bleeding' MCD (2002)

ORCA 018 Incoherence 'A World Without Heroes' MCD (2002)

ORCA 019 Instigators 'Dine Upon The Dead' (2002)

ORCA 020 Various Artists 'Thrash Or Be Thrashed: An International Tribute To Thrash' (2003)

BOSS TUNEAGE

Discography 1990-2000:

If there are missing catalogue numbers (BOSTAGE504 and BOSTAGE511 etc), these were released in 2001 or 2002.

BOSTAGE001 Goober Patrol/Vehicle Derek split 7-inch EP (1990)

BOSTAGE002 Damage 'TV Bible' MLP (1990)

BOSTAGE003 Wanton Thought 'Mustard Mit' 7-inch EP (1991)

BOSTAGE004 Goober Patrol 'Truck Off!' LP (1991)

BOSTAGE005 Various 'Floor 81' compilation LP (1992)

BOSTAGE006 Wordbug 'Losing It All' LP (1991) *co-release with Hometown Atrocities*

BOSTAGE007 Shutdown 'Shutdown' 12-inch (1992) *co-release with Off The Disk*

BOSTAGE008 Sofahead/Exit Condition split LP (not released)

BOSTAGE009 Goober Patrol 'Dutch Ovens' LP / CD (1992) *co-release with Lost And Found*

BOSTAGE010 Five Foot Nothing 'Pretty Nuclear' LP (not released)

BOSTAGE011 Rise 'Rise' LP/CD (1992) *co-release with RPN*

BOSTAGE012 Rise 'Where to Find' 7-inch (1992) *co-release with RPN*

BOSTAGE013 Loose 'Rocksalat' 7-inch (1992) *co-release with RPN*

BOSTAGE014 Life But How To Live It? 'Ugly' CD (1993) *co-release with RPN and Progress Records*

BOSTAGE015 Life But How To Live It? 'Burn Green' MCD (1992)

co-release with RPN and Fuck You All We're Making Our Own Records

BOSTAGE016 Asexuals 'Love Goes Plaid' 7-inch (1993) *co-release with RPN*

BOSTAGE017 Hooton 3 Car 'Spot Daylight' 12-inch (1993) *co-release with Rumblestrip and JSNTGM*

BOSTAGE018 Miranda Warning 'Twelve Speed Pop Blender' Cass / CD (1993)

BOSTAGE019 Rise 'Jack' CD (1993) *co-release with RPN*

BOSTAGE020 Wordbug / Byetail split 7-inch EP (1993) *co-release with Hometown Atrocities*

BOSTAGE021 Wordbug 'Locked In' 7-inch (1993) *co-release with Hometown Atrocities*

BOSTAGE022 Ran 'Beautiful Songs For Ugly Children' CD (not released)

BOSTAGE023 Wordbug 'Die' 7-inch (1994) *co-release with Hometown Atrocities*

BOSTAGE024 Annalise 'Fettered' CDEP (1995) (put out anonymously on Out Of Order records OOO-1)

BOSTAGE025 The Unknown 'Rocket Pop' CD (1995) *co-release with Jiffi Pop*

BOSTAGE501 Annalise 'You Can Dye Your Hair But Not Your Heart' CD (1999) *co-release with KYMF*

BOSTAGE502 Porcelain Boys 'Away Awhile' CD (2000) *co-release with Popkid*

BOSTAGE503 The Unknown 'Still Unknown' CD (1999) *co-release with Jiffi Pop*

BOSTAGE505 The Unknown 'Change' CD (1999) *co-release with Jiffi Pop*

BOSTAGE506 The Unknown 'Seems So Live' CD (1999) *co-release with Jiffi Pop*

BOSTAGE507 Jettison 'Search For The Gun Girl' CD (2000) *co-release with Popkid*

BOSTAGE508 Annalise 'Tour Issue' CD (2000) *co-release with Ding Dong Ditch*

BOSTAGE509 Various 'Year Zero: Exeter Punk 1977-2000' CD (2000) *co-release with Hometown Atrocities*

BOSTAGE510 Jelly Gun Jack 'Zarse' CD (2000)

BOSTAGE512 The Unknown 'Pop Art' CD (2000)

BOSTAGE513 Mulligan Stu 'Do The Kids Wanna Rock' CD (1999) *co-release with Rhetoric*

BOSTAGE514 Various 'Xanadu – Music For The Future' compilation CD (1999) *co-release with Rhetoric*

BOSTAGE515 Asexuals 'Greater Then Later' CD (2000)

BOSTAGE516 Asexuals 'Walts Wish' CDEP (2000)

BOSTAGE517 Eesch 'Candy Store' CD (2000)

BOSTAGE519 Shimmer 'Moonshine' CDEP(2000)

BOSTAGE520 Various 'Boss Samplerage' CD (2000)

BOSTAGE521 Rise 'Freezer Burn' CD (2000)

BOSTAGE522 Rise 'Jack' CD (2000) – *reissue of BOSTAGE019*

BOSTAGE523 Die Kunst 'Sweden' CD (2000)

BOSTAGE524 Brock Pytel 'Second Choice' CD (2000) *co-release with Scamindy*

BOSTAGE525 Asexuals 'Fitzjoy' CD (2000)

BOSTAGE527 Serpico 'Everyone Vs Everyone' CD (2000) *co-release with Waterslide Records*

BOSTAGE529 Pocket Genius ' Pocket Genius' CD (2000)

BOSTAGE530 Scarper! 'Every Turn' CD (2000)

BOSTAGE531 Tonka 'Discography' CD (not released)

BOSTAGE532 The Jones 'Gravity Blues' LP/CD (2000) *co-release with Waterslide, Flight 13, Rookie and Ding Dong Ditch*

BOSTAGE534 Raggity Anne 'Only Square People Think It's Cool To Be Cool' CD (2000)

BOSTAGE535 High Lo Fi 'Three Sided Single ' CDEP (2000)

BOSTAGE701 Annalise 'Signposts And Alleyways' 7-inch (1999)

BOSTAGE702 The Unknown 'Puzzles' 7-inch (1999)

BOSTAGE703 Wat Tyler 'The Vicar And I ' 7-inch (1999)

BOSTAGE704 Jelly Gun Jack 'Goomba' 7-inch (2000)

BOSTAGE705 Eesch 'Falling Down' 7-inch (2000)

RUCKTION

UKHC discography...

RUCK001 Area Effect 'Stand Strong' MCD (1998)

RUCK002 Area Effect/Knuckledust 'Split' 7-inch (1998) – *joint release with Black Up*

RUCK003 Ninebar '1999Bar' cassette (1999)

RUCK004 Special Move 'Dark Overlord' MCD (2000)

RUCK005 Knuckledust 'Time Won't Heal This' CD – *joint release with Blackfish*

RUCK006 Ninebar 'Urban Legends' MCD (2002)

RUCK007 BDF 'Family First' MCD (2002)

RUCK008 Six Ft Ditch 'Faces Of Death' MCD (2003)

RUCK009 Special Move 'Return Of The Three Swords' CD (2003)

RUCK010 Kartel/Diction/Ninebar 'Southbound' three-way split CD (2004)

RUCK011 TRC 'North West Kings' MCD (2004)

Rucktion band, Ninebar live, pic by Naki

RUCK012 Divide 'When All Else Fails' MCD (2004)

RUCK013 Blades Of Unity 'Backpack Full Of C4' MCD (2004)

RUCK014 Various Artists 'Time Fer Some Rucktion' CD (2005)

RUCK016 Six Ft Ditch 'Unlicensed Cemetary' CD (2005)

RUCK017 Taking Names 'This Guided Youth' MCD (2005)

RUCK019 Broken Oath 'Blood Cleanse The Streets' MCD (2005)

RUCK020 Ninebar 'Urban Legends' CD (2005)

RUCK021 Special Move 'Level 4: The Game Of Death' MCD (2005)

RUCK022 Diction 'From The Depths' CD (2006)

RUCK023 Ninebar 'Raising The Bar' CD (2006)

RUCK024 Bun Dem Out 'Self-titled' MCD (2007)

RUCK025 Injury Time/Wisdom In Chains 'Split' MCD (2007)

RUCK026 Knuckledust 'Dustography' CD (2007)

RUCK027 Broken Oath 'Given Half A Chance' MCD (2007)

RUCK028 Kartel 'Rise Of The Guttersnipe' CD (2007)

RUCK030 TRC 'Destroy And Rebuild' CD (2007)

RUCK031 Hellbent Diehard 'Self-titled' CD (2008)

RUCK032 Deal With It 'Endtime Prophecies' CD (2008)

RUCK033 True Valiance 'Hooked On Revenge' MCD (2008)

RUCK035 Special Move 'Curse Of The Blackwater' CD (2008)

RUCK038 Chains Of Hate 'Cold Harsh Reality' MCD (2009)

RUCK039 Ambush 'Forward Into Hell' MCD (2010)

RUCK040 Injury Time 'The Vex' CD (2010)

RUCK041 Prowler 'Strictly 3.5' CD (2010)

RUCK042 Deathskulls 'The Real Deal II' CD (2011)

RUCK043 Ninebar '900' CD (2011)

Also by Ian Glasper...

"Armed With Anger" is the latest in a highly acclaimed, definitive series of books by the author. You may also enjoy...

Burning Britain - A History Of UK Punk 1980 To 1984

"Featuring hundreds of new interviews and photographs, 'Burning Britain' tells the behind the scenes story of the UK's early eighties' punk scene in the words of the bands and labels who created it. Region by region, the author examines both the big names and those smaller artists who came and went almost un-noticed in what has quickly become a definitive text on the subject".

The Day The Country Died: A History Of Anarcho Punk 1980 To 1984

"If the bands featured in 'Burning Britain' were loud, political and uncompromising, those examined in 'The Day The Country Died' were even more so, and prepared to risk their liberty to communicate the ideals they believed in so passionately. All the scene's big names, and most of the small ones, are comprehensively covered by exclusive interviews and previously unseen photographs. A must for anybody even remotely interested in the punk scene".

Trapped In A Scene - UK Hardcore 1985-89

"Glasper digs deeper than anyone has previously dared into a subculture that was as manic, exciting, innovative and defiant as anything before or since. Constructed upon meticulously gathered first-hand accounts and heaving with exclusive never-seen-before photographs, 'Trapped In A Scene' is the definitive document on UKHC and essential reading for anyone with a passing interest in the convoluted evolution of genuinely challenging punk music".

www.cherryred.co.uk

FROCKCORE FESTIVAL '93!

Profound Victims *teencore*

Coping Saw *oddcore*

Witchknot *magicore*

Delicate Vomit *madcore*

Linus *grrrlcore*

Sister George *queercore*

Thistle Fairies *applecore*

Sat. 11/12/93
1 in 12 Club/Bradford
3 p.m. £3/£3.50 on door

BE WISE BEFORE THE EVENT!
MIDSUMMERS MADNESS
SAT 21st SEPT
ROCKIN & RAGIN
+OLDER THAN DIRT+
noisy herberts
SLEEP
BRIGHTONS FINEST - JOLLY GOOD P LP
£2
JUICE
LONDONS FAB FOUR
At
The Joiners Arms
BOYCOTT THE BUTCHER
GO VEGETARIAN
respect!
your clean fun
+ RAGING SOUTH-COAST HARDCORE +

THURSDAY 23rd NOV
noisebox PRESENTS:
GOOBER PATROL
TRAVIS CUT
HECTORS HOUSE 2 quid

NO MORE WEAKNESS PRESENTS

HC IN THE NINE-HATE

BORN FROM PAIN
HEAVY HC MOSH STYLE FROM HOLLAND

KNUCKLEDUST
OLD STYLE HC KINGS

SLAVEARC
BRUTAL SXE DEATHCORE

STAMPIN' GROUND
RETURN OF THE DARKSIDE

AREA EFFECT
MANCHESTER'S CRAZY YOUTH CREW

SPEAKEASY ABBEYDALE RD SHEFFIELD

SUNDAY FEBRUARY 22ND

£3 ON DOOR
FIRST BAND ON 7.30PM

STE 18!

SAT. SEPT. 29TH 8pm

SINK Ex Stupids-Hardcore/Blues/Country!

Can't Decide Ex Heresy/Ripcord-great LP!

Older than Dirt Intense Krishnacore!

The Joiners St Marys St

Southampton £3.00/2.50

Access-1 Step Cool Tunes & Record Stall! Come Early

YEP YOP OF THE RAVEHEADS

VAFFAN CULO

SKIN FLICK

GoT

THURS 14th MAY - NORMANDY

X.MAS BASH!

Urbcore

PUNK AS MACKEREL!

GABBA IS MY HERO

CHAOS U.K.

FARMYARD STOMPING BRISTOLIANS!

Haywire

WEYMOUTH'S ANARCHIC PUNK'S

+OLDER THAN DIRT+

FUNNY HAIR & FAT BELLIES!

cili--derr

TUES. 18TH DEC.

like in a dream...

AT THE JOINERS ST. MARY'S ST. SOUTHAMPTON

a journey into cider house

kipper trench

FREE FANZINES TO FIRST 20 PEOPLE

STE CHRISTMAS PARTY!

SAT. DEC. 18TH

CHICKEN BONE **CHOKED** **+OLDER THAN DIRT+**

THIRST!

Donation to Southampton AFA

The Joiners StMarys St

Southampton 8pm

Access 1 Step STE 60 Come Early!

The Winchester Gig Group presents......

snuff

The AB'S

+OLDER THAN DIRT+

SAT. 24th NOV
ALL SAINTS COMMUNITY
SCHOOL, HIGHCLIFFE
WINCHESTER

DOORS
7:30
£3
NO BAR

ADVANCE
TICKETS
VENUS RECORDS
TUBES RECORDS
£2·50

ALSO AVAILABLE FROM
CHERRY RED BOOKS:

Nina Antonia: Johnny Thunders – In Cold Blood

Andy Blade: The Secret Life Of A Teenage Punk Rocker: The Andy Blade Chronicles

Craig Brackenbridge: Hells Bent On Rockin': A History Of Psychobilly

Jake Brown: Tom Waits: In The Studio

Steve Bruce: Best Seat In The House – A Cock Sparrer Story

David Burke: Heart Of Darkness – Bruce Springsteen's 'Nebraska'

David Cartwright: Bittersweet: The Clifford T Ward Story

Jeremy Collingwood: Kiss Me Neck – A Lee 'Scratch' Perry Discography

Campbell Devine: All The Young Dudes: Mott The Hoople & Ian Hunter

Malcolm Dome / Jerry Ewing: Celebration Day – A Led Zeppelin Encyclopedia

Sean Egan: Our Music Is Red – With Purple Flashes: The Story Of The Creation

Sean Egan: The Doc's Devils: Manchester United 1972-77

Martin Elliott: The Rolling Stones: Complete Recording Sessions 1962-2012

Ian Glasper: The Day The Country Died: A History Of Anarcho Punk 1980 To 1984

Ian Glasper: Burning Britain – A History Of UK Punk 1980 -1984

Ian Glasper: Trapped In A Scene - UK Hardcore 1985-89

Stefan Grenados: Those Were The Days – The Beatles' Apple Organization

Phil Harding: PWL: From The Factory Floor

Colin Harper / Trevor Hodgett: Irish Folk, Trad And Blues: A Secret History

Dave Henderson: A Plugged In State Of Mind: The History of Electronic Music

Nick Hodges / Ian Priston: Embryo – A Pink Floyd Chronology 1966-1971

Jim Bob: Goodnight Jim Bob – On The Road With Carter USM

Barry Lazell: Indie Hits 1980 -1989

Mark Manning (aka Zodiac Mindwarp): Fucked By Rock (Revised and Expanded)

Mick Mercer: Music To Die For – International Guide To Goth, Goth Metal, Horror Punk, Psychobilly Etc

Alex Ogg: Independence Days – The Story Of UK Independent Record Labels

Alex Ogg: No More Heroes: A Complete History Of UK Punk 1976 To 1980

David Parker: Random Precision – Recording The Music Of Syd Barrett 1965 - 1974

Mark Powell: Prophets and Sages: The 101 Greatest Progressive Rock Albums

Terry Rawlings / Keith Badman: Good Times Bad Times – The Rolling Stones 1960-69

Terry Rawlings / Keith Badman: Quite Naturally – The Small Faces

John Repsch: The Legendary Joe Meek – The Telstar Man

John Robb: Death To Trad Rock – The Post-Punk fanzine scene 1982-87

Garry Sharpe-Young: Rockdetector: A To Zs of '80s Rock / Death Metal / Doom, Gothic & Stoner Metal and Power Metal

Garry Sharpe-Young: Rockdetector: Black Sabbath – Never Say Die

Garry Sharpe-Young: Rockdetector: Ozzy Osbourne

Mick Stevenson: The Motorhead Collector's Guide

Dave Thompson: Truth... Rod Stewart, Ron Wood And The Jeff Beck Group

Dave Thompson: Number One Songs In Heaven – he Sparks Story

Dave Thompson: Block Buster! – The True Story of The Sweet

Dave Thompson: Children of the Revolution: The Glam Rock Story 1970 -75

Paul Williams: You're Wondering Now – The Specials from Conception to Reunion

Alan Wilson: Deathrow: The Chronicles Of Psychobilly

Terry Wilson: Tamla Motown – The Stories Behind The Singles

PLEASE VISIT WWW.CHERRYREDBOOKS.CO.UK FOR FURTHER INFO AND MAIL ORDER

We're always interested to hear from readers, authors and fans - for contact, submissions, mail order and further information, please email books@cherryred.co.uk

www.cherryredbooks.co.uk